PATIENT FLOW: REDUCING DELAY IN HEALTHCARE DELIVERY

Recent titles in the **INTERNATIONAL SERIES IN OPERATIONS RESEARCH & MANAGEMENT SCIENCE**

Frederick S. Hillier, Series Editor, *Stanford University*

Maros/ *COMPUTATIONAL TECHNIQUES OF THE SIMPLEX METHOD*
Harrison, Lee & Neale/ *THE PRACTICE OF SUPPLY CHAIN MANAGEMENT: Where Theory and Application Converge*
Shanthikumar, Yao & Zijm/ *STOCHASTIC MODELING AND OPTIMIZATION OF MANUFACTURING SYSTEMS AND SUPPLY CHAINS*
Nabrzyski, Schopf & Węglarz/ *GRID RESOURCE MANAGEMENT: State of the Art and Future Trends*
Thissen & Herder/ *CRITICAL INFRASTRUCTURES: State of the Art in Research and Application*
Carlsson, Fedrizzi, & Fullér/ *FUZZY LOGIC IN MANAGEMENT*
Soyer, Mazzuchi & Singpurwalla/ *MATHEMATICAL RELIABILITY: An Expository Perspective*
Chakravarty & Eliashberg/ *MANAGING BUSINESS INTERFACES: Marketing, Engineering, and Manufacturing Perspectives*
Talluri & van Ryzin/ *THE THEORY AND PRACTICE OF REVENUE MANAGEMENT*
Kavadias & Loch/*PROJECT SELECTION UNDER UNCERTAINTY: Dynamically Allocating Resources to Maximize Value*
Brandeau, Sainfort & Pierskalla/ *OPERATIONS RESEARCH AND HEALTH CARE: A Handbook of Methods and Applications*
Cooper, Seiford & Zhu/ *HANDBOOK OF DATA ENVELOPMENT ANALYSIS: Models and Methods*
Luenberger/ *LINEAR AND NONLINEAR PROGRAMMING, 2nd Ed.*
Sherbrooke/ *OPTIMAL INVENTORY MODELING OF SYSTEMS: Multi-Echelon Techniques, Second Edition*
Chu, Leung, Hui & Cheung/ *4th PARTY CYBER LOGISTICS FOR AIR CARGO*
Simchi-Levi, Wu & Shen/ *HANDBOOK OF QUANTITATIVE SUPPLY CHAIN ANALYSIS: Modeling in the E-Business Era*
Gass & Assad/ *AN ANNOTATED TIMELINE OF OPERATIONS RESEARCH: An Informal History*
Greenberg/ *TUTORIALS ON EMERGING METHODOLOGIES AND APPLICATIONS IN OPERATIONS RESEARCH*
Weber/ *UNCERTAINTY IN THE ELECTRIC POWER INDUSTRY: Methods and Models for Decision Support*
Figueira, Greco & Ehrgott/ *MULTIPLE CRITERIA DECISION ANALYSIS: State of the Art Surveys*
Reveliotis/ *REAL-TIME MANAGEMENT OF RESOURCE ALLOCATIONS SYSTEMS: A Discrete Event Systems Approach*
Kall & Mayer/ *STOCHASTIC LINEAR PROGRAMMING: Models, Theory, and Computation*
Sethi, Yan & Zhang/ *INVENTORY AND SUPPLY CHAIN MANAGEMENT WITH FORECAST UPDATES*
Cox/ *QUANTITATIVE HEALTH RISK ANALYSIS METHODS: Modeling the Human Health Impacts of Antibiotics Used in Food Animals*
Ching & Ng/ *MARKOV CHAINS: Models, Algorithms and Applications*
Li & Sun/ *NONLINEAR INTEGER PROGRAMMING*
Kaliszewski/ *SOFT COMPUTING FOR COMPLEX MULTIPLE CRITERIA DECISION MAKING*
Bouyssou et al/ *EVALUATION AND DECISION MODELS WITH MULTIPLE CRITERIA: Stepping stones for the analyst*
Blecker & Friedrich/ *MASS CUSTOMIZATION: Challenges and Solutions*
Appa, Pitsoulis & Williams/ *HANDBOOK ON MODELLING FOR DISCRETE OPTIMIZATION*
Herrmann/ *HANDBOOK OF PRODUCTION SCHEDULING*
Axsäter/ *INVENTORY CONTROL, 2nd Ed.*

***** *A list of the early publications in the series is at the end of the book* *****

PATIENT FLOW: REDUCING DELAY IN HEALTHCARE DELIVERY

Edited by

Randolph W. Hall
Epstein Department of Industrial and Systems Engineering, University of Southern California, Los Angeles, California 90089-0193

Springer

Randolph W. Hall, (Editor)
University of Southern California
Los Angeles, CA, USA

ISBN-10: 0-387-33636-2 (e-book)
ISBN-13: 978-1-4419-4143-5
ISBN-13: 978-0387-33636-7 (e-book)

Printed on acid-free paper.

9 8 7 6 5 4 3 2

springer.com

Contents

Contributing Authors

David Belson
Epstein Department of Industrial and Systems Engineering, University of Southern California, Los Angeles, California

Emilio Cerdá
University Complutense of Madrid, Spain

Peter Congdon
Department of Geography, Queen Mary and Westfield College, Londdon

Maged Dessouky
Epstein Department of Industrial and Systems Engineering, University of Southern California, Los Angeles, California

Linda Green
Graduate School of Business, Columbia University, New York

Randolph Hall
Epstein Department of Industrial and Systems Engineering, University of Southern California, Los Angeles, California

Shane N. Hall
Department of Mechanical and Industrial Engineering, University of Illinois at Urbana-Champaign, Urbana, Illinois

Sheldon Jacobson
Department of Mechanical and Industrial Engineering, University of Illinois at Urbana-Champaign, Urbana, Illinois

Hongzhong Jia
Epstein Department of Industrial and Systems Engineering, University of Southern California, Los Angeles, California

Linda Kosnik
Overlook Hosptial, Summit, New Jersey

Lisa Kuramoto
Centre for Health Evaluation and Outcome Sciences, St. Paul's Hospital, Vancouver, British Columbia

Adrian Levy
Centre for Clinical Epidemiology and Evaluation, Vancouver Coastal Health Research Institute, British Columbia

Mark Lindsay
Mayo Health System, Eau Claire, Wisconsin

Pavan Murali
Epstein Department of Industrial and Systems Engineering, University of Southern California, Los Angeles, California

Fernando Ordóñez
Epstein Department of Industrial and Systems Engineering, University of Southern California, Los Angeles, California

Laura de Pablos
University Complutense of Madrid, Spain

Roger Resar
Institute for Healthcare Improvement, Boston

Maria V. Rodriguez
University of Oviedo, Spain

Sergei Savin
Graduate School of Business, Columbia University, New York

Zhihong Shen
Epstein Department of Industrial and Systems Engineering, University of Southern California, Los Angeles, California

Boris Sobolev
Department of Health Care and Epidemiology, the University of British Columbia, British Columbia

James R. Swisher
Mary Washington Hospital, Fredericksburg, Virginia

Jan Vissers
Institute for Health Policy and Management, Erasmus University Medical Centre, Rotterdam, Netherlands

Michael Warner
AtStaff, Inc., Durham, North Carolina

Michael Williams
The Abaris Group, Walnut Creek, California

Preface

Over the last 100 years, quality of life and human longevity have improved in most of the industrialized world as a result of advances in human health. We have benefited from reduced exposure to disease (through such measures as vaccinations and improved water quality), and developed treatments that reduce the consequences of disease once exposed. Nevertheless, humans continue to suffer because they do not have access to appropriate healthcare, or because healthcare is delivered in a manner that is confusing or inefficient. The gap between the science and the practice of healthcare is large.

This book is dedicated to improving healthcare through reducing the delays experienced by patients. One aspect of this goal is to improve the flow of patients, so that they do not experience unnecessary waits as they flow through a healthcare system. Another aspect is ensuring that services are closely synchronized with patterns of patient demand. Still another aspect is ensuring that ancillary services, such as housekeeping and transportation, are fully coordinate with direct patient care. Past experience shows that effective management of healthcare delays can produce dramatic improvements in medical outcomes, patient satisfaction, and access to service, while also reducing the cost of healthcare.

Within the 15 chapters of this book, readers will be exposed to a set of techniques and strategies that can be used by clinicians and administrators to substantially reduce delays in healthcare delivery. This is the first book to have reduction in patient delay as its sole focus, and this book provides the foundation by which hospitals can implement change. Reflecting the highly interdisciplinary nature of this book, the chapters have been written by doctors, nurses, industrial engineers, system engineers and geographers.

These perspectives provide the comprehensive view needed to address the problem of patient delay.

The book begins in Chapters 1 to 4 by examining healthcare as an integrated system. Chapters 1 and 2 provide hands-on methods for developing process models, using these models to identify and remove bottlenecks, and developing facility plans. Chapter 3 examines medical outcomes that result from waits for surgeries. Chapter 4 presents a set of breakthrough strategies that use real-time monitoring systems for continuous improvement.

Chapters 5 to 11 present techniques and methods that can be immediately implemented to improve healthcare operations. Chapter 5 focuses on the patient appointment system, particularly through the approach of advanced access, which makes appointments more immediately available to patients. Chapter 6 concentrates on management of waiting lists for surgeries and the allocation of available capacity to meet patient demands. Chapter 7 offers techniques for scheduling staff to match patterns in patient demand, and thus reducing predictable delays. The literature on simulation modeling, which is widely used for both healthcare design and process improvement, is surveyed in Chapter 8. Chapter 9 provides methods for forecasting demand for healthcare on a region-wide basis. Last in this group, Chapter 10 presents queueing theory as a general method for modeling waits in healthcare.

The last section of the book concentrates on achieving change. Chapter 11 focuses on the rapid delivery of medication in the event of a catastrophic event, such as a pandemic on terrorist attack. Chapter 12 provides a diagnostic for assessing the state of a hospital and using the state assessment to select improvement strategies. Chapter 13 demonstrates the importance of optimizing care as patients transition from one care setting to the next with an emphasis on clinical outcomes and the business case. Chapter 14 shows how to evaluate the overall portfolio of patient diagnostic groups to guide system changes. Lastly, Chapter 15 provides project management tools to guide the execution of patient flow projects.

This book is intended to motivate and guide change so that healthcare systems around the world give more priority to reducing patient delay and implement changes that dramatically improve healthcare. The chapters of this book illustrate that radical changes in the management of patient flow and patient delay are not only possible: they are essential to ensuring that advances in medical practice keep pace with advances in medical science.

Acknowledgments

This book was supported in part with a grant for the Department of Homeland Security through the Center for Risk and Economic Analysis of Terrorist Events, by LA Care and by the Los Angeles County Department of Health Services.

Chapter 1

MODELING PATIENT FLOWS THROUGH THE HEALTHCARE SYSTEM

Randolph Hall, David Belson, Pavan Murali and Maged Dessouky
Epstein Department of Industrial and Systems Engineering, 200 GER, University of Southern California, Los Angeles, California 90089-0193

Abstract: The system of health care can be evaluated from four perspectives: macro, regional, center, and department. In each case, reduction of patient delay depends on improving interfaces as patients are transferred from activity to activity or department to department. This chapter presents basic tools for resolving delays at interfaces, through mapping the processes by which patients are served, and by developing and implementing measures of system performance. These tools are demonstrated through a case study of the Los Angeles County/University of Southern California Hospital.

Key words: Process charts, performance measurement, healthcare systems

1. INTRODUCTION

Health care systems have been challenged in recent years to deliver high quality care with limited resources. In the United States, large segments of the population have inadequate health insurance coverage, forcing them to rely on an under funded public health system. At the national level, the National Institutes of Health has projected a steady increase in expenditures over the next 10 years, both in absolute terms and as a percentage of the gross-domestic-product (GDP). Total expenditures in year 2000 amounted to $1.3 trillion, or 13.2% of the GDP. While expenditures as a percentage of GDP held nearly constant between 1992 and 2000, they increased steadily from 5.2% to 13.1% in the 32-year period from 1960 to 1992. Due to aging of the population and increased costs of medical delivery, health-care costs are projected to increase to 15.9% of the GDP in 2010.

Given the pressures to contain costs, it is critical for hospitals and health care systems to develop systems that ensure the best possible patient care within limited resources. An important aspect of this objective is to develop procedures to improve patient flow, to provide timely treatment and maximum utilization of available resources. Patient flow analysis represents the study of how patients move through the health-care system.

1.1 Emergency Departments: Example of System Delays

Emergency Departments (ED) are perhaps the most challenged components of the health-care system with respect to patient delay. Patients arrive at the emergency department through multiple channels, including walk-in (or drive-in) and ambulance. Depending on the nature of the emergency, the patient may be served through an ambulatory or a non-ambulatory section of the emergency department. The patient (or a friend) meets with a receptionist to collect background and information, and a nurse to triage (prioritize and stabilize) the patient. Patients are served by physicians and nurses in treatment rooms, which may be specialized to particular injuries (e.g., orthopedics) or specialized by level of urgency. Before treating the patient, tests (X-ray, CT Scan, MRI, etc.) may be needed through a radiology department. In some cases patients must be moved to an operating room for surgery. Once emergency treatment is completed, it may be necessary to admit the patient to the hospital, in which case the patient is exposed to additional processes and delays. Eventually, the patient undergoes a discharge process, and his or her bed must be prepared for the next patient.

As stated in a recent study by the American College of Emergency Physicians (ACEP, 2002b), "A multitude of factors are responsible for crowding, including higher patient acuity, prolonged ED evaluations, inadequate inpatient bed capacity, a severe nursing shortage, problems with access to on-call specialists and the use of the ED by those with no other alternative to medical care, such as the uninsured". In 2000, 108 million ED visits occurred in the United States, representing 39.4 visits per 100 people. Growth in ED visits has resulted from the combined effect of a reduction in the number of people with insurance coverage (just 40% of visits were paid through private or commercial insurance; McCaig and Burt, 2001) along with the mandate under the Emergency Medical Treatment and Labor Act (EMTLA) that EDs not refuse service to any patient on the basis of ability to pay (ACEP, 2002a).

Emergency departments have been especially reliant on public sources, as people with no health insurance sometimes have no alternative for receiving medical care. In a recent survey, 78% of hospital administrators stated that their hospitals are inadequately reimbursed for emergency care, with 80% citing a "poor payer mix" (Greene, 1995). The mismatch between available funding and potential demand has made emergency departments particularly susceptible to patient delays, with their attendant consequences on quality of care (also see Derlet and Richards, 2000; Schneider *et al*, 2001, and Schull *et al*, 2001). For instance, Bindman et al (1991) found, in their study of San Francisco General Hospital, 15% had left the hospital before being called for their examination and that "almost twice as many patients who left without being seen reported at follow-up that their pain or the seriousness of their problem was worse." (Dershewitze and Paichel (1986), Buesching et al (1985), Derlet and Nishio (1990) and Shaw et al (1990) provide related studies.)

In this description, it should be apparent that medical care is delivered through a network of service stations, and that there is potential for delay in multiple locations. It should also be apparent that emergency departments, as a system, closely interact with other systems. Emergency departments are part of the "emergency medical system" (EMS), which includes the management of responders (fire, paramedic, ambulance), and the distribution of service among hospitals (e.g., the routing of an ambulance to a particular hospital). Emergency departments (EDs) also interact with general hospital care, as a frequent source of queueing is the inability to place a patient in a hospital bed once treatment is completed in the ED. Less obviously, emergency departments interact with clinical care, as ED demand is a byproduct of the patient's ability to receive treatment through a primary care provider, access preventive care and adopt a healthy lifestyle.

1.2 Goal of Book

This book presents strategies, concepts and methods that can radically improve the delivery of health care by reducing delays. Our supposition is that much of the delay accepted by the public is both unnecessary and costly. Patients are harmed in the process of delay, not only through wasted time, but through unnecessary suffering, and through adverse medical outcomes. Health care providers are harmed through the added cost and reduced efficiency resulting from the complications of handling delayed patients. For these reasons, it is imperative for all providers to seek out and implement solutions that reduce delay.

The study of health care delay is an application of the discipline of queueing theory (i.e., the study of lines and waits, Hall, 1989). Health care is similar to other forms of queueing in these respects:

- The demand for service is in part predictable (e.g., result of time-of-day patterns) and in part random.
- Health services require coordination of multiple resources, such as physicians, medications, and diagnostic equipment.
- Services are provided in multiple steps, through a network of services, with the attendant issues of "grid lock" and "bottlenecks."
- Delays can be reduced through careful forecasting, scheduling, process improvement and information management.

In these respects, reducing health care delays is similar to the efficient coordination of work in a factory. But health care has unique features, which demand specialized methods and research, as presented in this book.

- Services can usually only be provided when the patient is physically present (unlike a piece of work that can be dropped off and picked up later), which makes rapid service particularly important.
- A patient awaiting treatment may require significant continuing care (thus, waits translate into demand for more work).
- The outcome of the service – including survival, recovery time, and suffering -- is adversely affected by waits.
- Schedules and plans are likely to be disrupted due to the arrival of critical patients, who can both require an exceptional amount of attention, and be exceptionally urgent.
- A patient's condition may independently change while waiting and require more or different care.

Foremost, however, health care is a system that can be improved through a better understanding of the system components and their relationships to each other, as will be discussed in the following section.

1.3 Modeling Health Care as a System

As should be apparent from the prior sections, EDs are but one component of the entire health care system, which might be better characterized as a system of systems, as described below.

1.3.1 Macro System

The macro system, depicted in Figure 1-1, encompasses the set of activities that affect a person's well being, from birth to death. From the macro perspective an individual only leaves the health care system at the end of life because he or she is constantly making decisions and engaging in activities that affect his or her health, whether or not under the direct care of a health-care provider.

Figure 1-1 portrays six states of being, reflecting one's state of health, and reflecting whether (and for what purpose) one is present at a health care facility. The state of recuperation, for instance, is a period of recovery spent outside of health facilities (typically at home), with diminished health and likely under the supervision of a physician (necessitating occasional post-care visits).[1]

Broadly speaking, the goals of the macro system are simple:

- Maximize the years from birth to death (length of life).
- Maximize the proportion of one's life spent in the "well" state.
- Maximize the quality of life when not in the well state.

Reducing patient delay and improving patient flow accomplish these macro goals by: (1) improving access to care, we increase expected length of life; (2) minimizing the length of time spent in undesirable states (e.g., at a health care facility awaiting treatment, undergoing treatment or recuperating from treatment); and (3) reducing waiting time until treatment, we improve quality of life when not well.

By improving access to care, we also hope to minimize the frequency by which we enter into the undesirable states (e.g., minimize dotted line transitions shown in Figure 1-1, such as becoming ill or being readmitted for new treatment after beginning recuperation) and maximize the likelihood of transitioning to a desirable state (e.g., bold line transitions, such as becoming well after being ill). More broadly, personal health is optimized through an inter-related set of actions over the course of one's life, some of which are the consequence of health care delay, and some of which lead to changes in health care delay by changing societal demand for health services (Table 1-1).

[1] The model is a simplification as it does not explicitly account for co-morbidities. For certain chronic conditions, the patient may never be cured, but achieve an improved state of wellness, and patients may be cured of some conditions but not others.

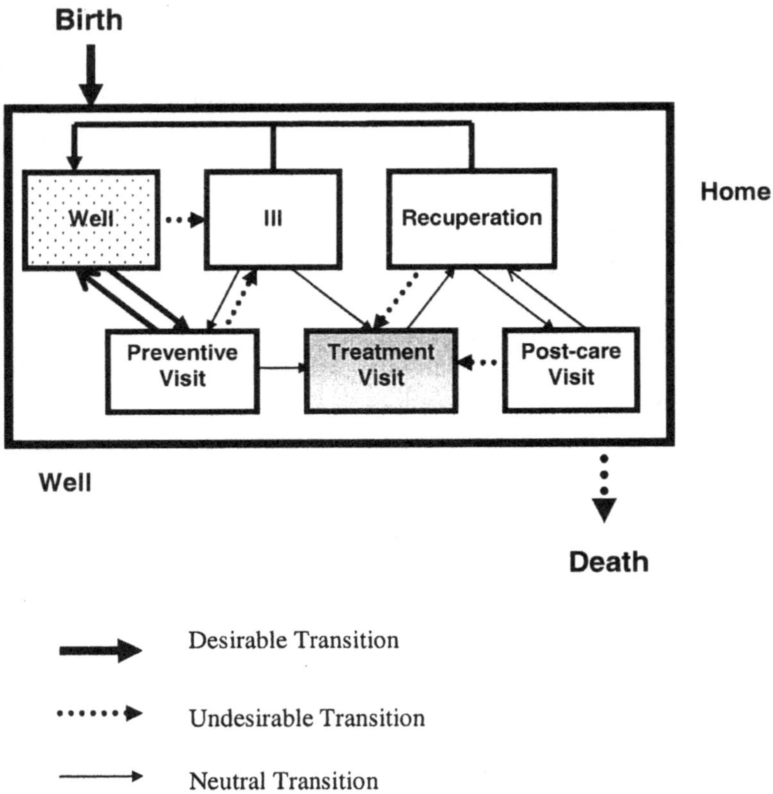

Figure 1-1. The Macro Health System

Table 1-1. Goals and Actions to Improve Macro Health

State	Goal	Actions	Examples
Well	Maximize time in state Minimize likelihood of presentinig well	Minimize Exposure, Personal Lifestyle, Reduce Societal Risks, self awareness of symptoms	Clean water and safe housing; stop smoking; no exposure to violence; patient education
Ill	Minimize time until well or treatment	Self awareness of symptoms, self care when appropriate	Patient education; non-prescription medication
Recuperation	Minimize time until well; Minimize likelihood of relapse	Home care, increase compliance; medication	Home nursing services; improved discharge instructions and assessment prior to discharge
Preventive Visit	Timely access to primary care Maximize likelihood of detection Apply appropriate care	Improve patient flow, apply appropriate diagnostics and preventive measures	Optimized appointments; apply appropriate tests based on risk factors; vaccinate on schedule
Treatment Visit	Timely access and minimimum length of stay Successful treatment or medications	Improve patient flow, correct diagnosis, apply appropriate medical care	Optimized scheduling; apply appropriate care
Post-treatment Visit	Timely access to care Apply appropriate care	Improve patient flow, apply appropriate medical care	Optimized appointments; apply approprate care

1.3.2 The Regional Health System

While the macro system represents the state of individual health, the regional system portrays the organizational and functional relationships among health care processes. This is invariably a hierarchy, beginning with primary care providers, through private practices and local clinics; moving to secondary care providers, through community hospitals; and then moving to tertiary providers, through regional medical centers (some highly specialized quaternary care is only available at a few national centers). As the geographical scale becomes larger, increasingly specialized care becomes available, a consequence of scale economies and a consequence of aggregated patient demand. On the other end of the spectrum, more routine care is conveniently obtained from primary care providers. The primary, secondary and tertiary providers are augmented by ancillary services, such as MRI centers, laboratories or dialysis facilities, which may support multiple providers (again influenced by scale economies); continuing care facilities, such as nursing homes; or, on a more basic scale, pharmacies.

Many variations exist within this general framework, which has evolved over time as more specialized treatments have become available, health care plans have changed, costs have changed and people have become more mobile. On one hand, by creating multiple layers of care, some delays are inevitably created due to increasing difficulty of access. On the other hand, without multiple layers, some types of specialty care would not be available at all due to insufficiently trained care-givers or simply cost. Yet it is clear that the regional/national system should be designed with three (somewhat conflicting) goals in mind:

- Minimizing the cost of providing desired services.
- Maximizing convenience and access to services that individuals need.
- Maximizing the likelihood of a positive health outcome from service.

Reducing health care delay contributes to all three goals by: (1) removing inefficiencies in the provision of services, thus reducing cost, (2) providing timely access to the services people need, and (3) reducing waits for needed services.

It should be recognized that the regional health system is in part the result of deliberate planning (e.g., design of the emergency medical system and designation of trauma centers), in part due to happenstance (e.g., where hospitals happened to develop many years ago), in part due to market pressures (e.g., competition for patients among facilities and health plans), and in part due to factors that originate from outside the region (e.g., regulations, medical discoveries, and medical training). Thus, it would be impossible to fully optimize such a system, though it might be steered in a desirable direction.

1.3.3 Health Care Center

The center is a grouping of geographically proximate facilities under the management of one organization. At a minimum, this entails two or more interacting departments, each with a distinct function (e.g., a laboratory and an outpatient clinic). At a maximum, this could encompass a larger tertiary care medical center with dozens of departments.

A health care center operates as a system of interacting departments, which must be coordinated through the flow of patients, specimens, employees, information, materials and pharmaceuticals. The center leadership, facility design, organizational design, employee training and recruitment are all important factors. Centers can sometimes represent enormous multi-billion dollar investments, and are frequently judged based on standards of financial return, quality of care and medical outcomes. Patient flow is particularly important for centers, as flow from department to department needs coordination; otherwise delays at the interfaces can be significant. During a typical center visit, the patient may separately encounter waits for these services:

- Information collection as part of admission
- Diagnostics and examinations

- Procedures, surgeries and therapies
- Education
- Rehabilitation and recuperation
- Transportation between departments
- Discharge processes

In the background, patients may be delayed waiting for ancillary services, many of which are invisible to patients:

- Transfer of medical records
- Transfer and analysis of laboratory specimens
- Filling prescriptions
- Housekeeping to prepare rooms for new patients
- Communication among departments, scheduling and decision-making in preparation for patient arrivals
- Movement and availability of wheel chairs, gurneys, and other portable equipment
- Completion of required paperwork for internal or governmental use.

Thus, patient delays depend in part how he or she physically flows through the center, and in part on how information, equipment and other objects flow through the center.

In summary, the system for managing patient flows in a center should be designed and operated to achieve these goals:

- Minimizing waits as patients transition from department to department.
- Achieving a high level of synchronization among patients, employees and resources, so that services begin promptly on patient arrival and are provided with high efficiency.
- Identifying and resolving system level bottlenecks that impede the flow of patients.

These goals can only be achieved through effective coordination and communication, combined with constant attention to patient service.

1.3.4 Department

The department is the most microscopic of the systems we consider. It represents a unit within a larger center oriented toward performing a single function, or a group of closely related functions. Examples include the ED, surgery, radiology, or an inpatient ward. A department could also be ancillary, such as house-keeping, medical records, or transportation. For the patient, departments typically have clearly defined points of entry and points of exit, which may be time-stamped and correspond to responsibilities for care. Like whole centers, departments are often judged based on financial return. Medical outcomes and quality of care, however, are often more difficult to assess at the department level, as these depend on the totality of service provided by the center over the entire duration of stay.

With respect to patient flow, departments must both support the mission of the center as a whole through effective coordination, and be effective in their own right. Neither should a department create unnecessary delay within, nor should they impose delay elsewhere (e.g., delays in accepting patients, or by failing to prepare a patient for transfer when he or she is needed elsewhere). The employees must be trained and rewarded for the priority of minimizing delays through prompt service; they should employ realistic appointment systems; they should ensure proper staffing, and advance planning prior to the arrival of patients.

Later in this chapter we will use a case study to explore, in depth, patient flow issues at the department and center levels.

1.4 Highly Congested Systems

Another unusual, though not entirely unique, property of health care systems is extreme congestion, meaning that patients have a high likelihood of encountering delay. In part, this is due to inattention to patient flow issues. However, it is also partly due to the financial structure of health care.

Again, we turn to EDs. For major public hospitals in particular, demand for service can be so large that the system rarely empties of waiting patients, either because the ED itself has insufficient capacity, or because the hospital's wards are not absorbing the inflow of patients, thus causing spillback into the ED. For this reason, contrary to conventional queueing models, the system arrival rate exceeds the system service capacity over extended periods – perhaps perpetually. As a result, the system resides in a state of dysfunctional equilibrium, where the only thing that keeps queues from growing without bound is the propensity of some patients to leave without being seen when waits are intolerable (Figure 1-2), some of whom may return later, possibly in a worsened state, and some of whom will never receive needed treatment. At times when waits become particularly long, more patients will opt to leave without being seen, either immediately at time of arrival, or subsequently after becoming frustrated with the wait, bringing waits back into balance. When waits become shorter, fewer patients leave, causing waits to gradually build again.

Highly congested queues exist in other contexts, such as Immigration/Naturalization Service Offices, Motor Vehicle Departments and public housing. A common characteristic is that the service provider has limited economic incentive to add capacity (because it is operated at a loss), or re-price service (because EMTALA prohibits financial screening). In fact, in some circumstances, the attraction of "latent demand" (customers who would otherwise leave) may mean that an increase in capacity causes cost to increase, but only slightly reduces average waits. To draw an analogy, expansion of highway capacity may have only small effects on congestion as overall traffic volumes increase.

Another important consideration in highly congested queueing systems is degradation in the ability to deliver quality service. Crowding in waiting rooms and treatment areas, loss in privacy, delays in accessing needed equipment, and delays in providing medication can all add to patient suffering. Continual queueing de-motivates employees, as no matter how hard they work patients will still be queued. And service will be unproductive, as patients must be shuttled in and out of treatment rooms as they wait for test results or resources. Crowding can also lead to diversion of ambulances to more distant hospitals, slowing the time until patients can be treated (ACEP, 1999; Litvak *et al*, 2001). For all of these reasons, it is impossible to fully address problems in patient flows without considering remedies for health care finance and pricing, topics that go beyond the scope of this book.

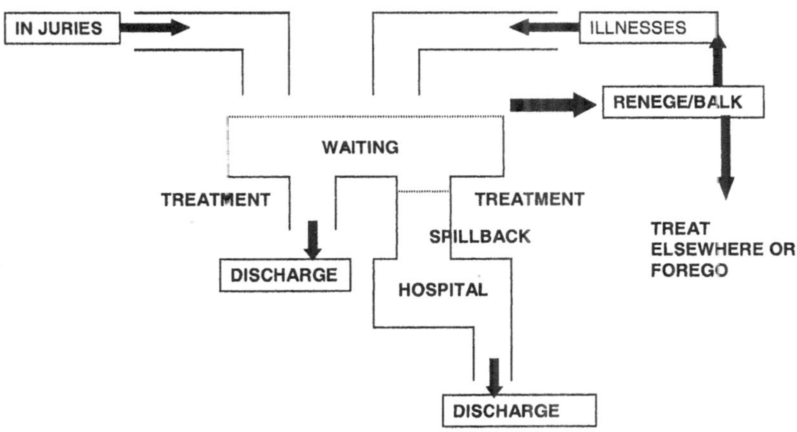

Figure 1-2. Highly Congested System Creates Spillback and Patients Who Leave Without Being Seen

1.5 Methods

Health care delays can be reduced through awareness of best practices, application of quantitative methods and a commitment to change. Organizations such as the Institute for Healthcare Improvement (IHI, 1996) and the American College of Emergency Physicians (ACEP, 2002b) have assembled numerous ideas for improvement. These and other new concepts are captured in this book. Most generally, the solutions to delay problems come in three forms (Hall, 1989):

Alter the service process: through scheduling, coordination, process changes, communication, automation, etc., increase the capacity for serving customers, and increase the synchronization between capacity and customer arrival patterns.

Alter the arrival process: through appointments, pricing, information, education programs, etc., influence the patterns by which patients present for service, improving the alignment between capacity and demand.

Alter the queueing process: through triage, moving waiting from the health care facility to the home, redesign of waiting areas, changes in prioritization, etc., ensure that the adverse consequences of waiting are minimized.

These three steps form a hierarchy, as the first priority should be optimizing service to meet the needs of patients; when this is infeasible or uneconomical, explore changes to patient patterns; and, if all else fails, focus on managing queues to maximum efficiency.

Within this chapter, we provide basic methods of industrial engineering that can be used to develop all three types of patient flow solutions. Our principal focus here is process planning (representing the steps needed to deliver service and the interactions between process steps), and performance measurement. These techniques are widely used to improve the performance of manufacturing, distribution and transportation systems, and are emerging as promising approaches to improve health care.

Process planning is an approach for documenting the steps entailed in delivering patient care (or an ancillary process), and redesigning the process for improved efficiency. We will show how to plan a series of process for patient service, and we will show how to plan for the physical movement of patients. Process planning can be an effective first step toward change as it can reveal the weaknesses and strengths of the current system, and identify methods of improvement.

Performance measurement entails identifying the system goals and the measures by which attainment of the goals are judged. To be effective, performance measurement should be embedded in the continuing operation of the system, so that key decisions are influenced and evaluated, according to established objectives (JCAHO Standard LD.3.11 recommends that management identify critical patient flow processes as well as monitor relevant measures.) Performance measurement should also be transparent to all involved, so that they can witness how their actions affect the overall performance of the system, so that they can be alerted to problems when they occur, and so that they are recognized for their accomplishments. Example measures include waiting time (by step or location), number of patients waiting, number of patients served, patient satisfaction, utilization of resources and costs. Performance measurement is ultimately useful as an approach for obtaining an accurate and meaningful picture of patient flow and helping determine where improvements can be made. Unfortunately, many hospitals have considerable difficulty making such measurements due to inadequate computer information systems or due to not having the financial resources to create and operate the necessary information system.

2. CASE STUDY: LOS ANGELES COUNTY HOSPITAL

The Los Angeles County/University of Southern California (LAC/USC) Hospital is used as a case study to demonstrate how the techniques of patient flow analysis can be used to create a system model of a center and its departments, and used to improve services (Belson et al, 2004). LAC/USC is a large urban health center serving a largely poor population. It is also the trauma center for central Los Angeles, with the busiest ED in the country, measured in admissions. Approximately 85% of the patients admitted to beds in the hospital enter through the ED.

LAC/USC, including the General Hospital (GH) and its allied Outpatient Department (OPD) and Community Health Centers (CHC), was studied as an integrated system, to identify bottlenecks and recommend improvements. This goal has been accomplished through a series of interviews with administration in 35 hospital departments, as well as focus groups with nurses, doctors, and analysts. Through these meetings we have documented the processes in place for resource scheduling, patient triage, and patient routing; and we have documented care-giver perceptions of critical issues and problems in serving patients.

Separately, we have obtained, reviewed and analyzed data sources to determine their usefulness for monitoring and evaluating patient flows. We have also performed sample analyses to demonstrate patterns of patient arrivals and interdepartmental flows.

These data sources were used to create process charts that show flows through the hospital as a whole, as well as flows within individual departments. Through our analysis of these charts, as well as our own observations, we developed a series of recommendations for improving patient flows within short-term and long-term time frames, with a focus on improving the coordination among hospital departments. Follow-up studies are in process, with focus on radiology and orthopedic surgery.

2.1 Process Map for Center and Aggregate Flows

Patient flow within the center can be viewed at several levels of detail. At the highest level, the center consists of four primary areas: Emergency, Inpatient, Outpatient and the Community Health Centers. Patients frequently move between them and some may visit all four in the course of a year. The patient flow and related costs are summarized in Table 1-2.

Table 1-2. Summary of Patient Workload (2003-04) and Costs

Area	Patients	Total Costs
Inpatient	40,000	475,000,000
Emergency	205,000	56,000,000
Outpatient	522,000	160,000,000
Total	749,000	691,000,000

Thus, the inpatient area serves relatively few patients but represents considerable cost. The emergency area serves five times as many patients, at 12% of the total inpatient cost. Some ED visits are brief and ambulatory while others entail complex trauma care prior to patients moving to an inpatient bed. Outpatient represents an even larger number of visits (about half of the total), with per patient costs similar to ED visits.

The ED is composed of three areas: 1050, 1060 and 1350. The 1350 is for the most critical patients and 1050 for the least critical or ambulatory patients. Inpatient areas in the GH are divided between surgery wards and other medical wards. The Outpatient Department (OPD) is composed of many clinics, each with a separate medical specialty.

The patient flow between areas is summarized in Figure 1-3, with more detail shown in Figure 1-4. In still more detail, important flows are shown for the General Hospital in Figure 1-5. In the following sections we will elaborate on patient flows, first illustrating processes that span departments, and then illustrating processes within departments. These descriptions are extracted from a much longer report (Belson et al, 2004) that provides detailed process maps for all of the major processes and departments in the center.

2.1.1 Service Process 1: Scheduling and Appointments

Patients begin their visit either as a scheduled or an unscheduled patient. Unscheduled patient visits include:

- Walk into the emergency department (these ambulatory patients represent the most common path into the hospital).
- Ambulance delivers patient at the emergency department.
- Walk into certain open clinics in the outpatient department that do not require an advance appointment.

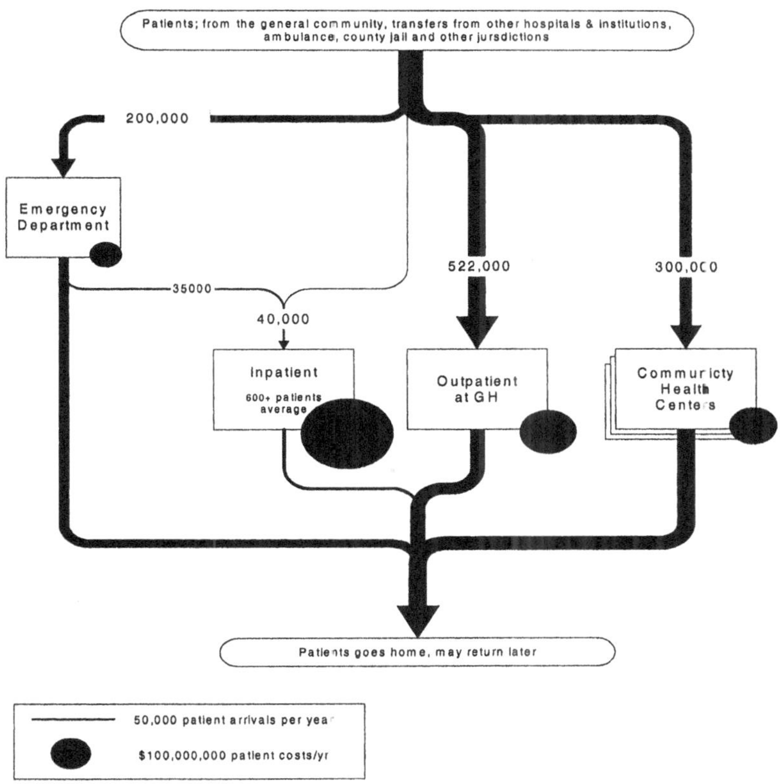

Figure 1-3. Overall Patient Flow and Costs

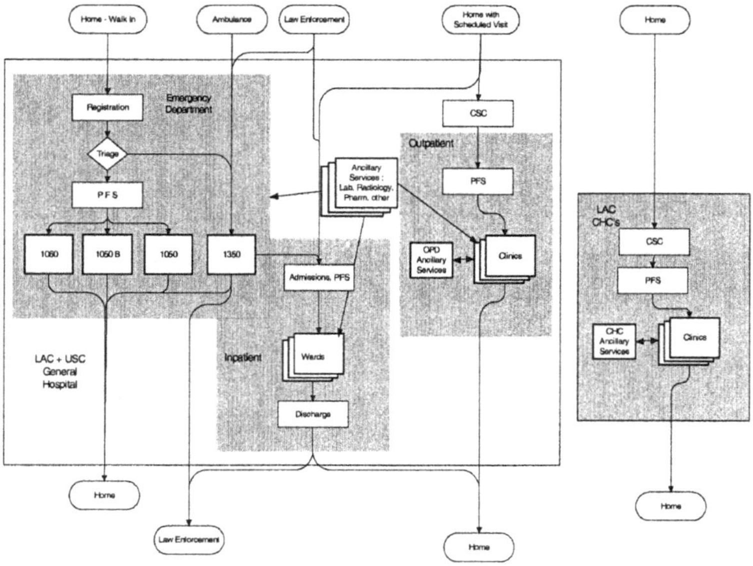

Figure 1-4. Flow Between LAC+USC Units

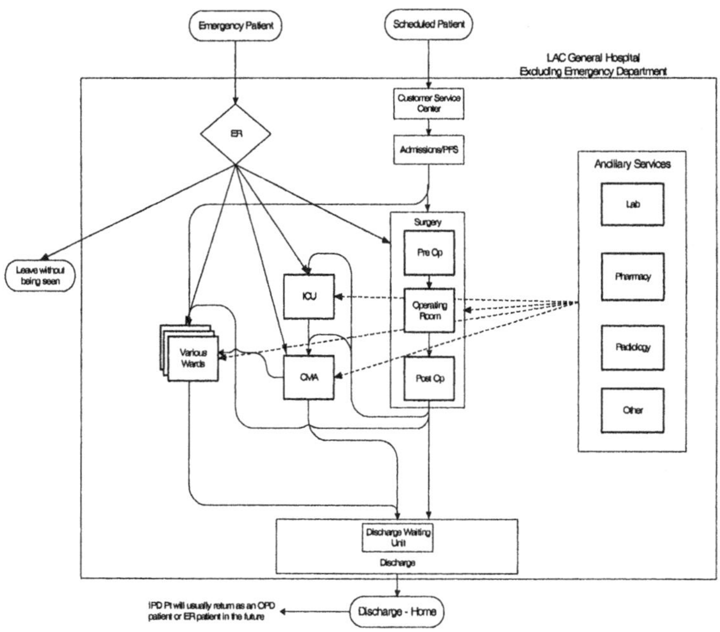

Figure 1-5. Intra Hospital Patient Flow

Scheduled patient visits include:

- Scheduled clinic visits which are arranged through the hospital's Customer Service Center (CSC) or the clinics themselves
- Appointments to an inpatient ward, such as scheduled day surgeries
- Scheduled returns to certain GH areas for visits of less than a day

The most common path into an inpatient bed is from the emergency area. This movement is recorded in the hospital's computer information system that is used throughout the hospital, which also tracks bed assignments and appointments.

2.1.2 Bed Management

Movement of patients from the emergency areas to inpatient beds is the responsibility of the Bed Control Unit (BCU). This is coordinated with the staff in the emergency room as well as the hospital wards. Moreover, the Nursing Department has assigned individuals to monitor bed availability; physicians are also consulted on the appropriateness of each movement. Therefore, the bed management process involves several jurisdictions and individuals. The bed control unit locates beds for ED patients based on diagnosis, and contacts the appropriate people in the ED and the wards as soon as a bed is made available. Information on bed availability and forthcoming discharges comes from the information system and informal communications among staff. The BCU staff has difficulty getting an overall picture of bed availability because they are not always told as soon as a bed is freed up, and because delays in housekeeping can hold up bed assignments.

An experienced patient flow manager, who is an Assistant Nursing Director, and other nurses who serve as census coordinators, walk the floors to assess the availability of beds resulting from discharging patients. The patient flow manager keeps a record of which patients are moved where and when. The manager walks through each ward and notes empty beds and potential discharges. After her rounds, she notifies the BCU of the results. She also calls up the Discharge Waiting Unit (DWU) to tell them whether any inpatients will be coming into their unit. This way she has discretion to send inpatients to the DWU and, in turn, make more beds available.

2.1.3 Discharge/Bed Preparation

Given the high percentage of beds occupied at all times, it is important to discharge patients as soon as possible. The GH has instituted several efforts to improve this aspect of patient flow, including creating committees charged with removing bottlenecks, implementing buffers between processes to reduce queuing, creating a housekeeping group specialized for making the rooms ready for new patients, and creating a discharge waiting room. The nursing staff records the availability of a bed within the information system, which provides automatic notification to housekeeping that a room needs to be cleaned, which then assigns cleaning staff. However, delays sometimes force nurses to clean rooms, and because there is some ambiguity as to when the cleaning is completed, there can be confusion as to when a new patient can be assigned to a bed.

2.1.4 Staffing

Nursing administration uses the number of patients and their levels of acuity in the various wards as a basis for its staffing decisions. Other than nursing, hospital staffing levels do not fluctuate greatly from day-to-day and are based on budgetary decisions concerning each functional area. A common issue is unfilled positions, as well as absenteeism.

The nursing organization is large; there are about 1,875 RNs and LVNs and a total of about 2,700 nurses. The director of nursing has a staffing office where they primarily accumulate the staffing information. Staffing, vacations and rotation are determined at the Nurse Manager level. The nursing department uses a computer system, which reports and records the daily staffing, but actual work schedules are largely planned manually. Staffing levels are based on an acuity system. A computer system processes acuity information on the mix of patients in each area and determines the desired level of staffing. Schedules for nurses are generally posted six weeks in advance but are adjusted more frequently. The staffing levels are fairly stable but the number of nurses available changes often – and is a major challenge. To manage the staff to patient ratio, which is monitored closely, there are several available options: (1) Overtime for nurses currently working, (2) Registry (the use of outside contractors), (3) Pool nurses, shared among departments, which is limited, (4) Close beds to reduce the requirement for staff.

2.1.5 Admission/Registration/PFS

A patient's entry to the hospital's data is recorded at a number of points for inpatients and outpatients. Generally this represents the entry of the patient into the information system to record a visit. Each patient is assigned a unique ID number (an "MRUN" number) on the initial visit that is used for all subsequent visits. Each visit of the patient is recorded as an "Account" in the information system.

Patient Financial Services (PFS) personnel are responsible for gathering information about the patient so that it can be reimbursed. They enter demographic data about a patient or "register" them in the system. If they detect an existing MRUN number, they locate it. If not, they generate a new one for the patient. PFS also explains financial obligations to patients.

PFS responsibilities are time consuming. They must get the general consent form completed for each patient, distribute brochures, work with triage nurses to complete patient registration, initiate the patient chart, complete a limited financial screening and provide insurance information. For outpatient areas, certain patients meet with PFS. They can determine PFS need by looking at the backside of the patient's ID card that they have received from a previous visit. Scheduled admissions and day surgery patients are financially screened by PFS prior to coming for surgery.

2.1.6 Transportation

LA County supplies patient transportation between the hospital and the outside by telephone requests by patients and by the hospital to the County's service, when the patients cannot provide it themselves. An internal transport unit sometimes supplies patient transportation by wheelchair or gurney within the hospital, but often nursing moves the patient when the transport group represents a delay. Transportation delays are common due to insufficient staffing and the difficulties in navigating through a crowded hospital. Elevator waits can also be long. These delays create a cascading effect, and have a significant impact on surgery, radiology and bed utilization, as resources can be left idle while waiting for patients, or because appointment systems cannot be followed due to delays.

2.1.7 Medical Records

Hospital Information Management (HIM) is responsible for storage and access to patient medical records (charts). They store a large volume of paper records in the hospital basement and use long-term storage off site. LAC/USC is moving to a more digital system with images of records and transcribed doctor notes. This should dramatically change the physical logistic issues, as well as provide more timely access to records, which can in turn reduce delays in surgery and other locations.

HIM has several functions: maintenance of medical records for each patient, assuring their completeness, copying the chart for several types of requests, and alerting clinicians for missing chart elements. They also make sure that the records follow professional and legal guidelines. They store about 1,000,000 charts at the hospital (basement) and 2,500,000 at an offsite warehouse. More information is stored in the paper chart than in the information system. The chart has the patient's laboratory results, radiology results, X-ray results, etc. These are all bound in the patient's chart folder.

The Central Discharge Unit (CDU) clerk checks through the information system three times a day for discharges. After the discharges have been identified, a clerk from the CDU visits the wards to pick up the patients' charts. This is done between 3.30 – 4.00 pm and 7.30 – 8.00 pm. The CDU keeps track of the records of the inpatients, scheduled admissions and day surgeries.

All charts go through a "coding" process where data are added to the record for statistical and research purposes. The next stage is "abstracting" information, such as length of state, the Rx, tests ordered, physician attending, etc. This is done within 24 hours of the time the chart is brought to the CDU. If a chart is deficient, then it is stacked on the shelves in the CDU for the physician to complete. Also, the HIM staff visits the wards three times a week to identify data deficiencies before a patient is discharged, reducing the time wasted in waiting for a physician to complete the chart.

Patients who have transferred from other hospitals have a copy of their chart brought to LAC GH. This copy is included in the chart at the GH. When they return to their initial clinic or hospital, GH sends a copy of their new GH records along with the patient. They also receive about 3,000-3,500 requests a month from patients requesting a copy of their records.

2.2 Flows for Key Departments

At this point we turn to patient flows within individual departments. Several key departments are used for illustration: (1) Emergency, (2) Radiology, (3) Pharmacy, (4) Laboratory and (5) Surgery

2.2.1 Emergency Department

The ED is organized into three areas: Major medical/trauma (Room 1350), Minor Medical/Trauma (Room 1060) and ED Walk-in (Room 1050). The room numbers are used as the departmental identifier. Each has a separate physical area (Figure 1-6 and Figure 1-7). Each also serves a different set of patients.

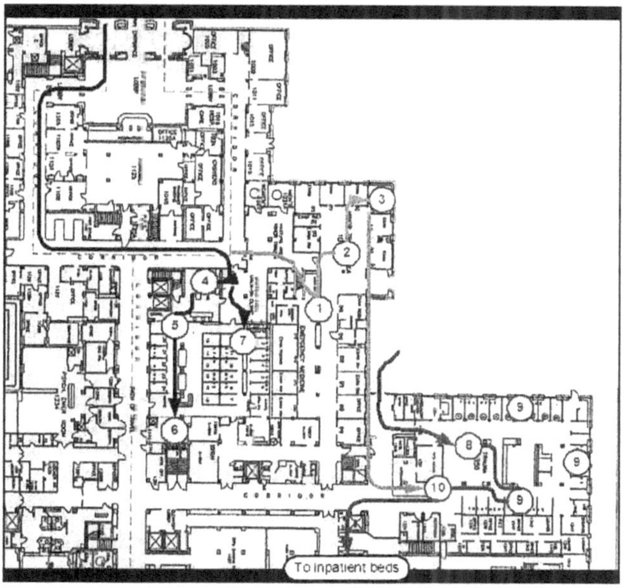

Figure 1-6. Department of Emergency Medicine Patient Areas.

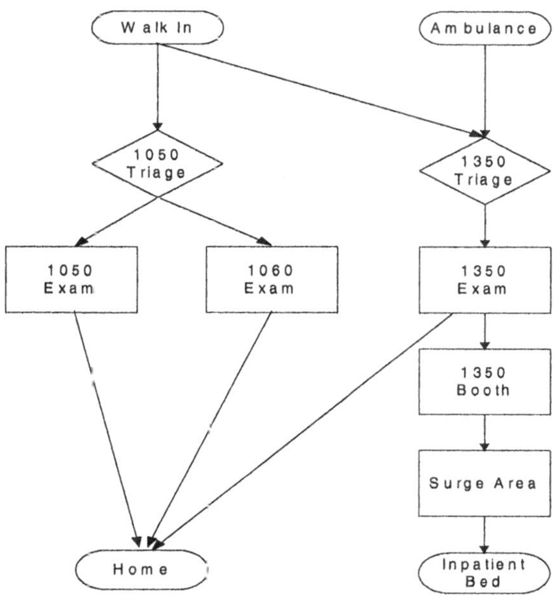

Figure 1-7. Typical Patient Flows in ER

When a patient enters the ED, he or she first sees a triage nurse, who determines the severity of the patient's condition. Immediately afterwards, the PFS assigns an MRUN number if the patient is new to the hospital. With the help of the patient's name, date of birth and mother's maiden name, PFS checks in the information system for previous medical records. In some cases a duplicate ID is created, but this is rare. Patients generally have previously received an ID card, which shows their MRUN number and their financial situation regarding hospital reimbursement.

The ED is extremely busy and crowded, and suffers long waits. This is due in part to waits for admission to inpatient beds. When inpatient beds are unavailable the ED patients often must wait in ED beds until then can be moved ("borders"). Also, processes are slowed in ED due to limited accessibility of certain ancillary services. Radiology, for example, is on a different floor and ED patients must sometimes be moved up to that floor for diagnostic services and then moved back down to the ED.

After the patient's condition has been stabilized, each patient is assigned one PFS worker who asks questions, enters data into the information system, takes printouts and puts this info next to the patient's bed for the doctor to see them. If the patient needs to be admitted into an inpatient bed, he/she is seen again by PFS. At the end of the ED visit, or if additional service is needed, such as admission to an inpatient bed, then the patient receives "financial screening" from PFS.

The 1350 area includes emergency admitting on a 24-hour, seven days a week, basis. It includes trauma care and services for other acute patients. When the other two ER areas are closed, it serves ambulatory patients as well.

Trauma patients are the most severe of the emergency patients that come into 1350. Most are victims of automobile accidents or violent crimes such as gunshots. Trauma represents about 7,500 patients per year. Virtually all trauma patients eventually become inpatients and represent a significant proportion of the total inpatient population. It has been growing at about 200 patients a year. The 1350 ER has one of the largest trauma centers in the USA. The trauma staff includes about eight faculty, nine residents and five physician assistants.

In the center of the 1350 area is the C-booth that serves critical trauma patients (Figure 1-8). The C-booth is a central resuscitation area that can hold four critical patients at one time. Surrounding the C-booth area are about 22 patient care booths that are used for less critical patients. When necessary, additional patients are handled on gurneys and chairs in the same physical area. Surges in demand occur, perhaps several days each month, when the capacity of the booths is exceeded.

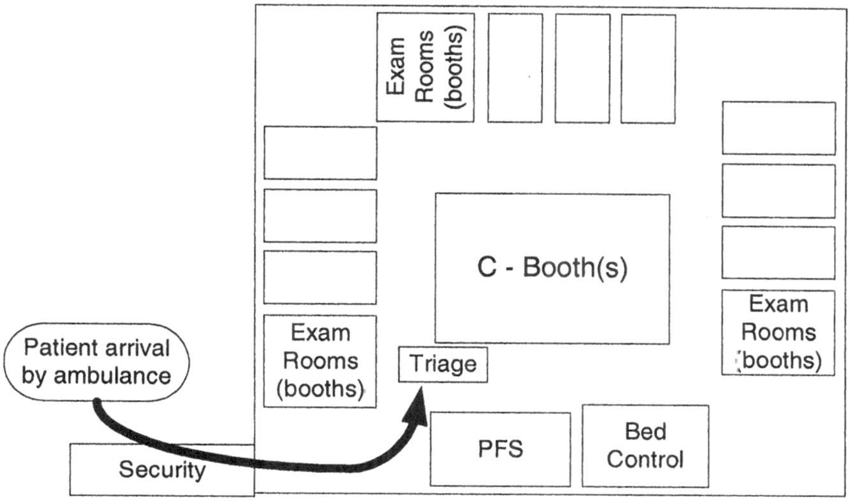

Figure 1-8. 1350 Area

The 1060 area includes minor trauma care on an ambulatory basis. This area is a sort of "mini ER" that focuses on skin and bone emergencies, lacerations, boils, fractures, sutures, etc. Patients cannot come directly into 1060 as they need to be referred from either 1050 or 1350. These patients have undergone triage in one of these two areas. However, registration takes place in 1060. There is a special hold area in 1060 for ambulatory patients. From here, patients either go home or go to an inpatient bed.

1060 handles a large volume throughout the year since it is open 24x7 while 1050 is not. It handles the most ED patients: 150 to 200 patients per day and about 15% to 20%, or 20 to 30 patients, go to inpatient beds.

The 1050 area is for walk-in patients that believe that they need immediate clinical help (Figure 1-9). Everyone goes through a common initial meeting with an RN for triage at a window and then may be seen right away or asked to wait or sent to 1350 if very critical. This initial window triage is followed by an additional triage with a nurse. If required, the patient will be moved to a booth in 1050A for a meeting with a doctor who will diagnose the patient and provide orders. Some patients are admitted from 1050 to inpatient beds, but this is relatively rare.

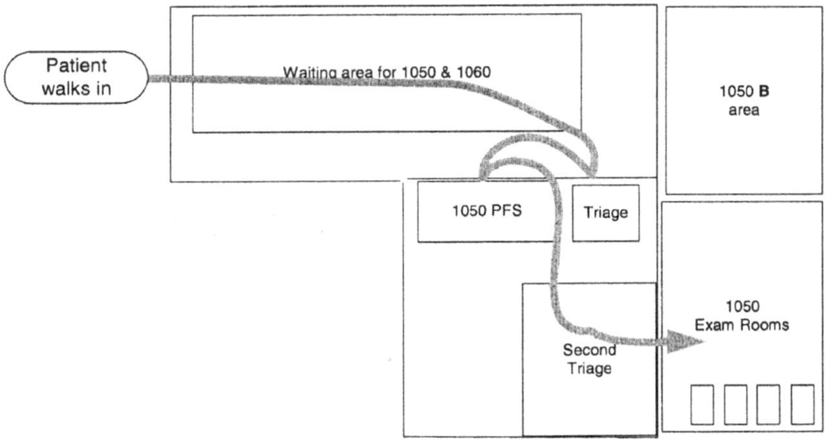

Figure 1-9. 1050 & 150B Areas

There are about 15 individual examination booths in 1050. Doctors see two or more patients per hour, and patients spend about 10 to 15 minutes per booth visit. A wait can be as much as eight hours. A standard triage form is used where criticality is determined as one of five levels, which defines the path of care to be provided.

The 1050 patient volume is about 150 patients per day. About 10% to 15% leave without being seen. About 1% of the 1050 arrivals are transferred to other inpatient services on the same day, about 10% are admitted to an inpatient bed and the remainder go home after being seen, some with an appointment for a return. If a 1050 patient can't be seen by the end of the day, they are sent to 1350.

Patients are sent to exam booths to meet with a doctor and doctors select which patient to see next. Doctors can select from the queue if they wish. A separate area (1050B) is for return and/or "Fast Track" patients. It's a type of primary care clinic where a patient returns for ongoing care or medication, such as follow-up for a broken limb. About 5% of 1050B patients are for medication refills. A Physician Assistant (PA), rather than an MD, staffs 1050B.

2.2.2 Radiology

Clinicians generate the patient flow into the radiology department. The clinician's orders are delivered to the radiology department much before the patient arrives. The various facilities in the radiology department include diagnostic X-ray, nuclear medicine, diagnostic ultrasound, off-site MRI, CT scan, various interventions and more. In addition to the services on the 3rd floor, three X-ray rooms are allotted to the ground floor ED. There is also a portable X-ray machine placed in the 1350 ER, which can X-ray the body parts that are most likely to need X-rays. For specialized X-rays, patients are taken to the 3rd floor. OPD also has its own radiology department.

Separate scheduling systems are used for each of the radiology services. Outpatient scheduling is separate from inpatient. Priority is given to ED patients then outpatients. Since inpatients are available for a greater time period they are given a lower priority. To avoid long delays arising from the radiology department waiting for an inpatient to be brought in, they call more inpatients than required. The inpatients are served on a first-come, first-served basis. The radiology waiting area is open and the inpatients and outpatients must wait along with the jail patients.

Figure 1-8 provides a detailed process map for the flow of inpatients through radiology (separate process maps have been created for outpatients and ED patients). Key steps in the chart include: (1) writing physician order, (2) review of request within radiology department, and review of available slots, (3) placing order for patient transport, (4) waiting for service upon arrival in radiology, (5) completion of scan, (6) transport of patient back to a ward, and (7) review of results. Through review of the full set of radiology processes, we have identified a set of bottlenecks and problems, which we are in the process of resolving.

- Out patients arrive hours before their appointment time, hoping to be served earlier. Thus, waiting rooms are full and the patient spends a longer time at the hospital
- Rather than send orders, physicians come to the 3rd floor (where the radiology department is located) to hand over the paper requisitions and check with the radiologist whether all the required information is present on the requisition sheet.
- Since there are many residents, considerable time is spent in teaching tasks that slow the availability of results.
- Staffing shortages and insufficiently experienced staff create idle equipment, even when there are patients waiting.
- Time between a doctor's order for a test and receipt of the results is lengthy.
- Patients are sometimes admitted to wards to gain priority over out patients for tests

We have found in radiology, and in other departments, that creating a process map, such as the one in Figure 1-10, helps reveal the bottlenecks to all participants, and leads to creative solutions.

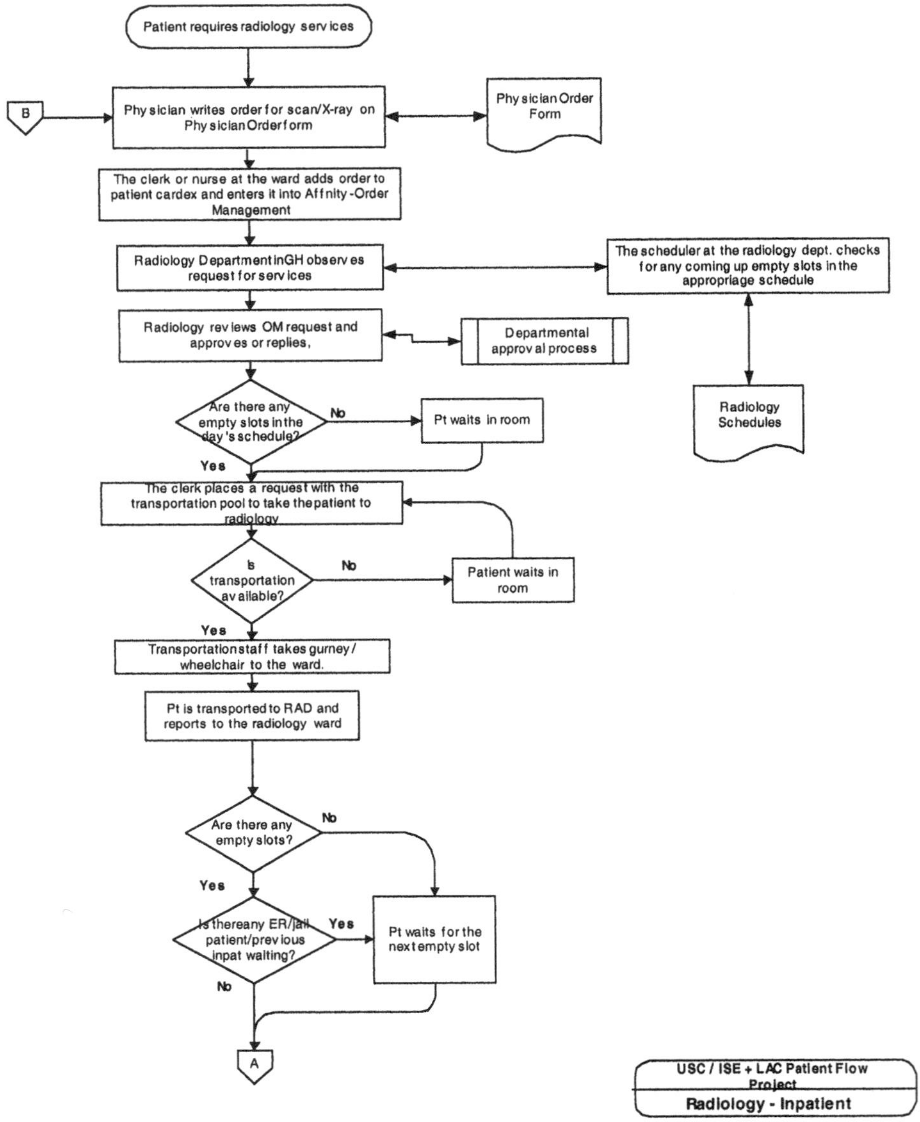

Figure 1-10a. Process Map for Inpatient Radiology, Part 1

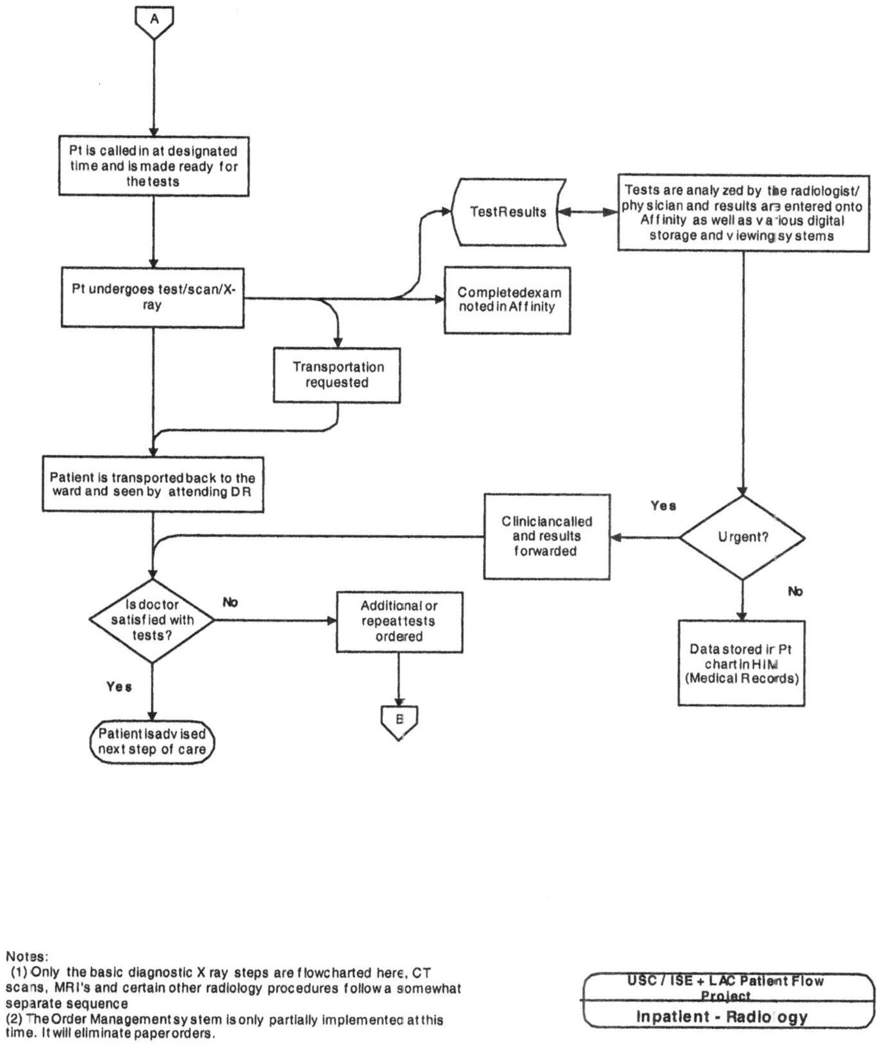

Figure 1-10b. Process Map for Inpatient Radiology, Part 2

2.2.3 Pharmacy

Pharmacy services are provided inpatients, outpatients and patient discharges. The GH has a 1st floor pharmacy, which operates 24x7; a 24x7 8th floor pharmacy, which is for inpatients, and an outpatient pharmacy in the OPD building. The first floor pharmacy also serves outpatients when the OPD pharmacy is closed and provides medications for patients when they are discharged.

The 1st floor pharmacy fills about 900 prescriptions per day, about 700 during the day shift. They get some prescriptions by fax but most are on paper. A ward nurse, a patient or a patient's family, brings prescriptions to the pharmacy. Refill orders are received by phone. The 8th floor pharmacy fills cassettes, which are one day supplies for inpatient beds. Many orders are received from wards to this pharmacy by fax.

Patients don't pay at the pharmacy in advance for their medicine. After the order is ready, patients are given a cash receipt and are sent to the cashier to pay. After payment, they come to pick up the medicines. Some are given a mail-in envelope for payment.

Pharmacy staff and other personnel noted bottlenecks and problems:

- Staffing shortages and insufficiently experienced staff
- Waiting for medications was said to contribute to delays in discharging patients from hospital inpatient beds.
- On IPD discharge the doctor is supposed to provide prescriptions in advance, on the day before, but they often don't write it until their morning rounds.

2.2.4 Lab

The GH lab provides a centralized service for a wide variety of tests. The primary flow is: specimens, mostly blood in tubes, are received in the lab area by pneumatic tube, hand carried to a receiving window or gathered by an outside transportation contractor to gather samples from CHC locations and various satellite locations. An initial set of steps involves receiving the material and paperwork; a second phase involves organizing the samples (for which they have automated equipment) and then doing the test itself. The tubes are generally bar coded and other information is printed as text on the tube.

The exact volume of work was said to be unknown, but in the central lab they do about 1,000 chemistry tests a day and about 700 of other tests a day. About 200 people work in the department, with about 80 test technicians and a number of open positions. The lab has a modern information system that is linked to the information system. Electronic orders from doctors are received through an order management system.

Some "outlying" lab people work in the ED and elsewhere, which do some of the receiving tasks. Lab turn-around time was targeted at one hour for stat work (30-40% of orders) and four hours for routine work. Results are often delivered electronically and paper results are sent to medical records for the patient's chart (seven days later for inpatients). Doctors must take the initiative to check lab results, so there is no certainty that they have been checked.

2.2.5 Surgery

The hospital has about 20 surgery suites (operating rooms) on several floors of the hospital. The exact number of rooms used on any day varies with staffing availability. Surgeries are of three basic types: emergency, inpatient and outpatient (or day surgeries). Non-emergency surgeries are scheduled one day in advance with a homegrown stand-alone computer system and priorities are set by various physicians responsible for their respective specialty. Surgery days are blocked out for various specialties on a two-week rotation pattern. Thus, a room is scheduled weeks in advance for a specific type of surgery (such as "cardiac") and may not be available for that type of surgery again for days or weeks. Doctors from each specialty define the sequence of patients within their specialty. Queues for each specialty may be weeks or months in length.

On the day before each surgery, the surgeon estimates duration of surgery, which is used to schedule the next day's use of the operating rooms. Surgeries often take longer than their estimated time. As a result, the last scheduled surgery for the day often is not done on the day scheduled. This missed surgery might not be done the next day due to what has already been blocked out and the surgery may be scheduled for sometime later in the month. This practice sometimes prolongs the number of days an inpatient occupies a bed, because an inpatient must stay in the GH until their surgery is completed. In the case of outpatients, they must then go home and come back for their re-scheduled surgery and repeat their pre op visit. Also, some scheduled surgery patients do not show up for their appointment. If a patient doesn't turn up at the scheduled time then another patient must be identified and prepared for surgery, which results in a delay.

The GH's 20 OR suites handle about 28 – 30 surgeries per day, out of which about 35% are outpatient and 65% inpatient. They generally use three ORs in the evening – one for red blanket patient (trauma), other two for scheduled or ED surgeries. A "white board" on the surgery floor lists pending emergency surgeries throughout the day.

Bottlenecks related to surgery include:

- Inpatient beds unavailable, which cause a back up of patients completing surgery.
- Scheduling which does not fully utilize the available surgery time.
- Patients for day surgeries who do not show up as expected.
- Incorrect or unavailable ancillary service results (Radiology, lab reports, Medical records).
- Staffing shortages resulting in fewer rooms or services available.
- Frequent rescheduling and bumping of surgeries for a variety of causes.
- Late start times and an early shift cutoff time.
- Slow clean-up between surgeries.
- Delays in transport service and waits for elevators.
- Allocation of rooms to specialties may not match the relative demand among specialties. Paperwork is not always available or correctly completed on time.

3. EVALUATION AND IMPROVEMENT STRATEGIES

We now turn to some of the methods for measuring system performance. It is important for every patient flow improvement project to develop quantitative measures of both problems and successes, to guide implementation of changes, and to create ongoing monitoring systems to make continual improvements. Unfortunately, desired data are not always collected, and are frequently not presented in a meaningful form. In this section we describe some of the more important measurements for patient flow, and describe our challenges in obtaining data.

3.1 Understanding Patient Arrival Patterns

Patient arrival patterns drive systems for scheduling staff and other resources. The patterns are somewhat predictable, even for the unscheduled ED. Hospital scheduling controls most of the other arrivals. The following time of day graphs for the 1350 and 1060 ER areas (Figures 1-11 and 1-12) show a strong peak early in the day (particularly 9-11:00 a.m.). The arrival pattern is somewhat different in 1350, with a peak in the evening hours, from about 5:00 p.m. until 1:00 a.m., which may reflect the severity and incidence of injuries resulting from accidents and violence.

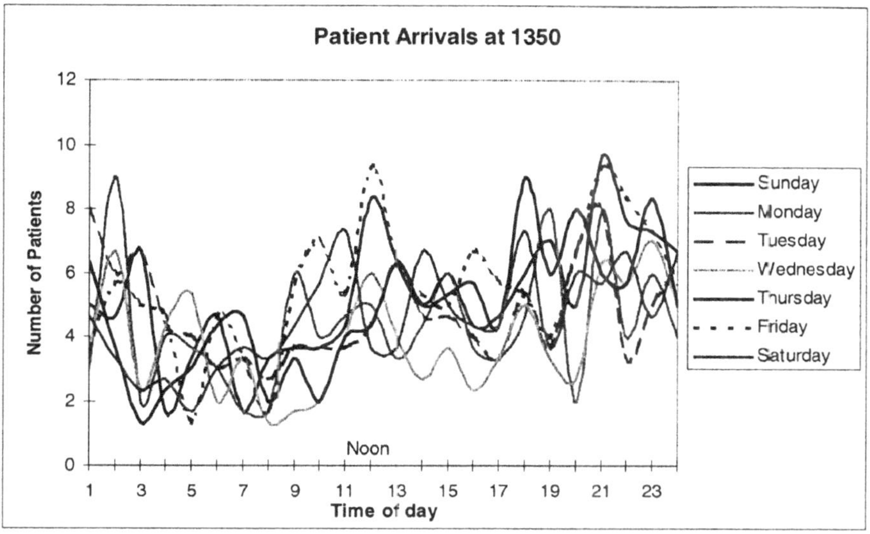

Figure 1-11. Hourly Arrivals in 1350

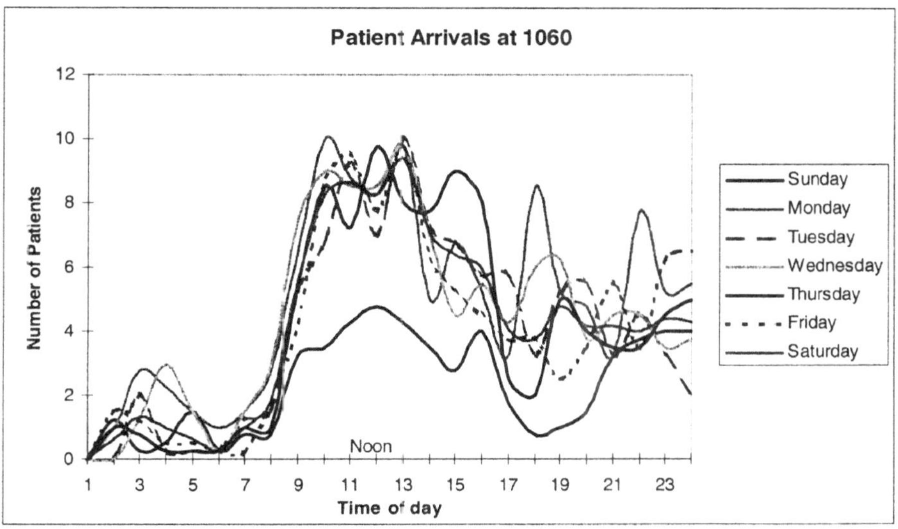

Figure 1-12. Hourly Arrivals in 1060

ED timing is important because 85% of inpatients arrive from the ED. ED arrival time has regular patterns over the typical day and week. However, all of these measures may be influenced by the ED being over busy (possibly on diversion) and by long waiting time in the less acute area of the ED discouraging additional patient arrivals. Typically, during the course of a week, Monday and Tuesday are busiest, and Sunday is the least busy, in the total ED (Figure 1-13). Overall inpatient volume has been decreasing during recent years with relatively flat seasonality (Figure 1-14).

The inpatient arrival time pattern is not a very meaningful measure since other issues, such as discharge times, which are more important for performance measurement, affect it. Thus, arrivals to inpatient are more a reflection of output than input. Admission to the inpatient area depends on bed availability and thus admission time depends on the previous patient's discharge time and the time to make the room and bed ready for a new patient. The transfer from ED to an inpatient ward may also be via a holding or surge area used when inpatient beds are unavailable.

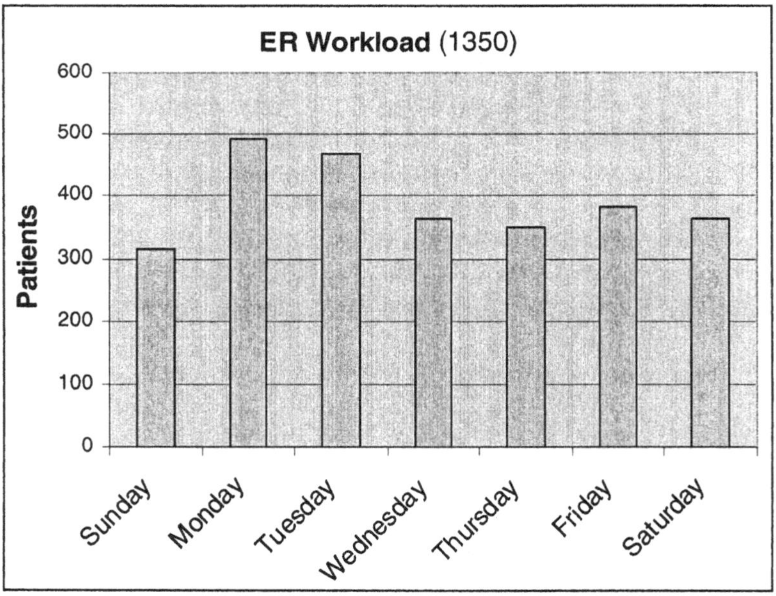

Figure 1-13. ER by Day of the Week

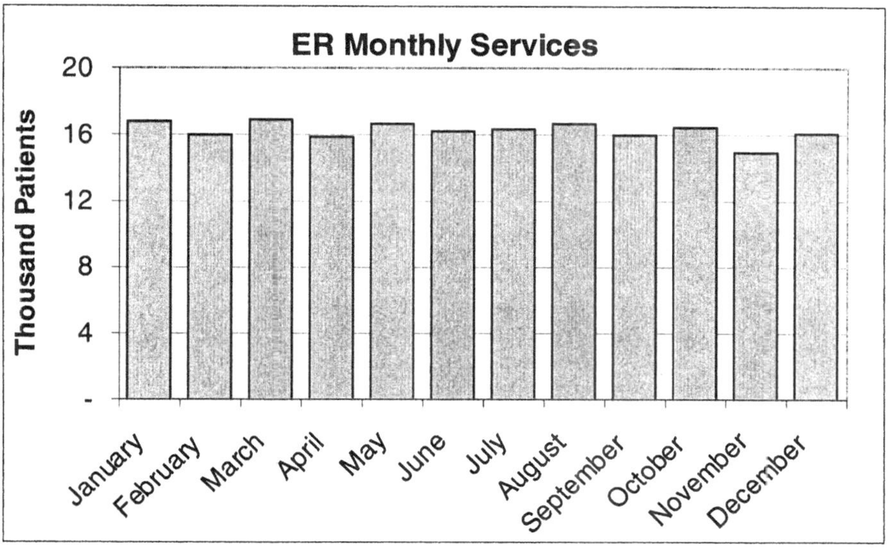

Figure 1-14. ER by Month of the Year

3.2 Tracking Patient Flow by Area

LAC/USC served 205,000 patients in its ED in 2003-2004, as well as 522,000 out-patients and 23,000 other services. 16,000 patients were admitted to surgical beds and 17,000 to medical beds. The hospital has detailed data for admissions into various areas, but patient flow between areas is not available. To quantify patient movement between major areas of the hospital, we developed a flow matrix by interpreting the sequence of transactions for a sample of 400 patients in April of 2004. This resulted in the input-output matrix in Table 1-3, which was extrapolated to annual flows between departments in Figure 1-15. The system flow chart helps identify where the focus should be with respect to improving department-to-department transfer of patients. It can also lead to subsequent analysis of patient delays on a input-output basis. Last, it is an example of a non-routine analysis, which could be imbedded in daily, weekly or monthly reporting through suitable modification of the center's MIS.

Table 1-3. Input-Output Table of Patient Movement

To \ From	1050 & 1050 B	1060	1350	wards	ICU	CMA	Surgery ward	OPD / Direct Admissions	Scheduled Admissions / Day Surgery
1050 & 1050 B		0.0%	3.2%						
1060	2.2%		1.9%						
1350	2.2%	0.8%		1.1%			1.4%		
Wards	8.6%	5.3%	19.6%	11.1%	16.7%	75.0%	17.4%	62.5%	42.9%
ICU	0.0%	0.8%	1.3%	2.2%	0.0%	0.0%	0.0%		14.3%
CMA	0.0%	0.0%	1.3%	1.1%	33.3%	0.0%	0.0%	0.0%	0.0%
Surgery ward	1.1%	5.3%	13.3%	5.6%	33.3%	0.0%	2.9%	37.5%	42.9%
OPD	4.3%	3.8%	2.5%	5.6%					
Day Surgery									
Discharge	81.7%	84.2%	57.0%	73.3%	16.7%	25.0%	78.3%		

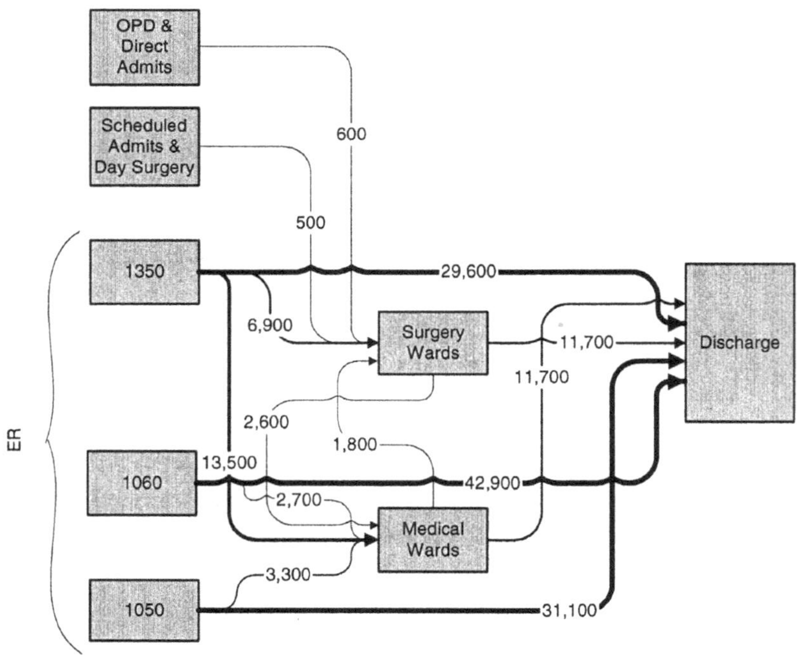

Figure 1-15. Patient Flows Between Areas on an Annual Basis

3.3 Defining Performance Measures

At this point we turn to measuring specific performance outcomes, such as waiting time, number of patients waiting, denied days, and utilization.

3.3.1 Time in System and Waiting Time

Time in system and wait time are reported in certain areas of the hospital but their accuracy is uncertain and may not provide a useful picture regarding patient flow. The basic problem is that the hospital does not time stamp events at the exact time when they occur. Event times are often recorded retrospectively (if at all), and exact times may get rounded to the nearest day, which is insufficient for tracking delays. Ideally, the time of every key event in the patient's stay should be recorded automatically as it happens, for instance with a simple bar code scan. With these data, it is possible to track waits by location and activity. It is also possible to optimize resource utilization, as staff can be alerted immediately when a resource is made available, thus eliminating idle time. We now turn to the actual data that we had available at LAC/USC.

3.3.1.1 ER Wait Time

ED wait time is an important patient flow measure since this is where many patients enter the hospital and delays can affect the clinical results. The hospital has only recently started recording the time of patient ED transactions. A problem is that recording methodology requires additional effort by nurses, doctors and clerical staff. Since they are already very busy with a backlog of patients, it is difficult to add data recording tasks or to assure that they are done accurately.

Some information on waits can be inferred from Figure 1-16, which shows the distribution of three events -- admissions, MD seen, and discharge – over the course of a day, for the month of November, 2004 for 1350. Wait times are reflected in the differences between event times. For instance, it appears that the backlog in patients waiting to be seen starts growing at 10:00 a.m. and reaches a maximum around 9:00 p.m., at which time the backlog shrinks. This is because the admissions percentages exceed the MD seen percentages during this time of day. The queue diminishes after midnight, and continues dropping until early morning. Adding staffing during this period of the day would be especially beneficial in reducing waits.

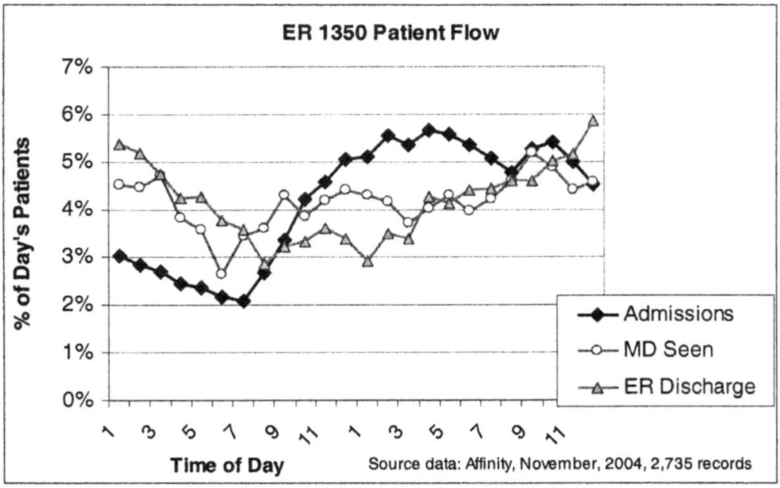

Figure 1-16. Patient Movement within 1350 ER

3.3.1.2 Outpatient wait time

Wait time in the Outpatient area involves two types of waiting: waiting for an appointment to see a doctor in a clinic and the wait time that the patient experiences once arriving at the clinic.

Wait time for an appointment is summarized in Table 1-4. The hospital works to keep these times as short as possible. A shorter wait time will often result in a better clinical result. Also, when wait times get longer, more missed appointments can be expected and the effect of the wait is compounded.

Table 1-4. Estimated Time to Wait for an OPD Appointment

OPD Clinic	**Days** **Average time until an appointment is available, calendar days, fall 2004**
Medical	15
Orthopedic	24
Primary Care, new outpatient	17
Primary Care, new outpatient	9
ENT	19
Dental	0 (walk in, no wait)
Surgery – Non-Emergency	Over 180 days
Ophthalmology	31

Patient wait time for an appointment is important and is often used by other hospitals as a measure of the performance of the outpatient function. However, there are important problems related to this measure.

In some sense the wait time of the clinic is different than what might be expected. If a clinic provides poor service few patients will apply and the wait time will be short. On the other hand, if the wait time is long, it may be an indication of the good quality of the service given. Another factor is the practically infinite outpatient demand at LAC GH. If the community senses good quality and a reasonable level of service, there will be a surge in demand and wait time will increase.

Wait time within the clinics themselves is not measured. Opinions seem to indicate three to four hours wait at the largest clinics (Medicine and Orthopedics), but it can vary greatly by type of clinic and time of day.

Individual patients may experience longer waiting times. Some patients arrive at the OPD building much earlier than their appointments with the expectation that this will improve their chances of being seen that day or reduce their total waiting time. In some cases early arrival at the clinic may actually result in their being seen earlier.

The sequence of three types of wait times is shown in the diagram below. We were told that in the Primary Care clinic the first wait time is about ½ to ¾ of an hour, the second ¾ to 1 hour and the last ½ to ¾ of an hour for a total of about 2 hours. Again, this will vary greatly by patient, time of day and particular clinic.

3.3.2 Number of Patients Waiting

The average number of patients waiting in ER, OPD and other parts of the hospital is generally unknown, as is the average wait time (though it could easily be derived if all critical events were time stamped and recorded). Based on visual observation, the number of ambulatory persons waiting in the 1050 & 1060 waiting room ranges from 50 to 150 during most of the daytime. The number waiting in 1350 is more difficult to evaluate since most of the waiting is in a bed and varies over the 24x7 operation. Also, it is impossible to determine which of the people waiting are patients and which are family members.

The number waiting in OPD is also highly variable. Some large clinics have many patients waiting at times but they have a number of doctors working simultaneously and the wait time and service times may be less than in other clinics where far fewer patients are waiting.

Waiting in the ED area is not simply at the entrance but occurs in several locations during the ED visit. These are shown in the following map with the locations for queues measured. It should also be noted that the queues are not independent. Waiting in one queue, such as waiting for PFS, reduces the flow to subsequent processes.

To understand where delay occurs within the ED, we conducted a special study in which we hand counted the number of patient charts by location over a two-day period. For this sample, the number of people waiting in booths in 1350 remained nearly constant from 10:00 a.m. to 3:00 p.m., as did the number of patients waiting for an inpatient bed assignment from the BCU. The waiting in 1350 for PFS, on the other hand, grew from about 5 to 30 patients during this period. However, this alone does not indicate that PFS is a system bottleneck, as the back-up may be more the result of waiting for beds or waiting to be seen by doctors, which spills back into other areas.

Based on these observations, Figure 1-17 was created to depict queue sizes at 10 locations over time. This graph shows that the queues grow over the course of the day, primarily due to an increasing backlog for PFS. Queues in booths do not grow, largely because there is a finite number of booths, which limits the total number of patients who can be waiting at this stage. It is unclear whether an increase in PFS staffing would reduce overall delay because booths may still be the constraining bottleneck in the system.

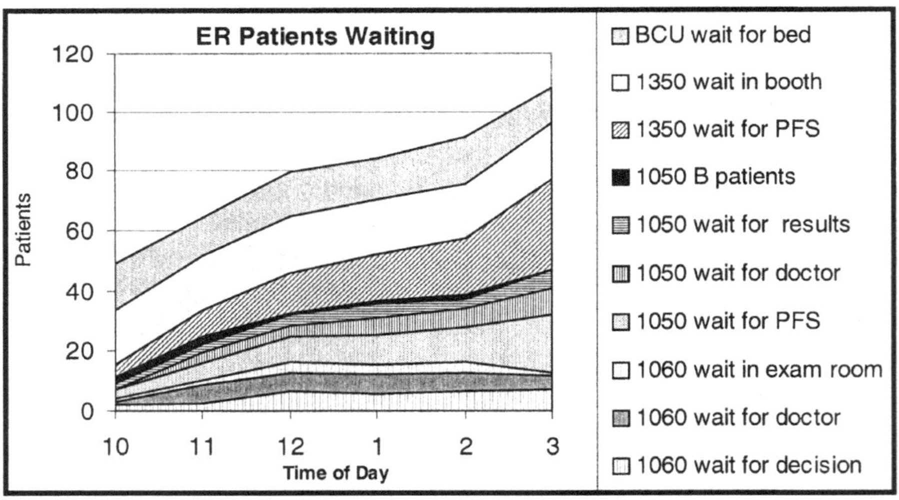

Figure 1-17. Patient Queue Size by ED Location

3.3.3 Productivity and Service Time

Productivity is defined as useful output divided by input or as work completed divided by resources used, such as the resource of labor. In the case of hospitals, output can be measured in terms of patient admissions, patient days or the number of specific services done. Input can be measured by staff size in FTEs or labor hours.

An alternative but indirect measure of productivity is hospital cost per patient day. This may be helpful on an overall basis in comparing the LAC GH to other similar institutions but probably not helpful when evaluating a functional area or a specific process. Service times, such as the time for a complete outpatient or ER visit, are a measure of how well the hospital is organized to provide prompt care. They can be compared to benchmarks from other hospitals or organizations. Service times at LAC GH are generally not measured with any useful precision by the hospital's HIS. Cycle times are known on a detailed level by technicians and other staff familiar with specific procedures. For example, the average scan time of 30 to 45 minutes for an MRI is known. Of greater interest is the time for an MRI appointment, and how this compares to benchmarks and historical data to measure trends in improvement.

Some anecdotal service times were reported but rarely were they based on a true independent measurement. Such details are particularly helpful in managing patient flow if they can be compared to benchmark times or be compared to the hospital's own past performance. Tracking of such time would be helpful as a component in managing and improving patient flow.

3.3.4 Denied Days

An important financial consideration of the hospital is "denied days". These represent days that are not reimbursed because the insurance provider does not view excessive inpatient days as appropriate. An example is inpatient days spent waiting for a surgery due to scheduling delays. This is a costly event exceeding 15% of total days and the hospital works to avoid such a situation. Improved patient flow will inevitably reduce denied days by assuring that patient movement is appropriate and prompt. Patient flow improvement is also important for patient satisfaction and the extent to which the hospital can serve the community. Long wait times and crowding are avoided by efficient patient flow throughout the hospital.

3.3.5 Utilization (Beds, OR, Staff) and Length of Stay

Utilization of beds in the GH is generally very high. The demand for beds exceeds the supply, which is determined by how many beds the hospital can open based on the availability of staff. The supply also depends on the ability to discharge patients rapidly, as well as to rapidly prepare the bed for the next patient, as well as transport that patient. Efficient utilization also depends on achieving a good match between the types of beds available and the population of patients waiting to be admitted.

More nursing staff also means more beds can be made available. Where there is a shortage of nursing staff, the hospital uses outside services, but this is costly and inefficient, so the use is limited. If staff cannot be gathered, beds are closed and patients must wait for beds to become available. However, bed utilization can be a misleading measure, as many inpatients are queued, waiting for surgery or waiting for tests. If these processes were completed more rapidly, the need for beds would diminish, which could in turn reduce delays in the ED. They could also significantly reduce the length of stay, which is in itself in part a measure of waiting time (i.e., wait for surgery, wait for test, wait for discharge). Though it is impossible to reduce length of stay to zero (as minimum times are needed for procedures and recuperation) much of the stay is devoted to costly waiting that should be eliminated.

Utilization is important in other areas, such as surgery and radiology. While an effort is made to keep these resources scheduled, resources are often left under utilized due to difficulties in predicting service times, cancellations or late arrivals, and slack times in preparing equipment or rooms. Thus, it is possible for a department to have a long backlog while simultaneously working below its capacity. In some instances long backlogs can cause efficiency to drop, as additional attention is needed to support waiting patients and service processes become disrupted.

Thus, an objective at LAC GH is to operate with prompt and efficient patient flow to process the maximum number of patients while maintaining high quality. Utilization of resources must be considered in regard to the inevitable backlog with no likelihood of idle time.

The average length of stay at the GH is about 6.5 days. This is considered long by the hospital administration, which is working to reduce it by one day. Utilization of hospital beds is high relative to other hospitals. At most times all beds are in use, in preparation to be used by the next patient, or closed due to shortage of staff. In 2005, while the hospital was typically staffed for 700 beds out of a theoretical capacity of 1,000 beds. Ancillary Performance Measures

In addition to patient wait time, non-labor resources should also be measured. For example, managers of ancillary services should have accessible and relevant measures of performance of their diagnostic equipment. The lab should monitor equipment related data such as downtime (time equipment is unavailable due to maintenance, failure, etc.) and idle time. The extent of downtime should be tracked and compared to past levels, trends and to industry benchmarks. Maintenance vendors should be required to provide such data if it is not readily available from the equipment itself.

Most service areas (Radiology, Pharmacy, etc.) have industry standards available to represent typical performance numbers. Error rates, cycle time, and throughput by equipment type should be compared to past performance and to figures typical for each type of equipment.

3.4 Improving System Performance

Our study of LAC/USC resulted in numerous recommendations that are in various stages of implementation. We summarize some of the major findings.

3.4.1 Improvement Process

Create a team of motivated, knowledgeable and empowered individuals to make needed changes related to patient flow. Provide them training and guidance in process mapping, analysis and operations improvement tools. Fact based data analysis must be a key ingredient and starting point. Give teams specific goals, deadline dates and incentives. Include necessary disciplines (nurses, clerical, administration and physicians) needed to implement changes.

3.4.2 Use Existing Data to Track Patient Flow

Patient arrivals, waiting time, service time and other measures can be created from existing data. Patient flow management requires facts that are best gathered from processes already in place. The current information system is not ideal, but it can provide additional information.

3.4.3 Discharge Waiting Unit Expansion

Continue expansion of this function so that it better serves the entire hospital and maximizes the utilization of inpatient beds while considering patient satisfaction. By evaluating the discharge workflow and facts concerning patient flow it is possible to determine the optimum size of the discharge waiting unit. Also, a training program for nursing staff focusing on the capabilities of the discharge unit and the steps that can be followed by wards to expedite discharge would be very useful.

3.4.4 Transportation Level Optimized

Determine a cost effective level of internal patient transportation and implement it. This must include the necessary staff, equipment and scheduling. It does not represent an added cost because the staff is already doing the transportation. The recommendation is to make it more efficient by analyzing the workflow and define the optimal assignment of staff.

3.4.5 Appointment/Scheduling Systems Using Simulations

Tools such as computer simulation and an optimized scheduling system will support better decisions. Scheduling requires complex tradeoffs and such decisions should be based on forecasts and determination of their likely impact before they occur.

3.4.6 Bed Management System

The bed control function is particularly critical to patient flow. As noted, the current system seems to need good information and has been criticized by users from all sides. Therefore, bed control related tools as well as communications must be improved. Various parties, including the inpatient wards and the emergency room staff, regularly criticize bed assignment decisions. Thus, a strong, clear and well publicized set of rules is needed to support prompt decisions. Also, part of the improvement to bed control is better information regarding bed availability. Discharge orders must be promptly entered into the information system and planned discharges should be frequently reported the day before the discharge is to occur.

3.4.7 Patient Tracking System and ID

By enforcing a system with a clear patient ID, costs can be avoided. Many computerized patient tracking systems, such as those the hospital is considering, have capabilities in electronic tracking. Operational data related to patient flow requires a clear, consistent and efficient patient identification system. A variety of alternatives is available, such as bar-codes and radio frequency ID, which will save operating costs and offer very useful data on patient flows.

3.4.8 Hospital Portal

Patient appointments and referrals are received by the hospital at a variety of points. This complicates the scheduling process and harms patient satisfaction through a lack of consistency and control. A single centralized point of access and a strengthened CSC would support a more efficient hospital operation and improve customer service.

4. CONCLUSIONS AND EXTENSIONS

Clinicians and administrators can form collaboratives to reduce health care delays. Success depends on an ability to understand health care as a system, including the many interactions between patients, clinicians, support services and other resources. Success also depends on an ability to pinpoint the bottlenecks and system failures, particularly with respect to interactions among departments as patients flow through the system.

This chapter presented process charting and performance measurement approaches, which have been used to model and evaluate patient flow delays at the LA County/USC health center. These tools can be used elsewhere, provided that hospital management is committed to improvement, and that it carries that message to its staff.

5. ACKNOWLEDGMENT

We gratefully acknowledge the Los Angeles County Department of Health Services, whose financial support enabled the completion of this study. Our work relied on the close cooperation and assistance of the staff of the LA County/USC Hospital. In particular, we would like to acknowledge the dedication and support of Mr. Pete Delgado, Mr. Cecil Clark, Dr. David Altman, Ms. Irene Recendez, RN, Ms. Shiela Mallete, RN and Ms. Behnaz Hekmatnia. We also acknowledge the support and guidance of Dr. Thomas Garthwaite and Ms. Paula Packwood of the Department of Health Services.

6. REFERENCES

American College of Emergency Physicians, ACEP (1999). Ambulance diversion policy statement).

American College of Emergency Physicians, ACEP (2002a). Emergency medical treatment and labor act policy statement.

American College of Emergency Physicians, ACEP (2002b). Responding to emergency department crowding: a guidebook for chapters.

Ancker, C.J. and A.V. Gafarian (1963). Some queueing problems with balking and reneging, I and II. *Operations Research*, V. 11, pp. 88-100; 928-937.

Belson, D., R. Hall, P. Murali and M. Dessouky (2004). Collaborative to improve patient flow at Los Angeles County/University of Southern California Hospital, Final Report, Epstein Department of Industrial and Systems Engineering.

Bindman, A.B., K. Grumbach, D. Keane, L. Rauch and J.M. Luce (1991). Consequences of queueing for care at a public hospital emergency department. *Journal of the Americal Medical Association*, V. 266, pp. 1091-1096.

Brewster, L.R., L. Rudell and C.S. Lesser (2001). Emergency room diversions: a symptom of hospitals under stress. Center for Studying Health System Change, Issue Brief N. 38.

Buesching, D.P., A. Jablonowski and E. Vesta (1985). Inappropriate emergency department visits. *Annals of Emergency Medicine*. V. 14, pp. 672-676.

Derlet, R.W. and D.A. Nishio. (1990). Refusing care to patients who present to an emergency department. *Annals of Emergency Medicine*. V. 19, pp. 262-267.

Derlet, R.W. and J.R. Richards (2000). Overcrowding in the nation's emergency departments: complex causes and disturbing effects. *Annals of Emergency Medicine*, V. 35, pp. 63-68.

Dershewitz, R.A., W. Paichel (1986). Patients who leave a pediatric emergency department without treatment. *Annals of Emergency Medicine*, V. 15, pp. 717-720.

Greene, J. (1995). Challenges entering the ER. *Modern Healthcare*, pp. 31-34.

Hall, R.W. (1989). *Queueing Methods for Services and Manufac*turing, Prentice Hall, Englewood Cliffs, New Jersey.

Institute for Healthcare Improvement (1995). Reducing Delays and Waiting Times Throughout the Healthcare System, IHI, Boston, MA.

Litvak, E., M.C. Long and A.B. Cooper (2001). Emergency department diversion: causes and solutions. *Academy of Emergency Medicine*. V. 8, pp. 1108-1110.

McCaig, L.F. and C.W. Burt (2001). National Hospital Ambulatory Medical Care Survey: 1999 Emergency Departmetn Summary. Centers for Disease Control and Prevention.

Schneider, S., F. Zwemer, A. Doniger (2001). New York: a decade of emergency department overcrowding. *Academy of Emergency Medicine*, V. 8, pp. 1044-1050.

Schull, M.J., J.-P. Szalai and B. Schwartz (2001). Emergency department overcrowding following systematic hospital restructuring: trends at twenty hospitals over ten years. *Academy of Emergency Medicine*, V. 8, pp. 1037-1043.

Shaw, K.M., S.M. Selbst and F.M. Gill. (1990). Indigent children who are denied care in the emergency department. *Annals of Emergency Medicine*. V. 19, pp. 59-62.

Chapter 2

HOSPITALS AND CLINICAL FACILITIES, PROCESSES AND DESIGN FOR PATIENT FLOW

Michael Williams
The Abaris Group, 700 Ygnacio Valley Road, Suite 270, Walnut Creek, California 94596

Abstract: This chapter discusses current trends and key drivers that affect patient flow and efficiency and analyzes the most common myths of resource allocation for healthcare. Providers are now finding that simply adding beds or staff will not solve the commonplace problems of long waits and delays. Contemporary physical design concepts that improve flow for healthcare are described in this chapter, and seven high-leverage steps that can significantly improve flow and expand capacity, and thus limit delays and waiting, are recommended.

Key words: Ambulance diversion, artificial variation, bed control, boarding, bottlenecks, capacity, crowding, design, discharge lounge, emergency department, fast track, flow, high impact teams (HIT), Just In Time, lean, random variation, rapid admission unit, rapid cycle testing (RCT), re-design, re-engineering, safety net, smoothing, staffing ratios, utilization, workforce shortages

1. THE CHALLENGE

Long waits, delays, cancellations and resource overloads have become commonplace in healthcare. For many years, healthcare providers have simply added more resources to solve the problem – building more beds, adding more staff. This approach has become increasingly impractical due to human-resource shortages and limited finances. Now healthcare providers have been forced to look at different approaches to solving the problem. In addition, many of the traditional approaches have only served to hide the real underlying problem: significant inefficiencies in timing and flow of resources during the delivery of healthcare.

The problems of healthcare crowding and waiting have become epidemic across the country. Nowhere is this more evident than with our country's emergency departments (ED). 45.5% of all hospital admissions come from the ED (McCaig and Burt, 2002). All too often when one thinks of an ED visit, one assumes there will be long waits. This is frustrating to the patient, their families and to the hospital staff as well. ED saturation and subsequent ambulance diversion has also reached crisis proportions in most urban communities. Ambulance diversion, or the sending of an ambulance to another hospital because the ED chosen is "closed", has a substantial backward effect on the ambulance industry as well. The ambulance industry is one healthcare provider that has experienced significant success with optimizing their resources and productivity to assure performance using traditional industrial engineering concepts (Stout, 1986). However, an October 2001 US Government study shows that:

> *"Ambulance diversions have impeded access to emergency services in metropolitan areas in at least 22 states since January 1, 2000. More than 75 million Americans live in areas affected by these ambulance diversions."* (US GAO, 2003)

These problems have arisen because of a dramatic increase in ED utilization and a perceived parallel decline in resources. The CDC reports that the number of ED visits for 2003 rose by 3.1% to 112 million patients while the total number of EDs declined during the past 10-year period by 12.2% (McCaig and Burt, 2002). In a survey they conducted on behalf of the American Hospital Association, The Lewin Group documented that 62% of the surveyed hospitals had reported being "at" or "over" capacity, with this proportion rising to 79% for urban hospitals and 90% for Level I trauma centers and hospitals over 300 beds (Lewin Group, 2002).

Hospital capacity is a major driver to the overall healthcare capacity and patient flow challenges across the country. In a recent report on ED crowding, the U.S. General Accounting Office (GAO) noted the connection between the ED and the rest of the hospital:

> *"While no single factor stands out as the reason why crowding occurs, GAO found that the factor most commonly associated with crowding was the inability to transfer emergency patients to inpatient beds once a decision had been made to admit them as hospital patients rather than to treat and release them. When patients "board" in the emergency department due to the inability to transfer them elsewhere, the space, staff and other resources available to treat new emergency patients are diminished."* (GAO, 2003)

The Lewin ED Study also noted that the lack of critical care beds was a factor for ED crowding. While staffing and other factors were also mentioned, the lack of critical care beds were cited as the most common cause in most of the regions studied.

Hospitals themselves are complex organizations and thus waiting and delays are also common and often a convenient explanation of the problem. Delays in scheduling a non-emergent surgery can be weeks. High patient admissions volumes in the morning at a hospital and patient discharges that occur in the afternoon assures that many patients will wait in a queue, whether that be at their home, in a physician's office, at the hospital's admitting department or perhaps in the ED.

Hospitals had historically responded to capacity problems by adding more staff and beds. However, frequently these changes only make the problem worse when the underlying processes and practices do not change and the new beds or staff eventually gets used with capacity problem ultimately returning. Limited physical capacity and staffing often results in the use of alternative but not the most desirable resources such as "boarding" patients in the ED. At best, these responses are just a band aid. Yet, in a survey conducted in 2004, approximately 51% of all hospitals in the country were rebuilding or expanding their EDs some of which are taking this step to simply accommodate the holding and boarding of patients (Healthcare Financial Management Association, 2004).

Due to the lack of space or the funds to expand or add staff, more and more hospitals are being forced to look at improving their flow of patients by studying bottlenecks and limitations in their process that artificially add to the problem. Unfortunately, many hospitals initially attempt to focus on the symptoms of the problem, the ED or in some cases the Emergency Medical System (EMS) delivery system that brings the patient to the hospital. The challenge is that the ED and inpatient capacity and flow are inextricably linked and resolving only the subsystems, such as the ED, will only have limited success. In fact, isolated achievements only serve to provide short-term successes but actually hurt the other departments by artificially growing the problems that they face. For example, ED initiatives often and appropriately prioritize getting ED patients that are being admitted to a hospital bed a priority and some simply set high performance standards to achieve their goal. But often, the hospital does not have a bed to send that patient to whether it is due to poor in-house staffing or the lack of contemporary in-house bed utilization and discharge practices. There is even some evidence that mandatory nurse ratios may increase patients risk for mortality and morbidity (Aiken et al, 2002).

To achieve a total and sustainable success to the patient flow and capacity problems, healthcare providers must embrace the interdependencies of their individual departments and services and accept solutions that view the entire continuum of care rather than the mere silos within.

2. KEY DRIVERS

The key drivers to hospital-wide capacity problems and their solutions are as follows:

Increasing Demand and Declining Capacity. It is clear from CDC data that demand for key services is rising and the overall number of hospitals is declining. While the total number of ED visits rose 3 to 5 percent per year during the five-year period from 1998-2003, the US population growth was only an averaged 1.1% per year for that same 5-year period (US Census, **YEAR**). As ED visits continue to rise, so do their associated hospital admissions. The number of uninsured Americans below 65 rose from 42 million to 48.1 million during 1998 to 2004 for the first six months of each year (AHRQ, 2004). As the number of uninsured increases, so does their impact on EDs and subsequent hospital care as the uninsured and underinsured tend to use the ED as their healthcare safety net. According to the Urgent Matters report: *Walking a Tightrope: The State of the Safety Net in Ten U.S Communities,* despite long waits for safety net populations in an ED, the ED was perceived to be more convenient and more accessible than for long waits for specialty care and multiple provider visits for testing and procedures (Regenstein et al, 2004).

Decreasing Revenues. The overall decline in Medicare and Medicaid reimbursement is not helping. Hospitals increasingly have to work harder with fewer resources. Budget pressures at state and federal government levels are resulting in decreases from these key funding sources.

Workforce Shortages. Hospitals are facing many challenges in recruiting and retaining key workforce positions. The nursing shortage is well documented and only expected to get worse. It has been reported that one in ten nursing positions remain unfilled (Sochalski, 2002). There are many other largely unrecognized workforce shortages including radiology technicians, pharmacists and even medical coders, all critical to the ability of a hospital to maintain and expand its capacity.

Rising Costs of Care. After nearly a decade of relatively stable costs of healthcare brought on by the mandates of managed care and consumerism, there has been much erosion and hospital costs are rising rapidly. The average adjusted expense of a hospital admission in 1997 was $1,031 and in 2002 it was $1,289, up 29% for this five-year period (AHA, 2005).

Limits in Technology and Informatics. Tight revenue often drives limits to capital expenditures with information technology (IT) resource acquisitions near the bottom of the list (Robeznicks, 2005). Key historical and forecasted data resources are missing in many hospitals. These resources are desperately needed to more precisely match resources to demand

Limited Industrial Engineering Wherewithal. Coupled to the IT challenge and the lack of data is the inability to study, interpret and respond to opportunities to improve the practices, policies procedures that limit demand. Without key data and the supporting tools of industrial engineering, a hospital is left to react to patient events rather than to respond to forecasted needs unlike the practice in many other industries (Chase et al, 2001). Contemporary principles of "Lean" and "Just in Time" introduced by the visions of Toyota and Federal Express are not embraced in a significant way by the healthcare industry.

3. KEY MYTHS OF HEALTHCARE DELIVERY

One of the most significant factors driving hospital capacity constraints are key myths held by many on their perception of the drivers for capacity challenges. For example, it is a long-held belief by hospitals and their providers that ED visits and inpatient admissions are isolated events that are dependant on variables out of the hospital's control. The fact is that ED visits and subsequent hospital admissions have significant predictability and thus the ability to forecast demand and the necessary resources to a very precise level.

The CDC has also reinforced a long-held belief that the number of EDs in this country is declining and thus driving excessive throughput times and excessive ED diversion. A recent California study reported that, while the number of EDs has declined in that state, the actual number of treatment stations or "beds" has increased substantially (Melnick et al, 2002). The article goes on to reinforce that total ED bed capacity, not the number of EDs themselves is the more appropriate metric for historical comparison of capacity.

Insufficient hospital beds are another myth held by many healthcare providers. A common hospital frustration is that they "do not have enough beds", but the fact is in most hospitals, even when there is waiting either in the ED, admitting area or a private physician's office for an inpatient bed, the patient ultimately gets to a hospital bed. Very few patients are transferred to another hospital in order to access an inpatient bed. This clearly demonstrates that actual capacity itself is not the problem but rather there is a misaligned capacity as compared to demand. Hospital demand for beds typically occurs early in the day but the patients that are being discharged do not go home until later in the day. Figure 1 provides the typical hospital admissions by hour of the day and compares that to the same hospital's discharges by hour of the day demonstrating the mismatch of capacity to demand for hospital beds over a 24-hour period.

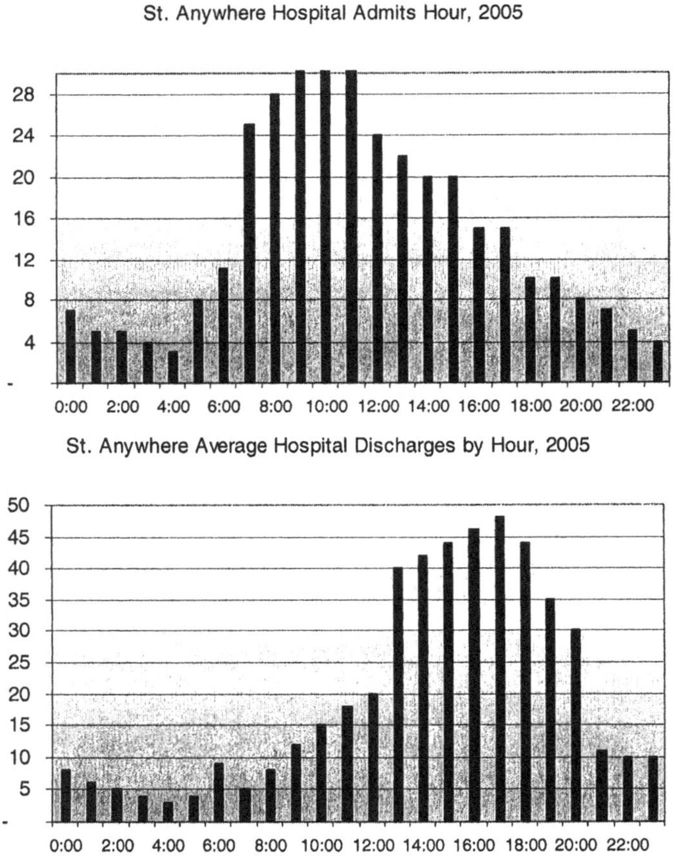

Figure 1. Typical hospital admissions and discharges by hour of the day

Another myth is the largely held belief that there is a nursing shortage in the country. While there may be pockets of shortages within the nation, quite the contrary is true nationwide. According to an American Nursing Association study, there is currently an excess number of nurses when compared to demand and there will not be an actual shortage until the year 2010 (Peterson, 2001). The fact of the matter is that many nurses do not want to work in a dysfunctional and seemingly unsafe healthcare environment, thus creating an artificial shortage.

Another common but mistaken myth is that ED visits and hospital admissions in general are isolated events. EDs commonly staff for the unknown. Individual hospital admissions from the ED are often interpreted from the in-house unit floor as a "surprise". The everyday bed management meetings that many hospitals have undertaken due to bed "shortages" (typically called Bed Control meetings) rarely value the predicted ED inpatient demand but rather inappropriately focusing on other hospital bed needs and only the present "boarders" in the ED.

These myths are perpetuated by a lack of appreciation of current data that already exists to make predictions, limited availability of forecasting tools, (e.g. ED arrival times, hospital patient discharge times) and the lack of knowledge about the nature and impact of artificial variation created by the healthcare delivery system itself and its impact on capacity and flow.

Knowing and valuing the factors that limit the rate of patient flow and increase waiting are essential steps to optimizing healthcare capacity and flow delivery. If the wrong problems are solved (e.g., adding staff and beds), as is the approach taken by many hospitals, then there will be much wasted resources and the problems will only get worse. For many hospitals, the solutions are not with building a bigger "sandbox" but rather building a more effective "sandbox."

Most healthcare providers with excessive waiting and bottlenecks do have a commitment to their organizations but do not realize they have the internal tools to solve the problem. The central source of problem resolution comes with a principal introduced by Dr. Donald Berwick, MD, President of the Institute of Health Improvement (IHI) wherein he published the first law of improvement: "Every system is perfectly designed to achieve the results that it achieves" (Berwick, 1996). Hospitals are at capacity and EDs are overcrowded because they have been incorrectly designed that way. That is, they have process, flow and sometimes physical design flaws. Thus, the answer to capacity and flow problems is likely to be with the fundamentally rethinking and redesigning of their entire healthcare delivery system that created the capacity and flow problems in the first place.

The goal of any healthcare provider is getting the right patient at the right time, with the right provider and with the right information all timed with the right interventions. When these elements are synchronized and waste is eliminated, it simply takes less staff, less space to provide healthcare services and thus this alone increases capacity and access for the next patient.

Using contemporary capacity and flow management principals will:

- Improve access
- Reducing waiting
- Lower costs
- Improve outcomes
- Improve staff satisfaction
- Improve the customer experience

Best practice improvement initiatives are now demonstrating that it is possible to reduce the stress of the healthcare system experiencing delays and waiting (e.g. ED diversion) and eliminate waiting and delays in access through the enhancement of flow of patients and their information through the care delivery system (see www.abarisgroup.org, www.ihi.org and www.urgentmatters.org).

These changes are occurring one provider at a time and also system-wide, as is the case of the 18 hospitals in the Sacramento County (CA) area that committed to a profound regional capacity and patient flow change process that ultimately resulted in the region's 73% drop in ED saturation and EMS diversion (Patel et al, 2006).

4. PHYSICAL PLANT CONSIDERATIONS

To put it mildly, healthcare physical plants are not known for their accomplished design. One only needs to think about an ED waiting room to conjure up images of uncomfortable chairs, painfully out-of-date color schemes and long delays while reading year-old magazines.

The physical plants for many healthcare sites are a long way from designs that are healing, efficient and promote patient flow. And yet it may seem trite to use the architectural principal that "form must follow function" but nothing could be closer to the truth. Thus for most architects, physical plant changes and new additions themselves are not likely to fix capacity and flow problems but if physical space is incorrectly designed or more importantly, designed to a flawed process or a hypothetical process, than the physical plant may in fact be the rate-limiting factor.

Healthcare delivery systems must be designed to support contemporary flow and capacity management functions. Poor design may have a substantial affect on patient capacity and flow. Key sources of physical plant bottlenecks include:

- Lack of long-range planning or a master plan, thus requiring a patchwork of architectural remodels or "solutions" that do not work well together.
- Excessive redundancies healthcare provider departments that drive duplicative spaces, excessive equipment, and excessive steps needed to move patients through the system.
- Inadequate use of technology and thus technology or technology related to a bed (e.g. telemetry) becomes the rate-limiting factor.
- Inadequate space management limiting the effective use of current space and the inability to appropriate use underutilized space.
- Multiple and duplicative recording and management systems thus resulting ineffective integration and fragmentation of patient information space.
- Designs that are a perfect fit for one style or philosophy of care or for a particular manager but quickly out of date for the next.
- Reluctance to automate from manual systems to computerized approaches.
- Departments that are landlocked due to inadequate planning.
- Narrow treatment bays inhibiting efficient operations or economies of scale.
- Gross-to-net-area ratios that are inadequate due to poor planning or being forced to use a limited footprint.
- Poor circulation patterns due to poor planning or a lack of expertise
- Poor proximities of essential functions resulting in long travel distances, inefficient flow and higher staffing ratios.
- Mechanical and electrical systems that have limited capacity to grow
- Seemingly random placement of vertical shafts, elevators and stairways inhibiting necessary expansions.
- Poor signage and flow design and thus assuring patients and families will have difficulty finding their way.
- Inadequate support space for staff and ancillary departments.
- New technologies that are difficult to accommodate due to inflexible infrastructures and a lack of master planned utilities.
- No phased replacement plan in existence for the gradual upgrade of a hospitals infrastructure.
- Inadequate safety and clinical care systems that are unable to advance for the changing environment of infections, bioterrorism and the like.
- Designs that are not welcoming, healing or do not act in a positive supportive way when there is waiting.

Traditional space planning and architectural design also tend to reinforce results that memorialize waiting, delays and inefficiencies. For example, a typical redesign of an ED will start with how large the waiting room should be. A common calculation for ED waiting space is 3 seats per treatment bed or 15 net square feet per seat (ACEP, 1993). For a 50,000 volume ED, that will represent approximately 28 treatment beds, using a common guide of 1,800 visits per treatment bed. This will generate a waiting area space of approximately 420 square feet, which if converted to treatment beds would be sufficient to generate two more beds and in some cases eliminate the need for a waiting room. Thus, waiting rooms tend to memorialize waiting.

To remove the traditional architectural biases will require leaving behind traditional architectural design concepts and replacing those with approaches that truly think "out of the box" and perhaps "out of the universe." The essential design strategies that will promote contemporary capacity and flow management strategies are as follows:

Flexibility

- Locate growth departments along open edges of the facility or adjacent to soft departments such as offices, storage or courtyards.
- Utilize structure systems that can be adapted.
- Organized infrastructure to allow new components to be plugged in.
- Develop a universal approach to examination and treatment rooms.
- Avoid locating several fast growing departments adjacent to each other unless there are outlets to permit growth.
- Build in shell space.
- Design in appropriate horizontal buffer zone space to allow for expansion of technology and thus allowing modification of electrical, mechanical and IT systems to support such.
- Do not short-change support space for supply, staff and logistical support such as education and IT services.
- Do not land-lock areas that will need replacement or additions in the future.

Efficiency

- Optimize functional internal relationships based on the highest frequency of need and intensity of use.
- Balance care needs with support departments but do not allow the support departments to drive the assumptions on space.
- Design circulation and infrastructure patterns so they can be adapted as needs change.

- Plan for facility development priorities that create logical sequencing for the future.
- Incorporate "smart" building planning to allow adapting to technology advances.
- Emphasize space planning that allow for a variety of models of care.
- Plan for bringing more services to the patient (e.g. radiology, point of care laboratory testing, etc).

Quality

- Create research environments that promote environments that promote healing and comfort (see www.planetree.org)
- Design around enhanced productivity and staff morale.
- Focus on designs that will have a positive effective for the customer and market share.
- Minimize traditional irritants such as noise, glare and privacy.
- Target opportunities to deinstitutionalize the facility and improving access such as parting, waiting areas and nutrition.
- Recognize patient imperatives of safety, comfort and privacy.
- Allow for space personalization for patients and staff.

Figure 2 provides a before and after picture of a traditional patient bed versus one that is designed for comfort and aesthetics in a "healing" environment. The key ingredient to enhance flow and capacity through design is to create flexibility, whether that is for care patterns, mix variations, new demographics, new technologies, or new modes of care or reimbursement. It is also helpful to develop physical configurations that are based on acuities and levels of care. For example, zones should be created that match urgent and outpatient care with diagnostics; specialized care needs such a psychiatric, pediatrics and geriatrics. Healthcare design should encompass physical planning to enhance the ability to achieve cost savings. With the advent of Just in Time (JIT) and LEAN manufacturing production strategies, excessive storage and hording will be a thing of the past (Williams, 2004). This kind of physical accommodation will also be necessary to support team configurations, care approaches and proximities that provide efficiencies and enhance flow. For example, if point-of-care laboratory testing is to be the future standard of practice for patient care, as it is becoming in some EDs, then there must be physical bedside space to accommodate this change.

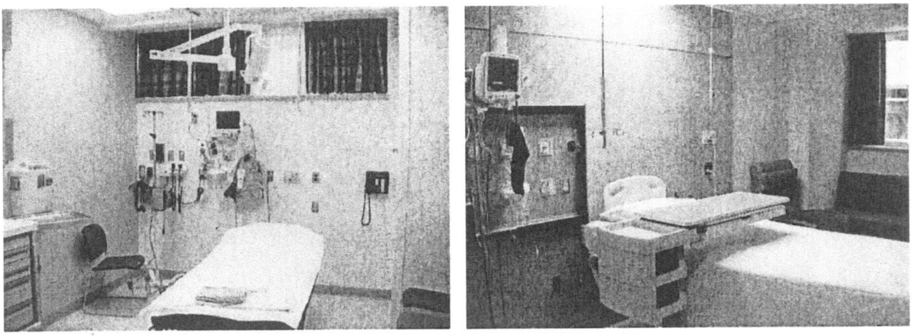

Figure 2 – Before and after photo of a patient treatment room moving from a technical and more austere design to a warm and healing environment. *Photos courtesy of Frank Zilm, AIA Zilm & Associates, Inc. Kansas City, MO*

Consideration should also be given to decentralizing space where appropriate and relocating non-essential services to improve treatment capacity. It is becoming a mantra in space-compromised hospitals to maintain "first floor space as patient care space" as a criterion for considering relocating administrative, PBX and other non-essential first-floor uses to improve access and expand patient care services. Remember also that privacy concerns continue to remain a priority in healthcare and this concept should always be at the forefront of healthcare space planning. Finally, taking from a Disneyland concept, the customer or guest experience goal should be "to make the best first impression and the best last impression" to the patient and their family and to design aesthetics and environmental quality into the planning process (Disney Institute, 2001).

5. KEY CONTEMPORARY SOLUTIONS FOR CAPACITY AND FLOW MANAGMENT

Through much trial and error, healthcare providers have learned the basic steps which must be taken to successfully and substantially improve patient flow. When speaking of conceptual approaches, it is important to think of high-leverage opportunities rather than attempting the universe of opportunities. Presented below are seven high-leverage steps that can be taken to dramatically and profoundly change the way a healthcare provider conducts it business and thus improve patient flow and enhance capacity.

5.1 Develop robust products that decompress ED and inpatient volumes.

Some hospitals have taken proactive steps to put patients in care delivery models that speed the care process itself, stage the patient for expedited care or reduce overall length of stay. Few hospitals, though, have all of the necessary models or product lines in place. Others have products that under perform and thus should be significantly re-engineered to create a true performance-based and high-leverage throughput delivery system.

5.1.1 Fast Track

One such product is an ED Fast Track. This product is typically located in a dedicated area of the ED designed to treat lower acuity patients in a speedier manner. However, most current ED Fast Tracks are slow, not producing anywhere near the 60-minute ideal throughput time that should be the goal for a Fast Track. For most EDs, 80% of their volume is considered non-urgent and therefore that volume would lend itself to more of a primary care treatment and flow model that provides faster services supported by more efficient tools (e g., checkbox clinical records, point-of-care testing, etc.). Most EDs should cycle approximately 40-50% of its patient volume through this care faster care model, thus dramatically reducing the total time on task, providing a protected and efficient care plan for those patients so that they do not get trumped by higher acuity patients, improving patient satisfaction and dramatically improving the bed capacity for the remaining higher-acuity patients.

5.1.2 Clinical Decision Unit (CDU)

A CDU should be considered for hospital admissions that do not truly need a traditional in-house bed. CDUs are 8-12 bed units designed for patients that would traditionally be admitted for conditions that simply need more therapy or care but do not necessarily need an inpatient bed. Most hospitals do not have a CDU. A typical CDU admission would include patients who have a need for longer diagnostic testing (e.g., rule-out cardiac chest pain), therapy (e.g., asthmatic) or other conditions that lend themselves to limited time protocols. These patients typically get admitted to the hospital and thus take up a hospital bed for up to two days. The average admission time for a CDU patient is 14 hours as compared to the 24 – 48 hours that their admission would have taken if the patient were in a traditional hospital bed. For most EDs, a CDU substantially reduces ED admissions to the hospital by up to 30% and the CDU also has a bonus of dramatically improving inpatient capacity as well. The overall length of stay for these CDU patients is dramatically less than their in-house counterpart patients. For a rule-out chest pain patient that is admitted to the hospital, their length of stay will range from for 23 – 48 hours but only 10 to 14 hours. For example a hypotensive patients needing fluid replacement might stay in the hospital an average 24 to 36 hours in-house but would likely only take 12 to 14 hours in CDU (Graff, 1998). These collective "saved" hours will dramatically open up inpatient beds due to the dropped overall utilization.

5.1.3 Rapid Admission Unit (RAU)

An RAU is a designated area for patients that are going to be admitted to the hospital but there is no available hospital bed to begin the admission workup, orders and paperwork. All hospitals should consider a RAU that provides peak weekday coverage for direct admissions and for staging inpatient admissions from the ED when there is no inpatient bed available. This model uses a two-hour throughput model for patients. The RAU is staffed only during peak weekday hours and thus not 24-hours or 7 days per week. The RAU area could accommodate the admission process, initiate early orders including taking the admission orders from the private physicians and evaluate the correct type of bed for the patient avoiding the common practice of further unnecessarily patient moves during their inpatient stay.

5.1.4 Discharge Lounge

Hospitals should also consider a discharge lounge that provides a quality location for discharge patients who would otherwise be waiting to be discharged from their hospital bed. With the discharge lounge, these patients wait in the discharge lounge for prescriptions, transportation home, care education or home healthcare scheduling. The patient that is going home but simply waiting for these logistical services is sent to an area of the hospital that is near the door where they will be picked up. Refreshments are served in a very nice area and perhaps a meal provided and they receive any final patient education or medications needed. This unit can dramatically speed the day-of-discharge times freeing up critical needed beds for that day's admissions.

5.2 Match staffing to demand.

Healthcare providers should take steps to precisely match staff to demand. For most providers, this is more of a guess than a precise process management tool. If the staffing has not been carefully studied or allocated to precise demand, a mismatch of service delivery will occur and there will be a resultant backlog of patient flow. This precise demand management review should be done for all core hospital functions including the ED, laboratory, radiology, housekeeping, central supply and inpatient care units.

The steps to matching demand to patient flow are as follows:

5.2.1 Analyze the staffing data

Collect and use historical data by month, day-of-week and hour-of-day to project needs and demand for services. Plotting the hospital admissions by various time periods is useful in identifying seasonal, weekly, or daily patterns and is the first step in understanding the demand/capacity ratio of services.

5.2.2 Adjust staffing to demand

Once the patterns of demand have been identified, the capacity of the system to handle the expected demand can be increased by arranging to have appropriate staff available during peak times. Staffing demand includes not only direct staff, but also ancillary services such as registration, laboratory and radiology services. A weight of 40 to 60% of technical versus nursing staff is recommended to sufficiently balance workload and to assure nurses are used primarily for their nursing responsibilities.

5.2.3 Prepare contingency plans

Even as patterns of peak demand are identified and staffing patterns adjusted, there will be times when unexpected demand occurs. The provider should establish back-up systems such as on-call systems or other contingency plans for meeting unanticipated demand. Having procedures in place wherein the unit or department can call on staff from other parts of the hospital to support them during unexpectedly high demand times can also be an effective method for reducing delays. It is also important to have formal and protected contingency plans for both nursing and ancillary staff and to establish these contingency plans for unpredictable delays.

5.2.4 Ensure the management team has sufficient resources, tools and ability to meet objectives

Creating precise demand management strategies requires managers to be surrounded with the right tools. What is often missing for the managers to create precise staffing is precise data. The data do not exist or access to the right data at the right level of details is limited. Key leadership positions should utilize the robust information systems and other resources available to them to make such calculations and adjustments to staffing to meet the needs and trends.

5.3 Reduce unnecessary utilization

One of the most potent sources of delay in hospitals, especially the ED, is a patient waiting for laboratory and radiological procedures and results. This is particularly a challenge in the ED environment, where primarily confirmatory tests are routinely ordered and are part of the accepted risk management process. Healthcare providers should identify diagnostic tests that neither contribute to the patient's diagnosis nor to the patient's treatment regime, but rather are primarily confirmatory in nature or to comply with perceived risk management objectives.

Studies on utilization and productivity and variations between physicians should also be refined and completed on an ongoing basis. This can be discreetly accomplished and should be considered as a place to start. Utilization standards for these tests should be developed with the overall goal of reducing unnecessary utilization.

5.4 Synchronize care delivery

For most healthcare providers, a significant source of delays is found within the inpatient unit or the ED itself. For example, most EDs have slow entry times from the time the patient arrives to the time the patient gets to a bed. Many hospitals have slow discharge times from when the physician writes the order to the time the patient leaves the hospitals. This is because many of the services and activities that are needed to complete the patient transaction are out of synch with the process.

Treating patients swiftly requires coordinating all processes as well as in ancillary departments, such as laboratory and radiology. It is important to standardize as many tasks as possible in order to achieve the synchronized and efficient care delivery system desired. Important steps for this effort follow.

5.4.1 Focus on getting the patient to the provider

Most patients want to see the physician so processes that interfere with that should be reexamined. In the ED, the point when the physician enters the exam room is the point around which everything else should revolve. Coming to an agreement on the importance of this point is crucial to achieving synchronization.

5.4.2 Evaluate, delete, or retime processes that do not enhance turnaround time

An example of this effort would be to continue to study the activities and behaviors of caregivers and eliminate unnecessary steps and activities or reschedule these activities. This includes streamlining triage when there is a delay due to a lack of beds, reducing assessment exams, and reducing duplicate questions between the registration/admitting staff and the physician nurse team (e.g. "why are you here today?"). Moving processes closer to the patient is important.

5.4.3 Establish protocols for top diagnoses

Hospitals and EDs should establish a number of protocols or care maps on care management. These protocols would provide a total set of agreed-upon steps to be taken in the diagnosis and treatment of particular types of patients. Protocols can greatly reduce delays by streamlining the transition of patients from one step in the treatment process to another. These protocols will also be effective in identifying steps in the treatment process that can be eliminated or provided by other professionals, rather than solely by nurses or physicians.

5.4.4 Based on protocols, initiate action

Once a protocol has been agreed upon, a patient who arrives at a hospital bed or in the ED with a condition for which a protocol is in place can be moved immediately through the steps, eliminating the delays that often occur in ordering appropriate tests. For example, with a patient who has an appropriate extremity injury (e.g., meeting the Ottawa extremity rules), with a pathway x-ray guideline can be moved directly from triage to radiology rather than waiting to be seen by a physician. Another example would be for known asthmatics to have their breathing treatments initiated by the nurses in a timely manner as a result of an established protocol.

5.5 Reconnect services within the hospital

It is not unusual to have a philosophical disconnect between the ED and the departments that support them. This is not uncommon for hospitals, as each department traditionally operates with their own "silo" accountable for the individual performance and service delivery standards. Many of the flow issues facing most EDs for example are manifestations of processes occurring elsewhere in the hospital, particularly in the flow of inpatients through the service system.

In reality, the each department is part of the larger system involving pre-hospital, hospital patient care units, other hospital departments, laboratory, radiology, other support services, community physicians, consultants (physician specialists and other professional disciplines), as well as patients, their families, and the communities in which they live. While a smooth-functioning unit depends on the services that others in the wider system of care provide for the unit, this level of functionality can be difficult to achieve since others may not see themselves as part of this wider vision of the unit's system. This "we" and "they" philosophy permeates most hospital cultures. Once the incentives are aligned, patient care managers held accountable and the patient is put into the center (e.g. not "your" patient or "my" patient but "our" patient) a significant breakdown of the silo mentality occurs. You then start seeing see breakthrough behaviors as this culture reverberates throughout the hospital. Some of this culture change occurs with a move away from the "push" methodology where patients have to push to the next unit versus a "pull" program where the accepting unit actually pulls the patient to the unit perhaps even coming to the ED to take "our" patient and to avoid further delays. One such "pull" model is the Adopt-a-Boarder Program at Stoneybrook Hospital in New York where unit nurses have agreed to accept patients in their hallways if there are no beds (see www.urgentmatters.org/enewsletter/vol1_issue4/P_adopt_boarder.asp). This breakthrough model was the brainchild of floor nurses trying to assist the ED with the flow of admitted patients.

5.6 Obtain the active engagement of hospital physicians in flow initiatives

No hospital will be completely successful in re-engineering their ED and inpatient throughput without active medical staff involvement. Nurses and managers can only re-engineer to a certain level of operations that they control. The key to medical staff collaboration on this topic is to look for the "win-wins." Being armed with good data is also a must.

Most physicians are aware that delays in hospital discharges are likely to be a reason for the shortage of inpatient beds on any given day. But what most physicians do not realize is that it is likely that less 5% of the medical staff account for 70% of the late discharges. In any hospital, a small number of physicians do not make their rounds until after 4:00 p.m., preferring instead to clear their office of scheduled patients or perform elective procedures in the morning. Most medical staff members, when presented with the data, are shocked that those few physicians are a substantial reason for why other physicians cannot get a bed for their patients or why patients are boarding for long hours in the ED.

Other common medical staff steps to improve capacity and flow include:

- Establishing a hospitalist program
- Creating inpatient care maps for common admission diagnoses
- Hiring nurse practitioners and physician assistants to assist with the discharge process
- Clinically based case managers to facilitate time drivers
- Establishing and enforcing admission and discharge policies for the telemetry and ICU units
- Conduct length of stay studies by physician to look for outliers
- Conduct time of discharge studies by physician to look for outliers
- Developing a "bed czar" position to bird dog key bed bottlenecks and to assure appropriate bed utilization
- Evaluate day-of-discharge ancillary test needs and adjust the schedule to assure results are on the chart during early morning discharge rounds
- Conduct "hallway" market research studies of medical staff members on what can be done to improve length of stay and day of discharge timing

5.7 Expedite the unit as a transition to other services

The most common complaint by ED practitioners is delays in the patient's admission, particularly in locating and moving a patient to a bed. The ED is merely a transitional treatment site, with the disposition of the patient to another treatment location or to discharge being the end point in the ED process. The same is true for an ICU patient that is waiting for a telemetry bed or the telemetry patient waiting for the medical/surgical bed. Delays occur not only with diagnosis and treatment of the patient, but also in moving the patient from the unit to another point of service in the hospital.

5.7.1 Create a Capacity Control and Communication Center

Most hospitals need more robust real-time capacity management strategies. Changes are needed to assure that all admissions and discharges are coordinated and the capacity managed through a single command center that is supported by real-time bed tracking software. A data-driven Capacity Command Center limits the existence of the so-called "phantom" bed process of patient needing beds but the unrecognized bed that has just been cleaned on one unit or a open bed being held all day for the surgery patient and therefore not listed as available will all be valued and appropriately used real time. Capacity Command Center with the appropriate IT technology interfaces can also identify the "mission-critical" beds that are the chief source of today's bottleneck (e.g. telemetry) and target resources to remove the bottleneck (e.g. STAT bed clean teams). This change should come in the form of a centralized Capacity Control Center that coordinates all bed requests, all discharges and monitors the bed turn and placement process. This center may also manage the logistics of tertiary referrals.

5.7.2 Establish discharge times from the patient care units ahead of the busy admit times from the ED

For most hospitals, the ED is the chief source of their admissions. Delays of inpatient beds result when discharge times on inpatient care units do not precede busy ED admits times. It is not unusual for hospital to have the bulk of their hospital discharges occurring after 3:00 in the afternoon and many not until 5:00 to 7:00 pm. Patients waiting for admission are queued and must wait to be transferred to a department where patients are still occupying beds. Analyzing data on the peak admit and discharge times and creating robust medical and nursing staff initiatives and product lines for the ED and patient floors can help to eliminate this problem. A new concept called "slotting" or scheduling discharges for specific times throughout the day may also be helpful as an adjunct to this effort.

5.7.3 Forecast inpatient bed needs

While the ED is often the chief source for admitted patients it is rarely valued as an important contributor to the overall hospital's function and more importantly the ED inpatient bed demand is rarely anticipated, forecasted or proactive bed control strategies utilized to respond to this predictable forecasted need. The unit staff of the anticipated destination for the patient admitted from the ED experiences the arriving patient as a new demand on its resources. This demand can be handled more smoothly if that unit can be given advance warning of the arriving patient. Staff at this arriving location can then prepare their system for the arrival of the patient. Establishment of a "bed-ahead" system is also an efficient way to transition patients when there is forecasted demand. With this system, the receiving unit anticipates demand and has an open bed available in advance of the request from the ED.

5.7.4 Develop refined bed control and surge protocols

Hospitals struggle with daily bed crunches but even if these were repaired, it is rare that hospitals, outside their disaster protocols, have conducted preplanned capacity to address temporary surges such is routinely the case during the annual flu season.

5.7.5 Establish bed control briefings and action plans

Hospitals should establish bed control briefings as a true empowered capacity management tool. This includes clearly defined meeting expectations, appropriate and timely attendance, with individual defined preparation steps and meeting response steps. Appropriate and consistent meeting start/stop times, attendance by key staff (case management), and staff attendance that is prepared and exits the meeting with a specific plan consistent with the bed needs of today, valuing predictable ED bed needs should also be goals. Logistical support for these meetings might include having an established form that calculates and dashboards beds needs and resources. A strongly reinforced characteristic and expectation of these meetings and the staff that attend would be a "pull" system mentality where each department is reaching out to compromised departments and "pulling" the patient or the resource (e.g. meals) to the next step. Success of this effort may require executive leadership attendance at the initial meetings and accountability for meeting goals for future meetings.

5.7.6 Establish a hospital activity barometer and surge action plan.

Hospitals should develop predefined roles for each department that measures current workload and functionality and also establishes preplanned activities should there be temporary surges. This barometer should assure drilled-down capacity-building strategies for each department within the hospital. This written action plan would have detailed steps to be taken by each department to proactively respond or react to key capacity variables based on the color-coded need at the time. This could even include fundamental changes such as dispensing with fundamental hospital-wide housekeeping functions (cleaning offices) to reallocate to resources to STAT

Bed Clean Teams or perhaps canceling routine meetings and having executive staff transport patients.

5.7.7 Revitalize the role of the house supervisor.

Most house supervisor roles were designed to assist with bed management and bed allocation process but so many duties have been added to that position and they are supported with so little technology that the bed allocation role itself often becomes the bottleneck. Hospitals should alter the house supervisor role to assure that capacity management is a priority and re-allocate routine functions to other appropriate staff. For example, if it is determined that the house supervisor is spending significant time on staffing challenges during compromised bed days, those functions should be permanently or temporarily reallocated to other staff. Routine bed requests that have predictable and protocol-driven responses could be delegated to the Bed Command Center with only conflicts and resource challenges brought to the attention of the house supervisor. The variability in house supervisor roles, skills and delivery should also be studies and addressed. Revising the communication devices should also be considered (e.g. cell phones versus pagers).

5.7.8 Develop improved interfaces with outside hospital resources

One of the sources of delays for many hospitals is getting access for discharged patients to nursing homes, rehabilitation centers, home health and other outpatient resources. The potential exists here to ‘slot’ or schedule a time for these nursing home admissions. There are even some hospitals that are leasing nursing home beds in advance to assure the forecasted patient demands are met. These interfaces need to be evaluated, barriers removed and access improved for the patient flow process to improve.

6. RESOLVING CAPACITY AND FLOW PROBLEMS DRIVERS

There are a variety of methodologies for assessing, developing a plan and implementing a change process that impact a healthcare provider's capacity and patient flow. The most effective methods typically center on the following key action steps.

6.1 Conducting a diagnostic study

Key to a healthcare provider's success to improving flow and thus increasing capacity it to know where the constraints and bottlenecks are. The Institute of Health Improvement (IHI) uses the mantra: "How much of the time do we get it right?" in terms of moving patients through the system (Haraden et al, 2004). The IHI model asks two questions:

- Do you park more than 2% of your admitted patients at some time during the day for at least 50% of the time? These patients may be "boarding" in the ED, waiting in the admitting office, holding in post anesthesia recovery or even in a private doctor's waiting room or even a nursing home waiting for an inpatient bed.

- Does your hospital have a midnight census of 90% or greater of your bed capacity more than 50% of the time? A high midnight census is likely to be symptomatic of a bottleneck for beds as there is limited capacity to admit new patients in the evening or morning hours, a considerably high bed demand period.

Parking patients and high midnight census are clear indicators that the hospital is struggling with flow problems. Sometimes the solution can be as simple as "smoothing" the capacity and demand, reducing workflow variations or better managing the rest of the chain of resources inside and outside the hospital (e.g. home healthcare, nursing homes, etc) to reduce peaks and take advantage of low-demand periods.

6.2 Measuring and Understanding Variation

Variation, while ever present in healthcare delivery systems, when left unchecked is tyranny. The key is to understand and manage the correct type of variation. Random or so called "natural" variation is the kind of variation that cannot be controlled. As an example, the types and severity of disease processes typically cannot be controlled unless the hospital is a specialty hospital. ED arrivals cannot be controlled unless the hospital is controlling a portion of those arriving by ambulance through ED diversion. Some forms of natural variation can be managed such as normal distribution of staff skill sets or care gaps that might be impacted by care maps or additional education.

Non-random variation or artificial "variation" can be controlled and in many cases must be eliminated for a healthcare delivery system to be optimized. This is variation that that is artificially introduced into the healthcare delivery system. Examples of artificial variation include the practice of scheduling elective surgeries to peak during the middle of the week but to dramatically decline on Friday afternoons. Practitioner skill sets outside the normal curve or methods or the delayed timing of physician discharge day rounding on patients will add artificial variation to the patient flow process. Hospitals that do not have published discharge times on the day of discharge or that do not manage their published time also add artificial variation and thus introduce bottlenecks into the discharge process and ultimately to the entire healthcare delivery flow process. Another common source of artificial variation in a hospital is liberal admission and discharge practices amongst physicians to the telemetry or intensive care units or the lack of published or managed admission/discharge criteria for those same units, which permits significant variation and artificially limits other appropriate patient access to these beds. Again, the resources are there but they are artificially being limited based on variations in practices, policies or procedures.

6.3 Develop interventions that drive to the key problems.

Understanding and measuring the constraints and bottlenecks within a healthcare delivery system is a critical first step but it key to the success of any effort to optimized flow and capacity. It is important that the providers solve the right problems with sufficient resources. However, it is not uncommon for a provider to try to solve a problem with the wrong intervention. It is also very common for a hospital to react to problems by merely adding beds or staff, only to find that theses beds get filled fast or the staff used more without solving the real problem. The real villain for many of the inpatient units is the lack of written and supervised clinical entry or exit criteria, thus inviting over utilization of these critical resources. Merely adding beds or staff invites continued over utilization. Another example in the ED is the frequently mention of slow laboratory or radiology test turnaround times. If the hospital is successful in changing its laboratory CBC turn-around time or speeding up the CT scan test results from radiology, it could find out that the problem was not within the laboratory or radiology departments but rather with delays and bottlenecks surrounding the laboratory or radiology process. For example, an ED physician may hold six patient care charts and write orders for all six patients before handing these six charts to the one unit secretary to "order" the test, thus artificially batching orders that can only be ordered through the computer one at a time. Another example might be test results that are sitting in the EDs printer waiting to be picked up and inserted into a chart for the physician to read. Another common problem is patient access. The laboratory may respond quickly to the ED but often cannot get to the patient because radiology is with the patient, or in another case the CT scanner may be available but there is no one to transport the patient.

6.4 Using accelerated implementation processes to assess the impact of interventions and then to roll out successes to the entire enterprise.

Many healthcare providers use traditional committee structures and protracted timeframes to implement their interventions on flow and capacity. While some of these providers have some limited success, often successes are not sustained or they are so fact specifics (e.g. based on today's volume or rate limiting factors) that once the underlying assumptions change, they intervention does not have the impact once hope for. In addition, traditional committees that can take a year or more to study the issues and implement their change processes are hampered by changing staff members, attendance issues and even having the underlying problem change.

Even as such, most of the process of change is not just changing the processes and policies but getting the people to move with these changes. To truly engage hospital staff requires a bottoms up and not a top down approach to problem identification, change implementation and sustenance. Most staff members will report the many consultant reports "that have sat on the shelf" or the many times that "administration did not listen" to them or have not made a commitment to "fixing the real problems".

Using an accelerated implementation process fundamentally addresses these issues by creating a stronger staff-driven change process and then empowering the staff to make the changes. In addition, the staff are given tools to implement small changes immediately and test these changes to make sure they are successful and solve the underlying problem.

The keys for rapid capacity and flow improvement are accelerated implementation teams called High Impact Teams (IT) using the Rapid Cycle Testing (RCT) method of change implementation.

6.4.1 High Impact Teams

High Impact Teams (HIT) teams are a hybrid version of other accelerated implementation teams (see www.teachmeteamwork.com/docs/top10team.pdf). The core structure of HIT teams is different from traditional healthcare committees in every way. First, they are not committees but small collaboratives of line and middle management staff who are representative to disciplines and the expertise of "real world" problems and solutions to solving specific issues (e.g., bottlenecks in the ED triage area, backups in surgery or late discharges of patients from the hospital to go home). Second, these teams are fully empowered to make change. They need not ask permission, seek authority or to go through a line of command to implement the small tests of change that they will be empowered to make. Typically these teams operate for a specific and abbreviated number of sessions (e.g. five to six meetings) perhaps over five days, five weeks or at the most, five months. Their job is to study, brainstorm bottlenecks and interventions, and roll out changes during the period of the five sessions. The reason for the limited number of sessions is that it eliminates much of the "fluff" of a traditional study and change process. With only five sessions, at most each team can only afford to do broad brainstorming of the problems for one or two sessions. Any more and the committee time erodes into precious intervention and implementation process time.

There are also a limited number of members on each team. Each team member is highly leveraged to represent their peers but also any closely associated peer group. (e.g. RN for LVNs and unit secretaries for patient care technicians, general diagnostic radiology technologists for CT and other specialty radiology staff). Why such limited attendance? In practical terms, limiting the numbers limits the number of late arrivals, risk for missed homework assignments and limits excessive dialogue and repeat memories during each HIT team session.

A typically ED HIT team that is looking to improve ED diagnosis and treatment process might include:

- ED nurses (2)
- ED physician
- Unit secretary
- Laboratory
- Radiology
- Case manager

For a typical inpatient team, the HIT team makeup might include:

- Charge nurse from a representative unit
- RNs from representative units (2)
- Hospitalist
- Case manager
- Housekeeping
- Bed control nurse

Typically each team adopts and operates within a type frame of ground rules that are designed to accelerate the process, limit delays and more important, to encourage breakthrough creativity. The ground rules have been assimilated by asking a number of HIT team participants what would make a session successful. A sample set of ground rules for a HIT team might look like the following:

- All sessions are just 90 minutes.
- Sessions start and end on time.
- All pagers and cell phones are turned off or set to vibrate mode. The team member's full attention at the sessions is essential.
- Encourage wild ideas.
- Respect everyone's opinion.
- All sessions are action oriented. There are no minutes, just action plans.
- All team members come prepared with all homework assignments completed.

All of the meetings are carefully scripted and supported with a coach to assure the progress on the goals of the meetings are being addressed and the ground rules are honored.

An emphasis for the HIT teams is identifying a small number of interventions that will have the highest yield whether that is impacting the bottleneck, ease of implementation or cost effectiveness to achieving the goals of the initiative. These are often refereed as the "low-hanging fruit." These four to six targets are designed to limit distraction and the so called "solver world hunger" appetite that these teams sometimes have and also further assists with the potential for success as there are likely to be a number of HIT teams in a hospital wide initiative. For example, if there are six HIT teams each delivering six interventions, this would equate to 36 interventions being rolled in a short period of time, a number that would test any sophisticated hospital's ability to absorb change and understand the results. The reality is that each HIT team works at its own pace and there generally is not a crunch of 30 plus interventions occurring at the same time.

Note there is very little executive management involvement at the HIT team level. Key management is typically involved at a steering team level to set broad project goals, to monitor the progress and to eliminate bottlenecks that might arise about the team's authority, responsibility and empowerment. For example, an ED HIT team may want to study and perhaps role out a trial of the use of point of care laboratory testing in the ED's Fast Track. Point of care tests might include bedside analysis and reporting of results of urine pregnancy, blood sugar, hematocrits and hemoglobins, certain chemical tests and in the cases of more significant clinical concerns, blood gases and cardiac enzymes. Let assume, hypothetically only, that the response from the laboratory leadership is "no" to the use of ED best side testing for a variety of perceived cost and quality controls reasons. If that bottleneck cannot be resolved by the HIT team members, the matter is referred to the Steering Team to remove the bottleneck because that team is empowered to study any option and use whatever tool is needed to reach the global goal established by the Steering Team. The HIT team would be allowed to trial the point-of-care testing process to see if it works and if the cost and quality concerns are a reality or perhaps can be mitigated. Figure 3 provides a typical organization chart for a HIT team. Table 1 provides sample ground rules for a HIT team.

6.4.2 Rapid Cycle Testing (RCT)

RCT is a contemporary industrial engineering concept designed to test changes on a small scale to assure clarity of the intervention's assumptions, intervention effectiveness to allow minor customization of the interventions to correct for found timing or intervention sizing issues that might make the intervention more effective. Another key reason for RCTs is to allow tests on a small change to minimize risk to patient care, flow or staff adoption. Another important reason for using the RCT process is to help scale the implementation process.

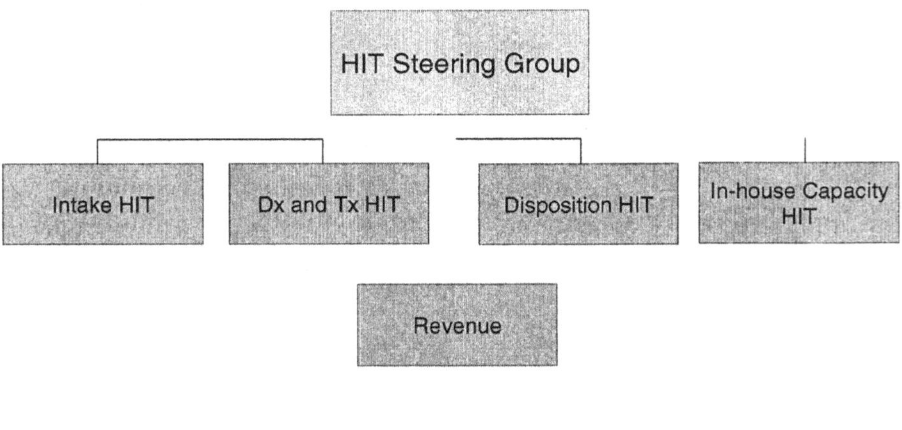

Figure 3. Typical HIT Teams and reporting structure

Table 1. Typical HIT Team meeting ground rules.
Source: The Abaris Group, Walnut Creek, CA

Typical HIT Team Ground Rules

Ground Rules (approved by each HIT Team):

1. All meetings will begin and end on time.
2. Meetings are limited to 90 minutes unless permitted by the committee members.
3. Beepers and phones are to be placed on "vibrate" mode during the meetings. Only emergencies should be responded to.
4. All team members will stay on track. A timekeeper will be used at each meeting and agenda items will have assigned time limits for discussion.
5. All team members will follow through with assignments and come prepared to the meetings.
6. All team members will regularly attend meetings. In the unlikely event they cannot attend a designee should be sent in their place.
7. No veto power or "sacred cows" during the brainstorming sessions.
8. Thinking "wildly" is encouraged during all brainstorming and action plan sessions.
9. One idea at a time
10. Defer judgment/respect all opinions
11. Build on the opinions of others
12. Stay focused
13. Titles stay outside the door.

For example, an ED might want to eliminate the patient triage process when beds are available in the back of the ED. The reason might be that the HIT team may have identified that triage itself adds 15 to 25 minutes of unnecessary delay to the care process, is a big patient dissatisfier and does not result in safer bed placement or elimination of care processes. In most EDs, if triage were simply and abruptly eliminated, there would be chaos throughout the department and substantial safety concerns among the clinical staff. Triage is also widely held to be a legally required step in the care process and many bedside nurses expect it to be completed in many EDs in a comprehensive way. Some nurses might even use the terms: "you're going to kill a patient if you eliminate triage."

Triage or "to sort" is often mistakenly associated with Napoleon but rather it was one of his key French surgeons, Dominque-Jean Laurey (Richardson, 2002), who invented the concept as a sorting tool to be used only when there were insufficient resources in the battlefield for the demand being presented. But triage, as deployed in most EDs, has been found to be a bottleneck itself when it is used when there are sufficient ED beds, for example early in the morning before the volume of ED patients begins to rise. The HIT team might desire to trial a "no-triage" protocol concept for a week, but would likely face a barrage of staff skepticism. Thus this might be trialed for a day, a shift or even just for several hours. Depending upon the perceived staff concerns, the time period for the trial can be customized, at the very least, to during the portion of a shift that HIT members are on duty, and thus willing to commit to the test of change during that period. This might be, for example, for the first three hours of the shift next Thursday that Dr. Smith and Nurse Jones, both HIT team members, are on duty. It is helpful that each team has a target or aim statement be used and that interventions be deployed using Nolan's Plan, Do, Check, Act (PDCA) model (Langley et al, 1996). Figure 6 provides a sample of an AIM statement.

RCTs are sequentially rolled out using small tests of change. Gradually, but over a relatively short period of time, the trial is adjusted and either abandoned or expanded based on the results of each trial. Figure 5 provides an ED example of an RCT to triage a new radiology protocol. RCTs, as a tool, can be applied to a wide variety of issues. For example, an inpatient HIT team -- after considerable analysis, research of best practices and brainstorming -- may wish to trial an Admission/Discharge Nurse concept on one of the floors to accelerate the time the patient is admitted or sent home, depending on the need at any given time. This is a published, best practice, concept. The concept might be trialed next Monday during the day shift, studying data acquired during the trial and then adjusting the role or duties on Tuesday for a Wednesday trial. The triage on Wednesday is successful, so it is expanded to include one more med/surgery area on Friday and further expanded until it is fully rolled out the following week. Although this process was changed through small tests, it was fully deployed hospital-wide in less than two weeks.

The key to a successful RCT trial is to have the following PDCA questions and supporting data in mind:

- What are we trying to change?
- What changes will have the biggest impact?
- How will we know if the change made a difference?
- Did the change make a difference and if not why not?

Having a clear understanding of the goal of the change is critical. Many healthcare providers, while building enthusiasm about a change process or a series of change processes, attempt to just implement changes without carefully thinking them out or having sufficient baseline data to know if the change will be effective or even if the change will affect the originally defined problem. It has often been witnessed that well-meaning health providers burn out in frustration due to:

- Tying to solve the wrong problem, or,
- Changing processes that won't impact the targeted problem, or,
- Insufficient use of the change process to impact the problem or, finally,
- Not knowing if they have solved the problem due to insufficient data collection.

Testing on a small scale also allows the collection of small data sets to define the baseline and to measure movement. Often times, staff may not feel they have access to baseline data, or data are perceived to be too difficult to get (e.g., ED time flow data from a complex patient tracking system). The solution is the manual collection of mini samples. In industrial engineering terms, you "collect big data for big decisions and little data for little decisions." This means, a small sample should suffice for testing on a small scale.

In industrial engineering circles, a sample of 30 events, if properly collected without bias (e.g. 30 consecutive events), should be sufficient to measure baseline current "as-is" status and 30 events during the RCT should measure impact. For example, a HIT team might wish to explore speeding up the process of when a patient leaves a hospital bed to when the bed is put into the computer for purposes of notifying housekeeping to clean the bed. Perhaps the trial intervention is to empower the charge nurse to also put the discharge order into the system due to a perceived bottleneck of a large number of discharge orders coming in at one during the peak discharge times. To obtain baseline data, the "patient departure time to time noted in the computer" is hand collected on 30 consecutive patients during Tuesday's peak discharge time and then the new charge nurse scope implemented on Wednesday, for 30 consecutive patients, those times are hand recorded and compared to the Tuesday baseline experience.

The concepts of HIT teams, RCTs and other accelerated implementation processes not only create a toolkit for radically improving the flow of patients and the capacity of a healthcare provider but also revolutionize and energize every aspect of the decision process and every stakeholder in that process. HIT teams are also simple to implement and can be used with a wide variety of issues, including revenue management, building designs and also major emergency response planning.

7. CONCLUSIONS AND EXTENSIONS

Healthcare providers are increasingly compromised with growing demand and limited resources. The resulting impacts are excessive waiting, prolonged patient flow and customer dissatisfaction. A key ingredient to improving the healthcare delivery system is to better understand the dynamics, the drivers and the myths that impact healthcare patient flow and capacity. In addition, healthcare providers should conduct independent and objective analyses of their particular bottlenecks and process and flow constraints to assure that steps are taken that will impact the real problems. Providers should also understand that key industrial engineering tools will create high-leverage solutions, many of which do not require more staff or beds but rather the reallocation of staff and beds to demand. Traditional change processes are often slow and ineffective and thus frustrating to providers who are trying to make a difference. Key to implementing and sustaining success is the use of accelerated implementation models, such as the HIT teams and RCT models noted in this article.

8. REFERENCES

Agency for Healthcare Research and Quality (2004). The Uninsured in America, 1996-2004, Rockville, Maryland.

American Hospital Association (2005). AHA Hospital Statistics 2005 Edition, Chicago, IL.

Aiken, L.H., Clark, S.P., Sloane, D.M., Sochalski, J., Silber, J.H. (2002). Hospital nurse staffing and mortality, nurse burnout and job dissatisfaction. *JAMA* **288** (16): 1987-93.

American College of Emergency Physicians, ACEP (1993). Emergency Department Design, Dallas, TX.

Berwick, D. M. (1996). A primer on leading the improvement of systems. *British Medical Journal*, **312** (March 9): 619-22.

Chase R, Aquilano N, Jacobs FR. (2001). *Operations Management for Competitive Advantage*. New York: McGraw-Hill Irwin.

Disney Institute (2001). Be Our Guest: Perfecting the Art of Customer Service, New York, NY.

Graff, L.G.(ed) (1998). Observation units: implementation and management strategies, American College of Emergency Physicians, Dallas TX,

Haraden, C., Resar, R., Henderson, D. et al, (2004). Capacity management breakthrough strategies for improving patient flow, frontiers of health services management, American College of healthcare Executives, Chicago, IL. **20**, No. 4,

Healthcare Financial Management Association. (2004). Financing the future survey. Westchester, IL.

Langley, C., K. Nolan, T. Nolan, C. Norman, and L. Provost (1996). The Improvement Guide: A Practical Approach to Improving Organizational Performance. *Jossey-Bass Publishers,* San Francisco.

McCaig LF, Burt CW. (2004). National Hospital Ambulatory Medical Care Survey: 2002 Emergency department summary. Advance data from vital and health statistics; **340**: Hyattsville, Maryland: National Center for Health Statistics.

Melnick, G., Bamezai, A., Green, L., Nawatje, E. (2002). California emergency department capacity and demand, California Healthcare Foundation, Oakland, CA.

Patel, P., MD, Derlet D, Vinson, D, Williams M, Wills, J. (2006). Ambulance diversion reduction: the Sacramento solution, *JEM*.

Peterson, C. (2001) Nursing shortage: not a simple problem - no easy answers., *Online Journal of Issues in Nursing*. **6**, No. 1.

Regenstein, M., Nolan, L., Wilson, M. Mead, H., Siegel, B, (2004), Walking a Tightrope: The State of the safety net in ten U.S. communities, George Washington University Medical Center Department of Health Policy, Washington DC.

Richardson R. 2002,. Surgeon to Napoleon's Imperial Guard. London, England: *Quiller Press Ltd.*

Robeznicks, A. (2005). A call to action, Modern Healthcare, Chicago, IL, October 24, 2005.

Sochalski, J. (2002). Nursing Shortage redux: turning the corner on an enduring problem, Health Affairs **21** 11: 157.

Stout, J. (1986) Ambulance Systems Design *JEMS*, **11**: 85-96.

The Lewin Group (2002). Analysis of AHA ED and hospital capacity survey. Chicago, IL

U.S. General Accounting Office (GAO).(2003). Hospital Emergency Departments: Crowded Conditions Vary Among Hospitals and Communities. Report No. GAO-03-460. Washington DC: U.S. GAO.

US Census Bureau, Population Division, Washington DC Population Division, US Census Bureau. For US population estimates from 1998 to 2000, Table CO-EST2001-12-00 - Time Series of Intercensal State Population Estimates: April 1, 1990 to April 1, 2000. Release Date: April 11, 2002. For US population estimates from 2001 to 2003, Table 1: Annual Estimates of the Population for the United States and States, and for Puerto Rico: April 1, 2000 to July 1, 2005 (NST-EST2005-01).Release Date: December 22, 2005. (http://www.census.gov/popest/archives/2000s/vintage_2001/CO-EST2001-12/CO-EST2001-12-00.html, http://www.census.gov/popest/states/NST-ann-est.html, last accessed January 11, 2006)

Williams, M. (2004). Materials management and logistics in the emergency department, M Rice (ed), *Emergency Medicine Clinics of North America*, Saunders February 2004, **22**, No.1. Philadelphia, PA.

Chapter 3

ACCESS TO SURGERY AND MEDICAL CONSEQUENCES OF DELAYS

Boris Sobolev,[1 2] Adrian Levy,[1 3] and Lisa Kuramoto[2]

[1]*Department of Health Care and Epidemiology, The University of British Columbia, Vancouver B.C., Canada,* [2]*Centre for Clinical Epidemiology and Evaluation, Vancouver Coastal Health Research Institute, 828 West 10th Avenue, Vancouver B.C. V5Z 1L8, Canada,* [3]*Centre for Health Evaluation and Outcome Sciences, St. Paul's Hospital, Vancouver B.C., Canada*

Abstract Wait lists are a common tool for managing access to elective surgery. However, little evidence is available on the health impact of delaying surgery for various conditions. Other than preoperative mortality, adverse events experienced by patients while on a wait list have not been systematically examined. Without these data, appropriate access time for surgery must be determined on the basis of expert opinion. When treatment is delayed, the condition of a patient on a surgical wait list may deteriorate and require urgent medical attention. In this case, emergency admission for the awaited procedure may be regarded as an adverse effect of waiting. In this chapter, we present the results of recent wait list studies that quantified the risk of delayed treatment in patients accepted for coronary artery bypass surgery and in patients awaiting elective cholecystectomy. Our results have implications for developing waiting-time limits for elective surgical procedure.

Keywords: Elective surgical procedures, access to care, wait lists, health effects

Wait lists are a common tool for managing access to elective – medically necessary, but non-emergency – surgery in publicly funded health systems (Naylor, 1991). While queuing according to urgency of intervention, or priority wait-listing, is perceived as a method for facilitating access to treatment within clinically appropriate times (MacCormick et al., 2003), waiting can adversely affect those delayed, causing worsening of symptoms or death (Ray et al., 2001).

When treatment is delayed, the condition of a patient on a surgical waiting list may deteriorate and require urgent medical attention, including emergency surgery. In this case, emergency admission for the awaited procedure may be regarded as an adverse effect of waiting.

Examples of clinical conditions which may require emergency surgery to be performed on patients who are on wait lists include inguinal hernia, spinal cord conditions, abdominal aortic aneurysm, and occlusive coronary artery disease (CAD). Also, routine operating room activity may be seriously disrupted by unexpected non-elective admissions of patients on wait lists (Buhaug, 2002).

Alternatively, the patient's condition may deteriorate to such an extent that surgery is no longer possible. In population-based studies, death before coronary artery bypass graft (CABG) surgery, for instance, has been reported to occur in 0.4 to 1.3 percent of patients for whom it is felt surgery can be safely delayed (Bernstein et al., 1997; Légaré et al., 2005; Morgan et al., 1998; Rexius et al., 2004). In addition, even if the surgery is still possible, a longer recovery may be necessary, or other complications may ensue.

Little evidence is available on the health impact of delaying surgery for various conditions (McGurran and Noseworthy, 2002; Turnbull et al., 2000; Derrett et al., 1999). Other than mortality, adverse events experienced by patients while on a wait list have not been systematically examined (Morgan et al., 1998). Even within the literature on mortality, data which identifies the risks for various waiting times are not widely available. Without such data, appropriate access times for surgery must be determined on the basis of expert opinion (Naylor et al., 1990).

In this chapter, we first provide an overview of the Canadian health care system and then present the results of two examples that quantified the risk of delayed treatment for patients awaiting elective cholecystectomy and for patients accepted for CABG surgery. At the end of the chapter, we describe statistical methods for studying the risks of adverse events associated with wait lists. Our results have implications for developing acceptable limits for waiting times for elective surgical procedures.

1. The Canadian health care system

Canada's health care coverage is universally available and publicly provided; it is funded through provincial and federal taxes and insurance premiums (Reinhardt, 1998). The legal basis of the Canadian health care system, the Canada Health Act, provides coverage for all medically necessary hospital and physician services. This means that Canadians seeking care go to a physician or hospital of their choice and present their health insurance cards.

Provincial governments are responsible for issuing health insurance cards to residents. Individuals do not pay directly for services and no dollar limits or deductibles apply. The Canada Health Act thereby ensures that health care services are made available on the basis of need rather than on an individual's ability to pay. However, while legislation creates national standards, the Canadian health care system is actually a complex arrangement of funding mechanisms worked out between the federal and provincial governments (Levy and Gagnon, 2002).

Most physicians and surgeons are paid on a fee-for-service basis, with the upper salary limits in some provinces. Patients are referred to specialists or surgeons by primary care physicians, who are considered the gatekeepers for access to specialized services.

Most Canadian acute care hospitals are operated as private non-profit organizations run by community boards of trustees, voluntary organizations, or municipalities. These hospitals receive global operating budgets established by provincial ministries of health and mostly determined annually by historical expenditures with some adjustments. Hospitals must look after their day-to-day allocation of resources within the operating budget (Klatt, 2000).

Wait lists are used extensively as part of hospital or regional responses to limited budgets. Naylor introduced the concept of wait lists as a management tool (Naylor, 1991) and a form of rationing (Naylor et al., 1993). In publicly funded health care, wait lists are commonly used to manage access to elective procedures, but the practice raises concerns about the delaying of necessary treatment (Naylor et al., 1995; Noseworthy et al., 2003).

2. Access to elective surgery

After a patient is referred, the surgeon assesses the patient and the severity of illness. The decision to operate is taken after surgery is indicated and the patient is deemed a suitable candidate. Patients are placed on the surgeon's wait list if they cannot be operated on immediately.

For non-life-threatening conditions, patients are enrolled on a first-come, first-served basis. For potentially live-threatening conditions, they are registered on a priority wait list. Patients are ranked by how urgently they need treatment, and a priority class is assigned to all patients to determine relative positions on the list. Patients with a higher priority will be selected for service ahead of those with a lower priority, regardless of when they are placed on the list. Patients in the same priority class are ranked in the order of arrival.

Patients are removed from the list if they reconsider the decision for surgery, if they accept surgery from another surgeon, if they decline admission, if they move out of the province, if they are deferred or suspended on medical grounds, if they are suspended for administrative reasons, if they die while awaiting surgery, if the physician decides to try a medical treatment instead of waiting for surgery, if their conditions preclude scheduling of surgery indefinitely, if their conditions improve and make the surgery unnecessary, if the operation is no longer possible, if the operation no longer offers the likelihood of improvement, or when surgery is done.

Access to surgical care in the hospital is usually managed through scheduling demands for service. Scheduling identifies patients available for the next service period and reserves hospital resources to ensure appropriate care before and after an operation (Blake and Carter, 1997).

To plan the utilization of the surgical suite resources, the hospital releases, on a periodic basis, blocks of operating room time to each surgical service, which then places patients on the operating room schedule (Magerlein and Martin, 1978). Some time slots are set aside for emergency cases. Any time which was not booked is made available to other services.

We use the term scheduling cycle for the sequence of events in surgical scheduling between two releases of operating time blocks. Within services, patients are selected from wait lists and scheduled for operation based on urgency, best use of allocated operating time, and the availability of hospital resources. However, an emergency case is sent to the operating room upon arrival, potentially causing cancelation of scheduled elective operations. On the other hand, if operating room time becomes available unexpectedly, patients may be added to the current schedule if they can come in at short notice. The service access is defined as immediate if patients are admitted within the scheduling cycle that had started at the time they were accepted for service. The access is said to be delayed if patients are admitted within a scheduling cycle that starts after their acceptance for service.

Before being added to the operating room schedule, all patients are assessed by an anesthesiologist as to suitability for surgery. If a patient's condition is not fit for surgery, scheduling of the operation may be postponed. Scheduling a patient for surgery may be also delayed for the following reasons: the patient decides to postpone surgery; a hospital ward, intensive care unit bed, or operating room is unavailable at the time scheduled; or, the doctor decides to send the patient for additional pre-operative investigation. The availability of other hospital resources is considered in selecting patients for scheduling the operation (Hamilton and Breslawski, 1994).

Patients might be reinstated on the list following medical deferral, administrative suspension, self-deferral, or failure to attend (Armstrong, 2000a).

3. Access to coronary artery surgery

A specific example of scheduling should clarify the process by which a patient arrives at surgery. In the Canadian province of British Columbia (B.C.), priority wait lists are commonly used to manage access to elective procedures according to urgency of treatment (Noseworthy et al., 2003). In particular, patients with CAD are prioritized according to angina symptoms, coronary anatomy, and left ventricular function impairment in order to facilitate access to surgical revascularization within clinically appropriate times (Levy et al., 2005).

Initially, a patient presenting with symptoms of CAD is referred to a cardiologist who assesses the need for revascularization. The cardiologist evaluates the results of coronary angiography and decides on treatment (Grech, 2003). If coronary angioplasty is not indicated, patients are referred to a cardiac surgeon who assesses their need and suitability for CABG.

When urgent assessment is required, patients are transferred to a hospital cardiac ward directly from the catheterization laboratory. If suitable for surgery, such patients remain in hospital until the operation.

Alternatively, patients are scheduled for an outpatient consultation with the cardiac surgeon at a later date. Following the consultation in which surgery is identified as necessary, surgeons register on their wait lists patients who require CABG and decide to undergo the operation in one of the four B.C. tertiary care hospitals at which the operation is performed, and at which the specific surgeon has admitting rights. A priority category is assigned to each patient according to the urgency of treatment.

The suggested time to surgery is three days for patients with left main coronary artery stenosis greater than 70% (urgent group); six weeks for patients with persistent unstable angina, impaired left ventricular function, and significant obstruction defined as left-main stenosis, triple-vessel disease or double-vessel disease with significant proximal left anterior descending stenosis (semi-urgent group); and 12 weeks for patients with intractable chronic angina, normal left ventricular function, and single-vessel disease or double-vessel disease with no lesion in the proximal left anterior descending artery (non-urgent group) (Levy et al., 2005).

At each hospital, the patient's access to surgery is managed through scheduling of operating room time. Patients are selected for scheduling both from hospital cardiac wards and from the surgical wait lists based on allocated operating room time-slots and priority.

Before being added to the operating room schedule, each patient is reassessed by an anesthesiologist as to suitability for surgery. The operation may be postponed for any of the reasons noted above, including if the anesthesiologist requests additional preoperative investigations, or when an emergency case comes in and scheduled operations are canceled. On the other hand, already scheduled patients may undergo surgery ahead of their scheduled dates if an operating room time slot becomes available.

A diagram showing the patient's path from presentation with symptoms of CAD to CABG can be found elsewhere (Sobolev et al., 2005a).

4. Two studies on adverse events while waiting for surgery

In order to understand the time-related nature of adverse events associated with wait lists, it will help to look at the results of recent studies of wait lists for elective surgical procedures. The full investigative methods are published elsewhere, so here we provide the most relevant elements for wait list outcomes (Sobolev et al., 2003; Sobolev et al., 2005c; Sobolev et al., 2005b).

Unplanned emergency admission while awaiting cholecystectomy

In the first example, that of patients with biliary colic caused by cholelithiasis, it can be seen that extended treatment delays may increase the probability that the patient will be admitted for cholecystectomy on an emergency basis. Emergency admission may be associated with more frequent or more severe attacks of biliary colic or other biliary complications such as acute cholecystitis, obstructive jaundice, cholangitis or pancreatitis (Friedman, 1993).

In order to assess the relationship between time spent on a wait list and the risk of emergency admission for this patient cohort, this study reviewed the timing and type of operations performed on patients on cholecystectomy wait lists maintained by the Department of Surgery, Queens University, Kingston, O.N. Canada. (Sobolev et al., 2003). In this setting, eight general surgeons performed cholecystectomy, and there was no system for ranking the urgency of the patient. Each surgeon's office managed its wait list independently.

Surgeons on call made the decision to operate on patients who presented to the emergency department by evaluating (a) the clinical presentation for symptoms of increased pain or fever and signs of persisting or worsening abdominal tenderness, guarding or rebound or (b) the ultrasonographic finding of a thick-walled gallbladder with pericholecystic fluid or a positive finding of hepatobilary iminodiacetic acid on radionuclide scan, or both (a) and (b).

Data on the timing and type of surgery were retrieved from the electronic hospital information system from fiscal years 1997 to 2000. The primary outcome investigated was emergency admission for cholecystectomy due to the worsening of symptoms while awaiting elective surgery. A wait list time was calculated for each patient based on the number of weeks from the last consultation visit to elective or emergency surgery. This approach assumes the last visit before surgery was the date when the decision to operate was made (DeCoster et al., 1999).

Elective patients spent a total of 5,712 person-weeks waiting to be admitted. The average weekly number of elective operations was 12.4 (95% confidence interval [CI] 11.6–13.3) per 100 patients on the list.

The rate differed across enrolment periods, from 10.3 (9.1–11.5) in fiscal year 1997/98 to 15.1 (13.4–16.9) in 1998/99 to 13.2 (11.5–15.0) in 1999/2000. The median length of stay on the list was 6 weeks. However, there was considerable variation in individual waiting times. At the present time, there is no recommended waiting time for cholecystectomy.

The probability of undergoing elective surgery increased rapidly from 25% within 3 weeks of the last clinic visit, to 50% at 6 weeks and 75% at 10 weeks, and then gradually reached a plateau. Although 90% of patients underwent surgery by 17 weeks, the remaining 10% waited another 1 to 35 weeks (total, 18 to 52 weeks) for their operation, Figure 3.1.

Surgeons with a low volume of cholecystectomies (less than 20 per year) operated on the majority of patients with extended delays. In general, low-volume surgeons had a primary interest in surgical oncology. This may explain the order in which their patients accessed cholecystectomy during the waiting period: the cholecystectomies were seen to be less medically necessary than oncological procedures.

Overall, 6.7% of the patients waiting for elective cholecystectomy underwent surgery through unplanned emergency admissions. The proportion varied significantly across the categories of patient and service characteristics. Women, the youngest (less than 25 years) and oldest (more than 75 years) patients, patients enrolled in 1999/2000, and pa-

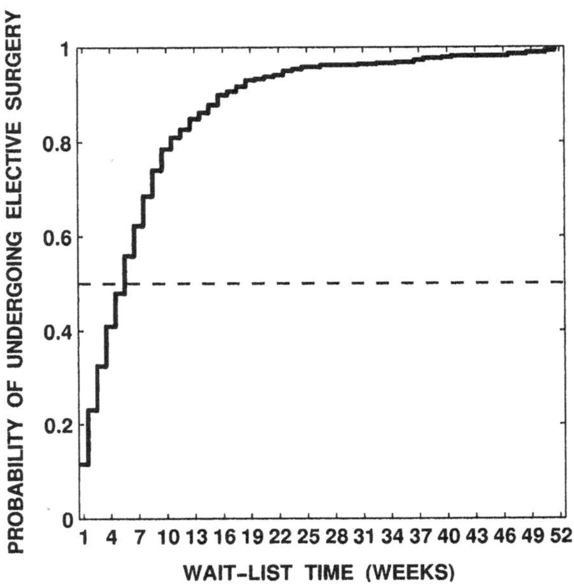

Figure 3.1. Estimated probabilities of elective surgery

tients operated on by lower volume surgeons were admitted as emergency cases more often.

The average weekly emergency admission rate of patients on the wait lists was 0.9 (95% CI 0.7–1.2) per 100 patients. However, the weekly emergency admission rate increased from 0.8 to 5.7 per 100 patients from the interval of the first 4 weeks to the interval of 40 to 52 weeks. See Figure 3.2.

When adjusted for sex, age decade, period, and surgeon volume, the emergency admission rate was more than 1.5 times higher after 20 weeks, 2 times higher after 28 weeks and 7 times higher after 40 weeks relative to the first 4 weeks of wait list time.

Patients waiting 20 weeks or more were more likely to undergo emergency admission than those waiting shorter times after adjustment for age, sex, period and surgeon volume. Table 3.1 shows the conditional probability of emergency admission during the 7 wait list intervals compared with the corresponding figures for elective admission. Although the probability of emergency admission during the first 19 weeks was low, after 20 weeks the probability started increasing and approached 40% in the interval of 40–52 weeks. Of 46 patients who waited for more than 20 weeks, 28% were admitted as emergency cases, compared with 5% of those who waited less than 20 weeks (715 patients).

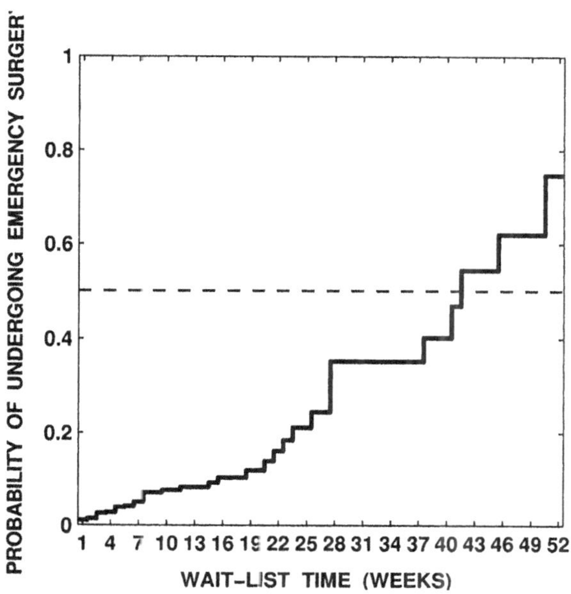

Figure 3.2. Estimated probabilities of emergency surgery

Table 3.1. Probabilities of elective and emergency admission by different wait list intervals, conditional on remaining on the list until the start of each interval

Interval, wks	Elective	Emergency
<4	0.32	0.02
4–7	0.44	0.02
8–11	0.49	0.03
12–19	0.53	0.03
20–27	0.43	0.11
28–39	0.33	0.19
40–52	0.60	0.40

The average weekly rates were 2.4 (95% CI 1.3–4.0) and 0.7 (95% CI 0.5–1.0) per 100 patients in these 2 groups, respectively, with the adjusted rate ratio being 2.7 (95% CI 2.0–3.7).

Risk of death while waiting for cardiac surgery

In the second example, we describe two studies which look at B.C. patients waiting for CABG. In these studies, delays in treatment are shown to be related to various measures of pre-operative mortality. For both investigations, we studied records of patients in whom surgical revascularization was indicated at the time of consultation with a cardiac surgeon. The primary outcomes were the occurrence of death from all causes and death related to CAD while awaiting surgery. Data were extracted from a prospective database of all patients who were accepted for isolated first-time CABG in B.C. between 1990 and 2001. We restricted the analysis to the first 52 weeks after registration on the wait list. Also, patients who underwent surgery in the week of registration (immediate access) were excluded from the analyses.

The analyses were conducted with adjustment for patient case-mix. Elderly patients are more likely to undergo revascularization as an urgent procedure. Their smaller coronary vessel diameters may account for a higher risk of adverse events seen among women. Co-existing medical conditions may delay scheduling surgery. Each patient was classified as 1) presenting with no co-existing conditions, 2) presenting with congestive heart failure, diabetes, chronic obstructive pulmonary disease, cancer or rheumatoid arthritis, or 3) presenting with other co-existing chronic conditions as defined in (Romano et al., 1993).

At 52 weeks of follow-up, 86% of patients had undergone surgery, 1% died while awaiting surgery, 5% of patients remained on the lists, and 8% dropped out during follow-up for various reasons: became unfit for surgery (2%), declined surgery (2%), transferred to another surgeon or hospital (1%), received other surgery (<1%), or removed from the list due to other reasons (2%). While the majority of the urgent patients had received surgery by 52 weeks, over one-tenth of non-urgent patients and less than 5% of semi-urgent patients were still on the list at 52 weeks. In the urgent group, 1% of patients had waits beyond 52 weeks: 0.2% were eventually removed due to patient request, for 0.4% urgency was downgraded at some point, and for 0.4% there were no records to identify the reasons for the delay.

In total, 1% (95% CI 0.82–1.23) of patients died before surgery. At 0.8% (95% CI 0.02–1.55), the urgent group had the smallest proportion of deaths on the wait list; whereas, 0.9% (95% CI 0.63–1.09) and 1.3% (95% CI 0.82–1.84) died before the operation in semi-urgent and non-urgent groups, respectively.

Overall, the rate of death from all causes was 0.67 (95% CI 0.53–0.81) per 1000 patient-weeks. The rate varied from 1.34 (95% CI 0.03–2.65) in the urgent group to 0.63 (95% CI 0.46–0.80) in the semi-urgent group and 0.58 (95% CI 0.36–0.80) in the non-urgent group. After adjustment for age, sex, and co-morbidity, the death rate in the non-urgent group was similar to that of the semi-urgent group (Odds ratio (OR) = 0.97, 95% CI 0.61–1.55), Table 3.2.

Table 3.2. Relationship between urgency and all-cause mortality in patients registered for bypass surgery, 1991-2000

Urgency	No. of deaths	Total wait*	Death rate† (95% CI)	OR‡ (95% CI)
Urgent	4	2994	1.34 (0.03, 2.65)	1.92 (0.70, 5.32)
Semi-urgent	55	87153	0.63 (0.46, 0.80)	1.00
Non-urgent	26	44719	0.58 (0.36, 0.80)	0.97 (0.61, 1.55)
All patients§	92	137139	0.67 (0.53, 0.81)	–

* measured in patient-weeks

† weekly rate was calculated as the number of all-cause deaths divided by the sum of observations periods (per 1000 patient-weeks)

‡ adjusted for age, sex, and comorbidity

§ includes additional patients with urgency not provided

One measure for summarizing the risk of death in a competing risk setting is the probability of death by a certain time (Pepe and Mori, 1993). Figure 3.3 shows the cumulative incidence of death while waiting for surgery in the semi-urgent and non-urgent groups. The non-urgent group had a greater probability of death before surgery than the semi-urgent group for almost all wait list weeks (Gray's two-sample test = 3.4, $p = 0.07$). Compared to the semi-urgent group, the odds of death before surgery was 1.6 times greater in the non-urgent group (OR = 1.63, 95% CI 1.01–2.63), after adjustment for age, sex, and co-morbidity.

The difference between the cumulative incidence functions became larger with time on the list, approaching respective proportions of deaths in each group by 52 weeks. Considering that death rates were similar in these two groups, the higher proportion dying among non-urgent patients suggests that the longer waiting times in this group contribute to a higher chance of death before surgery.

The rate of CAD death was 0.49 (95% CI 0.37–0.61) per 1000 patient-weeks. The rate decreased from 1.00 (95% CI 0.00–2.14) in the urgent group to 0.50 (95% CI 0.36–0.65) in the semi-urgent group and to 0.34

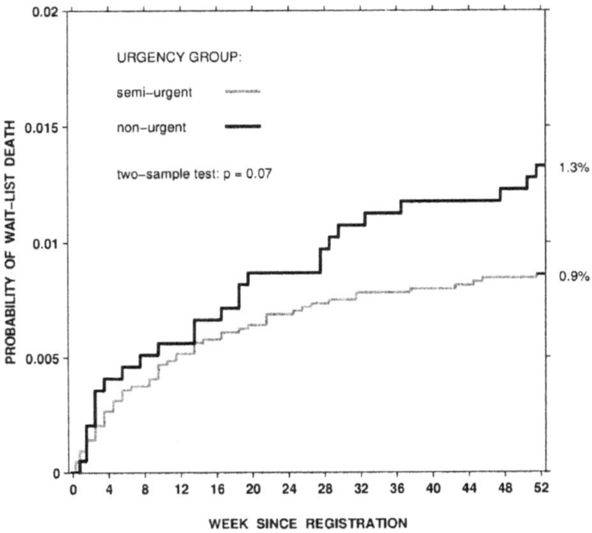

Figure 3.3. Estimated cumulative incidence of death by wait-list week since registration in semi-urgent and non-urgent groups

(95% CI 0.17–0.51) in the non-urgent group. After adjustment for age, sex, and co-morbidity, the death rate due to CAD in the non-urgent group was 30% lower than the semi-urgent group (OR = 0.70, 95% CI 0.39–1.26).

Figure 3.4 shows the probability of CAD death before surgery by a certain time in the semi-urgent and non-urgent groups. The semi-urgent group has a greater probability of death before surgery than the non-urgent group for 28 weeks since registration, but the difference between the cumulative incidence functions became smaller with time on the list (Gray's two-sample test = 0.13, p = 0.72). Considering that CAD death rate was higher in semi-urgent patients, similar proportions dying from CAD before surgery in both groups suggest that the waiting times in the non-urgent group equalized the risk of CAD death before surgery.

Another measure suggested for summarizing the risk of death over time in the competing-risk setting is the probability of death conditional on not having experienced the competing event by a certain time (Lin, 1997; Pepe and Mori, 1993). Using this approach, we sought to improve the estimates of the risk of death associated with delayed CABG for patients requiring and suitable for surgical revascularization. We therefore

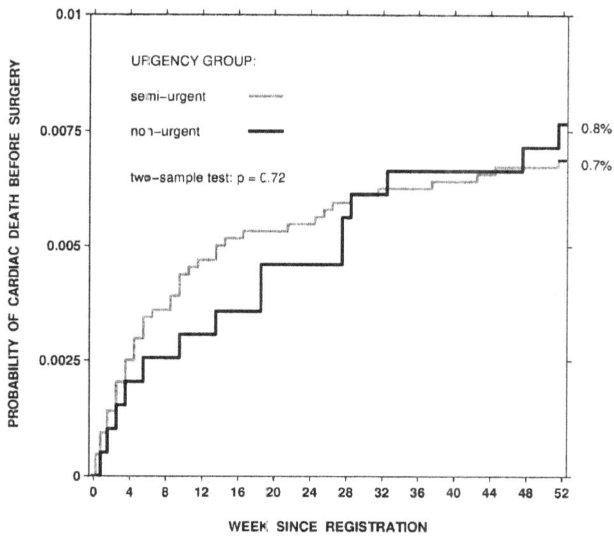

Figure 3.4. Estimated cumulative incidence of death due to cardiovascular disease by wait-list week since registration in semi-urgent and non-urgent groups

estimated the time-dependent probability of death, given that CABG was not performed by certain times.

The extent of disease was a major factor influencing time to surgery. The differences in the cumulative incidence of surgery were significant over time between groups with higher incidence in the semi-urgent group (Gray's two-sample test = 411.8, $p < 0.0001$), Figure 3.5. The average surgery rate was 6.5 per 100 patients per week of delay in the semi-urgent group compared to 3.3 in the non-urgent group, OR = 0.50 (95% CI 0.47–0.53), after adjustment for age, sex, and co-morbidity.

After adjustment for age, sex, and co-morbidity, the death rate in the non-urgent group was similar to the semi-urgent group (OR = 1.02, 95% CI 0.64–1.62). To compare proportions of patients dying by a certain time among those who had not received surgery by that time, we calculated the conditional probability of death from all causes in each group, Figure 3.6. The conditional probability of death from all causes was greater in the semi-urgent group than in the non-urgent group (Pepe's two-sample test = 2.8, $p = 0.002$).

Among patients whose delay to CABG exceeded 8, 16, 32 and 52 weeks, the probability of death from all causes was 0.6%, 1.8%, 6.8%

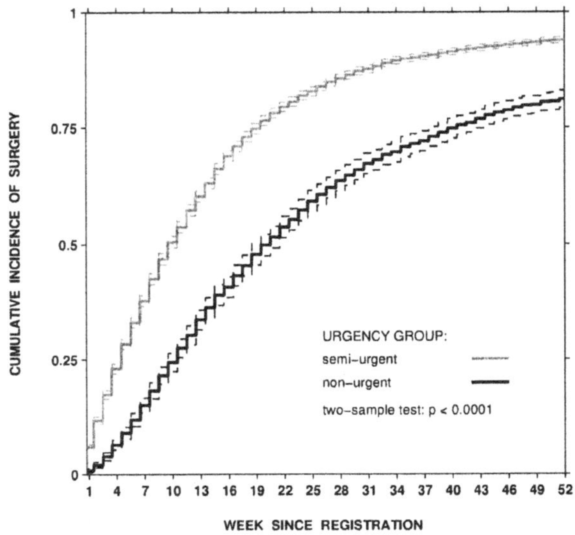

Figure 3.5. Estimated cumulative incidence of surgery and 95% CIs by week since registration in semi-urgent and non-urgent groups

and 14.9% in the semi-urgent group, and 0.6%, 1.2%, 3.6% and 7.9% in the non-urgent group.

The conditional probability of CAD death was greater in the semi-urgent group than in the non-urgent group (Pepe's two-sample test = 3.6, p = 0.0002), Figure 3.7. Among patients whose delay to CABG exceeded 8, 16, 32 and 52 weeks, the probability of death from all causes was 0.6%, 1.6%, 5.4% and 12.1% in the semi-urgent group, and 0.3%, 0.6%, 2.1% and 4.7% in the non-urgent group.

In each group, we estimated the time-dependent conditional probability that a patient, who may die or undergo surgery, dies if not operated by certain times. Among patients delayed without treatment for 52 weeks, an estimated 14.9% died in the semi-urgent group and 7.9% died in the urgent group from all causes. Similarly, an estimated 12.1% and 4.7% died from CAD in these two groups.

5. Discussion

Implicit in treatment delays is a risk that the health status of patients may worsen while they are awaiting treatment. Adverse events

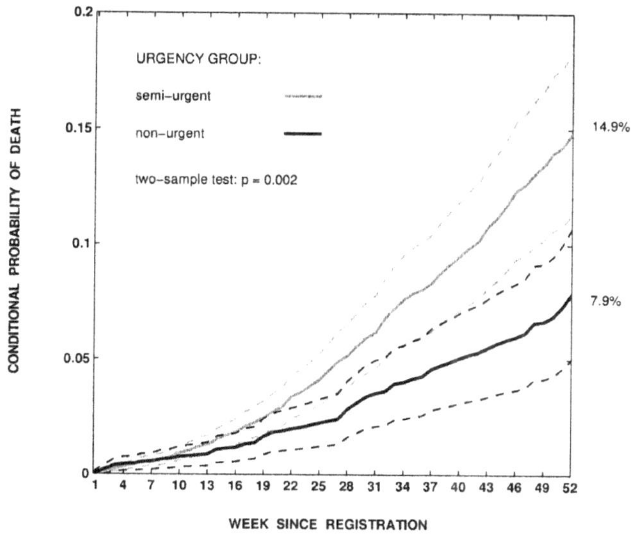

Figure 3.6. Estimated CPF of all-cause death and 95% CIs by week since registration in semi-urgent and non-urgent groups; two-sample test for all-cause deaths = 3.1, $p = 0.001$.

experienced by patients while on a wait list have not been systematically examined in the literature. Without these data, appropriate access times for surgery must be determined on the basis of expert opinion. Mortality is the main adverse event that has been examined; however, even within the literature on mortality, the risks associated with various waiting times have not been well-addressed. Other outcomes that should be considered include unplanned emergency admission, upgrade in severity, and cancelation of operation due to patient deterioration.

The research presented here is some of the first available that can be used to identify appropriate access times for patients waiting for elective operations. Our data included the health impact of delaying elective cholecystectomy and pre-operative death on CABG wait lists. For adverse events while waiting for cholecystectomy, the main findings are that (Sobolev et al., 2003):

- The greater the length of time to treatment, the more likely it is that the patient will have to be admitted as an emergency case.

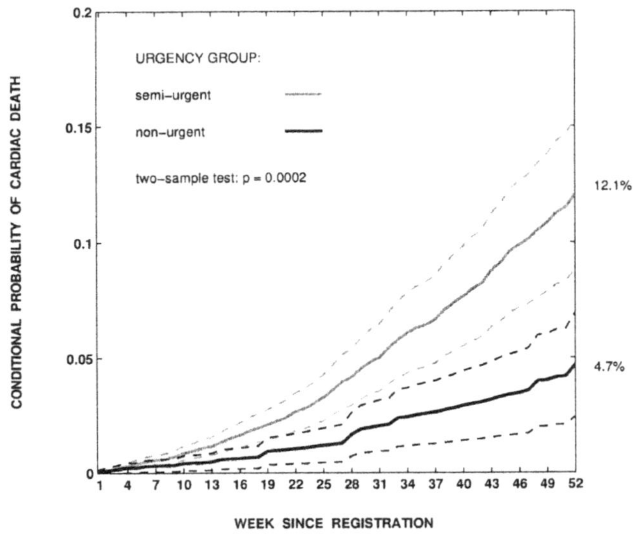

Figure 3.7. Estimated CPF of CAD death and 95% CIs by week since registration in semi-urgent and non-urgent groups; two-sample test for CAD deaths = 3.6, p = 0.0002.

The emergency admission rate in the population we studied increased 1.5 times at 20 weeks, and continued to rise thereafter.

- Nearly 7% of patients waiting for elective cholecystectomy underwent surgery through unplanned emergency admissions.
- Longer waiting times were associated with the surgeons who only did low volumes of cholecystectomies, less than 20 per year

These results have implications for developing target access times for elective surgery. The findings suggest that patients with biliary colic awaiting elective cholecystectomy for longer than 20 weeks have a substantially increased risk for development of acute symptoms that require an emergency operation. Therefore, an initial recommendation of 20 weeks might be considered as the maximum recommended waiting time for cholecystectomy. The 7% rate of unplanned surgeries is bound to have a large impact on operating room schedules and resources.

For adverse events while waiting for CABG, the main findings are that:

- The risk of death from all causes and from CAD was associated with longer wait list times.
- If patients remain unoperated by one year, 15% of semi-urgent patients and 8% of non-urgent patients die from all causes.
- Longer delays contributed to a higher proportion of CABG candidates dying before surgery from all causes in the non-urgent (1.3%) compared to the semi-urgent group (0.9%) despite similar rates of pre-operative death observed in both groups.
- The use of statistical methods for competing risks improved estimates of the probability of death associated with delaying surgery.

The contribution of the study on CABG is the estimated conditional probabilities of death while on a wait list derived from the population-based prospective database. These summary probabilities are not usually reported in prospective studies of mortality on wait lists. The appendix describes the rationale for this approach and lists previous studies that examined the risks of death while waiting for CABG. The findings suggest CABG operations should take place within the recommended 6 and 12 weeks for semi-urgent and non-urgent cases as the protracted delay for surgical revascularization when it is indicated carries a significant risk of death even in patients judged to be at low risk.

In both examples, cholecystectomy and CABG, we observed that specific populations – women and the elderly – have higher risks of adverse events while awaiting elective surgery. If confirmed in other studies, this may have implications for the acceptable wait list times in these groups.

Limitations

In the cholecystectomy example, the retrospective nature of the data may be considered an important limitation of the study. Prospective studies examine how long patients accepted for treatment wait for surgery, whereas retrospective studies examine how long the patients who were admitted were required to wait after enrolment (Armstrong, 2000b). If every wait ended in admission, the two study designs would generate equivalent results. However, patients accepted for treatment may expect to be removed from the wait list for reasons other than admission (Sobolev et al., 2000).

If patients removed from the list without surgery are not accounted for, the estimated probabilities of undergoing treatment may be biased toward a higher rate. Also, the analysis lacked data on co-morbid medical conditions. In general, a large number of co-morbid conditions may prevent aggressive treatment. Therefore, given its possible association with delay in treatment, co-morbidity is a potentially confounding factor for the observed relationship between time on the wait list and emergency admission.

In the CABG example, data were extracted from a prospective database, so there was less potential for bias in the results. Other limitations were the potential misclassification of dates and the priority assignment. Some assurance that procedure dates were recorded accurately comes from the finding that 99.3% of records were found to have the operation date recorded either between admission and separation dates (or within a few days) of discharge abstracts in the Hospital Separations File. Retrieved from the database, the priority category is a composite variable based on clinical information. The observation that higher priority patients were more likely to undergo CABG through the direct admission indicates that the degree of misclassification of priority was likely small.

Acknowledgments

This research was supported by the Canada Research Chair Program (B.S.), the Michael Smith Foundation for Health Research Scholar Program (A.L.), and Canadian Foundation for Innovation (B.S., A.L.). The following cardiac surgeons are members of the BCCR Surgical Research Committee: Drs. James Abel, Richard Brownlee, Larry Burr, Anson Cheung, James Dutton, Guy Fradet, Virginia Gudas, Robert Hayden, Eric Jamieson, Michael Janusz, Shahzad Karim, Tim Latham, Jacques LeBlanc, Sam Lichtenstein, Hilton Ling, John Ofiesh, Michael Perchinsky, Peter Skarsgard, and Frank Tyers.

Appendix

Marginal and conditional probability functions

Competing risks naturally arise in wait list settings. A competing event is "any event whose occurrence either precludes the occurrence of another event under examination or fundamentally alters the probability of occurrence of this other event" (Gooley et al., 1999). A subject on the wait list is considered at risk for an adverse event from registration time until a censoring event, surgery, or an adverse event before surgery. Other events will be classified as competing risk events if their occurrence precludes the subsequent development the primary event, or censoring events if their occurrence precludes observation, but not development of, the primary event. For example, relative to death before surgery, undergoing the planned operation is a competing risk, loss to follow-up is a censoring event.

In quantifying the risk of adverse events on wait lists, the Kaplan-Meier method is commonly used to estimate the cumulative probability of event by a certain time after registration for the operation (Ray et al., 2001; Jackson et al., 1999; Koomen et al., 2001). It has been established, however, that the complement of the Kaplan-Meier estimator overestimates the incidence of the event in the competing risks setting (Gooley et al., 1999).

As patients on wait lists are subject to the competing events of surgery, death, or removal for other reasons, the method produces probability estimates that are only valid in a hypothetical situation when all competing risks are removed prior to the event without altering the risk of the adverse event of interest (Gaynor et al., 1993). This approach implicitly assumes that time to surgery and time to the adverse event are independent. Without this assumption, the Kaplan-Meier estimator is not valid and should not be used (Alberti et al., 2003). Furthermore, the independence of wait list outcomes cannot be verified from data, and the assumption may not be realistic, as a low probability of the adverse event may indicate either a low risk of this event or a high surgery rate.

Other investigators have reported the incidence of preoperative death per time unit of waiting for CABG (Bernstein et al., 1997; Morgan et al., 1998; Rexius et al., 2004; Ray et al., 2001; Koomen et al., 2001; Cox et al., 1996; Seddon et al., 1999). Although accurately describing the instantaneous hazard, death rates cannot be converted into the probabilities of death without an unrealistic and unverifiable assumption that time to surgery and time to death are independent (Gooley et al., 1999). Plomp and colleagues have reported on the variation in time to deaths among those who died before surgery,(Plomp et al., 1999) but the proportion of CABG candidates dying over follow-up could not be derived from their figures.

The primary statistical instrument in those analyses was the incidence of preoperative death per time unit of waiting for CABG. Although they may accurately describe the instantaneous hazard, death rates cannot be converted into the probabilities of death without an unrealistic and unverifiable assumption that time to surgery and time to death are independent (Gooley et al., 1999).

Regression models

Regression methods for pseudo-values of CIF for death are used to estimate the effect of urgency group, while adjusting for age, sex, and comorbidity (Klein and Andersen, 2005). Pseudo-values of CIF for death are computed in the presence of surgery, and other competing events. In the absence of censoring, for each patient, pseudo-values of CIF for death correspond to a series of binary variables equal to 0 before and 1 at or after death. Using generalized estimation equations to adjust for subject-level correlation between pseudo-values, the CIF is modeled at all distinct, observed event times. The working weight matrix is fixed to be the estimated product-moment correlation matrix between pseudo-values of the CIF. The effect of urgency was measured by ORs, adjusted for age, sex, and comorbidity.

6. References

Alberti, C., Metivier, F., Landais, P., Thervet, E., Legendre, C., and Chevret, S. (2003). Improving estimates of event incidence over time in populations exposed to other events - application to three large databases. *Journal of Clinical Epidemiology*, 56:536–545.

Armstrong, P.W. (2000a). First steps in analysing nhs waiting times: avoiding the 'stationary and closed population' fallacy. *Statistics in Medicine*, 19:2037–2051.

Armstrong, P.W. (2000b). Unrepresentative, invalid and misleading: are waiting times for elective admission wrongly calculated? *Journal of Epidemiology and Biostatistics*, 5:117–123.

Bernstein, S. J., Rigter, H., Brorsson, B., Hilborne, L. H., Leape, L. L., Meijler, A. P., Scholma, J. K., and Nord, A. S. (1997). Waiting for coronary revascularization: a comparison between new york state, the netherlands and sweden. *Health Policy*, 42:15–27.

Blake, J.T. and Carter, M.W. (1997). Surgical process scheduling: a structured review. *Journal of Social and Health Systems*, 5:17–30.

Buhaug, H. (2002). Long waiting lists in hospitals. *BMJ*, 324:252–253.

Cox, J. L., Petrie, J. F., Pollak, P. T., and Johnstone, D. E. (1996). Managed delay for coronary artery bypass graft surgery: the experience at one canadian center. *Journal of the American College of Cardiology*, 27:1365–1373.

DeCoster, C., Carriere, K.C., Peterson, S., Walld, R., and MacWilliam, L. (1999). Waiting times for surgical procedures. *Medical Care*, 37:JS187–JS205.

Derrett, S., Paul, C., and Morris, J.M. (1999). Waiting for elective surgery: effects on health-related quality of life. *International Journal for Quality in Health Care*, 11:47–57.

Friedman, G.D. (1993). Natural history of asymptomatic and symptomatic gallstones. *American Journal of Surgery*, 165:399–404.

Gaynor, J. J., Feuer, E. J., Tan, C. C., Wu, D. H., Little, C. R., Straus, D. J., Clarkson, B. D., and Brennan, M. F. (1993). On the use of cause-specific failure and conditional failure probabilities. *Journal of the American Statistical Association*, 88:400–409.

Gooley, T. A., Leisenring, W., Crowley, J., and Storer, B. E. (1999). Estimation of failure probabilities in the presence of competing risks: New representations of old estimators. *Statistics in Medicine*, 18:695–706.

Grech, E.D. (2003). Pathophysiology and investigation of coronary artery disease. *BMJ*, 326:1027–1030.

Hamilton, D.M. and Breslawski, S. (1994). Operating room scheduling. factors to consider. *AORN Journal*, 59:665–680.

Jackson, N. W., Doogue, M. P., and Elliott, J. M. (1999). Priority points and cardiac events while waiting for coronary bypass surgery. *Heart*, 81:367–373.

Klatt, I. (2000). Understanding the canadian health care system. *Journal of Financial Service Professionals*, 54:42–51.

Klein, J. P. and Andersen, P. K. (2005). Regression modeling of competing risks data based on pseudovalues of the cumulative incidence function. *Biometrics*, 61:223–229.

Koomen, E. M., Hutten, B. A., Kelder, J. C., Redekop, W. K., Tijssen, J. G., and Kingma, J. H. (2001). Morbidity and mortality in patients waiting for coronary artery bypass surgery. *European Journal of Cardiothoracic Surgery*, 19:260–265.

Légaré, J.F., MacLean, A., Buth, K.J., and Sullivan, J.A (2005). Assessing the risk of waiting for coronary artery bypass graft surgery among patients with stenosis of the left main coronary artery. *CMAJ*, 173:371–375.

Levy, A., Sobolev, B., Hayden, R., Kiely, M., Fitzegrald, M., and Schechter, M. (2005). Time on wait lists for coronary bypass surgery in british columbia, canada, 1991 - 2000. *BMC Health Services Research*, 5:22.

Levy, A.R. and Gagnon, Y.M. (2002). Canadian formulary decisions: Does pharmacoeconomics matter? *Pharmaceutical News*, 9:47–55.

Lin, D. Y. (1997). Non-parametric inference for cumulative incidence functions in competing risks studies. *Statistics in Medicine*, 16:901–910.

MacCormick, A. D., Collecutt, W. G., and Parry, B. R. (2003). Prioritizing patients for elective surgery: a systematic review. *ANZ Journal of Surgery*, 73:633–642.

Magerlein, J.M. and Martin, J.B. (1978). Surgical demand scheduling: a review. *Health Services Research*, 13:418–433.

McGurran, J. and Noseworthy, T. (2002). Improving the management of waiting lists for elective healthcare services: public perspectives on proposed solutions. *Hospital Quarterly*, 5:28–32.

Morgan, C. D., Sykora, K., and Naylor, C. D. (1998). Analysis of deaths while waiting for cardiac surgery among 29,293 consecutive patients in ontario, canada. *Heart*, 79:345–349.

Naylor, C. D. (1991). A different view of queues in ontario. *Health Affairs*, 10:110–128.

Naylor, C. D., Levinton, C. M., Wheeler, S., and Hunter, L. (1993). Queueing for coronary surgery during severe supply-demand mismatch in a canadian referral centre: a case study of implicit rationing. *Social Science and Medicine*, 37:61–67.

Naylor, C. D., Sykora, K., Jaglal, S. B., and Jefferson, S. (1995). Waiting for coronary artery bypass surgery: population-based study of 8517 consecutive patients in ontario, canada. the steering committee of the adult cardiac care network of ontario [see comments]. *Lancet*, 346:1605–1609.

Naylor, C.D., Basinski, A., Baigrie, R.S., Goldman, B.S., and Lomas, J. (1990). Placing patients in the queue for coronary revascularization: evidence for practice variations from an expert panel process. *American Journal of Public Health*, 80:1246–1252.

Noseworthy, T.W., McGurran, J.J., and Hadorn, D.C. (2003). Waiting for scheduled services in canada: development of priority-setting scoring systems. *Journal of Evaluation in Clinical Practice*, 9:23–31.

Pepe, M. S. and Mori, M. (1993). Kaplan-meier, marginal or conditional-probability curves in summarizing competing risks failure time data. *Statistics in Medicine*, 12:737–751.

Plomp, J., Redekop, W. K., Dekker, F. W., van Geldorp, T. R., Haalebos, M. M., Jambroes, G., Kingma, J. H., Zijlstra, F., and Tijssen, J. G. (1999). Death on the waiting list for cardiac surgery in the netherlands in 1994 and 1995. *Heart*, 81:593–597.

Ray, A. A., Buth, K. J., Sullivan, J. A., Johnstone, D. E., and Hirsch, G. M. (2001). Waiting for cardiac surgery: results of a risk-stratified queuing process. *Circulation*, 104:I92–I98.

Reinhardt, U.E. (1998). Quality in consumer-driven health systems. *International Journal for Quality in Health Care*, 10:385–394.

Rexius, H., Brandrup-Wognsen, G., Oden, A., and Jeppsson, A. (2004). Mortality on the waiting list for coronary artery bypass grafting: incidence and risk factors. *Annals of Thoracic Surgery*, 77:769–774.

Romano, P. S., Roos, L. L., and Jollis, J. G. (1993). Adapting a clinical comorbidity index for use with icd-9-cm administrative data: differing perspectives. *Journal of Clinical Epidemiology*, 46:1075–1079.

Seddon, M. E., French, J. K., Amos, D. J., Ramanathan, K., McLaughlin, S. C., and White, H. D. (1999). Waiting times and prioritization for coronary artery bypass surgery in new zealand. *Heart*, 81:586–592.

Sobolev, B., Brown, P., and Zelt, D. (2000). Variation in time spent on the waiting list for elective vascular surgery: a case study. *Clinical and Investigative Medicine*, 23:227–238.

Sobolev, B., Levy, A., Hayden, R., and Kuramoto, L. (2005a). Does wait-list size at registration influence time to surgery? analysis of a population-based cardiac surgery registry. *Health Services Research.*

Sobolev, B., Mercer, D., Brown, P., FitzGerald, M., Jalink, D., and Shaw, R. (2003). Risk of emergency admission while awaiting elective cholecystectomy. *CMAJ*, 169:662–665.

Sobolev, B.G., Levy, A.R., Kuramoto, L., Hayden, R., Brophy, J.M., and FitzGerald, J.M. (2005b). The risk of death associated with delayed coronary artery bypass surgery. *unpublished manuscript.*

Sobolev, B.G., Levy, A.R., Kuramoto, L., Hayden, R., and FitzGerald, J.M. (2005c). Do longer delays for coronary artery bypass surgery contribute to pre-operative mortality in less urgent patients? *Medical Care.*

Turnbull, R.G., Taylor, D.C., Hsiang, Y.N., Salvian, A.J., Nanji, S., and OHanley G., et al. (2000). Assessment of patient waiting times for vascular surgery. *Canadian Journal of Surgery*, 43:105–111.

Chapter 4

BREAKTHROUGH DEMAND-CAPACITY MANAGEMENT STRATEGIES TO IMPROVE HOSPITAL FLOW, SAFETY, AND SATISFACTION

Linda Kosnik, RN, MSN, APN, CEN
Overlook Hospital, 99 Beauvoir Avenu, Summit, NJ 07902
Linda.Kosnik@ahsys.org

Abstract: Healthcare facilities are experiencing overcrowding and hospital-wide waits and delays. Potential bottlenecks must be identified and alleviated by matching demand to capacity. The matching of demand to capacity for the services of a hospital is a complex function of multiple variables and queues across the healthcare system. Achieving successful demand to capacity management requires a large-scale cultural change to support inter and intra department collaboration, which is paramount to the efficient functioning and flow of any healthcare organization. This chapter will outline the techniques and tools necessary for creating a successful demand to capacity system which is the results of identifying and implementing interventions to critical stressors in the environment. The intent of such approaches is not only to improve flow but also to support healthcare systems in their goals to become more reliable, safe, and satisfying for patients and providers.

Key words: Flow, demand to capacity matching, job satisfaction, recruitment and retention, customer satisfaction, emergency department overcrowding

1. INTRODUCTION

Healthcare facilities are experiencing overcrowding and hospital-wide waits and delays. Potential bottlenecks must be identified and alleviated by matching demand to capacity. The matching of demand to capacity for the services of a hospital is a complex function of multiple variables and queues. Healthcare units, services, and even professions have evolved in silos focused on meeting their own individual resource, expertise, customer, technology, and demand needs.

These silos are perfectly designed to support units to operate as individual business units striving to maintain autonomy. Therefore, collaborative, inter/intradepartmental matching of demand to capacity is a complex challenge, but one paramount to efficiency and flow across any healthcare organization.

The future of healthcare is dependent on the identification of change initiatives that create a synergy between the strategic goals of the healthcare organization and the professional goals of the care provider to afford safe, effective, individual-oriented patient care. Such change initiatives must be more user-friendly and focused on creating buy-in through staff empowerment, workload management and job satisfaction.

This chapter will outline the techniques and tools necessary for creating a successful demand to capacity system which is the result of identifying and implementing interventions to critical stressors in the environment. The intent of such approaches is not only to improve flow but also to support healthcare systems in their goals to become more reliable and safer, and more satisfying for patients and providers. Key system success factors will be discussed including real-time communication, inter/intradepartmental and inter-disciplinary collaboration, staff empowerment, standardization of best practices, and institutional memory. A dynamic, customizable color-coded demand to capacity management model will be discussed, which uses the tools and techniques from crew resource management (CRM) and microsystem thinking.

The deployment of a demand to capacity management system will be discussed with the web of work and examples cutting across the entire hospital system.

2. BACKGROUND

Pressures from regulatory and government agencies, consumer advocate groups, and insurance companies have forced hospitals to focus on cost containment (Holtom, 2004). Many consider this cost containment, although necessary, to create a significantly negative impact on employee satisfaction, driving a similar effect on patient care and outcomes. In addition, healthcare organizations are under pressure to bring on new technologies, processes and procedures to keep, if not increase, market share. This creates a conundrum of expectations for healthcare organizations, which must now strive to improve efficiency and cost containment while providing effective, safe patient care with maximal stakeholder satisfaction. As a result, healthcare organizations have implemented system-wide change initiatives under the guise of such terms as restructuring, re-engineering, TQM, and CQI.

The work of efficiency and cost containment frequently looks to personnel management as it makes up what is perceived to be the 'lion's share' of the controllable expenses. Therefore, such initiatives as 'restructuring' have the most impact on the work of nursing as integrated delivery systems are developed, reductions in length of stay are prioritized, and multifunctional workers are used as a solution for staffing issues (Tonges, 1998).

The United States is currently experiencing the most significant healthcare provider shortage in its history. It is expected that this shortage will intensify as healthcare personnel needs expand, the current work force continues to age, nurses continue to suffer the highest level of workplace stress of any profession (Laschinger, 2004), and universities and colleges struggle to meet rising demand with limited academic resources. With hospitals reporting an average annual nursing turnover rate of 21% and a cost of replacement to be 150% of a nurse's annual salary, recruitment and retention have become two of the greatest fiscal challenges facing the healthcare workplace (Holtom, 2004).

2.1 Job Satisfaction, Retention and Workload

The question of what decreases burnout and increases retention and job satisfaction has been widely studied. Empowerment and perceptions of organizational commitment are two factors that have been consistently positively correlated with job satisfaction (Kuokkanen, 2003). The concept of organizational commitment is core to retention in that it refers to employee job satisfaction as it applies to one's attachment, trust, and involvement in an organization (Kuokkanen et al., 2003). Empowerment can be divided into two categories: structural and psychological. Structural empowerment is perceived as access to support, supplies, opportunity and information necessary to do one's job. Psychological empowerment is viewed as autonomy and the meaningfulness of the work. Research suggests that individual behaviors are actually a response to factors in the workplace, making the structural or environmental variables the most critical (Hatcher & Laschinger, 1996). The more an individual perceives that he/she is empowered to control and drive his/her work experience, the greater the job satisfaction and the opportunity for the organization to retain that employee. Workers are empowered when they perceive that their environment provides access to power needed to get the job done. This perceived power is related to the individual's ability to access and mobilize support, information, and supplies. Therefore, there is opportunity to increase the sense of empowerment and autonomy by identifying factors that contribute to feelings of powerlessness and designing work environments and workloads that mitigate these factors.

The level of stress perceived to be experienced by a healthcare provider also directly correlates with job satisfaction.

In healthcare, stress management is a complex challenge. It is usually not one event that generates a stress response in an individual, unit, service or facility, but more likely multiple events. Different environments have different stressors and the sources of stress may even differ from individual to individual on the same unit. A shortage of resources and supports correlated with increased stress (French et al., 2000). Job satisfaction can provide the balance for stress, particularly in high stress areas such as Emergency Departments (ED) and Operating Rooms (OR). To a degree, stress can be positive and provide motivation or a sense of excitement, challenging an individual to function on a higher level, increasing efficiency, decision making and effectiveness. This is the stress that drives an individual to function outside their comfort zone creating greater job satisfaction through professional opportunity and growth. On the other hand, stress resulting from frustration and powerlessness to mitigate or implement coping mechanisms in the environment is negative stress. This type of stress is frequently associated with psychological and physiological manifestations as it escalates. Stress is dependent on the individual and the impact perceived from situations and events on one's physical or psychological well-being (French, et al., 2000). The factor most frequently correlated with workplace stress is workload (Tonges, 1998). Overload occurs when the demand exceeds the individual's ability to access resources or capacity (French et al., 2000). Developing supportive management, increasing opportunities for positive patient interactions, and creating a wide-spread sense of autonomy and empowerment have the potential to mitigate or diffuse stress (French et al., 2000).

2.2 Workload Management

Changing reimbursement and other economic factors in healthcare have led to higher patient acuity and hospital restructuring. These two factors have negatively impacted on workload, creating higher patient-to-nurse ratios, which compromises patient care and results in increased patient occurrences, complications and errors (Aiken et al., 2002).

As physicians spend less and less time in hospitals, the nurse's role has come to include not only surveillance, but health instruction, disease prevention and overall care of the patients and their families. As the role has become increasing complex, driven by advances in technology, documentation requirements, decreases in LOS and increased acuity, nurses have found they have less and less time to actually work with patients. In addition, these job changes have created a greater workload for the nurses who now require a broader spectrum of skills and experiences to be successful. As the sphere of nursing duties expands and the workload increases, nurses have begun to experience time constraints to providing optimal patient care. Workplace stress and overload occur when the job expectations are high and the ability to make decisions and problem-solve are low (Bojtor, 2003). Conflicts over time and expanding job expectations and duties have resulted in provider stress and, consequently, compromised patient care. These compromises drive patient and staff dissatisfaction. 86% of the nursing population believes that the nursing shortage has left little time for unexpected events or holistic patient care (Bojtor, 2003). This is worrisome since caring for patients is the reason many individuals went into healthcare professions, making this alienation a significant threat to recruitment and retention.

French (French et al , 2000) found that workload was the most significant work environment stressor, with higher levels of stress being associated with lower levels of job satisfaction. Workload issues include inadequate staffing levels, demanding patients, multiple tasks not completed by the previous shifts, insufficient time to complete necessary tasks, and concerns about the quality of care (French et al., 2000). These findings suggest that improvement in the work environment and the way the work is done may lessen the stress nurses experience and increase retention.

Managing resources and improving patient flow through demand to capacity management are not only strategies to manage workload but have become the focus of international concern for improving patient care, quality, and safety. According to the Institute of Medicine (IOM) report, 'Crossing the Quality Chasm', US healthcare should be safe, effective, patient centered, timely, efficient, and equitable (IOM, 2001). The Joint Commission's new standard LD.3.15, which went into effect for accreditation review in January 2005, focuses on the importance of identifying and mitigating impediments to efficient patient flow throughout the hospital. It suggests that improved management of processes and the matching of capacity to demand can support the appropriate use of limited resources and, thereby, reduce the risk of negative outcomes to patients from the delays in delivery of care (JCAHO, 2004).

The other catalysts for the focus of performance improvement initiatives on resource management and patient flow have been the nursing shortage and what was initially labeled as Emergency Department (ED) Overcrowding. The American College of Emergency Physicians (ACEP) defines (ED) overcrowding as "a situation in which the identified need for emergency services outstrips available resources in the ED. This situation occurs in hospital EDs when there are more patients than staffed ED treatment beds and wait times exceed a reasonable period" (JCAHO, 2004). Much of the problem is a result of EDs seeing an ever increasing volume of patients who do not meet the severity of illness that constitutes an emergency. This results from individuals using the services of the ED in lieu of other healthcare services, and is driven by convenience, lack of insurance or a primary care physician, or because the perception of what constitutes an emergency varies among individuals. Unfortunately, these non-emergent patients seek the services of the ED at peak periods, placing additional burden on the ED at a time when resources may already be overloaded (Siddharthan, Jones, & Johnson, 1996).

The outcomes of overcrowding include consumers experiencing problems with accessing care, deterioration in the community "safety net" and compromised patient and staff safety. The impact on safety can be measured by treatment delays, higher error rates, increases in mortality and negative clinical outcomes, patients leaving without treatment, and higher readmission rates (JCAHO, 2004).

Changes in reimbursement, competitive pricing, managed care, mergers and tightening of government spending have resulted in cost cutting that has shifted patient activity to the front end of a hospital stay where shorter stays can be better managed. As a result, the areas of the hospital that deliver this care, e.g. emergency departments, operating rooms and ICUs, began to experience long waits and delays for services. In response, hospitals that are already functioning in the red have been forced to focus on more efficient and effective operational performance. Many facilities have been driven to maximize resources and function with >90% occupancy and >95% productivity. Staffing coverage is often budgeted based on the average daily census (ADC), leaving few units with the resources to flex and maintain identified patient-to-nurse ratios when faced with unpredictable, fluctuating workloads, high vacancy and turnover rates, and high utilization of unplanned compensation time resulting from escalating stress and overload. It is estimated that six out of ten hospitals across the country are operating "at" or "over" capacity (JCAHO, 2004).

2.3 Communication, Silos and Queues

Current healthcare systems are under increasing stress loads. Current methods and practices of communication within these systems are less than ideal. Tools and strategies to manage flow and demand to capacity matching are not yet well understood. Since 1910, healthcare has evolved in silos. This resulted from extraordinary advances in healthcare technology which required each unit to develop unique areas of expertise which drove a sense of isolation or focus on monitoring and mitigating demand and capacity only within the 'silo'. Historically, communication across units has been challenging. It has been accomplished often by phone rather than face to face, allowing 'silos' to continue to function in isolation. Problems arise from departments or services acting independently and considering their own demand and capacity issues without consideration for the upstream and downstream impact on other departments and services. Traditional allocation of resources has resulted in a capacity imbalance in which specific systems and units have over-capacity while others strive to deal with the stress of under-capacity, resulting in bottlenecks or under-utilization (Mango and Shapiro, 2001).

From a patient's perspective, these 'silos' are all part of the system that makes up their healthcare experience. Patient flow is defined as the observable process a patient experiences during their healthcare delivery process (Nacey, 2004).

Attempts to solve the overcrowding problem with traditional change models has lead to increased episodes of ED diversion and waits and delays to access services. Significant analyses and process improvement initiatives targeted at EDs has forced healthcare administrators and consultants to identify overcrowding as actually being a hospital-wide system problem requiring a system-wide approach to managing waits and delays and resources (JCAHO, 2004).

Waits and delays in the ED are caused by the inability to access needed resources such as inpatient beds for admissions and lab and x-ray services. Patients waiting in the ED for the next level of care, often an inpatient bed, reduce the functional capacity of the ED, limiting its ability to care for new arrivals. Patients waiting for treatment create a queue, which is often manifested by the use of waiting rooms and hallways for extended periods. Queues occur whenever the current demand for services exceeds the current capacity to provide those services. For the ED, the total service time for patients is the sum of time spent for all medical care and ancillary services provided (Siddharten et al., 1996). Since patients consistently arrive at an uneven rate, multiple queues are a "constant state' for hospitals, particularly EDs. These queues identify the workload of the unit or service.

Queuing systems are defined by their input and arrival processes. Queuing defines the order in which patients entering a system are served. Use of queuing systems allows for the calculation of the average waiting time, the expected average number of patients waiting and the utilization of servers such as x-ray machines. Information drawn from studying queues supports long-term solutions including the addition of 'servers' such as inpatient beds, radiology equipment, and technicians to allow for volume fluctuations to avoid the development of excessive queues. Planning for variabilities in access and matching demand to capacity in real-time are also operational imperatives (Jones & Pearson, 2002). Much of this can be accomplished with some type of logistical communication across departments, which identifies the best use of valuable resources (Mango& Shapiro, 2001). The key indicator of the hospital's ability to provide a bed is the admission cycle time. The admission cycle time measures the time from the decision by the physician to admit to the time the patient leaves the ED for an inpatient bed. Resolving extended admission cycle times is an issue that requires collaboration and workload redesign across the facility. It is an excellent opportunity to apply the principles of demand to capacity management.

2.4 Change, Crew Resource Management (CRM) and Microsystem Thinking

System-wide demand to capacity management requires the ability to implement large-scale change. Large-scale change is defined as any change that results in organizational processes and routines being fundamentally altered, facilitating philosophical change in practice. This kind of change is also referred to as discontinuous or transformational as it often causes the organization to deviate from previous approaches. It challenges the organization to reevaluate its vision, mission, identity, values and its strategic plan; at times precipitating a complete change in organizational direction (Narine & Persaud, 2003). It should be noted that different cultural groups may require different approaches to communication and rewards to facilitate organizational change and job satisfaction. It is imperative that the large-scale change desired be congruent with the culture of the organization (Narine & Persaud, 2003).

The role of leadership in creating a cultural change cannot be under valued. Leaders must be visible; enforce the desired norms, vision and values, and encourage others to do the same. They are responsible for assuring that the unit has the resources, skills, and training to achieve the organization's goals (Hawkins & Kratsch, 2004).

Ultimately healthcare collaboration and teamwork are tied to the system's ability to work effectively and efficiently towards optimal patient flow and system outcomes across the healthcare experience. This is a result of a complex matrix of workload and resource management, staff empowerment, and effective communication targeted at matching demand to capacity in real-time.

2.4.1 Crew Resource Management (CRM)

One successful approach for supporting system-wide change, particularly clinical change based on best practices, is Crew Resource Management (CRM). CRM is a communication methodology focusing on team-centered decision–making systems which was developed by the aviation industry in 1979 in response to a NASA workshop that examined the role of human error in air crashes. When CRM is applied to healthcare, the communication space of healthcare practitioners caring for critically ill patients can be viewed as resembling that of an aircrew engaged in complex flight operations. Use of team-centered decision-making systems enables teams to perform more efficiently.

Use of the CRM model does not presuppose that adequate communication is enough but instead supports a combination of communication, technology, and process change. CRM's primary building blocks include the use of backup systems: team communication and coordination, adequate briefings, availability and use of resources, leadership and adequate supervision, system knowledge, personal readiness, planning, correction of known problems, and issues and management support (Kosnik, 2002).

Historically, effective medical practice depended on a small number of healthcare providers, which made communication and teamwork requirements simple. Today the healthcare system is composed of and dependent on many persons, each with unique knowledge and skill sets, which makes routine communication increasingly complex. With the emergence of patient safety, the importance of collaboration and a team approach to patient care has become paramount. Collaboration in providing patient care is more important than preserving an individual provider's professional boundaries or roles (IOM, 2001). All members of the healthcare team must communicate effectively to coordinate care and meet the patient's needs. This expectation correlates with IOM's "New Rule" number ten, which states that, "Clinicians and institutions should actively collaborate and communicate to ensure an appropriate exchange of information and coordination of care (IOM, 2001)".

CRM is all about shared knowledge and free flow of information. The model was specifically designed to promote team-based improvement initiatives and collaboration among clinicians for care that is safe and effective. This makes it an excellent tool to promote the behaviors necessary to create buy-in across multiple units and services towards matching demand to capacity.

2.4.2 Microsystem Thinking

Although CRM has been primarily used with teams and units, it has extraordinary potential to create synergy through communication and team building on the system level when coupled with the work of microsystem thinking. Microsystems are defined as the small, functional, front-line units that provide most healthcare to most people (Nelson et al., 2002). They are the place where patients and providers meet. Each microsystem has its own unique culture and customer population. From an operational perspective, it has clinical and business aims, policies and procedures, and shared information that produce the services and care measurable as performance outcomes. Macrosystems are the larger systems that are made up of microsystems. The emergency department and the radiology department are examples of microsystems. The average healthcare system is composed of a few basic parts: front-line clinical microsystems, overarching macrosystems, and patient subpopulations needing care (Godfrey et al., 2003). These systems evolve over time and are embedded in larger systems and organizations. As any living, adaptive, system, the microsystem must: (1) do the work, (2) meet staff needs, and (3) maintain itself as a clinical unit (Godfrey et al., 2003).

The microsystem framework provides practical steps to using microsystem thinking as strategic building blocks. Microsystem thinking makes several organizational assumptions. The first is that bigger systems (macrosystems) are made up of smaller systems (microsystems) which produce quality, safety, and cost outcomes at the front line of care (Nelson et al., 2002). Ultimately, the outcomes of the macrosystem can be no better than the outcomes of the microsystems of which it is composed. If strategically driven and the performance of each individual microsystem is optimized, a systematic transformation can be achieved to meet the organizational goals of the organization and the needs of the front line care providers. The greater the linkage and collaboration between the different clinical and support microsystems, the more seamless, timely, efficient, safe and reliable will become the operations of the macrosystem (Kosnik & Espinosa, 2003).

Microsystem thinking provides the structure and opportunity to drive strategic goals from the point where service is delivered to where the greatest value can be elicited. It is through the activation of the microsystems that there is the free-flow of information which drives the anticipation of needs supported by the collaboration of the providers. It is within the boundaries of the microsystem that the patient has the opportunity to meet with the providers and sculpt a common vision of the care desired and expected through shared decision making.

Integrating the concepts of CRM and Microsystems supports the creation of empowered teams who understand their position and relationship towards partnering with the organization (macrosystem) to achieving their mutual goals. For our purposes, this is the matching of resources and capacity to changing demand in a cost effective, efficient, patient oriented manner. The process of matching demand to capacity identifies the workload of a unit which drives patient flow.

3. DEMAND TO CAPACITY MANAGEMENT SYSTEM (DCMS)

Hospitals need to better understand the stress loads on their systems in order to identify, measure and mitigate stress loads. A system used to manage the relationship of demand on a system to the capacity of a system is called a Demand to Capacity Management System (DCMS). Mismatches between capacity and demand have significant consequences, including inpatient services meltdown, blocked patient flow, communication breakdowns, compromised patient safety, customer dissatisfaction, episodes of divert and bypass, and lost revenue.

A successful demand to capacity management system is a result of identifying and implementing interventions to critical stressors in the environment. The goals of a successful DCMS are to provide real-time communication, inter/intra-departmental and inter-disciplinary collaboration, staff empowerment, standardization of best practices, and institutional memory. The success of the work of matching demand to capacity is related to the success of six key factors:

1. Trust Making
2. Staff empowerment
3. Collaboration
4. Common vocabulary
5. Mitigation of constraints and barriers
6. Reciprocity.

A robust DCMS reduces incidents of overload, which is manifested by episodes of divert and bypass. These episodes are actually a result of inpatient services melt-down. A DCMS creates more reliable and stable systems with less variability because of the "smoothing" effect that can be achieved with monitoring, prevention and mitigation of stress loads and queues, returning control of the system (empowering) to the providers. It creates a synergy between the microsystems (units) and the macrosystems (hospital). Receptor sites become available, there are improved staffing rations and there is ready access to necessary supplies and processes that make the work of the microsystem efficient. The exciting by-products of demand-capacity matching include increased customer satisfaction from reductions in waits and delays, effective recruitment and retention from increased job satisfaction and new avenues of collaboration and inter/intradepartmental support resulting from collaboration. This collaboration is a result of the use CRM, the principles of which support the value, input and empowerment of all the team members. For example, through these principles the importance and input of the environmental person to the admission process as they own responsibility for preparing the bed for occupancy are recognized. This recognition becomes a driver for nurturing better communication between environmental services and bed management services with the common goal of improving admission cycle time.

Now let's imagine a system that operationalizes matching demand to capacity (DCMS). This system must empower the providers to measure and mitigate stress loads and queues in real time. There are five basic concepts to developing such a system which we call, grids, categories, criteria, interventions and statuses.

3.1 Categories and Criteria

The categories for a unit or service organize the key criteria or stressors that are central to getting the 'work' of the unit done. For this model, we use the categories of census, acuity, other and staffing (CAOS). Census is those criteria which describe what that unit or service "counts" to determine its workload. For example, an inpatient unit would count patients while a respiratory service might count treatments. Acuity criteria determine the level of stress associated with the population, procedure or specimens, which can be measured as workload and/or in time. This category often measures turn-around time. For example, an oncology inpatient unit may count the number of intravenous chemotherapy infusions scheduled while the laboratory may identify criteria around CBC turnaround. The oncology unit is using a number because from experience they know that each infusion takes a specific amount of time and requires a designated amount of resources. The laboratory, on the other hand, knows that CBC results can be routinely expected in a certain amount of time and are the most frequently ordered test. Therefore, for the laboratory, CBC is the test most likely to indicate the workload of the unit, in that an increase in turnaround time is most likely reflective of an increase in volume, a lack of resources or an access to information issue requiring mitigation.

'Other' criteria represent the factors that influence the productivity of the human services capacity such as availability of equipment, systems, and supplies. These criteria tend to center on access to information, particularly information systems downtime and on supplies, such as IV pumps. 'Staff' criteria represent the capacity of a unit in terms of labor or human services. It is specific to the status and matching of staff to fluctuating demand and for the mitigation of staffing discrepancies.

All criteria must have valid values that indicate a 'call to action'. It is also important to limit the number of criteria to only those items that are reoccurring, specific to a significant stressor or representative of a performance improvement initiative that warrants tracking and higher visibility. If a criterion does not drive a response or action then it should not be used for a DCMS.

3.2 Interventions

Interventions to mitigate demand to capacity mismatches are divided into two concepts, my interventions and other interventions. My interventions are those actions that a designated unit can perform for themselves. These actions have been identified by that microsystem to mitigate and deescalate the stress caused by the corresponding criterion. Other interventions are those that require supportive actions or responses from other units, departments or services. These interventions have been identified prior to the event and negotiated collaborative. The microsystem must be able to depend on the identified response from the designated support unit under the specific conditions that triggered the intervention. In order to facilitate buy-in, reciprocal responses should have also been identified to create what can be metaphorically called a "Fair Trade Agreement". The overarching goal of these interventions is to create a synergy or collaboration across all the microsystems within the macrosystem. By using the principles of CRM all individuals in the microsystem understand their value to the flow and 'work' of the microsystem and the macrosystem. In this way, the strategic goals of the macrosystem can be realized and a culture of collaboration and trust can be established. Much of the trust building that occurs is simply a result of mutually sharing issues and working collaborative to identify solutions. It is very difficult to support a rationale to creating barriers or be obstructive towards individuals that you now know and have partnered with. Mutual respect for the workload of other 'silos' drives positive relationships and the breakdown of silo thinking towards the use of CRM and microsystem thinking tools.

3.3 Status

The next step to developing a DCMS is to identify levels or statuses for each criteria, and to quantify the queues and the level of stress of the categories (CAOS). One of the most effective models is color coding, as promoted by the national security system --that of green, yellow, orange escalating to red with increased risk. This common vocabulary, derived mostly from everyday words, is the context of new or shared syntax. It encourages interactions and conversations about collaboratively seeking to solve problems and frames all activities as "shared". The color coding and terminology of the DCMS can become part of a common vocabulary that galvanizes the microsystems to the macrosystems.

Green reflects an optimally functioning system, a state of equilibrium, homeostasis. Demand and capacity are matched. Staff describes it as "a good day." *Yellow* reflects the status of early triggers, the first indications of demand without readily available capacity, and of developing queues. This is the most important status in that it allows for early intervention before the provider even recognizes escalating stress. This is the opportunity to mitigate -- even eliminate -- all the stressors that historically we ignore each day. If not mitigated, these stressors escalate in status and are compounded by each additional criterion triggered, ultimately creating work overload. It is usually not one event that generates a stress response in an individual, unit, service or facility, but more likely multiple events (French et al., 2000). Essentially, the goal is to act early before the system realizes it is under stress and while there is opportunity to match demand to capacity and maintain maximal system flow. *Orange* reflects escalating demand without readily available capacity. In this state, aggressive action is required to avoid system overload and ultimate gridlock. *Red* is a state of gridlock and system overload. This critical, high stress, status warrants the use of the organizations Disaster Plan, including such actions as canceling elective surgeries, admissions and procedures. This is the level manifested by significant waits and delays, admissions holding in the ED, customer dissatisfaction, high use of staff, unplanned benefit time, divert/bypass and loss of revenue and market share.

Categories, criteria, interventions and statuses come together in a unit or service grid. Our current DCMS is made of 44 grids representing the microsystems that currently support each other in identifying and mitigating stressors in real time to avoid demand to capacity mismatches. Table 4-1, shows an example of a generic DCMS grid.

Table 4-1. A Generic DCMS Grid.

UNIT NAME	CRITERIA	GREEN	YELLOW	ORANGE	RED
CENSUS		VALUES/ INTERVENTIONS	VALUES/ INTERVENTIONS	VALUES/ INTERVENTIONS	VALUES/ INTERVENTIONS
ACUITY		VALUES/ INTERVENTIONS	VALUES/ INTERVENTIONS	VALUES/ INTERVENTIONS	VALUES/ INTERVENTIONS
OTHER		VALUES/ INTERVENTIONS	VALUES/ INTERVENTIONS	VALUES/ INTERVENTIONS	VALUES/ INTERVENTIONS
STAFFING		VALUES/ INTERVENTIONS	VALUES/ INTERVENTIONS	VALUES/ INTERVENTIONS	VALUES/ INTERVENTIONS

Each criterion is given values that demonstrate escalating stress corresponding to each color or status (Table 4-2). Developing the interventions for each criterion and status is the core to real-time matching of demand to capacity. These interventions create the institutional memory. Institutional memory is those interventions that consistently produce the desired results. They are identified by looking at the behaviors, actions and collaboration demonstrated by the institution's best supervisors, managers and charge staff when challenged by specific constraints and barrier to "getting the work done". By memorializing these 'best practices' in DCMS unit grids, less experienced staff can be trained and empowered to utilize these practices successfully.

An example of escalating census criteria for the key criterion of the number of patients holding in the Emergency Department for an inpatient bed is displayed in Table 4-2.

Table 4-2. An Example of Escalating Census Criteria and Number of Patients Held for Inpatient Beds in the ED.

Emergency Department	Criteria	Green	Yellow	Orange	Red
Census	Patients holding for admission (>1 hour)	0-2	3-5	6-10	≥11

4. WHAT YOU DON'T MEASURE IS HARD TO IMPROVE!

The use of real-time data is necessary to demand to capacity management because it is real-time feedback that eliminates the use of intuition and supports the allocation of resources to the right place, at the right time in the right amount. By identifying queues the work of mitigating bottlenecks before they impact patient flow can be achieved.

Virtual instrumentation has been applied to almost every industry including telecommunication, automotives, semiconductors, factory management and essentially any industrial operations program. Still relatively new in healthcare, programs have been developed and implemented in a wide range of research-based clinical applications and executive information tools particularly as related to financial management (Rosow, et al. 2003). Unfortunately, healthcare has been slow to accept technological solutions and most institutions continue to manage complex processes such as patient flow using tradition methods such as paper, white boards and phone calls. Current "intuition" forecasting by managers is less than adequate, resulting in last minute adjustments to elective schedules, staffing and resources (Jones, Joy & persons, 2002). These approaches lack the timely information necessary to match resources to changing patient needs. The result is the exacerbation of hospital-wide waits and delays, loss of admissions, decreases in revenue, provider job dissatisfaction and an increase in all forms of healthcare resource wastes (Rosow, et al., 2003). In addition, it creates real-time barriers to patient access and flow as hospitals struggle to deal with unprecedented increases in the demand for services. User-defined, customizable solutions facilitate decision making from the big-picture to transaction-level detail, while providing real-time knowledge, information, access and resources that can empower all levels of the organization (Rosow et al., 2003).

Harper (Harper, 2002) demonstrated the effectiveness of an identified generic framework for modeling hospital resources. This framework was dynamic in that it used real-time data, patient flow and time-dependent demand profiles to support managerial decision making. The need for sophisticated, real-time tools is imperative to accurately reflect the complexity, uncertainty, variability and limited resources that drive the acute care facility's ability to respond to fluctuating demand. The ability to access data regarding a system is the foundation to the developing of "best practices" for the matching of demand to capacity. Best practices result from the analysis of the data over time and the development of management behaviors that predict the practices and processes support optimal outcomes.

Much of the success of our DCMS resulted from a paper system initiated in 1997. This system used a report sheet called the 'Bird's Eye View' (Figure 4-1) which was faxed to all participating units twice daily, with updates as needed. Since 2003 our system has been web based and increasingly interactive to facilitate timely completion of interventions. This system called Acute Care Operations Management Systems (ACOMS) is a collaborative effort between Atlantic Health System and Vistaar Technologies, Inc. It is suggested that a system for driving and measuring the DCMS in real time be considered, particularly for improving operational efficiency.

4.1 Our Results

A robust DCMS, particularly one that is able to generate real-time and retrospective trended data, can provide the impetus necessary for buy-in, particularly from administration and physicians. We have been fortunate to have greater than 92% retention, significantly decreased episodes of full divert (Figure 4-2) and support for supplies and resources needed for matching demand to capacity across the macrosystem.

There are commonalities that drive collaboration and the DCMS across the continuum of care. Some units and departments are natural partners for each other, for example environmental is the perfect partner for food services, volunteer services for transport. There also appears to be a hierarchy of impact with the first service to consistently become stressed being transport or the ability to deliver or return patients to and from services and procedures. It is also known that one service allowed to escalate in stress level and status will quickly cause the escalation of other services and units. For example, an increased turnaround to access laboratory results will delay diagnosis and treatment in the ED. The ability of services to provide support significantly decreases with the number of services in orange or red.

Birds Eye View

Date ______________

Time (circle one)

3AM 7AM 12N 3PM 7PM 11PM

House Census ______________

STAFFING RESOURCE: ______________

BEEPER #: ______________

UNIT	CENSUS	BEDS AVAILABLE	TELE AVAILABLE	APO/ MDS	*CAPPED*	CENSUS	ACUITY	OTHER	STAFF
10CD									
9CD									
8D									
5AB									
4AB									
3AB									
Critical Care									
ED									
CCU									
ICU 1									
ICU 2									
Maternal/ Child									
6AB									
L&D									
NICU									
Pediatrics									

Zone Key= G *(Green)*, Y *(Yellow)*, O *(Orange)*, R *(RED)*

Figure 4-1. Birds Eye View

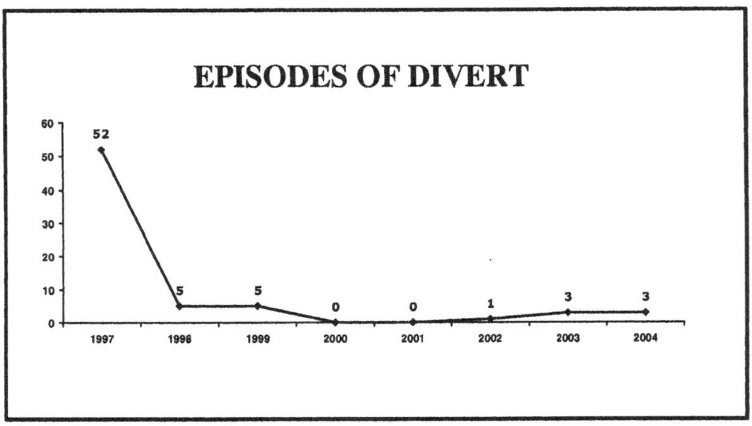

Figure 4-2. Episodes of Divert Since the Initiation of the DCMS in 1997.

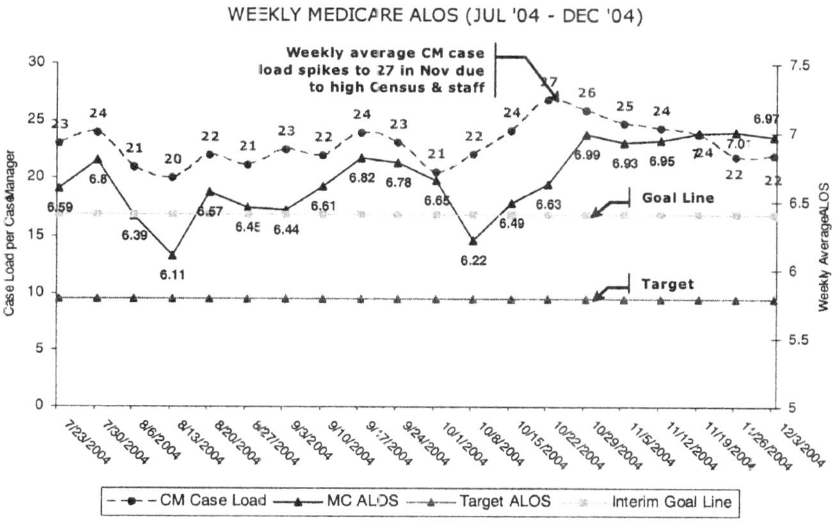

Figure 4-3. Graphs and Analysis provided by Vikas Phatak and Anik Roy. Base Demand & Capacity Data Captured by the ACOMS Software of Vistaar Technologies Inc. (WWW.Acoms.Vistaar.Com).

Some of the new programs initiatives that we have realized from demand capacity management include; developing bridge orders for admission from the ED, opening of additional intermediate beds to decompress ICU, additional FTEs for Case Management (Figure 4-3), additional transport staff, expedited ICU admissions, and additional ED staff for triage. ACOMS has also increased our ability to access capital dollars for purchasing equipment that had been found to negatively impact our ability to match demand to capacity including; IV pumps, PCA pumps and mini-infusers. Some of the most valuable results were those that improved communication across the system such as wireless phones and report sheets between the recovery rooms and the surgical units which were expanded to include components that improved antibiotic therapy (SIPS) compliance and pain management.

5. DISCUSSION

Much of the research done on healthcare restructuring suggest that while workload may increase during restructuring there are other factors that may actually drive job dissatisfaction, such as diminished resources with increasing demand for services. Distress may, in fact, be the result of the amount of work expected or the way restructuring changes were implemented. Change initiatives that include placing staff nurses on multidisciplinary, multi-departmental task forces and committees and providing access to education and learning resources, offer growth and promotional opportunities that support empowerment and job satisfaction (Laschinger, 2004). Better support, communication, resources and supervision during restructuring may be the key to increasing satisfaction with the change process (Burke, 2003).

The work of Aiken (Aiken et al., 2002) demonstrated substantial difference in patient mortality and nursing job satisfaction and burnout related to patient-to nurse ratios. This work did not, however, identify the workload expectations of nursing pre and post mandated ratios. Many hospitals have responded to mandated patient-to-nurse ratios by eliminating supportive resources and staff and creating a more complex workload for nurses. If, instead, their work was redesigned to optimize resources and productivity, would there be a similar impact on job satisfaction?

Additional research should be done to quantify the impact of mental and physical workloads on job satisfaction, taking into consideration such factors as fluctuations in census and patient visits, staffing and nurse-patient ratios, ancillary support, particularly transport and secretarial support, patient acuity and access to supplies and processes.

6. CONCLUSIONS

Efficiency demands on hospitals, driven by high costs and reimbursement and malpractice issues, have forced healthcare administrators to push operations to function at close to maximum capacity, resulting in a lack of resources, including staff, equipment and support services, particularly for accommodating unexpected surges in volume (Mango & Shapiro, 2001). These organizational pressures coupled with increased stress, workload and empowerment have been the impetus for wide-spread job dissatisfaction created the most significant healthcare provider shortage in history.

Nursing staffing has been cited as being the primary driver of high quality hospital care and optimal patient outcomes. Staffing shortages have resulted in higher workloads with hospital nursing leading the country with a forty percent burnout rate (Aiken et al, 2002).

The perceived level of stress experienced by a healthcare provider also directly correlates with job satisfaction drives burnout. Core to healthcare provider job satisfaction are empowerment and organizational commitment. Workload has been identified as a major source of workplace stressors.

Key to operational performance and workload management is identification of potential bottlenecks and development of an action plan that allows for mitigation or smoothing of demand and capacity mismatches in real-time. This involves identifying the varying demand for services at any one time and matching it to the necessary resources efficiently and effectively. The random fluctuations of demand can be analyzed to identify real patterns that can be managed. Limits can be placed on services or practices to facilitate process improvement. The most successful strategies empower the front-line worker to handle matching demand to capacity in real time and thus prevent bottlenecks, queues and stress from occurring.

Information technology is just beginning to be accepted as a strategy for managing workload and matching demand to capacity across the continuum in real-time. Greater use of technology has the potential to support the efficient use of human resources, which are a valuable commodity. There is opportunity to use a real-time demand to capacity matching system (DCMS), to empower staff to manage their workload towards optimizing patient flow, satisfaction and outcomes and to increase staff job satisfaction. A successful DCMS is dependent six key principles, trust making, staff, empowerment, mitigation of constraints and barriers to flow between microsystems, development of a common vocabulary, collaboration between microsystems ideally based on the principles of CRM, understanding of the value of the individuals within the microsystem not only within the microsystem but the macrosystem and development of a sense and support of reciprocal or "fair trade".

Ultimately it is the elimination of waits and delays that will truly distinguish a hospital (Mango & Shapiro, 2001). But it is the retention of our valuable human resources that will make it possible.

The right resources...in the right place...at the right time!

7. REFERENCES

Aiken, L.H., PhD, Clarke, S. P., PhD, Sloane, D. M., PhD, Sochalski, J., PhD, & Silber, J.H.,PhD. (2002). Hospital nurse staffing and patient mortality, nurse burnout, and job dissatisfaction. *JAMA*, 288(16), 1987-1993.

Bojtor, A. (2003). The importance of social and cultural factors to nursing status. *International Journal of Nursing Practice,* 9, 328-335.

French, S.E., PhD, Lenton, R.,PhD, Walters, V., PhD, & Eyles, J., PhD. (2000). An empirical evaluation of an expanded nursing stress scale. *Journal of Nursing Measurement,* 8 (2), 161-178.

Godfrey,M.M., Nelson, E.C., Wasson,J.H., Mohr, J.J., Batalden,P.B.,(2003). Microsystems in healthcare: Part 3.Planning patient-centered services. *The Joint Commission Journal for Quality Improvement,* 29 (4), 159-170.

Harper, P. R. (2002). A framework for operational modeling of hospital resources. *Healthcare Managemt Science, 5,* 165-173.

Hatcher, S., & Laschinger, H.K.S. (1996). Staff nurses' perceptions of job empowerment and level of burnout: A test of Kanter's theory of structural power in organizations. *CJONA,* 9 (4), 74-94.

Hawkins, A. L., Kratsch, L.S. (2004). Troubled units: Creating change. *AACN Clinical Iss*ues, 15 (2), 215-221.

Holtom, B.C., & PhD, O'Neill, B.S. (2004). Job embeddedness. *JONA,* 34 (5), 216-227.

Institute of Medicine. (2001). *Crossing the quality chasm.* Washington, DC: National Academy Press.

Joint Commission. (2004). *Joint Commission Resources: Managing Patient Flow.* Oakbrook Terrace, Illinois: Joint Commission on Accreditation of Healthcare Organizations.

Jones, S. A., Joy, M. P., & Pearson, J. (2002). Forecasting demand of emergency care. *Healthcare Manag. Sci., 5*(4), 297-305.

Kosnik, L.K. & Espinosa, J.A. (2003). Microsystems in healthcare: Part 7. The microsystem as a platform for merging strategic planning and operations. *Journal on Quality Improvement,* 29(9), 452-459.

Kosnik, L.K. (2002). The new paradigm of crew resource management: just what is needed to reengage the stalled collaborative movement? *Journal on Quality Improvement,* 28(5), 235-241.

Kuokkanen, L, MNSc, Leino-Kilpi, H., PhD, & Katajisto, J., MSSc. (2003). Nurse empowerment, job-related satisfaction, and organizational commitment. *J Nurs Care Qual.* 18(3), 184-192.

Mango, P. D., & Shapiro, L. A. (2001). *The McKinsey Quarterly: Number 2. Hospitals get serious about operations* (pp. 74-85). Pittsburgh, PA: McKinsey & Company

Nacey, G. E.. (2004). *Maximizing Hospital Capacity.* Pittsburgh, PA: Tele-Tracking Technologies, Inc.

Narine, L., & Persaud, D.D. (2003). Gaining and maintaining commitment to large-scale change in healthcare organizations. *Health Services Management Research,* 16, 179-187.

Nelson, E.C., Batalden, P.B., Huber, T.P., Mohr, J.J., Godfrey, M.M., Headric, L.A., Wasson, J.H. (2002). Microsystems in health care: Part 1. Learning from high-performing front-line clinical units. *The Joint Commission Journal for Quality Improvement,* 28(9), 472-493.

Radice, B. (1994). The relationship between nurse empowerment in the hospital work environment and job satisfaction: a pilot study. *Journal of the New York State Nurses Association,* 25 (2), 14-17.

Rosow, E., MS, Adam, J., MS, Coulombe, K., MS, Race, K., BSN, RN, & Anderson, R., RN, MPA, CNAA, FAAN. (2003). Virtual instrumentation and real-time executive dashboards. *Nursing Administration Quarterly, 27*(1), 58-76.

Siddharthan, K., Jones, W.J., & Johnson, J.A. (1996). A priority queuing model to reduce waiting times in emergency care. *International Journal of Healthcare Quality,* 9(5), 10-16.

Tonges, M. C., PhD., Rothstein, H., PhD. & Carter, H. K. (1998). Sources of satisfaction in hospital nursing practice. *JONA,* 28(5), 47-61.

Chapter 5

MANAGING PATIENT APPOINTMENTS IN PRIMARY CARE

Sergei Savin
Graduate School of Business, 404 Uris Hall, Columbia University, New York, NY 10027

Abstract: In recent years, many US health care establishments have found themselves under increasing pressure to improve the cost-effectiveness of their operations in the face of tight competition, while maintaining high standards of care. Finding the best trade-off between these competing objectives is not an easy task, since the efforts to keep costs under control often result in over utilization of existing resources and, as a consequence, increased patient delays. The Institute of Medicine report *Crossing the Quality Chasm: A New Health System for the 21st Century* identifies "timeliness" as one of six goals that should drive the redesign of the health care delivery system in the coming years. For many patients, primary care is one of the most important settings for their contact with the health care system. In this setting, an appointment mechanism directly determines "timeliness" of received care. In this chapter we introduce a simple model that describes the evolution of appointment backlogs in a primary office setting and describe how expected value and the variance of the daily demand for appointments influences backlog buildup. We also discuss the popular practice of advanced access, a newly proposed approach for reducing and eliminating appointment delays. In particular, we develop a set of guidelines that any primary care office should use in determining the patient panel size to support the advanced access approach. Our guidelines are illustrated through a set of examples based on the demand and supply data taken from the surveys of the American Academy of Family Practice as well as 2002 National Ambulatory Medical Care Survey.

Key words: Access to care, appointment scheduling, advanced access, optimal patient panel size.

1. INTRODUCTION: DELAYS IN ACCESS TO PRIMARY CARE

Primary care is the key part of any national health care system - a focal point of contact between an individual and health care professionals. The World Health Care Organization, in the Declaration of its International Conference on the Primary Health Care (1978), states that the primary care networks should ensure that "practical, scientifically sound and socially acceptable methods and technology" are "universally accessible to individuals and families ... at a cost that the community and country can afford to maintain..." A body of evidence based on cross-country comparisons reported in Starfield (1991) suggests that strong primary care results in higher patient satisfaction scores, lower health care expenses, and fewer drug prescriptions. American Academy of Family Physicians (AAFP, www.aafp.org) defines primary care as "care provided by physicians specifically trained for and skilled in comprehensive first contact and continuing care for persons with any undiagnosed sign, symptom, or health concern (the "undifferentiated" patient) not limited by problem origin (biological, behavioral, or social), organ system, or diagnosis."

Timely access to care is, simultaneously, a key characteristic of an effective primary care system, and a well-documented problem area for the US primary care system. Difficulty in getting an appointment to see a physician in a timely manner is a widespread phenomenon. In its recent milestone report on the quality of health care, *Crossing the Quality Chasm: A New Health System for the 21st Century*, the Institute of Medicine (IOM) identifies "the long waits for appointments which are common today" as a major factor increasing the probability of dangerous diagnosing delays and, consequently, "more advanced diagnosis". The same report defines "timeliness" as one of six characteristics that a working health care system should possess.

Timeliness is recognized as an important characteristic of service delivery in any service setting, including health care. However, it is hard to find any other business setting where the constraints on access to service are as persistent as they are in health care services. The IOM in *Crossing the Quality Chasm* characterizes prevalent practice as follows: "Lack of timeliness also signals a lack of attention to flow and a lack of respect for the patient that are not tolerated in consumer-centered systems in other service industries. It suggests that care has not been designed with the welfare of the patient at the center."

Patient delays in the primary care setting can be classified into two categories: *appointment* and *real-time*. Appointment delay can be defined as the number of days between the requested and scheduled appointment dates.

Clearly, not every appointment scheduled for some future date necessarily indicates the lack of access to care: in some cases, patient may find it desirable (due to some previous commitments) not to see a physician "today" (Murray and Tantau 2000 estimate that the fraction of such patients in the total patient pool does not exceed 25%). Such cases become a part of patient flow often characterized as a "good backlog" (another component of "good backlog" is formed by the appointments - such as follow-ups - which are pre-scheduled for a specific future date). On the other hand, when a patient is unable to obtain an appointment with her PCP on the day she selects, her access to service is clearly limited. The patient's service request has to be postponed and is forced to join the so-called "bad backlog". While the appointment delays can be as long as weeks or even months, the real-time delays that relate to the wait beyond the pre-specified appointment time on the day of actual service, are measured in minutes and hours. In addition, real-time delays can affect both the patient and the health-care provider.

The reasons behind these two types of service delays can be quite different. Appointment delays may be indicative of an overall strategic mismanagement of the demand-supply balance in the primary care environment. Such mismanagement could stem from a primary practice's excessively large patient panel to ineffective approaches for allocating patient demand to appointment slots. In this respect, appointment delays can be virtually eliminated by ensuring that the overall demand for care meets adequate supply of capacity, and that both are actively managed to deal with unexpected short-term mismatches. The real-time delays, on the other hand, have a more tactical nature, and are often a result of a complex combination of general service inefficiency, patient/provider lateness, potential mismatch between the average duration of an office consultation and the length of an appointment slot and, finally, due to sheer unpredictability of patient arrivals for their appointments and of actual consultation times. While there exist specific recipes aimed at minimizing the impact of most of these factors, the real-time delays cannot be entirely avoided due to the random, unpredictable nature of primary care service durations.

The focus of the majority of the operations research studies modeling delays in health care systems has been on the minimization of real-time delays (a comprehensive review of this literature stream is given in Cayirli and Veral 2003). At the same time, a more strategic (and, as one can argue, more practically important) task of appointment delay reduction has not received nearly as much attention. In this chapter we attempt to address this imbalance by focusing on the subject of appointment delays. In Section 2 we introduce a simple model that explains the role of patient demand characteristics in the creation and growth of appointment backlogs in primary care. Section 3 provides a detailed description of the advanced access, a recently developed approach to backlog elimination. In that section, our focus is on determining a patient panel size that is consistent with the practice of advanced access. We develop a set of practical guidelines that primary care offices can use to set their panel size targets and provide a number of examples based on the data reported in AAFP surveys and in the latest 2002 National Ambulatory Medical Care Survey.

2. APPOINTMENT BACKLOGS IN PRIMARY CARE: HOW ARE THEY CREATED

Long appointment backlogs in primary care are often a norm. In primary care facilities that employ traditional appointment systems, a patient with a "non-urgent" request may have to wait weeks and even months to be seen by a physician: 2004 National Healthcare Quality Report states that the fraction of patients who get timely appointments is only 43.8% for routine care and 57.3% for injury/illness related care (www.qualitytools.ahrq.gov/qualityreport/browse/browse.aspx?id=5080). Physicians' schedules are almost always full, and the truly urgent cases are either diverted to urgent care centers or emergency rooms, or attended to by double-booking, delaying other patients and working overtime. Patients perceive the appointment capacity as being strictly rationed and employ various tactics trying to "game the system" and gain an early access to care. At the same time, as an appointment backlog grows so does the probability of cancellations for those appointments scheduled far in advance of actual service. The overall level of tension and frustration on the part of all participants in such service system can be quite high: providers work long hours, but the backlogs remain stable, and patients still cannot get care when they want to. All of these signs seem to indicate that the demand for care exceeds the supply of appointment capacity. In fact, physicians may use these dysfunctional dynamics to justify their discomfort about adopting any changes threatening the existing appointment system, which is viewed as a wall protecting physician time against an overwhelming flood of care requests (Gordon and Chin 2004).

As our example below will demonstrate, the "obvious" conclusion about the demand/capacity imbalance may be incorrect: if the appointment backlogs remain stable (albeit long) and the actual daily patient demand for appointments is uncertain, then the average daily demand for care is likely to be *lower* than the available daily appointment capacity. The uncertainty of the daily appointment demand is the key to understanding this seemingly paradoxical statement.

It is often convenient to describe uncertain demand for appointments in terms of its average daily value (sometimes also called expected or mean value) and the demand uncertainty as measured, for example, by the value of the standard deviation of the actual demand around its average value. Given that the daily demand for appointments is uncertain, two general rules apply to a typical primary care setting:

1. A backlog of unserved appointment demand can build up even if the average daily demand for appointments is *less* than the available appointment capacity.

2. The value of the appointment backlog grows not only with the average value of daily appointment demand, but also with the value of its standard deviation.

Below we present simple examples that illustrate these rules. Consider a newly opened primary care office with daily appointment capacity of $C = 20$ slots and the average daily demand for appointments equal to 19. We assume that such an office starts its operation on some "day 1" with an empty appointment book, i.e., that all appointment slots on day 1 and on any other day in the future are open. For simplicity we assume that all patients requesting appointments will accept same-day appointments if presented with such an option (our conclusions will also remain valid in the case when some patients insist on later appointments). Such an office has enough capacity to serve the average number of daily appointment requests, so if there were no variation in daily demand the office would have no patient backlog. However, consider a situation in which the actual demand for appointments on any given day is uncertain and takes on two possible values, 16 or 22, each with 50% probability (we also assume that demands for appointments on different days are independent of each other). In this case, the average demand for appointments is $0.5\times16+0.5\times22 = 19$, but on each particular day the demand is either four below the available capacity or two above it. Demand uncertainty can be characterized by a standard deviation, which is computed as follows for the example:

$$\sqrt{0.5\times(22-19)^2+0.5\times(16-19)^2} = 3.$$

Suppose that on days when the demand for appointments exceeds the appointment capacity the "overflow" (appointment requests in excess of capacity) is pushed to the next available day, adding to "bad backlog". Figure 5-1 traces the possible values of patient backlog in such practice on days 1, 2, and 3 (numbers in the ovals show the actual appointment backlog values under each particular scenario): for example, at the end of day 1, the appointment backlog is either 2 (if demand for appointments on day 1 happens to be 22) or 0 (if demand for appointments on day 1 happens to be 16). Since each of these scenarios happens with 50% probability, the average appointment backlog at the end of day 1 is 0.5×2+0.5×0 = 1. As we can see, when the office starts with "empty" appointment books, the average backlog in the system *grows* from one at the end of day 1 to 1.75 at the end of day 3, despite the fact that average demand is *lower* than appointment capacity.

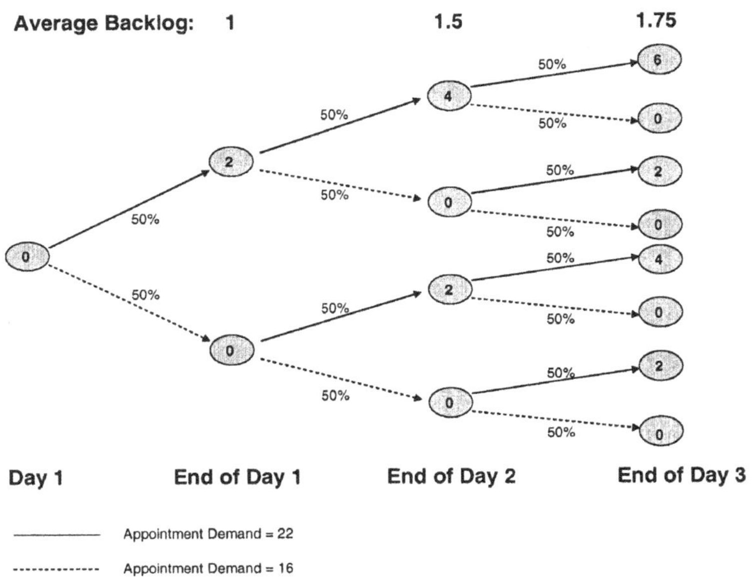

Figure 5-1. The appointment backlog scenarios when office starts with backlog = 0.

Will this backlog continue to grow indefinitely? Certainly not! Imagine that at the beginning of day X, the backlog of appointments happens to be equal to 10. Figure 5-2 shows all possible changes to such backlog over the period of next 3 days: the average backlog drops to 9 at the end of day X, and then continues to drop to 7.25 at the end of day X+2.

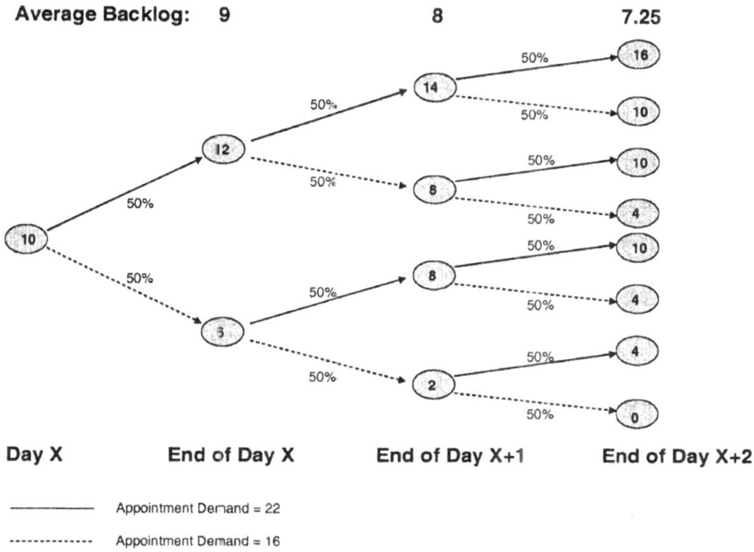

Figure 5-2. The appointment backlog scenarios when office starts with backlog = 0.

So far we have observed that the backlog grows when it is "too low" and drops when it is "too high". Perhaps, then, there should be a "medium" backlog level that remains *stable* over long period of time. In Figure 5-3 we extend the timeline depicted in Figures 5-1 and 5-2 and use simulation to show what happens to the average appointment backlog over a period of 40 days when the office starts with no backlog or with a backlog of 10 appointments. In both cases, the average backlog converges to the same value – approximately 3.25 appointments – the value that remains stable over a long period of time (we will call this value *long-term backlog*). Intuitively, it is not hard to rationalize why such long-term backlog builds up in a system in which average daily demand is below the capacity, even if such system starts "empty". On the "good" days, when the patient demand is less than the appointment capacity, the extra service capacity cannot be "stored" and "transferred" to the next day to serve future patient demand, such extra capacity is simply lost unless there is a backlog. On the other hand, on the "bad" days, when patient demand exceeds service capacity, the unserved demand is not lost and has to be satisfied in the future. So, if the system starts with no appointment backlog, the "good" days fail to clear the backlog created by the equal number of "bad" days.

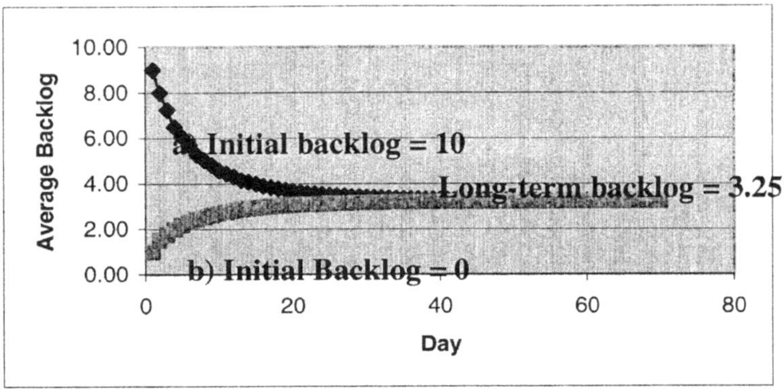

Figure 5-3. Average backlog as a function of time: a) initial backlog = 10, b) initial backlog = 0. Average demand = 19, standard deviation = 3.

The above example demonstrates the role of demand uncertainty in creating appointment backlogs. The greater is that uncertainty, the higher is the resulting long-term backlog. For contrast, Figure 5-4 evaluates a case with larger variation in demand. In the example demand takes two values, 15 and 23, with equal probability. The average daily demand is still 19 (0.5×15+0.5×23), but the demand uncertainty, as measured by the standard deviation, is $\sqrt{0.5\times(23-19)^2+0.5\times(15-19)^2} = 4$, which is higher than in the previous example. Correspondingly, the long-term appointment backlog value grows to about 6.3 (as compared to 3.2 for the standard deviation of 3).

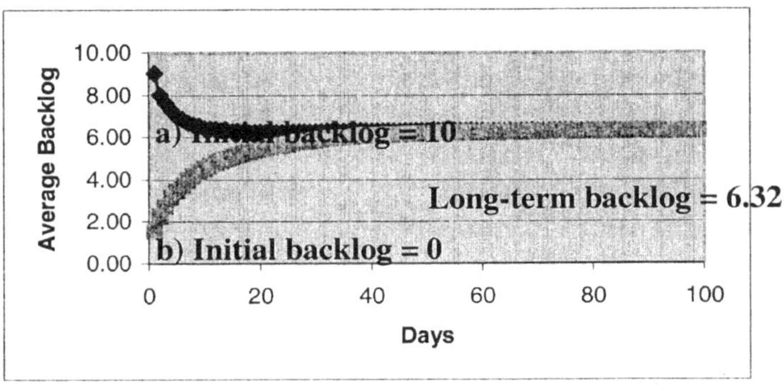

Figure 5-4. Average backlog as a function of time: a) initial backlog = 10, b) initial backlog = 0. Average demand = 19, standard deviation = 4.

As these examples indicate, the uncertainty in the daily demand for appointments (as measured, for example, by the standard deviation of daily demand around its average value) often creates a long-term appointment backlog, even in situations where the average daily demand is below the available appointment capacity. For a given value of the average demand, the larger the demand uncertainty, the longer is the resulting long-term backlog. An increase in the average daily appointment demand also leads to an increase in backlog. For instance, when the average value of uncertain demand is *equal to or larger than* the available appointment capacity, the appointment backlog continues to grow without limit. Figure 5-5 illustrates this fact by showing how the appointment backlog increases over the period of 100 days in cases when the initial backlog is equal to (a) 10 appointments, and (b) 0 appointments. Note the dramatic difference between this figure and Figure 5-3 (where the average demand was strictly below the appointment capacity): now the backlog grows without bound, no matter how small the initial value, exhibiting no signs of "converging" to any limit.

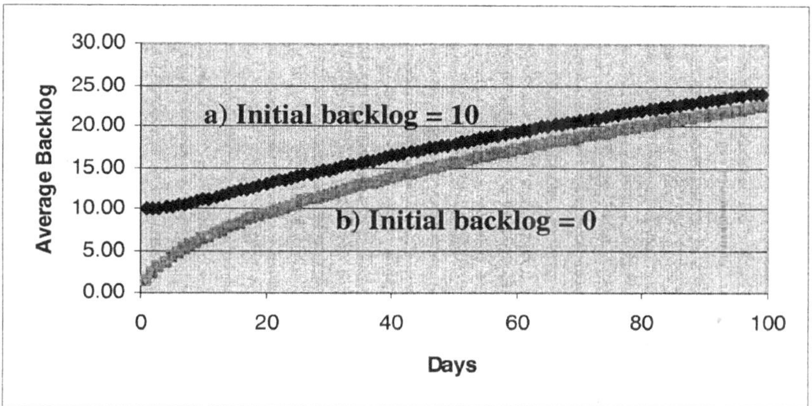

Figure 5-5. Average backlog as a function of time: a) initial backlog = 10, b) initial backlog = 0. Average demand = 20, standard deviation = 3.

The examples illustrate that appointment backlogs can occur in primary care practices even when appointment capacity is sufficient to serve average daily demand. However, appointment flexibility can eliminate this problem, as illustrated in the following section.

3. ELIMINIATING APPOINTMENT DELAYS THROUGH ADVANCED ACCESS

In a seminal paper, Murray and Tantau (2000) describe the "advanced access", a new system for handling appointments in primary care. At the heart of the "advanced access" approach is the patient-centric goal of ensuring that each patient can be seen by his or her PCP on the day of patient's choice, even if this choice is "today". A transition from a traditional backlog-ridden system to the advanced access appointment handling requires a set of steps that adjust the way a primary care office matches patient demand with appointment capacity. While the details of the implementation of the advanced access may differ from practice to practice, the general transition plan includes the following steps: estimating daily appointment demand, adjusting patient panel size, instituting demand control techniques, working down the appointment backlog, and post-introduction management. Below, we provide a detailed review of each of these steps and focus on developing an analytical model that connects the choice of the panel size and the frequency of the overtime work required to sustain advanced access.

3.1 Estimating Demand for Appointments

Demand classification schemes play an important role in shaping up the structure of appointment systems. The traditional appointment scheduling approach is greatly influenced by a classification scheme where all patient care requests go through a triage system that sorts them according to the perceived urgency of the request. "Urgent" (or "same day") requests are given priority and are often bumped-in on top of an already busy appointment schedule, while "non-urgent" requests are offered a future appointment slot. A commonly used alternative to this approach is the "carve out" appointment model, which explicitly reserves a fraction of daily appointments for urgent requests. A focus on urgency of care in these appointment systems is understandable. At the same time, a triage system is not perfect – and in many cases may disadvantage "stoic sick" (Murray and Berwick 2003) while yielding to the demands of "worried well". As a result, some of the demand that can and should be dealt without much of a delay is pushed into the future, giving rise to long appointment backlogs.

The advanced access approach, on the other hand, reduces the role of triage by eliminating, for appointment purposes, the distinction between urgent and non-urgent cases. On any day, every patient requesting an appointment is offered a "same-day" option, irrespective of how urgent the demand is or when a patient prefers to be seen (on the same day or on some future day). Thus, under the advanced access approach, patients are encouraged to see their PCP as soon as possible, and the classification of daily demand for appointments is not based on the urgency of an appointment request, but rather on when a patient wants to be seen by a physician. In particular, daily demand for appointments is usually split into four components: "same-day", "another-day", "walk-in" and "follow-up".

The "same-day" component consists of patients who accept the offer of a same-day appointment. It is likely that as the "advanced access" mentality sets in, this group of patients will constitute a strong majority. On the other hand, for some patients it may be impossible to adjust their schedules and visit their PCP on the same day. While the number of patients declining the same day offer can be expected to diminish with time, it is likely that even in the long run there will always be a fraction of patients who would prefer to be seen some time in the future rather than on the same day (this fraction can be as high as 25% according to Murray and Tantau 2000). These patients form an "another-day" component of the daily demand. "Walk-in" group consists of patients who "drop by" without contacting their primary care office in advance, while "follow-up" group is made up of patients who are seen on the *that day* and who require a follow-up appointment. Thus, daily demand for appointments is the total number of appointment requests *appearing* on a particular day, regardless of whether they are serviced on that same day or in the future. One important point to keep in mind is that the demand for appointments *cannot* be accurately estimated using past appointment data. Instead, a primary care office has to record all appointment requests as they happen for several weeks in order to establish repetitive daily demand patterns.

3.2 Finding the Right Panel Size

The process of establishing the right panel size for a particular primary care practice should proceed through the following five steps: 1) defining the current panel size, 2) estimating daily rate of appointment requests, 3) establishing the target number of daily appointment slots, 4) setting the target overflow frequency and 5) computing the appropriate panel size based on the overflow frequency trade-offs. Below we provide detailed guidelines on implementing each of these steps.

3.2.1 Defining current panel size

The estimation of patient panel size N in a managed care environment is easy: panel size is defined as a number of patients enrolled with a physician. On the other hand, in fee-for-service or mixed practices, the number of patients "on file" may be misleading since it is not uncommon to preserve files for patients who may no longer be using the practice's services. We suggest that in such an environment the panel size be estimated as a total number of distinct patients seen by a physician in the last 18 months (counting patients who visited practice over the last year may underestimate the effective panel size, while the two-year count typically produces an overestimated value). For example, if the number of patients who visited a physician over the last 18 months is 2500, we can use this number as an estimate of current panel size, N.

3.2.2 Estimating daily rate of appointment requests

Daily patient demand for care is based on the profile of the population served by the practice as well as the nature of the practice itself. To arrive at the most accurate assessment of total demand requires prospective measurement of the specific appointment dates that patients actually ask for including walk-ins (external demand) as well as the follow-up visit dates physicians request. This is accomplished by examining appointment logs for the last several months (it is best to look at the period of at least a year to capture all seasonal effects – we recommend 18 months, which is approximately equal to T=315 working days, assuming 210 Monday to Friday working days per calendar year) and count the total number of office visits over that period of time, A. Then, the average daily patient visit rate p is calculated as the ratio of the number of office visits A and the product of the number of patients on the current panel N and the number of days T in the period over which the appointments were counted (say, T=315 for a period of 18 months): $p = (A/(N \times T))$. For example, consider a general/family practitioner with a current panel of N = 2500 patients and suppose that the examination of her appointment log has established that the practice had A = 6500 office visits over the last 18 months (T=315 days). For this practice, we get $p = (A/(N \times T)) = (6500/(2500 \times 315)) = 0.008$ visits/day. Note that this value represents the average over a long period of time and is most appropriate for modeling long-term demand patterns. Over any short-term period, this value can underestimate or overestimate the actual demand rate. In section 3.2.7 we will discuss the effect of predictable short-term variations in the demand rate on the recommended panel size values.

3.2.3 Establishing the target number of daily appointment slots

To estimate the target supply of appointment slots C, the practice needs to decide upon the average length of an appointment slot and the average daily number of hours devoted to direct patient care. For example, if one assumes that a physician spends an average of 7 hours per day in direct patient care and that appointments are scheduled at 20-minute intervals, the target daily appointment capacity is C = 7 hours x 3 appointments/hour = 21 appointments. We use the term "target capacity" to reflect the subjective maximum length of the working day for a particular primary care physician. While under the advanced access approach daily fluctuations in patient demand may force a physician to work beyond this limit on any particular day, such extra work is considered undesirable.

3.2.4 Setting the target overflow frequency

In primary care, patient demand exhibits significant day-to-day variability. In part, this variability is predictable and can be attributed to changes in "calendar variables" (Batal *et al.* 2001): the expected number of daily patient requests to see a physician is often a *deterministic* function of the day of the week and time of the year. If such deterministic variability were the only source of day-to-day, changes in patient demand, a primary care practice would potentially be able to provide an exact match between the patient demand and the supply of service capacity. However, a substantial part of the observed demand variability is *random*, i.e., it cannot be predicted in advance. In this section, we use a simple model of daily demand which accounts for this random variability component. Later, in section 3.2.7, we extend our analysis to include the predictable weekly/seasonal demand variability.

In our demand model, we assume that for each patient a request for care is generated independently of any other patient's request, so that the total daily demand for primary care services can be modeled as a *binomial* random variable with the expectation equal to Np and the variance equal to $Np(1-p)$. The patient demand rate p is considered to be constant and not subject to day-to-day variations – in other words, it represents the long-term average demand rate estimated in section 3.2.2. Figure 5-6 illustrates this demand model by showing the distribution of binomial daily demand requests from a panel of N=2500 patients with p=0.008. We observe that while the expected number of patient appointment requests on any day is equal to 20, the actual number of requests can very well be anywhere between 15 and 25.

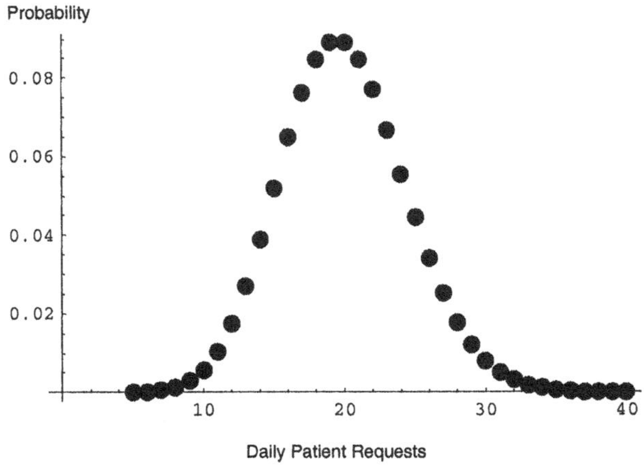

Figure 5-6. Daily patient demand distribution under binomial model: panel size $N = 2500$, demand rate $p = 0.008$.

Using our model and the target number of appointment slots available each day C, we can estimate the effect of panel size on the ability to offer same day appointments by calculating the probability that the demand for appointments exceeds the supply of appointment slots on any given day. We call this probability "overflow frequency". In particular, the overflow frequency for a primary practitioner who sets the target number of daily appointment slots to C and who serves a panel of size N with daily patient visit rate of p is equal to

$$f = 1 - \sum_{k=0}^{C} \frac{N!}{k!(N-k)!} p^k (1-p)^{N-k} \qquad (5\text{-}1)$$

The overflow frequency as expressed in (1) rapidly increases with the size of patient panel N and rapidly decreases with C. For $N = 2500$, $p = 0.008$ and $C = 21$, the calculated value of the current overflow frequency is 41.1%. This high value of overflow frequency indicates that with the given panel size a physician will not be able to "do today's work today" on a consistent basis without frequent overtime work. Clearly, the target level of overflow frequency should be much lower. In particular, a physician could consider setting it to 5% (approximately once a month), 10% (once in two weeks), or 20% (once in a week). When defining the overflow frequency, it should be kept in mind that high overflows are equivalent to long overtime work: in our example ($N = 2500$, $p = 0.008$ and $C = 21$, overtime frequency of 41.1%)

the average duration of overtime when it happens is more than an hour. Thus, limiting overflow frequency to 20% may be advisable.

3.2.5 Computing the appropriate panel size

The last step in calculating the appropriate panel size involves iterative adjustment of the trial panel size until the corresponding overflow frequency matches the target level. If the overflow frequency corresponding to the current panel size is higher than the target level, one should lower the panel size and repeat the overflow frequency calculation using (1). Similarly, if the computed overflow frequency turns out to be too low, the panel size should be increased. In our example, the computed initial value of the overflow frequency (41.1%) is much higher than the target level of 20%, so we need to diminish the panel size. Repeating the calculation of Equation 5-1 for the trial panel size of $N = 2000$, we obtain an overflow frequency of 15.9% - which is lower than the level of overtime work a physician is willing to tolerate. Adjusting panel size upwards to $N = 2250$ and recomputing the overflow frequency, we get the value of 32.9% - above the target level. Going down to the panel of $N = 2100$ patients, we get the overflow frequency of 21.8%. Repeating these panel size iterations several more times, we finally achieve the overflow frequency of 20.04% for the panel size of $N = 2072$. This overflow frequency is pretty close to our target level of 20% (due to discrete nature of the panel size it may not be possible to find the panel size that results in the overflow frequency of exactly 20%). Thus, a panel size of 2072 patients is recommended for the considered practice.

3.2.6 Examples based on NAMCS 2002 data

While the NAMCS 2002 survey (www.cdc.gov/nchs/about/major/ahcd/ahcd1.htm) reports the total number of annual visits to general and family practitioners in the United States (215,466,000), the annual visit rate per patient is not easy to estimate since we could not find reliable statistics on the number of people who actually use (or even have) a primary care physician. The rate of 0.761 annual office visits per person, reported in NAMCS 2002 survey, was obtained by dividing the total number of visits to general and family practitioners by the entire United States population (283,135,000), taken from 2000 Census data. Clearly, using this value would result in a gross underestimation of actual patient visit rates. The rate we use in our study (1.575 annual visits per patient) is calculated based on the assumption of 210 annual in-office days and on the assumption (used in Murray and Berwick 2003) that in an average patient panel not overly weighed with elderly and chronically ill patients, 0.7%-0.8% of patients will request visit on an average day. Table 5-1 shows the patient panel sizes (and attained capacity utilizations) for a "typical" general and family practitioner (on average, 1.575 annual visits per patient) and a "typical" pediatrician (on average, 1.98 annual visits per child according to 2002 NAMCS) which would result in an overflow frequency of 5% (approximately, once a month), 10% (twice a month), or 20% (once a week).

Table 5-1. Panel sizes (capacity utilizations) for different parameter values, primary care type: general and family practice and pediatrics.

Overflow Frequency	**General and Family Practice**		**Pediatrics**	
	Daily Slots = 24	Daily Slots = 20	Daily Slots = 24	Daily Slots = 20
5%	2294 (72%)	1852 (69%)	1475 (72%)	1191 (69%)
10%	2468 (77%)	2006 (75%)	1586 (77%)	1290 (75%)
20%	2697 (84%)	2211 (83%)	1734 (84%)	1421 (83%)

2002 NAMCS reported that the average duration of the "face-to-face" part of the office visit is 16.1 minutes for general and family practice and for pediatrics, 18.1 minutes for OB/GYN practice and 20.0 minutes for internal medicine practice. In our calculations we considered appointment intervals of 20 minutes, which is likely to be a realistic estimate for the duration of a typical appointment in a primary care setting. An 8-hour workday would produce 24 daily appointment slots (for a 5-day working week this number roughly corresponds to 40.2 hours spent by a family physician on direct patient care or patient-related service during a complete week of practice, according to a recent AAFP survey, http://www.aafp.org/x769.xml). Since the actual daily appointment capacity is likely to be somewhat lower than this optimistic estimate, in our calculations we also consider an alternative daily capacity of 20 appointment slots. The calculations were performed using Equation 5-1 under the assumption of 210 workdays per year. This value, in our estimate, is a good representation of the annual number of workdays for the majority of primary care practices.

3.2.7 Accounting for weekly and seasonal variations in patient demand

A recipe for setting the size of patient panel described above is based on the assumption that patient demand rate is the same every day. In practice, however, the expected demand for primary care is subject to weekly as well as seasonal variation. Consider a general/family practitioner who has the target number of daily slots equal to 20 and who is serving a panel of size N=2211 for which the long-term average demand rate is p=0.075, as defined in sections 3.2.1 and 3.2.2. This combination of parameters corresponds to one of the cells in Table 5-1 and results in an average overflow frequency of 20%.

Now, suppose that the daily demand rates change from day to day during each week as well as from month to month. In particular, let p_{ij} be the demand rate from any patient on the panel on day i in month j: for example, $p_{\mathrm{TUE,APR}}$ stands for the demand rate on a Tuesday in April. Under these assumptions, patient demand on day i in month j is a binomial random variable with the mean Np_{ij} and the variance $Np_{ij}(1\text{-}p_{ij})$. Thus, demand rate dynamics is described by 5x12=60 demand rate parameters, such that their average is equal to p:

$$\frac{1}{60}\sum_{i=\mathrm{MON}}^{\mathrm{FRI}}\sum_{j=\mathrm{JAN}}^{\mathrm{DEC}} p_{ij} = p. \tag{5-2}$$

For a given value of p, it is convenient to describe this demand rate dynamics in terms of the calendar adjustment factors, which are defined as ratios of the average demand value on a particular day and the long-term average demand over all days. In our model, the calendar adjustment factors can be computed as $q_{ij} = Np_{ij}/(Np) = p_{ij}/p$, so that the daily expected demand is Npq_{ij} and its variance is $Npq_{ij}(1\text{-}pq_{ij})$. Such adjustment factors reflect how much higher or lower the demand rate is on a particular day as compared to the long-term average demand rate. Figure 5-7 show the calendar adjustment factors computed from the appointment data at Scott and White Killeen Clinic (TX) as reported in Forjuoh *et al.* (2001).

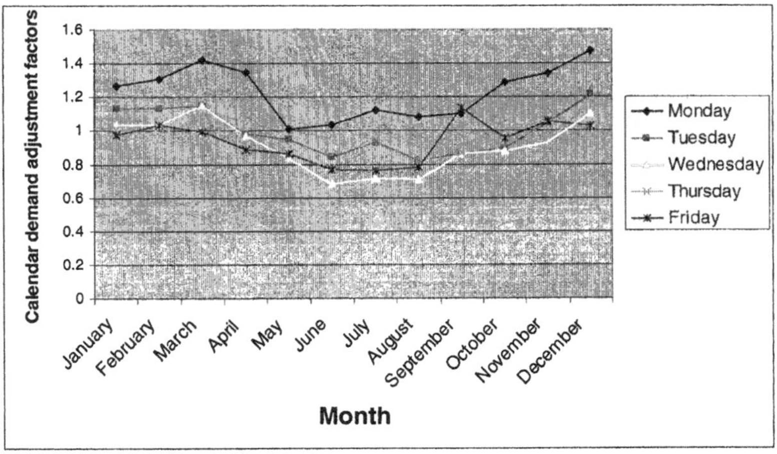

Figure 5-7. Calendar demand adjustment factors based on the data from Scott and White Killeen Clinic (TX) as reported in Forjuoh *et al.* (2001).

In this example, for most of the months, demand values are the highest on Mondays (average calendar adjustment factor is 1.234), sharply dropping on Tuesdays (0.998), before leveling off on Wednesdays (0.909), Thursday (0.921), and Fridays (0.938). Across months, daily demand rates follow mostly similar trajectories, reaching peak in colder months (average calendar adjustment factor from October through April is 1.088) and dropping in warmer months (average calendar adjustment factor in May through September is 0.887).

Given these variations in demand rates, the resulting overflow frequencies differ from day to day. In particular, on day i in month j the overflow frequency can be computed using the generalization of Equation (5-1):

$$f_{ij} = 1 - \sum_{k=0}^{C} \frac{N!}{k!(N-k)!} \left(pq_{ij}\right)^k \left(1 - pq_{ij}\right)^{N-k}. \qquad (5\text{-}3)$$

Then, the average overflow frequency can be obtained as follows:

$$f^* = \frac{1}{60} \sum_{i=\text{MON}}^{\text{FRI}} \sum_{j=\text{JAN}}^{\text{DEC}} f_{ij}. \qquad (5\text{-}4)$$

Would the resulting average overflow frequency f^* be far-away from the 20% value reported in section 3.2.6 for the case of time-independent demand rate? In the Table 5-2 below we show the overflow frequency values f_{ij} as well as the average f^*.

*Table 5-2.*Overflow frequency values for different days and months based on the data from Scott and White Killeen Clinic (TX) as reported in Forjuoh *et al.* (2001).

Overflow Frequency	Monday	Tuesday	Wednesday	Thursday	Friday	Average
January	0.59	0.39	0.25	0.22	0.17	0.32
February	0.64	0.39	0.25	0.18	0.25	0.34
March	0.77	0.41	0.41	0.30	0.19	0.42
April	0.69	0.18	0.16	0.08	0.08	0.24
May	0.22	0.14	0.05	0.07	0.06	0.11
June	0.25	0.05	0.00	0.02	0.02	0.07
July	0.37	0.12	0.01	0.02	0.02	0.11
August	0.31	0.04	0.01	0.01	0.02	0.08
September	0.34	0.06	0.06	0.07	0.39	0.19
October	0.62	0.09	0.08	0.13	0.15	0.21
November	0.68	0.26	0.12	0.12	0.28	0.29
December	0.82	0.52	0.34	0.45	0.24	0.47
Average	0.52	0.22	0.15	0.14	0.16	0.24

Two important observations can be made on the basis of the values in Table 5-2. First, uniform 20% overflow frequency is replaced by a wide range of values: from 82% on Mondays in December to 0% on Wednesdays in June. Second, the average value of the overflow frequency rises to 24%. The last observation indicates that in the presence of the demand rate variability advanced access approach cannot be sustained at the same level of overflow frequency. In this regard, primary care office will have to make certain adjustments – either in the size of patient panel it serves, or in the way the target appointment slot numbers are distributed across different days. Below we consider each of these possibilities in detail.

The downward revision of the patient panel size may be necessary in practices where a physician is unwilling to compromise on the daily target amount of work. In the presence of daily/seasonal demand variability, a physician may select one of several criteria to limit the patient panel size.

Generalizing the approach of sections 3.2.5 and 3.2.6, one can use the average overflow frequency f^* as the appropriate measure of overtime effort. As Figure 5-8 shows, a relatively small adjustment would be necessary to bring its value from the current 24% to the 20% level: panel size would have to be reduced from current 2211 to 2125 patients.

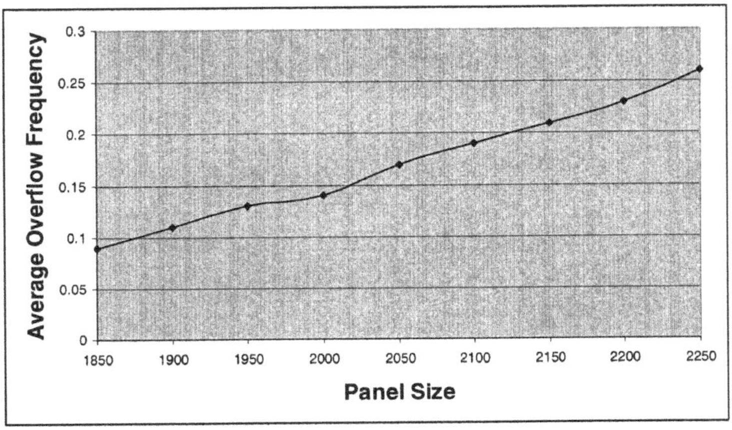

Figure 5-8. Average overflow frequency f^* as a function of patient panel size.

One possible downside of choosing the value of f^* as the guide for adjusting the panel size is that, as Table 2 shows, the daily overflow frequencies may be quite different from f^*: for example, when the panel size is set at 2125 patients (and the average overflow frequency is 20%), the maximum overflow frequency (namely, the one for Mondays in December) turns out to be 77%, which roughly corresponds to working overtime three out of four Mondays in December. Thus, while for panel size of 2125 the overtime work does not exceed the desired 20% limit on average, there could be some short-term runs of nearly certain overtime.

To decrease the chance of such short-term overtime runs, a physician may want to focus on controlling a different measure of overtime work, for example, the fraction of days for which the chance of overtime exceeds the desired target of 20%. An example of such measure is provided by Table 5-2, where out of 60 distinct day types we consider, the overflow frequency exceeds 20% on 28 days (which is 46.6% of 60 days). For the panel size of 2125, such number turns out to be 21 day, or 35% of all days. If such fraction is deemed too high, the panel size may have to be decreased further. Figure 5-9 shows how this overtime measure, the fraction of days for which the overflow frequency exceeds the target level of 20%, changes with panel size. We observe that if a physician would like to limit the fraction of days for which the overflow chance exceeds the target to, for example, 25%, the panel size should not exceed 2000 patients.

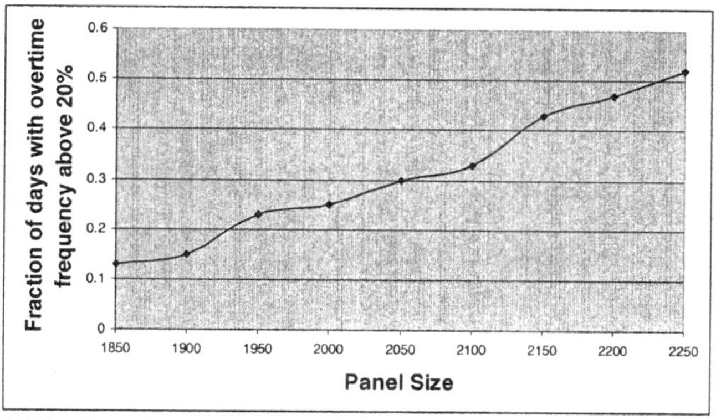

Figure 5-9. The fraction of days for which the overflow frequency is above the target level of 20%, as a function of patient panel size.

The analysis conducted above relies on the assumption that the primary care provider is willing to reduce the size of patient panel, but remains rather inflexible with respect to day-to-day changes in the target duration of daily work. An alternative assumption would describe an environment where provider would like to retain given panel by adjusting her day-to-day target work duration. In such environment, day-to-day demand rate variability is matched by the corresponding variability in the target appointment capacity. In particular, on day i in month j, this target C_{ij} has to be selected so that the overflow frequency

$$\overline{f}_{ij} = 1 - \sum_{k=0}^{C_{ij}} \frac{N!}{k!(N-k)!} \left(pq_{ij}\right)^k \left(1 - pq_{ij}\right)^{N-k} \qquad (5\text{-}5)$$

is as close as possible to 20% (due to the discrete nature of C_{ij} it may not be possible to exactly match this value). Table 5-3 shows the resulting values of the target appointment capacity for the panel size N=2211 and the demand rates taken from Forjuoh *et al.* (2001).

Table 5-3. Target values for appointment capacity for different days and months based on the data from Scott and White Killeen Clinic (TX) as reported in Forjuoh *et al.* (2001).

C_{ij}	Monday	Tuesday	Wednesday	Thursday	Friday	Average
January	25	23	21	20	20	21.8
February	26	23	21	20	21	22.2
March	28	23	23	21	20	23.0
April	26	20	19	18	18	20.2
May	20	19	17	18	17	18.2
June	21	17	14	16	16	16.8
July	22	19	15	16	16	17.6
August	22	17	15	15	16	17.0
September	22	17	17	18	23	19.4
October	25	18	18	19	19	19.8
November	26	21	19	19	21	21.2
December	29	24	22	23	21	23.8
Average	24.3	20.1	18.4	18.6	19.0	20.1

Appointment capacity values from Table 5-3 show how the target primary care capacity should be adjusted in order to match patient demand from a panel of 2211 patients for any day of the year. In particular, while the primary care provider can expect short office days on Wednesdays in June (14 appointments, or about 4 hours and 40 minutes), but very long days on Mondays in December (29 appointments, or 9 hours and 40 minutes). Note that, on average, the target length of the workday (20.1 appointments) is virtually the same as in the case of stationary demand considered in section 3.2.6.

In summary, significant day-to-day variability in the patient demand rates may require adjustments in either the panel size (as indicated in Figures 5-8 and 5-9) or in the distribution of the target appointment capacity (as shown in Table 5-3).

3.3 Demand Control Techniques

In the primary care setting, physician time is usually the most constrained resource. Effectiveness of any appointment scheduling approach depends on how this valuable resource is managed. Murray and Tantau (2000), Murray and Berwick (2003), and Oldham (2001) outline several approaches to improving the match between demand and supply in primary care settings: 1) enforcing the continuity of patient care, 2) increasing the effectiveness of each appointment, and 3) reducing the demand for face-to-face patient-physician interactions.

Continuity of care plays the major role in reducing the unnecessary demand for future care in advanced access settings. When a patient is attended by a physician who is not her PCP, the probability of an extra follow-up visit (for which patient requests to be seen by the PCP) increases, creating an avoidable future demand: Houck (2004) refers to data from Kaiser Permanente which indicate that as many as 48% of patients who were seen by a physician other than their PCP, return within 2 weeks to see "their" physician. In addition, continuity of care can increase profitability of primary care operations: O'Hare and Corlett (2004) report that the relative value unit (RVU) per patient visit was up to 17% higher for visits where patients were treated by their PCPs, with an average increase in physician's compensation of about $4.50 per visit.

Maximizing the value of each appointment ("max-packing") is another way of reducing the need for future appointments. Gordon and Chin (2004) describe a "combing" technique that could be used to facilitate max-packing of appointments. "Combing" is used every time a patient requests an appointment: the schedule is checked for any appointments and/or some anticipated needs (annual check-up, flu shots, etc.) for the same patient in the near future. This way, a single appointment can be used to attend to multiple patient needs. "Max-packing" is clearly appropriate in a managed-care environment but, as Murray and Tantau (2000) argue, it can also be useful in fee-for-service settings, since a more service-intensive appointment would correspond to a higher CPT code.

Effective demand reduction techniques may include broad use of phone and e-mail to substitute for various components of face-to-face interaction between patients and primary care office. It can be argued that advanced access reduces patients' "anxiety" about getting an appointment and, in a paradoxical way, reduces the need to book face-to-face appointments, opening the way to handling a larger fraction of demand through e-mail or phone interactions. E-mail can be used for repeat prescriptions, checking the test results, appointment reminders. In this regard, Oldham (2001) argues for the use of separate e-mail addresses for receptionists, nurses and physicians: some advanced access primary care offices report that patients use e-mail to query receptionists nearly as often as physicians (for example, see Patient Online system at Dartmouth-Hitchcock Medical Center in New Hampshire, www.dhmc.org). Phone consultations (with a nurse or a physician) may be used for managing same-day demand, follow up appointments, and other queries. Oldham (2002) reports as much as a 30-50% reduction in face-to-face consultations as a result of phone management of same day demand, and a 15-20% reduction in follow-up consultations.

Demand can also be reduced via increasing the length between patient visits as long as this does not contradict the requirements of medical necessity. Gordon and Chin (2004) describe an implementation of advanced access system under which some of the patients with chronic conditions are seen every three or four months instead of "standard" two months, in cases when a physician felt that a patient can manage her condition on her own through medication and monitoring. It could also be argued that patients do not necessarily associate an increase in inter-appointment intervals with lower service quality: a recent study by Wick and Koller (2005) indicates that patients prefer longer (by six days, on average) intervals for return visits than their physicians.

Finally, group patient consultations, or cooperative health care clinics (CHCC), can be used to combine visits for patients with similar chronic conditions. Houck et al. (2003) provides detailed instructions on how such group sessions have to be organized and run. Selecting the "right" type of patients for group visits is a key factor determining the effectiveness of this approach for overall reduction of the demand for appointments: group visits could work best for patients with chronic conditions characterized by potentially high rate of office visits (e.g., hypertension, asthma, diabetes, depression, etc) and/or geriatric patients with multiple comorbidities. CHCC can also be useful for patients without established chronic conditions who nevertheless generate high number of annual office visits. Existing empirical evidence points out that the use of group visits combines improved demand management with greater patient satisfaction, lower medical costs, and better medical outcomes: Beck et al. (1997) report the patients participating in group sessions had fewer emergency room visits, visits to sub-specialists, and repeat hospital admissions (on a per patient basis), and a higher rate of flu and pneumonia vaccinations. An important consequence of the use of group sessions is a decreased use of physician's time for services that can be delivered by other personnel: group participants made more visits and calls to nurses and fewer calls to physicians, while exhibiting higher overall satisfaction with care and reduced cost of care. Masley et al. (2000) report that the introduction of group sessions for patients with poorly controlled type 2 diabetes lead, after a year, to a 32% average reduction in total cholesterol/HDL ratios, a 30% average reduction in HbA_{1c} levels, and a 7% average reduction in medical expenses.

3.4 Working Down the Appointment Backlog

Before the advanced access can be effectively implemented, it is important that the "bad" appointment backlog accumulated in the system is eliminated. This one-time backlog clearing requires a temporary increase in service capacity that is needed to absorb new appointment demand, while working down a backlog. A "Backlog Reduction Worksheet" developed by Batalden, Godfrey and Nelson in 2003 and publicized by the Institute for Healthcare Improvement (www.ihi.org/IHI/Topics/OfficePractices/Access/Tools/, login required) outlines practical steps involved in successful implementation of this process. Typically, the extra capacity is gained by extending regular working hours; other strategies include the use of weekend appointment sessions, employing locum tenens, even (temporarily) rejecting new pre-scheduled (not same-day) appointments and off-loading other duties, such as teaching.

The length of this transition period varies from practice to practice and depends on how big the initial backlog is and how much extra appointment time can a practice afford. For one of the very first implementations of advanced access, Murray and Tantau (2000) report that it took six weeks to work down a two-month appointment backlog in a six-physician clinic. On the other hand, Grandinetti (2000) states that Community Pediatric and Adolescent Medicine section of Mayo Clinic in Rochester, MN had to use between three and six months to eliminate its appointment backlog; and in small practices, the transition period can be even longer.

3.5 Post-Introduction Management

Demand for primary care is inherently random and appointment capacity of a primary care office can change at a short notice. After the introduction of the advanced access approach, a set of robust contingency plans should be developed for dealing with both the expected as well as the unexpected temporary mismatches between supply and demand: staff sickness, vacations, demand surges (e.g., due to epidemics), etc. The UK National Primary Care Development Team (NPDT) advocates delegating the coordination and real-time management of such plans to a designated "contingency" person whose responsibilities include constant monitoring of the state of the appointment system, and activating a contingency plan when the situation warrants (www.npdt.org/Pre-Bookable.pdf). Contingency planning could include personnel cross-training (Nolan et al. (1996)) as well as the use of demand smoothing techniques before the predictable surge in appointment requests, such as "staggering" of demand for physicals near the beginning of a school year (Murray and Tantau 2000).

Monitoring the degree of mismatch between supply and demand is an important component of the overall management of advanced access. Oldham (2001) provides a detailed discussion on the practical use of two measures of patient access to primary care: time to third next available appointment (TTNAA) and percentage of patients receiving an appointment on the day of their choice, which we call "access fraction".

TTNAA is an access measure directly related to the length of the appointment backlog. When appointment cancellations are frequent, the position of the first and even second available appointments may not be indicative of the typical backlog. Third available appointment, on the other hand, is a much more stable measure of access, not easily affected by cancellations. According to the Institute for Healthcare Improvement, the goal of advanced access is to reduce the wait for the third next available appointment to 24 hours for general and family practices and to two days for specialty practices. An extensive set of reports on the achieved values of TTNAA for a number of different practices (primary as well as specialty) is available on the site of the Wisconsin Collaborative for Healthcare Quality (www.wiqualitycollaborative.org).

The fraction of patients obtaining an appointment on the day of their choice (whether it is the "same day" or some other day in the future) could serve as a proxy for patient satisfaction with the timeliness of the received care. While the exact relationship between this access fraction and TTNAA depends on the details of patients' preferences for the timing of their appointments, it is likely that high values of the access fraction correspond to the low values of TTNA. In this regard, Oldham (2001) suggests that a 90% value of access fraction would be roughly equivalent to TTNAA of 1 day.

4. CONCLUSIONS

The lack of timely access to primary care is a well recognized problem of the US health care system. In the United Kingdom, the National Primary Care Collaborative, the first program of the state-sponsored National Primary Care Development Team, has reached over 5,000 practices and more than 32 million patients in the effort to reduce patient waiting and to improve patient service. In the United States, the growing number of primary care offices is adopting the advanced access practice developed by Murray and Tantau in order to reduce or even eliminate appointment backlogs. One of the important enablers of the advance access approach is the overall match between the demand for primary care services and the supply of the appointment capacity. In our analysis, we explicitly model the connection between the patient panel size and the daily demand for appointments and develop analytical expressions for the frequency of overtime work which is required to sustain advanced access for a given level of appointment capacity. Using our model, we design a set of guidelines that can be used by primary care offices to determine the patient panel size to match the preset target level of overtime work.

The advanced access is quickly transforming itself from a new concept to a day-to-day routine. In our opinion, many primary care practices that contemplate adopting advanced access would greatly benefit from a decision support system that codifies the basic rules of advanced access and helps with its implementation and maintenance. Such a system could successfully complement the functionality of existing office management software (appointment recording, patient databases, billing, etc.) by adding new patient flow management capabilities.

5. REFERENCES

Batal, H., Tench, J., McMillan, S., Adams, J., and Mehler, P.S., 2001. Predicting patient visits to an urgent care clinic using calendar variables, *Academic Emergency Medicine* **8 (1)**: 48-53,

Beck, J., Scott, J., Williams, P., Robertson, B., Jackson, D., Gade, G., and Cowan P., 1997. A randomized trial of group outpatient visits for chronically ill older HMO members: the Cooperative Health Care Clinic, *Journal of American Geriatric Society*, **45(5)**:543-9.

Cayirli, T., and Veral, E., 2003. Outpatient scheduling in health care: a review of literature, *Production and Operations Management*, **12(4)**: 519-549.

Declaration of the International Conference on Primary Health Care, 1978. http://www.euro.who.int/AboutWHO/Policy/20010827_1.

Forjuoh, S.N., Averitt, W.M., Cauthen, D.B., Symm, B., and Mitchell M., 2001. Open-access appointment scheduling in family practice: comparison of a demand prediction grid with actual appointments, *Journal of the American Board of Family Practice*, **14 (4)**: 259-265.

Gordon, P., and Chin, M., 2004. Achieving a new standard in primary care for low-income populations: Case Study 2: Advanced Access Learning, *The Commonwealth Fund.*

Grandinetti, D., 2000. You mean I can see a doctor today? *Medical Economics*, March 20.

Houck, S., 2004. *What works: effective tools and case studies to improve clinical office practice*, HealthPress Publishing, Boulder, Colorado, p. 90.

Houck, S., Kilo, C., and Scott, J.C., 2003. Improving patient care. Group visits 101, *Family Practice Management*, **10(5)**:66-8.

Institute of Medicine, 2001. *Crossing the Quality Chasm: A New Health System for the 21st Century*. Washington, D.C.: National Academy Press; 51.

Masley, S., Sokoloff, J., and Hawes C., 2000. Planning group visits for high-risk patients, *Family Practice Management*, **7(6)**:33-7.

Murray, M., and Berwick, D.M., 2003 Advance access: reducing waiting and delays in primary care. *JAMA*, **289 (8)**: 1035-1039.

Murray, M., and Tantau, C., 2000. Same-day appointments: exploding the access paradigm, *Family Practice Management*, **7-8**: 45-50.

Nolan T.W., Schall M.W., Berwick D.M., and Roessner J., 1996.*Reducing delays and waiting times throughout the healthcare system*. Institute for Healthcare Improvement.

O'Hare, C. D., and Corlett, J., 2004. The outcomes of open-access scheduling, , *Family Practice Management*, **11(2)**:35-8.

Oldham, J., 2001. Advanced access in primary care, National Primary Care Development Team, http://www.npdt.org/AccesstoPrimaryCare/advancedaccess.pdf

Oldham, J., 2002. Telephone use in primary care, *British Medical Journal*, **325** (7363):547.
Starfield B., 1991. Primary care and health. A cross-national comparison, *JAMA*, **266**: 2268-2271.
Wick, A., and Koller, M.T., 2005. Views of patients and physicians on follow-up visits, *Swiss Medical Weekly*, **135**:139-144.

Chapter 6

WAITING LISTS FOR SURGERY

Emilio Cerdá [1,*], Laura de Pablos[1], Maria V. Rodriguez[2]
[1] University Complutense of Madrid. Spain. [2] University of Oviedo. Spain

Abstract: Health waiting lists in general and surgical waiting list in particular are a problem for the majority of the European countries with a National Health System. In this chapter, the problem of the waiting lists for surgery from a general perspective in the scope of the health management in the European Union (EU) is analyzed. Also, applying mathematical programming techniques, we intend to design the real performance of surgical services at a local general hospital offering the decision maker a suitable methodology that allows us to analyze whether or not it is possible to improve the running of the services, taking into account all the real constraints, e.g. space, staff availability, waiting time upper limit or financial support.

Key words: Waiting Lists, National Health Systems, Hospital Management, Mathematical Programming.

1. INTRODUCTION

The health systems in the European Union are aligned in two groups:

- The system inspired by the Beveridge Report of 1942, which formalized the health organization adopted by Sweden in the year 1930, establishing a National Health System. The United Kingdom, Denmark, Italy, Portugal, Finland, Sweden, Norway, Ireland, Greece and Spain can be considered in this group.

Corresponding author: Emilio Cerdá. Departamento de Fundamentos del Análisis Económico I. Universidad Complutense de Madrid. Campus de Somosaguas 28223 Madrid. Spain. E-mail: ecerdate@ccee.ucm.es. We thank B. Readman for the linguistic revision of the text.

- The Bismarck System, inspired in the social legislation of Germany in 1883, and which is traditionally known as Social Security. Austria, Belgium, France, Germany and the Netherlands can be considered in this group.

However, it is necessary to notice that neither of the models is strictly applied. Although each has its preponderant characteristics, each takes something from the other.

The existence of waiting lists is a usual fact in the countries with a National Health System. In some ways, lists are a method for managing the health services. In Spain the surgical waiting lists are a priority from both the political and social point of view.

This chapter is organized as follows: In Section 2, we review the dimension of waiting lists in some European countries, the main features of the Health Systems of the countries with and without waiting lists and the factors that could explain waiting time differences. In Section 3 we describe the major policies used to reduce waiting times. The issue of Section 4 is the choice between public and private sector in relation to waiting lists. The introduction of different standardized prioritization rules for waiting lists is discussed in Section 5. Section 6 proposes a specific model to manage the surgical waiting lists. This model has been applied to an important public hospital in Madrid, and is capable of adaptation to any other hospital. It is a mathematical programming program that has elements of linear programming, integer programming, dynamic optimization and multi-objective programming. Finally, Section 7 presents conclusions and future directions.

2. NATIONAL HEALTH SYSTEMS AND SURGERY WAITING LISTS IN EUROPEAN COUNTRIES

2.1 Waiting lists and health systems in some European countries

An important feature of EU countries is that while some countries report significant waiting times for non-emergency surgery, others do not. Waiting times are a serious health problem in Denmark, Finland, Ireland, Italy, Sweden, the United Kingdom, Spain, Portugal, Norway and Greece. However waiting times are not reported administratively because they are low and insignificant in a second group of countries, such as Germany, Belgium, Luxembourg, and France.

Table 6.1 and Table 6.2 show average and median waiting times in some European countries. The data were collected through a questionnaire submitted to 12 countries involved in the OECD Waiting Time Project (Hurst and Siciliani, 2003). The first question resolved in that project was the identification of a common definition of waiting time. This allows comparisons of waiting times across countries. In this sense, inpatient waiting time for patients admitted for treatment is defined by Hurts and Siciliani (2003) as "the time between specialists' assessment and the surgical treatment". A more comprehensive measure of waiting time for surgery would cover the whole period from the time a general practice refers the patients to a specialist, to the date they are admitted for the surgical procedure. This latter measure also will include any delay between a general practice referral and the specialist's treatment (outpatient waiting time). The data reported by the different countries are waiting time of patients admitted for surgical treatment.

Measures of waiting times are often aggregated through the utilisation of statistics. The most commonly utilised are the mean and the median. If the waiting time is distributed according to a normal (Gaussian) distribution, the two measures coincide. However, as is often observed, the waiting-time distribution tends to be positively skewed. This implies that there is a low proportion of patients with consistently long waits. In this case, using the median is usually recommended because the mean tends to be heavily influenced by the few patients with long waits.

Table 6.1. Mean inpatient waiting times of patients admitted for surgical procedure (days). Year 2000. (Source: Siciliani and Hurst, 2003.)

	Den.	**Finland**	**Norway**	**Neth.**	**Spain**	**Sweden**	**U.K.**
Hip replacement	112	206	133	96	123		244
Knee replacement	112	274	160	85	148		281
Cataract	71	233	63	111	104	199	206
Varicose veins	99	280	142	107			227
Hysterectomy		100	64	61	102		159
Prostatectomy		81	75	60	62		52
Cholecystectomy	75	159	103	71	107		156
Inguinal femoral hernia	73	125	109	75	102		150

Table 6.2. Median inpatient waiting times of patients admitted for surgical procedure (days). Year 2000. (Source: Siciliani and Hurst, 2003.)

	Denmark	Finland	Norway	United Kingdom
Hip Replacement	87	148	99	211
Knee replacement	90	202	132	262
Cataract	36	189	28	182
Varicose veins	69	155	110	178
Hysterectomy		70	37	110
Prostatectomy		39	47	37
Cholecystectomy	57	90	63	97
Inquinal and femoral hernia	46	74	74	95

The countries with highest waiting times are England and Finland, followed by Denmark, Norway and Spain. It is interesting to note how the waiting times for less urgent procedures are systematically higher than the waiting times for more urgent procedures.

The main characteristics of The Health System of the countries with waiting lists are:

- They have universal health coverage and are financed mainly through general taxation. Health care is provided by a National Health System. However: (1) In Ireland the health system is a mix of public and private institutions and funders. (2) In Norway, prior to 2002, the Health System was organised into three political and administrative levels: national government (legislation and regulation), counties (secondary care) and municipalities (primary care). The counties were responsible for financing and planning. Since January 2002, the responsibility for hospital care was removed from the counties to the state. Five regional enterprises have been established and the objectives and the basis for management of these enterprises are determined by central government. (3) In Spain the responsibility for provision of health services was, until 2002, partly centralised under INSALUD (the National Institute of Health), and partly decentralised to some Autonomous regions (Catalonia, Andalusia, Land of Valencia and Balearic Islands). From January, 2002, it has been wholly decentralised to all 17 Autonomous Regions. (4) In Sweden the health system is organised into three political and administrative levels. National government is responsible for legislation and control; county councils for primary and secondary care; and municipalities, for care of the elderly and nursing homes.

- Generally, in countries with waiting lists, the patients cannot access elective surgery without general practice referral.
- The majority of the hospitals are owned and financed by the public sector. The private sector plays a marginal role as a supplier of health care. Sometimes budgets for hospitals have been based on historical funding (Ireland, Denmark and Spain fix budget bases on past expenditure and the case mix of the hospital). In England public hospitals are remunerated according to contracts or arrangements that specify the services that must be provided. From 2002 Norway has been implementing the activity-based system for financing hospital care (this system is also applied in Sweden).
- Hospital doctors are salaried in the public sector. Often the specialists working in publicly funded hospitals are not allowed to treat patients within the same hospital as private doctors and have serious restrictions on working in the private sector. Only "part-time" specialists in publicly funded hospitals are allowed to work in privately funded hospitals (Sweden, Spain, Italy and England).
- Usually there are no co-payments for receiving publicly funded surgery. However: (1) In Finland, an outpatient visit costs 20 euros and each day in the ward costs 25 euros. (2) In Ireland, there are two categories of patients. The first category, public inpatients, receives services free of charge. The second one is subject to a daily overnight charge of 40 euros (in 2003), subject to an overall annual limit of 400 euros. (3) In Norway, patients pay 114 NOK for a general practice visit and 200 NOK for a specialist visit. The overall annual limit is 1350 NOK. (4) In Sweden, the patient usually pays a token daily fee for each day spent in the hospital. For a general practice, he/she pays 15 euros and, for a specialist visit, 20 euros. The overall annual limit for the last two treatments is 90 euros.
- The countries that do not report waiting time administratively, because it is low and insignificant, are Germany, Belgium, Luxembourg, and France. The health system of these countries is based on health insurance, generally composed of a basic compulsory public insurance and a supplementary insurance provided by private insurers. There is no universal coverage and the health system is also characterised by an important freedom for people to choose and use public and private health care services without a referral system. It is the patients who can access elective surgery without general practice referral. Public hospitals are important, but they are not the only ones: about 70% of beds are in public hospitals in France and around 55% in Germany, and they are funded through global budgets that are usually set annually during negotiations between the sickness funds. In Germany the budget specifies targets in terms of activity as well as per diems to be reached by the end of the

financial year. The hospital specialist can be salaried or paid by fee for service. This latter option is applied generally in private hospitals and in treatment. The countries without waiting times usually apply low co-payments. Some examples of co-payments in 1999 were:

France: 11 euros per day.
Germany: 7,16 euros per day.
Belgium: 250 FB per day.
Luxembourg: 5,43 euros per day.

- The Netherlands represents an interesting case for analysing waiting times because, despite the funding being based on a mix of public and private health insurance like France or Germany, waiting times for surgery are a significant problem. The reason could be the strong central control over the last two decades on total health expenditure fees.

2.2 The factors that may explain waiting time differences between European countries

The National Health System seems to have more problems with surgery waiting lists. We want to know which factors influence this question. Waiting time may be determined by demand factors, which affect the inflow to the waiting list, and by supply factors, which affect the outflow.

2.2.1 The demand for elective surgery depends on:

Health status of population. One of the main factors that could influence the health status is the share of the population that is elderly. In Europe, however, the population older than 65 is more or less the same in all countries. The age structure seems to be very similar in countries with and without waiting lists.

The proportion of population with private insurance, the price of private health insurance and the price of private surgery also influence public demand. In any case, there are feedback effects from prices to quantities demanded and supplied in private markets, so there are likely to be feedback effects from waiting times to quantities demanded and supplied in the public provision of elective surgery. For example: higher waiting time may encourage demand for private health (Besley et al. 1998). But also higher waiting times may discourage public demand for reducing referrals and deterring surgeons from adding patients to lists. At the same time, higher waiting times may raise supply by encouraging public authorities to allocate more money to public hospitals with longer queues (Gravelle et al. 2003).

Co-payments. Some financial measures, such as the extent of cost sharing, for example: co-payment can reduce demand. The countries with waiting times apply usually low co-payments but also countries without waiting times also have very low co-payments or no co-payments at all.

Doctors. It is also important to give a key role to the doctors in managing demand, the thresholds for referrals and addition to the list. General practitioners often act as gatekeepers in the countries with waiting times. The term gatekeeper suggests that the general practitioners should control the demand for access to specialists, avoiding unnecessary referrals. However, it may be that where there is a clear division of labour between generalists and specialists, general practitioners can consider that the best treatment is to pass on to surgeons any patients creating an upward pressure on demand. By contrast, where specialists can be approached directly by patients, they may become skilled at handling excess demand.

Most of the policies consider that waiting times can be reduced through supply-side policies because the volume of surgery is considered inadequate.

2.2.2 The supply of elective surgery depends on:

Public resources, mainly beds and surgeons (see Table 6.24 of the Appendix). In this sense, some evidence on the impact of waiting on public capacity is provided by Lindsay and Fetgenbaum (1984), Martin and Smith (1999) and Siciliani and Hurst (2003), who concluded that the waiting list is associated negatively with the number of beds and surgeons. A low endowment of acute beds may constitute a binding constraint for countries with waiting lists, limiting, in the short term, the opportunity to increase output. The number of doctors can also be essential on waiting times. However, authors like Siciliani and Hurst (2003) think that a larger staff is usually associated with lower waiting times if combined with other inputs. Also higher expenditure per capita is associated with a higher rate of surgery and with lower waiting time. Finland and England have low expenditure and report high waiting times. Countries such as Germany and the USA have high expenditures and do not report waiting times (see Table 6.22, and Table 6.23, of the Appendix). However, Norway is a high-expenditure country and reports high waiting times. The middle expenditure countries like Denmark, Netherlands, Austria, Belgium or France are also equivocal, while the first two report waiting times, the others do not. Consequently health expenditure may be important on waiting times but it is not the only factor.

Other differences. Another possibility is that other differences may play a role. For example, incentives and remuneration systems may encourage higher productivity in countries without waiting times, but induce a high propensity to add patients to the list. Productivity depends, among other things, on the way in which surgeons and hospitals are paid. There are some studies that have investigated the relationship between methods of paying physicians and productivity. The results suggest that fee-for-service payment shows better rates than the salaried staff model. Incentives to hospitals seem to be effective. Activity-based funding is likely to encourage higher productivity compared to funding based on fixed budgets (Clemmesen and Hansen, 2003). Some experiences support this idea (Spain, Norway, Denmark etc). Productivity also depends on the percentage of patients treated by day-surgery. Martin and Smith (1995) show that the waiting time is negatively associated with the percentage of day-surgery cases and the elasticity is -0,252.

Consequently, waiting times may be explained by these variables: health expenditure per-capita, the number of practising specialists and physicians, the number of acute care beds, and remuneration systems of hospitals and physicians.

3. THE MAJOR POLICIES USED TO REDUCE WAITING TIME

The main ways used to reduce waiting times are provided below.

Maximum waiting time guarantee. One of the most common policies introduced to reduce waiting time is the maximum waiting-time guarantee. These guarantees are intended to regulate waiting times so that patients should never wait beyond a certain time limit. Almost every country with waiting lists has regulated these guarantees, but the formulation of the guarantee differs substantially across countries. An alternative is an unconditional guarantee that is provided to patients (England and Sweden between 1992-1995). Another alternative is a conditional guarantee that is given only to a number of patients, for example "all the patients with most need should be treated within "x" months" (Norway 1990-2000, New Zealand and Sweden between 1992-1996). Another possibility of conditional guarantee is to regulate that a fixed percentage of patients should be treated within "x" months (Netherlands, Italy and Denmark).

A general point of criticism of a maximum waiting time guarantee is that it may be obtained at the expense of increasing the outpatient waiting time. In this sense some countries have also set maximum “outpatient waiting time guarantees”, such as Norway (between 1997 and 2000), Netherlands, Sweden and England. Also, as Siciliani and Hurst (2003) comment, the introduction of guarantees may produce conflicts between policy maker and surgical specialist, especially if they are not accompanied by extra resources. This and other problems have led to some countries, like Norway, to replace the maximum waiting time guarantee with a “right to necessary health care". In this case, the patient has the right to receive the treatment in an appropriate time and the waiting time for a specialist visit is 30 working days after the referral from the general practitioner.

Increasing productivity policies. There are a large number of policies whose main objective is to increase productivity. In many countries, public hospitals have been funded according to fixed budgets. In the Netherlands fixed budgets for specialists in replacement for service arrangements were piloted with bad results. Admission declined and waiting times increased. Several governments have tried to tackle high waiting times with extra funds. This fund has been tied to the achievement of waiting time objectives in several ways: (1) To raising the productivity of the hospitals in terms of number of treatments per surgeon or bed. (2) To fund hospitals which perform extra activity such as Sweden and the Netherlands.

Activity-based remuneration system. In Spain the concept of target population is important. It was introduced in 1996. The idea is to know what share of the target population could be treated in normal hours. In this way it is possible to calculate supplementary funding for the residual patient, who has not been treated in normal hours. The funds have been allocated to hospitals on the basis of the achievement of the different targets either in terms of the activity performance and achievement of maximum waiting time and mean time (monthly targets).

To encourage specialists to reduce waiting time to achieve maximum use of waiting time, Spain is using bonuses for specialists who have achieved waiting time reductions. In England from 2001, the "Performance Fund" has included rewards for staff, (new equipment, improved facilities and cash incentives) for individuals and teams.

Increasing resources. An alternative to increasing capacity in the public sector is to use the existing capacity in the private sector. Usually in these cases this can take the form of a purchaser of health services contracting out to privately-owned providers some volume of activity. This scheme presents some advantages: it may be the quickest way to increase capacity compared to other options. Second, contracting with private providers may introduce an element of competition with public providers.

Some countries, such as Norway, Denmark, Ireland, England and the Netherlands have increased elective health surgery services by purchasing extra activity abroad. Usually in these countries the private sector may be fairly small and already working at maximum capacity.

Reducing waiting times by improving management of the waiting list. Australia has introduced an important system: pre-admission services, optimisation of patient's health status prior to admission; education of the patient and family about hospital procedures; reducing cancellations and the number of unused sessions, and facilitation of day-surgery admissions.

Several governments (such as England) have taken steps to encourage *day surgery*. For example, England plans to introduce "Diagnostic and Treatment Centres" to increase the number of elective operations that can be treated in a single day. These centres will focus on routine hospital surgery and not on hospital emergency work so they can concentrate on reducing waiting times.

Reducing average hospitalization time. As can be seen in the data that appear in Table 6.25, in most of the countries of the European Union the average hospitalization time has declined progressively in the last 30 years. For example, in the United Kingdom the average hospitalization time was 25.7 days in 1970, 15.6 days in 1990, 10.2 days in 1998 and 8.1 in 2002. In Denmark the evolution of the average hospitalisation time went from 18.1 days in 1970 to 8.2 in 1990, 6.7 in 1998 and 5.7 in 2002. See Appendix, Table 6.25.

Increase patient choice. England, Denmark, Norway and Sweden have recently introduced more choice for patients often in conjunction with activity-based payment. It is possible that this kind of measure may encourage hospitals to compete for patients and revenues. A prerequisite of this type of policy is the dissemination of information on waiting times. In Denmark patients have had free choice of treatment in any publicly funded hospital. However, it has been estimated that only 5% of the patients exercised this right.

Reduce demand by subsidising voluntary "private health insurance". The main idea is that by lowering the price for private insurance, many citizens will be induced to purchase private health. However, this simple reasoning should be qualified. First, the substitution effect is likely to be strong when some dimension of the quality of the public provision is low (for example long waits) and it is the feature that induces a shift of patients from public to private; reducing waiting times may decrease the incentive for the population to buy voluntary private health insurance (feedback effect). Second, waiting times are very important in this decision but, in fact, there is some evidence that suggests that other factors like age, income and political affiliation are important. Third, if private hospitals have no ability to expand in the short or medium term to respond to increases in demand, due to markets access regulations or to shortages of capacity or medical workforce, the expected reductions in waiting times may be delayed.

4. WAITING TIME AND THE PUBLIC AND PRIVATE SECTOR

The concept of a private sector has several dimensions. One dimension is related to the ownership of the means of production. Another dimension is whether services are paid by the client or covered by the public sector. Generally it is considered as private provision if it is private in both aspects.

There are several possibilities as to how the existence of a queue might reduce the flow of the demand for health treatment, one of them is that the longer the waiting time, the more people choose the private alternative. In this sense, it could say the waiting time is an equilibrating mechanism making the demand for public treatment equal the supply. Theoretical models like the one developed by Besley and Coate (1991), suggest that the determinants of the demand for private health insurance must be investigated as a function of the quality of public sector provision and the individual characteristics, especially income. This theory has been contrasted by Besley et al. (1999) with an empirical specification in two stages. The first model that they consider does not differentiate between sources of health insurance. This was legitimate provided that the workers face the full cost of purchasing insurance or when the employers purchase insurance on their behalf. The general results of the model revealed that health insurance demand rises with age, tailing off for those older than age 65, it also depends strongly on income. Larger households are less likely to buy insurance, probably reflecting the equivalent income effect. Finally, and one of the most important factors is the long-term waiting list. The results suggest that if the long-term waiting list were to rise by one person per thousand, then there would be a 2% increase in the probability that an individual with the same characteristics would buy private insurance. The length of waiting lists is used as an indicator of health system quality and appears as one of the main factors demanding private health. This assumes that individuals know the length of the waiting list. This information is used as a barometer for the performance of the NHS.

It is supposed that the choice between public and private health services is an aspect with many consequences that have been studied by several authors. One consequence is that the public health system should improve because it would have fewer patients. However, a long-term system could go in the opposite direction, if there are feedback effects from private insurance demand to waiting lists through the political process. If the lobbying pressure to keep waiting times short declines in areas where there is a large privately-insured segment, then this could lead to a positive correlation between private insurance and waiting lists. Inversen, (1997) concluded that the effects on waiting time from the private causes are rather indeterminate. He developed a model with a long-term perspective: first the queuing model solution was applied; second, an elastic supply of health personnel was assumed.

The main conclusions can be summarized as follows: If the waiting times are not rationed, the effect of the private sector on a public hospital's waiting time is in general indeterminate. If the demand for public treatment is more elastic with respect to waiting time, more likely then it is that the private sector causes a longer waiting time for public patients. The reason is that a more elastic demand for public treatment makes possible a large reduction in public expenditure by increasing the waiting time (Inversen, 1997). When the admision to waiting time list is rationed, the waiting time will increase if the public sector consultants are permitted to work in the private sector (Inversen, 1997). Otherwise, waiting time will not change. Aaron and Schwartz (1984) also say the same. The private option motivates the consultants to reduce their work effort in the public sector and some patients probably choose the private sector. Other empirical studies came to the same conclusion. For example, in England Besley at al. (1998) have investigated the extent to which areas with high health insurance coverage had low waiting lists. Results were unexpected in the sense that areas with high private coverage had higher waiting lists. The authors suggest the government may under-fund public services in areas with private insurance coverage.

The choice of public or private sector also could have distributional implications. Individuals who opt out of public sector treatment free up resources for those who continue to rely exclusively on the National Health System. Assuming a fixed budget, the provision of public health should improve. However, as Besley et al. (1999) say, a significant fraction of the gain in any increased resources devoted to the National Health System could be taken by high income individuals who will choose to remove their private insurance coverage. Also, even high income individuals who are privately insured will continue to use the public service.

Hoel and Saether (2003) in the same line as Besley and Coate (1991) use a model describing the choice between treatment in the public and private sector. They use the model within a framework of standard welfare theory and the most important result is that if distributional objectives (equity) are sufficiently strong, it may be optimal to have waiting time for public treatment. There is a self-selection mechanism that gives the desired results, because the high-income persons choose to buy health in the private sector.

Another important issue in a system with predominantly public health care is how the government should treat the alternative private treatment. It is sometimes argued that the private alternative may undermine the public system. So the government ought to discourage any private alternative. There are different ways for discouraging the private alternative, such as regulation or taxes. Against this position one could think that those who choose the private alternative should be subsidized by the public sector. Cullis and Jones (1995) say that the argument above for subsidizing private health was based on fairness. This alternative is interesting from the point of view of the costs, because they are lower. The cost saved could be used to expand the treatment capacity of the public system. Australia has been the most active country in subsidizing voluntary private health insurance. For example, several policies have been included in the "1997 and 1998 private Health Insurers incentive schemes" and in 2000 "the lifetime health cover", which introduced tax rebates. As a result, the percentage of population covered by private health increased sharply from 30.5% in 1999 to 44.1% in 2002. The effects of these incentives still are unknown.

5. SETTING PRIORITIES FOR WAITING LISTS

Several countries -- Denmark, Finland, the Netherlands, Norway, Portugal, Spain, Sweden, New Zealand, Canada and the USA -- have introduced a profound debate in order to establish standardized prioritization rules for patients' admission to health waiting lists and in this sense, several actions have been carried out and many works have been developed in this field because it is a sensitive one (see Rodríguez Sendín, 2000, Pinto et al. 2000, Ortún-Rubio et al. 2001, Noseworthy, T. W. et al. 2003).

Traditionally, the usual prioritization rule for non-urgent patients was "first in, first out" but now new factors, such as doctors' opinions, are taken into account for the management of waiting lists in most of the developed countries. In this new context the necessity for the introduction of different standardized prioritization rules has been pointed out in order to preserve equity.

In principle, patients with more urgent conditions should receive services ahead of those with less urgent conditions, and patients with approximately the same degree of urgency should wait about the same length of time. Nevertheless, as has been stated by Hadorn et al. in 2000, standardized measures to assess patients' relative priority are needed.

Hadorn (2000) proposes several key concepts underlying the development of criteria for assessing patients' relative priority on waiting lists. These concepts are:

- **Severity:** the degree or extent of suffering, limits to activities or risk of death. The more a patient is suffering, the more severe is his/her condition, other factors being equal. But, how can severity be measured? How can we measure and compare pain and suffering? These last questions show how severity can not be the main prioritization criteria in health services.
- **Urgency:** extent to which immediate clinical action is required. Usually, in elective surgery severe cases are considered as urgencies but these two criteria can diverge in other situations, such as in the setting of many terminal conditions when there is no pain and no intervention is available to forestall death, in the presence of patients with a low or middle level of severity but which if not treated might become more severe. Therefore, urgency may be, in Hadorn's opinion, defined as severity in addition to considerations of the expected benefit and the natural history of the condition.
- **Need:** urgency.
- **Expected benefit:** extent to which desired outcomes are likely to exceed undesired outcomes.

Other key concepts appearing in the literature referring to the development of prioritization rules are the effectiveness and cost-efficiency of the treatment and some patients' social characteristics (employment status, for instance, is taken into account in some health systems).

The Council of Europe has published several recommendations related to the criteria for the management of waiting lists and waiting times in health care. Among them, there are several criteria for admitting patients to waiting lists which mainly coincide with the ones proposed by Hadorn in 2000. But, although priority is recommended to be given to patients with the greatest need for the services, "(...) waiting times should not be so long that the patients' health is at risk of deterioration". In this sense, acceptable waiting times have to be determined transparently trying if it is possible, to respect patients' preferences and principally patient necessities; but this is a key point because both concepts are difficult to define.

What seems to be clear in most of the public health systems is that the need and urgency for treatment should not be established on the basis of race, sex or religion of the patient. But, unlike what is happening in some health systems (see Kee et al. 1998), the Council of Europe does not recommend prioritizing patients on the basis of their socio-economic status or in general based on their age, although it could be taken into account as "an aspect of a patients' general medical condition and as a risk factor for particular treatments". The European Systems use a two-level to four-level classification system. In Spain high-priority and low priority; in Sweden very urgent, urgent and non-urgent; and in Italy admission within 30 days, within 90 days and 12 months.

Other kinds of prioritization have been considered in non-European countries. New Zealand recognised that the public resources are limited and it has been decided that patients on the waiting list should be prioritised according to need, and the public treatment is only provided for patients with the greatest need. One prerequisite is necessary to implement this policy, the introduction of guidelines to prioritise patients. These guides may also serve to pursue an efficiency goal.

6. A MODEL OF OPTIMAL MANAGEMENT

6.1 Introduction

In this section we will study the initial challenge that this research team faced some time ago, which would be the starting point for our line of work. The long stay of patients on waiting lists for surgery in public hospitals is a problem that worries the health authorities, public opinion and the professionals of health care in Spain. The health authorities of the different public administrations in our country have been taking steps and establishing requirement levels increasing over time. Specifically, in the year 1998, the maximum limit of stay of a patient on a waiting list for an operation changed from nine months to six months, implemented as follows: (1) For surgeries before the first of July of 1998, the maximum limit of stay was nine months. (2) Patients who entered a waiting list before the first of July of 1998, had to be off the list before the first of January of 1999; (3) Patients who entered a waiting list after the first of July of 1998 had six months as maximum limit of stay on the list.

By the end of 1997 a specific public hospital of Madrid had long waiting lists for the following surgical processes: Cataracts, Hallux Valgus, Knee Operations and Osteoarthritis. The first one depends on the hospital service of Ophthalmology and the rest on the service of Orthopedic Surgery and Traumatology. The authorities of the hospital, knowing the situation of the waiting lists for these four surgical processes and in the light of the new and larger requirements about the new limits of stay to be reached, were very worried. The four surgical processes had long waiting lists not only in the hospital we are considering but in all the public hospitals of Madrid. In fact, they were first place in the accumulation of patients, using aggregated data in Madrid.

When the Operations Research team went to work in 1998, the hospital had previously established its agreements for the year both at an internal level, with the different services, and at an external level with the Spanish National Health Service (SNHS) (INSALUD, in Spanish). In our Hospital, according to the decision maker, the bottleneck was neither in human resources nor in the number of beds available (at least initially), but in the operating rooms. The number of operating rooms in the hospital was appropriate from the point of view of the relationship with the rest of the facilities and teams.

The challenge for all hospitals involves getting waiting times down while maintaining costs within certain limits (Bitran et al. 1987, Chae et al., 1985). To attain the previously mentioned objectives, hospitals are allowed to use several methods of operating scheduling: (1) Within regular-operating hours, (2) Overtime, and (3) Private hospital contracts. Specifically, in our Hospital, in accordance with previously established agreements:

- Cataract surgeries could be in regular operating hours or in overtime, but private hospital contracts were not allowed (Methods 1 and 2, but not 3).
- Hallux Valgus: Methods 1 and 3 were possible, but not 2.
- Knee Operations: Methods 1 and 3 were possible, but not 2.
- Osteoarthritis: Method 1 was possible, but not 2 and 3.

The problem consisted of deciding how many operations can be performed in every month of the year 1998 for each of the four types, in regular time, overtime and private hospitals under contract, in such a way that all the constraints (to be introduced) are satisfied and the objective function (to be introduced) is optimized. Therefore, we have a problem of annual planning, to be solved with mathematical optimization. Before introducing the mathematical program we will point out several general features of the hospital in which the study was done.

6.2 General features of the Hospital

The data we consider correspond to the first of January of 1998, when the problem was solved. The general characteristics of the hospital are provided below, and in Tables 6-3 and 6-4.

- The Hospital is located in Madrid.
- Population dependent on the Hospital: 305 000 people.
- Number of beds available: 407.
- Number of operating rooms for planned operations: 8.
- Number of consulting rooms: 70.

Table 6-3. Structure of the Hospital in 1997

	Hospital	Global TSNHS
Beds/1000 inhabitants	1.34	2.67
Human resources/bed	3.62	2.96
Doctors/bed	0.62	0.48
Operat. rooms/100000 inh.	3.5	5.9
Surgeons/operating rooms	8.5	7.7
Anesthetists/operat. Rooms	1.4	1.4

Table 6-4. Activity in 1997

Activity	Number
Admissions	14 518
Stays	108 109
First examinations	132 821
Successive examinations	237 426
Total examinations	370 247
Urgencies	98 539
Planned surgical operations	3 111
Urgent surgical operations	2 061
Surgical operat. without stay for the night	4 935
Total surgical operations	10 107

6.3 The mathematical problem to be solved

In this section a mathematical programming problem is formulated in order to plan the surgical activity of the hospital for the four processes considered. First the decision variables will be defined, then the initial relevant data used in our work will be presented, the constraints and the objective functions will be defined and, finally, from the previous subsections, the mathematical problem to be solved will be defined.

We need to introduce considerable notation. Let

CL_1: Number of patients on the waiting list for cataracts the Jan, 1, 1998.
HL_1: The same for hallux valgus.
KL_1: The same for knee operations.
OL_1: The same for osteoarthritis.

These quantities are known for January 1, 1998.

6.4 Variables

Let us define the following state variables:

CL_k: Number of patients on the waiting list for cataracts the first day of month k.
HL_k: The same for hallux valgus.
KL_k: The same for knee operations.
OL_k: The same for osteoarthritis,

for $k = 2,3,\ldots,12,13$, where $k = 2$ corresponds to February, 1998, $k = 3$ to March, 1998, …, $k = 12$ corresponds to December, 1998, and $k = 13$ to January, 1999.

Let us define the following control variables:

CR_i: Number of cataract operations to be carried out in month i in regular-operation hours.
HR_i: The same for hallux valgus.
KR_i: The same for knee operations.
OR_i: The same for osteoarthritis.
CO_i :Number of cataract operations to be carried out in month i in overtime.
HP_i: Number of hallux valgus operations to be carried out in month i through private hospital contracts.
KP_i: The same for knee operations,

for $i = 1,2,\ldots,12$, where $i = 1$ corresponds to January of 1998, $i = 2$ to February of 1998, …, $i = 12$ to December of 1998.

Any month $i \in \{1,2,\ldots,12\}$ starts with a number of patients on the waiting list for each one of the four surgical processes CL_i, HL_i, KL_i, OL_i (using the terminology of Dynamic Optimization, these are the state variables, including then $i = 13$, but excluding $i = 1$ which are given). In month i the following operations will be carried out: CR_i, CO_i, HR_i, HP_i, KR_i, KP_i and OR_i (the control variables). Moreover, during the month i new patients will come on the waiting lists and some patients will leave the waiting lists without an operation for some reason (the forecast is among the data in the next subsection). The month i will finish (or equivalently the month $i + 1$ will begin) with the numbers of the waiting lists given by CL_{i+1}, HL_{i+1}, KL_{i+1} and OL_{i+1} . Therefore, we have a problem with the following number of variables:

- State variables: 4 x 12 = 48.
- Control variables: 7 x 12 = 84.
- Total number of variables: 132.

6.4.1 Data

In this subsection the relevant data for the problem are incorporated. We present the data in the way they were given by the Hospital. Table 6.5 contains, for each pathology, the number of patients on the waiting list by December, 31, 1997. Table 6.6 shows the month in which patients enter the waiting lists

Table 6.5. Patients on waiting list by December, 31, 1997

Cataracts	480
Hallux Valgus	199
Knee Operations	132
Osteoarthritis	128
Rest of processes of Traumatology	511
Rest of processes of Ophthalmology	97

Table 6.6. Month of entrance on the waiting lists

Process	Month of 1997									
	April	May	June	July	Aug.	Sept.	Oct.	Nov.	Dec.	Total
Catar.	11	15	24	66	37	71	85	89	82	480
H.V.	9	15	38	30	11	27	23	12	34	199
K.O.	4	19	12	14	10	23	18	19	13	132
Ost.	3	14	17	4	4	19	33	13	21	128
Rest T.	31	56	61	53	26	62	69	67	86	511
Rest O.	2	10	12	8	0	16	21	16	12	97

Table 6.7 contains the entries on the waiting lists estimated by the hospital for each month of 1998.

Table 6.7. Estimation of entries on the waiting lists

Pro.	Month of 1998												
	1	2	3	4	5	6	7	8	9	10	11	12	Total
C.	84	85	82	94	78	104	125	42	78	98	94	86	1050
H.V.	28	28	22	22	34	45	31	12	20	24	12	33	311
K.O.	21	22	18	15	30	18	15	12	24	18	21	13	227
O.	10	22	15	14	30	24	5	5	17	34	14	21	211
R.T.	130	145	120	122	159	169	116	65	151	162	122	57	1618
R.O.	111	113	100	112	107	139	144	50	102	137	119	104	1338

Table 6.8 contains the exclusions in the waiting lists (without an operation) estimated by the hospital for each month of 1998.

Table 6.8. Estimation of exclusions

Pro.	Month of 1998												
	1	**2**	**3**	**4**	**5**	**6**	**7**	**8**	**9**	**10**	**11**	**12**	**Total**
C.	8	13	16	16	20	37	53	12	19	20	17	7	238
H.V.	4	8	13	6	10	31	22	3	5	12	2	19	135
K.O.	3	5	4	3	10	14	4	0	7	9	1	5	65
O.	5	2	9	7	9	7	7	5	7	13	2	5	78
R.T.	26	37	56	58	42	72	105	17	61	75	26	61	636
R.O.	15	17	20	19	31	43	58	13	27	31	24	10	308

Table 6.9 contains the distribution of surgical sessions for the year 1998 (within regular-operating hours).

Table 6.9. Distribution of surgical sessions

Service	Month											
	1	**2**	**3**	**4**	**5**	**6**	**7**	**8**	**9**	**10**	**11**	**12**
Traum.	26	27	28	24	27	28	21	19	18	31	27	24
Ophtha.	19	20	20	17	20	20	9	11	9	23	20	16

Table 6.10 contains the operating room time necessary for each operation. Is the time that elapses from the moment when the patient enters the operating room until the moment when he or she leaves.

Table 6.10. Operating room time

Process	Time (in minutes)
Cataracts	60
Hallux Valgus	65
Knee Operations	100
Osteoarthritis	140

Table 6.11 contains the number of operations and the total time of operating room used in the hospital in 1997, for each process under study.

Table 6.11. Number of operations and total time of operating room

Process	Number of operations	Total time (in minutes)
Cataracts	450	26 557
Hallux Valgus	27	1 795
Knee Operations	68	6 868
Osteoarthritis	105	15 173
Total Traumatology	1 018	102 506
Total Ophthalmology	904	54 749

We have to point out that some of these operations were not on any surgical waiting list, being urgent operations but carried out in programmed operation rooms. Table 6.12 contains the maximum number of possible operations in each month, for each one of the possibilities out of the regular-operating hours

Table 6.12. Maximum number of possible operations

	Month											
	1	2	3	4	5	6	7	8	9	10	11	12
C.o	0	0	68	40	64	72	0	0	44	52	48	24
H.p	0	20	25	35	35	35	35	35	35	35	35	35
K.p	0	0	8	21	21	20	20	20	20	10	10	0

C.o: Cataracts Overtime. H.p: Hallux Valgus in private hospital contracts. K.p: Knee Operations in private hospital contracts.

These maximum limits correspond to previously established agreements (with financing guaranteed) between the management of the hospital and the service of ophthalmology of the hospital (for cataracts in overtime) and the regional health direction of the SNHS (for hallux valgus and knee operations in private hospital contracts).

Table 6.13 contains the costs for this hospital, for each process, both in regular time and in overtime. The hospitalization costs are included.

Table 6.13. Costs for the hospital

Process	Cost in regular time	Cost in overtime
Cataracts	110 852 pesetas	123 733 pesetas
Hallux Valgus	125 899 pesetas	138 781 pesetas
Knee Operations	287 338 pesetas	313 273 pesetas
Osteoarthritis	853 338 pesetas	887 071 pesetas

The costs of the processes to be carried out in private hospitals with contracts are considered maximum rates for 1997 (rates of the SNHS for 1997), in accordance with the order of the government published the day May, 8, 1997. These are presented in Table 6.14

Table 6.14. Rates of the SNHS for 1997

Process	Rates for the SNHS for 1997
Cataracts	146 971 pesetas
Hallux Valgus	106 605 pesetas
Knee Operations	141 120 pesetas
Osteoarthritis	925 000 pesetas

6.4.2 Constraints

6.4.2.1 State equations

For each one of the surgical processes under study, the number of patients on the waiting list on the first day of month $i+1$ is equal to the number of patients that were on the list on the first day of month i plus those who came on the list during the month i minus those excluded from the list without operation during the month i, minus those operated (in regular time, overtime or in a private hospital under contract), during the month i. That is, for $i = 1,2,\ldots,12$,

$$CL_{i+1} = CL_i + CA_i - CE_i - CR_i - CO_i,$$

$$HL_{i+1} = HL_i + HA_i - HE_i - HR_i - HP_i,$$

$$KL_{i+1} = KL_i + KA_i - KE_i - KR_i - KP_i,$$

$$OL_{i+1} = OL_i + OA_i - OE_i - CR_i,$$

subject to the following initial conditions:

$$CL_1 = 480,\ HL_1 = 199,\ KL_1 = 132,\ OL_1 = 128.$$

6.4.2.2 Operating rooms allocated to each service

Ophthalmology

$$80\ CR_i \leq OCQ_i \qquad \text{for } i = 1,2,\ldots,12.$$

The previous inequality shows that for each month the number of minutes of operating room needed to operate cataracts in regular time has to be smaller or equal to the number of minutes of operating room available to operate cataracts. It is assumed that each operation requires 80 minutes (60 minutes of operation plus 20 minutes to clean the operating room). The amount of time available in each month for operations of cataracts in regular time (OCQ_i) is collected in Table 6.15.

Traumatology

$$85\ HR_i + 120\ KR_i + 160\ OR_i \leq TEQ_i \qquad \text{for } i = 1,2,\ldots,12.$$

The previous inequality shows for each month the operating room time (in minutes) needed to operate on hallux valgus, knee operations and osteoarthritis in regular time (where to the required time for each operation 20 minutes have been added for the cleaning of the operating room) has to be smaller or equal to the operating room time that the traumatology service of the hospital has to carry out these three types of surgical processes (TEQ_i). The values of OCQ_i and TEQ_i appear in Table *6.15*.

Table 6.15 Parameter values

Month	OCQ_i	TEQ_i
$i = 1$	5 520	3 255
$i = 2$	5 840	3392
$i = 3$	5 920	3 486
$i = 4$	4 880	2 982
$i = 5$	5 840	3 392
$i = 6$	5 840	3 486
$i = 7$	2 560	2 572
$i = 8$	3 040	2 384
$i = 9$	2 400	2 247
$i = 10$	6 720	3 892
$i = 11$	5 840	3 434
$i = 12$	4 560	3 024

In the Table 6.15, time (the numbers that appear in columns 2 and 3) is expressed in minutes. It is very important to explain how the values that appear in Table *6.15* have been obtained.

Ophthalmology: Let us see how the values OCQ_i have been obtained. Every surgical session is assumed to (theoretically from 8 to 15 hours) last six hours and a half, which is more realistic than the seven theoretical hours. In this way, as Ophthalmology has for example 19 sessions in January, it has initially 19x390 = 7410 minutes of operating room in January. In the same way the initial available minutes of operating room are worked out for each month of the year. The time contained in some of these sessions coincides with time reserved for scientific sessions and during this time operations are not carried out. Therefore, from the previously obtained minutes, it is necessary to subtract the time devoted to scientific sessions. We have been checking day-by-day for each month, ensuring that we have to subtract 480 minutes in January, February, April, May, June, August, September, October, November and December, 360 minutes in March and 240 minutes in July. From the remaining time we have deduced that 80% of time is devoted to cataract operations, thus obtaining the values of OCQ_i.

Traumatology: Let us see how the values TEQ_i have been obtained. In the same way as for the other service, we start multiplying for each month the number of sessions for Traumatology by 390 minutes (which correspond to six hours and thirty minutes) and subtracting the minutes devoted to scientific sessions, which correspond to surgical sessions of Traumatology. Specifically, we have to subtract 840 minutes in January, February, April, May and July; 960 in March, June and October; 600 in August and September and 720 in November and December. From this time we have to keep the 70% that the service devotes to programmed operations that are on the waiting list (the remaining 30% is devoted to "delayed urgencies"). From the remaining time we have deduced that it is necessary to give 50% to these three traumatology operations, thus obtaining the values of TEQ_i.

If it were possible to pool the operating room times devoted to Cataracts and the set of hallux valgus plus knee operations plus osteoarthritis, the following constraint would substitute the constraints 6.4.2.2:

$$80\ CR_i + 85\ HR_i + 120\ KR_i + 160\ OR_i \leq OCQ_i + TEQ_i \text{ for } i = 1,2,\ldots,12.$$

6.4.2.3 Limits to the number of processes in private and overtime scheduling

The following constraints have to be satisfied:

$CO_i \leq l_i$,

$HP_i \leq m_i$,

$KP_i \leq n_i$,

for $i = 1,2,\ldots,12$, where the values for l_i, m_i and n_i appear in Table 6.16

Table 6.16. Limits to the number of processes

	1	**2**	**3**	**4**	**5**	**6**	**7**	**8**	**9**	**10**	**11**	**12**	**Total**
l_i	0	0	68	40	64	72	0	0	44	52	48	24	412
m_i	0	20	25	35	35	35	35	35	35	35	35	35	360
n_i	0	0	8	21	21	20	20	20	20	10	10	0	150

6.4.2.4 Waiting list time upper limit: no more than nine months

With the following constraints we reflect that throughout the year the maximum time for patients to be on the waiting list should be nine months.

$$(CR_1 + CO_1) + (CR_2 + CO_2) + \ldots + (CR_k + CO_k) \geq a_k,$$

$$(HR_1 + HP_1) + (HR_2 + HP_2) + \ldots + (HR_k + HP_k) \geq b_k,$$

$$(KR_1 + KP_1) + (KR_2 + KP_2) + \ldots + (KR_k + KP_k) \geq c_k,$$

$$OR_1 + OR_2 + \ldots + OR_k \geq d_k,$$

for $k = 1,2,\ldots,12,$ where the values for a_k, b_k, c_k and d_k appear in Table 6.17.

The values contained in Table 6.17 are constructed from Table 6.6. The meaning of these values is the following: in January, at least the 11 patients that entered the waiting list for cataracts in April on 1997 (and are on the waiting list on January 1st) have to be operated on. In the same way, the nine patients that entered the waiting list for hallux valgus in April, 1997, have to be operated on January. The same for the four patients that entered the list of those needing knee operations and the three patients that entered the list for osteoarthritis in April, 1997. In February, at least the 15 patients that entered the waiting list for cataracts in May, 1997, and have not been operated on in January. That is the reason why the number of cataract operations in January and February has to be greater than or equal to the number of patients who entered the waiting list for cataracts in April and May, which is equal to 26. Reasoning in this way, the values that appear in Table 6.17 are obtained.

Table 6.17. Waiting time upper limit: no more than nine months

	1	2	3	4	5	6	7	8	9	10	11	12
a_k	11	26	50	116	153	224	309	398	480	556	628	694
b_k	9	24	62	92	103	130	153	165	199	223	243	252
c_k	4	23	35	49	59	82	100	119	132	150	167	181
d_k	3	17	34	38	42	61	94	107	128	133	153	159

6.4.2.5 No more than six months waiting at the end of 1998

The following constraints have to be satisfied:

$$CL_{13} \leq 395,$$

$$HL_{13} \leq 69,$$

$KL_{13} \leq 77,$

$OL_{13} \leq 57.$

These values are obtained from the addition of the estimated entries minus the estimated exits without operations corresponding to the last six months of 1998, Tables 6.7 and 6.8.

6.4.2.6 All the variables have to be non-negative integers

6.4.3 Objective functions

The problem has two objective functions.

First Objective. Minimize the waiting list pending by the end of 1998 (measured in operating room time).

$$\text{Min } f_1 = 80\ CL_{13} + 85\ HL_{13} + 120\ KL_{13} + 160\ OL_{13}.$$

It is clear that a fundamental objective of the planning to be done is to leave the waiting list by the end of the year as small as possible. Specifically, the objective function to minimize is the operating room time (in minutes) that remains on the waiting list by the end of the year we are planning.

Second Objective. Minimize costs.

$$\begin{aligned} \text{Min } f_2 = {} & 110852\ (CR_1 + \ldots + CR_{12}) + 125899\ (HR_1 + \ldots + HR_{12}) + \\ & + 287973\ (KR_1 + \ldots + KR_{12}) + 853338\ (OR_1 + \ldots + OR_{12}) + \\ & + 123733\ (CO_1 + \ldots + CO_{12}) + 106605\ (HP_1 + \ldots + HP_{12}) + \\ & + 141120\ (KP_1 + \ldots + KP_{12}) + 90584\ CL_{13} + 58035\ HL_{13} + \\ & + 148157\ KL_{13} + 537603\ OL_{13}. \end{aligned}$$

Let us explain how this second objective function was obtained. We have to add the costs of the operations carried out in the hospital in regular time (the unit values of which appear in Table 6.13), the costs of the cataract operations carried out in the hospital in overtime (the unit values also appear in Table 6.13), the costs of the operations carried out in private hospitals with contracts (for which it has been assumed that the unit values are those given in Table 6.14) and an assessment, in costs terms, of the operations pending for the next year, where for each process an expected approximated unit cost has been introduced, bearing in mind that some entries on the list will leave the list without an operation and that there are several possibilities for operation (regular time, overtime and private contracts).

6.4.4 The mathematical program

In previous sections the elements of a mathematical program have been introduced. It is a program with two objectives and several constraints, where the decision variables are integer. Among the different possibilities to broach the bi-objective program, one of the more immediate is to ask the decision maker (in this case, the manager of the hospital) if it was possible to give weighting to the objectives in accordance to their importance from the hospital's perspective. The reply of the decision maker was emphatic: give a weighting of 0.8 to the first objective (to minimize the waiting list by the end of 1998) and a weighting of 0.2 to the second one (to minimize costs).

After the introduction of the usual technical adjustments in multiobjective programming, specifically

$$0.8\,(f_1 / \left| f_1^* - f_{*1} \right|) + 0.2\,(f_2 / \left| f_2^* - f_{*2} \right|),$$

where f_1^* and f_2^* are the ideal of the first and second objective and f_{*1} and f_{*2} are the anti-ideal of the first and second objective, respectively,

$$f_1^* = 34379, \qquad f_{*1} = 55825,$$

$$f_2^* = 431561300, \quad f_{*2} = 462946208.$$

We have the following objective function:

$$\begin{gathered}\text{Min } 0.0706\,(CR_1 + \ldots + CR_{12}) + 0.0802(HR_1 + \ldots + HR_{12}) + \\ + 0.1835\,(KR_1 + \ldots + KR_{12}) + 0.05437\,(OR_1 + \ldots + OR_{12}) + \\ + 0.0788\,(CO_3 + \ldots + CO_6 + CO_9 + \ldots + CO_{12}) + 0.0679\,(HP_2 + \ldots + HP_{12}) + \\ + 0.0899\,(KP_3 + \ldots + KP_{12}) + 0.3561\,CL_{13} + 0.3539\,HL_{13} + \\ + 0.5420\,KL_{13} + 0.9393\,OL_{13}.\end{gathered}$$

The problem is subject to the constraints given in 6.4.2. It is a linear program with integer variables, 132 variables and 160 constraints (apart from the non-negativity of the variables).

6.4.5 Results

The program HIPERLINDO has been used to solve the problem. We introduced the data of the mathematical programming problem in

HIPERLINDO, and found that no feasible solution exists. That is, it is not possible to satisfy all the requirements of maximum limit of permanence on the waiting list with the resources of the hospital, with the established agreements and with the hospital's usual way of working.

After the analysis of the problem and its solution we found that the problem has an optimal solution if the following constraint is removed,

$$OL_{13} \leq 57.$$

Therefore the hardest constraint is the maximum limit of 6 months of permanence on the waiting list for osteoarthritis, which occupies the most operating room time and is the most expensive; which cannot be done in overtime and which cannot be sent to a privately contracted hospital (as had been previously decided in the agreements of the hospital). We have studied the problem without that constraint, obtaining the minimum limit for OL_{13} in order to assure feasibility. All requirements can then be satisfied if it is possible to renegotiate, and if it is possible to send 30 processes of osteoarthritis to privately contracted hospitals.

A second possibility consists of transferring some planned operating room sessions from ophthalmology to traumatology. In that case, an optimal solution is obtained, satisfying all the constraints, and the hospital could satisfy all the requirements without the necessity of renegotiating with the Spanish National Health Service to send 30 osteoarthritis processes to privately contracted hospitals. Specifically, 13 operating room sessions initially allocated to ophthalmology should be allocated to traumatology in the following way: 1 in January, 1 in February, 1 in March, 2 in May, 1 in June, 1 in July, 1 in August, 2 in September, 2 in October and 1 in November.

The results obtained with the first option, to have the Spanish National Health Service finance 30 operations of osteoarthritis in private hospitals, appear in Table 6.18.

Table 6.18. Results obtained with the first option

Process	**Month**											
	1	**2**	**3**	**4**	**5**	**6**	**7**	**8**	**9**	**10**	**11**	**12**
Cat RT	69	73	74	61	73	73	32	38	30	84	73	57
Cat OT	0	0	68	40	64	72	0	0	44	52	48	24
HV RT	10	1	6	0	0	0	0	0	0	0	0	0
HV PC	0	20	25	35	35	35	35	35	35	35	35	35
KO RT	15	10	2	2	0	1	8	1	0	23	0	5
KO PC	0	0	8	21	21	20	20	20	20	10	10	0
O RT	4	13	17	17	21	21	10	14	14	7	21	15

In this situation the evolution of the waiting list is as recorded in Table 6.19, where for each process there appears the number of patients on the waiting list for the first day of the corresponding month. The optimal value of the objective function is equal to 404.9.

Table 6.19. Evolution of the waiting list with the first option

Process	Month											
	2	**3**	**4**	**5**	**6**	**7**	**8**	**9**	**10**	**11**	**12**	**13**
Cataracts	487	486	410	387	308	230	270	262	247	189	145	143
H.V.	213	212	190	171	160	139	113	87	69	46	21	0
K.O.	135	142	146	135	134	117	100	91	88	64	74	77
Osteoar.	129	136	125	115	115	111	99	85	81	95	86	87

With the second option (rearranging the allocation of operating rooms to the different services of the hospital), the results are recorded in Table 6.20.

Table 6.20. Results obtained with the second option

Process	Month											
	1	**2**	**3**	**4**	**5**	**6**	**7**	**8**	**9**	**10**	**11**	**12**
Cat RT	65	69	70	61	65	69	28	34	22	76	69	57
Cat OT	0	0	63	40	64	72	0	0	44	52	48	24
HV RT	10	0	7	0	0	0	0	0	0	0	0	0
HV PC	0	20	25	35	33	35	35	35	35	35	35	35
KO RT	5	18	14	4	0	4	2	19	1	0	1	1
KO PC	0	0	8	21	21	20	20	20	20	10	10	0
O RT	14	10	10	15	26	21	17	3	18	29	23	18

In this situation the evolution of the waiting list is as recorded in Table 6.21, where for each process there appears the number of patients on the waiting list for the first day of the corresponding month. The optimal value of the objective function is equal to 407.2.

Table 6.21. Evolution of the waiting list with the second option

Process	Month											
	2	**3**	**4**	**5**	**6**	**7**	**8**	**9**	**10**	**11**	**12**	**13**
Cataracts	491	494	422	399	328	254	298	294	287	23	197	195
H.V.	213	213	190	171	160	141	115	89	69	46	21	0
K.O.	145	144	136	123	122	102	91	64	60	59	68	75
Osteoar.	119	129	125	117	112	108	89	86	78	70	59	57

7. CONCLUSIONS AND FUTURE DIRECTIONS

The revision of the health systems in operation in Europe permits us to affirm that the problem of waiting lists is usual in countries that have a National Health System. However, these systems also have important advantages. For example, they permit good control of costs; they are less expensive than the systems based on health insurance; and they permit high levels of coverage in all benefits. In the European Union the countries that apply this kind of health system, mainly characterized by supplying universal coverage and obtaining financing via taxes, are increasingly numerous. To England and the Northern Countries have been added little by little some countries from Southern Europe, such as Italy, Portugal, Greece and Spain. In these systems waiting lists work as management instruments for health resources. They have always been the object of special attention, particularly if certain waiting times are exceeded or some kind of collapse is produced. It is for that reason that waiting lists are always on the agenda of health reforms. Some measures have been used to try to shorten the waiting time and the number of patients in queues. For example: maximum waiting time guarantee, trying to diminish the length of stay of hospitalized patients, increasing productivity policies, increasing resources, improving the management of the waiting lists, increasing patient choice or reducing public demand by subsidising voluntary private health insurance.

Continuous and appropriate management of the waiting lists is essential. The operations research techniques used to control the waiting lists can be enumerated: queuing theory (Worthington, 1987), simulation (H&SSSG, 1994, Wisniewski, 1997), data envelopment analysis (DEA) (O'Neill and Dexter, 2004), mathematical programming (Cooper, 1981) and multicriteria decision making (Arenas el al., 2002).

One important factor in demand for private health insurance seems to be the long-term waiting lists. At the same time, the choice between public and private health services should be an aspect with many consequences for waiting lists. One consequence of high private coverage could be that the public health system should improve because it would have fewer patients. However a long-term system could go in the opposite direction, if there are feedback effects from private insurance demand to waiting lists. In this empirical sense it has been observed that some areas with high private coverage had higher waiting lists because the government may under-fund public services in areas with private insurance coverage.

The choice of public or private sector could also have distributional implications. Individuals who opt out of public sector treatment free up resources for those who continue to rely exclusively on the National Health System.

Another important scheme is to establish priorities for managing waiting lists. Traditionally, the usual prioritization rule for non-urgent patients was "first in, first out", but now new factors are taken into account for the management of waiting lists in most of the developed countries. In this new context the necessity of the introduction of different standardized prioritization rules has been pointed out in order to preserve equity. Some of these rules are based on: severity, urgency, need, expected benefit, etc. Another kind of prioritization has been considered in some non-European country. For example, New Zealand recognises that the public resources are limited and the public treatment is only provided for patients with the greatest need.

Section 5 contains the application of a mathematical problem of dynamic optimization to the management of the surgery waiting lists in a public hospital of Madrid. This model is adapted to the particular circumstances of that hospital, being capable of adaptation to any other hospital. The mathematical program has elements of linear programming, integer programming, dynamic optimization in discrete time and multi-objective programming. The computer program HIPERLINDO has been used to solve the problem. An important property in our model is that it can easily be made adaptive, in the sense that in every month in the year, where we have new information about current waiting lists or updated forecasting for admission/exit of patients, it is possible to adapt the model in such a way that it incorporates the new information in substitution of the old and we can obtain updated values after optimization, from that month to the end of the year. The results obtained confirm our belief that this kind of mathematical technique is very useful in the management of surgery waiting lists.

In the work presented in Section 5, the agreements of the hospital, both with external authorities and between the different services of the hospital, were given. In future research it would be interesting to study the problem in two stages: first, a model as an aid to the decision maker of the hospital in the negotiations both internal and external; second, take the results of the negotiations as given (as is the case in the model presented here). In other situations it will be necessary to include the number of available beds as an additional constraint. Also it would be interesting to improve the forecasting of demand, entries of new patients to the waiting lists and patients that leave the waiting lists without an operation. It would also be interesting to introduce random elements in the model, especially when the operating room time of some of the surgical processes to be considered has high variance. Finally, it would be interesting to introduce in the model different criteria about priorities for waiting lists.

8. REFERENCES

Aaron, H.J. and Schwartz, B., 1984, The painful prescription: Rationing hospital care, Brookings Institution, Washington, D.C.

Arenas, M., Bilbao, A., Caballero, R., Gómez, T., Rodríguez, M.V., Ruiz, F., 2002, Analysis via goal programming of the minimum achievable stay in surgical waiting lists, *Journal of the Operational Research Society,* **53** (4): 387-396.

Besley, T., and Coate, S., 1991, Public Provision of private goods and the redistribution of income, *American Economic Review* **81** (4): 979-984.

Besley, T., Hall J. and Preston I., 1999, The demand for private health insurance: do waiting lists matter?, *Journal of Public Economics*, **72**: 155-181.

Bitran, G.R., Valor-Sabatier, J., 1987, Some Mathematical Programming Based Meassures of Efficiency in Health Care Institutions, *Advances in Mathematical Programming and Financial Planning,* **1**: 61-84.

Chae, Y., Suver, J., Chou, D., 1985, Goal programming as a capital investment tool for teaching hospitals, *HCM Review,* Winter: 27-35.

Cooper, R.C., 1981, A linear programming model for determining efficient combinations of 8, 10 and 12-hour shifts, *Respiratory Care,* **26**: 1105-1108.

Council of Europe, 1998, Recommendation No R(99) 21 on the criteria for the management of waiting lists and waiting times in health care. Available online on http://www.coe.int

Cullis, J.G. and Jones, P.R., 1985, National Health Service waiting list: a discussion of competing explanations and a policy proposal, *Journal of Health Economics,* **4**: 119-135.

Cullis, J.G. and Jones, P.R., 1986, Rationing by waiting list: an implication, *American Economic Review* **76**(1): 250-256.

Gravelle, H., Smith, P.C. and Xavier, A., 2003, Waiting lists and waiting times: a model of the market for elective surgery, *Oxford Economic Papers*, **55**(1): 81-103.

Hadorn, D. C. and the Steering Committee of the Western Canada Waiting List Project, 2000, Setting priorities for waiting lists: defining our terms, *Canadian Medical Association Journal*, **163**(7): 857-60.

Hoel, M. and Saether, E.M., 2003, Public health care with waiting time: the role of supplementary private health care, *Journal of Health Economics*, **22** (4): 599-616.

Hurst, J. and Siciliani, L., 2003, Tackling Excessive Waiting Times for Elective Surgery: A Comparison of Policies in Twelve OECD Countries, *OECD Health Working Papers* n. 6.

H&SSSG, 1994, *Simulation in Health Care Management,* Operational Research Society.

Iversen, T., 1997, The effect of a private sector on the waiting time in a National Health Service, *Journal of Health Economics*, **16**: 381-396.

Kee, F., Mcdonald, P., Kirwarn, J. R., Patterson, C. and Love, A. H. G., 1998, Urgency and priority for cardiac surgery: a clinical judgment analysis, *BMJ*, **316**: 925-9.

Lindsay, C.M. and Feigenbaum, B., 1984, Rationing by waiting list, *American Economic Review* **74** (3): 404-417.

Martin, S. and Smith, P., 1999, Rationing by waiting lists: an empirical investigation, *Journal of Public Economics* **71**: 141-164.

Noseworthy, T. W., McGurran, J. J. and Hadorn, D. C., 2003, Waiting for scheduled services in Canada: development of priority-setting scoring systems, *Journal of Evaluation in General Practice*, **9**(1): 23-31.

O.C.D.E.., 2005, Health data.

Office of Health Economics, 1997, *Compendium of Health Statistics*. OHE. London.

O¨Neill, L. and Dexter, F., 2004, Evaluating the Efficiency of Hospitals´ Perioperative Services Using DEA. In Brandeau, M.L., Sainfort, F. and Pierskalla, W. P. : *Operations*

Research and Health Care. A Handbook of Methods and Applications. Kluwer Academic Publishers, Boston.

Ortún-Rubio, V., Pinto-Prades, J. L. and Puig-Junoy, J., 2001, *El establecimiento de prioridades en al cirugía electiva.*, Ed. Ministerio de Sanidad y Consumo, Madrid.

Rodríguez Sendín, J. J., 2000, Responsabilidad y listas de espera. El problema de las listas de espera en el SNS. Discordancias, ética y equidad, *Actas del VII Congreso de Derecho Sanitario*, Madrid.

Siciliani, L. and Hurst, J., 2003, Explaining Waiting Times Variations for Elective Surgery across OECD Countries, *OECD Health Working Papers* n. 7.

Wisniewski, M., 1997, *Quantitative Methods for Decision Makers,* Pitman Publishing.

Worthington, D.J., 1987, Hospital waiting list management models, *Journal of Operational Research Society* **42** (10): 833-843.

APPENDIX: ADDITIONAL DATA

Table 6.22. Total and Public Health expenditure
(Source: O.C.D.E., 2005: Health data.)

	Total expenditure on Health per capita US$ PPP			Public expenditure on Health per capita US $ PPP		
	1998	**2000**	**2002**	**1998**	**2000**	**2002**
NO WAITING TIMES						
Austria	1953	2147	2220	1362	1495	1551
Belgium	2041	2288	2515	1433	1613	1790
France	2231	2416	2736	1696	1832	2080
Germany	2470	2640	2817	1942	2080	2212
Luxembourg	2291	2682	3065	2117	2406	2618
WITH WAITING TIMES						
Portugal	1290	1493	1646	866	1091	1201
Denmark	2141	2351	2580	1755	1940	2142
Finland	1607	1698	1943	1225	1276	1470
Ireland	1487	1774	2367	1138	1300	1779
Italy	1880	2001	2166	1293	1474	1639
Norway						
Spain	1371	1493	1646	990	1056	1176
Sweden	1961	2243	2517	1682	1904	2148
United Kingdom	1607	1839	2160	1292	1392	1801
Greece	1517	1617	1814	743	810	980
The Netherlands	2016	2196	2843			

*Table 6.23.*Total public health expenditure, % GDP; and public expenditure on in-patient care, % GDP (Source: O.C.D.E. 2005: Health data)

	Total expenditure on health %GDP			**Public expenditure on In-patient health %GDP**		
	1998	**2000**	**2002**	**1998**	**2000**	**2002**
NO WAITING TIMES						
Austria	5.4	5.4	5.4	2.9	2.9	
Belgium	6	6.2	6.5	2.2		
France	7.1	7.1	7.4	3.8	3.6	3.7
Germany	8.3	8.3	8.6	3.3	3.2	3.3
Luxembourg	5.4		5	1.7	2.1	2.1
WITH WAITING TIMES						
Portugal	5.6	6.4	6.5			
Denmark	6.9	6.9	7.3	4.3	4.2	4.2
Finland	5.3	5	5.5	2.6	2.4	2.7
Ireland	4.7	4.7	5.5		3.3	
Italy	5.6	6	6.4	3.9	3.2	3.3
Spain	5.4	5.3	5.4	1.9	1.8	1.8
Sweden	7.2	7.2	7.9	3.5	3.9	2.8
United Kingdom	5.5	5.9	6.4			
Greek	4.9	5.2	5			
Netherlands						

Table 6.24. Resources of the Health Systems
(Source: O.C.D.E., 2005: Health data.)

	Acure care beds/1000pop.		Hospital Physicians		Total hospital employment	
	1998	2002	1998	2002	1998	2002
NO WAITING TIMES						
Austria	6.40	6.1	3.3	3.3		
Belgium			3.7	3.9		
France	4.3		3.3	3.3	18.7	
Germany	9.2		3.2	3.3	15	15
Luxemburg	6	5.8	2.4	2.6		
WITH WAITING TIMES						
Portugal	3.2		3.1		10.1	
Denmark	3.6		3.1	3.3		18.1
Finland	2.6	2.3	3	3.1		
Ireland	3.1	3	2.2	2.4	14	16.7
Italy	5		4.1	4.4		
Norway						
Spain	2.9		2.8	2.9	10	
Sweden	2.6					
United Kingdom	4.1	3.9	1.9	2.1	22.4	23
Greece	4		4.3		9.5	
The Netherlands	3.7		2.9	3.1	16.6	16.6

Table 6.25. Total surgical cases/1000p and average length of stay (Source:O.C.D.E. 2005: Health data.)

	1998	2002	1970	1990	1998	2002
NO WAITING TIMES						
Austria			2.2	13	10.9	8.1
Belgium				13.8	11.4	
France			18.3	13.3	14.1	
Germany			23.7	17.2		
Luxembourg	216.6	214.1	27	17.6	15.3	
WITH WAITING TIMES	**1998**	**2002**	**1970**	**1990**	**1998**	**2002**
Portugal	48	58	23.8	10.8	9.8	
Denmark	170	207.6	18.1	8.2	6.7	5.7
Finland	89	91.2	24.4	18.2	11.8	
Ireland	136.7	197.8	13.3	7.9	7.8	7.6
Italy	64.4	73.3	19.1	11.7	10.1	
Norway					10	
Spain	63.6			12.2		
Sweden			27.2	18	6.7	6.2
United Kingdom	124.9	125.3	25.7	15.6	10.2	8.1
Greece			15	9.9	8.2	
The Netherlands	71.8	75.1	38.2	34.1	32.8	

Chapter 7

PERSONNEL STAFFING AND SCHEDULING

Michael Warner, Ph.D., Chief Scientist
AtStaff,Inc., 3000 Croasdaile Drive, Suite 100 Durham, North Carolina 27705

Abstract: Not only do personnel make up approximately 2/3 of the cost of hospital health care, but they account for an even higher percentage of the quality of care delivered and patient safety. Additionally, they, with physicians, are the major determinate of how quickly a patient moves through a hospital. The key factor for throughput, quality, and safety, is that the correct number of personnel, with the correct qualifications and correct motivation, be present at the right times and places of the patient's stay. This is the goal of the personnel staffing and scheduling processes and systems in hospitals. This chapter first briefly reviews the history of the use of modeling for more efficient and effective scheduling and staffing. Then it presents in some detail modeling work to move staff management decisions from the present, where intervention options are severely limited, into the near future (several days) where intervention options are numerous. This significantly improves not only throughput, but quality, safety, and staff satisfaction. This new effort involves: (1) Forecasting demand for staff into the near future, (2) Predicting no-shows of prescheduled personnel, and (3) A robust decision support system to include professional judgment and "best practices" allowing the hospital to be able to take advantage of the significant increase in intervention options for staffing (for example) four days ahead rather than four hours ahead. How this effort fits into the larger aspects of staff management is discussed, along with possible future opportunities to use modeling to improve staff management in hospitals.

NOTE: The concepts, techniques, procedures and computer systems for (1) moving staffing decisions into the future and (2) Event Driven Workload have Patent Pending status owned by AtStaff Inc. of Durham, NC.

Key words: Scheduling, staffing, forecasting

1. INTRODUCTION

A critical element in a patient's moving through the health care system as quickly as possible is that the correct number of caregivers, with the correct qualifications, and with the correct attitudes and motivations are available at each phase of the patient's stay. Caregivers are the assembly line managers of health care. Institutions and physicians set protocols to follow, procedures to be performed, etc., but the minute by minute execution of healthcare is primarily performed and managed by caregivers.

Thus if there's a theoretical "shortest time" that a patient A must stay in the system, achieving such time is largely a function of the environment the patient is in, a set of things that must be done (correctly and at the right time), plus a set of things that must not be done (that can cause delays). Having the right number of motivated caregivers who set the environment, know what to do (and how to do it) and not do is critical to minimizing delay.

In addition to throughput, correct matching of the supply of caregivers to demand also affects patient care quality, patient safety, and staff satisfaction (Litvak, 2005; Needleman, 2002; Kovner, 1998). These three critical outcomes in turn affect throughput.

Having the optimal number and skill of caregivers available at the right time and place is the goal of good scheduling and staffing. While shift-by-shift staffing is where the real action is, there are a number of steps that must take place to set the stage. The better these earlier decisions are done, the better the chance that optimal shift-by-shift staffing can occur.

2. DEFINITIONS

Before introducing the several aspects of Personnel Management, it will be useful to define certain terms as they are used in this chapter.

- "Nurse" will be used as a stand-in for all types of caregivers and other personnel in hospitals, such as pharmacists, radiologists, transport people, etc. Nurses are indeed the most numerous caregivers, plus they are the most difficult to schedule and staff.
- "Skill" will refer to the care-giving abilities of the nurse. At its most basic, it refers to what they are licensed for – registered nurse, nursing aide, senior technician, etc. But for our purposes, when possible it will also cover qualifications, experience, attitudes, motivation, etc.

- "Unit" will refer to a logical unit or cost center of the hospital, where a group of personnel call "home". Examples are the ICU, the ER, the OR, a medical nursing unit, the pharmacy, etc. Again, most examples will be nursing units, but the methodologies discussed apply to any unit.
- "Shift" will refer to an interval of time within the day. Most typical for nursing units are 8-hour shifts, or 12-hour shifts, but 10-hour, 4-hour, or other length of time might make up a "shift". Personnel may work a combination of shifts within a unit (such as 12-hour and 8-hour), and different personnel may be working different Shifts at the same time (some on 4-hour, some on 8-hour, etc.). When measuring demand for care, time slices as short as an hour may be needed (e.g., the ER), or variable time slices defined by events (see end of chapter). All such "time slices", whether variable or fixed, will be referred to as "shift" in this chapter.
- "Demand" for personnel refers not only to the number of people needed, but also the mix of skills, qualifications, attitudes, and experience that together is needed to give optimal care to a patient or a set of patients.
- "Supply" has the same dimensions as demand, but will usually include the actual personnel who make up the team that will provide care.

Additional definitions will be provided prior to the discussions in later sections of this chapter.

3. THE STAGES LEADING TO STAFF SCHEDULING

There are several stages involved in determining the correct number of qualified caregivers being present to care for a particular set of patients on a particular shift.

3.1 Determining a measure of Demand for Staff

The first step is to establish a method of measuring the demand for caregivers based on the number and type of patients present to be cared for. The most basic measure is Nursing Hours per Patient Day ("NH/PD"), different at least by the type of Unit (Medical, ICU, Peds, etc.) where the patient is staying. (In radiology, it would be minutes of each skill or type of personnel required for each type of procedure). NH/PD may then be divided within the day by percentages per shift to create Nursing Hours per Patient Shift (NH/PS).

A step up in refinement on NH/PD and NH/PS is to classify patients into several (typically between three and seven) patient classes, where Class 1 requires X amount of time during the day shift (for example), Class 2 requires Y (Y>X), etc. For long-term (seasonal, annual) decision making, a typical mix of patients by class is then forecasted for a unit and shift to move to the next step (immediately below). (An even more granular method for measuring demand called "Event Driven Workload" is discussed at the end of the chapter).

3.2 Determination of Core Staffing ("Core Staffing")

Core staffing for a unit (such as a nursing unit) is the number of personnel by skill needed to provide optimal care to the average number of patients at an average acuity or need level, or an average mix of patients by class. For example, it may be determined that on nursing unit 6-West, on the day shift weekdays in the winter, on average we need a head nurse, three RNs, an LPN, three nurse aids, and a unit secretary. (Core staff will be different on the other shifts, probably different on weekends, and possibly different in other seasons). Of course, core staffing is to meet average demand: adjusting to a known level of demand is addressed below.

3.3 Determining Positions that Provide Core Staffing (Position Control")

In order to have staff available to meet core staffing 24 hours a day and seven days a week, a certain number of positions (by skill and unit) must be budgeted. This number includes the fact that coverage is 24/7, full time staff work 40 hours a week, some will be part time, vacation, orientation, professional development, sick time, turnover, etc. The result of this phase is a list of positions needed, by skill and unit, into which personnel are hired.

3.4 Recruiting and Hiring

Staff must be recruited and hired to fill those positions (a not insignificant task!).

3.5 Long Range Scheduling ("Scheduling")

Approximately three weeks before it is to start, the long range (four to eight weeks) schedule is determined, considering a host of factors such as equal weekend time, shift rotation, number of days worked in a row, special requests, scheduled vacation, etc. Typically, making the long range schedule manually can take a week, and it is typically published two weeks before it starts, so the best scheduling can do to try to have the right number and skill of staff is to schedule to fixed core staffing, knowing that actual demand will be different once that future day and shift arrives. Most typically for nursing, a new long range schedule must be rebuilt every four weeks (or the length of the schedule), although some institutions use "cyclical" schedules that cycle repeat over some cycle (multiple of length of schedule). For non-nursing, cyclical or fixed schedules are common.

3.6 Shift Staffing ("Shift Staffing")

Typically, several hours before a shift begins, a nurse manager attempts to determine the need for staff for that shift (or perhaps for the next two or three Shifts). She compares this with who is scheduled (from the long rage schedule) to come in, and makes decisions on how to adjust supply to meet demand. Recall that a shift may be of any length of time, so shift staffing takes place on whatever schedule the decision maker must use to ensure that demand is met by how shifts are defined for that unit.

This decision process - shift staffing - is the main topic of this chapter. After a brief history of the modeling of the scheduling problem and automation of staffing, we will focus on the difficulties of determining demand in the near future, and the difficulties of adjusting supply to meet demand (calling extra nurses in, moving a nurse from one unit to another, or arranging for a nurse to not come in).

4. MODELLING THE SCHEDULING AND STAFFING DECISIONS

Viewed from a modeling perspective, the scheduling and staffing decisions are quite different.

4.1 Scheduling

For scheduling, demand is well defined: it is core staffing, and has been previously determined. Supply is also known, defined as the 30 or so individuals that will be available to work these four weeks, their workloads (full time or part time), and their special rules such as only work on day shift or evening shift, no more than 40% on evenings, work a maximum of four days in a row ("work stretch"), every other weekend off, etc. This makes scheduling a difficult problem to fit into an optimization solution technique, but does make it possible to formulate for optimization.

Four Week Schedule for 8/1/2005 - 8/28/2005

Emp	Skill	8/1 Mo	8/2 Tu	8/3 We	8/4 Th	8/5 Fr	8/6 Sa	8/7 Su	8/8 Mo	8/9 Tu	8/10 We	8/11 Th	8/12 Fr	8/13 Sa	8/14 Su
Aroh, Kerry	LPN	7a-3p LPN	7a-3p LPN						7a-3p LPN	7a-3p LPN					
Arn, Kelly	RN		7a-3p RN	7a-3p RN	3p-11p	3p-11p Charg	11p-7a Charg		11p-7a Charg	7a-3p RN	11p-7a	3p-11p Charg			3p-11p
Cambell, Chris	NA		7a-3p NA	7a-3p NA	7a-3p NA	7a-3p NA	7a-3p NA		7a-3p NA	7a-3p NA	7a-3p NA	7a-3p NA	7a-3p NA		
Entz, Mark	NA	7a-3p NA			7a-3p NA				7a-3p NA	7a-3p NA					
Favro, Jill	LPN	7a-3p LPN		7a-3p LPN	3p-11p LPN	7a-3p LPN			3p-11p LPN	3p-11p LPN	3p-11p LPN	7a-3p LPN			
Gonzalez, Marbella	NA		11p-7a NA			3p-11p NA		7a-3p NA		11p-7a NA	11p-7a NA			7a-3p NA	
Hansen, Jane	LPN	7a-3p LPN	7a-3p LPN	7a-3p LPN				3p-11p LPN						7a-3p LPN	7a-3p LPN
Hiebert, Maurene	NA	11p-7a NA			3p-11p US	3p-11p US	7a-3p US	7a-3p US		3p-11p NA	3p-11p NA	3p-11p NA		7a-3p US	7a-3p US
Higgins, Rebbeca	RN	3p-11p			11p-7a	11p-7a	7a-3p RN	7a-3p RN						Off Off	Off Off
Jaderborg, Joy	RN	11p-7a Charg	3p-11p	3p-11p			7a-3p RN	7a-3p RN		3p-11p	7a-3p RN	3p-11p	3p-11p	Off Off	Off Off
Jankord, Anna	RN		3p-11p	3p-11p		11p-7a	Off Off	Off Off	11p-7a		11p-7a			7a-3p RN	7a-3p RN
Jansen, Silvia	RN		3p-11p	11p-7a	11p-7a		Off Off	Off Off	11p-7a	11p-7a	11p-7a			7a-3p RN	7a-3p RN

Emp	Skill	8/15 Mo	8/16 Tu	8/17 We	8/18 Th	8/19 Fr	8/20 Sa	8/21 Su	8/22 Mo	8/23 Tu	8/24 We	8/25 Th	8/26 Fr	8/27 Sa	8/28 Su
Aroh, Kerry	LPN	7a-3p LPN	7a-3p LPN						7a-3p LPN	7a-3p LPN					
Arn, Kelly	RN			11a-3p RN	3p-11p Charg	7a-3p Charg	3p-11p Charg	3p-11p	11p-7a Charg	7a-3p Charg	11p-7a Charg	11a-3p RN		3p-11p	
Cambell, Chris	NA	7a-3p NA	7a-3p NA	7a-3p NA	7a-3p NA	7a-3p NA			7a-3p NA	7a-3p NA	7a-3p NA	7a-3p NA	7a-3p NA		
Entz, Mark	NA	7a-3p NA	7a-3p NA						7a-3p NA	7a-3p NA					
Favro, Jill	LPN			3p-11p LPN	7a-3p LPN				3p-11p LPN		7a-3p LPN		3p-11p LPN		
Gonzalez, Marbella	NA	3p-11p NA			7a-3p NA	11p-7a NA	7a-3p NA	3p-11p NA	3p-11p NA	11p-7a NA		7a-3p NA	11p-7a NA	3p-11p NA	
Hansen, Jane	LPN		3p-11p LPN			3p-11p LPN		3p-11p LPN						7a-3p LPN	
Hiebert, Maurene	NA	3p-11p US	3p-11p US	3p-11p US			7a-3p US	7a-3p US		3p-11p US	3p-11p US	3p-11p US		7a-3p US	7a-3p US
Higgins, Rebbeca	RN	11p-7a	11p-7a				7a-3p RN	7a-3p RN			3p-11p	11p-7a		Off Off	Off Off
Jaderborg, Joy	RN	11p-7a Charg	11p-7a Charg	11p-7a			7a-3p RN	7a-3p RN		11p-7a Charg	3p-11p	7a-3p RN		11p-7a Charg	11p-7a
Jankord, Anna	RN			11p-7a	3p-11p		Off Off	Off Off	11p-7a			11p-7a	3p-11p	7a-3p RN	7a-3p RN
Jansen, Silvia	RN			11p-7a		3p-11p	Off Off	Off Off	11p-7a	3p-11p			11p-7a	7a-3p RN	7a-3p RN

Figure 7-1: Four week schedule showing when each employee (left column) is scheduled to work. This is the first page of a three-page schedule, for approximately 30 employees on a particular unit.

Figure 7-1 shows a four-week schedule generated by software that "solves" the scheduling problem. Variables are Nurse N (by name) working on Shift B on Day D, and constraints are 1) a minimum and maximum number of nurses of Skill S for each shift and day, 2) that Nurse N works exactly her workload (e.g. five times a week), 3) that she works only on <u>her</u> shifts (e.g. day and evening), 4) no more than four days in a row, and 5) a host of other work constraints. The objective function is a combination of minimizing how far off actual staffing is to core staffing, and maximizing the "quality" of the nurses' individual schedules as defined in terms of things such as work stretch, rotation (working on a shift other than her "home" shift), requests, etc. Formulated correctly, the objective function contains many non-linear items (e.g. a shortage of two nurses is much greater than twice the shortage of one, a work stretch of 8 days in a row is much worse than twice 4 days in a row, etc.), variables are integer, and thus the problem does not readily fit a optimization solution technique. Most often an individualized heuristic solution technique (usually of the "branch and bound" type) is designed to find several "good" solutions, if not the optimal to the scheduling problem.

4.2 Shift Staffing

The shift staffing decision, on the other hand, is much fuzzier, and is stochastic rather than deterministic. Here we're dealing with many aspects that are unknown, the three most difficult being 1) what actual demand will be the next shift or two or three, 2) who is able (and willing) to be called in, and 3) who among those Scheduled to come in will not "show" (for whatever reason). The most difficult of these is what demand will be next shift (or two or three shifts).

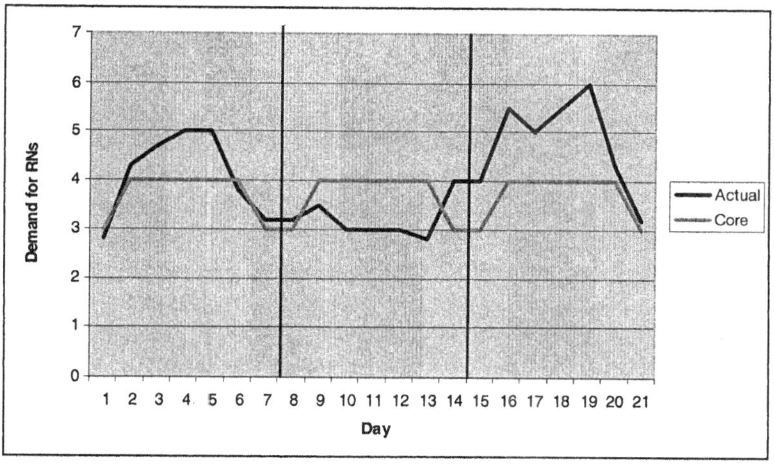

Figure 7-2: Demand for RNs for the day shift over a three week period. Core staffing follows a "fixed" pattern, dipping on the weekends. Actual demand follows the number of patients actually on the unit and for each a measure of how much RN time they require.

Figure 7-2 shows the actual behavior of demand, versus core staffing, for RNs for the day shift over a three week period for a typical nursing unit in a hospital. (This is actually a "moderately" variable example such as a medical or surgical unit: an ICU would show much more variation and a psych unit much less). Clearly core staffing, while useful for approximating demand for recruiting, position control, and scheduling, is not going to closely match actual demand for the shift staffing decision.

The shift staffing decision in hospitals today is typically done for the next shift or two (sometimes a weekend), using best professional estimates of what demand will be, what supply will be, and calling in nurses from previously established pools of employees or free agents to fill expected holes in staffing. What results is a fair amount of chaos, and unhappy employees being called in at the last minute. More seriously, compromises in staffing must be endured because of the lack of choices of nurses to come in, based on lack of knowledge of demand beyond this shift.

The modeling of the shift staffing decision will require dealing with the uncertainty of demand and supply, will be limited to the "near future" (zero to eight days ahead), and will require building in professional judgment to supplement what will always be estimates (projections and predictions) of supply and demand.

5. HISTORY OF AUTOMATED SCHEDULING AND STAFFING

The scheduling problem was initially modeled and solved in the late seventies (Warner, 1976; Warner, 1991), and by the early eighties two companies were offering automated staff scheduling systems on personal PCs that included position control, a scheduler that "generated" a good quality four week schedule (saving many hours of unpopular work by nurse managers), and a framework for shift staffing. This framework was a huge help by providing accurate data, accurate calculations, and numerous "roster" type reports of who will work when and where. The weakness remained the reliance of a mildly retrospective (four to twelve hours old) measurement of demand, and no support for pushing the decision more than a shift or two into the future.

The automation of scheduling and support for staffing was a large success – by the nineties, some 60%-70% of hospitals over 100 beds were using some sort of computer system. Scheduling took much less time, was accurate and more "fair" to those scheduled, and very useful reports were produced. Staffing support was also a hit, increasing accuracy and communications with easily printed rosters and reports.

But until 2005 none of the commercially available systems had approached the shift staffing problem as a probabilistic model, required for pushing the decisions into the near future. Even with a helpful (deterministic) framework, decision makers were stuck in the present.

New computer technology has of course played a significant role in automated staff scheduling systems. The first systems were on PCs with dual floppies, then hard disks (with 10MB of storage!). In the mid to late eighties, systems became networked. Then in the late nineties the Internet added new value by allowing access to individual employees, managers, and executives wherever they happened to be. One current system is designed in a "job centric" mode, where employees "see" the system on the Internet in a way that's relevant to them, managers "see" another view, and there are separate views or "dashboards" for the staffing office and for executives.

6. MOVING SHIFT STAFFING INTO THE NEAR FUTURE

The remainder of this chapter focuses on a significant improvement to the shift staffing decision – moving shift staffing from its present four to eight hours ahead to four to eight days ahead. The benefits of this redefinition of the problem are:

1) Much greater flexibility in deciding who will be called in: there may be only one or two possible staff to call in with a four-hour notice, where there may be 20 or 30 who can be called in with a four-day notice. This flexibility allows the decision maker to use criteria such as skills, experience (on this unit or total experience), cost, qualifications, attitudes, willingness to come in, how often a person was called before, etc.
2) Higher satisfaction of staff that are called in: they now get notice in time to arrange work time with personal time, which is difficult with short notice. It gives staff much more of a say in their work time – a major concern of 24/7 employees.

This redefinition will involve three elements that will be discussed in turn:

1) Forecasting demand into the near future
2) Predicting "no shows" (staff scheduled to come in but for some reason will not show up)
3) A decision support system that supports the probabilistic nature of the environment of the decision, allowing professional judgment and "best practices" to balance the accuracy of the forecasts and predictions.

7. FORECASTING DEMAND: PROJECTION AND PREDICTION

The model uses a "best information available" approach to forecasting demand, combining projecting the behavior of need by current patients until they leave the system, and as they leave backfilling with new admissions based on available future information (where available) and predicted census. The result is a simulation of what is expected to happen in terms of demand for caregivers.

7.1 Projecting Demand

Projecting demand is the use of information about what "phase" each patient is in within their typical "care pattern of need over time" within the hospital (their "care pattern"), and then projecting that patient through the remaining phases of their care pattern. For example, a total hip replacement might have a typical "caregiver need" care pattern defined in terms of need for RN care, as in Figure 3.

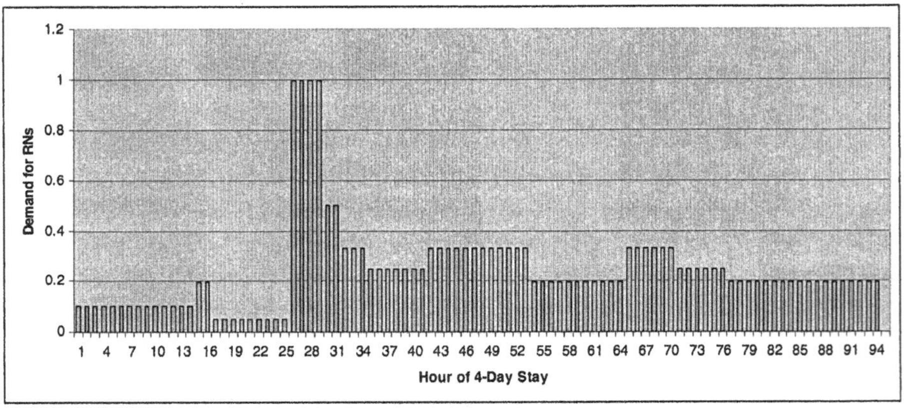

Figure 7-3: "Total Hip" demand care pattern. Demand for RNs of a typical total hip replacement, by hour of a four-day stay. Hours 1-14 (Phase 1) have low care need as patient is admitted in PM for surgery next day. Hours 15-16 (Phase 2) are OR prep, then patient is out of unit between hours 17-25. Hours 26-29 are immediately after arriving back on unit, etc.

At any point in time from Figure 7-3, the remaining care pattern will project the care needed for this patient type until this patient is discharged or transferred out. By projecting each patient by their predetermined care pattern, and summing over a time slice (such as a shift or an hour on the second day in the future), the total demand for RNs can be projected for that time slice for all present patients who have yet to leave the system.

The predetermined care patterns are established by:

1) Defining discrete "types" of patients (for example, total hip replacement for patients under 70 years old).
2) Using a suitable sample of patients of this type to define the phases they go through, how much caregiver time is needed at each phase, and building a "typical" care pattern for patients of this type.

As many patient types as desired can be defined, with accuracy improving (with diminishing returns) with more types. For a surgical unit, between 6 and 12 types may return sufficient accuracy for the application described herein.

Each phase in the care pattern of need will be in terms of caregiver demand measured (from less to more granular) by:

- Nursing hours per patient day for that phase (corrected for the length of each state – eight hours, four hours, etc.)
- What patient "Class" this type of patient can be expected to be in this phase
- A measurement based on events that are expected to happen to this type of patient over time, where changing from one need level to another is an event, as well as certain procedures, etc. (See Event Driven Workload at the end of the chapter).

The above measure of demand will give direct care. To direct care must be added caregiver time on the unit not devoted to any one patient. This is typically done as a percentage of time, or a fixed number of minutes per person.

(The "care pattern" type of projection will give the best results in terms of projecting demand, but a less precise "length of stay" model may be used where care patterns cannot be established. This model will again look at all patients currently on a unit, but instead of a demand care pattern, only an estimate of the remaining length of stay is made. This is used to project the census of current patients until they leave, and is blended with the census prediction model below to forecast total census. Then a NH/PD or NH/PS or other method can be applied to transform census into demand).

7.2 Predicting Census and Admissions

Using the projection of a given number of patients starting at time zero, the unit will "lose" patients as they are discharged or transferred out. These will be "replaced" in the simulation model with a certain number of new admissions (and in-transfers) each shift. The number of new admissions and in-transfers is determined by either:

- Using pre-scheduled admissions data (including the OR schedule and other schedules – see discussion below), or
- Predicting census (Figure 7-4) for that unit and shift, and comparing predicted census to projected census (total patients still in some phase of their care pattern this shift), and base predicted admissions on the difference. For example, if predicted census is 33 and projected census is 30, the model "admits" three more patients. These new admits have their own care pattern definition ("new admit"), and the model then projects (simulates) this patients care pattern as it does for the other patients.

Even if pre-scheduled admission data is available, emergency admissions will need to be predicted to add to scheduled admissions. The model for predicting emergency admissions is the more accurate of:

- Correlating emergency admissions to projected (simulated) census, subject to minimum and maximum emergency admissions based on historical data, or
- Predicting total census directly (see below) and subtracting from it projected census (including the pre scheduled admissions).

The census prediction model is a bit more complex than projection, as there is a host of factors that influence census. Considering that the model will be predicting census for the near future of a few days, many variables that are typically used to predict census for longer periods (growth, changes in length of stay, seasonality, weather, etc.) were deemed to not be appropriate. Instead, the census prediction model uses pattern and autocorrelation type methods.

No one predictor method fits each unit (think of the difference between ICU and psych), or even how far out the prediction is being made (autocorrelation methods are superior in the very near future, while pattern type predictors – such as day of week correctors – are superior after a few days.) The "best" census prediction model for Unit U on Shift S on a future Day D is determined by:

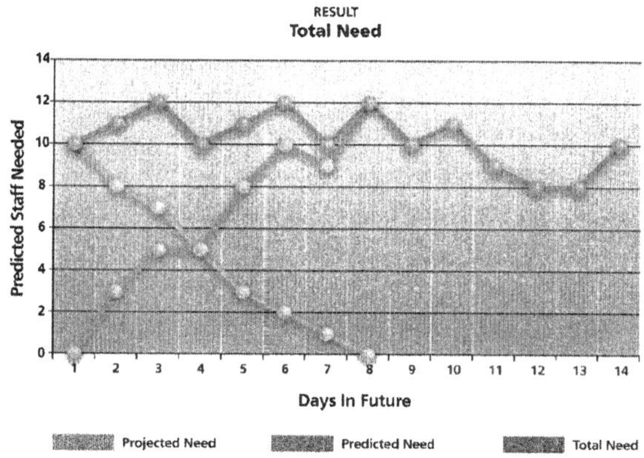

Figure 7-4: Contribution of projection of current patients and prediction of new admissions over forecasting horizon. In Days 1-3, most of the forecast is from current patients. After Day 4, when many have been discharged, more of the forecast is from predicted new admits (following their need behavior). At some point (Day 8), all current patients have left the system.

1) Establishing a measure of "better". In this case, a weighted "score" of how often a particular method generates demand from its census prediction that is within 0.5 caregivers, is within 1.5 caregivers, is within 2.5 caregivers, or is off by more than 2.5 caregivers is calculated. The weights placed on the errors to make up a "score" are established using professional judgment of the "cost" of a projection being off that much. This cost is a balance of making decisions too soon (possibly wasting money) versus making them too late (and not having as many choices).
2) Establishing a "pool" of "candidate" predictors that an evaluation program can use as variables. For example, average census is a "candidate", as is average census corrected for day of week. So is the prior day's census, the average of the last x days (x varying between 2 and, say 7), and a weighted average of the last x days, where the weights themselves define a new variable.
3) Using a special-purpose branch-and-bound search algorithm that intelligently "tries" thousands of possible <u>combinations</u> of candidate predictors on one or two years of past data for this unit, and picks the one that would have produced the best score on this data using the criteria of one).

More specifically, candidate engines to be evaluated for a Unit u for a particular Shift s in the future are in the form of:

$$F_{u,s}= \quad A_{u,s}*OA_{u}*DOW_{,u,s} + B_{u,s}*(Z_{i=1,T}\, W_{u,s.i}C_{u,s.i}/DOW_{u,,i})*DOW_{u,s}$$

Where:

$F_{u,s}=$ the forecasted census for a Shift s on Unit u in a future forecasting horizon

Subject to:

$F_{u,s} < MAX_{u,s,}$ where $MAX_{u,s,}$ is the maximum census should be for Shift s on Unit u

$F_{u,s} > MIN_{u,s,}$ where $MIN_{u,s,}$ is the minimum census should be for Shift s on Unit u

A and B are weights that balance the day-of-week ("DOW") effect with the autocorrelation effect, such that:

A and B are between 0 and 1, and A+B=1

OA_{u} is the overall average census for the Unit for this "season"

$DOW_{u,s}$ is a day of week factor which "corrects" OA_{u} for DOW on which s falls

$i=1,T$ is a shift in the immediate past, and T the number of such shifts looking "backward" from today on which an autocorrelation estimate is to be based

$W_{u,s.i}$ is a weight placed on the DOW corrected census for past Shift i, i=1,T

$ZW_{u,s.i=1,T}= 1$

$C_{u,s.i}$ is the census for that past Shift i

$DOW_{u,,i}$ is the DOW "corrector" for the DOW of past Shift i

OA and DOW are constants based on a year or so of data from this unit, and the C is available to the search algorithm from past data. A candidate engine is defined by different values for A, B, and $W_{i,\, i=1,T}$. Thus there are an infinite number of candidate engines. The branch-and- bound search engine "intelligently" evaluates different combinations of A, B, and W, and picks the one that produces the best "score" (defined above). The search engine looks "intelligently" at a finite number of candidates for evaluation.

The result is a census predictor "engine" for each unit, and shift of each day in the forecasting horizon (i.e. a three-day predictor engine for the ICU is different than the two-day predictor engine). Accuracies of these engines vary widely with the type of unit (not too good for ICU, great for psych, very useful for units in between like medical units and surgical units). In all cases, the predictor is significantly superior to average census, on which core staffing is based.

7.1 Simulation: Combining Projection and Prediction

Thus forecasting (or simulating) demand for a unit for several days ahead is performed by

1. Projecting all present patients out one shift on their care patterns
2. If known, adding prescheduled admissions for this shift with their expected care patterns
3. Predict emergency (or otherwise unknown) admissions by either:
   - Predicting census for that shift, comparing it with projected census, and admitting the difference (subject to minimum and maximum admissions by day of week), or
   - Predicting admissions directly
4. Place each new admission into the care pattern that best represents the admission
5. Sum across all patient care patterns (projected, pre-scheduled admissions and emergency admissions) to get total demand
6. Add in indirect time, if appropriate
7. Project all patients (the Projected plus the new admits) another shift
8. Repeat steps 2-7 until end of horizon.

7.4 Predicting Admissions Directly from Other Sources

As indicated above, a more accurate prediction of admissions may be available from other sources within the hospital rather than predicting census and subtracting projected census. Fortunately, much of this information is easily obtainable from the hospital's HL7 interface system. For example the Admissions Discharge Transfer (ADT) system may have future information on pre-scheduled admissions. Scheduled admissions to certain units (elective surgery, etc.) may be a good source for admission predictions, as well as the OR schedule. As mentioned above, to the pre- scheduled admissions must be added a prediction piece for emergency admissions. Many units mostly serve emergencies to start with, so that scheduled admissions will be less help. The key here is to use the best information available, and to be able to fit the model to the data available.

8. PREDICTING NO-SHOWS

No-shows are predicted by applying the probability that each scheduled individual does not show up for that particular day of week and shift. This probability is calculated from the known number of times a person did not show in the past, divided by the times they were supposed to show. If the sample size by DOW and shift is not large enough to get an accurate probability for an individual, the fall back is the individual by DOW. The next fall back is the overall probability of a no show for this individual, followed by the average no show by DOW and shift for nurses of her skill on the unit. Such data are readily available from staff scheduling systems, and often from personnel or time and attendance systems.

9. PROACTIVE PROTOCOLS

Each decision to place a nurse on duty involves hundreds of dollars, and serious implications on quality, safety, and throughput. So in a probabilistic environment like this one, professional judgment and "best practices" must be incorporated as part of the decision support system.

In this case, proactive protocols are developed for each unit, shift, skill, shortage and day in the forecasting horizon which spells out the "optimal" action to be taken. For example, when looking four days out on the medical unit, the night shift is forecasted to be short three RNs. (This is from the projection plus prediction of section 7.4, added to the prediction of no shows of Section 9.) The proactive protocol for this situation (which is displayed for the decision maker) might be:

1) Call one RN in for the shift.
2) Develop a list of four candidates that could come in if you need another
3) Flag this shift and check again tomorrow

Tomorrow, the forecast will cover three days, with higher expected accuracy, and only two RNs may be projected to be needed. In that case, the Protocol may say secure the second one, or wait. The Protocols are constructed by the expert staffers in the hospital to balance the cost of calling in too many with the costs of waiting until the last minute. By publishing such Protocols for the decision maker, "best practices" will evolve over time as lessons are learned.

10. THE STAFFING SYSTEM

Recall that the traditional staff scheduling system has available most of the information needed to make the shift staffing decision:

1) Who is scheduled to come in each day and shift.
2) Their skills, qualifications, etc.
3) Minima and maxima of how many to staff by skill
4) A framework for adding to or adjusting rosters on screen
5) Lists of staff by skill, availability, with telephone numbers, etc.
6) Other personnel data to make the decisions

What is added here is the demand forecasting and no show predictions, along with the proactive protocols to enhance the framework and allow it to be "pushed" into the near future.

Figures 7-5 shows projected staffing need (incorporating demand forecasting and no show predictions) for the ICU unit for three days ahead. The decision maker can look at all three shifts (Figure 7-5a), or drill down to one shift by skill (Figure 7-5b), then bring up the proactive protocol for this situation (Figure 7-5c). From this screen certain actions may be taken such as pulling up lists of nurses by criteria (availability, qualifications, etc.), and posting the need to the internet dashboards of certain staff members. Call-ins are made by phone or email (and/or through the system's communication system), and adjustments made to staff on the screen. Any adjustments immediately update the situation, bringing up a new proactive protocol for the new situation

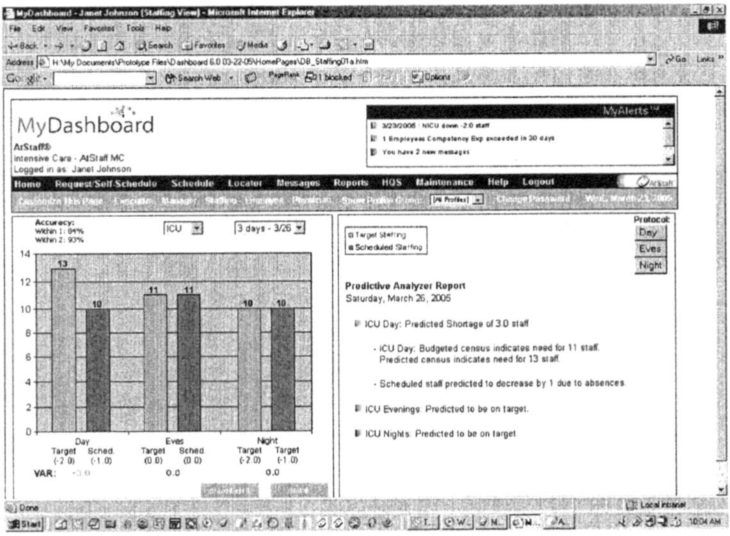

Figure 7-5a: Forecasted staffing three days ahead for the ICU. To left is a comparison, by Shift, of forecasted need (in blue), versus what is predicted to come in (red). For the day shift, the system is predicting being short three nurses.

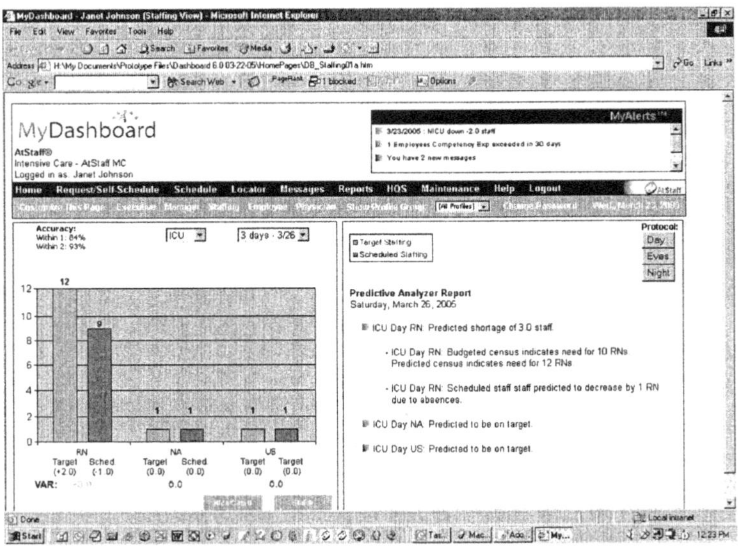

Figure 7-5b: Forecasted demand for the day shift "drilled down" to skill. The three forecasted needed nurses are all RNs.

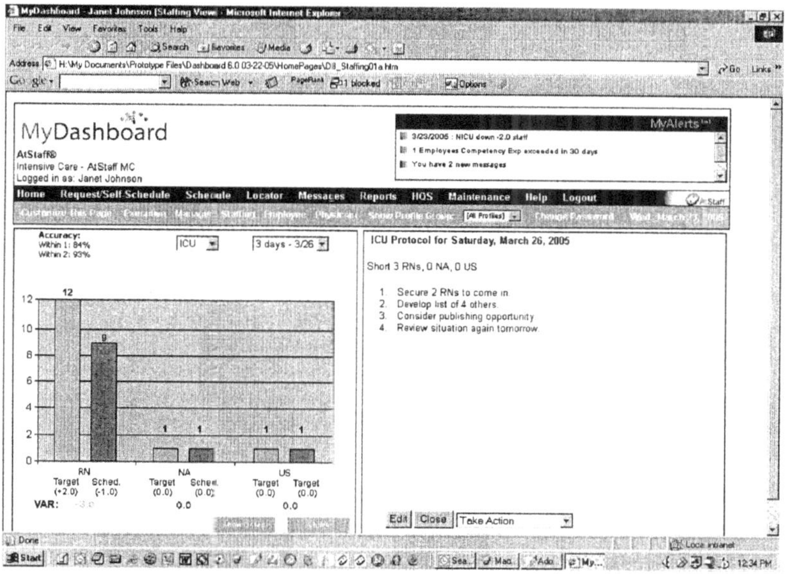

Figure 7-5c: Proactive Protocol for this situation pulled up (right of screen)

11. CONCLUSIONS AND FUTURE EXTENSIONS

The above discussion attempts to place staff management as a critical process for not only optimal throughput of patients in hospitals, but also cost, quality, safety, and staff satisfaction.

11.1 Conclusions

Significant improvements can be made to traditional staff management by moving the staffing decision from the present to the near future. Benefits are improved balance between supply and demand in terms of the number of staff, but perhaps more importantly in the quality, qualifications, motivation, and other less quantitative measures of quality and efficiency. Moreover, by placing the decision out four days rather than four hours, staff satisfaction increases. To move the decision into the near future requires a rather complex mixture of

- Projecting (simulating) current patients and their staff needs into the future
- Predicting (or otherwise obtaining) new admissions

- A decision support system that performs the projections and predictions, displays all options and information to the decision maker, and offers a professional "best practices" framework for those decisions that balance the cost of waiting too late with the costs of acting too early.

Two important side effects of moving staffing decisions from the present to the near future are:

- The establishment of a "mindset" within staff management that things and acts calmly in the near future rather than in chaos in the present, and
- Elevating staff management at the executive level by displaying the effects of staffing in the future to them in the form of executive "dashboards" from the decision support system.

11.2 Extensions

One extension to the work discussed above includes a finer measure of demand for staff using event driven workload, where instead of assuming a patient stays in a "class" or "level" of need for an entire shift, demand is established by "time stamped" events (such as a procedure, return from or, accident, change of condition, etc.) That happens within the shift.

An event driven approach "sharpens" all levels of staff management, from determination of core staffing straight through to shift staffing. In addition, retrospectively, it allows a feedback loop to continually refine how well the different parts of staff management perform, as a finer measurement of demand improves decisions at every level.

A second "extension" is represented by improved sources of information about pre-scheduled admissions and events. These may come through the HL7 interface from the ADT system, for OR schedules, bed control, or other sources. The more information of this type that is available to the simulation, the more accurate the forecasts, and the more aggressive the proactive protocols can be, providing more options to improve the matching of supply to demand, and enhancing employee satisfaction.

12. REFERENCES

Kovner, C., Gergen, P.J. (1998). Nurse staffing levels and adverse events following surgery in U.S. Hospitals. *Image J Nurs Sch,* 30 (4).

Litvak, E., et al. (2005). Managing unnecessary variability in patient demand to reduce nursing stress and improve patient safety, *Journal on Quality and Patient Safety*, June.

Needleman, J, et al. (2002). Nurse-staffing levels and quality of care in hospitals in the United States. *New England Journal of Medicine*, 346, May, 30.

Warner, M., et al. (1991). Automated nurse scheduling. *Journal of the Society for Health Systems*, V2#2.

Warner, M. (1976). Scheduling nursing personnel according to nursing preference: A mathematical programming approach. *Operations Research,* V.24.

Chapter 8

DISCRETE-EVENT SIMULATION OF HEALTH CARE SYSTEMS

Sheldon H. Jacobson[1], Shane N. Hall[2] and James R. Swisher[3]
[1,2]Department of Mechanical and Industrial Engineering, 1206 West Green Street (MC-244), University of Illinois at Urbana-Champaign, Urbana, IL 61801-2906
[3]Mary Washington Hospital, 1001 Sam Perry Boulevard, Fredericksburg, VA 22401

Abstract: Over the past forty years, health care organizations have faced ever-increasing pressures to deliver quality care while facing rising costs, lower reimbursements, and new regulatory demands. Discrete-event simulation has become a popular and effective decision-making tool for the optimal allocation of scarce health care resources to improve patient flow, while minimizing health care delivery costs and increasing patient satisfaction. The proliferation of increasingly sophisticated discrete-event simulation software packages has resulted in a large number of new application opportunities, including more complex implementations. In addition, combined optimization and simulation tools allow decision-makers to quickly determine optimal system configurations, even for complex integrated facilities. This chapter provides an overview of discrete-event simulation modeling applications to health care clinics and integrated health care systems (e.g. hospitals, outpatient clinics, emergency departments, and pharmacies) over the past forty years.

Key words: discrete-event simulation health care services, hospitals, clinics

Acknowledgements: The authors wish to thank Dr. R.W. Hall for his comments and feedback on an earlier draft of this chapter, resulting in a significantly improved final version. The first author has been supported in part by the National Science Foundation (DMI-0222597, DMI-0457176).

1. INTRODUCTION

Over the past 40 years, escalating health care costs have provided researchers and health care professionals with the impetus to identify new approaches to improve the efficiency of health care operations and to reduce delivery costs. Discrete-event simulation has become a popular tool for health care decision-makers to support their efforts in achieving these objectives. Discrete-event simulation is an operations research modeling and analysis methodology that permits end-users (such as hospital administrators or clinic managers) to evaluate the efficiency of existing health care delivery systems, to ask "what if?" questions, and to design new health care delivery system operations. Discrete-event simulation can also be used as a forecasting tool to assess the potential impact of changes on patient flow, to examine asset allocation needs (such as in staffing levels or in physical capacity), and/or to investigate the complex relationships among different system variables (such as the rate of patient arrivals or the rate of patient service delivery). Such information allows health care administrators and analysts to identify management alternatives that can be used to reconfigure existing health care systems, to improve system performance or design, and/or to plan new systems, without altering the existing system.

The application of discrete-event simulation in the analysis of health care systems has become increasingly more accepted by health care decision-makers as a viable tool for improving operations and reducing costs. This is due in part to the large number of successful discrete-event simulation health care studies reported in the literature, as well as ongoing enhancements to simulation software packages that make their application to health care less arduous. This chapter surveys the large body of discrete-event simulation modeling and analysis efforts that have been reported to address health care delivery system problems and provides an up-to-date, comprehensive collection of articles describing these applications.

This chapter focuses on articles that analyze single or multi-facility health care clinics, including outpatient clinics, emergency departments, surgical centers, orthopedics departments, and pharmacies. An extensive taxonomy of the literature over the past 30 years is presented (though some relevant earlier articles are also referenced). Discrete-event simulation studies on wide area or regional health care community planning, ambulance location service, gurney transportation, disease control planning, and studies that do not address some aspect of patient flow are not discussed. For a complete review of the literature in health care prior to the mid-1970s, see England and Roberts (1978) and Valinsky (1975).

Several excellent review articles have appeared that examine conducting a discrete-event simulation study in health care clinics. England and Roberts (1978) provide a thorough and comprehensive survey on the application of discrete-event simulation in 21 health care settings (including laboratory studies, emergency services, and the national health care system). Their detailed survey cites 92 discrete-event simulation models out of 1,200 models reviewed, including all published models through 1978. Klein et al. (1993) present a bibliography that includes operational decision making, medical decision making, and system dynamics planning models. Smith-Daniels et al. (1988) present a literature review pertaining to acquisition decisions (e.g., facility location, aggregate capacity, and facility sizing) and allocation decisions (e.g., inpatient admissions scheduling, surgical facility scheduling, and ambulatory care scheduling), including several operations research methodologies, such as heuristics, Markov chains, linear programming, and queuing theory, as well as discrete-event simulation. Jun et al. (1999) present a survey of discrete-event simulation applications to clinic design and analysis. Note that this chapter builds upon the Jun et al. survey and provides new updates that have been reported since 1999.

2. FUNDAMENTALS OF DISCRETE-EVENT SIMULATION IN HEALTH CARE

An important advantage of using discrete-event simulation, over other modeling techniques like linear programming or Markov chain analysis, when modeling a health care clinic is the capacity to model complex patient flows through health care clinics, and to play "what if" games by changing the patient flow rules and policies. The success or failure of a discrete-event simulation study within a health care environment often depends on a standard sequence of carefully followed steps. Law and Kelton (2001) outline the key steps necessary to undertake a successful simulation study. These steps include the formulation of the problem and the plan of study, the collection of data and the conceptual model design, the validation of the model, the constructions of the computer representation of the model, the verification of the model, the design of experiments needed to address the problem being studied, production runs using the computer model, the statistical analysis of the data obtained from the production runs, and the interpretation of the results with respect to the system under study. Eldabi and Paul (2001) notes that a key issue in the success of health care simulation studies is the careful formulation of the problem statement, and the buy-in of all stakeholders. In manufacturing simulation studies, modeling and data errors may lead to unexpected costs and poor performance. However, in health care simulation studies, such errors can ultimately lead to lives lost and the associated liabilities surrounding such events. Therefore, the tolerable margin for error in the design and application of health care simulation models is significantly more limited. Such restrictions provide obstacles and barriers that can only be overcome through the highest attention to detail and accuracy, as well as fluid communization between all stakeholders.

The additional references that follow address the fundamental principles for performing a discrete-event simulation study of a healthcare system. These are excellent references that provide detailed methodologies for a successful simulation study in the context of healthcare. Hence, for brevity, these methodologies are omitted here. Banks and Carson (1987) and Mahachek (1992) provide structured tutorials on the steps that should be followed when conducting a health care system discrete-event simulation study. Mahachek (1992) also provides details of a discrete-event simulation study on hospital patient flow. Kanon (1974) shows how one could use sample data to build a discrete-event simulation model of a simplified problem in a hospital setting. Eldabi and Paul (2001) discuss an iterative approach to modeling health care systems, while Harper (2002) and Vissers (1998) discuss the general framework and process for operational modeling in heath care. Isken et al. (1999) present a general simulation modeling framework for outpatient obstetrical clinics that is applicable to other types of outpatient clinics. Finally, Morrison and Bird (2003) detail a simulation methodology for improving patient care in ambulatory heath care.

Lowery (1998, 1996) and Standridge (1999) discuss issues facing an analyst when using discrete-event simulation to study a health care system, such as what type of problems are appropriate to be addressed using simulation, the degree of model complexity, the definition of input distributions, model documentation and validation, and the interpretation and reporting of findings. Sanchez et al. (2000) discuss other emerging issues that affect a successful health care discrete-event simulation study, such as the expansion of information technology and the combining of information technology with traditional process models. Baldwin et al. (2004) discuss an iterative approach to health care simulation modeling that is meant to increase the understanding of the problem to decision-makers and enhance communication between stakeholders of the health care system that is being modeled. All of these articles provide useful information for practitioners interested in using discrete-event simulation to study health care systems and issues. Moreover, these articles stress the ability of discrete-event simulation to aptly address the unique factors inherent to health care systems.

Discrete-event simulation models that have been used to analyze health care delivery systems have primarily focused in two areas: (1) optimization and analysis of patient flow and (2) allocation of assets to improve the delivery of services. The first area considers patient flow through hospitals and clinics, with the primary objective of identifying efficiencies that can be realized to improve patient throughput, reduce patient waiting times, and improve medical staff utilization. The second area considers the number of beds and staffing requirements necessary to provide efficient and effective health care services. This section reviews the breadth of studies and approaches taken in these two distinct, though related, areas.

2.1 Patient Flow Optimization and Analysis

As hospitals and clinics face ongoing competition for their services, they must be able to provide fast and efficient health care in order to attract new patients and retain their existing patients. High quality, efficient patient flow is a function of high volume patient throughput, low patient waiting times, short total visit times, and low levels of staff overtime coupled with the maintenance of reasonable staff utilization rates and low physician idle times. Three areas that have a significant impact on patient flow are patient scheduling and admissions, patient routing and flow schemes, and appointment scheduling and availability of resources.

2.1.1 Outpatient Scheduling

Outpatient scheduling focus on procedures for setting the timetable to match patients with caregivers, both in terms of when these appointments are set and their length of time. This involves rules or policies that determine when appointments can be made (such as morning versus afternoon) and the length of time (or spacing) between appointments. This may also include the specific types of caregiver who will be responsible for treating patients and the physical space that will be required to deliver the necessary care and treatment. All these issues have a significant impact on how health care personnel and facility resources can be optimally used such that patient flow is maximized without incurring additional costs or excessive patient waiting.

The majority of discrete-event simulation studies that focus on patient scheduling and admissions are focused on outpatient clinics. Guo et al. (2004) outline a simulation framework for analyzing scheduling rules for outpatient clinics. This framework, termed Patient Scheduling Simulation Model (PSSM), addresses four key components of an outpatient clinic scheduling system: demand for appointments, supply of physician time blocks, patient flow, and the scheduling algorithm. The study provides a demonstration of the framework for a pediatric ophthalmology clinic and discusses some challenges for adapting the framework to other settings. Outpatient clinics typically schedule appointments over some future time horizon. A discrete-event simulation study of rolling horizon appointment scheduling is presented by Rohleder and Klassen (2002). This study considers two common management policies: Overload Rules and Rule Delay. The Overload Rules policy considers scheduling methods such as overtime and double booking that are used when demand is high, while the Rule Delay policy determines when to implement Overload Rules. The authors conclude that determining the "best" scheduling policy depends on the measures of performances that are deemed most important by decision-makers.

Fetter and Thompson (1965) present one of the earliest discrete-event simulation studies conducted in the area of individual clinical facility operations for outpatient clinics. They analyze physician utilization rates with respect to patient waiting time by using different input variables (such as patient load, patient early or late arrival patterns, no-show rates, walk-in rates, appointment scheduling intervals, physician service times, interruptions, and physician lunch and coffee breaks). They concluded that if the physician appointment load increases from 60% to 90% (capacity), the physician idle time decreases by 160 hours and patient waiting time increases by 1600 hours (cumulative over a fifty day period). With such a capacity increase, they suggest that the physician's time would have to be worth ten times the patient's time to justify such a shift in patient scheduling and admission policies.

Smoothing the distribution of patient demand has been used to improve patient throughput and patient waiting times in outpatient clinics. Smith and Warner (1971) compare patients arriving according to a uniformly scheduled arrival pattern versus patients arriving in a highly variable manner. They show that the uniformly scheduled arrival pattern can decrease the average length of stay at the clinic by over 40% (from 40.6 minutes to 24 minutes), due to the more predictable use of resources when patient arrivals are uniformly spaced. Similarly, Rising et al. (1973) show that increasing the number of appointments slots in an outpatient clinic on those days that had the least number of walk-ins smoothed the demand on the physician, resulting in a 13.4% increase in patient throughput and less clinic overtime. Kho and Johnson (1976) and Kachhal et al. (1981) show that in a radiology department and in an ear, nose, and throat clinic, respectively, performance can be improved when demand for outpatient services is evenly distributed.

In contrast to uniform scheduling, a number of alternative scheduling rules have been studied. Bailey (1952) studies an outpatient clinic scheduling rule (where two patients are scheduled at the beginning of every session, morning or afternoon, with all other patients scheduled at equal intervals) that yields acceptable results for both patients (in terms of waiting times) and staff (in terms of utilization), assuming that all patients have the same service time distributions and that all patients arrive at their designated times. Smith et al. (1979) use a modified-wave scheduling scheme (where more patients are scheduled at the beginning of each hour and less towards the end of the hour, thus allowing the physician to absorb unexpected delays and return back to schedule at the end of each hour) for an outpatient clinic to find the maximum number of patients a physician could see while minimizing patient waiting time. They show that this schedule is superior to the uniform scheduling scheme, in terms of patient flow and patient waiting times. Williams et al. (1967) study the relationship between physician utilization and patient waiting time in an outpatient clinic using a staggered block scheduling system (i.e., eight patients arriving every half hour) versus the single block scheduling system (i.e., sixteen patients arriving simultaneously). The single block system emphasizes the physician's idle time, while the staggered block system emphasizes the patient's waiting time, resulting in a substantial decrease in the patient waiting times (with no decrement in the utilization of the physician).

2.1.2 Inpatient Scheduling and Admissions

Inpatient scheduling and admissions focus on procedures for matching patients with caregivers (e.g., surgeons, infectious disease specialists) within a hospital or similar health care facility. This involves rules or policies that determine when healthcare providers must see and provide services for inpatients, as well as matching specific types of caregiver with the needs of patients and the necessary treatments.

Surgical (operating room) center scheduling has also been studied using discrete-event simulation. Magerlein and Martin (1976) review the literature on using discrete-event simulation for scheduling surgical centers. Murphy and Sigal (1985) examine surgical block scheduling, where a block of operating room time is reserved for one or more surgeons. Fitzpatrick et al. (1993) study the use of first-come-first-serve, fixed (scheduling the same block of time in the same time slot each day of the week), variable (scheduling under the influence of seasonal fluctuation in demand), and mixed block scheduling (a combination of fixed and variable) for hospital operating rooms. They observed that variable block scheduling is superior to all scheduling policies, in terms of facility utilization, patient throughput, average patient waiting time, and patient queue length.

Klassen and Rohleder (1996) use discrete-event simulation to study the best time to schedule patients with large patient service time means and variances. They analyze several rules and arrive at the best result (which is to schedule such patients towards the end of the appointment session) that minimizes the patient's waiting time and the physician's idle time. Additionally, they analyze the best position for unscheduled appointment slots for potentially urgent calls and found no conclusive scheduling rule. Swisher et al. (1997) consider scheduling more patients with larger mean service time distributions in the morning session, rather than the afternoon, in an outpatient clinic. They found that staff overtime is sharply reduced, with a corresponding reduction in the physician's lunch time period. Steward and Standridge (1996) report the results of an overtime study using a discrete-event simulation model of a veterinary practice. The veterinary domain is very similar to the larger human medical systems domain, since both involve the challenge of varying flow and service rates, as well as resource utilization, staffing, demand, and scheduling. In this study, the performance measure of interest is the average time interval between the closing time of the clinic and the time the last client is discharged after clinic hours, which serves as an indicator of overhead cost and client satisfaction. They report that performance can improve if the clinic disallows the scheduling of appointments less than 90 or 120 minutes prior to closing, rather than 60 minutes, as was the current practice.

Hancock and Walter (1979) attempt to use discrete-event simulation to reduce the variance in occupancy levels in a hospital inpatient facility, with the goal of increasing patient throughput and maximizing average occupancies. Unfortunately, they were unsuccessful in achieving their stated objective, since the staff was accustomed to admitting patients on the date of the requests 90% of the time, and they refused to schedule over four weeks in advance. Hancock and Walter (1984) attempt to smooth the daily patient loads of nineteen hospital departments by varying the admission days of urgent inpatient and outpatient loads. The variation in average load for each of the departments suggested that no one single admission policy could provide a stable workload for all the departments, since each department had its own unique patient arrival patterns and treatment requirements, including different inpatient and outpatient requirements.

Lim et al. (1975) apply two admission policies (quickcall and maximum queue lengths) to a discrete-event simulation model of an inpatient orthopedics unit. "Quickcall" is defined as a patient willing to enter the hospital on very short notice; whereas, maximum queue lengths is a concept in which the physicians are required to maintain a maximum number of patient requests on a waiting list. Both systems improved system performance, in terms of patient waiting times and staff utilization. Similarly, Groothuis et al. (2001) investigate two patient scheduling procedures (the current procedure where no patient is scheduled after 4:00 PM, versus scheduling a fixed number of patients each day) for a hospital cardiac catheterization lab. Both scheduling procedures were applied to the current configuration and three additional experimental configurations, with patient throughput and working day duration as the measures of performance. A discrete-event simulation was designed using Medmodel and showed that the third experimental configuration under the current scheduling procedure could, on average, accommodate two additional patients with fewer working days that exceed eight hours.

Walter (1973) describes several aspects of a queuing system in a radiology department, using several different appointment schemes. By segregating patients into inpatient and outpatient sessions with a similar examination time distribution, Walter observed that a substantial staff time savings was possible. He also found that the practice of giving multiple bookings for a given appointment time (i.e., overbooking) yields a small increase in staff utilization while substantially increasing the patient waiting time, and that efficiency always improves when the proportion of patients with appointments increases, resulting in a smoothing of the arrival rate. Goitein (1990) obtained similar conclusions using Monte Carlo simulation to examine factors such as physician idle time relative to patient waiting time. He found that if the physician overbooked the schedule (even slightly), patients would experience very long waiting times. His model provides insights into how delays build up as a result of commonly-observed statistical fluctuations. Everett (2002) suggests using a simulation model to help match patient needs with hospital availability (in a public hospital system) by scheduling patients waiting for elective surgery.

In conclusion, patient scheduling and admission rules along with patient appointment timing can have significant impacts on physician utilization and patient waiting. In general, studies using discrete-event simulation as discussed here suggest that rules and policies can be employed that will help to balance the tradeoff between physician utilization rates and patient waiting times, though the unique features of each clinic environment need to be taken into account to determine the exact extent of these tradeoffs. External market factors often dictate how health care facilities must prioritize the tradeoff between patient convenience and caregiver utilization. For example, in highly competitive markets, clinics may favor patient convenience over staff utilization in an effort to retain market share. Obviously, the unique factors that determine optimality must be elicited from each decision-maker given his/her environmental factors. The studies presented herein also point to the importance of, when possible, smoothing patient arrival rates and service times. As in most systems, reducing variability facilitates performance improvement.

2.1.3 Emergency Room Simulation Models

Discrete-event simulation models can capture complex patient flows through health care clinics, as well as analyze the effect of new patient flow rules and policies. Such flows are typical in emergency room settings, where patients arrive (nearly always without appointments), and require treatment over a large and varied set of ailments and conditions, ranging from the benign (e.g., mild sports injuries) to the fatal (e.g., heart attacks, gunshot wounds). Although the patient arrival patterns are highly unpredictable, the treatment sequence can be controlled by clinical staff. Therefore, by altering patient routing and flow, it may be possible to minimize patient waiting times and increase staff utilization rates.

Limited access to primary care has led to extreme increases in emergency department usage across the United States. Emergency department overcrowding has been recognized by national health industry groups and regulatory bodies like the American Hospital Association (AHA) and the Joint Commission on the Accreditation of Healthcare Organizations (JCAHO) as a significant public health issue. All of this has led to a significant increase in the use of discrete-event simulation in modeling emergency departments in the past decade. General guidelines for analyzing an emergency department using discrete-event simulation exist in the literature. Takakuwa and Shiozaki (2004) propose a procedure for planning emergency room operations that minimize patient waiting times. Sinreich and Marmor (2004) develop a general emergency department simulation tool that is "flexible, intuitive, simple to use and contains default values for most of the system's parameters." Miller et al. (2004) describe steps for building a discrete-event simulation tool meant to determine the best emergency room configuration.

A key service metric used by hospital emergency departments is patient waiting time. Garcia et al. (1995) analyze the impact of a fast track queue on reducing waiting times of low priority patients in an emergency room. Emergency room patients are typically prioritized according to patient acuity (the level of sickness), hence low acuity patients regularly wait for excessively long periods of time. A fast track queue is used to treat a particular patient acuity level (in this case, non-urgent patients). They found that a fast track lane that uses a minimal amount of resources could result in significantly reduced patient waiting times. A similar study to assess the effect of fast care processing routes for non-critical patients on waiting times in an emergency department is presented by Mahapatra et al. (2003). This study showed that the addition of an alternate care unit (such as a fast track unit) improved average waiting times by at least 10%. In a discrete-event simulation model of the emergency department at the University of Louisville Hospital, Kraitsik and Bossmeyer (1993) suggest that patient throughput can be improved using a fast track queue and a "stat" lab for processing high volume tests. Kirtland et al. (1995) examine eleven alternatives to improve patient flow in an emergency department and identified three alternatives (using a fast track lane in minor care, placing patients in the treatment area instead of sending them back to the waiting room, and the use of point-of-care lab testing) that can save on average thirty eight minutes of waiting time per patient. Blake and Carter (1996) also analyze an emergency department at the Children's Hospital of Eastern Ontario using discrete-event simulation. Their study led to the implementation of a fast track queue for treating patients with minor injuries.

Another important measure for emergency department efficiency is the overall time a patient spends in the emergency room (i.e., the patient length of stay). McGuire (1994) uses MedModel to determine how to reduce the length of stay for patients in an emergency service department in a SunHealth Alliance hospital. The results from the study resulted in several alternative recommendations, including adding an additional clerk during peak hours, adding a holding area for waiting patients, extending the hours of the fast track queue, and using physicians instead of residents in the fast track area. Miller et al. (2003) use a discrete-event simulation of an emergency department of a large hospital in the southeast United States to show that significant process changes would be required to meet specified goals for patient length of stay. Samaha et al. (2003) describe how discrete-event simulation was used by the Cooper University Hospital to reduce patient length of stays in their emergency department. Their study determined that length of stay was a process related problem rather than resource dependent. For example, the study showed that adding square footage or beds would not shorten the length of stay, which resulted in significant cost avoidance. Another discrete-event simulation study of patient flow to reduce emergency department length of stay is presented by Blasak et al. (2003). This study also simulates an inpatient medical telemetry unit to see how the processes of other units impact the emergency department. El-Darzi et al. (1998) and Martin et al. (2003) present additional patient flow simulation studies that seek to increase patient throughput and decrease patient length of stay. Both studies, however, model a hospital geriatric department.

Ritondo and Freedman (1993) show that changing a procedural policy (of ordering tests while in triage) results in a decrease in patient waiting times in the emergency room and an increase in patient throughput. Edwards et al. (1994) compare the results of simulation studies in two medical clinics that use different queuing systems: serial processing, where patients wait in a single queue, and quasi-parallel processing, where patients are directed to the shortest queue to maintain flow. They show that patient waiting times could be reduced by up to 30% using quasi-parallel processing. Johnson (1998) uses a MedModel discrete-event simulation model to examine the effect of new legislation (requiring a minimum length of stay) and physician practices on patient flow and census of the maternity unit at Miami Valley Hospital in Dayton, Ohio, USA. The study led to minor changes in the maternity unit configuration that resulted in a 15-20% increase in patient volume and more balanced utilization of all areas within the unit. Also, the model results supported decisions to construct new facilities, such as a larger perinatal intensive care unit.

2.1.4 Specialist Clinics

Specialists bring their own unique set of issues when scheduling patients and allocating space within health care facilities. Sepúlveda et al. (1999) use discrete-event simulation to evaluate improvement in patient flow at a cancer treatment center under three different scenarios: 1) a change in the layout of the clinic, 2) different patient scheduling options, and 3) a new facility with increased capacity. The simulation of all three scenarios identified key patient flow bottlenecks and provided insights to improve patient flow and utilization. In particular, under the layout scenario, the simulation was used to identify a facility layout that allowed for a 100% increase in chair capacity. Simulating different patient scheduling options showed a 20% increase in the number of patients seen per day, without any change in the operating time of the treatment center. Finally, the new facility scenario showed that one of the waiting rooms did not have the capacity to support patient flow.

Ramakrishnan et al. (2004) describe a discrete-event simulation model used to analyze different "what-if" scenarios for the Wilson Memorial Regional Medical Center in Broome County, New York USA. The center recently implemented a digital image archiving system within its radiology services department and with this implementation wanted to identify patient flow changes in the computerized tomography (CT) scan area that would maximize patient throughput and minimize report generation time. Using simulation, the researchers identified changes within the CT scan area that would increase patient throughput by 20%, while simultaneously reducing report generation time by over 30%. Likewise, Alexopoulos et al. (2001)

describe a discrete-event simulation used by Partnership of Immunization Providers to study "what-if" scenarios for immunization clinics serving the poor. Such scenarios included narrowing/expanding appointment slots and the impact of bilingual versus monolingual staff on patient throughput.

Groothius et al. (2002) describe a systematic approach for analyzing the effects on patient flow when a hospital department is relocated. This approach is demonstrated with a MedModel simulation model of relocating a hospital phlebotomy department, which assesses the resulting impact on the average patient turn around time. They observed that this time could be reduced by as much as 50% (from 12 minutes down to 8 minutes).

2.1.5 Physician and Health Care Staff Scheduling

The majority of discrete-event simulation models for scheduling health care clinics are directed at patient scheduling (so as to optimally distribute patient demand to physicians and clinical staff). A number of studies, however, have addressed the reverse problem; namely, scheduling physician and clinical staff to satisfy patient demand, given a collection of patient arrivals. For example, walk-in clinics, which are unable to control the arrival rate of patients, must schedule their staff accordingly. Incorporating this idea, Alessandra et al. (1978) study both the staffing levels and patient arrival rates to ease bottlenecks and to improve patient throughput. Eight alternatives that varied the staffing pattern and the patient scheduling scheme were analyzed. The best alternative identified was to keep the staffing and arrival rate the same, but to distribute the current morning appointment patients to the afternoon shift. Mukherjee (1991) identifies a staffing mix that reduces patient waiting time and increases patient throughput, while controlling resource costs in a pharmacy.

There have also been discrete-event simulation studies that address physician scheduling. Rossetti et al. (1999) use discrete-event simulation to test alternative physician-staffing schedules at the emergency department at the University of Virginia Medical Center. For each staffing alternative, they analyzed the impact on patient throughput and resource utilization. Tan et al. (2002) present a discrete-event simulation study of an urgent care center that simulates the current physician schedule and a proposed schedule to test if the proposed schedule reduces the average total time patients spend at the facility. The simulation showed an 18% reduction in total visit time using the proposed schedule. Likewise, using a discrete-event simulation, Lach and Vázquez (2004) study a telemedicine program in Mexico that provides medical assistance to those living in extreme poverty. This study analyzes the effect on patient throughput and resource (tele-consult) utilization when an extra physician is scheduled; both tele-consult utilization and patient throughput increase when the extra physician is scheduled. Osidach and Fu (2003) study the staffing of technicians required to perform medical exams on scheduled survey participants in a mobile examination center. Configurations of three, four, and five technicians for a batch arrival of seven survey participants were simulated to minimize the technicians' idle time and average time spent in the system by the survey participant. The best configuration for utilization was a three technician configuration, whereas a five technician configuration was the most time-effective; however, the five technician configuration also resulted in an overly crowded examination center.

Several discrete-event simulation models of nursing staff scheduling in emergency departments have been developed. Emergency room staff scheduling has its own unique challenges, due to the high volume of visits, significant variability in patient arrival patterns, and the urgency of the care required. Draeger (1992) studies nurse workload in an emergency room and its effect on the average number of patients, average time in system, average number of patients waiting, and average patient waiting time. Comparing the current schedule's performance to those of two alternative staffing schedules, the author found an alternative that could reduce both the average patient time in system (by 23%) and the average patient waiting time (by 57%), without any increase in costs. Similarly, Evans et al. (1996) reduce a patient's length of stay by finding the optimal number of nurses and technicians that should be on duty during four shifts in an emergency room. Kumar and Kapur (1989) examine ten nurse scheduling policy alternatives, selecting and implementing the policy yielding the highest nurse utilization rate.

Lambo (1993) applies a recursive linear programming and discrete-event simulation methodology to examine staffing problems in a health care center in Nigeria. In the study, the clinic was observed to be at 50% capacity due to the misallocation of (rather than the inadequacy of) personnel. After making changes to the staffing patterns and other policy changes, capacity increased by 60% and patient waiting times were reduced by 45 minutes. In a similar study, Chan et al. (2002) uses integer programming and discrete-event simulation to study a medical records department to determine the optimal staff schedule and understand the workflow of the transcription function.

All of these discrete-event simulation studies suggest that when patient flow patterns cannot be controlled, staffing strategies can be employed to smooth some of the unavoidable variability in the systems. This can result in improved patient throughput, while keeping staff utilization rates and total staffing costs at acceptable levels. It may also act as an important public relations and marketing tool. Health care is unique in that quality is not always readily identifiable by its customers. A patient whose condition improves may have received quality care; however, if services were delivered inefficiently, the patient's perception of quality may be greatly diminished. Efficient patient flow, then, often acts as a surrogate for quality of care in the patient's mind. Given a choice, patients will tend to a health care provider they perceive to offer higher quality services. Moreover, facilities that minimize the obstacles to the provision of care for health care providers (e.g., physicians, nurses) are better able to attract and retain the best and brightest. In short, patient flow is not just important to the bottom line, but it can serve as a major competitive advantage.

2.2 Health Care Asset Allocation

Hospital and clinic administrators have approached cost containment within their operations by working to minimize expenditures for health care provisions while simultaneously providing quality health care services. Such situations pervade the health care community as indicated by the large number of papers and studies that analyze the allocation of scarce health care assets. Discrete-event simulation modeling is an attractive method to help make such allocations since it can be used to estimate the operational characteristics of a health care system operation and to observe the impact of changes in planning or policies prior to the implementation of such changes, and thereby mitigate financial risks. The allocation of health care assets can be broken down into three general areas where assets most directly impact health care delivery: bed sizing and planning, room sizing and planning, staff sizing and planning.

2.2.1 Bed Sizing and Planning

The demand for hospital beds can be classified as either routine (e.g., scheduled) or emergency (e.g., unscheduled) admissions. Both of these admission types impact how many beds are needed to meet demand, while maintaining reasonable bed utilization rates. In the literature, most bed planning discrete-event simulation models attempt to overcome bed shortages or policies that lead to patient misplacement, bumping, or rejection. Hospitals are typically faced with the tradeoff between having available beds to service patient demand versus keeping bed occupancy (utilization) rates high.

Butler et al. (1992a) use discrete-event simulation to study patient misplacements, where patients are scheduled and assigned to an alternative unit within a hospital due to a shortage of beds in the preferred hospital area.

They examine the sensitivity of patient misplacement with respect to a variety of modifications in their bed allocation policy, including patient transfers, bed scheduling, and assignments, and found that reducing a patient's length of stay and reallocating rooms among the different services within a hospital could substantially decrease patient misplacement. Furthermore, the smoothing of routine patient arrivals only marginally reduced patient misplacement. In another study designed to reduce patient misplacement, Butler et al. (1992b) use a two-phase approach involving a quadratic integer programming model and a discrete-event simulation model to evaluate bed configurations and to determine optimal bed allocations across a number of hospital service areas. Vasilakis and El-Darzi (2001) use discrete-event simulation to identify the possible cause for a hospital bed crisis that occurs each winter in United Kingdom National Health Services hospitals. Using simulation, they demonstrate a "breakdown in the discharge of dependent patients from the medium stay (or rehabilitative) stream" because during the Christmas and New Year holiday season surgeons are not performing routine operations. However, once surgeons return to work after the holidays, the resulting surge in the number of surgeries scheduled results in an insufficient number of beds for incoming medical emergencies. The study suggests that the UK winter bed crisis is likely due to staff scheduling, the holidays, and ineffective management of non-acute (longer stay) patients. Note that US hospitals typically experience such "winter census" crises, as well.

Lowery (1992, 1993) and Lowery and Martin (1992) consider the use of discrete-event simulation in a hospital's critical care areas (e.g., operating rooms, recovery units, intensive care units, and intermediate care units) to determine critical care bed requirements. Their literature review reveals that most models do not fully consider the interrelationships between different hospital units and few models have been validated using actual hospital performance data. Focusing on these deficiencies, they demonstrate improvements in their methodologies over previous models. Dumas (1984, 1985) also focuses on the interrelationships between several units within a hospital by comparing two bed planning rules (vacancy basing and home basing) for locating a bed within different hospital units when a patient cannot be allocated a bed at the preferred unit. Vacancy basing rules employ a ranked list of alternative misplacement possibilities, while home basing prohibits off-service misplacements, and hence, is more restrictive with respect to patient placement. They show that home basing policies result in better overall performance but lessen patient days and thereby reduce hospital revenues. Note that in the mid-1980s (the time of Dumas' publications) most hospitals were still paid by third party providers based on the patient's overall length of stay, so reducing patient days was seen as a potentially negative outcome. In contrast, modern reimbursement systems tend to favor case rates that encourage shorter lengths of stay, ultimately resulting in an incentive for hospitals to reduce patient days.

Cohen et al. (1980) present a bed planning model of a progressive patient care hospital, where patients are moved between units within a hospital as their condition changes. In this form of demand-matching, hospitals attempt to apply resources commensurate with patients' condition during their stay by "stepping the patient down" as their conditions improve. The authors demonstrate that the probability of inappropriate patient placement is a function of the capacities of all the units, as well as the policies for handling priority patients and bumped patients.

By considering individual units within a hospital, Zilm et al. (1983) use a discrete-event simulation model to analyze a surgical intensive care unit for various bed levels and future demand. They observe that most of the unit's volume consists of weekday cases (routine admissions), and hence, attempts to maintain a high overall average occupancy level would not be possible without straining the entire system. Similarly, Cahill and Render (1999) study proposed changes to the intensive care unit (ICU) at the Cincinnati Veterans Administration Medical Center. Using discrete-event simulation, they show that creating a respiratory care unit and increasing bed levels in other units closely associated with the intensive care unit would resolve the ICU access problems. However, an increase in ICU bed availability increased bed utilization in other units, which in turn increased the overall length of stay. Therefore, modeling in advance helped the hospital identify policy changes to lessen the impact on length of stay. Masterson et al. (2004) discuss the optimization of the military health system for all military health facilities. They present a case study based on a simulation analysis of the intensive care unit at the US Air Force's Wilford Hall Medical Center, to determine the appropriate ICU size, bed mix, and staffing level.

Romanin-Jacur and Facchin (1987) use discrete-event simulation to study the facility dimensioning problem and the sizing of the assistance team in a pediatric semi-intensive care unit. They compare several different priority-based models by using peak admission conditions to find the optimal number of beds and the best choice of the nurse's care assignment. Other bed sizing discrete-event simulation models can be found in Hancock et al. (1978), Wright (1987), Harris (1985), Wiinamaki and Dronzek (2003), and Akkerman and Knip (2004). Harris (1985) compares the difference in the number of surgical suites needed in a surgical center for three physicians under two operating timetable scenarios. Under the first (and current) scenario, each physician scheduled his/her patients independently of the other two physicians, while in the second scenario, the physicians pooled their resources to schedule their patients and consequently reduced the number of surgical suites required by over 20%. Wiinamaki and Dronzek (2003) show how simulation was used in determining the bed requirements for the new emergency care center at the Sarasota Memorial Hospital in Sarasota, Florida. Akkerman and Knip (2004) show that the number of beds could be reduced in a cardiac surgery center if recovering patients are transferred once they no longer require the center's specialized care services.

Gabaeff and Lennon (1991) use an extensive time-motion study to collect data on the mix of patient types, patient characteristics (such as x-ray requirements), and staffing mix for emergency admissions in an emergency department feasibility study at Stanford University Hospital. Using discrete-event simulation models, they highlight deficiencies in several key areas, including maximum bed utilization exceeding current bed availability (which would cause displacement of minor care patients). Vassilacopoulos (1985) develops a discrete-event simulation model to determine the number of beds with the following constraints: high occupancy rates, immediate (emergency admission) patients, and low length of waiting lists. He shows that by using a waiting list and smoothing the patient demand, it is possible to achieve high occupancy rates. Emergency department bed planning discrete-event simulation models are also discussed by Altinel and Ulas (1996) at the Istanbul University School of Medicine, Freedman (1994) at St. Joseph Hospital and Washington Adventist Hospital in Maryland, USA, Lennon (1992) at the Stanford University Hospital, and Williams (1983) at the University of Pennsylvania Hospital. All these studies suggest that discrete-event simulation modeling and analysis provides a valuable "what if" tool for hospital planners when deciding how many beds are needed to meet demand and maintain profitability. It also assists decision-makers in judiciously allocating precious financial resources. The ever-increasing costs of medical equipment (e.g., CT scanners) mean that health care administrators must preserve capital for technology that historically could have been allocated to brick-and-mortar expansions. Simulation modeling can play an important role in this effort. Moreover, simulation models allow hospital administrators to experiment with different bed allocation rules to help optimally utilize hospital facilities and improve bed occupancy rates.

2.2.2 Room Sizing and Planning

The ongoing movement towards freestanding surgicenters, as well as the shift to deliver health care services away from inpatients facilities and towards outpatient facilities, has put increased pressure upon hospital management to expand their outpatient services and/or to build new facilities to handle these additional patient demands. Discrete-event simulation has become an important tool for the planning of future expansion, integration, and/or construction of new outpatient facilities and health service departments, by significantly enhancing the hospital administration decision-maker's ability to find the most cost-effective and efficient solutions to such problems.

The number and use of operating rooms is often an important resource in maintaining hospital profitability and patient services. Currie et al. (1984) study operating room utilization, vertical transportation needs, radiology staffing, and emergency medical system operations at the West Virginia University Hospital. They use discrete-event simulation to estimate the number of operating rooms and recovery beds needed to handle a 20% increase in future demand. Kwak et al. (1975) use discrete-event simulation to determine the capacity of a recovery room needed to support an operating room expansion. Similarly, Kuzdrall et al. (1981) use a discrete-event simulation model of an operating and recovery room facility to determine and assess the facility utilization levels and facility needs under different scheduling policies. Olson and Dux (1994) apply discrete-event simulation modeling to study and evaluate the decision to expand the Waukesha Memorial surgicenter from seven to eight operating rooms. Their study reveals that an eighth operating room would only serve to meet the hospital's needs for no more than two years, at a cost of $500,000 (USD). However, an analysis of the cross-departmental and administrative needs reveal that an ambulatory surgery center that separates the inpatients and outpatient procedures would better serve the hospital's future health care delivery needs. Similarly, Amladi (1984) uses discrete-event simulation to help size and plan a new outpatient surgical facility, by considering patient wait time (quality) and facility size (resource). Lowery and Davis (1999) developed a discrete-event simulation to assess the impact of a proposed renovation to the surgical suite of Brigham and Women's Hospital in Boston, Massachusetts, USA. Hospital administrators wanted to ensure that the renovations would be sufficient to handle a projected increase in the number of inpatient surgeries. The simulation showed the projected increases could be met with 30 or less operating rooms (32 operating rooms were planned in the renovation) provided scheduled block times were extended to include the addition of a Saturday block.

Ferrin et al. (2004) apply discrete-event simulation to help St. Vincent's Hospital in Birmingham, Alabama, USA, a not-for-profit hospital, determine the value of implementing an incentive program for their operating room environment. The simulation showed that improving the room turnaround process by 20% would result in a 4% improvement in the operating rooms case volume and a 5% increase in utilization of same day surgical rooms.

This increase in volume provided enough increase in revenue to justify an incentive to improve the operating room turnaround process. In addition to evaluating the value of incentives, St Vincent's administration used the simulation to determine the required number of operating rooms, number of beds in the Post Anesthesia Care Unit (PACU), and changes in physician scheduling blocks.

Meier et al. (1985) use discrete-event simulation to compare and evaluate eleven scenarios in varying the number of exam rooms and demand shifts of both a hospital ambulatory center and a freestanding surgicenter. They found that existing room capacity is adequate to handle demands over the next five years. Iskander and Carter (1991) use discrete-event simulation to show that current facilities were sufficient for future growth in a study of a same day (outpatient) health care unit in an ambulatory care center. However, they suggest a threefold increase in the size of the waiting room. Using discrete-event simulation, Ramis et al. (2001) evaluate a proposed future center for ambulatory surgery by evaluating several process alternatives. The results determined the bed resources and scheduling rule required to maximize daily surgical throughput. Similarly, Stahl et al. (2003) seek to optimize the management and financial performance of ambulatory care clinics used for teaching medical students. Here they use discrete-event simulation to determine that a teaching ambulatory care clinic runs optimally (where optimality is defined as the policy that minimizes patient flow time and wait time while maximizing revenue) when the trainee-to-preceptor ratio is between 3 and 7 to 1.

Kletke and Dooley (1984) use discrete-event simulation to examine the effects on service level and utilization rates in a maternity unit to determine if the current number of labor rooms, delivery rooms, post-partum rooms, nursery, and nurses are able to meet future demands. Their study recommends increasing the number of labor rooms and the number of post-partum rooms, while maintaining four full-time nurses. Levy et al. (1989) use discrete-event simulation to analyze the operational characteristics of an outpatient service center at Anderson Memorial Hospital to determine whether to merge this service with an off-site outpatient diagnostic center. They collected data on the utilization of the servers, the total number of patients in the center, the maximum and average times spent in the center, the maximum and average times spent in each service queue, and the total number of patients in each queue. This information was used to specify staffing and facility sizing requirements. In another facility integration plan, Mahachek and Knabe (1984) use discrete-event simulation to evaluate a proposal to cut costs by combining an obstetrics clinic and a gynecology clinic into a single facility. The analysis found that this proposal would not be successful due to the shortage of exam rooms. All these studies illustrate the value provided by discrete-event simulation modeling and analysis to determine how to set the size of key hospital facilities (such as operating rooms). As the health care industry continues to move more towards outpatient delivery systems, and away from traditional inpatient health care facilities, discrete-event simulation will continue to assist health care decision-makers in leveraging their resources in undertaking such transitions.

2.2.3 Staff Sizing and Planning

The medical community requires highly skilled staff to delivery quality health care services, making staff sizing and planning an important factor in designing health care delivery systems (such as those found in hospitals). Moreover, the tradeoff between insufficient clinical staff to meet demand (hence unacceptable patient waiting times) and underutilization of clinical staff can have an enormous impact on the economic viability and sustainability of a medical facility. Discrete-event simulation has played an important role in addressing the issues inherent in this trade-off.

Several discrete-event simulation studies have been conducted to determine the staff size or the number of physicians for emergency departments (e.g. Carter et al. 1992). Badri and Hollingsworth (1993) analyze the impact of different operational scenarios on scheduling, limited staffing, and changing the patient demand patterns in an emergency room of the Rashid Hospital in the United Arab Emirates. These scenarios included using a patient priority rule based on severity of ailment, not serving a category of patient that does not belong in the emergency room, eliminating one or more doctors on each shift, and a hybrid scenario that combines the last two scenarios. The results from this hybrid scenario were accepted and implemented. Klafehn and Owens (1987) and Klafehn et al. (1987) address the problem of determining the relationship between patient flow and the number of staff available in an emergency department. They conclude that moving one nurse from the regular emergency area to a triage position significantly reduces patient waiting lines and waiting times. Furthermore, they found that the addition of a second orthopedic team in the emergency department increases patient throughput, though utilization levels were lower and the average length of stay remains virtually the same (since the number of patients flowing through the orthopedic area was relatively small). Liyanage and Gale (1995) formulate an M/M/n queuing model of the Campbelltown Hospital emergency facility to estimate and develop patient arrival time distributions, patient waiting times, and patient service times. These parameters were then used in a discrete-event simulation model to estimate the expected patient waiting times, the expected physician idle times, and the optimal number of doctors. Baesler et al. (2003) use a discrete-event simulation model to predict a patient's time spent in the emergency room of a private hospital in Chile. These results were then used in a design of experiments to minimize the number of resources (four full-time physicians and one part-time physician) required to meet patient demand. Similarly, Centeno et al. (2003) combine discrete-event simulation with integer programming to develop an optimal schedule for emergency room staff. The study showed a 28% improvement over the current method of staffing which offers a potential significant savings in hospital labor costs. Lopez-Valcarcel and Perez (1994) use discrete-event simulation to evaluate the staffing levels, the arrival rates, and the service times of diagnostic equipment (alterable by purchasing better equipment) in an emergency department. They recommend that the arrival rate should not exceed twelve patients per hour. Moreover, they recommend that investments in human resources would be more effective than investments in newer (better) equipment. In contrast, Bodtker et al. (1992) and Godolphin et al. (1992) determine that a reduction in staff by at least one staff member could be achieved if better equipment were purchased.

O'Kane (1981), Klafehn (1987), and Coffin et al. (1993) use discrete-event simulation to analyze staff allocations to improve patient flow in a radiology department. Klafehn and Connolly (1993) model an outpatient hematology laboratory and compare several configurations. They observed that if the staff is cross-trained (and hence, can be more fully utilized), then patient waiting times can be reduced. Vemuri (1984) and Ishimoto et al. (1990) use discrete-event simulation to identify the optimal medical staff size and mix that reduces patient waiting times in a hospital pharmacy. Weng and Houshmand (1999) simulate a general hospital outpatient clinic to find the optimal staff size that maximizes patient throughput and minimizes patient flow time.

Jackson Memorial Hospital (JMH) in Dade County, Florida, USA uses discrete-event simulation to model hospital operations. Centeno et al. (2001) present a simulation study of the labor and delivery rooms at JMH. This study used historical data for all simulation inputs and identified ways to improve physician scheduling and better staffing levels. A simulation study of the radiology department at JMH is discussed in Centeno et al. (2000). Six different scenarios, that vary staff and physical resources, are studied to determine the impact on patient flow and utilization of the department staff and operating rooms. This study determined the most cost-effective staff level for each procedure and identified additional revisions to improve process and service efficiencies.

Hashimoto and Bell (1996) conduct a time-motion study to collect data for a discrete-event simulation model of an outpatient (general practice) clinic. They show that increasing the number of physicians, and consequently the number of patients, without increasing the support staff, would significantly increase patient length of stay. By limiting the number of physicians to four and increasing the number of dischargers to two, they were able decrease the patient's average total time in the system by almost 25%. Wilt and Goddin (1989) use discrete-event simulation to evaluate patient waiting times to determine appropriate staffing levels in an outpatient clinic. McHugh (1989) uses discrete-event simulation to examine hospital nurse-staffing levels and their impact on cost and utilization. This analysis shows that 55% of the maximum workload produces the best results based on these measures. Swisher et al. (2001) discuss a discrete-event simulation model of the Queston Physician Practice Network where individual family outpatient clinics are modeled and integrated into a network of clinics that uses a central appointment scheduling center. Performance measures such as patient throughput, patient waiting time, staff utilization, and clinic overtime are analyzed for various numbers of exam rooms and staff mixes. In certain cases, adding support personnel had negligible effects on the performance measures. Swisher and Jacobson (2002) use an object-oriented visual discrete-event simulation to evaluate different staffing options and facility sizes for a two physician family practice health care clinic. They describe a clinic effectiveness measure that is used to evaluate the overall effectiveness of a given clinic configuration. This clinic effectiveness measure integrates clinic profits, patient satisfaction, and medical staff satisfaction into a single performance measure.

Rossetti et al. (1998) use discrete-event simulation to study clinical laboratory and pharmacy delivery processes in a mid-size hospital environment. The study specifically assesses the costs and performance benefit of procuring a fleet of mobile robots to perform delivery functions. The study found that a fleet of six mobile robots improved the turn-around time by 33% and reduced costs by 56% compared to the current system of three human couriers. Similarly, Wong et al. (2003) use simulation "to quantify the advantages of an electronic medication ordering, dispensing, and administration process" at an academic acute care center. The automated system had an average turnaround time of 123 minutes versus the current manual system turnaround time of 256 minutes. Dean et al. (1999) also study a hospital pharmacy distribution system, where they use simulation to help determine when a pharmacist should visit each nursing unit to minimize the mean time delay between the time when a prescription is filled and its arrival to the ward.

Stafford (1976) and Aggarwal and Stafford (1976) develop a multi-facility discrete-event simulation model of a university health center that incorporates fourteen separate stations (e.g., receptionist area, injections, dentist, gynecology, physical therapy, radiology, and pharmacy). Using student population figures and seven performance measures, they were able to estimate the level of demand for services in the clinic. They also show that patient inter-arrival times are distributed negative exponential with the mean changing according to the time of day, and patient service times are distributed Erlang-K. Using these data, they investigate the effects of adding another pharmacist to the pharmacy. A multi-factor experimental design was developed to examine the relationships between the controllable system variables and the system performance variables. They show that different calling population sizes and different levels of staffing can impact the performance measures at each station. Additionally, the aggregation of two or more similar facilities can cause an increase in the average number of patients waiting at each of the remaining facilities and the average patient waiting times, though these increases were offset by a significant decrease in the staff idle times and staff costs. These studies suggest that staffing levels and staff distributions have a significant impact on patient throughput and waiting times. As with facility sizing and planning, discrete-event simulation can be an effective tool to study various staffing strategies for a wide variety of health care facilities and systems. As the national shortage of skilled clinicians (particularly nurses) deepens, such studies will become increasingly important to health care organizations as they attempt to optimally deploy scarce human resources.

3. RECENT INNOVATIONS AND FUTURE DIRECTIONS

There is a growing amount of literature on using discrete-event simulation to study the design and operation of health care delivery systems. Publications based on such studies have steadily increased from eight in 1973-1977 to twenty-eight in 1993-1997 to over fifty in 1998-2004. This positive trend can be attributed to the increasing demand for cost-cutting in health care coupled with an increase in the ease-of-use and power of discrete-event simulation software packages (especially over the past decade). A growing number of these studies attempt to apply optimization techniques to analyze discrete-event simulation models. Despite the increase in health care simulation studies and the integration of discrete-event simulation and optimization techniques, few studies focus on complex integrated systems. This may be a result of the associated complexity issues and resource requirements required for such studies. Moreover, no matter how complex modeled systems are or what techniques are applied, it will continue to be a challenge to implement the results of such studies. However, recent advances in discrete-event simulation software may help to overcome some of these obstacles.

Most discrete-event simulation models focus on individual units within multi-facility clinics or hospitals. Using a macroscopic analysis of multi-facility systems, discrete-event simulation can be used to estimate patient demand (directly related to arrival rates), utilization of staff, and overall costs. The estimation of these performance measures may not be possible in a microscopic, single level model, due to the duplication of and overlapping of facilities and services. Discrete-event simulation models that capture the interaction of major service departments and support services in a hospital, and the information that can be gained from analyzing the system as a whole, can be invaluable to hospital planners and administrators.

To remain competitive in today's market, the health care industry is being forced to integrate hospitals and clinics, especially the ever-growing number of ambulatory care facilities, into health maintenance organizations (HMO), multi-hospital, or multi-clinic organizations. This presents a challenging application for discrete-event simulation: to operate these networks of clinics or departments efficiently and cost effectively. Studies in multi-facility simulation models have been conducted by Rising et al. (1973), Aggarwal and Stafford (1976), Hancock and Walters (1984), Swisher et al. (1997, 2001), and Lowery and Martin (1992).

A benefit from simulating integrated systems is the more realistic representation of the system under study, hence greater confidence in the results. Though this may not be significant when analyzing a small system, the consequences of invalid results or the lack of a thorough study may potentially be a costly decision for large multi-million dollar organizations. With this potential benefit, the question that has to be asked is: Why is there a lack of literature in this area? The answer may lie in one or both of two issues: (1) the level of complexity and resulting data requirements of the simulation model and/or (2) the resource requirements, including time and cost.

A widely recognized guideline in discrete-event simulation modeling is to keep the model as simple as possible while capturing the necessary measures of interest. This is reiterated by Dearie et al. (1976) who stress the importance of capturing only relevant performance variables when creating a simple, though not necessarily the most complete model. They suggest that it is best to depict the various subsystems at the lowest level of complexity such that the model is accurate while providing information that is easily interpreted. Moreover, Lowery (1996) suggests using simple analytical models if they can provide the necessary level of detail. However, when analyzing integrated systems, the level of detail that is required far exceeds the complexity and demands of analytical techniques. Therefore, care must be taken when determining the required level of detail (since more detail typically means that more data must be collected). The soft system methodology (SSM), an approach that aids in determining the level of detail, identifying system boundaries, and ascertaining system activities, is suggested by Lehaney and Paul (1994, 1996) and Lehaney and Hlupic (1995). Through increased participation of the users/customers, SSM encourages acceptability of the model, its results, and eventually the model's implementation.

Resource requirements, such as the length of time, the cost, and the skills necessary to complete the project must be fully considered before commencing such a large-scale project. Today's health care delivery environment is rapidly changing and if the process of developing and searching for a solution requires a large investment in time and resources, the system may be outdated before the results from the simulation study can be implemented. Consequently, an adequate amount of resources must be dedicated to the project to ensure completion of the study in a reasonable length of time. For example, the cost of collecting the required data (in terms of time and money), the cost of purchasing a discrete-event simulation software package that would ease the development of complex models, and the cost of skilled consultants or in-house engineers may all be prohibitive.

Given that discrete-event simulation is not an optimization tool, it can only provide estimates of performance measures for various system alternatives. Moreover, discrete-event simulation models typically have several output performance measures upon which to optimize, hence creating a multi-criteria objective function environment. There are several advantages and disadvantages of using either discrete-event simulation methodologies or optimization techniques to model complex systems. Karnon (2003), Davies and Davies (1994) and Stafford (1978) compare discrete-event simulation modeling to several techniques, such as Markov chain analysis, semi-Markov chain analysis, input-output analysis, and queuing analysis of an outpatient clinic. They find that discrete-event simulation is particularly well suited for modeling health care clinics due to the complexity of such systems, whereas many optimization techniques, such as linear programming, have a limited capacity for characterizing the complexities of medical systems. An optimization technique may require too many unrealistic assumptions about the process, hence rendering the solution invalid and unrealistic. For example, optimization models cannot be used to study the details of the day to day operations of a medical clinic, such as appointment scheduling, service routing, and service priorities, which can be easily captured by a discrete-event simulation model. On the other hand, many optimization models require only one experimental run to produce optimal or near optimal solutions, though the complexity of the model may result in an intractable solution; whereas, discrete-event simulation models require a large amount of effort in time, cost, and data collection. For all of these reasons, operations researchers have attempted to combine simulation with deterministic operations research techniques, such as linear programming, to simultaneously exploit the advantages of using both techniques.

Several studies have reported success in combining these techniques to find the best staffing allocations and facility sizes. A common technique when applying an optimization methodology to discrete-event simulation models of health care clinics is a recursive method employed by Carlson et al. (1979), Kropp et al. (1978), and Kropp and Hershey (1979). First, an optimization technique is used to analyze and reduce the number of alternatives of the system at an aggregate level (i.e., the total system level). These results are then used in a more complex and detailed discrete-event simulation model of the same system, which is then used to identify additional information and validate the results. Finally, these additional constraints are passed back into the optimization model and this process is iteratively repeated. Similarly, Butler et al. (1992b,c) employ a two phase approach by first using quadratic integer programming for facility layout and capacity allocation questions, and then a discrete-event simulation model to capture the complexities of alternative scheduling and bed assignment problems. Baesler and Sepúlveda (2001) extend the study of Sepúlveda et al. (1999) by using a simulation model of a new cancer treatment facility as a case study for solving a multi-objective (minimize patient waiting time, maximize chair utilization, minimize closing time, maximize nurse utilization) simulation optimization problem.

All of these studies use a variety of optimization techniques to arrive at parameters for the discrete-event simulation models. In general, recursive simulation optimization techniques can be very difficult, and therefore, costly to implement in the health care sector. However, a growing number of simulation software packages have appeared that provide an optimization add-on (Carson and Maria 1997). Instead of an exhaustive, time-consuming, and indiscriminate search for an optimal alternative, discrete-event simulation software companies are now starting to provide special search algorithms to guide a simulation model to an optimal or near-optimal solution. Examples of these include an add-on to MicroSaint 2.0 called OptQuest, that uses a scatter search technique (based on tabu search) to find the best value for one or multiple objective functions (Glover et al. 1996). Other optimization simulation software includes ProModel's SimRunner Optimization (Benson 1997) and AutoStat for AutoMod (Carson 1996).

Since their introduction, discrete-event simulation software packages have gone through a series of technological leaps and advances. First, the introduction of visually-oriented graphical outputs has greatly aided in the verification and validation of models and results (Gipps 1996, Sargent 1992), though this does not necessarily guarantee model correctness (Paul 1989). Moreover, discrete-event simulation model animation is primarily used to present movie-like images of the actual operation of the model and system which, in essence, helps to sell insights into the system under study. Second, the wide use of the object-oriented paradigm (OOP) in discrete-event simulation software design enables analysts to model a system without writing a single line of code (Banks 1997). Numerous companies are developing general-purpose software packages incorporating the latest technologies (Banks 1996), with packages like MedModel (Harrell and Lange 2001, Harrell and Price 2000, Price and Harrell 1999, Heflin and Harrell 1998, Carroll 1996, Keller 1994) and ARENA with a health care template (Drevna and Kasales 1984) specifically aimed to serve the health care industry.

Jones and Hirst (1986) present one of the early articles on using visual simulation, using the discrete-event simulation software package See-Why. The visualization of different policies in the visual simulation of a surgical unit and surrounding resources plays an integral part in assisting managers in identifying the best solutions. Paul and Kuljis (1995) use CLIMSIM, a generic discrete-event simulation package, to illustrate how clinic appointments and operating policies can influence patient waiting time. Evans et al. (1996) use ARENA to model an emergency department using thirteen patient categories. They reduce patients' length of stay using alternative scheduling rules for the number of nurses, technicians, and physicians on duty during each particular hour of the simulation run. In addition to these studies, several other visual simulation modeling project of interest have been conducted (including McGuire, 1994 and Ritondo and Freedman, 1993).

The number of health care organizations and government agencies using advanced discrete-event simulation software packages has grown, with much of their work and the results of their efforts not available in the open literature. Considering the number of easy to use discrete-event simulation software packages available today, it seems unusual to find that such a small number of visually-oriented simulation models of health care clinics have been published. This may be attributed to the shifting face of simulation modelers. As discrete-event simulation models have become easier to build with new software packages, the type of users have also changed. Since it is no longer necessary to have an advanced technical degree to use discrete-event simulation software packages (due largely to the drag-and-drop operation of such packages), numerous non-technical (and typically non-publishing) users have emerged. However, this development does not diminish the importance of contributions from operations research professionals to the health care field, since such individuals will continue to be needed to provide technical expertise when conducting or managing critical or large-scale discrete-event simulation projects.

Discrete-event simulation modeling of health care clinics has been extensively used to assist decision-makers to identify areas of service where efficiencies can be improved. For discrete-event simulation to reach its full potential as the key tool for analyzing health care clinics, the results from such simulation studies must be implemented. Unfortunately, in a survey of two hundred papers reporting the results of discrete-event simulation studies in health care, Wilson (1981) found that only sixteen projects reported successful implementations. A number of recommendations were given to increase the opportunities for and likelihood of implementation success. These recommendations include: the system being studied is actually in need of a decision, the project must be completed before a deadline, data must be available, and the organizer or the decision-maker must participate in the project.

Lowery (1998, 1996, 1994) addresses some additional implementation barriers, as well as solutions to help overcome the resistance to implementation. Some of the suggestions include animating the simulation model execution to more easily communicate the problem and the solution to the decision-maker, making sure management stays involved throughout the project, and avoiding too many assumptions or making the model too complex. She also suggests that management engineers must simplify the simulation process and improve their sales skills. Marsh (1979) lists three key elements necessary for the successful implementation of simulation results: total commitment and support from the users, credibility of the model, and the analyst must work with the real operations under study rather than any esoteric studies.

Despite the lack of implementation observed in the literature, other benefits can still be gained from conducting a discrete-event simulation study. The procedure and methodology of applying discrete-event simulation requires decision-makers and managers to work closely with the simulation analyst to provide details of the system, often for the first time. As a result, the manager is likely to gain a new perspective on the relationships between the available resources and the quality of health care services offered by the system. Rakich et al. (1991) study the effects of discrete-event simulation in management development. They conclude that conducting a simulation study not only develops a manager's decision-making skills, but also forces them to recognize the implications of system changes. Moreover, as also noted Wilson (1981), in the cases where managers developed their own discrete-event simulation models, implementation occurred much more frequently. Finally, Lowery (1996) notes that there are benefits, such as identifying unexpected problems unrelated to the original problem, which arise even if implementation fails.

4. SUMMARY AND CONCLUSIONS

In conclusion, this chapter surveys the literature (focusing primarily on the past thirty years) on the application of discrete-event simulation modeling and analysis to understand the operations of health care facilities. A significant amount of research has been conducted in the area of patient flow and asset allocation. The multiple performance measures associated with health care systems makes discrete-event simulation particularly well-suited to tackle problems in these domains. A large number of discrete-event simulation studies reported in the literature have the common theme that they attempt to understand the relationship that may exist between various inputs into a health care delivery system (e.g., patient scheduling and admission rules, patient routing and flow schemes, facility and staff resources) and various output performance measures from the system (e.g., patient throughput, patient waiting times, physician utilization, staff and facility utilization). The breadth and scope of units within hospitals and clinics makes it impossible to undertake a single comprehensive study that simultaneously addresses all of these issues.

The aforementioned observations, together with the dearth of literature in the area of complex integrated multi-facility systems, suggest the need to develop a comprehensive simulation modeling framework for determining clinical performance measures and interdepartmental resource relationships. Furthermore, this survey identified a number of continuing trends in discrete-event simulation software such as: the development of optimization add-ons, increased visualization, and the shift to an object-oriented paradigm. These powerful features will have the greatest impact when educating decision-makers on what changes need to be made and weakening the resistance to implementation. The outlook for discrete-event simulation in health care looks promising. The further development of more powerful high speed processing, distributed simulations (Baezner et al. 1990), and object-oriented simulation, will facilitate the creation of complex, but tractable, models of large integrated systems. Greater decision-maker buy-in will lead to model results being implemented more easily and frequently, providing greater opportunities for success. Twenty-first century health care decision-makers are faced with a complex and challenging environment. Costs are rising, human and fiscal resources are becoming scarcer, consumer expectations are rising, and technology is becoming more complex. It is crucial that health care managers make informed decisions on health care policies and the application of resources. Discrete-event simulation offers perhaps the most powerful and intuitive tool for the analysis and improvement of complex health care systems.

5. REFERENCES

S.C. Aggarwal and E.F. Stafford, 1976, A simulation study to identify important design parameters of a typical outpatient health system and to analyze measures of its performance, *Proceedings of the 1976 Summer Computer Simulation Conference*, Simulation Council, Washington, DC, USA, 12-14 July, 544-553.

R. Akkerman and M. Knip, 2004, Reallocation of beds to reduce waiting time for cardiac surgery, *Health Care Management Science*, **7**:119-126.

A.J. Alessandra, T.E. Grazman, R. Parameswaran, and U. Yavas, 1978, Using simulation in hospital planning, *Simulation*, **30**(2): 62-67.

A. Alexopoulos, D. Goldsman, J. Fontanesi, M. Sawyer, M. De Guire, D. Kopald, and K. Holcomb, 2001, A discrete-event simulation application for clinics serving the poor, *Proceedings of the 2001 Winter Simulation Conference* (B.A. Peters, J.S Smith, D.J. Medeiros, M.W. Rohrer, Editors), Institute of Electrical and Electronics Engineers, Arlington, Virginia, USA, 9-12 December, 1386-1391.

I.K. Altinel and E. Ulas, 1996, Simulation modeling for emergency bed requirement planning, *Annals of Operations Research*, **67**:183-210.

P. Amladi, 1984, Outpatient health care facility planning and sizing via computer simulation, *Proceedings of the 1984 Winter Simulation Conference* (S. Sheppard, U.W. Pooch, C.D. Pegden, Editors), Institute of Electrical and Electronics Engineers, Dallas, Texas, USA, 28-30 November, 705-711.

M. Badri and J. Hollingsworth, 1993, A simulation model for scheduling in the emergency room, *International Journal of Operations and Production Management*, **13**(3):13-24.

F.F. Baesler, H.E. Jahnsen, and M. DaCosta, 2003, The use of simulation and design of experiments for estimating maximum capacity in an emergency room, *Proceedings of the 2003 Winter Simulation Conference* (S. Chick, P.J. Sánchez, D. Ferrin, D.J. Morrice, Editors), Institute of Electrical and Electronics Engineers, New Orleans, Louisiana, USA, 7-10 December, 1903-1906.

F.F. Baesler and J.A. Sepúlveda, 2001, Multi-objective simulation optimization for a cancer treatment center, *Proceedings of the 2001 Winter Simulation Conference* (B.A. Peters, J.S. Smith, D.J. Medeiros, M.W. Rohrer, Editors), Institute of Electrical and Electronics Engineers, Arlington, Virginia, USA, 9-12 December, 1405-1411.

D. Baezner, G. Lomow, and B.W. Unger, 1990, Sim++^{TM}: The transition to distributed simulation, *Proceedings of the 1990 SCS Western Multiconference on Simulation:*

Distributed Simulation (D Nicol, Editor), Society for Computer Simulation, San Diego, California, USA, 17-19, January, 211-218.

N.T. Bailey, 1952, A study of queues and appointment systems in hospital outpatient departments, with special reference to waiting times, *Journal of the Royal Statistical Society*, **A14**:185-199.

L.P. Baldwin, T. Eldabi, and R.J. Paul, 2004, Simulation in healthcare management: a soft approach (MAPIU), *Simulation Modelling Practice and Theory*, **12**:541-557.

J. Banks, 1996, Software for Simulation, *Proceedings of the 1996 Winter Simulation Conference* (J.M. Charnes, D.M. Morrice, D.T. Brunner, J.J. Swain, Editors), Institute of Electrical and Electronics Engineers, Coronado, California, USA, 8-11 December, 31-38.

J. Banks, 1997, The future of simulation software: A panel discussion, *Proceedings of the 1997 Winter Simulation Conference* (S. Andradottir, K.J. Healy, D.E. Withers, B.L. Nelson, Editors), Institute of Electrical and Electronics Engineers, Atlanta, Georgia, USA, 7-10 December, 166-173.

J. Banks and J.S. Carson, 1987, Applying the simulation process, *Proceedings of the 1987 Winter Simulation Conference* (A. Thesen, H. Grant, W.D. Kelton, Editors), Institute of Electrical and Electronics Engineers, Atlanta, Georgia, USA, 14-16 December, 68-71.

D. Benson, 1997, Simulation modeling and optimization using ProModel, *Proceedings of the 1997 Winter Simulation Conference* (S. Andradottir, K.J. Healy, D.E. Withers, B.L. Nelson, Editors), Institute of Electrical and Electronics Engineers, Atlanta, Georgia, USA, 7-10 December, 587-593.

J.T. Blake, M.W. Carter, and S. Richardson, 1996, An analysis of emergency room wait time issues via computer simulation. *INFOR* **34**(4):263-273.

R.E. Blasak, W.S. Armel, D.W. Starks, and M.C. Hayduk, 2003, The use of simulation to evaluate hospital operations between the emergency department and a medical telemetry unit, *Proceedings of the 2003 Winter Simulation Conference* (S. Chick, P.J. Sánchez, D. Ferrin, D.J. Morrice, Editors), Institute of Electrical and Electronics Engineers, New Orleans, Louisiana, USA, 7-10 December, 1887-1893.

K. Bodtker, L. Wilson, and W. Godolphin, 1992, Simulation as an aid to clinical chemistry laboratory planning, *Proceedings of the 1992 Conference on Simulation in Health Care and Social Services* (J. Anderson, Editor), Newport Beach, California, USA, 20-22 January, 15-18.

T. Butler, G. Reeves, K. Karwan, and J. Sweigart, 1992a, Assessing the impact of patient care policies using simulation analysis, *Journal of the Society for Health Systems*, **3**(3):38-53.

T.W. Butler, K.R. Karwan, and J.R. Sweigart, 1992b, Multi-level strategic evaluation of hospital plans and decisions, *Journal of the Operational Research Society*, **43**(7):665-675.

T.W. Butler, K.R. Karwan, J.R. Sweigart, and G.R. Reeves, 1992c, An integrative model-based approach to hospital layout, *IIE Transactions*, **24**(2):144-152.

W. Cahill and M. Render, 1999, Dynamic simulation modeling of ICU bed availability, *Proceedings of the 1999 Winter Simulation Conference* (P.A. Farrington, H.B. Nembhard, D.T. Sturrock, G.W. Evans, Editors), Institute of Electrical and Electronics Engineers, Phoenix, Arizona, USA, 5-8 December, 1573-1576.

R.C. Carlson, J.C. Hershey, and D.H. Kropp, 1979, Use of optimization and simulation models to analyze outpatient health care settings, *Decision Sciences*, **10**:412-433.

D. Carroll, 1996, MedModel-Healthcare simulation software, *Proceedings of the 1996 Winter Simulation Conference* (J.M. Charnes, D.M. Morrice, D.T. Brunner, J.J. Swain, Editors), Institute of Electrical and Electronics Engineers, Coronado, California, USA, 8-11 December, 441-446.

J.S. Carson, 1996, AutoStat output statistical analysis for AutoMod Users, *Proceedings of the 1996 Winter Simulation Conference* (J.M. Charnes, D.M. Morrice, D.T. Brunner, J.J. Swain, Editors), Institute of Electrical and Electronics Engineers, Coronado, California, USA, 8-11 December, 492-499.

Y. Carson and A. Maria, 1997, Simulation optimization: Methods and applications, *Proceedings of the 1997 Winter Simulation Conference* (S. Andradottir, K.J. Healy, D.E. Withers, B.L. Nelson, Editors), Institute of Electrical and Electronics Engineers, Atlanta, Georgia, USA, 7-10 December, 118-126.

M.W. Carter, L.L. O'Brien-Pallas, J.T. Blake, L.McGillis, and S. Zhu, 1992, Simulation, scheduling, and operating rooms, *Proceedings of the 1992 Simulation in Health Care and Social Services Conference* (J.G. Anderson, Editor), Simulation Council Inc., San Diego, California, USA, 28-30.

M.A. Centeno, C. Albacete, D.O. Terzano, M. Carrillo, and T. Ogazon, 2000, A simulation study of the radiology department at JMH, *Proceedings of the 2000 Winter Simulation Conference* (J.A. Joines, R.R. Barton, K. Kang, P.A. Fishwick, Editors), Institute of Electrical and Electronics Engineers, Orlando, Florida, USA, 10-13 December, 1978-1984.

M.A. Centeno, R. Giachetti, R. Linn, and A.M. Ismail, 2003, A simulation-ILP based tool for scheduling ER staff, *Proceedings of the 2003 Winter Simulation Conference* (S. Chick, P.J. Sánchez, D. Ferrin, D.J. Morrice, Editors), Institute of Electrical and Electronics Engineers, New Orleans, Louisiana, USA, 7-10 December, 1930-1938.

M.A. Centeno, M.A. Lee, E. Lopez, H.R. Fernandez, M. Carrillo, and T. Ogazon, 2001, A simulation study of the labor and delivery rooms and JMH, *Proceedings of the 2001 Winter Simulation Conference* (B.A. Peters, J.S. Smith, D.J. Medeiros, M.W. Rohrer, Editors), Institute of Electrical and Electronics Engineers, Arlington, Virginia, USA, 9-12 December, 1392-1400.

S.-Y.E. Chan, J. Ohlmann, S. Dunbar, C. Dunbar, S. Ryan, and P. Savory, 2002, Operations research methods applied to workflow in a medical records department, *Health Care Management Science*, **5**:191-199.

M.A. Coffin, G. Lassiter, B. Killingsworth, and J.W. Kleckley, 1993, A simulation model of an X-ray facility, *1993 SCS Western Multiconference on Simulation: Simulation in the Health Sciences and Services* (J.G. Anderson, M. Katzper, Editors), Society for Computer Simulation, La Jolla, California, USA, 17-20 January, 3-7.

M.A. Cohen, J.C. Hershey, and E.N. Weiss, 1980, Analysis of capacity decisions for progressive patient care hospital facilities, *Health Services Research*, **15**:145-160.

K. Currie, W. Iskander, L. Michael, and C. Coberly, 1984, Simulation modeling in health care facilities, *Proceedings of the 1984 Winter Simulation Conference* (S. Sheppard, U.W. Pooch, C.D. Pegden, Editors), Institute of Electrical and Electronics Engineers, Dallas, Texas, USA, 28-30 November, 713-717.

R. Davies and H. Davies, 1994, Modeling patient flows and resource provision in health systems, *Omega*, **22**(2):123-131.

B. Dean, A. van Ackere, S. Gallivan, and N. Barber, 1999, When should pharmacists visit their wards? An application of simulation to planning hospital pharmacy services, *Health Care Management Science*, **2**:35-42.

D. Dearie, J. Gerson, and T Warfield, 1976, The development and use of a simulation model of an outpatient clinic, *Proceedings of the 1976 Summer Computer Simulation Conference*, Simulation Council, Washington, DC, USA, 12-14 July, 554-558.

M.A. Draeger, 1992, An emergency department simulation model used to evaluate alternative nurse staffing and patient population scenarios, *Proceedings of the 1992 Winter Simulation Conference* (J.J. Swain, D. Goldsman, R.C. Crain, J.R. Wilson, Editors),

Institute of Electrical and Electronics Engineers, Arlington, Virginia, USA, 13-16 December, 1057-1064.

M.C. Drevna and C.J. Kasales, 1984, Introduction to Arena, *Proceedings of the 1984 Winter Simulation Conference* (S. Sheppard, U.W. Pooch, C.D. Pegden, Editors), Institute of Electrical and Electronics Engineers, Dallas, Texas, USA, 28-30 November, 431-436.

M.B. Dumas, 1984, Simulation modeling for hospital bed planning, *Simulation*, **43**:69-78.

M.B. Dumas, 1985, Hospital bed utilization: An implemented simulation approach to adjusting and maintaining appropriate levels, *Health Services Research*, **20**(1): 43-61.

R. Edwards, J. Clague, J. Barlow, M. Clarke, P. Reed, and R. Rada, 1994, Operations research survey and computer simulation of waiting times in two medical outpatient clinic structures, *Health Care Analysis*, **2**:164-169.

J. El-Darzi, C. Vasilakis, T. Chaussalet, and P.H. Millard, 1998, A simulation modeling approach to evaluating length of stay, occupancy, emptiness, and bed blocking in a hospital geriatric department, *Health Care Management Science*, **1**:143-149.

T. Eldabi and R.J. Paul, 2001, A proposed approach for modeling healthcare systems for understanding, *Proceedings of the 2001 Winter Simulation Conference* (B.A. Peters, J.S. Smith, D.J. Medeiros, M.W. Rohrer, Editors), Institute of Electrical and Electronics Engineers, Arlington, Virginia, USA, 9-12 December, 1412-1420.

W. England and S. Roberts, 1978, Applications of computer simulation in health care, *Proceedings of the 1978 Winter Simulation Conference* (H.J. Highland, L.G. Hull, N.R. Neilsen, Editors), Institute of Electrical and Electronics Engineers, Miami Beach, Florida, USA, 4-6 December, 665-676.

G.W. Evans, T.B. Gor, and E. Unger, 1996, A simulation model for evaluating personnel schedules in a hospital emergency department, *Proceedings of the 1996 Winter Simulation Conference* (J.M. Charnes, D.M. Morrice, D.T. Brunner, J.J. Swain, Editors), Institute of Electrical and Electronics Engineers, Coronado, California, USA, 8-11 December, 1205-1209.

J.E. Everett, 2002, A decision support simulation model for the management of an elective surgery waiting system, *Health Care Management Science*, **5**:89-95.

D.M. Ferrin, M.J. Miller, S. Wininger, and M.S. Neuendorf, 2004, Analyzing incentives and scheduling in a major metropolitan hospital operating room through simulation, *Proceedings of the 2004 Winter Simulation Conference* (R.G. Ingalls, M.D. Rossetti, J.S. Smith, B.A. Peters, Editors), Institute of Electrical and Electronics Engineers, Washington, D.C., USA, 5-8 December, 1975-1980.

R.B. Fetter and J.D. Thompson, 1965, The simulation of hospital systems, *Operations Research*, **13**(5): 689-711.

K.E. Fitzpatrick, J.R. Baker, and D.S. Dave, 1993, An application of computer simulation to improve scheduling of hospital operating room facilities in the United States, *International Journal of Computer Applications in Technology*, **6**(4):215-224.

R.W. Freedman, 1994, Reduction of average length of stay in the emergency room using discrete simulation, *Proceedings of Simulation in the Health Sciences* (J.G. Anderson, M. Katzper, Editors), Society for Computer Simulation, Tempe, Arizona, USA, 24-26 January, 6-8.

S.C. Gabaeff and J. Lennon, 1991, New computerized technology for the design and planning of emergency departments, *Proceedings of the American Hospital Association*, American Hospital Association, Anaheim, California, USA, July, 1-15.

M.L. Garcia, M.A. Centeno, C. Rivera, and N. DeCario, 1995, Reducing time in an emergency room via a fast-track, *Proceedings of the 1995 Winter Simulation Conference*

(C. Alexopoulos, K. Kang, W.R. Lilegdon, D. Goldsman, Editors), Institute of Electrical and Electronics Engineers, Washington DC, USA, 3-6 December, 1048-1053.

P.J. Gipps, 1986, The role of computer graphics in validating simulation models, *Mathematics and Computers in Simulation*, **28**(4): 285-289.

F. Glover, J.P. Kelly, and M.L. Laguna, 1996, New advances and applications of combining simulation and optimization, *Proceedings of the 1996 Winter Simulation Conference* (J.M. Charnes, D.M. Morrice, D.T. Brunner, J.J. Swain, Editors), Institute of Electrical and Electronics Engineers, Coronado, California, USA, 8-11 December, 144-152.

W. Godolphin, K. Bodtker, and L. Wilson, 1992, Simulation modeling: A tool to help predict the impact of automation in clinical laboratories, *Laboratory Robotics and Automation*, **4**(5): 249-255.

M. Goitein, 1990, Waiting patiently, *The New England Journal of Medicine*, **323**(9): 604-608.

S. Groothuis, H.M.J. Goldschmidt, E.J. Drupsteen, J.C.M. de Vries, A. Hasman, and G.G. van Merode, 2002, Application of computer simulation analysis to assess the effects of relocating a hospital phlebotomy department, *Annals of Clinical Biochemistry*, **39**:261-272.

S. Groothuis, G.G. van Merode, and A. Hasman, 2001, Simulation as decision tool for capacity planning, *Computers Methods and Programs in Biomedicine*, **66**:139-151.

M. Guo, M. Wagner, and C. West, 2004, Outpatient clinic scheduling—A simulation approach, *Proceedings of the 2004 Winter Simulation Conference* (R.G. Ingalls, M.D. Rossetti, J.S. Smith, B.A. Peters, Editors), Institute of Electrical and Electronics Engineers, Washington, D.C., USA, 5-8 December, 1981-1987.

W.M. Hancock, D.B. Magerlein, R.H. Storer, and J.B. Martin, 1978, Parameters affecting hospital occupancy and implications for faculty sizing, *Health Services Research*, **13**:276-289.

W. Hancock and P. Walter, 1979, The use of computer simulation to develop hospital systems, *Simuletter*, **10**(4): 28-32.

W. Hancock and P. Walter, 1984, The use of admissions simulation to stabilize ancillary workloads, *Simulation*, **43**(2): 88-94.

P.R. Harper, 2002, A framework for operational modelling of hospital resources, *Health Care Management Science*, **5**:165-173.

C.R. Harrell and R.N. Price, 2000, Healthcare simulation modeling and optimization using MEDMODEL, *Proceedings of the 2000 Winter Simulation Conference* (J.A. Joines, R.R. Barton, K. Kang, P.A. Fishwick, Editors), Institute of Electrical and Electronics Engineers, Orlando, Florida, USA, 10-13 December, 203-207.

C.R. Harrell and V.R. Lange, 2001, Healthcare simulation modeling and optimization using MEDMODEL. *Proceedings of the 2001 Winter Simulation Conference* (B.A. Peters, J.S. Smith, D.J. Medeiros, M.W. Rohrer, Editors), Institute of Electrical and Electronics Engineers, Arlington, Virginia, USA, 9-12 December, 233-238.

R.A. Harris, 1985, Hospital bed requirements planning, *European Journal of Operational Research*, **25**:121-126.

F. Hashimoto and S. Bell, 1996, Improving outpatient clinic staffing and scheduling with computer simulation, *Journal of General Internal Medicine*, **11**:182-184.

D.L. Heflin and C.R. Harrell, 1998, Healthcare simulation modeling and optimization using MEDMODEL, *Proceedings of the 1998 Winter Simulation Conference* (J.D. Medeiros, E.F. Watson, J.S. Carson, M.S. Manivannan, Editors), Institute of Electrical and Electronics Engineers, Washington, D.C., USA, 13-16 December, 185-190.

K. Ishimoto, T. Ishimitsu, A. Koshiro, and S. Hirose, 1990, Computer simulation of optimum personnel assignment in hospital pharmacy using a work-sampling method, *Medical Informatics*, **15**(4): 343-354.

W.H. Iskander and D.M. Carter, 1991, A simulation model for a same day care facility at a university hospital, *Proceedings of the 1991 Winter Simulation Conference* (B.L. Nelson, W.D. Kelton, G.M. Clark, Editors), Institute of Electrical and Electronics Engineers, Phoenix, Arizona, USA, 8-11 December, 846-853.

M.W. Isken, T.J. Ward, and T.C. McKee, 1999, Simulating outpatient obstetrical clinics, *Proceedings of the 1999 Winter Simulation Conference* (P.A. Farrington, H.B. Nembhard, D.T. Sturrock, G.W. Evans, Editors), Institute of Electrical and Electronics Engineers, Phoenix, Arizona, USA, 5-8 December, 1557-1563.

W.C. Johnson, 1998, Birth of a new maternity process, *Proceedings of the 1998 Winter Simulation Conference* (J.D. Medeiros, E.F. Watson, J.S. Carson, M.S. Manivannan, Editors), Institute of Electrical and Electronics Engineers, Washington, D.C., USA, 13-16 December, 1429-1432.

L.M. Jones and A.J. Hirst, 1986, Visual simulation in hospitals: A managerial or a political tool? *European Journal of Operational Research*, **29**:167-177.

J.B. Jun, S.H. Jacobson, and J.R. Swisher, 1999, Applications of discrete-event simulation in health care clinics: A survey, *Journal of the Operational Research Society*, **50**(2): 109-123.

S.K. Kachhal, G.A. Klutke, and E.B. Daniels, 1981, Two simulation applications to outpatient clinics, *Proceedings of the 1981 Winter Simulation Conference* (T.I. Oren, C.M. Delfosse, C.M. Shubl, Editors), Institute of Electrical and Electronics Engineers, Atlanta, Georgia, USA, 9-11 December, 657-665.

D. Kanon, 1974, Simulation of waiting line problems in a hospital setting, *Proceedings of the 1st World Conference on Medical Information* (J. Anderson, J.M. Forsythe, Editors), North-Holland, Stockholm, Netherlands, 5-10 August, 503-507.

J. Karnon, 2003, Alternative decision modelling techniques for the evaluation of health care technologies: Markov processes versus discrete-event simulation, *Health Economics*, **12**: 837-848.

L.F. Keller, 1994, MedModel-Specialized software for the healthcare industry, *Proceedings of the 1994 Winter Simulation Conference* (J.D. Tew, S. Manivannan, D.A. Sadowski, A.F. Seila, Editors), Institute of Electrical and Electronics Engineers, Lake Buena Vista, Florida, USA, 11-14 December, 533-537.

J.W. Kho and G.M. Johnson, 1976, Computer simulation of a hospital health-care delivery system, *Proceedings of the 1976 Bicentennial Winter Simulation Conference* (R.G. Sargent, H.J. Highland, T.J. Schriber, Editors), Institute of Electrical and Electronics Engineers, Gaithersburg, Maryland, USA, 6-8 December, 349-360.

A. Kirtland, J. Lockwood, K. Poisker, L. Stamp, and P. Wolfe, 1995, Simulating an emergency department is as much fun as..., *Proceedings of the 1995 Winter Simulation Conference*, (C. Alexopoulos, K. Kang, W.R. Lilegdon, D. Goldsman, Editors), Institute of Electrical and Electronics Engineers, Washington DC, USA, 3-6 December, 1039-1042.

K.A. Klafehn, 1987, Impact points in patient flows through a radiology department provided through simulation, *Proceedings of the 1987 Winter Simulation Conference* (A Thesen, H Grant, WD Kelton, Editors), Institute of Electrical and Electronics Engineers, Atlanta, Georgia, USA, 14-16 December, 914-918.

K.A. Klafehn and M. Connolly, 1993, The simulation/animation of a new outpatient hematology laboratory, *1993 SCS Western Multiconference on Simulation: Simulation in the Health Sciences and Services* (J.G. Anderson, M. Katzper, Editors), Society for Computer Simulation, La Jolla, California, USA, 17-20 January, 12-15.

K.A. Klafehn and D. Owens, 1987, A simulation model designed to investigate resource utilization in a hospital emergency room, *Proceedings of the Eleventh Annual Symposium on Computer Applications in Medical Care* (W. Stead, Editor), Institute of Electrical and Electronics Engineers, Washington DC, USA, 1-4 November, 676-679.

K.A. Klafehn, D. Owens, R. Felter, N. Vonneman, and C. McKinnon, 1989, Evaluating the linkage between emergency medical services and the provision of scarce resources through simulation, *Proceedings of the 13th Annual Symposium on Computer Applications in Medical Care* (L. Kingsland III, Editor), Institute of Electrical and Electronics Engineers, Washington DC, USA, 5-8 November, 335-339.

K.J. Klassen and T.R. Rohleder, 1996, Scheduling outpatient appointments in a dynamic environment, *Journal of Operations Management*, **14**:83-101.

R.W. Klein, R.S. Dittus, S.D. Roberts, and J.R. Wilson, 1993, Simulation modeling and health-care decision making, *Medical Decision Making*, **13**(4):347-354.

M.G. Kletke and T.E. Dooley, 1984, A simulation model of a maternity ward: A key planning tool for hospital administrators, *Proceedings of the Conference on Simulation in Health Care Delivery System*, San Diego, California, USA, 2-4 February, 35-39.

M.J. Kraitsik and A. Bossmeyer, 1993, Simulation applied to planning an emergency department expansion, *1993 SCS Western Multiconference on Simulation: Simulation in the Health Sciences and Services* (J.G. Anderson, M. Katzper, Editors), Society for Computer Simulation, La Jolla, California, USA, 17-20 January, 19-27.

D. Kropp, R.C. Carlson, and J.V. Jucker, 1978, Use of both optimization and simulation models to analyze complex systems, *Proceedings of the 1978 Winter Simulation Conference* (H.J. Highland, L.G. Hull, N.R. Neilsen, Editors), Institute of Electrical and Electronics Engineers, Miami Beach, Florida, USA, 4-6 December, 195-201.

D. Kropp and J. Hershey, 1979, Recursive optimization-simulation modeling for the analysis of ambulatory health care facilities, *Simuletter*, **10**(4): 43-46.

A.P. Kumar and R. Kapur, 1989, Discrete simulation application-scheduling staff for the emergency room, *Proceedings of the 1989 Winter Simulation Conference* (E.A. MacNair, K.J. Musselman, P. Heidelberger, Editors), Institute of Electrical and Electronics Engineers, Washington DC, USA, 4-6 December, 1112-1120.

P.J. Kuzdrall, N.K. Kwak, and H.H. Schmitz, 1981, Simulating space requirements and scheduling policies in a hospital surgical suite, *Simulation*, **27**:163-171.

N. Kwak, P. Kuzdrall, and H. Schmitz, 1975, Simulating the use of space in a hospital surgical suite, *Simulation*, **24**(5): 147-152.

J.M. Lach and R.M. Vázquez, 2004, Simulation model of the telemedicine program, *Proceedings of the 2004 Winter Simulation Conference* (R.G. Ingalls, M.D. Rossetti, J.S. Smith, B.A. Peters, Editors), Institute of Electrical and Electronics Engineers, Washington, D.C., USA, 5-8 December, 2012-2017.

E. Lambo, 1983, An optimization-simulation model of a rural health center in Nigeria, *Interfaces*, **13**(3): 29-35.

A.M. Law and W.D. Kelton, 2000, *Simulation Modelling and Analysis*, 3rd Ed., McGraw-Hill.

B. Lehaney and V. Hlupic, 1995, Simulation modeling for resource allocation and planning in the health sector, *Journal of the Royal Society of Health*, **115**(6): 382-385.

B. Lehaney and R.J. Paul, 1994, Using soft systems methodology to develop a simulation of out-patient services, *Journal of the Royal Society for Health*, **114**:248-251.

B. Lehaney and R.J. Paul, 1996, The use of soft systems methodology in the development of a simulation of outpatient services at Watford General Hospital, *Journal of the Operational Research Society*, **47**:864-870.

J. Lennon, 1992, Simulation in the design and planning of emergency departments, *1992 SCS Western Multiconference: Simulation in education for business, management, and MIS*, Society for Computer Simulation, Newport Beach, California, USA, January, 93-97.

J.L. Levy, B.A. Watford, and V.T. Owen, 1989, Simulation analysis of an outpatient services facility, *Journal of the Society for Health Systems*, **1**(2): 35-49.

T. Lim, D. Uyeno, and I. Vertinsky, 1975, Hospital admissions systems: A simulation approach, *Simulation and Games*, **6**(2): 188-201.

L. Liyanage and M. Gale, 1995, Quality improvement for the Campbelltown hospital emergency service, *1995 IEEE International Conference on Systems, Man, and Cybernetics*, Institute of Electrical and Electronics Engineers, Vancouver, British Columbia, Canada, 22-25 October, 13: 1997-2002.

B.G. Lopez-Valcarcel and P.B. Perez, 1994, Evaluation of alternative functional designs in an emergency department by means of simulation, *Simulation*, **63**(1): 20-28.

J.C. Lowery, 1992, Simulation of a hospital's surgical suite and critical care area, *Proceedings of the 1992 Winter Simulation Conference* (J.J. Swain, D. Goldsman, R.C. Crain, J.R. Wilson, Editors), Institute of Electrical and Electronics Engineers, Arlington, Virginia, USA, 13-16 December, 1071-1078.

J.C. Lowery, 1993, Multi-hospital validation of critical care simulation model, *Proceedings of the 1993 Winter Simulation Conference* (G.W. Evans, M. Mollaghasemi, E.C. Russell, W.E. Biles, Editors), Institute of Electrical and Electronics Engineers, Los Angeles, California, USA, 12-15 December, 1207-1215.

J.C. Lowery, 1994, Barriers to implementing simulation in health care, *Proceedings of the 1994 Winter Simulation Conference* (J.D. Tew, S. Manivannan, D.A. Sadowski, A.F. Seila, Editors), Institute of Electrical and Electronics Engineers, Lake Buena Vista, Florida, USA, 11-14 December, 868-875.

J.C. Lowery, 1996, Introduction to simulation in health care, *Proceedings of the 1996 Winter Simulation Conference* (J.M. Charnes, D.M. Morrice, D.T. Brunner, J.J. Swain, Editors), Institute of Electrical and Electronics Engineers, Coronado, California, USA, 8-11 December, 78-84.

J.C. Lowery, 1998, Getting started in simulation healthcare, *Proceedings of the 1998 Winter Simulation Conference* (J.D. Medeiros, E.F. Watson, J.S. Carson, M.S. Manivannan, Editors), Institute of Electrical and Electronics Engineers, Washington, D.C., USA, 13-16 December, 31-35.

J.C. Lowery and J.A. Davis, 1999, Determination of operating room requirements using simulation, *Proceedings of the 1999 Winter Simulation Conference* (P.A. Farrington, H.B. Nembhard, D.T. Sturrock, G.W. Evans, Editors), Institute of Electrical and Electronics Engineers, Phoenix, Arizona, USA, 5-8 December, 1568-1572.

J.C. Lowery and J.B. Martin, 1992, Design and validation of a critical care simulation model, *Journal of the Society for Health Systems*, **3**(3): 15-36.

J.M. Magerlein and J.B. Martin, 1976, Surgical demand scheduling: A review, *Health Services Research*, **11**:53-68.

A. Mahachek, 1992, An introduction to patient flow simulation for health-care managers, *Journal of the Society for Health Systems*, **3**(3): 73-81.

A.R. Mahachek and T.L. Knabe, 1984, Computer simulation of patient flow in obstetrical/gynecology clinics, *Simulation*, **30**:95-101.

S. Mahapatra, C.P. Koelling, L. Patvivatsiri, B. Fraticelli, D. Eitel, and L. Grove, 2003, Pairing emergency severity index5-level triage data with computer aided system design to improve emergency department access and throughput, *Proceedings of the 2003 Winter Simulation Conference* (S. Chick, P.J. Sánchez, D. Ferrin, D.J. Morrice, Editors), Institute of Electrical and Electronics Engineers, New Orleans, Louisiana, USA, 7-10 December, 1917-1925.

J. Marsh, 1979, Simulation as a decision aid: A management perspective, *Simuletter*, **10**(5): 47-49.

E. Martin, R. Grønhaug, and K. Haugene, 2003, Proposals to reduce over-crowding, lengthy stays and improve patient care: Study on the geriatric department In Norway's largest hospital, *Proceedings of the 2003 Winter Simulation Conference* (S. Chick, P.J. Sánchez, D. Ferrin, D.J. Morrice, Editors), Institute of Electrical and Electronics Engineers, New Orleans, Louisiana, USA, 7-10 December, 1876-1881.

B.J. Masterson, T.G. Mihara, G. Miller, S.C. Randolph, M.E. Forkner, and A.L. Crouter, 2004, Using models and data to support optimization of the military health system: A case study in an intensive care unit, *Health Care Management Science*, **7**:217-224.

F. McGuire, 1994, Using simulation to reduce length of stay in emergency departments, *Proceedings of the 1994 Winter Simulation Conference* (J.D. Tew, S. Manivannan, D.A. Sadowski, A.F. Seila, Editors), Institute of Electrical and Electronics Engineers, Lake Buena Vista, Florida, USA, 11-14 December, 861-867.

M.L. McHugh, 1989, Computer simulation as a method for selecting nurse staffing levels in hospitals, *Proceedings of the 1989 Winter Simulation Conference* (E.A. MacNair, K.J. Musselman, P. Heidelberger, Editors), Institute of Electrical and Electronics Engineers, Washington DC, USA, 4-6 December, 1121-1129.

L. Meier, E. Sigal, and F.R. Vitale, 1985, The use of simulation model for planning ambulatory surgery, *Proceedings of the 1985 Winter Simulation Conference* (D.T. Gantz, G.C. Blais, S.L. Solomon, Editors), Institute of Electrical and Electronics Engineers, San Francisco, California, USA, 11-13 December, 558-563.

M.J. Miller, D.M. Ferrin, and M.G. Messer, 2004, Fixing the emergency department: A transformational journey with EDsim, *Proceedings of the 2004 Winter Simulation Conference* (R.G. Ingalls, M.D. Rossetti, J.S. Smith, B.A. Peters, Editors), Institute of Electrical and Electronics Engineers, Washington, D.C., USA, 5-8 December, 1988-1993.

M.J. Miller, D.M. Ferrin, and J.M. Szymanski, 2003, Simulating six sigma improvement ideas for a hospital emergency department, *Proceedings of the 2003 Winter Simulation Conference* (S. Chick, P.J. Sánchez, D. Ferrin, D.J. Morrice, Editors), Institute of Electrical and Electronics Engineers, New Orleans, Louisiana, USA, 7-10 December, 1926-1929.

B.P. Morrison and B.C. Bird, 2003, A methodology for modeling front office and patient care processes in ambulatory health care, *Proceedings of the 2003 Winter Simulation Conference* (S. Chick, P.J. Sánchez, D. Ferrin, D.J. Morrice, Editors), Institute of Electrical and Electronics Engineers, New Orleans, Louisiana, USA, 7-10 December, 1882-1886.

A.K. Mukherjee, 1991, A simulation model for management of operations in the pharmacy of a hospital, *Simulation*, **56**(2): 91-103

D.R. Murphy and E. Sigal, 1985, Evaluating surgical block scheduling using computer simulation, *Proceedings of the 1985 Winter Simulation Conference* (D.T. Gantz, G.C. Blais, S.L. Solomon, Editors), Institute of Electrical and Electronics Engineers, San Francisco, California, USA, 11-13 December, 551-557.

P.C. O'Kane, 1981, A simulation model of a diagnostic radiology department, *European Journal of Operational Research*, **6**:38-45.

E. Olson and L.E. Dux, 1994, Computer model targets best route for expanding hospital surgicenter, *Industrial Engineering*, **26**(9): 24-6.

V.Z. Osidach and M.C. Fu, 2003, Computer simulation of a mobile examination center, *Proceedings of the 2003 Winter Simulation Conference* (S. Chick, P.J. Sánchez, D. Ferrin, D.J. Morrice, Editors), Institute of Electrical and Electronics Engineers, New Orleans, Louisiana, USA, 7-10 December, 1868-1875.

R.J. Paul, 1989, Visual simulation: Seeing is believing, *Impacts of Recent Computer Advances on Operations Research*, **9**:422-432.

R.J. Paul and J. Kuljis, 1995, A generic simulation package for organizing outpatient clinics, *Proceedings of the 1995 Winter Simulation Conference* (C. Alexopoulos, K. Kang, W.R. Lilegdon, D. Goldsman, Editors), Institute of Electrical and Electronics Engineers, Washington DC, USA, 3-6 December, 1043-1047.

R.N. Price and C.R. Harrell, 1999, Healthcare simulation modeling and optimization using MEDMODEL, *Proceedings of the 1999 Winter Simulation Conference* (P.A. Farrington, H.B. Nembhard, D.T. Sturrock, G.W. Evans, Editors), Institute of Electrical and Electronics Engineers, Phoenix, Arizona, USA, 5-8 December, 215-219.

J.S. Rakich, P.J. Kuzdrall, K.A. Klafehn, and A.G. Krigline, 1991, Simulation in the hospital setting: Implications for managerial decision making and management development, *Journal of Management Development*, **10**(4): 31-37.

S. Ramakrishnan, K. Nagarkar, M. DeGennaro, K. Srihari, A.K. Courtney, and F. Emick, 2004, A study of the CT scan Area of a healthcare provider, *Proceedings of the 2004 Winter Simulation Conference* (R.G. Ingalls, M.D. Rossetti, J.S. Smith, B.A. Peters, Editors), Institute of Electrical and Electronics Engineers, Washington, D.C., USA, 5-8 December, 2025-2031.

F.J. Ramis, J.L. Palma, and F.F. Baesler, 2001, The use of simulation for process improvement at an ambulatory surgery center, *Proceedings of the 2001 Winter Simulation Conference* (B.A. Peters, J.S. Smith, D.J. Medeiros, M.W. Rohrer, Editors), Institute of Electrical and Electronics Engineers, Arlington, Virginia, USA, 9-12 December, 1401-1404.

E.J Rising, R. Baron, and B. Averill, 1973, A systems analysis of a university-health-service outpatient clinic, *Operations Research*, **21**(5): 1030-1047.

M. Ritondo and R.W. Freedman, 1993, The effects of procedure scheduling on emergency room throughput: A simulation study, *1993 SCS Western Multiconference on Simulation: Simulation in the Health Sciences and Services* (J.G. Anderson, M. Katzper, Editors), Society for Computer Simulation, La Jolla, California, USA, 17-20 January, 8-11.

T.R. Rohleder and K.J. Klassen, 2002, Rolling horizon appointment scheduling: A simulation study, *Health Care Management Science*, **5**:201-209.

G. Romanin-Jacur and P. Facchin, 1987, Optimal planning of a pediatric semi-intensive care unit via simulation, *European Journal of Operational Research*, **29**:192-198

M.D. Rossetti, A. Kumar, and R.A. Felder, 1998, Mobile robot simulation of clinic laboratory deliveries, *Proceedings of the 1998 Winter Simulation Conference* (J.D. Medeiros, E.F. Watson, J.S. Carson, M.S. Manivannan, Editors), Institute of Electrical and Electronics Engineers, Washington, D.C., USA, 13-16 December, 1415-1421.

M.D. Rossetti, G.F. Trzcinski, and S.A. Syverud, 1999, Emergency department simulation and determination of optimal attending physician staffing schedules, *Proceedings of the 1999 Winter Simulation Conference* (P.A. Farrington, H.B. Nembhard, D.T. Sturrock, G.W. Evans, Editors), Institute of Electrical and Electronics Engineers, Phoenix, Arizona, USA, 5-8 December, 1532-1540.

S. Samaha, W.S. Armel, and D.W. Starks, 2003, The use of simulation to reduce the length of stay in an emergency department, *Proceedings of the 2003 Winter Simulation Conference* (S. Chick, P.J. Sánchez, D. Ferrin, D.J. Morrice, Editors), Institute of Electrical and Electronics Engineers, New Orleans, Louisiana, USA, 7-10 December, 1907-1911.

S.M. Sanchez, T. Ogazon, D.M. Ferrin, J.A. Sepúlveda, and T.J. Ward, 2000, Emerging issues in healthcare simulation, *Proceedings of the 2000 Winter Simulation Conference*

(J.A. Joines, R.R. Barton, K. Kang, P.A. Fishwick, Editors), Institute of Electrical and Electronics Engineers, Orlando, Florida, USA, 10-13 December, 1999-2003.

R.G. Sargent, 1992, Validation and verification of simulation models, *Proceedings of the 1992 Winter Simulation Conference* (J.J. Swain, D. Goldsman, R.C. Crain, J.R. Wilson, Editors), Institute of Electrical and Electronics Engineers, Arlington, Virginia, USA, 13-16 December, 104-114.

J.A. Sepúlveda, W.J. Thompson, F.F. Baesler, M.I. Alvarez, and L.E. Cahoon, III, 1999, The use of simulation for process improvement in a cancer treatment center, *Proceedings of the 1999 Winter Simulation Conference* (P.A. Farrington, H.B. Nembhard, D.T. Sturrock, G.W. Evans, Editors), Institute of Electrical and Electronics Engineers, Phoenix, Arizona, USA, 5-8 December, 1541-1548.

D. Sinreich and Y.N. Marmor, 2004, A simple and intuitive simulation tool for analyzing emergency department operations, *Proceedings of the 2004 Winter Simulation Conference* (R.G. Ingalls, M.D. Rossetti, J.S. Smith, B.A. Peters, Editors), Institute of Electrical and Electronics Engineers, Washington, D.C., USA, 5-8 December, 1994-2002.

S.R. Smith, B.J. Schroer, and R.E. Shannon, 1979, Scheduling of patients and resources for ambulatory health care, *Proceedings of the 1979 Winter Simulation Conference* (H.J. Highland, M.G. Spiegel, R. Shannon, Editors), Institute of Electrical and Electronics Engineers, San Diego, California, USA, 3-5 December, 553-562.

E.A Smith and H.R. Warner, 1971, Simulation of a multiphasic screening procedure for hospital admissions, *Simulation*, **17**(2): 57-64.

V.L. Smith-Daniels, S.B. Schweikhart, and D.E. Smith-Daniels, 1988, Capacity management in health care services: Review and future research directions, *Decision Sciences*, **19**:889-918.

E.F. Stafford, Jr, 1976, A General Simulation Model for Multifacility Outpatient Clinics, M.S. Thesis, Pennsylvania State University, Pennsylvania.

E.F. Stafford, Jr., 1978, Simulation vs. mathematical analysis for systems modeling: a comparison of techniques, *Proceedings of the 1978 Summer Computer Simulation Conference*, AFIPS Press, Los Angeles, California, USA, 24-26 July, 53-159.

J.E. Stahl, M.S. Roberts, and S. Gazelle, 2003, Optimizing management and financial performance of the teaching ambulatory care clinic, *Journal of General Internal Medicine*, **18**:266-274.

C.R. Standridge, 1999, A tutorial on simulation in health care: Applications and issues, *Proceedings of the 1999 Winter Simulation Conference* (P.A. Farrington, H.B. Nembhard, D.T. Sturrock, G.W. Evans, Editors), Institute of Electrical and Electronics Engineers, Phoenix, Arizona, USA, 5-8 December, 49-55.

D. Steward and C.R. Standridge, 1996, A veterinary practice simulator based on the integration of expert system and process modeling, *Simulation*, **66**:143-159.

J.R. Swisher and S.H. Jacobson, 2002, Evaluating the design of a family practice healthcare clinic using discrete-event simulation, *Health Care Management Science*, **5**:75-88.

J.R. Swisher, B.J. Jun, S.H. Jacobson, and O. Balci, 1997, Simulation of the Queston physician network, *Proceedings of the 1997 Winter Simulation Conference* (S. Andradottir, K.J. Healy, D.E. Withers, B.L. Nelson, Editors), Institute of Electrical and Electronics Engineers, Atlanta, Georgia, USA, 7-10 December, 1146-1154.

J.R. Swisher, S.H. Jacobson, J.B. Jun, and O. Balci, 2001, Modeling and analyzing a physician clinic environment using discrete-event (visual) simulation, *Computers and Operations Research*, **28**(2): 105-125.

S.T. Takakuwa and H. Shiozaki, 2004, Functional analysis for operating emergency department of a general hospital, *Proceedings of the 2004 Winter Simulation Conference*

(R.G. Ingalls, M.D. Rossetti, J.S. Smith, B.A. Peters, Editors), Institute of Electrical and Electronics Engineers, Washington, D.C., USA, 5-8 December, 2003-2011.

B.A. Tan, A. Gubaras, and N. Phojanamongkolkij, 2002, Simulation study of Dreyer urgent care facility, *Proceedings of the 2002 Winter Simulation Conference* (E. Yücesan, C.H. Chen, J.L. Snowdon, J.M. Charnes, Editors), Institute of Electrical and Electronics Engineers, San Diego, California, USA, 8-11 December, 1922-1927.

D. Valinsky, 1975, Simulation, *Operations Research in Healthcare: A Critical Analysis* (L.J. Shuman, R.D. Speas, J.P. Young, Editors), The Johns Hopkins University Press: Baltimore, Maryland, USA.

C. Vasilakis and E. El-Darzi, 2001, A simulation study of the winter bed crisis, *Health Care Management Science*, **4**:31-36.

G. Vassilacopoulos, 1985, A simulation model for bed allocation to hospital inpatient departments, *Simulation*, **45**(5): 233-241.

S. Vemuri, 1984, Simulated analysis of patient waiting time in an outpatient pharmacy, *American Journal of Hospital Pharmacy*, **41**:1127-1130.

J.M.H. Vissers, 1998, Health care management modelling: A process perspective, *Health Care Management Science*, **1**:77-85.

S.D. Walter, 1973, A comparison of appointment schedules in hospital radiology department, *British Journal of Preventive and Social Medicine*, **27**:160-167.

M.L. Weng and A.A. Houshmand, 1999, Healthcare simulation: A case study at a local clinic, *Proceedings of the 1999 Winter Simulation Conference* (P.A. Farrington, H.B. Nembhard, D.T. Sturrock, G.W. Evans, Editors), Institute of Electrical and Electronics Engineers, Phoenix, Arizona, USA, 5-8 December, 1577-1584.

A. Wiinamaki and R. Dronzek, 2003, Using simulation in the architectural concept phase of an emergency department design, *Proceedings of the 2003 Winter Simulation Conference* (S. Chick, P.J. Sánchez, D. Ferrin, D.J. Morrice, Editors), Institute of Electrical and Electronics Engineers, New Orleans, Louisiana, USA, 7-10 December, 1912-1916.

S.V. Williams, 1983, How many intensive care beds are enough? *Critical Care Medicine*, **11**(6): 412-416.

W.J. Williams, R.P. Covert, and J.D. Steele, 1967, Simulation modeling of a teaching hospital clinic, *Hospitals*, **41**(21): 71-75.

J.C.T. Wilson, 1981, Implementation of computer simulation projects in health care, *Journal of the Operational Research Society*, **32**:825-832.

A. Wilt and D. Goddin, 1989, Health care case study: Simulating staffing needs and work flow in an outpatient diagnostic center, *Industrial Engineering*, **21**(5): 22-26.

C. Wong, G. Geiger, Y.D. Derman, C.R. Busby, and M.W. Carter, 2003, Redesigning the medication ordering, dispensing, and administration process in an acute care academic health sciences centre. *Proceedings of the 2003 Winter Simulation Conference* (S. Chick, P.J. Sánchez, D. Ferrin, D.J. Morrice, Editors), Institute of Electrical and Electronics Engineers, New Orleans, Louisiana, USA, 7-10 December, 1894-1902.

M.B. Wright, 1987, The application of a surgical bed simulation model, *European Journal of Operational Research*, **32**:26-32.

F. Zilm, D. Arch, and R.B. Hollis, 1983, An application of simulation modeling to surgical intensive care bed need analysis in a university hospital, *Hospital & Health Services Administration*, **28**(5): 82-101.

Chapter 9

FORECASTING DEMAND FOR REGIONAL HEALTHCARE

Peter Congdon
Department of Geography, Queen Mary and Westfield College, Mile End Road, London E1 4NS

Abstract: Trends in developed nations point to increased demand for acute inpatient care across most age groups, though especially at older ages. Demand growth has also been differentiated by specialty, with evidence of a major rise in demand for medical rather than surgical hospital care. This growth has occurred despite new emphasis on siting appropriate care in primary and community settings. Building on existing work relating to spatial perspectives on changing health demand, the present analysis develops a Bayesian approach to modeling the generation of health demand in a region and its allocation to health providers. At the first stage projections of acute demand are made by specialty, patient age and area of residence, with the allocation to providers then determined by a gravity model. A case study considers trends in health demand during the 1990s as a basis for forecasting during 2000-2010. The study region comprises North East London and South Essex. In this application, projections of specialty referral rates (usage rates) by age are based on national data, and are applied to regional population projections to give a forecast health demand. The allocation of this demand to hospitals then takes account of projected changes in the configuration of hospital beds in the region.

Key words: Health Demand Gravity Model.

1. INTRODUCTION

There is growing awareness of the impact of changing age structures on demand for health care. In terms of demand for hospital care (i.e. the acute health sector) there is a pronounced age gradient of usage in many health specialties. With increasing proportions of the very old in the total population as life expectancy extends, this raises issues about growing morbidity and hence health demand from this age group (Kane, 1994; Metz, 1999).

Combined with population ageing are trends in the demand for health care. National evidence in the UK and other developed nations points to increased demand for acute inpatient care (via inpatient referrals) across most age groups, though especially at older ages. Demand growth for hospital care has also been differentiated by specialty and method of admission, with evidence of a major rise in demand for medical rather than surgical care, in part through a rise in emergency admissions (Hull et al, 1997; Puig-Junoy et al, 1998). Growth in acute demand has occurred despite the potential for compressing morbidity, namely reducing cumulative lifetime morbidity through success in lifestyle risk prevention, so postponing the age of onset of morbidity (Fries et al, 1998).

Demand for hospital care will also be affected by the performance of health care systems, and success or otherwise of strategies regarding the appropriate balance of care between community and acute settings. The Department of Health in the UK undertook a Hospital Beds Inquiry to investigate future bed needs in acute hospitals (Dept of Health, 2000). This inquiry included in its remit the impact of demographic change and policy initiatives on demand, as well as reviewing changing patterns of bed usage in hospitals in terms of reduced lengths of stay and increased day case rates. Day cases may involve temporary use of hospital beds but not overnight stays, and have been increasing as a proportion of all hospital admissions (Sibbritt, 1992).

Policy initiatives to manage demand and plan capacity are aimed at containing the increase in hospital admissions. They include targets to increase day case rates, provide community based rehabilitation and intermediate care in residential and nursing home settings (so acting against 'bed blocking' by certain patient categories), and efforts to boost primary care in order to reduce avoidable admissions, especially those classified as emergencies. Strategies within hospital include improved bed management and reductions in length of inpatient stay. These initiatives are set against longer term strategic objectives to raise health expectancies by preventive measures and encouragement of healthier lifestyles.

Against such a background of demographic and service provision change, the present analysis considers projections of demand for hospital care in 2005-6 in a study region covering 2 million people in North East London and parts of the adjacent county of Essex. The study region includes socially deprived parts of inner East London (the East London and City Health Authority), suburban and rural South Essex, and four suburban boroughs in outer North East London (Redbridge, Waltham Forest, Barking, and Havering). Altogether there are 13 Local Authority areas considered, with the small City of London area merged with the London Borough of Tower Hamlets. There are ten hospitals ('providers') considered in the analysis, accounting for over 90% of the regions hospital referrals (Figure 9-1). The hospital sites considered are general or District hospitals including Accident and Emergency facilities (i.e. special hospitals, such as psychiatric hospitals are not considered).

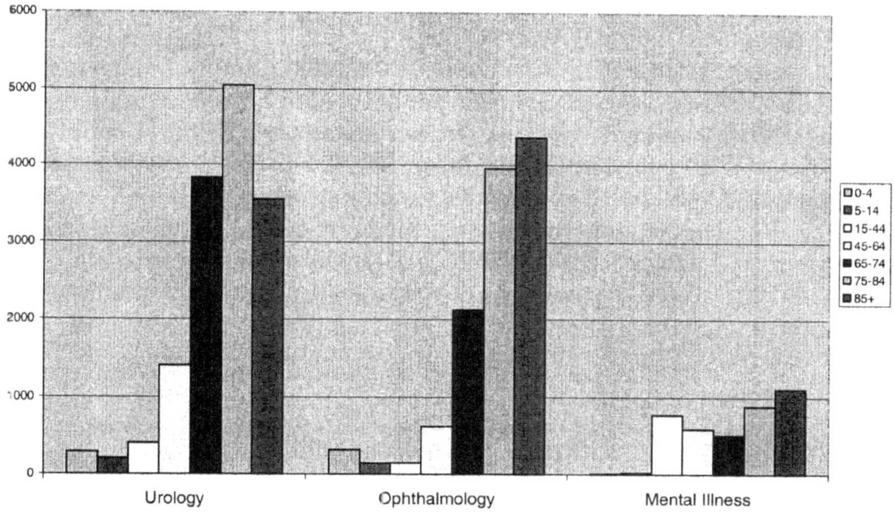

Figure 9-1. Referral Rates in Selected Specialties

2. MODELLING ISSUES

The analysis focuses especially on the impact of changing population totals and age compositions, and of changes in referral rates (i.e. health demand) on levels of acute referrals by specialty and provider within the context of the publicly funded UK National Health Service.

Spatial perspectives on changing health demand have been discussed before (Clarke and Wilson, 1984; Lowe and Sen, 1996). The modeling of future demand and its impact on acute care provision is complicated by the interplay of factors involved. These include demographic change in different residential areas (e.g. changing age and ethnic structure), changes in demand for different categories of acute care (e.g. specialties), the blurred interface

In the present analysis, projections of acute demand for future years (t) are made in terms of specialty (s), hospital provider (h), patient age (a) and local authority of residence (i). Other variables might potentially be included in such an analysis, such as patient's sex, income group or social class. The latter two variables are not available routinely in UK health records but might be especially relevant in projections of health care which also involved a split between private and public health care.

Because study region data on specialty use by age are not available on an extended time series basis, the analysis includes retrospective analysis of England wide specialty referral trends (from 1991-92). These data are analysed with a view to establishing past trends and projecting likely future growth in specialty specific referral rates by age. The study region health demand data pertains to a single year (1997-98) and contains hospital referral data by specialty, patient age, patient area of residence and hospital provider. Also available for the study region are projections of the population and its age structure in the year 2005-6. These two sources of data, combined with the England wide projections of specialty use, form the basis for future projections of health demand by local authority area and specialty, and of the way it is distributed across the ten acute providers.

In summary terms the model involves a demand generation sub-model which predicts numbers of referrals by area, age, specialty and year $n_{i,a,s,t}$. This model uses national data on past specialty trends by age N_{ast} to project likely specialty demand, together with regional projections of population by age and area p_{iat}. With sufficient regional data on specialty trends the need to involve national reference data might be avoided. The projected referrals $n_{i,a,s,t}$ are then allocated to providers via an extended gravity model formulation (i.e. with areas as origins and hospitals as destinations but with additional stratification by specialty).

The allocation stage may be based simply on projections of existing activity, with referrals serving as mass measures in the gravity allocation. This may be broadly termed a demand led projection. Alternatively, the gravity model may be adjusted to allow for new hospital sites, closure of sites or the expansion or contraction of bed numbers at existing sites (Congdon, 2000). Under this option, total acute beds (for example) may provide the mass measure in the gravity model.

between acute and community care for many chronic conditions (for example, hospital admissions may be avoidable given suitable community care and case management), the interaction between residence area and hospital location (e.g. in terms of travel mode and choice between providers), and questions of hospital capacity management to meet demand. Models will tend to be at best partial and to involve simplifying assumptions. They also tend either to be statistical models aiming at best fit to observed data with forecasts based on extrapolating to the future, or simulation models which generate future scenarios based on realistic input values without necessarily considering issues of fit.

Much statistical work has focussed on the less predictable emergency care element of hospital workload, or on particular care areas (e.g. geriatric care), or on making demand estimates for single providers. This work may have a regional focus but often concentrates on simple summary measures (e.g. total emergency admissions from an entire region to a single provider), rather than providing a disaggregated overview of demand for different demographic groups, different residential areas, multiple providers, and different areas of care (e.g. specialties). Thus Milner (1988) presents an ARIMA model of attendances at emergency units, while Farmer et al (1990) use such a model to forecast need for surgical beds; a later review of such work appears in Milner (1997), with Jones et al (2002) using a GARCH model for emergency bed occupancy at one provider. Operational research models based on queuing theory include Utley et al (2003), Gilchrist (1985) and a number of papers by Millard and co-workers (e.g. Millard et al, 2000; McKay and Millard, 1999). Downing and Wilson (2002) present a descriptive analysis of temporal and demographic variations in A&E attendances, describing variations over broad age groups. By contrast, Harper et al (2005) present a simulation model for patient flows that includes area of residence and travel mode but without allowance for patient demography.

The present analysis contributes to these developments using a Bayesian modeling approach which includes both demand generation and allocation to specialties and providers using a gravity model, and extends to forecasting medium term acute health demand. The model provides a demand overview in the sense of being disaggregated by age group, specialty, provider, area of residence and potentially other stratifiers. The model may be extended to include supply changes or to allow for capacity parameters (length of stay, occupancy) – see sections 8 and 10. In this connection, Taket and Mayhew (1981) develop an earlier gravity model of patient flows in London (though without including demographic group or specialty) while Tebaldi and West (1998) illustrate a Bayesian gravity model approach to transportation flows.

3. PROJECTING REFERRAL PATTERNS BY AGE AND SPECIALTY

Referrals for the study region illustrate the pronounced age gradients of inpatient usage rates, and therefore the potential impact in the next decade of an increasing proportion of elderly populations. Table 9-1 shows the high rates of usage by persons over 75 for specialties such as urology, ophthalmology and general medicine. For the broad categories of general surgery and general medicine, which together account for around a third of all regional referrals (i.e., around 150,000 in an annual total of 450,000), the referral rate among the over 75s is 3 to 4 times the average rate for all ages (Figure 9-2). The main objectives of the generation stage of the analysis are to project these usage profiles by age and specialty at local authority area level to mid-decade.

Table 9-1. Hospital Referrals, Numbers and Rates, in Study Region, by Age Band and Specialty 1997-98

Numbers of Episodes	0-4	5-14	15-44	45-64	65-74	75-84	85+	All ages	
Total Episodes	51619	20996	154752	87685	59699	55269	24313	454333	
Total Population of Region	158073	293474	946915	444862	163639	103451	35030	2145444	
Age specific referral rates per 100,000 population (Specialties with all ages rate over 500/100,000)	0-4	5-14	15-44	45-64	65-74	75-84	85+	All ages	***Ratio of 75+ rate to average***
General Surgery	621	870	1707	2975	4657	5687	5161	2249	3.3
Urology	289	206	405	1404	3826	5048	3548	1112	5.6
Trauma & Orthopaedics (T&O)	631	969	1001	1487	2207	3331	4799	1337	3.7
Ear Nose and Throat (ENT)	1313	1488	565	561	599	508	474	744	0.9
Ophthalmology	317	146	152	624	2121	3955	4373	664	8.2
General Medicine	288	206	2238	6135	12793	13563	14705	4179	4.4
Paediatrics	21379	1655	68	-	-	-	-	1832	-
Geriatric Medicine	-	-	94	347	2132	13282	28510	1382	-
Gynaecology, Obstetrics	5138	29	7389	1296	645	587	468	3997	0.2
Mental Illness	9	18	774	590	510	888	1108	567	2.2
Total (including minor specialties)	32655	7154	16343	19711	36482	53425	69406	21177	3.6

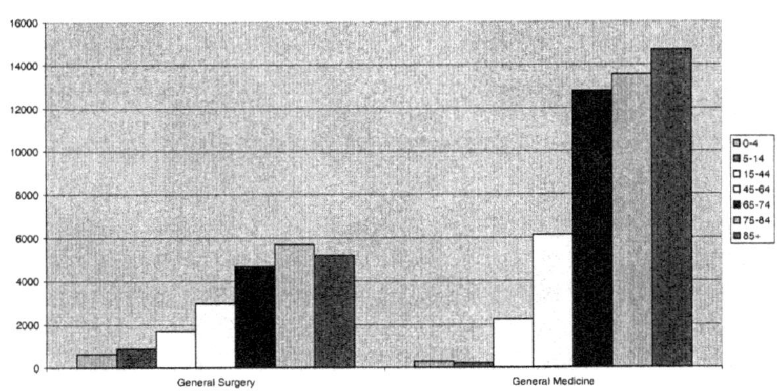

Figure 9-2. Annual Referral Rates per 100,000 (1997-98) by Age Group, Study Region

Let $n_{ias} = \Sigma_h n_{i,a,s,h}$ denote the pattern of referrals in a particular year, aggregating over hospitals h. Here the year concerned is 1997-98. The ages are as in Table 9-1, and there are S=18 specialties. Since these are count data, with potentially small numbers of events involved, a Poisson model is assumed in relation to age specific populations by area, denoted p_{ia}, for the same year. Thus for a given year

$$n_{ias} \sim \text{Poi}(\mu_{ias})$$
$$\mu_{ias} = p_{ia} \times \rho_{ias}$$

where ρ_{ias} are age and specialty specific usage rates by local area, (i=1,..13; a=1,..7; s=1,..18). These in turn are modeled in terms of two factors:

- age and specialty effects across the region γ^R_{as};
- area and specialty specific effects δ_{is}.

Both sets of effects are taken to be random. They reflect, respectively, the contrasts in age usage rates within and between specialties (as illustrated in Table 9-1), and area level departures from regional norms in terms of specialty use.

The analysis may therefore be seen 'provision constrained' as it incorporates current variations between areas in their referral rates to different specialties. Some of the differences δ_{is} may be related to patient need (e.g. populations may differ in their need for maternity services or cancer services because of social factors), others to variations in supply of services.

Adding main effects for specialty and age was found to make little difference to outputs from subsequent stages of the model, such as the final projections of regional hospital activity by specialty. So the model for region wide referral rates in the base year t=B (here 1997-98) is

$$\log(\rho_{ias}) = \alpha + \delta_{is} + \gamma^R_{as} \qquad (9\text{-}1)$$

We assume that the first component of this model, namely area differences in specialty usage rates δ_{is}, remains constant in future years, but anticipate that demand growth is likely to vary by specialty and by age also. Hence the element γ^{R}_{as} will be subject to change and need to be projected on the basis of past trends. Projections will be facilitated if these trends are consistent and provide a clear basis for forecasting.

4. PROJECTING NATIONAL SPECIALTY REFERRAL RATES

The national evidence indeed provides clear trends in acute hospital referrals. Thus referral rates (per 100,000 population) across all specialties have been increasing throughout England at around 6% annually for the over 75s and around 3.5% for all ages – see Table 9-2. The all-ages referral rate, aggregating over all specialties, has grown from 19400 in 1991-2 to 24100 in 1998-9. However, the highest increase in referral rates is for the age groups 65-74, 75-84 and 85+. These changes are purely an effect of increased usage, and not a reflection of ageing population except in so far as a more long-lived elderly population may generate extra morbidity. In terms of annual numbers, England-wide referrals have risen from 9.4 to 12 million for all ages, and from 1.4 million to 2.2 million among the over 75s.

Table 9-2. Trends in England Wide Specialty Referral Rates by Age (per 100,000 population)

	Age Group								*Annual growth*	
1998/99	0-4	5-14	15-44	45-64	65-74	75-84	85+	All Ages	All Ages	Ages 75+
General Surgery	569	686	2051	3803	6116	6902	6230	2870	0.8	2.1
Urology	191	143	465	1375	3564	4419	3115	1141	9.0	11.7
T&O	686	992	1226	1747	2530	3676	5243	1602	1.6	2.8
ENT	1341	1499	602	587	633	642	551	765	0.0	6.5
Ophthalmology	369	157	170	671	2273	4605	5333	813	8.0	11.2
General Medicine	156	154	2473	6522	13836	17390	19428	5049	9.9	18.8
Paediatrics	29722	2556	114	1	2	4	20	2226	0.9	-
Geriatric Medicine	1	1	62	193	1881	9371	20536	1135	0.3	0.1
Obstetrics & Gynaecology	1552	46	7775	1477	713	623	422	3817	0.0	0.0
Mental Illness	53	185	588	394	659	1145	1573	513	-1.7	-2.7
Total	***38370***	***8163***	***18142***	***22399***	***40540***	***57189***	***70644***	***24097***	***3.5***	5.9
1991-92										
General Surgery	961	1007	2012	3462	5339	6225	5258	2720		
Urology	179	134	333	842	2017	2504	1632	699		
T&O	728	1023	1190	1483	2041	3089	4362	1443		
ENT	1601	1864	559	484	524	457	363	763		
Ophthalmology	455	200	127	439	1344	2662	2909	522		
General Medicine	121	130	1652	4265	8145	8437	7481	2985		
Paediatrics	28417	2006	97	44	74	100	106	2090		
Geriatric Medicine	5	1	24	105	1862	9936	19811	1114		
Obstetrics & Gynaecology	1552	46	7775	1477	713	623	422	3817		
Mental Illness	49	187	639	492	702	1443	1904	584		
Total	***36715***	***8057***	***16335***	***16336***	***27260***	***40439***	***49965***	***19404***		

Changes in demand are also differentiated by specialty. All types of medical referral have risen appreciably both for the over 85s and for all ages combined (Figures 9-3 and 9-4). The highest growth rates for surgical specialties are for urology and ophthalmology.

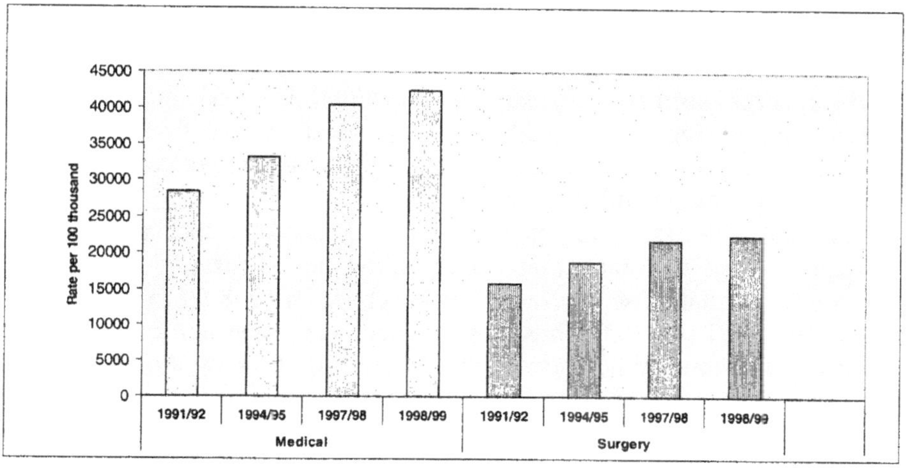

Figure 9-3. Trend in Medical & Surgical Referral Rate for Ages over 85 (England)

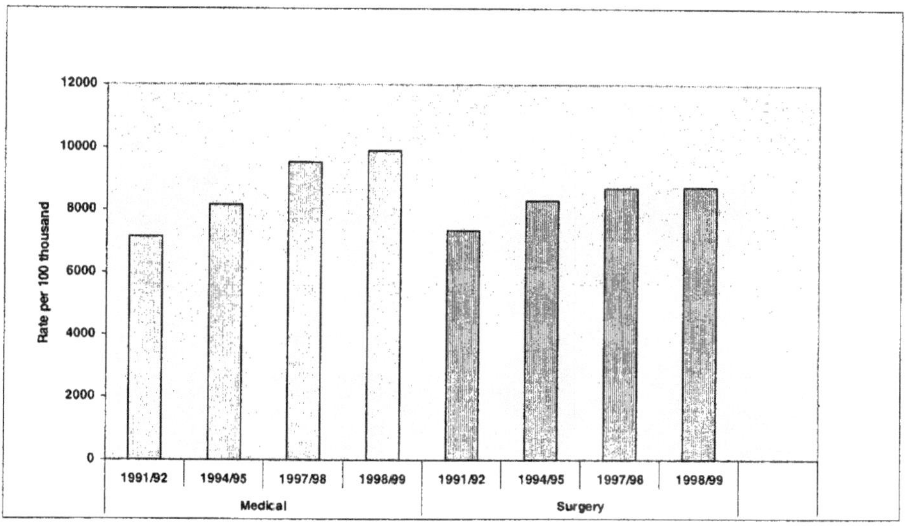

Figure 9-4. Trend in Medical and Surgical Referral Rate (All ages, England)

We use such national trends in specialty activity as a basis for projections of future demand by age and specialty in the study region, i.e., we consider time trends in national age and specialty referral rates, denoted γ^{N}_{ast}, and project them to a future year T. Such trends reflect many factors, including changing patterns of illness, reductions in length of overnight stays, increases in day case referrals, and changes in technology and service provision across sectors. They may also reflect clinical policies (e.g. on age related criteria) regarding suitability of surgical interventions for older people, and improved procedures for managing risks associated with such interventions (Chalfin and Nasraway, 1994).

Changes in the study region in terms of demand by specialty and age between now and 2005-6 are assumed to follow the forecast national trend in age specific specialty use, the results of which (from 1998-99 to 2005-6) are summarized in Table 9-3. Thus general medicine usage across all ages is forecast to increase by 36% over 1998-99 to 2005-6 or by around 5% per year. These forecasts allow for changing referral over time by age group and by specialty, and so for the increase in usage in many specialties observed up to 1998-99. However, the increase observed between 1991-2 and 1998-99 is 'damped down' in the extrapolation from 1998-99 to 2005-06. This damping produces a greater compatibility with the National Beds Inquiry age usage forecasts (from 1998/99 to 2003/4) which in a sense provide a guide forecast.

Table 9-3. Forecast change in population hospitalization rate, 1998-99 to 2005-6, (Ratios of rates, later to earlier period)

	Age Group							
Specialty	0-4	5-14	15-44	45-64	65-74	75-84	85+	*All Ages*
General Surgery	1.13	1.10	0.98	1.02	1.10	1.17	1.23	1.04
Urology	1.21	1.24	1.30	1.33	1.41	1.44	1.52	1.31
T&O	0.94	0.95	1.05	1.07	1.16	1.24	1.31	1.06
ENT	0.99	1.01	1.02	1.06	1.15	1.11	1.17	1.04
Ophthalmology	1.33	1.39	1.22	1.25	1.31	1.34	1.41	1.27
Oral/Dentistry	1.06	1.03	1.22	1.16	1.23	1.06	1.16	1.16
Other Surgery	1.00	1.06	1.14	1.18	1.28	1.27	1.37	1.15
Plastic Surgery	1.12	1.13	1.30	1.34	1.45	1.48	1.55	1.30
General Medicine	1.34	1.37	1.35	1.39	1.39	1.29	1.27	1.36
Audiological etc.	1.17	1.02	1.18	1.23	1.30	1.18	1.22	1.18
Cardiology	1.66	1.66	1.46	1.55	1.54	1.47	1.51	1.53
Medical Oncology	2.12	1.95	1.51	1.48	1.53	1.59	1.65	1.61
Neurology	1.32	1.28	0.94	1.02	1.07	1.20	1.12	1.06
Rheumatology	0.71	0.76	1.14	1.19	1.24	1.22	1.18	1.09
Paediatrics	1.05	1.03	1.05	-	-	-	-	1.05
Geriatric Medicine	1.27	0.67	0.63	0.73	0.95	1.08	1.07	0.76
Obstetrics and GP Maternity	0.54	0.61	1.06	1.29	1.56	0.67	0.55	1.03
Gynaecology	1.32	1.32	1.00	1.09	1.12	1.06	1.18	1.10
Mental Illness, Old Age Psychiatry	0.82	0.85	0.86	0.98	0.98	1.21	1.32	0.92
Oncology/Radiology	2.13	2.14	2.02	2.09	2.20	2.35	2.77	2.10
Other Specialties	0.59	0.43	1.03	1.10	1.23	1.44	1.60	0.99
Total	1.03	1.04	1.11	1.27	1.32	1.27	1.26	1.16

Specifically, let N_{ast} denote the observed England wide specialty referral totals by specialty s, age group a and year t, and let national age specific populations for year t be denoted P_{at}. Then referrals by specialty s, age a and year t (=1,8) from 1991-2 to 1998-9 are binomial as follows

$$N_{ast} \sim \text{Bin}(\gamma^N_{ast}, P_{at})$$

$$\text{logit}(\gamma^N_{ast}) = A + a_s + b_a + c_{sa} + d_{st} + e_{at} \qquad (9\text{-}2)$$

The prior for the intercept is $A \sim N(0,10)$, and the age, specialty and age-specialty effects, a_s, b_a and c_{sa} are assumed to be random:

$$a_s \sim N(0,\tau_a), \quad s=1,..21$$
$$b_a \sim N(0,\tau_b), \quad a=1,..7$$
$$c_{sa} \sim N(0,\tau_c).$$

The precisions $1/\tau_a$, $1/\tau_b$ and $1/\tau_c$ are taken to have gamma priors G(1,0.001).

The forecasting element of the model for England specialty rates is based on the time specific parameters d_{st} and e_{at}, namely trends in usage by specialty and by age. The year 1 parameters d_{s1} and e_{a1} are distributed randomly as $N(0,\tau_d)$ and $N(0,\tau_e)$ respectively. Subsequent years of the $d_{s,t}$ are modeled in terms of specialty specific growth rates δ_s with damping when taken into future years:

$$d_{s,t} = d_{s,t-1} + \delta_s \times \log(t) \qquad t=2,..8$$
$$d_{s,t} = d_{s,t-1} + \delta_s \times \log(t)*(0.75)^{t-8} \qquad t=9,..15 \qquad (9\text{-}3a)$$

The parameters δ_s are random effects, with prior $N(0,\tau_f)$. Trends in use by age are similarly forecast using age specific growth rates ε_a

$$e_{a,t} = e_{a,t-1} + \varepsilon_a \times \log(t) \qquad t=2,..8$$
$$e_{a,t} = e_{a,t-1} + \varepsilon_a \times \log(t)*(0.75)^{t-8} \qquad t=9,..15 \qquad (9\text{-}3b)$$

The ε_a are also random effects, with prior $N(0,\tau_g)$.

Table 9-4 shows the estimates of the growth rate parameters by age and specialty, ε_a and δ_s, together with 95% credible intervals. Interpretation may need to reflect demographic demand: thus growth in pediatrics may have outpaced the growth in demographic demand per se, so that the age group parameter ε_1 is negative. On the other hand growth in geriatric referrals may have been less than implied by demography (as efforts are made to reduce bed blocking by older patients and improve community care transfers).

Table 9-4. Specialty and Age Groups, Referral Growth Rate Parameter Estimates

Specialty Demand Growth Parameters	Mean	2.5%	97.5%
General Surgery	-0.80	-0.81	-0.78
Urology	2.43	2.40	2.45
T&O	-0.19	-0.21	-0.17
ENT	-0.40	-0.43	-0.36
Ophthalmology	2.00	1.97	2.04
Oral/Dentistry	1.07	1.03	1.10
Other Surgery	1.12	1.08	1.16
Plastic Surgery	2.48	2.41	2.52
General Medicine	3.47	3.46	3.48
Audiological etc.	1.62	1.58	1.65
Cardiology	4.64	4.60	4.69
Medical Oncology	4.35	4.31	4.40
Neurology	-0.81	-0.88	-0.74
Rheumatology	0.75	0.67	0.81
Paediatrics	1.70	1.66	1.73
Geriatric Medicine	-2.63	-2.66	-2.60
Obstetrics and GP Maternity	-0.73	-0.74	-0.71
Gynaecology	0.22	0.19	0.24
Mental Illness, Old Age Psychiatry	-2.59	-2.62	-2.55
Oncology/Radiology	9.40	9.36	9.43
Other Specialties	0.02	-0.03	0.06
Age Group Demand Growth Parameters			
0-4	-0.71	-0.73	-0.65
5-14	-0.55	-0.57	-0.52
15-44	0.57	0.56	0.58
45-64	1.29	1.27	1.30
65-74	2.13	2.11	2.14
75-84	2.56	2.55	2.57
85+	3.25	3.22	3.28

Evaluations of these forecasts involved prediction of 1998-99 observations using the data for the first seven years only. The performance of the model above (denoted model N1) was compared to two more highly parameterized variants. The first involves forecasting at each age and specialty combination, so that (9-2) is replaced by

$$\text{logit}(\gamma^N_{ast}) = A + a_s + b_a + c_{sa} + f_{ast} \qquad (9\text{-}4)$$

with the evolution of f_{ast} based on logarithmic growth rates specific for age and specialty

$$f_{a,s,t} = f_{a,s,t-1} + \eta_{as} \times \log(t) \qquad t=2,..8 \qquad (9\text{-}5a)$$

and with $f_{a,s,1}$ modelled as a separate set of random effects (this may be termed model N2). The second variant extends this approach by allowing the power of t (implicitly zero for a trend in log time) to be a free parameter at specialty level. Thus in model N3

$$f_{a,s,t} = f_{a,s,t-1} + \eta_{as} \times t^{\xi_s} \qquad t=2,..8 \qquad (9\text{-}5b)$$

Comparisons are made between actual referral rates by age and specialty in 1998-99, namely $R_{as9} = 1000N_{a,s,9}/P_{a,9}$, and predictions for $\hat{R}_{as9}$. A chi-square statistic is accumulated over the 147 specialty-age combinations, and shows the models N2 and N3 with age-specialty combination forecasting to have lower prediction error. This is especially so when combined with the model (5b) with different growth rate scales. Whereas the chi square for N1 is 207, that for model N2 is 103 and that for N3 is 39.

More heavily parameterized models will generally improve on the fit of the model to observed data and on the accuracy of cross-validatory predictions within the observed data. On the other hand, there is no reason why incorporating the forecasts from N2 or N3 should lead to 'better' forecasts for the future year 2005-6 (i.e. for out of sample rather than cross-validatory predictions) at a regional level. Therefore we might view alternative methods to obtain national forecasts as one scenario to adopt in a sensitivity analysis of the regional activity forecasts.

5. COMPARISON WITH THE UK NATIONAL BEDS INQUIRY

Table 9-5 shows the match between the activity growth assumptions (to 2003-4) made in the UK National Beds Inquiry, which are not specialty specific, and those resulting from the modeling the analysis here (with model N1), when aggregated over specialties. There is a 22% growth in the all ages usage rate here as compared to 27% (seven year equivalent) in the National Beds Inquiry.

Table 9-5. Forecasts to 2005-6 of England Specialty Referral Rates by Age

Specialty	0-4	5-14	15-44	45-64	65-74	75-84	85+	All Ages
General Surgery	642	758	2014	3886	6745	8072	7656	3031
Urology	232	178	602	1826	5031	6364	4723	1569
T&O	645	943	1289	1877	2926	4540	6857	1761
ENT	1322	1516	614	620	728	711	643	791
Ophthalmology	490	219	206	836	2983	6186	7497	1069
General Medicine	209	211	3350	9088	19250	22470	24580	6848
Paediatrics	31250	2636	120	9	18	26	39	2338
Geriatric Medicine	1	1	39	141	1785	10110	22060	1175
Obstetrics & Gynaecology	1536	42	8157	1790	1012	949	726	4097
Mental Illness	43	156	507	386	647	1390	2071	495
All Specialties	***36369***	***6659***	***16898***	***20459***	***41124***	***60817***	***76852***	***28728***
Change in all specialties rate, 1998-99 to 2005-6	0.957	0.804	0.933	0.943	1.057	1.109	1.126	1.217
National Beds Inquiry Change	1.113	1.054	1.137	1.386	1.384	1.332	1.267	1.268
Age Group Trends in Usage Rates and Average Length of Stay (National Beds Inquiry)								
	0-4	5-14	15-44	45-64	65-74	75-84	85+	All Ages
1989-90 to 1998-99 (annual change rate)								
Length of stay (excl Day cases)	-4.1	-5	-3.1	-3.9	-4.3	-6	-9.1	-4
Usage Rate per 100000	0.6	0.2	1.6	5.3	7.0	5.9	5.9	3.5
1998-99								
Length of Stay	3.34	2.21	3.12	5.86	8.75	12.34	16.29	7
Usage Rate per 100,000	22400	7800	13300	20300	35400	47200	56600	19300
1998-99 to 2003-04 (annual change rate)								
Length of stay	-2.8	-2.0	-1.6	-1.9	-2.5	-2.5	-2.5	-1.9
Usage Rate per 100,000	1.6	0.8	2.0	5.5	5.5	4.7	3.8	3.8
2003-04								
Length of stay	2.87	1.99	2.87	5.3	7.65	10.79	14.28	6
Usage Rate per 100,000	24200	8100	14600	25900	45100	58400	67400	23000

These projected demand growth rates are lower than in the recent past in England. However, to simply extrapolate past trends would neglect efforts being made in England (as in other countries) to manage demand for acute care by encouraging community and primary care, especially policies to reduce avoidable admissions and bed blocking. Also much of the rise in admissions has been due to reduced length of stay and an increase in day cases, and national projections are for a slower fall in average length of stay in the next five years.

In this context, Table 9-5 presents the assumptions of the National Beds Inquiry over the period 1998-99 to 2005-06. It shows the smaller decline in average length of stay expected to occur in that period as compared to the 1990s, together with the expected increase in age specific usage of all kinds.

6. PROJECTIONS OF TOTAL REGION WIDE ACUTE ACTIVITY

The national projections of age and specialty specific usage rates (as summarize in Tables 9-3 and 9-4) are now incorporated in forecasts of region wide activity by specialty. These region wide forecasts also take account of projected population change p_{iat} in areas i, up to a future forecast year T. Let $\kappa_{as} = \gamma^{R}_{asB} / \gamma^{N}_{asB}$ denote the ratio, comparing the study region to England, of age–specialty usage in the base year B. We assume (in the absence of data to confirm differential national-regional trends) that this differential remains constant between years B and T.

Projected study region referral rates in a future year T are modeled as

$$\log(\rho_{iasT}) = \alpha + \delta_{is} + \kappa_{as} \gamma^{N}_{asT} \quad (9\text{-}6)$$

So the expected total referrals in the future year T are given by

$$\mu_{iasT} = p_{iaT} \times \rho_{iasT}$$

where p_{iaT} are regional population projections. To allow fully for sampling variability we can sample projected referrals, conditional on these projected means:

$$n_{iasT} \sim \text{Poi}(\mu_{iasT})$$

With regard to expected population changes p_{iat} up to the year T (i.e. 2005-6), two sources are available for London boroughs, and a single source for S.Essex areas. One source for the London boroughs (the UK Office of National Statistics projections) do not take account of planned housing development, whereas projections from the Greater London Authority do. In the analysis below, an *average* of the two sets of population projections is taken for NE London local authorities. This option is chosen in preference to making variant activity forecasts according to GLA or ONS projections.

7. MODELLING THE DISTRIBUTION OF TOTAL ACTIVITY TO ALTERNATIVE SITES; EXTENDED GRAVITY MODEL FOR PATIENT FLOWS

At the allocation stage, a patient flow model is established for age and specialty specific patient flows from area i (origins) to hospital sites h (destinations). This is therefore a version of the gravity model for health demand (e.g. Taket and Mayhew, 1981), but with an additional dimension of medical specialty. To this end the 'destination' mass effect of the gravity model may be taken as specific to both provider and specialty, and so the model includes specialty specific mass parameters λ_s which are applied to a mass given by the total number M_{sh} of referrals to different specialties in each hospital from the entire region. The model also includes distance decay effects in terms of distance d_{ih} (between grid references) from the area i to the hospital h. The decay parameters are specific both to origin and specialty, since some specialties occur at all sites but some at only one or two – so that the latter will have less steep decay.

Developments of this stage may also include the overall impact of beds, and other types of contiguity or association between areas and hospitals. A distinction may be made between allocation models which are based on

- (a) existing referral patterns relating areas to providers but taking account of changing health demands across demographic groups and specialties (demand led models)
- (b) allowing a change in spatial supply patterning as well as in health demand by including changes in mass (e.g. beds, staff) at different hospitals (composite demand and supply models). Major changes in provider configuration (e.g. openings of new hospital sites or closures of existing sites) may also be included (Congdon, 2000).

The former demand-led model can be translated into bed requirements corresponding to an ageing population or increased demand for different types of care. Thus with LOS denoting length of stay in hospital we can use the standard relationship (at specialty level)

$$\text{Projected Beds} = (\text{Average LOS} \times \text{Projected Episodes}) / (\text{Occupancy Rate} \times 365)$$

to project numbers of non-day beds. Day beds may be projected by assuming an average number of days worked each week, and the average number of patients (e.g. 1.5) occupying a day bed in each day worked.

The supply-led model (b) may, by contrast, be used in conjunction with modeling methods which allow for opening new hospitals, and closing existing ones, as well as for simple changes in bed numbers. With the first approach we therefore translate changes in the demographic structure of catchment populations to the demands for different acute care (e.g. implied bed numbers). In the latter we convert projected changes in health demand *and* adjustments in supply to predict a reconfiguration of spatial flows.

Under either option, the impact of changes in age structure on specialty demand by hospital depends on the catchment area of each hospital, since areas differ in their overall population growth rates and the extent of their ageing populations In 1998/99 total referrals from the 13 areas were around 455,000, of which 90% (402,000) were to the ten study hospitals - so emphasizing the high self-containment of the 'region' defined by the 10 hospitals. Just as the impact on hospital workload of demographic change depends on the trusts' catchment areas, so the impact of changing specialty referral rates depends in part on the specialty profile of the trusts. Table 9-6 shows the distribution of specialty referrals by patient area and hospital in 1998-99 for patient flows originating in the study region. Certain specialties only figure significantly at one or two provider sites, and that some providers have a more restricted specialty range than others. To reflect local patterns of supply, hospital and specialty specific effects α_{sh} are included in the allocation model.

Table 9-6. Trust Workload by Specialty, 1998-99 (Numbers of Referrals from Study Region)

Specialty	Southend Acute	Basildon & Thurrock	Forest Health Care	Redbridge Health Care	Havering Hospitals	Newham Health Care	Royal London	Mid Essex	Princess Alexandra	Homer-ton	Total
General Surgery	12.0	12.2	8.9	13.3	13.6	14.6	7.6	2.4	24.4	13.7	11.5
Urology	5.2	6.7	4.8	6.1	8.2	3.4	6.1	1.1	4.9	1.9	5.6
Trauma/Orthopaedics	7.9	8.6	4.6	6.5	7.7	6.1	4.5	1.8	15.7	5.1	6.4
ENT	3.6	5.9	4.9	0.0	5.2	0.6	3.4	0.5	3.6	0.1	3.3
Ophthalmology	7.8	0.0	5.1	0.2	2.3	0.0	0.7	0.2	1.8	0.0	2.4
Oral/Dentistry	1.2	2.8	1.3	0.0	1.9	0.0	4.4	0.4	4.0	0.8	1.7
Other Surgery	2.2	0.6	4.1	0.3	1.8	0.0	7.3	0.7	0.0	0.0	2.4
Plastic Surgery	1.0	0.0	0.0	0.0	0.3	0.0	2.2	72.3	2.2	0.3	2.1
General Medicine	21.1	19.2	19.5	20.6	22.2	21.3	23.7	3.4	15.2	23.9	21.0
Audiological etc.	0.5	0.6	2.6	1.4	1.6	4.9	5.7	0.2	0.0	5.5	2.5
Cardiology	0.2	3.3	1.4	0.0	0.4	0.0	7.8	0.0	0.0	0.0	1.9
Medical Oncology	0.0	0.0	0.0	2.9	0.0	0.6	3.6	0.3	3.3	0.0	1.0
Paediatrics	3.1	10.3	13.5	14.3	3.8	10.0	6.2	6.5	0.0	15.7	8.5
Geriatric Medicine	10.3	9.4	8.4	3.7	6.4	10.0	0.0	0.4	0.0	1.4	6.2
Maternity etc.	19.5	18.9	18.1	20.5	23.3	28.3	15.7	9.7	17.8	31.6	20.7
Mental Illness + Old Age Psychiatry	0.3	0.0	2.6	5.8	0.0	0.0	0.0	0.0	0.1	0.0	1.0
Oncology/Radiology	4.1	0.0	0.0	0.0	0.9	0.0	1.0	0.0	0.0	0.0	1.0
Other Specialties	0.0	1.4	0.2	4.3	0.5	0.3	0.0	0.1	0.9	0.0	0.7

8. INCORPORATING SUPPLY CHANGE

In the present analysis option (b) above is adopted, in that a change in provider configuration in the study region is also included in the model calibration. Thus, following a review of health care in London (Dept of Health, 1999), a major planned change affecting this part of London is a centralization of acute services in the outer North East London. This involves an expanded and more central Oldchurch site and conversion of the Harold Wood site on the London boundary to an outpatient facility only (see Figure 1). Actual 1998/99 beds and future assumed bed numbers B_h (2005/6) at the 10 providers are as follows

Hospital Provider	*1998/99*	*Projection Year*
Newham	362	362
King Georges (Redbridge Health Care)	395	416
Whipps Cross (Forest Health Care)	446	446
OldChurch Hospital	400	722
Harold Wood Hospital	300	-
Royal London	1116	1150
Broomfield (Mid-Essex Acute Trust)	601	601
Basildon & Thurrock	440	440
Southend	495	495
Homerton	321	321
Princess Alexandra	329	329

To see how these factors are included in the allocation stage, we assume for simplicity that all age groups are subject to the same allocation model. Accordingly consider the total observed referrals by area and specialty in the base year B

$$n_{i,s} = \Sigma_a n_{iasB}$$

To model allocations of this total between sites we consider the data

$$n_{i,s,h} = \Sigma_a n_{i,a,s,B,h}$$

as a multinomial response

$$n_{i,s,1:H} \sim \text{Mult}(\theta_{i,s,1:H}, n_{is})$$

where the choice probabilities are parameterized as

$$\theta_{ish} = \phi_{ish}/\Sigma_h \phi_{ish}$$

The effects ϕ_{ish} take account of distances from areas i to hospitals h, the sizes of different specialties in different hospitals (in terms of annual referrals M_{sh}) and the total acute bed mass B_h in hospital h. Thus we take

$$\log(\phi_{ish}) = b_0 + \alpha_{sh} + \beta_{is}\times\log d_{ih} + \lambda_s\times\log(M_{sh}+1) + b_1\times S_{ih} + b_2\times\log(B_h) \qquad (9\text{-}7)$$

Note that under option (a) above (i.e. under a demand led projection) we would omit mass factors at hospitals which are potentially subject to deliberate strategic revision, such as the term in B_h in (7) - as opposed to the M_{sh}. As well as the impact of area-hospital 'similarity' through distances between them, there may be a secondary effect of a hospital being in the same Health Authority as the patient (represented by dummy indices S_{ih}=1 if this applies and S_{ih}=0 otherwise).

Given that there are 18 specialties, and 10 hospitals to consider, we have 180 specialty and hospital effects α_{sh} to estimate (their impact in practice is illustrated in practice in Table 9-7). We assume these are drawn from a population of effects and therefore are random with

$$\alpha_{sh} \sim N(0,\tau_\alpha) \qquad (9\text{-}8a)$$

The remaining effects are taken as fixed and specified in terms of prior assumptions about the likely nature of mass effects and distance decay. Thus the mass parameters have priors

$$\lambda_s \sim N(1,1) \qquad s=1,..18 \qquad (9\text{-}8b)$$

$$b_2 \sim N(0.5,1) \qquad (9\text{-}8c)$$

Table 9-7.. Parameter Estimate Summary, Allocation Mode

		Mean	2.5%	97.5%
Distance Decay (by Patient Origin Area)				
Barking & Dagenham	$\beta_{1.}$	-3.33	-3.46	-3.22
Hackney	$\beta_{2.}$	-3.61	-3.80	-3.43
Havering	$\beta_{3.}$	-1.35	-1.45	-1.28
Newham	$\beta_{4.}$	-2.76	-2.90	-2.61
Redbridge	$\beta_{5.}$	-2.34	-2.42	-2.26
TH +City	$\beta_{6.}$	-1.47	-1.60	-1.33
Waltham Forest	$\beta_{7.}$	-1.97	-2.07	-1.88
Basildon	$\beta_{8.}$	-2.57	-2.73	-2.43
Brentwood	$\beta_{9.}$	-4.66	-4.84	-4.49
Castle Point	$\beta_{10.}$	-2.16	-2.32	-2.00
Rochford	$\beta_{11.}$	-2.30	-2.49	-2.13
Southend-on-Sea	$\beta_{12.}$	-1.43	-1.52	-1.34
Thurrock	$\beta_{13.}$	-5.79	-5.98	-5.61
Specialty Mass Effects				
General Surgery	λ_1	0.45	0.29	0.65
Urology	λ_2	0.63	0.50	0.76
Trauma/Orthopaedics	λ_3	0.41	0.17	0.62
ENT	λ_4	0.80	0.55	1.02
Ophthalmology	λ_5	1.64	1.19	2.12
Oral/Dentistry	λ_6	1.13	0.95	1.42
Other Surgery	λ_7	1.63	1.45	1.82
Plastic Surgery	λ_8	2.82	2.58	3.00
General Medicine	λ_9	2.02	1.84	2.20
Audiological etc.	λ_{10}	2.22	1.83	2.58
Cardiology	λ_{11}	2.22	2.05	2.36
Medical Oncology	λ_{12}	1.60	1.14	1.99
Paediatrics	λ_{13}	0.51	0.17	0.83
Geriatric Medicine	λ_{14}	1.59	0.81	2.22
Maternity etc.	λ_{15}	0.45	0.26	0.65
Mental Illness + Old Age Psychiatry	λ_{16}	1.56	1.20	2.03
Oncology/Radiology	λ_{17}	1.82	1.48	2.22
Other Specialties	λ_{18}	1.33	0.94	1.82
Other Factors				
Hospital and LA in same HA	b_1	1.19	1.16	1.21
Beds	b_2	0.53	0.41	0.73

and the distance decay parameters have priors

$$\beta_{is} \sim N(-2,1) \qquad i=1,13;\ s=1,..18 \qquad (9\text{-}8d)$$

We would expect the effect of hospital being in the same health region as the patient's home to raise referral rates but take a vague prior on the associated parameter

$$b_1 \sim N(0,100) \qquad (9\text{-}8e)$$

The predicted mean flows are then

$$\nu_{ish}=\theta_{ish} \times R_{is}$$

and may be compared (e.g. in terms of deviance fit measures) with the actual flows $n_{i,s,h}$.

The model of (7) is based on analyzing current flows. Changes in total bed mass ($B_{h.new}$) or in the specialty balance at hospitals (e.g. via bed loads by specialty $B_{sh.new}$) may, however, be incorporated in the model to derive forecasts of allocation parameters for year T, denoted $\phi_{ish.new}$

$$\log(\phi_{ish.new}) = b_0 + \alpha_{sh} + \beta_{is}\times \log d_{ih} + \lambda_s \times \log(M_{sh}+1) + b_1 \times S_{ih} + b_2 \times \log(B_{h.new}) \qquad (9\text{-}9)$$

Table 9-7 shows the estimates of λ_s, b_1, b_2 and of the average distance decay parameters in model (7) by patient area of residence $\beta_{i.}$ (averaging over specialties). Local authorities without a major hospital within their boundaries (e.g. Brentwood, Thurrock) but with a high dependence on a few sites have more highly negative values of $\beta_{i.}$. Specialty specific supply effects λ_s are greater for those specialties (e.g. plastic surgery) which are located at only a minority of the ten hospitals. The secondary effect of a hospital being in the same Health Authority as the patient is also clear, which may in part reflect referral preferences among primary care practitioners. The positive impact of bed numbers is consistent with the conventional gravity model.

With new bed numbers and revised health demand by specialty we therefore are in a position to predict health flows in the 'new' situation of 2005-6. Specifically, we use the predicted allocation rates

$$\theta_{ish.new} = \phi_{ish.new}/\Sigma_h \phi_{ish.new}$$

to predict new mean flows

$$\nu_{ish.new} = \theta_{ish.new} \times n_{isT}$$

where $n_{isT} = \Sigma_a n_{iasT}$ and the n_{iasT} are projected as in Equation 9-6 using the England wide specialty forecasts. To allow for sampling variability we can then sample new flows

$$n_{i,s,h,new} \sim Poi(\nu_{ish.new})$$

9. FORECASTS AND THEIR SENSITIVITY

The resulting forecasts of specialty demand by age in the study region in 2005-6 are given in Table 9-8. They show a projected growth of around 75 thousand episodes across the region by 2005-2006 as compared to 402,000 to the 10 providers in 1998-99. Note that the latter total relates to the ten providers excluding flows to non-study hospitals.

Table 9-8. Patient Flow Forecasts in 2005-6 by Specialty and Hospital

	Hospital										
Specialty	Southend Acute	Basildon & Thurrock	Forest Health Care	Redbridge Health Care	Havering Hospitals	Newham Health Care	Royal London	Mid Essex	Princess Alexandra	Homer-ton	Total
General Surgery	8448	6944	4802	4936	9575	5691	5171	319	241	3384	49512
Urology	4765	5122	3341	2825	7459	1723	5396	179	59	632	31501
Trauma & Orthopaedics (T&O)	5762	5092	2582	2644	5432	2462	3152	219	142	1294	28781
Ear Nose and Throat (ENT)	2409	3172	2528	-	3383	208	2226	54	27	30	14037
Ophthalmology	7040	-	3342	79	1830	-	554	32	19	0	12898
General Medicine	18970	14270	13610	9398	20310	10870	20830	586	208	7770	116821
Paediatrics	2020	5019	6591	5275	3045	3708	4181	674	0	3753	34266
Geriatric Medicine	6963	5540	4009	1140	4593	3468	0	60	0	319	26092
Gynaecology, Obstetrics	12770	9616	9033	7072	16070	10580	10370	1198	164	7181	84054
Mental Illness	212	-	1259	2327	-	-	-	-	-	-	3798
Total	79457	60748	57242	40469	78185	41464	79641	11823	1022	26257	476309

The expanded Oldchurch site has a growth of around 15,000 episodes as compared to the 1997-8 totals in Table 9-6. The fast growing general medicine specialty increases by around 6,000 episodes at this site.

The repercussions on neighboring hospitals of an expansion at one site are important to consider. Thus the workload of King George Hospital, relatively close by to the expanded Oldchurch hospital, is forecast to be static, despite the region wide growth in demand.

Impacts of population ageing by contrast are greater in areas of suburban Essex, most notably in post war New Towns (of which Basildon was one). These experienced a major influx of young families in the 1950s and 1960s and consequent cohort ageing is apparent in increased demand at Basildon and Thurrock Trust (from 48 thousand episodes in 1997-8 to around 60 thousand in 2005-6).

As a sensitivity analysis of these forecasts we may consider first a modification of the above prior model assumptions, as in (8a) to (8e). To this end, we adopt a heavy tailed alternative to (8a), namely a t density with 5 degrees of freedom, and replace priors (8b) to (8d) by normal priors with zero mean and variance 10. This has little impact on the overall forecasts of total hospital workload, as given in the last row of Table 9-8. The set of average workloads and the 2.5% and 97.5% forecast limits are in Table 9-9.

Table 9-9. Forecast Trust Workload under Variant Priors

		Credible Interval	
Hospital Trust	Mean	2.5%	97.5%
Southend Acute	79410	78590	80260
Basildon & Thurrock	60740	60020	61490
Forest Health Care	57410	56770	58050
Redbridge Health Care	40160	39590	40740
Havering Hospitals	78430	77610	79250
Newham Health Care	41520	40970	42080
Royal London	79430	78700	80310
Mid Essex	11850	11540	12170
Princess Alexandra	1035	963.6	1111
Homerton	26340	25900	26700
Total	476325	470654	482161

A second sensitivity analysis involves using the model N3 for national usage forecasts, without damping as in (3). These should be compared to the forecast N1 summarized in Tables 9-3, 9-4 and 9-5, and show a much higher growth rate in demand, especially at older ages. The overall growth rates (2005-6 vs 1998-99) are 57%, 51% and 53% at ages 65-74,75-84 and 85+ respectively. These compare to growth implied by the National Beds Inquiry of 38%, 33% and 27% (see Table 9-5). The resulting prediction of the total regional flow in 2005-6 is around 520 thousand (see Table 9-10), as compared to around 475,000 using model N1 with damping.

Table 9-10. Forecast Trust Workload under Variant National Model

Hospital Trust	Mean	Credible Interval 2.5%	Credible Interval 97.5%
Southend Acute	89270	88400	90230
Basildon & Thurrock	65660	64910	66330
Forest Health Care	61280	60650	61930
Redbridge Health Care	43200	42640	43890
Havering Hospitals	84620	83610	85410
Newham Health Care	45180	44440	45820
Royal London	88010	87210	88820
Mid Essex	11480	11120	11790
Princess Alexandra	1076	985	1162
Homerton	28380	27860	28930
Total	518156	511825	524312

10. IMPLICATIONS FOR CAPACITY PLANNING

Hospital planning focuses especially on providing an adequate number of beds while making efficient use of those available to avoid operational overload (Gallivan et al, 2002). Bed numbers need to reflect total demand (referrals to hospitals) and length of stay distributions, and to be sufficient to avoid excess occupancy rates and high refusal rates (referrals not admitted because sufficient beds are not available), and also meet daily and seasonal fluctuations in referrals (Harper & Shahani, 2002). The gravity model approach considered in this chapter, with adjustment for supply as in Section 8, is only a preliminary to an extended model framework that allows for hospital dynamics. For example, instead of assuming an externally set number of beds as in Section 8, one may model bed requirements in terms of length of stay and occupancy rates. Thus a deterministic calculation for beds B involves an average length of stay L times admitted referrals R, and an allowance for beds days not used though notionally available, via the occupancy rate O. Thus,

$$B = R \times L/(365 \times O).$$

More ideally, one should disaggregate bed requirements according to patient groups with similar broad diagnosis or sub-specialty, and allowing for admission method (emergency vs elective in-patient and day case). In this way excessively broad specialty groups (e.g. medical, surgical) are sufficiently differentiated in terms (for example) of different length of stay distributions (Harper & Shahani, 2002). Denoting groups by g and differentiating also by hospital leads to a deterministic equation that allows also for group specific occupancy and length of stay, namely

$$B_{gh} = R_{gh} \times L_{gh}/(365 \times O_{gh}).$$

Such a model might incorporate forecasts of average lengths of stay by specialty and hospital (i.e. a statistical forecasting approach as in Farmer and Emami, 1990), or allow for varying scenarios over future lengths of stay and occupancy under a simulation based approach. A model might also allow for refused referrals, which will occur when there is under-capacity, and excess length of stay (including bed blocking) (Harper & Shahani, 2002). Several papers have argued that the impact of length of stay on bed requirements ideally requires a probabilistic approach, whereby simulation of bed requirements using skew length of stay densities (e.g. mixed exponential, Weibull, lognormal) improves in predicting bed requirements compared to using average length of stay (Costa et al, 2003; Harrison, 2001). This would require forecasts of some or all parameters of such densities.

11. AVENUES FOR FURTHER RESEARCH

Much discussion has focussed on national impacts of population ageing on health care costs and demand for medical staff (Metz, 1999; Kane 1994). However, impacts of ageing on health care are likely to be spatially differentiated. There have been a number of advances in spatial allocation modeling as applied to health care which facilitate a regional perspective. The gravity model approach has been applied to modeling patient flows between areas and hospitals, but disaggregation to patient demographic groups or specialties has not generally been a feature of such models.

The present paper has developed an estimation and simulation model which takes account of changing age structure in 13 local authority areas, and the differential provision of care over hospitals and specialties in a region of two million people in England. The forecasting element of the model is consistent with the assumptions made in the national Hospital Beds Inquiry but introduces an extra specialty dimension, and reflects the clear patterning of demand by specialty according to patient age.

Assessment in terms of alternative national forecasts of specialty use by age and in terms of the prior assumptions of the allocation stage was carried out. This shows the forecast of hospital workload to be more sensitive to the method adopted for national forecasting of specialty usage by age than to variant prior assumptions about the allocation model. It may be noted that the model N1 for national specialty usage forecasting comes closer (in the scenario period) to the 'guideline' provided by the National Beds Inquiry than the more parameterized model N3. The latter, by contrast, has better fit within the period 1991/92 to 1998/99 and in a one-step-ahead validation using seven years data to predict 1998/99. Such contradictions emphasize the possible problems involved in extrapolating a best fit model for current data to the future.

There is obvious scope for further sensitivity analysis using different population projections or different bed numbers at the study hospitals. One might also differentiate hospital episodes by their mode of admission (e.g., emergency vs. elective) or their destination at discharge (e.g., return to home, nursing home, community care). Such disaggregation will add to the potential strategic and planning potential of such models. On the other hand extensive disaggregation may make modeling unwieldy, especially at broader regional or even national scales.

A Bayesian modeling perspective may assist in simulation (i.e., prediction) of new flows in the face of multiple sources of uncertainty, and in allowing for information from prior studies (e.g. on the likely degree of distance decay or direction of mass effects) to be used in guiding parameter estimation.

Application of the modeling framework here to other locations might, as in this chapter, involve a full perspective on acute health demand. Alternatively a modified version of it might focus on one type of care (e.g. geriatric or maternity care), might add certain classifications (e.g. method of admission), and perhaps drop others (e.g. only consider one provider). Despite the potential for such modification, the framework rests essentially rests on the following: demographic projections for a set of residential areas, projections of future need by area of care (e.g. by specialty or case-mix group), and a flow model that 'allocates' patients to providers. As in Section 10, bed capacity parameters may also be introduced. The ideal data requirement would be a regional panel of patent flow observations n_{iasth} over providers h and times t=1,..B. Often such data are not available because of changes in area definitions or because providers are subject to restructuring. In this case national guideline projections of demand in different care areas are one option, as in the work described here. If a full regional panel is available then one may estimate a dynamic flow model, which extends equations (9-7) and (9-9) to include time varying data on beds B_{ht} and area-hospital specialty mix M_{sht}, as well as allowing some parameters to be time specific.

12. REFERENCES

Chalfin D, Nasraway S (1994) Preoperative evaluation and postoperative care of the elderly patient undergoing major surgery. Clin Geriatr Med,10(1):51-70.

Clarke, M, Wilson, A (1984) Health services planning: an outline and an example, pp 22-56 in Planning and Analysis in Health Care Systems (edited by M Clarke), Pion. London Papers in Regional Science 13.

Congdon P (2000) A Bayesian approach to prediction using the gravity model, with an application to patient flow modeling, Geographical Analysis, 32: (3) 205-224.

Costa A, Ridley S, Shahani A, Harper P, De Senna V, Nielsen M (2003) Mathematical modelling and simulation for planning critical care capacity. Anaesthesia. 58, 320-7.

Department of Health (1999) Modernising the NHS in London, HMSO.

Department of Health (2000) Shaping the future NHS: Long Term Planning for Hospitals and Related Services, HMSO.

Downing, A, Wilson, R (2002) Temporal and demographic variations in attendance at accident and emergency departments. Emerg Med J, 19, 531–535.

Farmer R, Emami J (1990) Models for forecasting hospital bed requirements in the acute sector. J Epidemiol Community Health, 44, 307-12.

Fries J, Koop C, Sokolov J, Beadle C, Wright D (1998) Beyond health promotion: reducing need and demand for medical care. Health Affairs, 17: (2), 70-84.

Gallivan S, Utley M, Treasure T, Valencia O (2002) Booked inpatient admissions and hospital capacity: mathematical modelling study. Brit Med J, 324(7332), 280-2.

Gilchrist, R (1985) Some aspects of modeling operational problems in the National Health Service. The Statistician 34, 209–214.

Harper P, Shahani A (2002) Modelling for the planning and management of bed capacities in hospitals. Journal of the Operational Research Society. 53, 11-18.

Harper, P, Shahania, A, Gallagher, J, Bowie, C (2005) Planning health services with explicit geographical considerations:a stochastic location–allocation approach. Omega, 33, 141 – 152.

Harrison, G (2001) Implications of mixed exponential occupancy patient flow models for health. Health Care Management Science 4: 37–45.

Hull, S, Rees Jones, I, Moser, K (1997) Factors influencing the attendance rate at accident and emergency departments in East London: the contributions of practice organization, population characteristics and distance, Journal of Health Services Research & Policy, 2, 6-13.

Jones, S, Joy, M, Pearson, J (2002) Forecasting demand of emergency care. Health Care Management Science 5, 297–305.

Kane V (1994) An older America: strategic challenges for the acute-care hospital. Health Manage Quarterly, 16(4) :9-12.

Lowe J, Sen A (1996) Gravity model applications in health planning: Analysis of an urban hospital market, J Reg Sci: (3) 437-461.

Metz D (1999) Can the impact of ageing on health care costs be avoided? J Health Serv Res Policy, 4(4):249-52.

Mackay, M, Millard, P (1999) Application and comparison of two modelling techniques for hospital bed management Australian Health Review, 22, 118–143.

Millard, P, Mackay, M, Vasilakis,C, Christodoulou, G (2000) Measuring and modelling surgical bed usage. Annals of the Royal College of Surgeons of England, 82, 75–82.

Milner, P (1988) Forecasting the demand on accident and emergency departments in health districts in the Trent region, Statistics in Medicine, 10 , 1061–1072.

Milner, P (1997) Ten year follow-up of ARIMA forecasts of attendance at accident and emergency departments in the Trent region. Statistics in Medicine, 16 , 2117–2125.

Puig-Junoy J, Saez M, Martinez-Garcia E (1998) Why do patients prefer hospital emergency visits? A nested multinomial logit analysis for patient-initiated contacts. Health Care Manag Science;1(1):39-52.

Sibbritt D (1992)Trends and projections for day only admissions in NSW acute hospitals. Aust Clin Rev, 12(3):115-24.

Taket, A, Mayhew, L (1981) Interactions between the supply of and demand for hospital services in London, Omega, 9, 519-526.

Tebaldi C, West M (1998) Bayesian inference on network traffic using link count data, Journal of the American Statistical Association, 93, 557-573.

Utley, M, Gallivan, S, Davis, K, Daniel, P , Reeves, P, Worrall, J (2003) Estimating bed requirements for an intermediate care facility. European Journal of Operational
Research, 150, 92–100.

Chapter 10

QUEUEING ANALYSIS IN HEALTHCARE

Linda Green
Graduate School of Business, Columbia University, New York, New York 10027

Abstract: Many organizations, such as banks, airlines, telecommunications companies, and police departments, routinely use queueing models to help determine capacity levels needed to respond to experienced demands in a timely fashion. Though queueing analysis has been used in hospitals and other healthcare settings, its use in this sector is not widespread. Yet, given the pervasiveness of delays in healthcare and the fact that many healthcare facilities are trying to meet increasing demands with tightly constrained resources, queueing models can be very useful in developing more effective policies for bed allocation and staffing, and in identifying other opportunities for improving service. Queueing analysis is also a key tool in estimating capacity requirements for possible future scenarios, including demand surges due to new diseases or acts of terrorism. This chapter describes basic queueing models as well as some simple modifications and extensions that are particularly useful in the healthcare setting, and give examples of their use. The critical issue of data requirements is also be discussed as well as model choice, model- building and the interpretation and use of results.

Key words: Queueing, capacity management, staffing, hospitals

1. INTRODUCTION

1.1 Why is queueing analysis helpful in healthcare?

Healthcare is riddled with delays. Almost all of us have waited for days or weeks to get an appointment with a physician or schedule a procedure, and upon arrival we wait some more until being seen. In hospitals, it is not unusual to find patients waiting for beds in hallways, and delays for surgery or diagnostic tests are common.

Delays are the result of a disparity between demand for a service and the capacity available to meet that demand. Usually this mismatch is temporary and due to natural variability in the timing of demands and in the duration of time needed to provide service. A simple example would be a healthcare clinic where patients walk in without appointments in an unpredictable fashion and require anything from a flu shot to the setting of a broken limb. This variability and the interaction between the arrival and service processes make the dynamics of service systems very complex. Consequently, it's impossible to predict levels of congestion or to determine how much capacity is needed to achieve some desired level of performance without the help of a queueing model.

Queueing theory was developed by A.K. Erlang in 1904 to help determine the capacity requirements of the Danish telephone system (see Brockmeyer et al. 1948). It has since been applied to a large range of service industries including banks, airlines, and telephone call centers (e.g. Brewton 1989, Stern and Hersh 1980, Holloran and Byrne 1986, Brusco et al 1995, and Brigandi et al 1994) as well as emergency systems such as police patrol, fire and ambulances (e.g. Larson 1972, Kolesar et al 1975, Chelst and Barlach 1981, Green and Kolesar 1984, Taylor and Huxley 1989). It has also been applied in various healthcare settings as we will discuss later in this chapter. Queueing models can be very useful in identifying appropriate levels of staff, equipment, and beds as well as in making decisions about resource allocation and the design of new services.

Unlike simulation methodologies, discussed in Chapter 9, queueing models require very little data and result in relatively simple formulae for predicting various performance measures such as mean delay or probability of waiting more than a given amount of time before being served. This means that they are easier and cheaper to use and can be more readily used to find "optimal" solutions rather than just estimating the system performance for a given scenario.

Timely access has been identified as one of the key elements of healthcare quality (Institute of Medicine 2001) and consequently, decreasing delays has become a focus in many healthcare institutions. Given the financial constraints that exist in many of these facilities, queueing analysis can be an extremely valuable tool in utilizing resources in the most cost-effective way to reduce delays. The primary goal of this chapter is to provide a basic understanding of queueing theory and some of the specific queueing models that can be helpful in designing and managing healthcare systems. For more detail on specific models that are commonly used, a textbook on queueing theory such as Hall (1991) is recommended.

Before discussing past and potential uses of queueing models in healthcare, it's important to first understand some queueing theory fundamentals.

1.2 Queueing System Fundamentals

A basic queueing system is a service system where "customers" arrive to a bank of "servers" and require some service from one of them. It's important to understand that a "customer" is whatever entity is waiting for service and does not have to be a person. For example, in a "back-office" situation such as the reading of radiologic images, the "customers" might be the images waiting to be read. Similary, a "server" is the person or thing that provides the service. So when analyzing delays for patients in the emergency department (ED) awaiting admission to the hospital, the relevant servers would be inpatient beds.

If all servers are busy upon a customer's arrival, they must join a queue. Though queues are often physical lines of people or things, they can also be invisible as with telephone calls waiting on hold. The rule that determines the order in which queued customers are served is called the queue *discipline*. The most common discipline is the familiar first-come, first-served (FCFS) rule, but other disciplines are often used to increase efficiency or reduce the delay for more time-sensitive customers. For example, in an ED, the triage system is an example of a *priority* queue discipline. Priority disciplines may be preemptive or non-preemptive, depending upon whether a service in progress can be interrupted when a customer with a higher priority arrives. In most queueing models, the assumption is made that there is no limit on the number of customers that can be waiting for service, i.e. there is an *infinite waiting room*. This is a good assumption when customers do not physically join a queue, as in a telephone call center, or when the physical space where customers wait is large compared to the number of customers who are usually waiting for service. Even if there is no capacity limit on waiting room, in some cases new arrivals who see a long queue may "balk" and not join the queue. This might happen in a walk-in clinic. A related characteristic that is incorporated in some queueing systems is "reneging" which occurs when customers grow inpatient and leave the queue before being served. An example of this behavior is found in some EDs where the patients who renege are often referred to as "left without being seen".

Finally, queues may be organized in various ways. In most cases, we will consider a *single line* that feeds into all servers. But sometimes each server has his/her own queue as may be the case for a primary care office in which patients have their own physician. This is usually referred to as queues in *parallel*. In other situations, we may want to consider a *network* design in which customers receive service from different types of servers in a sequential manner. For example, a surgical inpatient requires an operating room (OR), then a bed in the recovery unit, followed by a bed in a surgical intensive care unit (ICU), and/or other part of the hospital. However, it might still make sense to analyze a single queue in these situations to determine the capacity requirements of a single type of resource, particularly if there is reason to believe that the resource is a bottleneck.

A queueing model is a mathematical description of a queuing system which makes some specific assumptions about the probabilistic nature of the arrival and service processes, the number and type of servers, and the queue discipline and organization. There are countless variations possible, but some queueing models are more widely used and we will focus on these in this chapter. For these models, as well as many others, there are formulae available that enable the fast calculation of various performance measures that can be used to help design a new service system or improve an existing one.

2. BASIC QUEUEING PRINCIPLES AND MODELS

Most of queueing theory deals with system performance in *steady-state*. That is, most queueing models assume that the system has been operating with the same arrival, service time and other characteristics for a sufficiently long time that the probability distribution for the queue length and customer delay is independent of time. Clearly, there are many service systems, including health care systems, for which there are time-of-day, day-of-week or seasonality affects. In this section, we will assume that we are looking at systems in steady-state and in subsequent sections, we will discuss how to deal with systems that have some time-varying characteristics.

2.1 Delays, Utilization and System Size

In queueing theory, utilization, defined as the average number of busy servers divided by the total number of servers times 100, is an important measure. From a managerial perspective, utilization is often seen as a measure of productivity and therefore it is considered desirable for it to be high. For example, in hospital bed planning, utilization is called occupancy level and historically, an average hospital occupancy level of 85 percent has been used as the minimum level for the states to make a determination under Certificate of Need (CON) regulations that more beds might be needed (see Brecher and Speizio 1995). Since the actual average occupancy rate for nonprofit hospitals has recently been about 66 percent, there has been a widely held perception in the health care community that there are too many hospital beds. Largely because of this perception, the number of hospital beds has decreased almost 25 percent in the last 20 years.

But determining bed capacity based on occupancy levels can result in very long waiting times for beds (Green 2003). In all queueing systems, the higher the average utilization level, the longer the wait times. However, it is important to note that this relationship is nonlinear. This is illustrated in Figure 1 which shows the fundamental relationship between delays and utilization for a queueing system. There are three critical observations we can make from this figure. First, as average utilization (e.g. occupancy rate) increases, average delays increase at an increasing rate. Second, there is an "elbow" in the curve after which the average delay increases more dramatically in response to even small increases in utilization. Finally, the average delay approaches infinity as utilization approaches one. (It's important to note that this assumes there is no constraint on how long the queue can get and that customers continue to join and remain in the queue.)

The exact location of the elbow in the curve depends upon two critical characteristics of the system: variability and size. Variability generally exists in both the time between arrivals and the duration of service times and is usually measured by the ratio of the standard deviation to the mean, called the coefficient of variation (*CV*). The higher the degree of variability in the system, the more to the left the elbow will be so that delays will be worse for the same utilization level. System size is defined as the ratio of the average demand over the average service time, which is a determinant of the number of servers needed. The larger the system, the closer the elbow will be to 100%, so that delays will be smaller for the same utilization level.

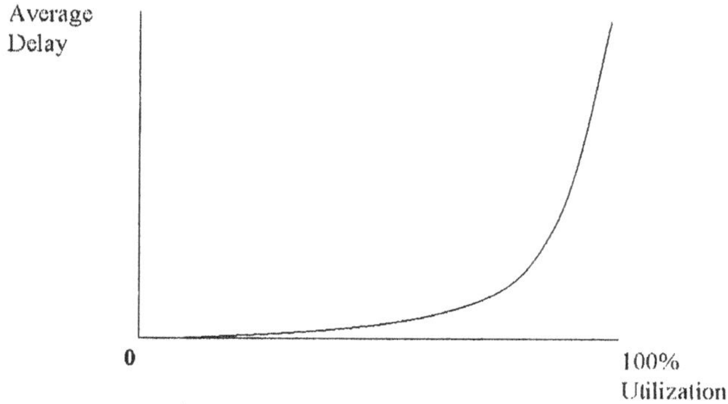

Figure 10-1 Tradeoff between average delay and utilization in a queueing system

These basic queueing principles have several important implications for planning or evaluating capacity in a service system. First, the average total capacity, defined as the number of servers times the rate at which each server can serve customers, must be strictly greater than the average demand. In other words, unless average utilization is strictly *less than* 100%, the system will be "unstable" and the queue will continue to grow. Though this fact may appear counter-intuitive on the surface, it has been well known by operations professionals for decades. So if an emergency room has ten patients arriving per hour on average and each healthcare provider (physician or physician assistant) can treat 2 patients per hour, a minimum of six providers is needed. (Of course, in many contexts, if arrivals see a long queue they may not join it or they may renege after waiting a long time. If so, the system may stabilize even if the average demand exceeds the average capacity.) Second, the smaller the system, the longer the delays will be for a given utilization level. In other words, queueing systems have economies of scale so that, for example, larger hospitals can operate at higher utilization levels than smaller ones yet maintain similar levels of congestion and delays. Finally, the greater the variability in the service time (e.g. length-of-stay), the longer the delays at a given utilization level. So a clinic or physician office that specializes in e.g. vision testing or mammography, will experience shorter patient waits than a university based clinic of the same size and with the same provider utilization that treats a broad variety of illnesses and injuries. These properties will be more specifically illustrated when we discuss applications of queueing models.

2.2 Some simple but useful queueing models

2.2.1 The Poisson process

In specifying a queueing model, we must make assumptions about the probabilistic nature of the arrival and service processes. The most common assumption to make about arrivals is that they follow a *Poisson* process. The name comes from the fact that the number of arrivals in any given time period has a Poisson distribution. So if $N(t)$ is the number of arrivals during a time period of duration t and N(t) has a Poisson distribution,

$$\text{Probability } \{N(t) = n\} = e^{-\lambda t} (\lambda t)^n / n!$$

where λ is called the *rate* and is the expected number of arrivals per unit time. For example, if $\lambda = 10$ customers per hour, then the expected number of arrivals in any 60 minute interval is 10 and the expected number to arrive in a 15 minute interval is 2.5. Notice that these are averages so that λ need not have an integer value. Another way to characterize the Poisson process is that the time between consecutive arrivals, called the interarrival time, has an *exponential* distribution. So if *IA* is the interarrival time of a Poisson process with rate λ,

$$\text{Probability }\{IA \leq t\} = 1 - e^{-\lambda t}$$

and $1/\lambda$ is the average time between arrivals.

An important property of the exponential distribution is that it is "memoryless". This means that the time of the next arrival is independent of when the last arrival occurred. This property also leads to the fact that if the arrival process is Poisson, the number of arrivals in any given time interval is independent of the number in any other non-overlapping time interval. Conversely, it can be shown analytically that if customers arrive independently from one another, the arrival process is a Poisson process. For this reason, the Poisson process is considered the most "random" arrival process.

In determining whether the Poisson process is a reasonable model for arrivals in a specific service system, it is useful to consider its three defining properties:

1. Customers arrive one at a time.
2. The probability that a customer arrives at any time is independent of when other customers arrived.
3. The probability that a customer arrives at a given time is independent of the time.

In most contexts, customers generally do arrive one at a time. Though there may be events, such as a major accident, that trigger multiple simultaneous arrivals, this is likely to be an exceptional circumstance which will not significantly affect the usefulness of this modeling assumption. Intuitively, the second property is also often a reasonable assumption. For example, in an emergency room, where the population of potential patients is very large, it is unlikely that someone arriving with a broken arm has anything to do with someone else's injury or illness, or that the fact that the number of patients who arrived between 9am and 10am was four provides information about the number of patients that are likely to arrive between 10am and 11am. Again, there may be occasional exceptions, such as a flu outbreak, for which there is an exogenous factor responsible for generating multiple arrivals over a time period. However, this assumption is still likely to be a reasonable one in most situations. The third property may be more suspect. More typically, the average arrival rate varies over the day so that, e.g., it is more likely for an arrival to occur in the morning than in the middle of the night. Certain days of the week may be busier than others as well. However, we may be able to use the standard Poisson process as a good model for a shorter interval of time during which the arrival rate is fairly constant. We will discuss this in more detail in a subsequent section.

So the assumption of a Poisson process will generally be a good one when the three properties above are a reasonable description of the service system in question. However, it is possible to perform more rigorous tests to determine if it is a good fit. The simplest tests are based on the relationship of the standard deviation to the mean of the two distributions involved in the Poisson process. Since the variance (square of the standard deviation) of the Poisson distribution is equal to its mean, we can examine the number of arrivals in each fixed interval of time, (e.g. 30 minutes) and determine whether the ratio of the mean to the variance is close to one. Alternatively, since the exponential distribution is characterized by its standard deviation being equal to its mean, we can look at the interarrival times and compute the ratio of the standard deviation to the mean to see if it's close to one. Hall (1991) describes goodness of fit tests in greater detail.

Many real arrival and demand processes have been empirically shown to be very well approximated by a Poisson process. Among these are demands for emergency services such as police, fire and ambulance, arrivals to banks and other retail establishments, and arrivals of telephone calls to customer service call centers. Because of its prevalence and its assumption of independent arrivals, the Poisson process is the most commonly used arrival process in modeling service systems. It is also a convenient assumption to make in terms of data collection since it is characterized by a single parameter – its rate λ. In healthcare, the Poisson process has been verified to be a good representation of unscheduled arrivals to various parts of the hospital including ICUs, obstetrics units and EDs (Young 1965, Kim et al 1999, Green et al 2005).

2.2.2 The *M/M/s* model

The most commonly used queueing model is the *M/M/s* or *Erlang delay* model. This model assumes a single queue with unlimited waiting room that feeds into *s* identical servers. Customers arrive according to a Poisson process with a constant rate, and the service duration (e.g. LOS or provider time associated with a patient) has an exponential distribution. (These two assumptions are often called Markovian, hence the use of the two "M's" in the notation used for the model.)

One advantage of using the *M/M/s* model is that it requires only three parameters and so it can be used to obtain performance estimates with very little data. Given an average arrival rate, λ, an average service duration, $1/\mu$, and the number of servers, s, easy-to-compute formulae are available to obtain performance measures such as the probability that an arrival will experience a positive delay, p_D, or the average delay, W_q:

$$p_D = 1 - \sum_{n=0}^{s-1} p_n \qquad 10\text{-}1$$

$$W_q = p_D / [(1 - \rho s \mu)] \qquad 10\text{-}2$$

for

$$\rho = \lambda / s\mu \qquad 10\text{-}3$$

and

$$p_n = \begin{cases} \dfrac{\lambda^n}{n!\,\mu^n} p_0 & (1 \leq n \leq s) \\ \dfrac{\lambda^n}{s^{n-s} s!\,\mu^n} p_0 & (n \geq s) \end{cases} \qquad 10\text{-}4$$

where

$$p_0 = \left[\sum_{n=0}^{s-1} \frac{(\rho s)^n}{n!} + \frac{\rho^s s^{s+1}}{s!(s - \rho s)} \right]^{-1} \qquad \rho < 1 \qquad 10\text{-}5$$

Note that ρ is the average utilization for this queueing system and the equation is only valid when the utilization is strictly less than one. Also note that average delay increases as utilization approaches one. These quantitative observations support the discussion of utilization and delays in the previous section.

Many other measures of performance can be calculated as well and many of the formulae for both the *M/M/s* and other common queueing models are available in software packages or are easily programmable on spreadsheets. One common performance constraint is often referred to as the *service level* – a requirement that x% of customers start service within y time units. For example, many customer call centers have a target service level that 85% of calls be answered within 20 seconds. The delay is always measured from the time of the demand for service (e.g. patient registered in the ED) to the time at which service begins (e.g. a provider is available to treat that patient). It's important to note that the model's delay predictions pertain only to waiting times due to the unavailability of the server.

2.2.3 Some useful extensions of the M/M/s model

There are several variations on the basic *M/M/s* queueing model. One important one for many healthcare organizations is the *M/M/s* with priorities. While the fundamental model assumes that customers are indistinguishable and are served FCFS, the priority model assumes that customers have differing time-sensitivities and are allocated to two or more service classes $i = 1,2,\ldots N$, and that customers are served in priority order with 1 being the highest priority and N the lowest. Within any given class, customers are served FCFS. But when there is a queue and a server becomes available, a customer belonging to class i will be served only if there are no waiting customers of class $1,\ldots,i$-1. A priority queueing model would be appropriate if a facility is interested in identifying the capacity needed to assure a targeted service level for the highest priority customers. For examples, in an ED, while many arriving patients would not incur any particular harm if they had to wait more than an hour to be seen by a physician, some fraction, who are emergent or urgent, need a physician's care sooner to prevent serious clinical consequences. In this case, a priority queueing model could be used to answer a question like: How many physicians are needed to assure that 90% of emergent and urgent patients will be seen by a physician within 45 minutes?

There are two types of priority queueing disciplines: preemptive and non-preemptive. In the preemptive model, if a higher priority customer arrives when all servers are busy and a lower priority customer is being served, the lower priority customer's service will be interrupted (preempted) so that the higher priority customer can begin service immediately. The preempted customer must then wait for another server to become free to resume service. In the non-preemptive model, new arrivals cannot preempt customers already in service. While priority queueing models are usually either purely preemptive or non-preemptive, it is possible to model a service system that has both preemptive and non-preemptive customer classes. This might be appropriate for a hospital ED where the normal triage system which classifies patients as emergent, urgent or non-urgent is usually assumed to be non-preemptive, but will use a preemptive discipline for certain urgent patients whose conditions are extremely time-sensitive, such as stroke victims. In addition to the usual input parameters for the *M/M/s* model, priority models also require the fraction of customers in each of the priority classes.

Another common variant of the *M/M/s* model assumes a finite capacity $K \geq s$ and is notated as *M/M/s/K*. In this model, if a customer arrives when there are K customers already in the system (being served and waiting), the customer cannot join the queue and must leave. A common application of this would be a telephone trunk line feeding into a call center. Such a system has a finite number of spaces for calls being served or on hold and when a new call comes in and all the spaces are already taken, the new arrival hears a busy signal and hangs up. A similar phenomenon might occur in a walk-in health clinic which has a waiting room with a fixed number of seats. Though some patients may choose to wait even if there is no seat available upon arrival, many patients may leave and try to return at a less busy time. Customers who are "blocked" from joining the queue are called "lost" and may show up again or never return. In these types of systems, queueing analysis might be used to help determine how large the waiting or holding area should be so that the number of customers who are blocked is kept to an acceptably low level.

A specific special case of these finite capacity models is the one where $K = s$ so that there is no waiting room for those who arrive when all servers are busy. These are called pure "loss" models and they are often used to analyze service systems in which it is considered either impractical or very undesirable to have any customers wait to begin service. For example, Kaplan, Sprung and Shmueli (2003) used a loss model to analyze the impact of various admissions policies to ICU facilities.

2.3 The *M/G/1* and *G/G/s* models

An important characteristic of the exponential distribution used in the *M/M/s* is that the standard distribution equals the mean and so the CV of the service time equals one. If the actual CV of service is a bit less than or greater than one, the *M/M/s* will still give good estimates of delay. However, if the CV is substantially different than one, the *M/M/s* may significantly underestimate or overestimate actual delays. (Recall that if variability is lower, the model will overestimate delays while the converse is true if variability is greater.) In this case, if the arrival process is Poisson, and there is only one server, the average delay can still be calculated for any service distribution through use of the following formula for what is known as the *M/G/1* system:

$$W_q = [\, \lambda\rho / (1 - \rho) \,]\, [\, (1 + CV^2(S)) / 2 \,] \qquad \text{10-6}$$

where $CV^2(S)$ is the square of the coefficient of variation of the service time. Clearly, this formula requires knowledge of the standard deviation of the service time in addition to the mean in order to compute $CV^2(S)$. This formula also illustrates the impact of variability on delays. Notice that, as mentioned previously, as the coefficient of variation of the service time increases, so does the average delay.

Though there are no exact formula for non-Markovian multi-server queues, there are some good, simple approximations. One such approximation (Allen 1978) is given by:

$$W_q = W_{q,M/M/s}\ [CV^2(A) + CV^2(S)]\ /\ 2 \qquad \text{10-7}$$

where $CV^2(A)$ is the square of the coefficient of variation of the arrival time and $W_{q,M/M/s}$ is the expected delay for an *M/M/s* system, eq. (2). So this formula requires the standard deviation of the interarrival time as well and again demonstrates that more variability results in longer delays.

3. ANALYSES OF FIXED CAPACITY: HOW MANY HOSPITAL BEDS?

Many resources in health care facilities have a fixed capacity over a long period of time. These are usually "things" rather than people: beds, operating rooms, imaging machines, etc. Queueing models are not always appropriate for analyzing such resources. In particular, if the patients for a resource are scheduled into fixed time slots, there is little or no likelihood of congestion unless patients routinely come late or the time slots are not large enough to accommodate most patients. An example of this would be a magnetic resonance imaging (MRI) facility which is only used by scheduled outpatients. It should be noted that the use of an appointment system can be an effective way to minimize or eliminate variability in the arrival stream of a service system and therefore minimize delays. See Chapter for more on appointment systems.

However, the difficulty of managing many healthcare facilities is that the demand for resources is unscheduled and hence random, yet timely care is important. This is the case for many parts of a hospital that deal primarily with non-elective admissions. In these cases, queueing models can be very helpful in identifying long-term capacity needs.

3.1 Applying the *M/M/s* model

To illustrate the use of a queueing model for evaluating capacity, consider an obstetrics unit. Since it is generally operated independently of other services, its capacity needs, e.g. number of postpartum beds, can be determined without regard to other parts of the hospital. It is also one for which the use of a standard *M/M/s* queueing model is quite good. Most obstetrics patients are unscheduled and the assumption of Poisson arrivals has been shown to be a good one in studies of unscheduled hospital admissions (Young 1965). In addition, the *CV* of length of stay is typically very close to 1.0 (Green and Nguyen 2001) satisfying the service time assumption of the *M/M/s* model.

A queueing model may be used either descriptively or prescriptively. As an example of the descriptive case, we can take the current operating characteristics of a given obstetrics unit: arrival rate, average LOS, and number of beds; and use these in equation (10-1) to determine the probability that an arriving patient will not find a bed available. Let's assume that Big City Hospital's obstetrics unit has an average arrival rate of $\lambda = 14.8$ patients per day, an average LOS of $1/\mu = 2.9$ days, and $s = 56$ beds. Then the *M/M/s* formula for probability of delay (10-1) produces an estimate of approximately 4%. To use the *M/M/s* prescriptively to find the minimum number of beds needed to attain a target probability of delay, we can enter equation (10-1) in a spreadsheet and produce a table of results for a broad range of bed capacities to find the one that best meets the desired target. Table 10-1 is a partial table of results for our example obstetrics unit.

Table 10-1 Probability of (Delay) and utilization for obstetrics unit

No. Beds	Pr(Delay)	Utilization
45	0.666	0.953
46	0.541	0.933
47	0.435	0.913
48	0.346	0.894
49	0.272	0.875
50	0.212	0.858
51	0.163	0.841
52	0.124	0.825
53	0.093	0.809
54	0.069	0.794
55	0.051	0.780
56	0.037	0.766
57	0.026	0.753
58	0.018	0.740
59	0.013	0.727
60	0.009	0.715
61	0.006	0.703

62	0.004	0.692
63	0.003	0.681
64	0.002	0.670
65	0.001	0.660

Though there is no standard delay target, Schneider (1981) suggested that given their emergent status, the probability of delay for an obstetrics bed should not exceed 1%. Applying this criterion, Table 10-1 indicates that this unit has at least 60 beds. Table 10-1 also shows the utilization level for each choice of servers and that at 60 beds, this level is 71.5%. This is what hospitals call the average occupancy level and it is well below the 85% level that many hospitals and healthcare policy officials consider the minimum target level. It is also below the maximum level of 75% recommended by the American College of Obstetrics and Gynecology (ACOG) to assure timely access to a bed (Freeman and Poland 1992). So does this example show that as long as an obstetrics unit operates below this ACOG occupancy level of 75%, the fraction of patients who will be delayed in getting a bed will be very low?

3.2 The problem with using target occupancy levels

Hospital capacity decisions traditionally have been made, both at the government and institutional levels, based on target occupancy levels - the average percentage of occupied beds. Historically, the most commonly used occupancy target has been 85%. Estimates of the number of "excess" beds in the United States, as well as in individual states and communities, usually have been based on this "optimal" occupancy figure (Brecher and Speizio 1995, p.55). In addition, low occupancy levels are often viewed as indicative of operational inefficiency and potential financial problems. So hospital administrators generally view higher occupancy levels as desirable. However, as we saw previously in this chapter, higher occupancy levels result in longer delays and so basing capacity on target occupancy levels can lead to undesirable levels of access for patients.

In Green (2002), the basic *M/M/s* model is used to demonstrate the implications of using target occupancy levels to determine capacity in both obstetrics and ICU units in New York State. Figure 1 from that paper (shown below as Figure 10-2) shows the distribution of average occupancy rates for 148 obstetrics units in New York State for 1997. These data, representing nearly all obstetrics units in New York, were obtained from Institutional Cost Reports (ICRs), and unlike most other published data, reflect staffed beds rather than certified beds. The graph shows that many maternity units had low average occupancy levels with the overall average occupancy level for the study hospitals was only 60%, which, based on the ACOG standard, would imply significant excess capacity. Applying this 75% standard to the 1997 data, 117 of the 148 New York state hospitals had "excess" beds, while 27 had insufficient beds.

However, if one considers a bed delay target as a more appropriate measure of capacity needs, the conclusions can be quite different. Now the number of beds in each unit becomes a major factor since, for a given occupancy level, delays increase as unit size decreases. While obstetrics units usually are not the smallest units in a hospital, there are many small hospitals, particularly in rural areas, and the units in these facilities may contain only five to 10 beds. Of the New York state hospitals considered here, more than 50% had maternity units with 25 or fewer beds.

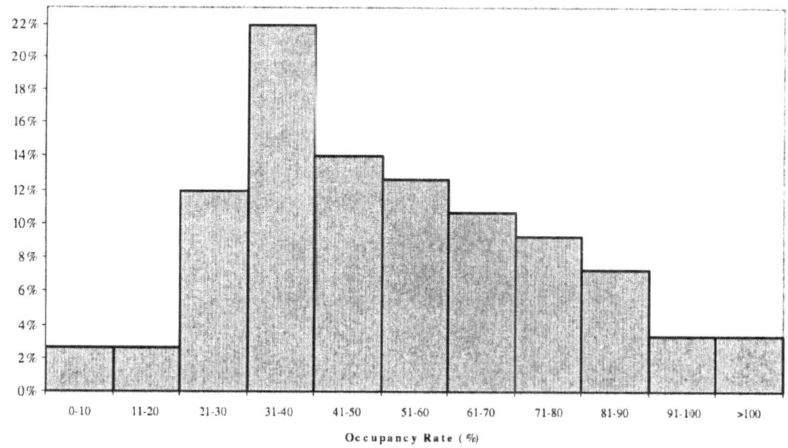

Figure 10- 2 Average Occupancy Rates of New York State Maternity Units, 1997

In the *M/M/s* model, probability of delay is a function of only two parameters: s and ρ, which in our context is the number of beds and occupancy level. Each of the three curves shown in Figure 10-3 represents a specific probability of delay as a function of these two variables as generated by equation (10-1). Thus, using the unit size and occupancy level reported on the ICR report for a given maternity unit, we can determine from this figure if the probability of delay meets or exceeds any one of these targets.

For example, if a maternity unit has 15 beds and an occupancy level of 45%, it would fall below all three curves and hence have a probability of delay less than .01 or 1%, meeting all three targets.

Doing this for every hospital in the database, 30 hospitals had insufficient capacity based on even the most slack delay target of 10%. (It is interesting to note that two of the hospitals that would be considered over utilized under the 75% occupancy standard had sufficient capacity under this delay standard.) Tightening the probability of delay target to 5%, yields 48 obstetrics units that do not meet this standard. And adopting a maximum probability of delay of 1% as was suggested in the only publication identified as containing a delay standard for obstetrics beds (Schneider 1981), results in 59, or 40%, of all New York state maternity units with insufficient capacity.

How many hospitals in New York State had maternity units large enough to achieve the ACOG-suggested 75% occupancy level and also meet a specified probability of delay standard? Using Figure 10-3, we see that for a 10% target, an obstetrics unit would need to have at least 28 beds, a size that exists in only 40% of the state hospitals. For a 5% standard, the minimum number of beds needed is 41, a size achieved in only 14% of the hospitals; for a 1% standard, at least 67 beds are needed, leaving only three of the 148 or 2% of the hospitals of sufficient size.

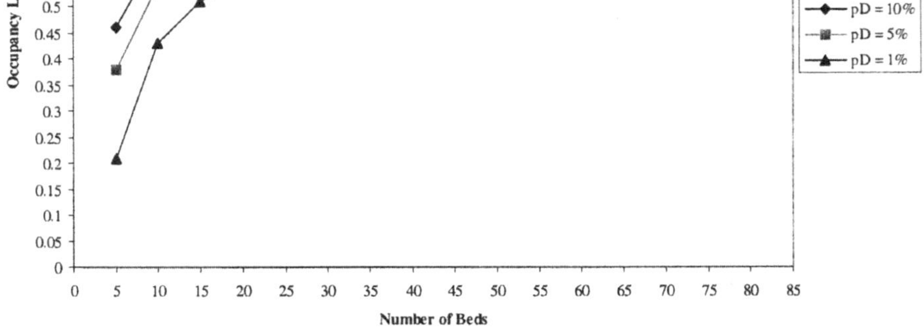

Figure 10-3 Probability of Delay (pD) by Occupancy and Size

3.3 Choosing a delay standard

As the previous analysis illustrates, the number of required beds can change substantially depending upon what level of delay is considered tolerable. There is no single right choice and in choosing a delay standard, several factors are relevant.

First, what is the expected delay of those patients who experience a delay? This performance measure can be easily calculated once both the probability of delay (equation 10-1) and the average or mean delay (equation 10-2) are known. Specifically,

$$\text{Expected delay of delayed customers} = W_q / p_D \qquad 10\text{-}8$$

So returning to our obstetrics example above, Table 10-1 shows that the average delay is .008 days (note that since the input was expressed in days, so is the output) which multiplying by 24 gives us .19 hours. So dividing this by the probability of delay of .04 results in an expected delay for delayed patients of about 4.75 hours. This may indicate that the probability of delay standard should be lower. This, of course, should be considered in light of what this level of congestion means for the particular hospital.

What are the possible consequences of congestion? In the obstetrics case, while patients in some hospitals remain in the same bed through labor, delivery, recovery, and postpartum, in most maternity units, there are separate areas for some or all of these stages of birth. Therefore, a delay for an obstetrics bed often means that a postpartum patient will remain in a recovery bed longer than necessary. This, of course, may cause a backup in the labor and delivery areas so that newly arriving patients may have to wait on gurneys in hallways or in the emergency room. Some hospitals have overflow beds in a nearby unit that is opened (staffed) when all regular beds are full. (This is likely the case for the five hospitals that reported average occupancy levels exceeding 100%.) While these effects of congestion likely pose no medical threat for most patients who experience normal births, there could be adverse clinical consequences in cases in which there are complications. In particular, whether patients are placed in hallways or overflow units, the nursing staff is likely to be severely strained, thereby limiting the quantity and quality of personal attention. Even if a hospital is able to obtain additional staffing, it is usually by using agency nurses who are more expensive and not as familiar with the physical or operating environment, thereby jeopardizing quality of patient care. In addition, telemetry devices, such as fetal monitors that are usually in labor and delivery rooms, may be unavailable in other locations, thus compromising the ability to monitor often need the resources of an intensive care vital body functions of both mother and baby. Finally, it is worth noting that such results of congestion may negatively affect patients' perceptions of service quality.

Of course, all major capacity decisions need to be made in light of financial constraints, competing demands, and predictions concerning future demands for the service.

3.4 Planning for predictable changes in demand

When making capacity decisions about resources that will be used over several years, it is clearly necessary to consider how conditions may change over that period of time. So in determining the choice of arrival rate or average LOS for a queueing analysis of a hospital unit, it would be important to engage in analyses and discussion to gauge how these parameters may change and then run the model to determine the sensitivity of capacity levels to these changes.

However, what may not be so obvious is the need to consider the changes in the arrival rate that are likely to occur on a regular basis due to predictable day-of-week or time-of-year patterns. For example, obstetrics units often experience a significant degree of seasonality in admissions. An analysis performed on data from a 56-bed maternity unit at Beth Israel Deaconess Hospital in Boston (Green and Nguyen 2001) revealed that the average occupancy levels varied from a low of about 68% in January to about 88% in July. As indicated by Figure 10-4, the *M/M/s* model estimate of the probability of delay of getting a bed for an obstetrics patient giving birth in January is likely to be negligible with this capacity. However, in July, the same model estimates this delay to be about 25%. And if, as is likely, there are several days when actual arrivals exceed this latter monthly average by say 10%, this delay probability would shoot up to over 65%. The result of such substantial delays can vary from backups into the labor rooms and patients on stretchers in the hallways to the early discharge of patients. Clearly, hospitals need to plan for this type of predictable demand increase by keeping extra bed capacity that can be used during peak times, or by using "swing" beds that can be shared by clinical units that have countercyclical demand patterns.

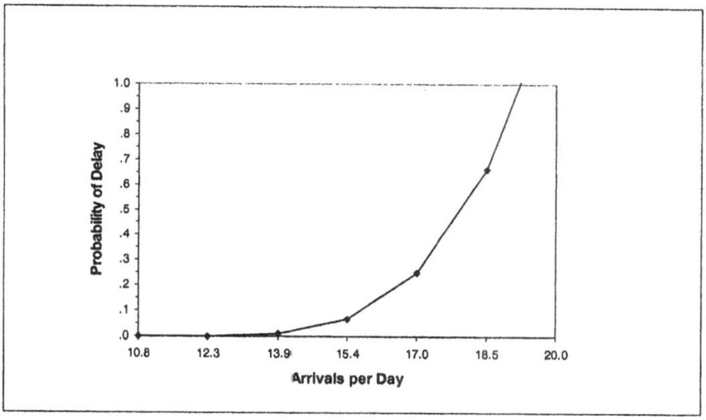

Figure 10-4 Probability of Delay as a function of arrivals per day for a 56 bed obstetrics unit

Most hospital units experience different arrival rates for different days of the week. For example, in one surgical intensive care unit, the average admissions per day over a six month period varied from a low of 1.44 for Sundays to a high of 4.40 for Fridays. Using the average arrival rate over the week of 3.34 in a queueing model would indicate that given the 12 bed capacity of this unit, the probability of delay for a bed was about 39%, indicating serious congestion. However, this is very misleading because delays will be significantly greater in the middle of the week and quite small earlier in the week due to the large differences in the admissions rates (Green and Nguyen (2001). This illustrates a situation in which a steady-state queueing model is inappropriate for estimating the magnitude and timing of delays and for which a simulation model will be far more accurate.

It's important to note that while in the obstetrics unit case, most arrivals are unscheduled and cannot be controlled, in the surgical unit case, the converse is true since most surgeries are elective. So while there is little that can be done to minimize the seasonal variability in arrivals for the former, the intra-week variability of the surgical unit could be reduced by adjusting the scheduling of surgeries so as to smooth out the demand over the week. This would result in higher average levels of bed occupancy and shorter delays for beds.

3.5 Using queueing models to quantify the benefits of flexibility

Healthcare facilities often have to make a choice as to the extent to which resources should be dedicated to specific patient types. For example, should there be a imaging facility just for the use of inpatients, or for emergency patients? Should there be a "fast-track" unit in the emergency room to deal with simpler, non-urgent cases. How many distinct clinical service units should be used for hospital inpatients? In many of these situations, a queueing analysis can be useful in evaluating the potential trade-offs between more flexible and more specialized facilities.

For example, seriously ill patients arriving to a hospital ED often experience serious delays in being admitted due to highly variable patient demands and insufficient inpatient bed capacity. Yet, hospitals are often reluctant or unable to add capacity because of cost pressures, regulatory constraints, or a shortage of appropriate personnel. This makes it extremely important to use existing capacity most efficiently. Increasing bed flexibility can be a key strategy in alleviating congestion. For example, hospitals vary in the degree to which they segregate patients by diagnostic type. While all hospitals have separate units for pediatrics, obstetrics and psychiatric patients, some also have distinct units for clinical services such as cardiology, neurology, oncology, urology, neurosurgery, etc. Other hospitals may make no such distinctions and simply designate all of these as medical/surgical beds. What are the implications of these differing bed assignment policies on delays for beds?

As mentioned in section 2.1, service systems have economies of scale and so in general, the less specialized the beds, the larger the pool of beds that can be used for any type of patient, and therefore the fewer beds should be needed to achieve a given standard of delay. In other words, if one hospital has 100 general medical/surgical beds, and another has the same 100 beds, but allocated into 10 distinct clinical services, each of which can only be used for patients falling into the appropriate category, the second hospital will likely have considerably longer delays for beds (which usually show up as longer stays in the ED) and lower average occupancy levels than the first. This is pretty clear once you consider that by creating separate categories of beds, there is the possibility of patients waiting for beds even when beds are available if they are the "wrong" kind. This also happens when beds are distinguished by capability, for example, telemetry beds.

Clearly, there are many instances in which there are compelling clinical and/or managerial reasons for maintaining particular patient types in specialized units. From a medical perspective, there may be benefits derived from having patients clustered by diagnostic categories in dedicated units managed and staffed by specialized nurses. These include shorter LOS, fewer adverse events and fewer readmits. Yet, many hospital managers believe that nurses can be successfully cross-trained and that increasing bed flexibility is ultimately in the best interests of patients by increasing speedy access to beds and minimizing the number of bed transfers. By incorporating waiting times, percentage of "off-placements" and the effects on LOS, queueing models can be used to better evaluate the benefits of greater versus less specialization of beds or any other resource. This would be done by simply modeling the general-use unit as a single multi-server queueing system fed and comparing the results to those from modeling each distinct service as an independent queue. In the latter case, the overall patient delay can be obtained from an arrival rate weighted average of the individual queue delays (see e.g. Green and Nguyen 2001).

4. ANALYSES OF FLEXIBLE CAPACITY: DETERMINING STAFFING LEVELS TO MEET TIME-VARYING DEMANDS

As mentioned previously, health care facilities generally experience very different levels of demand over the day, over the week, and even over the year. Many facilities adjust their staffing – e.g. physicians, nurses, technicians, housekeeping staff – in order to respond to the demands in a timely fashion at minimal cost. This is often done without the help of a quantitative model and can lead to an inefficient and ineffective allocation of resources. Here we use the example of determining physician staffing levels in an ED to illustrate how queueing models can be used to improve performance in these types of situations.

4.1 Data collection and model choices

In order to use a queueing model to determine how to adjust staffing to meet time-varying demands, it is first necessary to collect fairly detailed data on the volume of demand that must be handled by that staff by time-of-day and day-of-week. In collecting demand data, the goal is two-fold. First, and most obviously, the data will be used to parameterize the queueing model. However, before that can be done, it must first be determined how many staffing models are needed. That is, will staffing be identical for all days of the week or vary from day to day? For example, in a study conducted in the ED of a mid-size urban hospital in New York City (Green et al 2005), the overall volume varied from a low of 63 patients per day on Saturdays to a high of 72 per day on Monday. This degree of variation indicated that the then-current policy of identical staffing levels for all days of the week was likely suboptimal. However, it was deemed impractical to have a different provider schedule every day and so it was decided to use queueing analyses to develop two schedules: weekday and weekend. This required aggregating ED arrival data into these two groups. For each, demand data was then collected for each hour of the day using the hospital's admissions database to understand the degree of variation over the day (see Figure 10-5). This level of detail also allows for the use of queuing analysis to determine the impact of different shift starting times on delays and/or staffing levels.

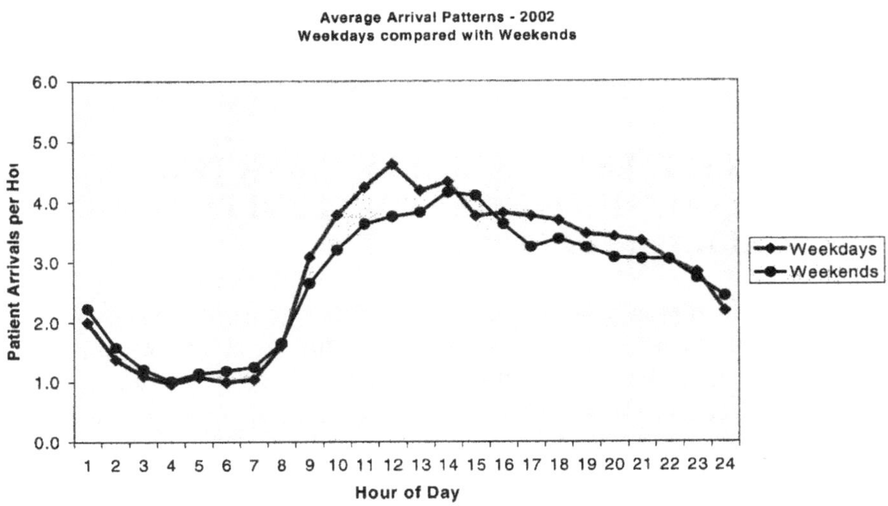

Figure 10-5 Average Arrival Patterns for the Allen Pavilion

A queueing model also requires an average provider service time per patient, which must include the times of all activities related to a patient. In the ED, these activities include direct patient care, review of x-rays and lab tests, phone calls, charting, and speaking with other providers or consults. In many, if not most, hospitals, these data are not routinely collected. At the time of the study, provider service times were not recorded and had to be estimated indirectly from direct observation and historical productivity data.

4.2 Constructing the queueing models

Since the *M/M/s* model assumes that the arrival rate does not change over the day, actual service systems that have time-varying demands typically use this model as part of a *SIPP* (stationary independent period-by-period) approach to determine how to vary staffing to meet changing demand. The *SIPP* approach begins by dividing the workday into staffing periods, e.g. one, two, four or eight hours. Then a series of *M/M/s* models are constructed, one for each staffing period. Each of these period-specific models is independently solved for the minimum number of servers needed to meet the service target in that period. The service target might be a desired maximum mean delay or probability of delay standard. However, recent research has shown that the *SIPP* approach is often unreliable, particularly when average service times are 30 minutes or more, and that a simple modification, called *Lag SIPP*, is often more effective in identifying staffing levels that achieve the desired performance standard (Green et al 2001). This is because in many service systems with time-varying arrival rates, the time of peak congestion significantly lags the time of the peak in the arrival rate (Green et al 1991). While the standard *SIPP* approach ignores this phenomenon, the *Lag SIPP* method incorporates an estimation of this lag and thus does a better job of identifying staffing levels to limit delays. For the *M/M/s* model, the lag can be well-approximated by an average service time.

4.3 Choosing a delay standard and applying the queueing results

In our ED physician staffing study, the *Lag SIPP* approach was applied by first advancing the arrival rate curve by our estimate of the average physician time per patient, 30 minutes. We then constructed a series of *M/M/s* models for each 2-hour staffing interval, using the average arrival rate for each based on the time-advanced curve and the average 30 minute service time. The delay standard we choose was that no more than 20% of patients wait more than one hour before being seen by a provider. The use of one hour is consistent with the time standards associated with emergent and urgent patient groups used in the National Hospital Ambulatory Medical Care Survey (McCaig and Burt 2002). The 20% criterion reflects the approximate percentage of non-urgent arrivals at the study institution.

The modeling results gave the number of ED physicians needed in each of the 2-hour staffing intervals to meet the delay standard. In total, 58 physician-hours were needed on weekdays to achieve the desired service standard, which represented an increase of 3 hours over the existing staffing level of 55 hours. Model runs for the weekend indicated that the target performance standard could be achieved with a total of 53 provider-hours. In both these cases, the queueing analyses suggested that some physician hours should be switched from the middle of the night to much earlier in the day. A more subtle change suggested by the model was that the increase in staffing level to handle the morning surge in demand needed to occur earlier than in the original schedule. Though resource limitations and physician availability prevented the staffing suggested by the queueing analyses from being implemented exactly, the insights gained from these analyses were used to develop new provider schedules. More specifically, as a result of the analyses one physician was moved from the overnight shift to an afternoon shift, 4 hours were moved from the weekends and added to the Monday and Tuesday afternoon shifts (since these were the two busiest days of the week) and a shift that previously started at noon was moved to 10 AM. These changes led to shorter average delays and a reduced fraction of patient that left before being seen by a physician.

5. USING QUEUEING MODELS TO IMPROVE HEALTHCARE DELIVERY: OPPORTUNITIES AND CHALLENGES

As this chapter has illustrated, service systems are very complex due to both predictable and unpredictable sources of variability in both the demands for service and the time it takes to serve those demands. In healthcare facilities, decisions on how and when to allocate staff, equipment, beds, and other resources in order to minimize delays experienced by patients are often even more difficult than in other service industries due to cost constraints on the one hand and the potentially serious adverse consequences of delays on the other hand. Therefore, it is imperative that these decisions should be as informed as possible and rely upon the best methodologies available to gain insights into the impact of various alternatives.

Queueing theory is a very powerful and very practical tool because queueing models require relatively little data and are simple and fast to use. Because of this simplicity and speed, they can be used to quickly evaluate and compare various alternatives for providing service. Beyond the most basic issue of determining how much capacity is needed to achieve a specified service standard, queueing models can also be useful in gaining insights on the appropriate degree of specialization or flexibility to use in organizing resources, or on the impact of various priority schemes for determining service order among patients.

On the other hand, though queueing models don't require much data, the type of operational data needed as input to a queueing model is often unavailable in healthcare settings. Specifically, though demand or arrival data are often recorded, service times are usually not documented. So a queueing analysis might require a data collection effort to estimate, for example, the time that a care provider spends with a patient. However, as information technology systems become more prevalent in healthcare, this type of data will be increasingly available.

In developing the data inputs for a model, it's also very important to make sure that all of the data needed for the model is collected and/or estimated. On the demand side, this means including all demands for care, including the ones that may not have been met in the past because of inadequate capacity. For example, in a hospital ED, some patients who are forced to wait a long time before seeing a physician leave the ED before being seen. If these are not captured in the data collection system that is being used to measure demands, the model will underestimate the capacity needed to meet the desired performance standard. On the service side, it's important to include all of the time spent by the servers that is directly associated with caring for the patient. For a physician, this may include reviewing medical history and test results in addition to direct examination of the patient.

In addition to data, a queueing analysis of a particular healthcare system requires the identification of one or more delay measures that are most important to service excellence for that facility. These measures should reflect both patient perspectives as well as clinical realities. For example, though hospital ED arrivals with non-urgent problems may not require care within an hour or so from a clinical perspective, clearly very long waits to see a physician will result in high levels of dissatisfaction, and perhaps even departure, which could ultimately lead to lost revenue. Trying to decide on what might be a reasonable delay standard in a specific healthcare facility is not trivial due to a lack of knowledge of both patient expectations as well as the impact of delays on clinical outcomes for most health problems.

In summary, healthcare managers are increasingly aware of the need to use their resources as efficiently as possible in order to continue to assure that their institutions survive and prosper. This is particularly true in light of the growing threat of sudden and severe demand surges due to outbreaks of epidemics such as SARS and avian flu, or terrorist incidents. As this chapter has attempted to demonstrate, effective capacity management is critical to this objective as well as to improving patients' ability to receive the most appropriate care in a timely fashion. Yet, effective capacity management must deal with complexities such as tradeoffs between bed flexibility and quality of care, demands from competing sources and types of patients, time-varying demands, and the often differing perspectives of administrators, physicians, nurses and patients. All of these are chronic and pervasive challenges affecting the ability of hospital managers to control the cost and improve the quality of healthcare delivery. To meet these challenges, managers must be informed by operational and performance data and use these data in models to gain insights that cannot be obtained from experience and intuition alone. Queueing analysis is one of the most practical and effective tools for understanding and aiding decision-making in managing critical resources and should become as widely used in the healthcare community as it is in the other major service sectors.

6. REFERENCES

Allen, A.O., 1978, *Probability, statistics and queueing theory, with computer science applications*. New York, Academic Press.

Brecher, C. and Speizio, S., 1995, *Privatization and Public Hospitals*, Twentieth Century Fund Press, N.Y.

Brewton, J.P., 1989, Teller staffing models, *Financial Manager's Statement*, July-August: 22-24.

Brigandi, A.J., Dargon, D.R., Sheehan, M.J. and Spencer III, T., 1994, AT&T's call processing simulator (CAPS) operational design for inbound call centers, Interfaces 24: 6-28.

Brockmeyer, E., Halstrom, H.L., and Jensen, A., 1948, The life and works of A.K. Erlang, *Transactions of the Danish Academy of Technical Science* 2.

Brusco, M.J., Jacobs, L.W., Bongiorno, R.J., Lyons, D.V. and Tang, B., 1995, Improving personnel scheduling at airline stations, Operations Research, 43: 741-751.

Chelst, K. and Barlach, Z., 1981, Multiple unit dispatches in emergency services, *Management Science*, 27: 1390-1409.

Cobham, A., 1954, Priority assignment in waiting line problems, *Operations Research*, 2: 70-76.

Freeman, R.K., and Poland, R.L., 1997, Guidelines for Perinatal Care, 4th ed., American College of Obstetricians and Gynecologists, Washington, D.C.

Green, L.V., Giulio, J., Green, R., and Soares, J., 2005, Using queueing theory to increase the effectiveness of physician staffing in the emergency department, *Academic Emergency Medicine*, to appear.

Green, L.V., 2003, How many hospital beds? *Inquiry*, 39: 400-412.

Green, L.V., Kolesar, P.J., Svoronos, A., 2001, Improving the SIPP approach for staffing service systems that have cyclic demands, *Operations Research*, 49: 549-564.

Green, L.V. and Nguyen, V., 2001, Strategies for cutting hospital beds: the impact on patient service. *Health Services Research*, 36: 421-442.

Green, L.V., Kolesar, P.J., and Svoronos, A., 1991, Some effects of nonstationarity on multi-server Markovian queueing systems. *Operations Research*, 39: 502-511.

Green, L.V., and Kolesar, P.J., 1984, The feasibility of one-officer patrol in New York City, *Management Science* 20: 964-981.

Hall, R.W., 1990, *Queueing Methods for Service and Manufacturing*. New Jersey: Prentice Hall.

Holloran, T. J. and Byrne, J.E., 1986, United Airlines station manpower planning system, *Interfaces*, 16: 39-50.

Green, L.V., 2003, How many hospital beds? *Inquiry*, 39: 400-412.

Institute of Medicine, Committee on Quality of Health Care in America, 2001, *Crossing the quality chasm: a new health system for the 21st century*. Washington, D.C.: National Academy Press.

Kaplan, E.H., Sprung, C.L., Shmueli, A., and Schneider, D., 1981. A methodology for the analysis of comparability of services and financial impact of closure of obstetrics services. *Medical Care*, 19: 395-409.

Kim, S., Horowitz, I., Young, K.K., and Buckley, T.A., 1999, Analysis of capacity management of the intensive care unit in a hospital, *European Journal of Operational Research* 115: 36-46.

Kolesar, P.J., Rider, K., Crabill, T., and Walker, W., 1975, A queueing linear programming approach to scheduling police cars, *Operations Research*, 23: 1045-1062.

Larson, R.C., 1972, *Urban Police Patrol Analysis*, MIT Press, Cambridge.

McCaig, L.F., and Burt, C.W., 2004, National hospital ambulatory medical care survey: 2002 emergency department summary. *Advance Data from Vital and Health Statistics*, 340: 1-35.

Stern, H.I. and Hersh, M., 1980, Scheduling aircraft cleaning crews, *Transportation Science*, 14: 277-291.

Taylor, P.E. and Huxley, S.J., 1989, A break from tradition for the San Francisco police: patrol officer scheduling using an optimization-based decision support system, Interfaces, 19: 4-24.

Worthington, D.J., 1987, Queueing models for hospital waiting lists. Journal of the *Operations Research Society*, 38: 413-422.

Young, J.P., 1965, Stabilization of inpatient bed occupancy through control of admissions, *Journal of the American Hospital Association*, 39: 41-48.

Chapter 11

RAPID DISTRIBUTION OF MEDICAL SUPPLIES

Maged Dessouky, Fernando Ordóñez, Hongzhong Jia, and Zhihong Shen
Daniel J. Epstein Department of Industrial and Systems Engineering, University of Southern California, Los Angeles, California, 90089-0193

Abstract: Some important issues in the design of an efficient pharmaceutical supply chain involve deciding where to place the warehouses/inventories and how to route distribution vehicles. Solving appropriate facility location and vehicle routing problems can ensure the design of a logistic network capable of rapid distribution of medical supplies. In particular, both these problems must be solved in coordination to quickly disburse medical supplies in response to a large-scale emergency. In this chapter, we present models to solve facility location and vehicle routing problems in the context of a response to a large-scale emergency. We illustrate the approach on a hypothetical anthrax emergency in Los Angeles County.

Key words: Emergency supply, facility location, and vehicle routing

1. INTRODUCTION

Rapid distribution of medical supplies plays a critical role in assuring the effectiveness and efficiency of the healthcare system. The medical supply distribution involves the movement of a large volume of different items that usually must be delivered rapidly. For example, in the United States, the distribution system must serve more than 130,000 pharmacy outlets every day on demand and a typical pharmacy relies on the distributors to have more than 10,000 SKUs accessible for delivery, often within 12 hours (HDMA, 2005).

In broad terms, most pharmaceuticals distributed in the United States go through a supply chain that comprises the following steps (Belson, 2005):

- Manufacturers produce various pharmaceuticals necessitated by demand;
- Distributors manage large warehouses and control the movement of supplies from manufacturers to the retailers;
- Retailers, including hospitals, clinics, independent pharmacies, chain pharmacies, and grocery stores, sell or dispense the pharmaceuticals to customers.

The pharmaceutical supply chain is relatively complex compared to the supply chains for other products, particularly when considering the strict deadline and sufficiency requirements. Different information technologies such as product identification, bar coding, usage related information, and electronic identification have been applied to facilitate the rapid distribution of the pharmaceuticals in the supply chain (Belson, 2005). Furthermore, logistic and inventory control of the pharmaceuticals have also been widely investigated in the research community in the past decades; for example, see Rebidas et al. (1999), Rubin and Keller (1983), and McAllister (1985).

It is the design of the distribution system in particular, that most significantly affects the rapid disbursement of pharmaceuticals, directly impacting the quality of healthcare. The design of an effective distribution system comprises the careful consideration of two strategic planning issues:

- Where to place the facilities including warehouses and inventories in support of rapid distribution of the medical supplies, and
- What is the best strategy to distribute the medical supplies and what routes need to be used?

Operations research models play an important role in addressing these logistical problems for distribution systems. At the heart of both questions there is a transportation network to distribute the medical supplies. The question of where to place warehouses/inventories is essentially a facility location problem within this supply network, while the disbursement of supplies can be posed as a vehicle routing problem (VRP) on this network. The benefits of modeling and solving the facility location problem and vehicle routing problem are two-fold. First, from a planning perspective, the models and solutions can aid planners to optimally determine the facility locations and vehicle routes and thus maximize the efficiency and effectiveness of the pharmaceutical supply chain system as a whole. Second, these plans can become well tested operating policies, which can further improve performance. Clearly, the plans need to be flexible enough to accommodate contingencies of daily operations. For the plans to be robust, they must take into consideration the stochastic nature of the problem such as uncertain demand, traffic conditions, etc.

Large-scale emergencies create situations that demand a rapid distribution of medical supplies and thus require an efficient and coordinated solution to both the facility location and vehicle routing problems. In particular, the response to a large-scale emergency must take into consideration that:

- A huge demand for medical supplies appears within a short time period and thus large quantities of medical supplies must be brought to the affected area;
- The local first-responders and resources will be overwhelmed;
- Although tremendous in their magnitude, large-scale emergencies occur with low frequency.

An additional parallel distribution system is envisioned in response to large-scale emergencies such as earthquakes, terrorist events, etc. as massive supplies that are brought to the affected area have to be rapidly disbursed among the affected population. Indeed, many countries maintain national stockpiles of medical supplies that can be delivered in push packages to the Emergency Staging Area (ESA) in case of a large-scale emergency. For example, to address emergencies of infectious disease outbreak, the federal government of the United States maintains a Strategic National Stockpile (SNS) which contains about 300 million doses of smallpox vaccines and enough antibiotic to treat 20 million people for anthrax (CDC website, 2005). Furthermore, a vendor managed inventory system (VMI) has also been developed to augment the SNS from pharmaceutical vendors to ESAs within 21-36 hours. During a large-scale emergency, the medical supplies at the national stockpile and VMI require direct delivery and disbursement to ESAs and dispensing centers from which the population could receive the medical supplies. Rapid delivery and disbursement of the large volume of supplies need careful planning and professional execution to save lives, particularly in high-density urban regions like Southern California.

In this chapter, we analyze the facility location and vehicle routing problems, which are crucial for a rapid distribution of medical supplies in response to large-scale emergencies. We use the anthrax disease as an emergency example to investigate the problems of determining where to locate the staging areas to receive the national stockpile and how to route the vehicles to distribute the medical supplies. The rest of the chapter is organized as follows: Section 2 presents a literature review of the facility location and vehicle routing problems that are related to emergency services. In Section 3, we describe an anthrax emergency example in a metropolitan area and then analyze the requirements for locating the facilities and routing the vehicles for rapid medical supply distribution. In Section 4, we propose a facility location model and a vehicle routing model that address the characteristics of an anthrax emergency. In Section 5, we demonstrate how the proposed models can be used to solve the facility location problem and the VRP. The solutions, including the selected staging areas and vehicle routes to store and distribute the medical supplies, are discussed. Finally, we conclude the chapter and give future research directions in Section 6.

2. LITERATURE REVIEW

Facility location problems and VRPs have been extensively investigated by different researchers and practitioners. In this section, we review the prior work that is related to different emergencies settings.

2.1 Review of Facility Location Problems

Various location models have been proposed to formulate different facility location problems for emergency services. Based on the objectives, these location models can be classified into covering models, *P*-median models, and *P*-center models.

2.1.1 Covering Models

Covering models are the most widespread location models for formulating the emergency facility location problem. The objective of covering models is to provide "coverage" to the demand points. A demand point is considered as covered only if a facility is available to service the demand point within a distance limit. Figure 11-1 presents an illustration of an infeasible covering problem, where the coverage area of a facility is indicated by circles around the four selected locations.

Toregas et al. (1971) first proposed the location set covering problem (LSCP), aiming to locate the least number of facilities to cover all demand points. Since all the demand points need to be covered in the LSCP, the resources required for facilities could be excessive. Recognizing this problem, Church and ReVelle (1974) and White and Case (1974) developed the MCLP model that does not require full coverage to all demand points. Instead, the model seeks the maximal coverage with a given number of facilities. The MCLP, and different variants of it, have been extensively used to solve various emergency service location problems (see e.g., Benedict 1983, and Hogan and ReVelle 1986).

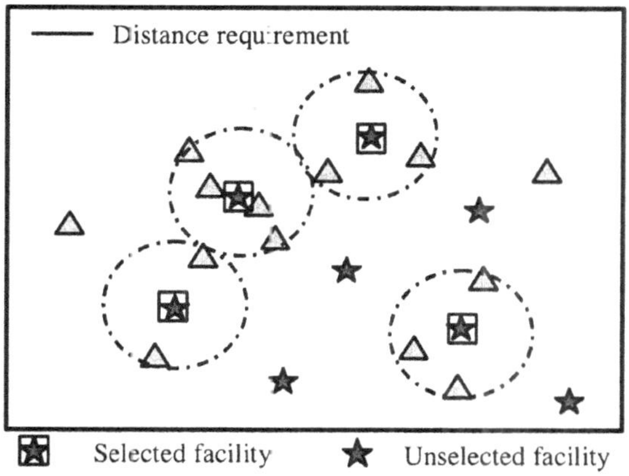

Figure 11-1. Covering Problem Example

Research on emergency service covering models has also been extended to incorporate the stochastic and probabilistic characteristics of emergency situations so as to capture the complexity and uncertainty of these problems. Examples of these stochastic models can be found in recent papers by Goldberg and Paz (1991), ReVelle et al. (1996), and Beraldi and Ruszczynski (2002). There are several approaches to model stochastic emergency service covering problems. The first approach is to use chance constrained models (Chapman and White, 1974). Daskin (1983) used an estimated parameter (q) to represent the probability that at least one server is free to serve the requests from any demand point. He formulated the Maximum Expected Covering Location Problem (MEXCLP) to place P facilities on a network with the goal to maximize the expected value of population coverage. ReVelle and Hogan (1986) later enhanced the MEXCLP and proposed the Probabilistic Location Set Covering Problem (PLSCP). In the PLSCP, a server busy fraction and a service reliability factor are defined for the demand points. Then the locations of the facilities are determined such that the probability of service being available within a specified distance is maximized. The MEXCLP and PLSCP later were further modified to tackle other EMS location problems by ReVelle and Hogan (MALP) (1989a), Bianchi and Church (MOFLEET) (1988), Batta et al. (AMEXCLP) (1989), Goldberg et al. (1990), and Repede and Bernardo (TIMEXCLP) (1994). A summary and review to the chance constrained emergency service location models can be found in ReVelle (1989).

Another approach to modeling stochastic emergency medical service (EMS) covering problems is to use scenario planning to represent possible values for parameters that may vary over the planning horizon in different emergency situations. A compromise decision is made to optimize the expected/worst-case performance or expected/worse-case regret across all scenarios. For example, Schilling (1982) extended the MCLP by incorporating scenarios to maximize the covered demands over all possible scenarios. Individual scenarios are respectively used to identify a range of good location decisions. A compromise decision is made to the final location configuration that is common to all scenarios in the horizon.

2.1.2 *P*-median Models

Another important way to measure the effectiveness of facility location is by evaluating the average (total) distance between the demand points and the facilities. When the average (total) distance decreases, the accessibility and effectiveness of the facilities increase. This relationship applies to both private and public facilities such as supermarkets, post offices, as well as emergency service centers, for which proximity is desirable. The *P*-median problem takes this measure into account and is defined as: minimize the average (total) distance between the demands and the selected facilities. We illustrate a *P*-median model in Figure 11-2. The total cost of the solution presented is the sum of the distance between demand points and selected locations represented by the black lines.

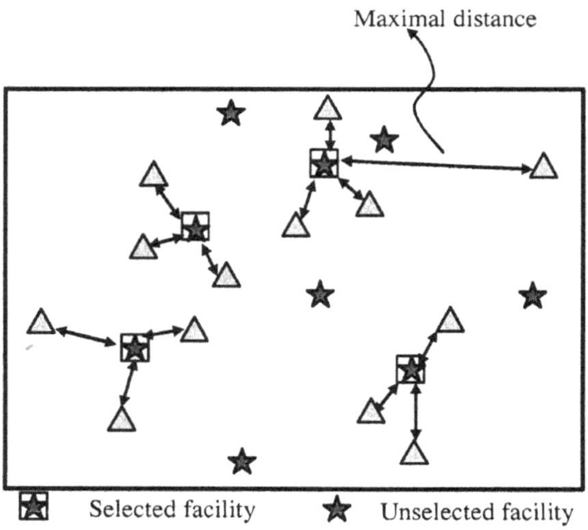

Figure 11-2. *P*-median / *P*-center Problem Example

Since its formulation, the *P*-median model has been enhanced and applied to a wide range of emergency facility location problems. Carbone (1974) formulated a deterministic *P*-median model with the objective of minimizing the distance traveled by a number of users to fixed public facilities such as medical or day-care centers. Recognizing the number of users at each demand node is uncertain, the author further extended the deterministic *P*-median model to a chance constrained model. The model seeks to maximize a threshold and meanwhile ensure the probability that the total travel distance is below the threshold is smaller than a specified level α. Paluzzi (2004) discussed and tested a *P*-median based on a heuristic location model for placing emergency service facilities for the city of Carbondale, IL. The goal of this model is to determine the optimal location for placing a new fire station by minimizing the total aggregate distance from the demand sites to the fire station.

One major application of the *P*-median models is to dispatch EMS units such as ambulances during emergencies. For example, Carson and Batta (1990) proposed a *P*-median model to find the dynamic ambulance positioning strategy for campus emergency service. Mandell (1998) developed a *P*-median model and used priority dispatching to optimally locate emergency units for a tiered EMS system that consists of advanced life-support (ALS) units and basic life-support (BLS) units.

Uncertainties have also been considered in many *P*-median models. Mirchandani (1980) examined a *P*-median problem to locate fire-fighting emergency units with consideration of stochastic travel characteristics and demand patterns. Serra and Marianov (1999) implemented a *P*-median model and introduced the concept of regret and minmax objectives. The authors explicitly addressed in their model the issue of locating facilities when there are uncertainties in demand, travel time or distance.

2.1.3 *P*-center Models

In contrast to the *P*-median models, which concentrate on optimizing the overall (or average) performance of the system, the *P*-center model attempts to minimize the worst performance of the system and thus is also known as minimax model. The *P*-center model considers a demand point is served by its nearest facility and therefore full coverage to all demand points is always achieved. In the last several decades, the *P*-center model and its extensions have been investigated and applied in the context of locating facilities such as EMS centers, hospitals, fire station, and other public facilities. The objective function for the *P*-center model of the location solution in Figure 11-2 quantifies only the longest distance between a demand point and a selected location.

In order to locate a given number of emergency facilities along a road network, Garfinkel et al. (1977) examined the fundamental properties of the *P*-center problem. He modeled the *P*-center problem using integer programming and the problem was successfully solved by using a binary search technique and a combination of exact tests and heuristics. ReVelle and Hogan (1989b) formulated a *P*-center problem to locate facilities so as to minimize the maximum distance within which EMS service is available with α reliability. System congestion is considered and a derived server busy probability is used to constrain the service reliability level that must be satisfied for all demands. Stochastic *P*-center models have also been formulated for EMS location problems. For example, Hochbaum and Pathria (1998) considered the emergency facility location problem that must minimize the maximum distance on the network across all time periods. The cost and distance between the locations vary in each discrete time period. The authors used *k* underlying networks to represent different periods and provided a polynomial time 3-approximation algorithm to obtain the solution for each problem. Talwar (2002) utilized a *P*-center model to locate and dispatch three emergency rescue helicopters to serve the growing EMS demands from accidents of tourist activities such as skiing, hiking and climbing at the north and south end of the Alpine mountain ranges. One of the model's aims is to minimize the maximum (worst) response times and the author used effective heuristics to solve the problem.

2.2 Review of VRPs

Routing vehicles in response to a large-scale emergency typically include various uncertainties such as stochastic demands and/or travel times. In this section, we first review the literature on the stochastic vehicle routing problem (SVRP). We then review other vehicle routing/dispatching problems in the literature that have been formulated for emergency situations.

2.2.1 Stochastic Vehicle Routing Problems (SVRPs)

SVRPs differ from the deterministic VRPs in several aspects, such as problem formulations and solution techniques. SVRPs are usually divided, according to the uncertainties in consideration, into SVRPs with stochastic customers and/or demands, and SVRPs with stochastic travel time and/or service time.

The VRP with stochastic customers (VRPSC) addresses the probabilistic presence of customers (see e.g., Jezequel (1985), Jaillet (1987) and Jaillet and Odoni (1988)). Bertismas (1988) gave a systematic analysis to this problem. The properties, bounds and the heuristics to solve the problem were also presented.

The VRP with stochastic demand (VRPSD) captures the uncertainty of customer demands (i.e. the demands at the individual delivery (pickup) locations behave as random variables). An early investigation on the VRPSD comes from Stewart and Golden (1983), who applied the chance constraint modeling and resource methods to model the problem. Dror (1986) later illustrated the effects of route failure on the expected cost of a route, as well as the impact that a re-direction of the pre-designed route has on the expected cost. In the late 80's and early 90's, along with the conventional stochastic programming framework, Markovian Decision Processes for single-stage and multi-stage stochastic models were introduced by Dror (1989,1993) to investigate the VRPSD. Another major contribution to the study of VRPSD comes from Bertsimas (1988, 1992). Their work illustrates different recourse policies that could be applied to re-optimize the routes. More recently, a re-optimization based routing policy for the VRPSD was demonstrated by Secomandi (2001). In their work, a rollout algorithm is proposed to improve a given a priori solution.

The vehicle routing problem with stochastic customers and demands (VRPSCD) combines the VRPSC and the VRPSD. Early work on this topic includes Jezequel (1985), Jaillet (1987), and Jaillet and Odoni (1988). Motivated by applications in strategic planning and distribution systems, Bertsimas (1992) constructed an a priori customer visit sequence with minimal expected total distance and analyzed the problem using a variety of theoretical approaches. Gendrueau, Laporte and Seguin (1995) proposed a L-shaped method for the VRPSCD and solved it to optimality for instances of up to 46 customers. Another strategy to account for the demand uncertainties is to develop a waiting strategy for vehicles to strategically wait at pre-determined locations in order to maximize the probability of meeting any future anticipated demand (Branke et al. 2005).

VRP with stochastic travel time (VRPSTT) addresses the unknown knowledge of the road conditions. Systematic research on the VRP with service time and travel time (VRPSSTT) has been done by Laporte, Louveaux and Mercure (1992). They proposed three models for the VRPSTT: chance constrained model, 3-index recourse model, and 2-index recourse model. The VRPSSTT model was also applied by Lambert, Laporte and Louveaux (1993), and Hadjiconstrantinou and Roberts (2002) to optimize the customer service in the banking and other commercial systems. Jula, Dessouky, and Ioannou (2005) develop an approximate solution approach for random travel times with hard time windows. Their approximation approach is based on developing estimations for the first two moments of the arrival time distribution.

2.2.2 Vehicle Locating/Routing/Dispatching for Emergency Services

Emergency service systems (e.g., police, fire, etc.) need to dispatch their response units to service requests. In an emergency, the primary objective is to save lives, and thus sending response units to the incident site at the earliest time has the highest priority. However the requests for emergency services are usually unpredictable and furthermore they come with a relatively low frequency. Therefore the planner is generally faced with two major problems. First, an allocation problem in which the response units that are sent for service need to be determined; and second, a re-deployment problem in which the available response units need to be deployed at the potential sites in preparation to incoming requests needs to be determined.

One important thrust and cornerstone in vehicle locating/routing/dispatching for emergency services is the development and application of the queuing approach. The most well known queuing models for emergency service problems are the hypercube and the approximated hypercube by Larson (1974, 1975), which consider the congestions of the system by calculating the steady-state busy fractions of servers on a network. The hypercube model can be used to evaluate a wide variety of output performance such as vehicle utilization, average travel time, inter-district service performance, etc. Particularly important in the hypercube models is the incorporation of state-dependent interactions among vehicles that preclude applications of traditional vehicle locating/routing/dispatching models. Larson (1979) and Brandeau and Larson (1986) further extended and applied the hypercube models with locate-allocate heuristics for optimizing many realistic EMS systems. For example, these extended models have been successfully used to optimize the ambulance deployment problems in Boston and the EMS systems in New York. Based on the hypercube queuing model, Jarvis (1977) developed a descriptive model for operation characteristics of an EMS system with a given configuration of resources and a vehicle locating/dispatching model for determining the placement of ambulances to minimize average response time or other geographically based variables. Marianov and ReVelle (1996) created a realistic vehicle locating/dispatching model for emergency systems based on results from queuing theory. In their model, the travel times or distances along arcs of the network are considered as random variables. The goal is to place a limited numbers of emergency vehicles, such as ambulances, in a way as to maximize the calls for service. Queueing models formulating other theoretical and practical problems have also been reported by Berman and Larson (1985), Batta (1989), and Burwell et al. (1993).

3. A LARGE-SCALE EMERNGECY -- AN ANTHRAX ATTACK

In this section, we use an anthrax attack emergency to demonstrate the characteristics of a large-scale emergency. We then derive the requirements for the facility location problem and vehicle routing problem for the medical supply distribution in a large-scale emergency. Note that different emergency scenarios may require different response plans. The area in which we consider the anthrax attack emergency is Los Angeles (LA) County, which consists of 2054 census tracts and a total population of 9.5 million. In addition, we identify a number of potential eligible medical supply facility sites (see Figure 11-3) and the goal is to select some of these eligible facility sites as the staging areas to dispense the vaccinations.

3.1 Characteristics of an Anthrax Emergency

Anthrax is an acute infectious disease caused by a spore-forming bacterium. The anthrax spores can be used as a bioterrorist weapon, as was the case in 2001, when *Bacillus anthracis* spores had been intentionally distributed through the postal system causing 22 cases of anthrax emergency, including 5 deaths (CDC website, 2005). If the anthrax spores had been disseminated in an airborne manner through airplanes or from high buildings, thousands of people and hundreds of blocks would have been severely affected. Anthrax causes disease after inoculation of open or minor wounds, ingestion, or inhalation of the spores. At the earliest sign of disease, patients should be treated with antibiotics and other necessary medications to maximize patient survival. Otherwise, shock and death could ensue within 24 to 48 hours. Although no cases of person-to-person transmission of inhalation anthrax have ever been reported, cutaneous transmissions have occurred. Early treatment of anthrax disease is usually curative and significant for recovery. For example, patients with cutaneous anthrax have reported case fatality rates of 20% without antibiotic treatment and less than 1% with it (CDC website, 2005).

The impact of an anthrax attack to the population can be tremendous. First, thousands of people could be directly infected by the disease at the incident site. Second, the affected area could quickly spread from the original incident site to a much larger region by the movement of the infected but unaware people because the anthrax attack is usually covert and the appearance of the disease symptom may lag the attack from hours to days. Third, after an anthrax disease emergency becomes known in public, people may panic and become scared. They may request medical treatment or vaccination even if they are not actually infected or not in a high-risk situation.

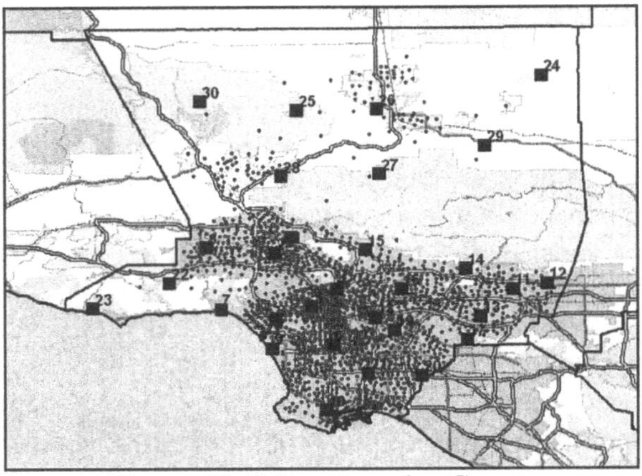

Figure 11-3. Los Angeles County

Huge demands for medical supplies could occur in a short time period after the anthrax attack. Blanket medical service coverage and mass vaccination may be necessary to all the population in a region. As such, a large amount of vaccines may be required. However an anthrax emergency has a low occurrence frequency and it is very expensive for any local region to maintain massive medical supplies for such a rare event. Therefore, large volumes of medical supplies for such an emergency are usually not stored at local sites. Instead, they are inventoried by the government at national stockpiles which consist of large quantities of medications, vaccines, and antibiotics to protect the public. The national stockpile is organized as push packages for flexible response and immediate deployment to a designated site within 12 hours (e.g. the SNS of the United States). Once delivered to the local areas, the stockpiles can be repackaged and distributed to various demand points though the local dispensing centers (staging areas). The overall process of a rapid medical supply distribution for a large-scale emergency can be depicted as follows in Figure 11-4. The details for each procedure in this process are described in the following sections.

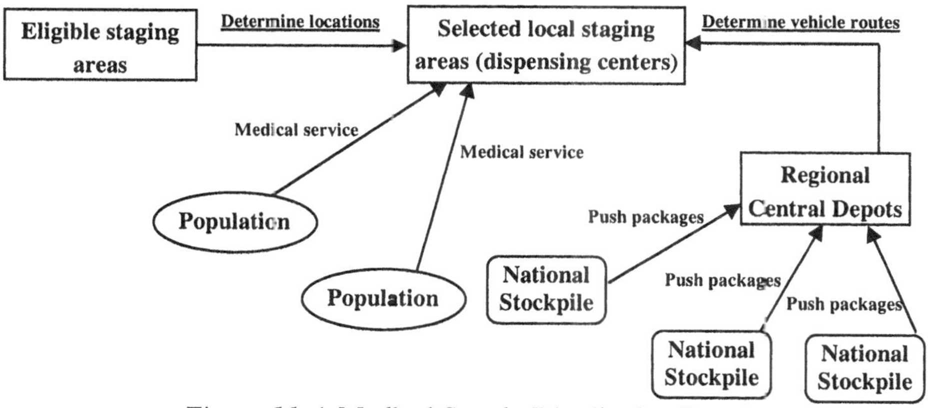

Figure 11-4. Medical Supply Distribution Process

It should be noted that anthrax is not contagious from person to person and the medical service coverage should depend on the actual disease spreading pattern. For example, if the attack can be detected at an early stage and the infected people can be identified and quarantined in a timely manner, then only the areas near the incident site need to be serviced with medical supplies. In this example we consider the worst case scenario and assume that the delayed detection of the attack has caused intractable population movements, and thus a blanket medical service coverage to all the areas is required. The logistical problem for such a worst case scenario is much more challenging than other scenarios in which only a portion of a region needs to be provided with medical supplies. Also note that the blanket medical service coverage is similarly applicable to contagious emergencies such as smallpox. During a contagious disease outbreak, it is possible that some areas are more critical than others due to certain disease spreading pattern. However, a mass vaccination to all the areas may be desired since it could effectively stem the disease transmission among the population (CDC, 2005).

3.2 Requirements to Facility Location Deployment

As mentioned in the last section, the medical supplies are usually not stored at the local level, and during an anthrax emergency the national stockpile will be called to service the demands at the local areas. Therefore, the primary goal of the facility location problem is to determine a number of local staging areas so that the supplies from the national stockpile can be received, re-packaged and distributed.

The deployment of medical facility sites (staging areas) in response to a large-scale emergency must account for massive service requirements. In most traditional facility location problems, each individual demand point is covered only by one facility given the fact that demand does not appear in large amounts. However, in the event of an anthrax emergency, if a mass vaccination to the population is necessary, the demands for medical services will be significant. As a result, a redundant and dispersed placement of the facilities (staging areas) is required so that more medical supplies could be mobilized to service different demand points to reduce mortality and morbidity.

Another important aspect of the facility locations for the anthrax emergency is the fact that given the occurrence of the emergency at an area, the resources of a number of facilities will be applied to quell the impact of the emergency, not only those located closest to the emergency site. This implies that there are different types of coverage, or quality of coverage, which can be classified in terms of the distance (time) between facilities and demand points. Thus, a facility that is close to a demand point provides a better quality of coverage to that demand point than a facility located far from that demand point. When planning the emergency medical services, it is important to consider adequate staging areas of various qualities for each demand point.

Furthermore, potential demand areas for medical services need to be categorized in a different way than other regular emergencies. Each demand area has distinct attributes, such as population density, economic importance, geographical feature, weather pattern, etc. Therefore, different requirements of facility quantity and quality should be assigned for each demand point so that all demand points can be serviced in a balanced and optimal manner. For example, for the demand points at a downwind and populous downtown area, a larger quantity of facilities should be located at a relatively better quality level, as opposed to the demand points at an upwind and/or less populous area.

Moreover, the facility location objective for an anthrax disease emergency should be carefully defined. An anthrax emergency is bound to impact lives regardless of the solution. Thus care should be taken in prioritizing one solution over another. Since the blanket medical service coverage and mass vaccination may be carried out, all the demand points in the affected areas need to be serviced simultaneously. To optimize the overall performance of the medical distribution system, it is desirable that the total (average) distance from all demand points to the staging areas be minimized. Thus, a *P*-median model with multiple facility quantity-of-coverage and quality-of-coverage requirements is applicable. It is important to note the model that is selected should be in accordance with the characteristics of the emergency, and different models may be suitable for different emergency scenarios. For example, for the emergency of a dirty bomb attack in which only a portion of a region needs be serviced by the medical supplies, the covering model may be more applicable since the model ensures a maximal population coverage by the medical supply facilities.

Finally, the selection of eligible staging area sites for the anthrax emergency must consider a different set of criteria that are used for regular emergencies. For instance, the facilities should have easy access to more than one major road/highway including egress and ingress. The sites should be secure and invulnerable to damages caused by the emergencies. In this paper we consider eligible staging area sites as given.

3.3 Requirements to Vehicle Routing

In an anthrax emergency, the primary goal of vehicle routing is to deliver the medical supplies to the affected areas as soon as possible. To reach this goal, a fast and efficient vehicle routing/dispatching plan needs to be executed. To maximize life-saving in an anthrax emergency, medications, antibiotics, and vaccines should be administered to the affected population within a specified time limit (within 24 hours to 36 hours). This implies that vehicles need to have a hard time-window for medical supply delivery. To minimize the loss of life at any demand area, the medical supplies must be sent to the demand area within this hard time-window. Note that although a hard time-window is used to model the VRP for the anthrax emergency, it may not always be applicable to other emergencies. For example, for a contagious disease outbreak, such as smallpox, the demand for medical supplies could be a continuous function of time. In such a case, a soft time-window approach may be more suitable to model the VRP.

The input parameters to the vehicle routing problem in the anthrax emergency have a probabilistic/stochastic nature. For example, the traffic conditions may change and therefore the vehicle travel times can be highly uncertain. In addition, the demands for medical services may be stochastic because of the way the disease disseminates, the wind direction, the geographic conditions, etc. As such, the vehicle routing problem needs to capture the demand uncertainties and provide a robust solution that performs well in a variable environment.

Moreover, because of the massive service requirements, the demand at a location is not necessarily satisfied by a single truckload. As such, the vehicle routing problem for the anthrax emergency should allow for split delivery (i.e., a point can be visited more than once if the demand exceeds the load capacity of available vehicles). Also, the VRP for the anthrax emergency should be a multi-depot problem since many local depots are dispersed across a region. However, unlike the traditional multi-depot VRP, which requires each vehicle to return to its origination depot, the vehicles are now allowed to return to any depot for reloading and then continue serving other demand points. This requirement enables the vehicles to distribute the medical supplies in a more flexible manner.

Finally, the primary objective of the vehicle routing problem during the emergency should be the minimization of loss of lives, which is caused by minimizing the unmet demands for the medical service.

As mentioned before, the facility location and vehicle routing models can be used as a planning tool to determine the optimal staging areas and vehicle routes considering the probabilistic/stochastic nature of the emergency. These plans can serve as practical drills for the first responders to prepare and train them for a possible emergency, and they may be to be altered in the event that an emergency has occurred once the characteristics of the emergency become known.

4. MATHEMATICAL MODEL FORMULATIONS

Based on the analysis stated in the last section, we now formulate a facility location model and a vehicle routing model that take into account the characteristics of the anthrax disease emergency. Generalizations of the models discussed in this section can found in Jia et al. (2005) for the facility location problem and Shen et al. (2005) for the vehicle routing problem.

4.1 Formulation of the Facility Location Model

To formulate the facility location model, we use I to denote the set of demand points and J to denote the set of eligible facility sites (staging areas). Indexed on these sets we define two types of integer variables:

Decision variables:

$$x_j = \begin{cases} 1 & \text{if a facility is placed at site } j; \\ 0 & \text{otherwise.} \end{cases}$$

$$z_{ij} = \begin{cases} 1 & \text{if a facility } j \text{ services demand point } i; \\ 0 & \text{otherwise.} \end{cases}$$

Furthermore, we define the following parameters:

Input Parameters:

Pop_i = the population of demand point i.

d_{ij} = the distance between demand point i and facility location j

D_i = the distance limit within which a facility could service demand point i.

$N_i = \{j \mid d_{ij} \le D_i\}$, the set of eligible facility sites that are located within the distance limit and thus are able to service demand point i.

Q_i = the required number of facilities that must be assigned to demand point i so that i is considered as covered.

P = the maximal number of facilities that can be placed in J.

We can now formulate the model to locate P facilities to service the population during an anthrax emergency, requiring that Q_i facilities service demand point i with the same quality.

$$\text{Minimize} \sum_{i\in I} \sum_{j\in J} Pop_i d_{ij} z_{ij} \qquad 11\text{-}1$$

Subject to:

$$\sum_{j\in J} x_j \le P \qquad 11\text{-}2$$

$$\sum_{j\in N_i} z_{ij} \ge Q_i \qquad \forall i \in I, \qquad 11\text{-}3$$

$$z_{ij} \le x_j \qquad \forall i \in I, j \in J, \qquad 11\text{-}4$$

$$x_j, z_{ij} = \{0,1\} \qquad \forall i \in I, j \in J, \qquad 11\text{-}5$$

The objective (11-1), as mentioned in Section 3.2, is to minimize the total demand-weighted distance between the demand points and the facilities. Constraint (11-2) states that there are P facilities to be located in a set J of possible locations. Constraint (11-3) ensures that demand point i is assigned with a required quantity (Q_i) of facilities servicing it. This constraint also requires that all the facilities assigned to demand point i need to be located within the given distance limit. Constraint (11-4) allows assignment only to the sites at which facilities have been located. Finally constraint (11-5) enforces the integrality of variables z_{ij} and x_i.

Consider now the problem with multiple quality-of-coverage requirements at each demand point. Let us assume that at demand point i we must have Q_i^1, Q_i^2,..., Q_i^q, facilities for each quality from 1 to q, where quality Q_i^1 represents the facilities that are closest to demand point i, Q_i^2 are the facilities located farther than those of quality 1, and so on. Thus the facility location model needs to be modified as follows:

(1) *Objective function*: Since multiple quality-of-coverage is considered, the objective function needs to be optimized across different quality levels. Because the facilities with a higher quality level (i.e. closer to the demand points) are usually considered to be more crucial in servicing the demand points, as opposed to the facilities with lower quality levels (i.e. farther from the demand points), we introduce a weight parameter, h^r, to prioritize the importance of the facilities at each different quality level r. Also we modify z_{ij} to z_{ij}^r in order to differentiate the facilities that are servicing the demand points at different quality levels. Thus, we obtain the modified objective function:

$$\text{Minimize} \sum_{r} \sum_{i \in I} \sum_{j \in J} h^r Pop_i d_{ij} z_{ij}^r \qquad 11\text{-}6$$

(2) *Constraints*: First, the group of constraints (11-3) needs to be changed to:

$$\sum_{j \in N_i^r} z_{ij}^r \geq Q_i^r \qquad \forall i \in I, r = 1,\dots,q \qquad 11\text{-}7$$

The modified constraints state that, for each demand point, there must be more than a required quantity of facilities at each quality level so that this demand point can be considered as properly serviced. In addition, to avoid repeated assignment of a facility to any demand point for different quality requirements, we introduce another group of constraints:

$$\sum_{r} z_{ij}^r \leq 1 \qquad \forall i \in I, j \in J \qquad 11\text{-}8$$

As such, the modified objective (11-6), together with the constraints (11-2), (11-4), (11-5), (11-7), and (11-8), can be used to formulate the facility location problem for the anthrax emergency with multiple facility quantity-of-coverage and quality-of-coverage requirements. Note that in the problem formulation, all the z_{ij}, Q_i, and N_i need to be correspondingly changed to z_{ij}^r, Q_i^r, and N_i^r.

Exact algorithms have been developed in the literature to solve different facility location problems; for example, see Holmberg (1999). However exact algorithms can only solve small problem instances in a reasonable computational time. Therefore, to solve the location problems for large-scale emergencies, efficient heuristics, such as greedy algorithms, genetic algorithms, or Tabu search, should be used. References to the heuristics for traditional location problems can be found in Jain et al. (2002) and Jaramillo et al. (2002).

4.2 Formulation of the Vehicle Routing Model

To formulate the vehicle routing model, we use *K*, *I*, *J*, and *A* to denote the sets of vehicles, demand points, facility sites, and medical supply items. In addition, we use node 0 as a dummy node to represent a virtual/imaginary central depot that is linked to each real depot (facility site). The cost or travel times on these links is set to be a large number. The dummy node is useful in representing the availability of vehicles. To conveniently denote different node combinations in the medical supply network, we further define set $C = I \cup J \cup \{node\_0\}$, and set $RO = I \cup J$. Furthermore, indexed on these sets, we define the following deterministic parameters. Note that different from the facility location problem, in which the index i is defined as demand point i and the index j is defined as facility site j, here the indices i and j are defined as any node from set C, which could be either a demand point or a facility site (depot).

Deterministic Parameters:

n_i = the initial number of vehicles at facility site (depot) i.

w_a = the unit weight of medical supply item a.

$c_{a,k}$ = the load capacity of vehicle k for medical supply item a.

$e_{a,i}$ = the earliest service start time for medical supply item a at demand point i.

$l_{a,i}$ = the latest service start time for medical supply item a at demand point i.

$s_{a,I}$ = the amount of medical supply item a supplied at facility site (depot) i.

r_i = the service (loading/unloading) time at node i, including both the demand points and the facility sites.

We use M as a large constant to transform nonlinear terms to linear ones for the time window constraints. In addition, the parameter α_D is used to represent the upper bound of unsatisfactory rate for demands at each demand point and α_T is used to denote the upper bound of total traveling time for each vehicle. These two parameters represent the probabilistic violation on the demand and travel time constraints.

As mentioned in the pervious section, uncertainties exist in the anthrax emergency. We consider the following two parameters as stochastic variables.

Stochastic Parameters:

$\tau_{i,j,k}$ = the time required for vehicle k to travel from point i to j.

$\zeta_{a,i}$ = the demand for medical supply item a at demand point i.

Finally, four groups of decision variables are defined as follows:

Decision variables:

$$X_{i,j,k} = \begin{cases} 1 & \text{if vehicle } k \text{ traverses arc } (i,j); \\ 0 & \text{otherwise.} \end{cases}$$

$Y_{a,i,j,k}$ = the amount of medical supply item a traversing arc (i, j) using vehicle k.

$U_{a,i}$ = the amount of unsatisified demand for medical supply item a at demand point i.

$T_{i,k}$ = the service start time for vehicle k at demand point i.

Based on these parameters and variables, we are now in a position to formulate the stochastic vehicle routing problem, with the objective to minimize the unmet demands over all the demand points.

$$\text{Minimize} \sum_{a\in A}\sum_{i\in I} U_{a,i} \qquad \text{11-9}$$

Subject to:

$$\sum_{k\in K} X_{0,i,k} \le n_i \qquad \forall i \in J \qquad \text{11-10}$$

$$\sum_{j\in I} X_{i,j,k} = 1 \qquad \forall i \in J, k \in K, \qquad \text{11-11}$$

$$\sum_{j\in I} X_{j,i,k} = 1 \qquad \forall i \in J, k \in K, \qquad \text{11-12}$$

$$\sum_{j\in RO} X_{i,j,k} = \sum_{j\in RO} X_{j,i,k} \qquad \forall i \in I, k \in K, \qquad \text{11-13}$$

$$P\{\tau \mid (T_{i,k} + r_i + \tau_{i,j,k} - T_{j,k}) \le (1 - X_{i,j,k})M\} \ge 1 - \alpha_T \qquad \forall i, j \in C$$

11-14

$$s_{a,i} - \sum_{k\in K}\left[\sum_{j\in C} Y_{a,i,j,k} - \sum_{j\in C} Y_{a,j,i,k}\right] \geq 0 \qquad \forall a\in A, \forall i\in J \qquad 11\text{-}15$$

$$Y_{a,0,i,k} + Y_{a,i,0,k} = 0 \qquad \forall a\in A, \forall i\in RO, k\in K \qquad 11\text{-}16$$

$$X_{i,j,k}c_k \geq \sum_a w_a Y_{a,i,j,k} \qquad \forall\{i,j\}\subseteq RO, k\in K, a\in A \qquad 11\text{-}17$$

$$e_{a,i}\sum_{j\in\Delta^+(i)} X_{i,j,k} \leq T_{i,k} \leq l_{a,i}\sum_{j\in\Delta^+(i)} X_{i,j,k} \qquad \forall a\in A, \forall i,j\in C \qquad 11\text{-}18$$

$$P\left\{\zeta \mid \sum_{k\in K}\left[\sum_{j\in C} Y_{a,j,i,k} - \sum_{j\in C} Y_{a,i,j,k}\right] - U_{a,i} - \zeta_{a,i} \geq 0\right\} \geq 1-\alpha_D$$

$$\forall a\in A, \forall i\in I \qquad 11\text{-}19$$

$$X_{i,j,k} = \{0,1\}; \qquad Y_{a,i,j,k} \geq 0; \qquad U_{a,i} \geq 0; \qquad T_{i,k} \geq 0; \qquad 11\text{-}20$$

Constraints (11-10)-(11-14) characterize the vehicle flow on the medical distribution network. Constraint (11-10) states that the number of vehicles in service should not exceed the number of vehicles available at each depot at the beginning of the planning horizon. The number of vehicles in service is the total number of vehicles flowing from the dummy central depot 0 to each facility site. Constraints (11-11) and (11-12) specify that each vehicle can flow from and to only one facility site (depot). Constraint (11-13) states that all vehicles that flow into any demand point must also flow out of it. Constraint (11-14) is a chance constraint for the service start times at the demand points. The inner part, $(T_{i,k} + r_i + \tau_{i,j,k} - T_{j,k}) \leq (1 - X_{i,j,k})M$, guarantees the schedule feasibility with respect to time considerations. Constraint (11-15) gives the balanced material flow requirement for the facility sites. Constraint (11-16) prohibits the medical supply items flow from and to the dummy node. Constraint (11-17) allows the medical supply item to flow as long as there are sufficient vehicle capacities. It establishes the connection between the medical supply flow and vehicle flow. Constraint (11-18) gives the hard time window constraint on each demand point. Chance constraint (11-19) enforces the balanced material flow requirement for the demand points from a probabilistic perspective. It states that a small probability of unmet demands at each demand point is allowed within a threshold level. Finally constraint (11-20) enforces the integrality and non-negativity constraints on the variables.

5. PROBLEM SOLUTION AND ANALYSES

In the preceding section, the facility location problem and the VRP for the anthrax disease emergency have been formulated. In this section, we first specify illustrative values for the input parameters and then we show how these proposed models could be applied to solve the facility location problem and the VRP for the anthrax emergency.

5.1 Facility Location Problem

5.1.1 Parameter Specification

There are 2054 census tracts and 9.5 million people in Los Angeles County. To define the demand distribution for medical services during an anthrax disease emergency, we use the day-time population density pattern that is available for Los Angeles County (ESRI website, 2005). Furthermore, we use the centroid of each census tract as a demand point to represent the aggregated population in this tract. Thus we obtain 2054 discrete demand points that have different population densities. We assume that, in the anthrax emergency, the people at different demand points need to visit the selected facilities (staging areas) for vaccination. Note that although we assume that all the population at the demand points need to be serviced by the medical supplies, during an emergency, a more accurate demand pattern for medical supplies can be obtained by using schools, shopping malls and offices as indicators to assess the actual disease exposure.

To determine the staging areas that can be used to receive, re-package, and distribute the medical supplies from the national stockpile to the demand points, we identify 30 eligible facility sites. We assume that the resource limitation allows only 10 eligible facility sites to be selected to services the demand points (P = 10). To ensure effective and efficient medical supply distribution, each demand point needs to be serviced by a required quantity of facilities that are located at each quality level. In practice, different quality levels should be defined for different demand points, based on the attributes of each point such as population density, political/economic importance, etc. In this example, for simplicity, we define a uniform quality requirement for all demand points; that is, each demand point needs two quality levels and the distance requirements for the first and second quality levels are 35 miles and 60 miles, respectively.

Furthermore, we specify the facility quantity requirement at each quality level for each demand point as follows:

(1) $Q_i = 1$, if the population of demand point i is less than 4,000;
(2) $Q_i = 2$, if the population of demand point i is between 4,000 and 8,000;
(3) $Q_i = 3$, if the population of demand point i is greater than 8000.

Finally, we specify the distances (times) between each pair of demand point and facility site. In practice, the roadway system should be used to define the distances since the medical supplies will be transported by vehicles during the emergency. However, for simplicity, in this illustrative example, we use the straight line distances between the demand points and facility sites.

5.1.2 Solution and Analyses

Based on the input parameters defined above, we solve the facility location problem for the anthrax emergency. The solution is depicted in Figure 11-5. The problem was solved to optimality using a commercial integer program solver, CPLEX 8.1. The stars in the diagram represent the selected facilities.

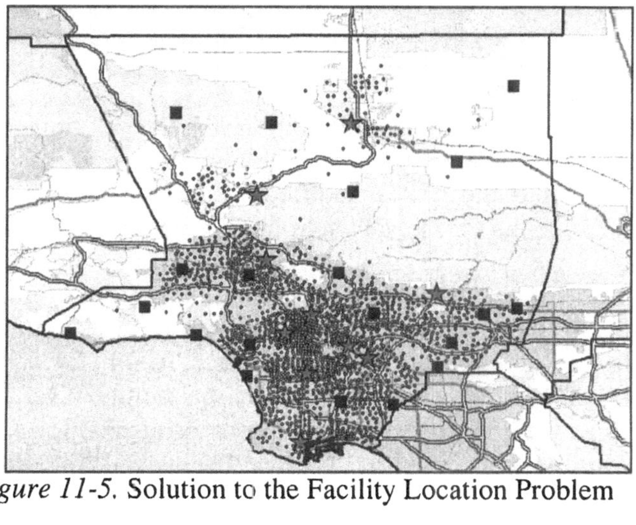

Figure 11-5. Solution to the Facility Location Problem

In this solution, each demand point is covered by a required quantity of facilities at each of the two quality levels. Therefore, the demand points can be sufficiently serviced by the facilities in an efficient manner. The average distance from the demand points to their servicing facilities at quality level 1 is 25.8 miles; and the average distance at quality level 2 is 50.2 miles. Since the weighted total distance between the demand points and the facilities has been minimized (as defined by the objective function), the effectiveness of facility service performance is optimized.

It should be noted that a tight definition of the input parameters may lead to the facility location problem being infeasible; that is, no subset of P facilities is able to service all demand points within the defined quality levels (distance requirements). In this case, any one of the following four adjustments in the parameters can be made to make the problem feasible:

(1) Increase the parameter P, i.e. the number of facilities that can be selected;
(2) Relax the distance requirements, within which the facilities need to be located to service the demand points;
(3) Drop the insignificant demand points (e.g. the ones with a low population density) from the problem constraints so that the limited resources (facilities) can be leveraged to the other demand points.

5.2 Vehicle Routing Problem (VRP)

5.2.1 Parameter Specification

After the facility sites (staging areas) have been determined, the solution is used as input parameters for the vehicle routing problem. In the anthrax emergency example, the 10 selected facility sites from the location problem are the demand points for the vehicle routing problem. To illustrate the VRP, for simplicity, we will use a single depot (i.e. Los Angeles International Airport as the central distribution warehouse) and a uniform capacity for each of a total of three vehicles to route and service the 10 staging facilities.

We calculate the demand on each selected facility by summing up the population in the tracts that are covered by the facility. The population size will be used as the criterion to specify the demand size; for example, 1 box of 100000-dose anthrax vaccine is needed for every 100000 people. As we stated in the previous section, the demand of each facility is stochastic. The exponential distribution, $p(x) = e^{(A-x)/B} / B$ (where the mean is $A+B$ and variance is B^2), is assumed with the mean value set according to the population density. The standard deviation is set to be 20 percent of its mean value at each facility.

Furthermore, we assume an exponential distribution for the travel times between each pair of facility and central depot. Their mean values are specified as proportional to the Euclidean distances between them. We also set the standard deviation to be 20 percent of the mean value of the travel time on each leg of the connection. Such an exponential distribution gives a lower bound and an upper bound for the travel time, which reasonably reflects the fact that travel time is constrained by the physical distance and the maximal speed of the vehicle, and could be prolonged by different traffic conditions.

Shock and death caused by untreated anthrax exposure could ensue within 24 to 48 hours, and the dispatching from the central warehouse to the 10 selected local staging facilities is just one chain of the whole process of dispensing medical supplies. Hence we use a hard time window constraint of up to half of the required time for treatment (i.e. 12 hours) to finish this placement.

Finally, we assume the total supply at the depot can meet 120 percent of the summation of the mean value of the demand quantity at all points. However, since the demand is stochastic, it is possible that the demand cannot be fully satisfied in some cases.

5.2.2 Solution and Analyses

The routing problem is solved based on the parameters specified in the previous section and its result is compared with that of a deterministic formulation to show the advantage of our chance-constraint model.

The CPLEX solver was used to optimally solve both the deterministic and chance-constraint models to optimality with the given parameters. The deterministic model uses the mean value of the demand quantity and travel time to eliminate uncertainties.

To compare the routing solutions, we generate exponential random variables with the mean and variance specified above for the demand and travel time. For each generated scenario we solve a linear optimization problem to obtain the quantities of supply that minimize the total unmet demand with fixed routing solutions obtained above and constrained by the deadline and the total available quantity at the depot. The comparison shows that out of the 50 test cases, the deterministic routes generate 18 unmet demand cases with an average unmet demand of 9.94 while the chance-constraint routes only generate 2 unmet demand cases with an average unmet demand of 5.50. The chance-constraint routes outperform the deterministic ones because of the conservative nature of the chance-constraint model, which leads to balanced routes with similar number of nodes. The deterministic routes are more prone to have uneven number of nodes on different paths. We observe that this property makes the chance-constraint solution more robust and competitive than the deterministic one especially for the test cases that deviate far away from the mean value.

6. CONCLUSIONS AND FUTURE DIRECTIONS

Facility location and vehicle routing are important issues in designing the medical supply distribution system, particularly for large-scale emergencies. This chapter has two primary goals. The first is to review different location models and vehicle routing models in the literature that are related to regular emergency services such as police, fire, etc. The second goal is to present tailored location and vehicle routing models to design rapid distribution systems of medical supplies in response to a large-scale emergency. An illustrative example of an anthrax emergency was discussed to show how the proposed models can be used to determine the facilities locations and vehicle routes for rapid medical supply distribution during the emergency.

In this chapter, we consider an emergency due to an anthrax attack as a representative large-scale emergency. We discuss the characteristics of large-scale emergencies and their requirements for the facility location and vehicle routing problems in the context of this particular emergency. However, other types of emergencies (e.g. chemical incident, dirty bomb attack, contagious disease outbreak, etc.) may involve different characteristics and thus will lead to different requirements on the problem formulations and solutions. For example, an emergency caused by a dirty bomb attack may impact not only the population, but also the medical supply facilities themselves. Therefore, reduced service capability of the facilities needs to be taken into account. A chemical incident may need instantaneous medical service to the infected people, and therefore medical supplies may need to be pre-positioned at a local level for immediate deployment. An open research question is how to develop an overall response plan that takes into consideration all the different possible scenarios. Is it more efficient and cost effective to develop a single strategy that is robust to the different possibilities or is it better to develop a separate plan for each possible emergency?

Another research direction is to develop efficient algorithms to solve the facility location and vehicle routing problems. In this chapter, the formulated problems were of relatively small size (i.e. 30 eligible facility sites, 10 selected staging areas, 1 central depot, and 3 vehicles) so the optimal solutions could be readily found using commercially available optimization software. However, for modeling more realistic and larger scenarios, the problem size of the models will increase significantly so that it becomes computationally prohibitive to obtain an optimal solution. Future research direction should also focus on developing efficient heuristics which can identify near optimal solutions to the large problems within a reasonable computational time.

7. ACKNOWLEDGEMENT:

This research was supported by the United States Department of Homeland Security through the Center for Risk and Economic Analysis of Terrorism Events (CREATE), grant number EMW-2004-GR-0112. However, any opinions, findings, and conclusions or recommendations in this document are those of the authors and do not necessarily reflect views of the U.S. Department of Homeland Security. Also the authors wish to thank Richard Larson, Harry Bowman, and Terry O'Sullivan for their valuable input and comments for the improvement of this paper.

8. REFERENCES

Batta, R., 1989, A queueing-location model with expected service time-dependent queueing disciplines, *European Journal of Operational Research*, 192-205.

Batta, R., Dolan, J. and Krishnamurthy, N., 1989, The maximal expected covering location Problem: Revisited, *Transportation Science*, **23:** 277-287.

Belson, D., 2005. Storage, distribution and dispensing of medical supplies, CREATE Interim Report.

Benedict, J., 1983, Three hierarchical objective models which incorporate the concept of excess coverage for locating EMS vehicles or hospitals, MSc thesis, Northwestern University.

Beraldi, P. and Ruszczynski, A., 2002, A branch and bound method for stochastic integer problems under probabilistic constraints, *Optimization Methods and Software*, **17:** 359-382.

Berman, O. and Larson, R.C., 1985, Optimal 2-facility network districting in the presence of queuing, *Transportation Science*, **19:** 261-277.

Bertsimas., D., 1988, *Probabilistic combinational optimization problems*, PhD thesis, Operation Research Center, Massachusetts Institute of Technology, Cambridge, MA.

Bertsimas, D, 1992, A vehicle routing problem with stochastic demand, *Operation Research*, **40**: 574-585.

Bianchi, C. and Church, R., 1988, A hybrid FLEET model for emergency medical service system design, *Social Sciences in Medicine*, 163-171.

Brandeau, M. and Larson, R. C., 1986, Extending and applying the hypercube queueing model to deploy ambulances in Boston. In: Swersey, A. and Ignall, E. (ed.), *Delivery of Urban Services*, New York: North Holland.

Branke, J., Middendorf, M., Noeth, G., and Dessouky, M. M., 2005. Waiting strategies for dynamic vehicle control, *Transportation Science*, **39**: 298-312.

Burwell, T., Jarvis, J. and McKnew, M., 1993, Modeling co-located servers and dispatch ties in the hypercube model, *Computers and Operations Research*, 113-119.

Carbone, R., 1974, Public facility location under stochastic demand, *INFOR*, 12

Carson, Y. and Batta, R., 1990, Locating an ambulance on the Amherst campus of the State University of New York at Buffalo, *Interfaces*, **20:** 43-49.

Chapman, S.C. and White, J.A., 1974, Probabilistic formulations of emergency service facilities location problems, *Paper Presented at the ORSA/TIMS Conference*, San Juan, Puerto Rico.

Church, R. and ReVelle, C., 1974, The maximal covering location problem, *Papers of the Regional Science Association*, **32:** 101-118.

Daskin, M., 1983, The maximal expected covering location model: Formulation, properties and heuristic solution, *Transportation Science*, **17-1:** 48-70.

Dror, M., 1989, Vehicle routing with stochastic demands: properties and solution framework, *Transportation Science*, **23:** 166-176.

Dror, M., 1993, Modeling vehicle routing with uncertain demands as a stochastic program: properties of the corresponding solution, *European Journal of Operational Research*, **64:** 432–441.

Dror, M. and Trudeau, P., 1986, Stochastic vehicle routing with modified savings algorithm, *European Journal of Operational Research*, **23:** 228–235.

Garfinkel, R. S., Neebe, A. W. and Rao, M. R., 1977, The m-center problem: Minimax facility location, *Management Science*, **23:** 1133-1142.

Gendreau, M., Laporte, G. and Seguin, R., 1995, An exact algorithm for the vehicle routing problem with stochastic demands and customers, *Transportation Science*, **29:** 143-155.

Goldberg, J. and Paz, L., 1991, Locating emergency vehicle bases when service time depends on call location, *Transportation Science*, 264-280.

Goldberg, J., Dietrich, R., Chen, J.M. and Mitwasi, M.G., 1990, Validating and applying a model for locating emergency medical services in Tucson, AZ, *European Journal of Operational Research*, **49:** 308-324.

Hadjiconstrantinou, E. and Roberts, D., 2002, Routing under uncertainty: an application in the scheduling of field service engineers. In: Toth, P. and Vigo, D. (ed.), *The Vehicle Routing Problem,* 331-352, SIAM Monographs, Philadelphia.

HDMA, Healthcare Distribution Management Association, http://www.healthcaredistribution.org/

Hochbaum, D.S. and Pathria, A., 1998, Locating centers in a dynamically changing network and related problems, *Location Science*, **6:** 243-256.

Hogan, K. and ReVelle, C., 1986, Concepts and applications of backup coverage, *Management Science*, **32:** 1434-1444.

Holmberg, K., 1999, Exact solution methods for uncapacitated location problems with convex transportation costs, *European Journal of Operational Research*, **114:** 127-140.

Jaillet, P., 1987, Stochastic routing problem. In: Andreatta, F. and Mason, P. S. (ed.), *Stochastics in Combinatorial Optimization World Scientific*, Oxford University Press, Oxford.

Jaillet, P. and Odoni, A., 1988, The probabilistic vehicle routing problem. In: Golden, B. L. and Assad, A. A. (ed.), *Vehicle Routing: Methods and Studies,* North-Holland, Amsterdam.

Jain, K., Mahdian, M. and Saberi, A., 2002, A new greedy approach for facility location problems, *Proceedings of the 34th ACM Symposium on Theory of Computing*, 731-740.

Jaramillo, J. H., Bhadury, J. and Batta, R., 2002, On the use of genetic algorithms to solve location problems, *Computers and Operations Research*, **29:** 761-779.

Jarvis, J. P., 1977, Models for the location and dispatch of emergency medical vehicles, In: Willemain, T. R. and Larson, R. C. (ed.), *Emergency Medical Systems Analysis*, Lexington, MA: Lexington Books.

Jezequel, A., 1985, Probabilistic vehicle routing problems, Master's thesis, Department of Civil Engineering, Massachusetts Institute of Technology.

Jia, H., Ordonez, F. and Dessouky, M. M., 2005, A modeling framework for facility location of medical services for large-scale emergencies, USC ISE Working paper #2005-01. Under revision in *Special Issue IIE Transactions on Homeland Security*

Jula, H., M. M. Dessouky, and P. Ioannou, 2005, An approximate solution for the TSPTW with stochastic travel and service times, to appear *IEEE Transactions on ITS*.

Lambert, V., Laporte, G. and Louveaux, F., 1992, Designing collection routes through bank branches, *Computers and Operations Research*, **20:** 783–791.

Laporte, G., Louveaux, F and Mercure, H., 1992, The vehicle routing problem with stochastic travel times, *Transportation Science*, **26:** 161-170.

Larson, R.C., 1974, A hypercube queuing model for facility location and redistricting in urban emergency services, *Computers and Operations Research*, **1:** 67-95.

Larson, R.C., 1975, Approximating the performance of urban emergency service systems, *Operations Research*, 845-868.

Larson, R. C., 1979, Structural system models for locational decisions: an example using the hypercube queueing model, In: Haley, K. B. (ed.), *Operational Research '78, Proceedings of the Eighth IFORS International Conference on Operations Research*, North-Holland Publishing Co., Amsterdam, Holland

Mandell, M.B., 1998, A *P*-median approach to locating basic life support and advanced life support units, *Presented at the CORS/INFORMS National Meeting*, Montreal, April, 1998.

Marianov, V. and ReVelle, C., 1996, The queueing maximal availability location problem: A model for the siting of emergency vehicles, *European Journal of Operational Research*, 93, pp.110-120.

McAllister, J. C., 1985, Challenges in purchasing and inventory control, *American Journal of Hospital Pharmacy,* **42:** 1370-1373.

Mirchandani, P.B., 1980, Locational decisions on stochastic networks, *Geographical Analysis*, **12:** 172-183.

Paluzzi, M., 2004, Testing a heuristic *P*-median location allocation model for siting emergency service facilities, *Paper Presented at the Annual Meeting of Association of American Geographers*, Philadelphia, PA.

Rebidas, D., Smith, S. T. and Denomme, P., 1999, Redesigning medication distribution systems in the OR, *AORN Journal*, **69:** 184-190.

Repede, J.F. and Bernardo, J.J., 1994, Developing and validating a decision support system for locating emergency medical vehicles in Louisville, Kentucky, *European Journal of Operational Research*, **40:** 58-69.

ReVelle, C., 1989, Review, extension and prediction in emergency service siting models, *European Journal of Operational Research*, **40:** 58-69.

ReVelle, C. and Hogan, K., 1986, A reliability constrained siting model with local estimates of busy fractions, *Environment and Planning*, B15, 143-152.

ReVelle, C. and Hogan, K., 1989a, The maximum availability location problem, *Transportation Science*, **23:** 192-200.

ReVelle, C. and Hogan, K., 1989b, The maximum reliability location problem and a-reliable p-center problem: Derivatives of the probabilistic location set covering problem, *Annals of Operations Research*, **18:** 155-174.

ReVelle, C., Schweitzer, J. and Snyder, S., 1996, The maximal conditional covering problem, *INFOR*, **34:** 77-91.

Rubin, H. and Keller, D. D., 1983, Improving a pharmaceutical purchasing and inventory control system, *American Journal of Hospital Pharmacy*, **40:** 67-70.

Secomandi, N., 2001, A rollout policy for the vehicle routing problem with stochastic demands, *Operation Research*, **49:** 796–802.

Serra., D and Marianov, V, 1999, The *P*-median problem in a changing network: The case of Barcelona, *Location Science*, 4.

Schilling, D.A., 1982, Strategic facility planning: The analysis of options. *Decision Sciences*, **13:** 1-14.

Shen, Z., Dessouky, M., and Ordonez, F., 2005, Stochastic Vehicle Routing Problem for Large-scale Emergencies, ISE Working paper #2005-02.

Stewart, W. and Golden, B., 1983, Stochastic vehicle routing: a comprehensive approach, *European Journal of Operational Research*, **14:** 371–385.

Talmar, M., 2002, Location of rescue helicopters in South Tyrol, *Paper Presented at 37th Annual ORSNZ Conference*, Auckland, New Zealand.

Toregas, C., Swain, R., ReVelle, C. and Bergman, L., 1971, The location of emergency service facility, *Operations Research*, **19:** 1363-1373.

White, J. and Case, K., 1974, On covering problems and the central facility location problem, *Geographical Analysis*, 281.

CDC website, http://www.bt.cdc.gov/agent/anthrax/, 2005.

ESRI website, http://reports.esribis.com/, 2005.

Chapter 12

USING A DIAGNOSTIC TO FOCUS HOSPITAL FLOW IMPROVEMENT STRATEGIES

Roger Resar, MD

Institute for Healthcare Improvement, 20 University Road, 7th Floor, Cambridge, MA 02138

(The work presented here is from the efforts of the IHI Innovation Team.)

Abstract: Current methods to evaluate hospital flow primarily measure micros-system issues, such as numbers of diversions from the ED, or how many patients are boarded in some way somewhere in the hospital, or specific delays in hospital units and annual admissions. The narrow focus on delays, although appropriate, generally leads to attempts at fixing a large system problem from the viewpoint of a micro-system. A newly developed hospital diagnostic that utilizes a broader view of flow can be used to evaluate how a hospital might best respond to delays, but also how to maximize the number of turns each bed generates in a year. The diagnostic utilizes easily obtainable and commonly collected hospital metrics. The diagnostic allows a hospital to categorize itself depending on the number of bed turns and the efficiency of using those beds. Based on a self-evaluation a hospital can determine which improvement strategies would be most useful, or if ongoing improvement strategies are properly focused to achieve an ultimate goal of reduced delays and increased bed turns (the goal of 90 or more adjusted turns and a bed use efficiency of around 90%). A business case for improvements can be based on increasing turns either by accommodation of more demand or by decreasing unneeded capacity. Improvements in throughput per bed allow leadership to justifiably focus resources on the appropriate change concepts. Serial measurements of the bed turns and bed utilization metric allow the organization to measure the effects of flow improvement strategies over time.

Key words: Bed turns, hospital efficiency, flow streams, delays, flow diagnostic

1. INTRODUCTION

In 2002 the Institute for Healthcare Improvement (IHI) Innovation Team started work on hospital flow and the hospital flow diagnostic. Although the characteristics of the diagnostic and how the diagnostic is used continue to develop, it has become an important focus for the direction of flow improvement work for many hospitals. Initially the diagnostic was designed to direct hospitals towards specific change concepts that would be most appropriate for their particular flow problems. Currently the diagnostic is first being used as a high-level hospital evaluation and then second as an entry point to improvement strategies. The diagnostic can validate a given approach to flow improvement in a hospital and provide a measurement overtime of eventual success of the improvement work. Prior to the use of the diagnostic it was far too easy to tackle hospital delays as isolated unit specific problems. Trying to solve a system problem by working on a single unit has proven to be very wasteful and foolhardy since the best plans of a single unit redesign (since they are connected to the rest of the hospital) can be ruined by changing practices of upstream or downstream units. For example, the best of efforts in the ICU can be totally discounted by changing policies on admissions or transfers to a step down telemetry unit. So rather than making the ICU responsible for delays, the hospital flow system needs to be accountable for delays. It is now clear hospital flow is a system problem and needs to be looked at from a more global point of view.

The chapter will describe the methodology of the hospital diagnostic, demonstrate the degree of variability in the number of bed turns and bed utilization, and lastly suggest strategies for improvement and introduce the use of flow streams to work on delays. Patient flow management is a very complex problem not limited to just patient flow within the hospital. It also includes study of pre-hospital patient flow (e.g., why patients use the ED rather than their primary care physicians) post-hospital patient flow (e.g., availability of rehabilitation or skilled nursing facility beds). Comprehensive coverage of all these issues would not be possible in this chapter. Those who are interested in those issues are referred to the references at the end of this chapter.

2. HISTORY

Characteristically most hospital flow solutions relate to fixing the "squeaky wheel", commonly entwined with demands from high producers, or by looking at isolated unit problems with solutions from a narrow point of view. Both usually accomplish nothing in terms of overall hospital flow.

Both solutions, however, usually assume demand is greater than capacity by measuring delays. One only has to look at the building boom in hospitals to understand the agreement to the general assumption that demand is far greater than capacity. These approaches might lead an occasional hospital to the right solution, but luck or happenstance not deliberate design would be responsible. Another possible solution to hospital flow has been the approach of the flow communities working with the Institute for Healthcare Improvement. The hospital diagnostic was used by each hospital as a self-evaluation. A description of the hospital flow problem was generated. Next each hospital was encouraged to select appropriate strategies for improving hospital flow. In this scenario new or interesting ideas, such as discharge appointments or extending the flow chain, are tested knowing the appropriateness of the intervention based on the hospital diagnostic and how in many cases how it will be applied specifically to a high volume flow stream.

The hospital diagnostic was developed by the IHI Innovation Team with a specific set of outcomes around bed turns. For those hospitals with a high number of turns (greater than 90), the goal is to maintain or increase turns, but with minimal delays. For those hospitals with low bed turns, increasing the number of bed turns by capturing deflected demand or reducing unneeded capacity is the goal.

The hospital diagnostic views flow from a viewpoint of the whole system including beyond the walls of the hospital in some cases. One viewpoint that will not be examined is how adequately the hospital services are fulfilling the needs of the community as a societal resource. Hospital throughput will be measured as bed turns and revenue per bed, as well as bed utilization (different than occupancy rate). The strategy will demand minimal delays as an adjunct to any improvement in turns and utilization.

The methodology, tools and other documents related to the topic of hospital flow can be found on the IHI website (www.ihi.org). The following definitions are used in the diagnostic calculation:

- **Unadjusted Bed Turns** = (Admissions + OIIB)/ by functional beds.
- **OIIB** Stands for any outpatient in an inpatient bed. These may include the standard observation patients in an inpatient bed, in addition to any other use of an inpatient bed without being an actual admission. Common uses might be post heart catheterization observation, post outpatient endoscopy procedure observation, etc. Since the bed is being used even for a short period of time, it does force admissions to compete for the bed and must be counted. (A good method to determine this is to

take several weeks and just survey each unit once each 24 hours for any outpatient use of an inpatient bed and average it out for the year.)

- **Adjusted Bed Turns** = (Admissions x case-mix-index)/functional beds + OIIB/functional beds
- **Utilization** (efficiency) = unadjusted bed turns divided by potential bed turns. This number is different than occupancy, since occupancy is measured at midnight and usually only once per day.
- **Potential Bed Turns** = 365 divided by aggregate average length-of-stay (LOS)
- **Average Length of Stay (LOS)**: Average overall length of stay for inpatient admissions. This does not include the standard observation classification and should exclude newborns, which most hospitals do automatically.
- **Admissions:** The number of inpatient admissions (excluding newborns)
- **Observations:** Those patients defined by billing purposes as not being an admission, but being cared for in the hospital for 24 hours or less. If they become an admission they should not be counted twice when the OIIB calculation is made.
- **Case Mix Index (CMI)**: All payer case mix as defined by CMS (Center for Medicare and Medicaid Services)
- **Bed Turns**: Number of times (to the nearest whole number) an inpatient bed is used by a patient whether for admission or for any type of OIIB.
- **Functional Beds**: The number of beds normally open and staffed in a hospital over a year on average, excluding newborn and delivery beds, but including all other beds. The beds must be staffed around the clock which would exclude admission units etc. For rehab beds they are counted if under the same Medicare number.

The performance metrics from Section 3 are now demonstrated with example calculations.

Unadjusted Bed Turns = (admissions + OIIB) divided by functional beds. Example:

Admissions:	10,000/yr
Observations:	1,000/yr
Functional beds:	200

10,000 + 1000 = 11,000/200=55 turns on average per bed per year

Adjusted Bed Turns = ((Admissions x Case Mix Index) + OIIB)/functional beds. Example:

Admissions	10,000/yr
Observations	1,000/yr
Functional beds	200
Case Mix Index	1.4

10,000x1.4 = 14,000 + 1,000 = 15,000/200=75 turns on average/bed/year

Potential Bed Turns = 365/LOS. Example:

LOS 4.0 days
365/4.0 = 91 potential bed turns per year

Utilization = Unadjusted Bed Turns/Potential Bed Turns.
In the above example:

Unadjusted Bed Turns = 55
Potential Bed Turns = 91
Utilization = 55/91 = 60.4%

3. OBSERVATIONS

Figure 12-1 shows the data submitted by hospitals in the IHI Flow Community in 2004. The plot uses adjusted bed turns versus bed utilization percentage. None of the hospitals were unique specialty hospitals, although there was a mixture of academic and non-academic hospitals. The number of actual turns adjusted by the case mix index attempted to level the field by consideration of severity. Even with the adjustment for severity of illness considerable variation exists between these hospitals. The IHI team looked at the plot and selected 90 adjusted bed turns and 90% utilization as desirable goals. The turns and utilization goals were based on reviewing best performers and using the knowledge of queuing theory. Based on these guidelines, the data collected from the hospitals place each hospital into one of four quadrants. Representative samples of hospitals from each quadrant were studied and some visited to learn about the characteristics of the hospitals in each of the quadrants.

One obvious observation needing an explanation is utilization well over 100%. Obviously consistent over 100% utilization is difficult to imagine. The partial answer is the fact that the calculation for utilization uses bed turns. The bed turns associated with OIIB do not have a LOS measure since many of the stays are only for a few hours. Hospitals with very high OIIB fractions commonly will have unusually high utilization rates. If a hospital has a very high OIIB rate with significant delays, this particular flow stream needs to be examined for opportunity.

Figure 12-1 also gives the visual representation of tremendous variability between hospitals in terms of flow and utilization. Yet each of these hospitals have a common problem of significant flow delays otherwise they would not have joined the collaborative. It is hard to imagine how a hospital with only 40 turns and a utilization of 60% should have delays, while it is very understandable why a hospital with 140 turns and 100% utilization should have delays. Those questions and the subsequent quest for the answers will form the basis for the rest of the chapter but should also tempt the reader to "find their dot".

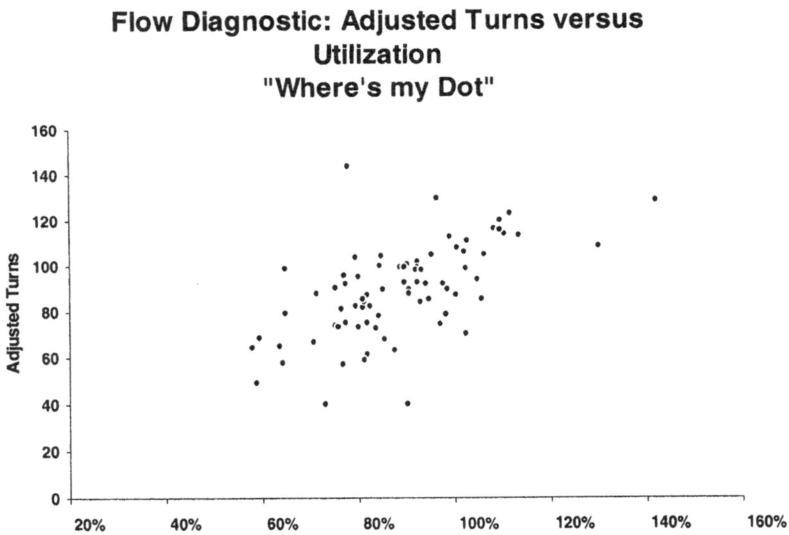

Figure 12-1. Flow Diagnostic: Adjusted Turns Versus Utilization, "Where's My Dot"

4. UNDERSTANDING DELAYS FROM THE FLOW DIAGNOSTIC

Figure 12-2 demonstrates the four quadrants and the relationship between capacity, demand and delays in each of the quadrants, in addition to the 90 turn and 90% utilization goals.

Figure 12-3 portrays the expectation of delays. Quadrants 2 and 4 because of the high utilization should expect delays. Quadrants 1 and 3, because of the low utilization, should be surprised by delays. The utilization is given a window, as shown by the dotted lines.

Using Figure 12-4, we see quadrant 1 has a good balance between capacity and demand, but certain hospitals may still have significant inefficiency in utilization of varying degrees; all in our series still have delays. Quadrant 3 is an inefficient hospital in terms of utilization and also has low turns and delays. Both of these quadrants need to question delays from the viewpoint of "why". With low utilization, one should expect no or minimal delays.

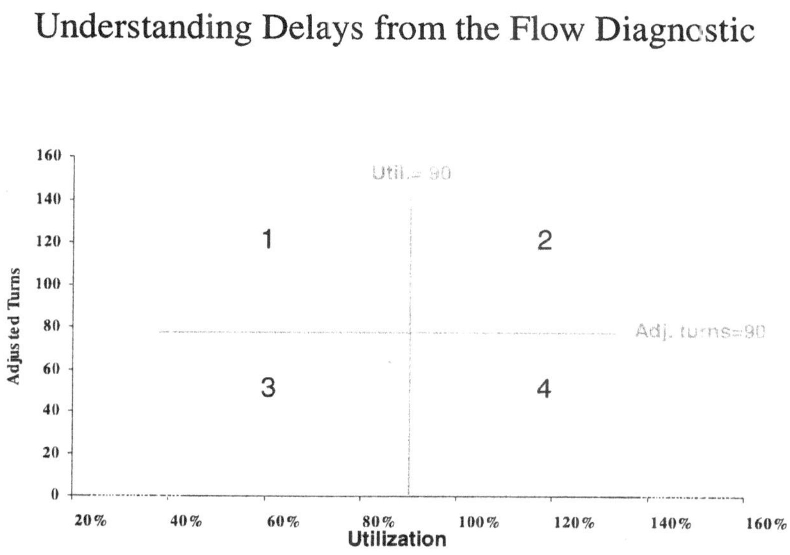

Figure 12-2. Flow Diagnostic: Understanding Delays

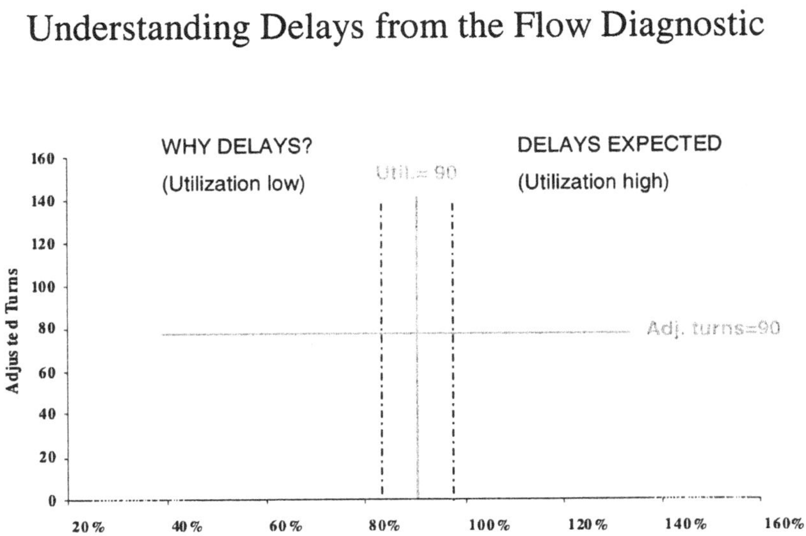

Figure 12-3. Understanding Delays From The Flow Diagnostic

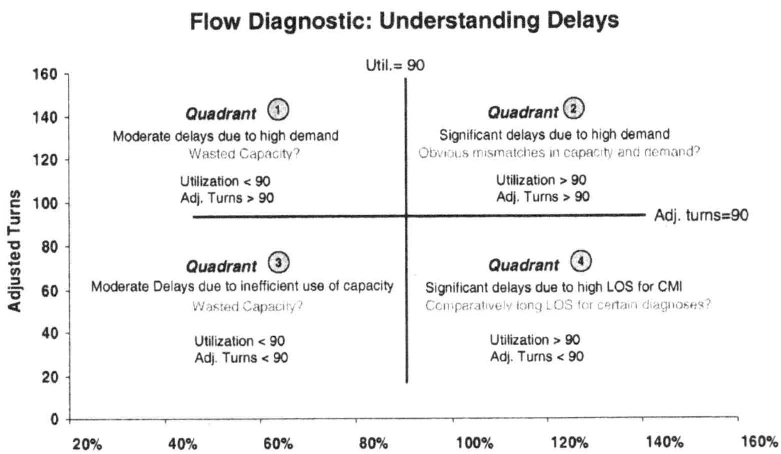

Figure 12-4. Flow diagnostic: understanding delays

Again using Figure 12-4 Quadrant 2 hospitals are highly functional systems, but with delays. Quadrant 4 also high-functioning, in terms of utilization, but in both quadrants we should not be surprised to find delays -- in fact they might be expected.

No one quadrant is without it's own set of problems that need to be solved, but from a business case, being in quadrant 1 or 2 would be preferable, with quadrant 1 in the long run best from a queuing theory point of view. Participants in the flow collaborative -- because of the nature of the hospitals that joined a collaborative on flow – all experienced significant delays and lost opportunity in one way or another, no matter in which quadrant their dot was placed.

Figure 12-5 shows hospitals in the IHI flow community. Each hospital is represented by a dot and the y axis is unadjusted turns. The x axis is the case mix index divided into four categories. The finding of wide variation within any given case mix grouping is extremely interesting. In category 1, for example, the unadjusted turns range from 40 to 120 turns/bed/year. Explaining this variation is very difficult. The assumption is that competent managers and executives work in each of these hospitals. In addition to the variation within a grouping, how can we explain a hospital with a case mix index of 1-1.22 and bed turns/year of 60, when another hospital with a case mix of 1.71 and obviously much sicker patients has the same number of bed turns? The answer may well be the proportionality in how specific hospitals handle streams of flow. The defining of the flow streams and the change concepts to improve the flow stream efficiency can be extrapolated in part from understanding the flow diagnostic.

5. STEPS TO USING THE HOSPITAL DIAGNOSTIC

This section provides a step-by-step explanation of how to apply the diagnostic.

Step 1

Collect the OIIB (remember these are any outpatients using inpatient beds), admissions (excluding newborns), case mix index for all payers, functional beds (see methodology below) and LOS. The data should be collected for a full year. If multiple years of data are available, you may wish to use this to establish a trajectory.

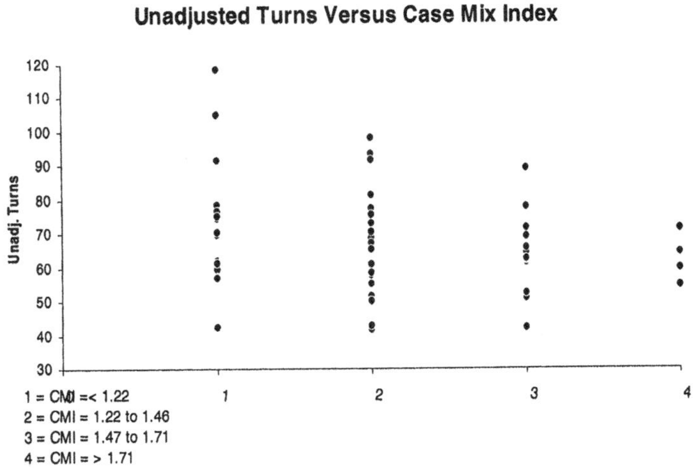

Figure 12-5. Unadjusted Turns Versus Case Mix Index

SideBar on methodology to determine functional beds. Most hospitals have licensed beds, staffed beds and even functional beds as different numbers. Usually the actual beds in use on a daily basis are less than the licensed beds. Functional beds can best be described as over a three or four month average how many beds are actually staffed. Difficulty arises when there is a great fluctuation with seasonality. Since seasonality usually is a recurring phenomenon, the three or four month average should include both high and low season. (Many hospitals could just average out the staffed beds for a whole year and get the functional bed number). Absolute accuracy is less important than stability in this measure. If stable over time, the change in bed turns can then be measured to reflect actual change.

Step 2

Calculate bed turns with and without adjustment for case severity using the case mix index, and calculate utilization.

SideBar Since the functional beds affects the bed turns fairly dramatically, the leeway within any quadrant allows this to be an average over months and then allows the comparison over time as a trajectory to be helpful.

SideBar: An alternative method to measure utilization, rather than actual bed turns divided by potential bed turns, is to directly measure the bed utilization. Each bed in the hospital is numbered. A random number generator for the total number of beds is created, and each hour for one week a bed number is generated and a determination is made as to whether the bed is filled or not. The resulting utilization is then calculated as a simple total filled over the total number of observations. A few rules apply, however:

1. Beds held for a patient in surgery is not a filled bed.
2. If patient is no longer alive, bed is not a filled bed
3. Patient not in room but down for procedure is a filled bed, but patient needed to be in the room prior to the procedure or test
4. Room being cleaned is not a filled room

Step 3
Place your hospital into a quadrant based on your calculations. Be careful if you are at the dividing lines since there is some overlap.

Step 4
Evaluate your current flow improvement strategy and see if it is consistent with the quadrant recommendations

Step 5 (Optional)
Evaluate previous years and determine the trajectory of your change based on bed turns and utilization. Is it going in the right direction? In this case, is it moving to the left upper quadrant as improvements are being made in both bed turns and delays?

6. STRATEGIES

Although the aim of the chapter is not to provide a detailed discussion of the specific strategies associated with flow improvement, the appropriate use of the diagnostic still demands an understanding of the approaches to be taken for the specific strategies. In that light, the specific strategies need to be at least understood. The overall aim is to increase throughput (as measured by bed turns) and minimize delays (as measured by time) while assuring that high performance in flow is not at the expense of poor quality. The specific delay measurements commonly used in the Flow Collaborative are:

- Time from entering the Emergency Department to the floor (Using a door to floor concept)
- Diversions from the Emergency Department (Or alternatively hours on diversion)
- Left without being seen from the Emergency Department

In those hospitals with turns already high, the goal is to maintain or increase turns but now with minimal delays. In those hospitals with low bed turns the goal is to increase turns by capturing deflected demand or reducing capacity. Figure 12-6 presents strategies for quadrants 1 and 3

Quadrants 1 and 3 have poor utilization in common. The best quadrant is 1 but without delays. The worst quadrant situation is 3. Both need to determine whether beds are available and since in all likelihood they are the change concepts need to be related to recapture of wasted capacity. Large volume flow streams are essential starting points. These might include the cardiac service or the orthopedic service as examples. Ultimately those in quadrant 3 will need to increase turns and this might be done by increasing utilization and closing unneeded capacity. Figure 12-7 presents strategies for quadrants 2 and 4

Flow is a property of the entire system and can only be optimized at a system level. Understanding this fact has led to the idea of streams of flow that are then optimized by the specific change strategies.

In order to start the work on flow, a sound administrative system that manifests a bed management process that incorporates planning based on predictions of capacity and demand should be an overarching design in any improvement strategy. The chapter by Linda Kosnik demonstrates an hour by hour evaluation of capacity and demand with explicit processes designed to specific changes in demand or capacity. Some organizations are using bed huddles several times a day in addition to trying to understand larger issues of variation such as seasonality to adjust capacity and demand. A bed administrative system may or may not incorporate an electronic bed board product.

The process of where to go from the diagnostic can best be described in three steps:

1. Determine the major flow stream that will be subjected to the flow change strategies.
2. Rather than working on a given unit look at the project as a system problem crossing multiple silos of interest. A stream of flow should manifest a large volume, exhibit significant delays and flow from at least the admission through the discharge, although the work done by Mark Lindsay would suggest moving this out to the pre-admission and the post-discharge
3. Once a major flow stream has been identified, the specific flow improvement strategies now need to be applied, particularly those that are demonstrated as useful for the hospital's quadrant.

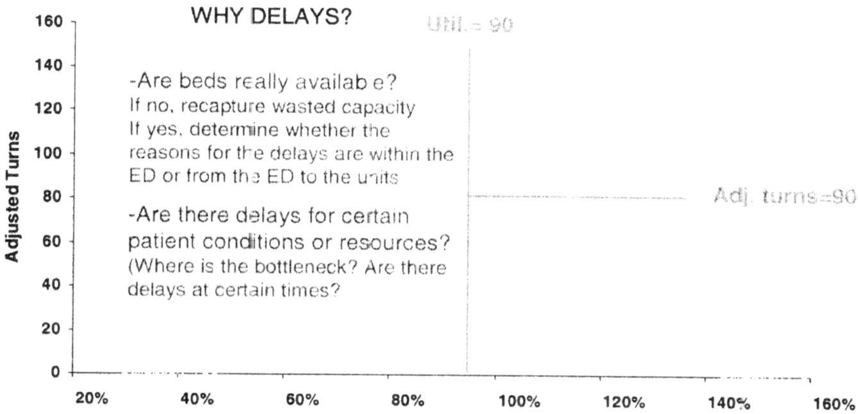

Figure 12-6. Understanding Delays from the Flow Diagnostic

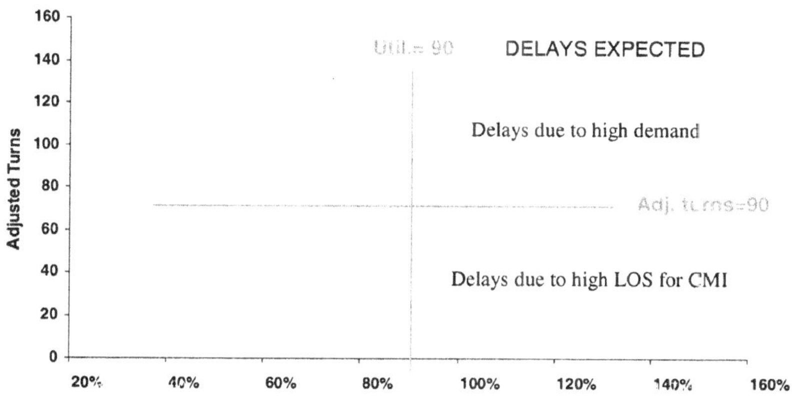

Figure 12-7. Understanding Delays from the Flow Diagnostic, Quadrants 2 And 4

6.1 Quadrant 1 (Left upper quadrant)

The quadrant has, in general, adequate turns and reasonable utilization, but still has moderate delays due to high demand. Adjusted bed turns are greater than 90 and utilization is less than 90%. The primary problem is waste of capacity. Any bed use variant could contribute to the wasted capacity. The wasted capacity would be easiest to pinpoint by looking at several large volume flow streams. Examples of a large volume stream might be orthopedic surgery or heart disease requiring medical telemetry. Obviously, the large volume stream work should focus on reducing wasted capacity by identifying and remove bottlenecks in the flow stream. The bottlenecks are commonly admissions, transfers or discharges and specific change concepts for each of these interfaces. For example, the use of discharge appointments could be linked to either transfers or admissions. Detailed information on this and other concepts can be found at www.ihi.org.

6.2 Quadrant 2 (Right upper quadrant)

The quadrant has adequate turns, but the utilization is so high that staff burnout and safety issues need to be considered. These are super high functioning hospitals. Adjusted turns are greater than 90% and utilization is greater than 90%. Significant delays are seen due to mismatch of capacity with a high demand, more than wasted capacity. Hospitals in this quadrant may truly have a need to add more capacity, but only after significant efforts have been made to correct the mismatch between capacity and demand. The mismatch is significant enough that use of electronic bed tracking systems may have tremendous utility for organizations in quadrant 2. Poor habits need to be purged from the system such as holding beds, lack of good discharge planning and lack of pre-admission planning for elective surgery. Again, the emphasis should be to start with larger flow streams and apply these change concepts.

6.3 Quadrant 3

Hospitals in quadrant 3 present a very unique opportunity. They experience moderate delays due to inefficient use of capacity. In most cases they have more beds than necessary, but due to the inefficient use of the capacity staff keep too many beds open. The result is adjusted turns less than 90 and utilization less than 90%. Again, the concept of isolating several major flow streams and applying some of the change principles would be the strategy. Those change concepts include eliminate bed holds, developing bed cleaning and turnaround strategies, reducing internal transfers, decreasing use of inpatient beds by outpatients or decreasing capacity. Most hospitals have an initial response of shock when a suggestion is made to reduce capacity, but the reduction in capacity reduces the staffed beds and immediately increases turns per bed and utilization of the beds remaining.

6.4 Quadrant 4

Quadrant 4 has significant delays due to a high LOS for the case mix index. Adjusted turns are less than 90 and utilization is greater than 90. Almost all the hospitals studied have a comparatively long length of stay for multiple high volume diagnoses. The utilization of flow streams would necessarily need to focus on one of those high volume diagnoses. The focus should be on conditions that have a long LOS compared to other hospitals. The strategy needs again to look at the bottlenecks. A commonly found bottleneck is the inability to work outside the hospital for certain chronic disease states, such as chronic ventilator use. An easy measurement is to look at the LOS for all patients admitted to a nursing home. Hospitals average five to seven days around the country. Longer than seven days suggests that flow efforts need to extend outside the walls of the hospital.

The business case for increasing turns can be illustrated in the following example. The data are from a real hospital.

- Admissions: 16,704 with 4,246 observations
- Case mix index: 1.49
- LOS: 4.7
- Average functional staffed beds 432
- Average revenue (actual collections) from an admission = $7,525

- Unadjusted Turns = (Admissions + Observations)/Average Functional Beds = 48 Turns/year
- Adjusted Turns = (Admissions x CMI + Observations)/Average Functional Beds = 67 Turns
- Potential Bed Turns = 365/LOS = 77 Turns
- Hospital efficiency = Adjusted Turns/Potential Turns = 74%

High performing hospitals have 90 or more adjusted turns and an efficiency of 90%. Adding 10 turns per year per bed produces $32,000,000 in revenue per year, assuming same average revenue per admission. Increasing turns to the level of high performing hospitals (89 turns) produces $60,000,000 in revenue per year.

Figure 12-8 is an example of using the diagnostic retrospectively to determine whether the appropriate flow improvement strategies were selected and the impact on turns. Initially the hospital was near the intersection of quadrant 2 and 4. Turns were reasonably high and LOS was actually low for the case mix index. Since the demand was high existing capacity needed to be optimized. An effective administrative system was added with an hour-by-hour response system. Discharge appointments were synchronized. Extensive collaboration with nursing homes was highly developed to provide continuum of care. Over the four years of measurement turns increased by 20 per bed, while at the same time the case mix index edged up slightly. At the same time the utilization decreased into a more reasonable sustainable pace from a little over 100% to 86%. The financial benefit was approximately $11 million to the organization.

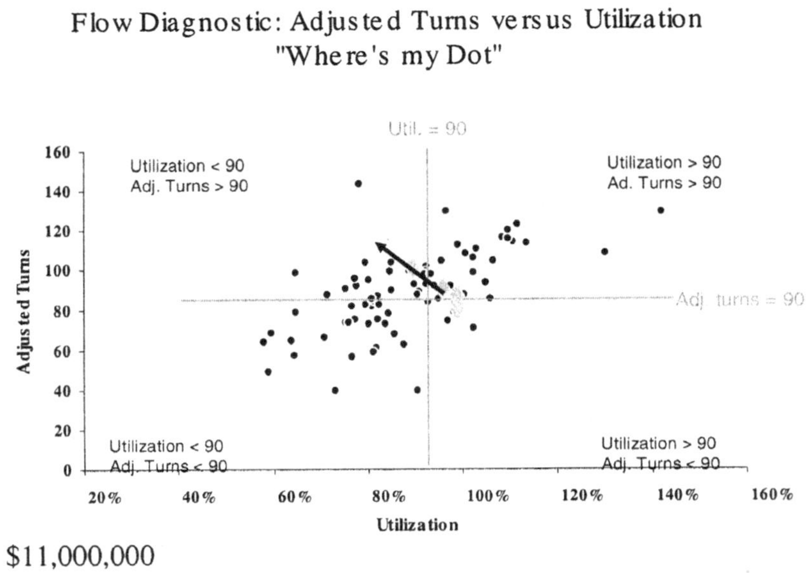

Figure 12-8. Flow Diagnostic, Adjusted Turns Versus Utilization

7. CONCLUSIONS

The hospital diagnostic can be used to initially determine a hospital's status in regard to utilization and throughput. General high level conclusions regarding these measures will set up the next step, which is the determination of high volume flow streams and the application of specific change concepts. The diagnostic in itself is not a change strategy. It allows for an initial evaluation and a methodology to follow a trajectory over time. The business case for increasing turns (throughput) is very compelling.

8. ACKNOWLEDGMENTS

The author would like to acknowledge the contribution of the IHI Innovation Team particularly the flow design team: Tom Nolan, Carol Haraden, Kirk Jensen, Diane Jacobsen, Eugene Litvak and Kevin Nolan

9. REFERENCES

Institute for Healthcare Improvement. Patient Flow, (http://www.ihi.org/IHI/Topics/Flow/PatientFlow/

Institute for Healthcare Improvement. Patient flow. Discussion, (http://www.ihi.org/ihi/forums/ShowPost.aspx?PostID=1691

Joint Commission on Accreditation of Healthcare Organizations, (2004). *Managing Patient Flow. Strategies and Solutions for Addressing Hospital Overcrowding*. Joint Commission Resources.

Chapter 13

CONTINUUM OF CARE PROGRAM

Mark Lindsay MD, MMM

Mayo Health System 1221 Whipple Street Eau Claire WI, 54702

Abstract: The Continuum of Care Program promotes innovation of new processes and systems to ensure high compliance of evidence based care. It emphasizes teamwork, staff empowerment, collaboration across care settings and the development of new pathways outside the Intensive Care Unit (ICU) and hospital. The program eliminates the notion of discharge, and promotes high quality programs in each care setting as patients are most vulnerable in the transition from one setting to the next. New innovative programs will be developed to ensure patients have the opportunity to reach their highest level of independence in the most appropriate care setting. The home setting will be emphasized, recognizing this is the most desirable care setting and preferable to institutional care. The Continuum of Care Program will provide the most cost-effective, safe, patient-centered health care.

Key words: Continuum of Care, transitional care units, ventilator units, cost-effective, critical access hospitals, long-term acute care hospitals, collaboration, multidisciplinary rounds.

1. INTRODUCTION

Healthcare in the United States is fragmented with silos that do not allow for optimizing care across care settings. The Institute of Medicine (IOM) reports highlighted the concerns with our present healthcare system that contributes to numerous errors and preventable deaths (IOM, 1999, 2001). Many of these errors may be attributed to lack of standardization and poor compliance implementing evidence based care (McGlynn and Asch, 2003). The spiraling costs of healthcare reached $1.5 trillion dollars in 2002, almost 15% of the country's GDP (National Healthcare Expenditures). This is significantly more than other industrialized nations. Hospital care has accounted for the largest component of healthcare costs.

Elderly patients are a particularly vulnerable patient population. They account for a significant proportion of hospital admissions and prolonged hospital stays. Older patients may have readmission rates as high as 66% within six months post discharge. Hospital admissions have inherent risk for elderly patients, which include delirium, nosocomial infections, malnutrition, pressure ulcers, and adverse drug events (Callahan, 2002).

The healthcare concerns for our elderly population are magnified in skilled nursing facilities. Patients admitted to skilled nursing facilities are at high risk for urinary and lower respiratory tract infections, decubitus ulcers, etc. The high prevalence of these infections and complications may be related to high staff turnover, lack of attention to infection control practices as well as other factors (Garibaldi, 1981). Nursing staff turnover may be as high as 100% (Decker and Gruhn, 2002). Clinical outcomes that reflect the transition of high-risk patients from the acute care setting to skilled nursing facilities demonstrate results that are less than desirable. Cook found that 45% of patients discharged from a surgical Intensive Care Unit (ICU) to an extended care facility died within 2 years (Cook and Martin, 1999). Carey reported that over 13% of CABG (coronary artery bypass graft) patients in his report that were transferred to other healthcare facilities died (Carey and Parker, 2003). Ankrom reported outcomes from a nursing home ventilator unit with 15% of patients liberated from the ventilator and 19% were alive at one year (Ankrom and Barofsky, 1998). Most reporting of outcomes does not reflect outcomes across care settings, but rather focuses on outcomes at time of discharge, or at 30 days. One must question whether these undesirable outcomes would be positively affected by improved collaboration across care settings, development of standardized systems and processes of care, and the empowerment of frontline workers.

The quality of care provided in skilled nursing facilities and the lack of pathways designed to care for patients in the home is frequently an obstacle for physicians, patients and families' acceptance of timely discharge. Medicare Diagnostic Related Group (DRG) payments do not compensate adequately for prolonged hospitalizations. The costs of this discounted care are increasingly passed on to employers' insurance costs. It is not surprising that there is a growing uninsured working population. Our present healthcare system provides fragmented, poor quality, uncoordinated, unsafe healthcare that is ridden with errors, complications, and spiraling costs. Clearly our present healthcare system is not a sustainable model.

Because of DRG payment and because Medicare patients account for a high percent of patients requiring prolonged hospitalization and rehabilitative care, there is a very strong financial incentive for acute care facilities to collaborate with efforts to expand and optimize the alternatives to acute care hospitalization to proactively decrease length of stay, reduce costs, increase revenues and improve hospital flow. One of the greatest opportunities in healthcare is outside of the hospital.

The Continuum of Care Program is an attempt at creating a model and framework that encourages breaking down healthcare silos. It encourages the design and innovation of new systems and processes of care that will achieve the highest quality, cost-effective, safe healthcare promoting the patient receiving the right care in the right place. In attempting to design an ideal model for healthcare, it is helpful to learn from other highly successful corporations in the business industry. Two corporations that will be highlighted in this chapter include Toyota, the most profitable respected corporation in the auto industry and IDEO, one of the largest design and innovation firms (Liker, 2004); (Kelley, 2001).

Some of the key components that led to Toyota's successful business model can be applied to healthcare. Toyota's emphasis on standardized processes, lean thinking and reducing waste, empowered employees, pull systems with an investment in their network of partners and suppliers are essential elements that are applicable to a successful healthcare model (Liker, 2004). Toyota has identified seven types of waste, which include overproduction, waiting, unnecessary transport, over or incorrect processing, excess inventory, unnecessary movement, and defects. Jeffrey Liker the author of the "Toyota Way", identified an eighth type of waste: unused employee creativity (Liker, 2004). Certainly in the healthcare industry there are numerous examples of ineffective care, poor access, poor quality outcomes and excess costs that are associated with all eight types of waste.

Toyota's leadership empowers their frontline employees to work effectively as a team to make timely adjustments and improvements in their work processes to optimize the Toyota product. This represents an untapped opportunity for healthcare leaders and administrators to empower their frontline employees to develop systems and processes that achieve the results that our healthcare consumers deserve. Toyota also gives tremendous value to the development of "pull" systems to avoid excess inventory and overproduction. They also place very high expectations on their partners and suppliers to commit to equally high quality standards. In Liker's "The Toyota Way", there is a description of a fire that destroyed a large factory of Toytota's only supplier of a brake part that was used in all of their vehicles. Within a few days other suppliers had filled in the need with the development of the brake part. This emphasizes Toyota's collaboration with their partners and suppliers (Liker, 2004). There are significant opportunities for acute care hospitals to collaborate with skilled nursing facilities, rural hospitals, long-term acute care hospitals (LTACs), and other key stakeholders to develop effective "pull" systems.

IDEO, a highly respected design and innovation company, uses several strategies to innovate and develop new products that have included the Apple Mouse, Palm handheld device, and the Polaroid Instant Camera. IDEO promotes a high energy, rapid turnaround approach that relies on brainstorming sessions, creativity, teamwork, and functionality. IDEO has five basic steps in their process: understand, observe, visualize, evaluate and refine, and implement (Kelley, 2001). Many of the processes and systems that are presently in place in healthcare are not designed to achieve the outcomes that we would desire. The IDEO and Toyota strategies can energize key stakeholders in healthcare to collaborate and innovate new processes and systems of care to achieve the desired outcomes.

2. CONTINUUM OF CARE PROGRAM

Continuum of Care Program emphasizes achieving the highest compliance of evidence-based care, standardization, and optimizing coordination of care as patients transition from the acute care to alternate care settings. This program creates a "Pull" system, aggressively expanding the alternatives to acute care hospitalization with the development of state-of-the-art transitional care rehabilitative programs that emphasize socialization, patient-centered and clinical outcomes. The program will also focus on increasing the ability to care for patients in the home setting through homecare, hospice and new innovative programs utilizing advance practice providers. It will emphasize the importance of optimizing utilization through "providing the right care in the right place" through aggressive partnering with the essential stakeholders in the healthcare industry. The "Continuum of Care House" is structured to highlight the strengths of the Toyota House, recognizing the tremendous power and strength of how each component reinforces and complements the other components (Liker, 2004) (see Figure 13-1). Any weak link can negatively impact the healthcare product. The Continuum of Care Program emphasizes the importance of empowering frontline workers to innovate, redesign and revitalize our healthcare delivery system. New processes and systems of care will ensure high reliability outcomes. We must eliminate the concept of patient discharge rather promote the concept of collaboration and continuity as patients safely transition from one care setting to the next. This chapter will briefly describe the "hospital push" that includes efforts to safely navigate patients through the acute care hospital. It will describe the "out of hospital pull", expanding the capabilities to care for patients outside the acute care hospital. We will then describe the other supporting structures to the program. A few cases will be used to highlight the strength of this model.

3. THE VIRTUAL BED TOWER WITHOUT BRICKS AND MORTAR

One may choose to view the Continuum of Care structure as a virtual hospital bed tower, however without the costs of bricks and mortar. The Medicare DRG reimbursement method provides a fixed payment for most diagnoses regardless of the length of stay (LOS). Certain transfer DRGs will result in a per diem rate when transferred to a post acute care provider within a designated length of stay (Law Watch). The ability to reduce length of stay for Medicare DRG patients, including Transfer DRG patients, beyond the designated time frame will result in reduced variable costs and will free up hospital beds. If we assume that the costs of caring for the Medicare patient being discharged is equivalent to the costs of caring for a new patient who can now occupy that bed, we will add one fully staffed bed to the virtual bed tower for every 365 Medicare bed days that are saved through optimizing the inpatient care and through alternative pathways outside the hospital. The virtual bed tower is now available to receive new patients with new associated revenues. An acute care hospital that runs a high hospital census and is considering building expansion to address increasing demands may preferentially choose to invest in the Continuum of Care Program, which will improve outcomes, reduce variable costs, increase revenues through increasing capacity for new admissions and avoid new building costs. The cost of a new hospital bed may be as high as 1.5 million dollars in some markets (San Francisco Business Times, 2005).

4. HOSPITAL PUSH

We will briefly review the three components of the hospital push, which includes ICU Redesign, Acute Care Redesign and Patient Care Team Redesign. Important strategies in each of these redesign efforts include the development of systems and processes to ensure high compliance of evidence based care, empowerment of frontline workers to initiate timely interventions within the scope of their training, and to look outside the geographic boundaries to ensure that there is appropriate standardization from one hospital unit to the next. Table 13-1, below, includes a few of the many key efforts in each redesign effort that should be managed. Each redesign team should have appropriate stakeholder representation, leadership

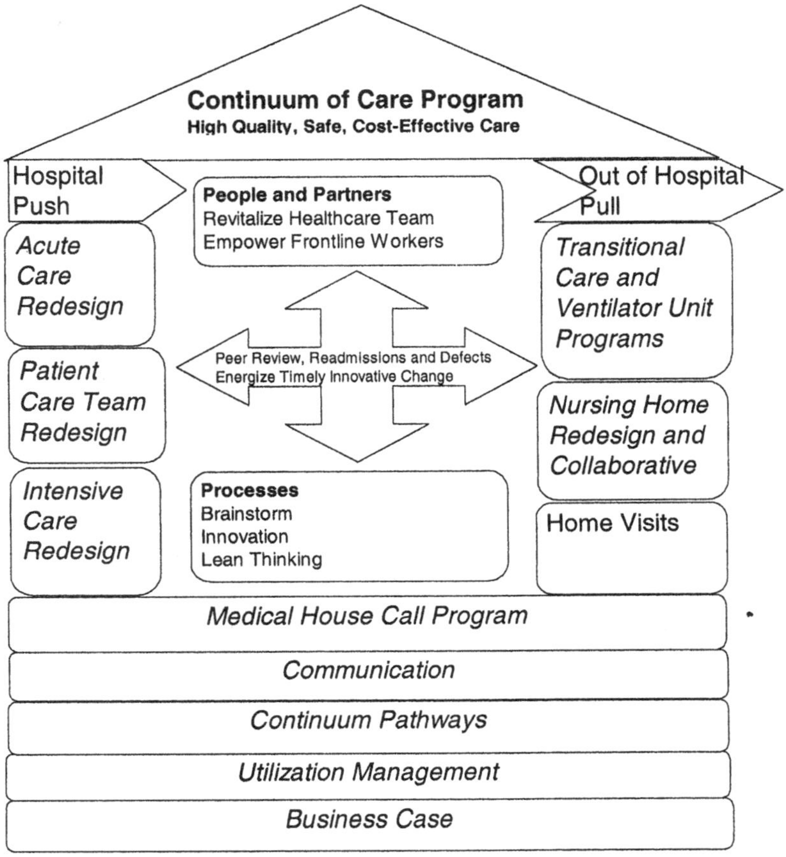

Figure 13-1. Model of the Continuum of Care Program

Table 13-1. Hospital Push: Example Of Efforts That Should Be Managed

ICU Redesign	Acute Care Redesign	Patient Care Redesign
Intensive Glucose Management	JCAHO Core Measures	Patient Care Team Order Set
NPPV and Weaning Protocols	DVT Prophylaxis	Bedside Multidisciplinary Rounds
Ventilator Bundle	Advance Directives	Case Management
Rapid Response Team	Decubitus Ulcer Prevention	
Pain and Sedation Protocols	Diabetes Management	

and administrative support. The management of these efforts should include outcome measures, with an attempt at achieving best practice. This may include a champion or expert team to oversee each effort.

5. INTENSIVE CARE UNIT REDESIGN

The goal of Intensive Care Redesign is to optimize the care of critically ill patients, emphasizing expanding the capabilities to care for patients inside and outside of the ICU and providing the appropriate care in the appropriate setting. ICU Redesign Team members should include key stakeholders from the emergency room, medical surgical floors, the ICU, and key physician providers. We are going to review one organization's efforts to implement three projects.

5.1 Noninvasive positive pressure ventilation (NPPV)

NPPV has been demonstrated to reduce mortality, nosocomial pneumonia, ICU bed days, endotracheal intubations in subsets of patients with acute respiratory failure (Keenan and Sinuff, 2004; Plant and Owen, 2000). There is literature to support that respiratory therapy and nurse led weaning leads to earlier extubation and liberation from mechanical ventilation in comparison to physician led weaning (Kollef and Shapiro, 1997; Marelich and Murin, 2000). Luther developed a respiratory therapy and nurse led weaning protocol in 1997.

In 1997, Luther Midelfort implemented a respiratory therapy directed NPPV protocol. Establishing a respiratory therapy driven protocol at Luther Midelfort has resulted in a dramatic increase in NPPV use (Figure 13-2), which is largely performed outside the ICU (Table 13-2). An essential element to this program is the ability for respiratory therapists to initiate the protocol and the nurse education program. Both of these elements allow for patients to be managed outside the ICU, avoiding unnecessary transfer and associated resources. In a Luther Midelfort respiratory therapy staff survey, 94% of the staff believed the NPPV protocol reduced intubations, provided more timely interventions, and improved job satisfaction. This impacts recruitment and retention of high quality staff.

Figure 13-2. Implementation and Growth of a Respiratory Therapy Directed Noninvasive Positive Pressure Ventilation (NPPV) Protocol in a Community Hospital

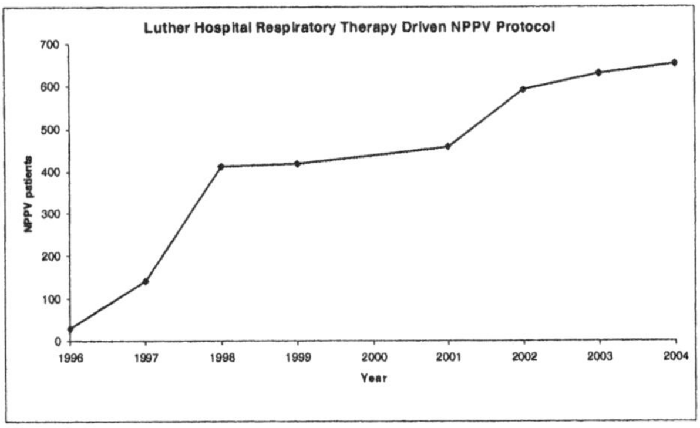

Table 13-2. 50 Consecutive NPPV cases in 2003, Impact on outcomes. Most of the NPPV is Initiated Outside the ICU.

*50 Consecutive NPPV Patients 2003	Number (%)
2 Signs or Symptoms Respiratory Failure	37/50 (64%)
NPPV Initiated Outside ICU	37/50 (74%)
Did Not Require Intubation	43/50 (86%)
NPPV Initiated in the ER	19/50 (38%)
* excludes routine NPPV for OSA	

5.2 Preventing Nosocomial Pneumonia

It is well recognized that ventilator patients are at high risk for complications including deep vein thrombosis, stress ulcers and nosocomial pneumonia. Resar and others reported that hospital units that obtained high compliance on four prevention measures, (stress ulcer prophylaxis, deep vein thrombosis prophylaxis, holding sedation, and head of bed elevation), had a significant reduction in nosocomial pneumonia (Resar and Pronovost, 2005). They reported units that had 95% compliance on the four prevention measures and a 59% reduction in nosocomial pneumonia. When we looked at Luther Midelfort's results, consistently less than 50% of our patients had documented evidence that all four measures were implemented. The poor results led to a concerted team approach to design a process to achieve the desired results. A standardized protocol was developed that allowed the nursing staff to implement the prevention measures if the physician did not write the order. Additional checks, balances and redundancies were implemented utilizing the respiratory therapists and nursing to optimize the compliance. Figure 13-3 demonstrates very high compliance on the four prevention efforts for ventilator patients in our ICU. These outcome measures are displayed in our ICU for families and staff to view. This transparency is another key feature that is quite powerful.

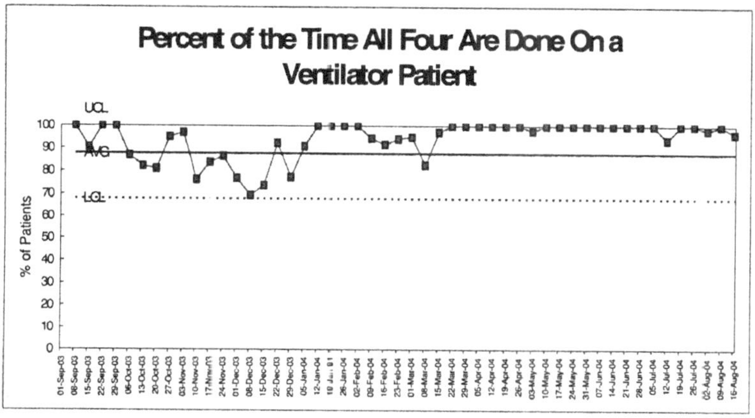

Figure 13-3. Near 100% Compliance on Ventilation Prevention Efforts

5.3 Rapid Response Teams

Emergency Teams have demonstrated significant reductions in cardiac arrests and post code ICU and hospital bed days (Bellomo and Goldsmith, 2004). This is based on the concept that patients will have warning signs hours prior to a cardiac arrest. The rapid response team can implement earlier intervention resulting in improved outcomes. Luther Midelfort's development of a rapid response team has also demonstrated through survey data that the program is viewed as an important resource to floor nurses who may not have the expertise or dedicated time to care for a critically ill patient.

5.4 Aggressive Glucose Management

Aggressive glucose management has been linked to improved outcomes and reduced complications (Van den Berghe and Bouillon, 2003) In Van den Berghe's report, intensive insulin therapy was associated with a 34% reduction in mortality, significant reductions in bloodstream infections, prolonged mechanical ventilation, acute renal failure, and intensive care. Luther Midelfort demonstrated a significant reduction in sternal wound infections in cardiovascular surgery patients and has dramatically improved blood sugars in intensive care unit patients with the use of an intensive insulin protocol. Importantly, Luther Midelfort's intensive insulin protocol can be implemented inside and outside the ICU. This avoids unnecessary delays in patient transfers out of the ICU.

5.5 End of Life Care

There are data to support that the ICU is frequently utilized to care for patients at the end of life (Goldstein, 2003) There are data to support use of palliative care and hospice programs as an alternative to ICU care when comfort care and the ability to be cared for in the home or alternate care setting is preferred. As few as 25% of patients with serious chronic disease have an advance directive (Goldstein, 2004; Smucker, 2004). A dedicated community effort in LaCrosse, Wisconsin demonstrated significant success on increasing compliance of advanced directives. Eighty five percent of their decedents had an advance directive and 95% of the advance directives were in the medical record (Lynne, 2003). Luther Midelfort adapted the LaCrosse efforts and participated with other healthcare entities to develop a community video "Choices" that educated healthcare providers and community members on the importance of advance directive and advance care planning. Providing inappropriate end of life care in the ICU is frequently dissatisfying to physicians, nurses, patients and families and can be avoided through concerted efforts to educate the community on their choices related to advanced directives and end of life care. Such efforts can also increase access to a very expensive limited resource.

6. ACUTE CARE REDESIGN

The key elements of acute care redesign are standardizing processes, education, and applying checks, balances and redundancies to ensure the highest compliance of evidence based practices. It replicates the process demonstrated in the ventilator prevention efforts, which has achieved close to 100 % compliance and applies these concepts to other efforts, including the Joint Commission on Accreditation of Healthcare Organizations (JCAHO) core measures that focus on important diagnoses, such as pneumonia, congestive heart failure, myocardial infarction, tobacco use, etc.

The medical literature would strongly support efforts to ensure high compliance of evidence based care. Malone reported that when patients were not treated with established pneumonia guidelines, they had a more than 4 fold increase in mortality and significantly increased length of stay (Malone and Shaban). Patients with severe congestive heart failure treated with enalapril had a 31% reduction in mortality at one year (Consensus Trial Study Group). Pfeffer reported that patients with left ventricular dysfunction after myocardial infarction treated with captopril had a 21% reduction in cardiovascular deaths (Pfeffer and Braunwald). RAND research conducted one of the largest studies on healthcare quality in the United States. (Rand Health) They reported in the largest study performed that only 55% of participants received the recommended care. These findings were consistent in all geographic areas studied. They determined that diabetics received only 45% of the recommended care, hypertensive patients less than 65% of recommended care, coronary artery disease patients received 68% of recommended care, and pneumonia patients 39% of recommended care. The report concluded that there were significant gaps in the medical knowledge and the actual care provided.

Acute Care Redesign recognizes that new processes and systems of care will be needed to ensure high compliance of evidence based care. We can no longer rely on individual physicians to implement appropriate standards. Other healthcare disciplines can partner with physicians to provide a team approach to accomplish the desired outcomes.

It makes good strategic sense for like acute care hospitals to participate in larger collaborative efforts to promote broader standardized implementation across our healthcare environment, avoiding duplication. An acute care redesign team should be a permanent fixture of an acute care hospital. A process owner or expert team should be assigned to monitor each effort. Efforts should be implemented to standardize the education of disciplines and providers to maximize efficiency.

One of the greatest potential obstacles in this effort is the potential loss of physician autonomy. However, with higher compliance with desired outcomes, decreased physician liability and improved efficiencies, these potential obstacles can be overcome. It is essential to have influential physician leadership to help drive these processes.

7. PATIENT CARE TEAM REDESIGN

The largest patient survey ever conducted by Press Ganey demonstrated that the top two factors that were associated with a patient recommending a hospital was how well the staff worked together to care for the patient and the cheerfulness of the staff. This is an invitation from our most important stakeholder to optimize the multidisciplinary care team and empower staff (Wolosin, 2003).

Dodek reported that rounds in the ICU improve communication and satisfaction of the ICU staff (Dodek, 2003). Young reported that a multidisciplinary approach to care for ventilator patients resulted in a significant reduction in ICU length of stay, and costs (Young et al, 1998).

Leape reported that pharmacists on rounds in the ICU can reduce adverse drug events by 66%. Importantly, 99% of the pharmacist recommendations were accepted by a physician (Leape and Cullen, 1999). Bedside multidisciplinary care team rounds can improve communication among team members as well as update the patient and family. Luther Midelfort has promoted bedside multidisciplinary care team rounds that occur at a set time with inclusion of the patient and family for patients in the intensive care unit, transitional care unit, and the offsite ventilator unit. Table 3 demonstrates survey results after implementation of ICU bedside rounds. Present efforts are in place to expand these efforts to all patient care areas.

Luther Midelfort recently initiated a brainstorm session using a template adapted from the "Toyota Way" and "The Art of Innovation" (Liker, 2004; Kelley, 2001). The effort included key stakeholders from the patient care team. The brainstorm session identified a number of opportunities, including the need to integrate nurse case workers on rounds, develop and implement a "Patient Care Team Order Set" that would empower disciplines to implement timely interventions within the scope of their training. Scripted huddles, increased physician involvement, as well as assessing high risk patients on rounds were also emphasized in the brainstorm sessions. The brainstorm sessions are an effort to engage the frontline healthcare workers to participate in the redesign efforts.

The patient care team can play an important role to ensure that standardized protocols are implemented and provide checks and balances, which is one of the key factors that led to near 100% compliance on the ventilator prevention efforts for ICU patients.

Optimizing bedside multidisciplinary care team rounds in various care settings is one of the most important opportunities in healthcare to identify and address patient needs in a timely manner and to include the patient and family as important members of the care team and to empower staff to their highest level of training.

Table 13-3. Patient, Family and Staff Surveys after Implementation of ICU Bedside Multidisciplinary Care Team Rounds with Intensivist.

Intensivist Multidisciplinary Care Team Rounds	
Patient/Family Surveys After Implementation	**Percent %**
Overall positive experience	86%
Increased ability to get questions answered	82%
Increased understanding of my family member's condition	86%
Understood what was discussed at bedside rounds	88%

Intensivist Led Multidisciplinary Care Team Rounds	
Staff Surveys After Implementation	**Percent %**
Better understanding of plan for the day	100%
Increased communication among team members	100%
Increased timeliness of tasks being performed	75%
Increased patient/family understanding	95%
Increased education of team members	85%

8. OUT OF HOSPITAL PULL

An aging population with increasing co-morbidities is increasing demands on acute care hospitals. Acute care hospitals have an alternative to adding new fixed costs with bricks and mortar and can aggressively implement the Toyota approach of developing "Pull" systems by partnering with other healthcare stakeholders. Expanding "out of hospital" pathways can significantly reduce costs, improve hospital flow, increase new revenues from opening up new beds, avoid new building costs and improve clinical outcomes. To optimize the opportunity, it is essential to invest in the quality of the pathways and partners in the same way Toyota has created very high expectations for the quality and service of their suppliers and partners. This is likely one of the most untapped opportunities in healthcare. Three "out of hospital pull" pathways will be discussed which include ventilator unit programs and transitional care units, and the most desired "home" care setting.

8.1 Transitional Care and Ventilator Unit Program

Transitional care and ventilator units can provide an important alternative to acute care hospitalization. There are significant opportunities to standardize post acute care pathways. It is important to recognize that a small subset of patients may be accounting for a large use of the resources. In one report from a medical surgical ICU, patients who stayed for 14 or more days accounted for 7.3% of the admissions but accounted for more than 40% of the total patient days (Weissman, 2005). Physicians must be engaged to participate in the development of these pathways. This will also likely require realignment of incentives.

Patients on mechanical ventilation account for less than 10 percent of admissions to intensive care units but they account for over 30% of bed days and resources (Lindsay and Bijwadia, 2004). Chronic ventilator dependent units have been developed to optimize the care for chronic ventilator patients (Gracey et al, 2000; Scheinhorn et al, 1997; Bagley and Cooney, 1997). Many of these reports have demonstrated reduced costs as well. Chronic ventilator dependent units, largely representing long-term acute care (LTAC) facilities, provide an important mechanism to improve flow through acute care facilities, thereby improving access for new admissions and associated revenues. One of the greatest concerns is the lack of pathways to care for chronic ventilator patients in the home and skilled nursing facilities. This creates a bottleneck and significant financial deterrent for LTAC facilities to accept patients, which may have poor weaning potential, resulting in difficulty in placing these patients. Medicaid ventilator patients are a very difficult subset of patients to place due to financial reimbursement.

Kindred Healthcare and Select Medical Corporation are the largest healthcare companies that specialize in long-term acute care facilities. Long-term acute care facilities provide services for Medicare patients who require care of at least 25 days on average. Select Medical Corporation has had rapid growth since 1997 and now operates 83 long-term acute care facilities, 75 of the 83 are "hospitals within hospitals". In 2002, Medicare began shifting reimbursement for LTAC facilities from cost basis to prospective payment system (Levin Associates).

8.2 Luther Midelfort Mayo Health System Nursing Home Ventilator Unit: The Patient's Perspective

In 1997, Luther Midelfort implemented several efforts to optimize care for ventilator patients in a skilled nursing facility. Key features in the success of the Lakeside Nursing Home Ventilator program, which has cared for over 23,000 ventilator patient days since 1997, include an emphasis on training and education, empowerment of staff, multidisciplinary approach to care, standardization, protocol development, and emphasis on socialization. We believe social engagement has a significant impact on the outcomes of our ventilator patients (Lindsay and Bijwadia, 2004). Most of the patients utilize their talking valve the majority of waking hours. Patients will eat their meals around a common table, engage in conversation, and participate in off-site outings. The majority of patient referrals had been residing in an ICU prior to transfer. This can result in depression, sleep wake disruption, and the loss of hope. We encourage hospital referrals to visit the unit prior to admission. We believe the socialization significantly impacts outcomes, provides hope for patients and families, and increases acceptance of a nursing home vent unit transfer. Socialization may be the single most important factor in the success of our ventilator model. We have promoted socialization for other rehabilitative patients in the Continuum of Care Program.

The pulmonary physician led weekly multidisciplinary bedside rounds focus on establishing the plan for the week. A nurse practitioner is dedicated to the unit and is available as needed. Respiratory therapy and nurse led weaning and the development of a "vent unit specialist program" for certified nurse assistants reflect the emphasis on empowerment of staff. We have reported outcomes that surpass any published report with over 100 patients and at reduced costs (Lindsay and Bijwadia, 2004). Table 13-4 demonstrates outcomes of the Lakeside ventilator unit relative to other reports in the literature. 67% of the patients admitted to the unit were liberated from mechanical ventilation. This is critically important as this success maintains the flow through the unit that positively impacts flow through the hospital. This is further facilitated through the Medical House Call Program, which provides the nurse practitioner who participates in the vent unit care and subsequent follow-up care post discharge. 28% of patients that presented to Lakeside Nursing Home Ventilator Unit had a neuromuscular diagnosis, which is significantly higher than other reports (Lindsay and Bijwadia, 2004). This subgroup of patients is the least likely to be liberated from mechanical ventilation. Through the use of an innovative protocol, many of these patients were converted to noninvasive positive pressure ventilation, allowing them to be discharged home. This results in significant patient satisfaction, cost savings and maintains flow through the ventilator unit and acute care hospitals. Establishing "pull" systems that match best practices will drive patient, family and physician support for an early discharge from the acute care hospital.

The establishment of the nursing home ventilator unit has resulted in a cost savings to more than 20 referring facilities of approximately $18.5 million. More than 50% of the admissions to the unit were from the Mayo Health System. These cost savings do not take into account the new revenues generated from new admissions as a result of opening up thousands of bed days at the referring facilities. It also does not take into account avoided new building costs. In contrast to other reports, this was implemented in a nursing home setting that is not part of Luther Midelfort.

Table 13-4. Lakeside Nursing Home Ventilator Unit Comparison to Other Reports in the Literature.

Ventilator Unit	% Weaned	Survival to Discharge	% Neuro	Cost per day
Lakeside NH	67	80	27	303
Scheinhorn 97	56	71	7.8	980
Bagley 97	38	53	19	630

8.3 Luther Midelfort' Mayo Health System Transitional Care Units at Bloomer and Osseo

The success of Luther Midelfort's Ventilator Program led to proposals to develop rehabilitative programs within underutilized rural critical access hospitals. The 1997 Budget Act gave rural hospitals with a critical access hospital designation the ability to receive cost based reimbursement for swing bed admissions to their facility (Greene, 2002). Transitional care units in rural hospitals can provide higher staffing ratios than skilled nursing facilities, allowing the rural facility to care for more complex patients. Other efforts that may help attract patients may include emphasis on socialization, music therapy, patient-centered and clinical outcomes, and the ability to be cared for close to home. There are financial gains for the acute and rural hospitals with these programs. These programs may help provide long-term financial viability for the rural hospitals, maintaining access for the community to healthcare, and providing jobs.

Key stakeholders from the acute and rural hospitals meet regularly to establish pathways and new programs, develop outcome measures, optimize coordination of care, develop needed educational programs for the transitional care unit staff, and break down obstacles that interfere with the success of the program. Figure 13-4 demonstrates growth of the Bloomer Transitional Care Unit. Figure 13-5 demonstrates patient satisfaction survey results that demonstrate patients strongly recommend the program to others.

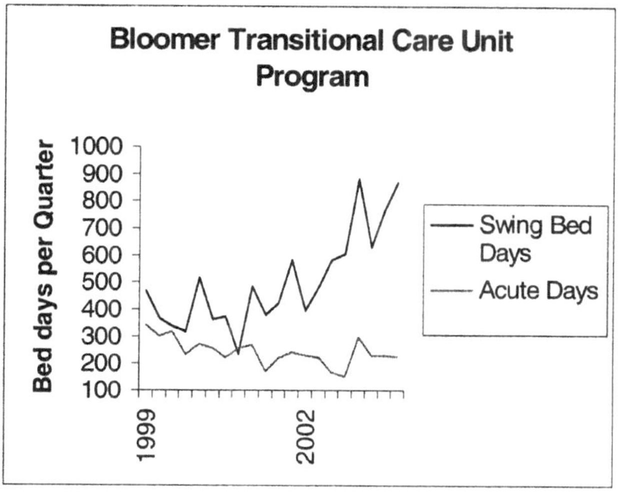

Figure 13-4. Growth of Bloomer Transitional Care Unit. Before mid 2001, Bloomer Hospital had ten consecutive quarters with negative net operating income. After implementation of the transitional care program in Mid 2001, nine of the next ten quarters had a positive net operating income.

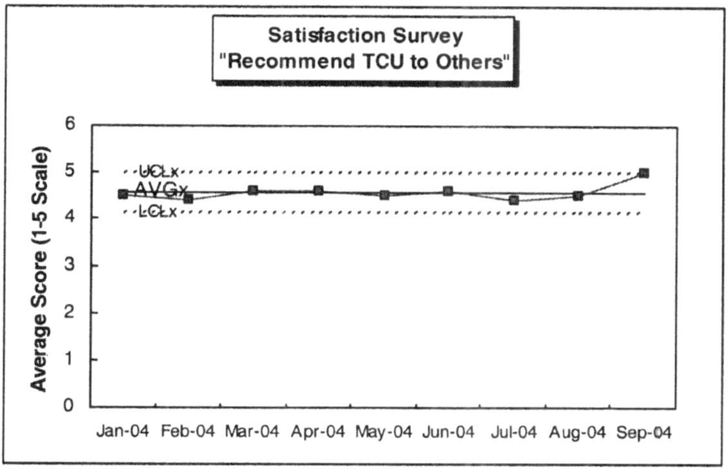

Figure 13-5. Patient-centered Outcome Measure that is Displayed on the Bloomer Transitional Care Unit dashboard

The Osseo Transitional Care Unit (TCU), which opened in January of 2004, developed a specialized focus on post cardiovascular surgery patients in addition to other diagnoses. The Osseo TCU staff and Luther Cardiovascular Surgery department have worked in collaboration to participate in bedside multidisciplinary rounds, peer review and the development of new pathways. Figure 13-6 demonstrates the growth of the Osseo TCU program.

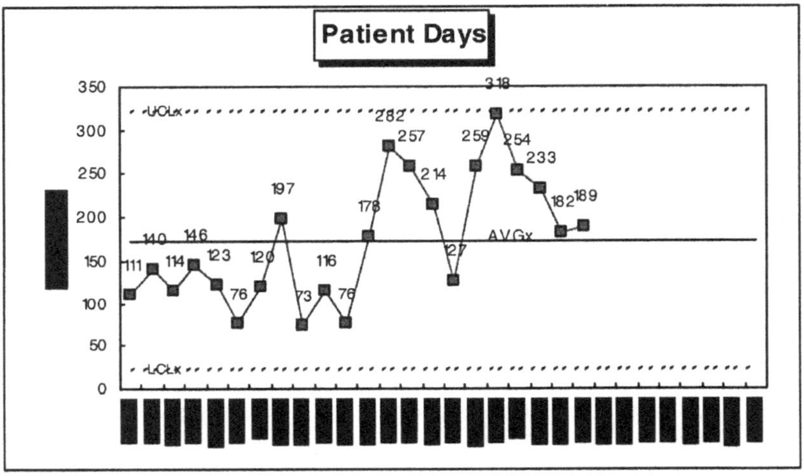

Figure 13-6. Growth of the Osseo Transitional Care Unit Program

It is important to note that Luther Midelfort's transitional care units use the same standardized protocols, multidisciplinary bedside care rounds and outcome measures. The Luther Transitional Care Program has cared for over 13,000 TCU bed days since 2001, expanded the ability to care for complex patients in our rural hospitals, improved the collaboration of our acute and rural hospitals, positively impacted the financial status and most importantly demonstrated excellent patient-centered and clinical outcomes.

9. NURSING HOME REDESIGN

There are several opportunities to positively impact the "pull" system in skilled nursing facilities. Factors that negatively impact the ability to utilize the skilled nursing facility as an effective "pull" system include concerns with high staff turnover, high infection and decubitus rates, poor acceptance of this care setting by patients, families and physicians. A study by the American Health Care Association demonstrated that, in 2002, turnover for certified nurse assistants was 71%. Turnover rates in 2002 were also very high for other positions: Director of Nursing positions 49.7%, Administrative RNs 35.5%, Staff RNs 48.9%, and LPNs 48.9% (American Health Care Association).

Involvement in interdisciplinary care and opportunities for advancement can positively impact staff turnover for certified nurse assistants (Banazsak-Hall and Hines, 1996; Maier, 2002). Other studies have demonstrated that advance practice providers can positively impact outcomes in long-term care facilities (Ryden et al, 2000). The Wellspring model was developed as a collaborative effort involving 11 non-profit organizations that are committed to empowered workforce, staff education, and implementation of best practices. They have demonstrated reduced staff turnover, improved federal survey performance, and Wellspring facilities had lower costs than other facilities. There were also observations of more proactive staff and improved resident and staff interaction (Stone and Reinhard, 2002).

We will go back and revisit our nursing home ventilator effort to further emphasize some important opportunities that can be broadly applied to other skilled nursing facilities. Table 13-5 below demonstrates two reports in the literature on ventilator outcomes in skilled nursing facilities. Table 6 demonstrates dashboard measures for our off-site nursing home ventilator unit.

Table 13-5. Nursing Home Ventilator Unit Comparison

Nursing Home Ventilator Comparison	% liberated from Vent	One Year Survival
Lakeside NH Vent Unit	67%	>80%
Ankrom	15	·9

Table 13-6. Nursing Home Ventilator Dashboard

Nursing Home Ventilator Dashboard 2005	Outcome Measure
Total Ventilator Bed Days since 1997	23,427 bed days
Hospital bed days/1000 NH vent bed days	3.0/1000 NH bed days
New Decubitus, stage 2 or higher/1000 vent bed days	.54/1000 NH bed days
Received Excellent Care by the Vent Unit Team	4.75/(Scale of 5)
Recommend the Vent Unit to Others	4.75/(Scale of 5)

It is clear that there are dramatic differences in the results from the two studies. Certainly patient mix or patient selection may contribute to some of the results. It is more likely that the disparity in results can be attributed to a number of factors that include the effective implementation of multi-disciplinary rounds, respiratory therapy and nurse directed weaning, empowerment of staff (including certified nurse assistants), training and education of the staff, 24 hour seven days per week pulmonary physician staff coverage, nurse practitioner participation, and emphasis on patient socialization. It would not be likely that pulmonary physicians, other staff, patients and family would likely promote transfer of a ventilator patient in an acute care hospital to a skilled nursing facility that has 19% survival at one year and liberation from mechanical ventilation of 15%. Clearly, the quality of the program will significantly impact the effectiveness of the "pull" system.

Table 13-7 demonstrates staff turnover in the ventilator unit relative to the facility as a whole. The ventilator unit staff turnover is significantly lower than the facility as a whole. The ability to retain highly trained staff impacts the confidence of the care team to care for complex patients.

Table 13-7. Staff Turnover in the Nursing Home Ventilator Unit

Ventilator Unit Staff Turnover	% Turnover/ year
Certified Nurse Assistant Turnover in the Entire Facility	76%
Certified Nurse Assistant Turnover in the Ventilator Unit	47%
Registered Nurse Staff Turnover in the Entire Facility	36%
Registered Nurse Staff Turnover in the Ventilator Unit	22%
Total Staff Turnover in the Entire Facility	64%
Total Staff Turnover in the Ventilator Unit	41%

In summary, there are significant opportunities to improve collaboration of acute care hospitals and skilled nursing facilities and develop effective "pull" systems. The success of these efforts will require significant investment of the strategies discussed above. There are also opportunities for skilled nursing facilities to develop collaboratives to ensure broad implementation of best practices.

10. HOME SETTING

The home setting is the most desired care setting, which should necessitate increased efforts and resources to ensure this option is available to our patients. The ability to design and innovate new cost-effective programs to care for patients in this care setting is critically important. In

2002, Luther Midelfort reviewed 100 consecutive readmissions to their acute care hospital. It was determined that 70% of the readmissions came from home, 19% from nursing homes. Importantly 54% of the patients had not been seen prior to their readmission and 40% of the readmissions were determined by the physician reviewers to have been preventable. In a *JAMA* study in 1999, patients that had one of the following risk factors -- age greater than 80, inadequate support systems, multiple active health problems, history of depression, moderate to severe functional impairment, multiple hospitalizations in prior six months, hospitalization in the past 30 days, fair or poor self rating of health, or history of non-adherence to therapeutic regimen -- had a significant reduction in readmissions when a nurse practitioner participated in the discharge planning and follow-up care (Naylor and Brooten). Importantly there was an approximately 50% reduction in Medicare dollars spent in the intervention group.

Several diagnoses can be cared for at home with good outcomes and at reduced costs including congestive heart failure, chronic obstructive pulmonary disease, deep vein thrombosis, and pneumonia (Leff and Burton, 1999; Leff and Burton, 1996; Koopman and Prandoni, 1996; Stewart and Horowitz, 2002). Comprehensive multidisciplinary home care programs can increase the rate of advance directives, decrease the rate of admissions to nursing homes, hospital, and deaths in the hospital (Morrison and Meier, 2004). The Continuum of Care Program promotes this care setting, most importantly as it is the most desired care setting and preferable to institutional care.

10.1 Supporting Structure and Foundation of the Continuum of Care Program

We will now review the supporting structures and foundation for the Continuum of Care Program. The supporting structures include Medical House Call Program, Continuum Pathways, communication, utilization management and the business case. These components of the Continuum of Care largely support the ability to care for patients across care settings and help provide the glue for the hospital "push" and hospital "pull" pathways. The business case will provide the motivation for leadership and administration to support efforts that may result in investments with partners and other stakeholders that do not share the same financial statement.

10.2 Luther Midelfort's Mayo Health System's Medical House Call Program

The Medical House Call Program is a new innovative effort that was developed to optimize the care as patients transition from the acute to alternate care settings through the use of advance practice providers. Clinical studies have demonstrated the positive impact that advance practice providers and outreach nurses can have on improving clinical outcomes in the home and nursing home. (Ryder et al, 2000; Stone and Reinhard, 2002, Naylor and Brooten, 1999; Stewart and Horowitz, 2002; Allen and Hazelett, 2004) The Medical House Call Program is an attempt at providing the needed network of advance practice providers and the commitment to develop effective multidisciplinary care teams to implement best practices across care settings. Luther Midelfort advance practice providers participate in numerous Continuum of Care Program components with a variety of responsibilities including participating in patient care team rounds in the acute care hospital, nursing home, and rural hospitals, and ventilator unit. The risk factors that have been identified from the *JAMA* study are utilized to identify hospital patients who are at risk for readmission. This will result in a Medical House Call consultation and appropriate follow-up as patients transition through the various care settings (Naylor and Brooten, 1999).

The Medical House Call Program has been developed as a non-profit corporation within an existing homecare company. The revenues for the program are generated from the billable services from the patient visits as well as from the hospital and departments for time committed to patient care efforts. Medicare reimburses 85% of the physician rate for advance practice provider visits in the hospital, home and nursing home.

Skilled Nursing Facilities welcome the ability for the Medical House Call providers to come to the patients and avoid the unnecessary and costly use of their nursing home staff to participate in the transportation and outpatient clinic visits that leave their facility understaffed and patients with increased vulnerability.

10.3 Continuum Pathways

Studies have demonstrated that concerted efforts to care for certain diagnoses or patient populations across care settings can improve clinical outcomes, reduce risk for readmission, and reduce costs. Concerted efforts across care settings have been linked to improved outcomes for stroke, congestive heart failure and other high risk patient populations (Ryder et al, 2000; Stone and Reinhard, 2002, Naylor and Brooten, 1999; Stewart and Horowitz, 2002; Allen and Hazelett, 2004). The goals of the Continuum

Pathways work effort are to engage the essential stakeholders in work teams to implement best practices of care for various diagnoses and high-risk patient populations across the various care settings. Most of these teams are linked with the Medical House Call advance practice providers who will follow patients as they transition from the hospital to home, nursing home and other settings. Luther Midelfort Continuum Pathway teams have included the following areas: nephrology, neurology, palliative care, cardiology, cardiovascular surgery, pulmonary, and orthopedics. Luther Midelfort's Pulmonary Continuum of Care Pathways work team has standardized educational efforts and competency training for nurses to increase the ability to care for complex respiratory patients including education on noninvasive positive pressure ventilation, and tracheostomy care. These efforts have resulted in discharge of home ventilator patients with follow-up from the advance practice providers. It has also increased our ability to accept tracheostomy and noninvasive positive pressure ventilation patients at our transitional care units, opening up new beds at our acute care hospital.

10.4 Communication

Communication is a critical component to fully implement the Continuum of Care model. To provide the most optimal care it is essential to ensure timely sharing of data and communication with all relevant stakeholders, especially the patient and family. Patients and families should also receive very clear discharge instructions in patient friendly language as they transition from one care setting to the next. It is also critically important to provide clear education and communication of the Continuum of Care Program, allowing patients to anticipate timely discharge and improving the acceptance of new programs and pathways outside the hospital designed to provide the highest quality, safe, patient-centered, cost-effective healthcare. Additional opportunities include the ability to optimize information technology, recognizing that patients will frequently transition from one facility to the next that may be utilizing alternate informational technology products that may not communicate.

Health care providers have differing views as to reasons for delayed discharge. In a survey of healthcare providers, nurses believed that discharge was frequently delayed because discharge plans were not in place. Physicians more likely attributed delays in lab tests, procedures, and availability of sub-acute beds (Minichiello and Auerback, 2001). This gap in communication reflects the importance of efforts to increase collaboration, teamwork and communication in optimizing coordination of patient care.

10.5 Utilization Management

Utilization management is providing the appropriate care in the appropriate setting. Traditional utilization management uses criteria, such as the McKesson's Interqual Criteria, to encourage appropriate utilization. However, Kalant reported that these criteria did not reflect well against a panel of experts (Kalant and Berlinguet, 2000). Therefore, it is critical for acute care hospitals to complement traditional utilization management. Optimizing evidence-based care through preventing unnecessary complications, and providing alternatives in less expensive care settings, avoiding unwanted end of life ICU care, and preventing cardiac arrests through rapid response teams will have far greater impact on optimizing utilization than providing individual feedback to physicians on their utilization data. The essential role of utilization management in the Continuum of Care Model is to engage physicians and look for opportunities based on the utilization data to develop new pathways. Luther Midelfort utilization data has led to the development of new Continuum Pathway teams to work on optimizing care for cardiology, nephrology, and pulmonary patients.

As we previously discussed, a small percent of admissions may be accounting for a large percent of the resources (Weissman, 2005). This is highlighted in the following case study.

10.6 Case Study: A Small Percent of Admissions May Account for a Large Percent of Bed Days and Resources.

Luther Midelfort facilitated and developed the off-site nursing home ventilator unit in 1997. The Lakeside Nursing Home Ventilator Unit has cared for 61 Luther ventilator admissions as well as numerous other complex respiratory and tracheostomy admissions. As the patients who could not wean took up a disproportionate number of the Lakeside Ventilator beds, there was decreased capacity for new admissions. This resulted in insufficient capacity to match demand leading to an increase in the average LOS for DRG 483 and 475 at Luther (See Table 13-8). This contributed to diversion of patients from our emergency room, cancellation of elective surgical cases and inability to accept new admissions. The table below demonstrates the relationship between inadequate capacity in the ventilator unit and the increase in average length of stay.

Table 13-8. Inadequate "Pull" System to Match Demand

Continuum of Care Case Study			
DRG 483 Vent 96 hours +	2001	2002	2004
Average LOS Luther Midelfort	23	26	36.5
Number of Cases Luther Midelfort	33	28	21
Number of New Vent Admissions Lakeside	21	19	1
DRG 475 Respiratory Dx with Ventilator			
Average LOS Luther Midelfort	6	9.2	13.4
Number of Cases Luther Midelfort	41	56	43

Luther Midelfort is now aggressively pursuing the development of a second off-site nursing home ventilator unit as well as considering the development of an LTAC hospital in the region. A pulmonary continuum pathways team has been formed, standardizing Luther Midelfort's respiratory protocols to allow our TCUs and skilled nursing facilities to have the skill set to care for tracheostomy and complex respiratory cases. We have developed pathways to care for ventilator patients at home.

Utilization management may play an important role in the monitoring of key DRGs and providing appropriate feedback into the Continuum of Care Program to ensure resources and "pull" systems are adequately developed. A virtual bed tower is far less expensive than bricks and mortar. Figure 13-7 demonstrates Luther's severity adjusted length of stay. It is evident that Luther's severity adjusted length of stay improved from 2000 to 2003, reflecting improvements in the "hospital push" and "hospital pull" pathways. The sharp increase in the severity-adjusted length of stay in 2004 was likely affected by inadequate capacity to match demand for respiratory patients, as well as other factors. Aggressive implementation of the Continuum of Care Program can positively impact the severity-adjusted length of stay. Utilization management should be closely linked to Continuum of Care efforts.

Table 13-9 represents a summary of evidence-based literature supporting various components of the Continuum of Care Program. Acute care hospitals that aggressively implement the following programs will realize improved patient survival, reduced hospital length of stay, reduced costs, and increased revenues.

Luther Midelfort has aggressively implemented a number of evidence based efforts and Continuum of Care components that will result in improved hospital flow (See Table 13-10).

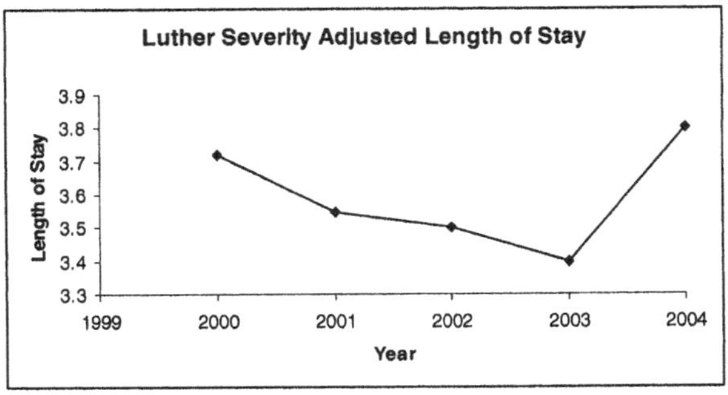

Figure 13-7. Luther's Severity Adjusted Length of Stay

10.7 Business Case

The development of a business case for the implementation of the Continuum of Care Program will be an important driver for leadership and administrative support of these efforts. Luther Midelfort's finance department performed an in-depth analysis looking at the financial impact of two components of the Continuum of Care Program in 2003. The financial analysis focused solely on the financial impact of these programs on our acute care facility, Luther Hospital. The Bloomer Transitional Care Unit and the off-site nursing home ventilator unit had a positive financial impact to Luther Hospital of $2.99 million in 2003. This did not take into account the impact the ventilator program had on other complex respiratory patients, such as tracheostomy and NPPV patients that were cared for in the ventilator unit.

The Continuum of Care Program, if aggressively implemented, can have a very positive financial impact for acute care facilities. Each component of the program should be valued on the benefits and impact that it provides to the other components and the Continuum of Care Program as a whole.

The Continuum of Care model, when fully implemented, will improve the financial impact on all care settings. Resources will be shifted to the home setting, the most desirable and least expensive care setting. The comprehensive implementation of the Continuum of Care Program should reduce hospital, Medicare, Medicaid, insurance and employer costs. Most importantly, the ability to improve outcomes and reduce costs increases the value of our healthcare product.

Table 13-9. Literature to Support Continuum of Care Components and Reduced Length of Stay

Component	Medical Literature Supporting Continuum of Care Program
Patient Care Team	Multidisciplinary team rounds reduce length of stay (LOS)
ICU	Intensive insulin reduces mortality, prolonged mechanical ventilation and intensive care NPPV reduces intubation, ICU LOS and ICU mortality Medical emergency team (MET) reduces mortality and LOS Respiratory therapy and RN directed weaning reduces time to extubation
Acute	Hospital based palliative care improves symptoms, reduces ICU and hospital LOS and costs Elevated blood sugars can increase hospital LOS and decrease likelihood of home discharge Patients with congestive heart failure, myocardial infarction, and community acquired pneumonia have significantly improved survival when established evidence based care is provided.
Ventilator/TCU	Chronic ventilator dependent units can improve outcomes, decrease hospital bed days and costs
Nursing Home	Nursing home collaborative efforts, use of advance practice providers, engaging certified nurse assistants in care rounds improve outcomes and reduce staff turnover.
Home	A number of diagnoses can be treated at home with similar outcomes of reduced costs, avoiding hospitalization Multidisciplinary home care programs can result in higher rates of advanced directives, decreased rate of admission to nursing home, hospital and death in the hospital,
Medical House Call and Continuum Pathways	Advance practice providers caring for high risk patients can reduce readmissions and Medicare dollars spent Concerted efforts across care settings can improve outcomes, reduce readmissions for a number of diagnoses

Table 13-10. Luther Midelfort's Virtual Bed Tower

Luther Midelfort Implementation of Continuum of Care Program Components	
NPPV Protocol Cases 97-04	3304
Transitional Care Unit Bed Days 01 to Mid 05	13,625
Lakeside NH Bed Days Vent 97-04	23,424
Medical House Call Encounters	1619
Continuum Pathway Teams Initiated	7

10.7.1 People and Processes

It is essential to empower our frontline workers to innovate and actively participate in redesigning our healthcare system. The Continuum of Care Program will aggressively utilize the concepts offered by Toyota as well as the IDEO Corporation. People will be empowered to their highest level of training. Processes will be developed with checks and balances to ensure high compliance of evidence based care. Efforts to reduce waste and avoid unnecessary paperwork and other non-valued steps will be encouraged (Liker, 2004; Kelley, 2001).

10.7.2 Leadership and Administrative Support

The successful implementation of the Continuum of Care Program depends on the proper alignment and administrative structure that support collaboration across all care settings and components of the Continuum of Care Program. It must be recognized that silos in healthcare are the greatest obstacles to providing safe, cost-effective, patient-centered healthcare. Leadership can help facilitate innovation and redesign of our healthcare system through empowerment of frontline workers, rewarding and celebrating successes, breaking down silos and recognizing that physician autonomy can be a significant obstacle to designing and innovating new processes and systems of care that are desperately needed in our healthcare system. Figure 13-8 demonstrates the factors that need to be addressed to successfully implement the Continuum of Care Program.

11. CASES TO DEMONSTRATE TO DEMONSTRATE THE STRENGTH OF THE CONTINUUM OF CARE PROGRAM.

11.1 Case 1: Avoiding the ICU and Improving Outcomes

Patient with Chronic Obstructive Pulmonary Disease (COPD) and pulmonary edema, was seen in the emergency room at 8 am in severe respiratory distress. Arterial blood gas studies at 8 am demonstrated a pH of 7.23, pCO_2 of 79 (on 15 liters of oxygen). The respiratory therapist initiated the respiratory therapy directed NPPV protocol. The patient clinically improved with a follow-up ABG at noon, demonstrating a pH 7.41, pCO_2 36, and pO_2 78 (eight liters of oxygen). The patient was admitted to telemetry avoiding the ICU.

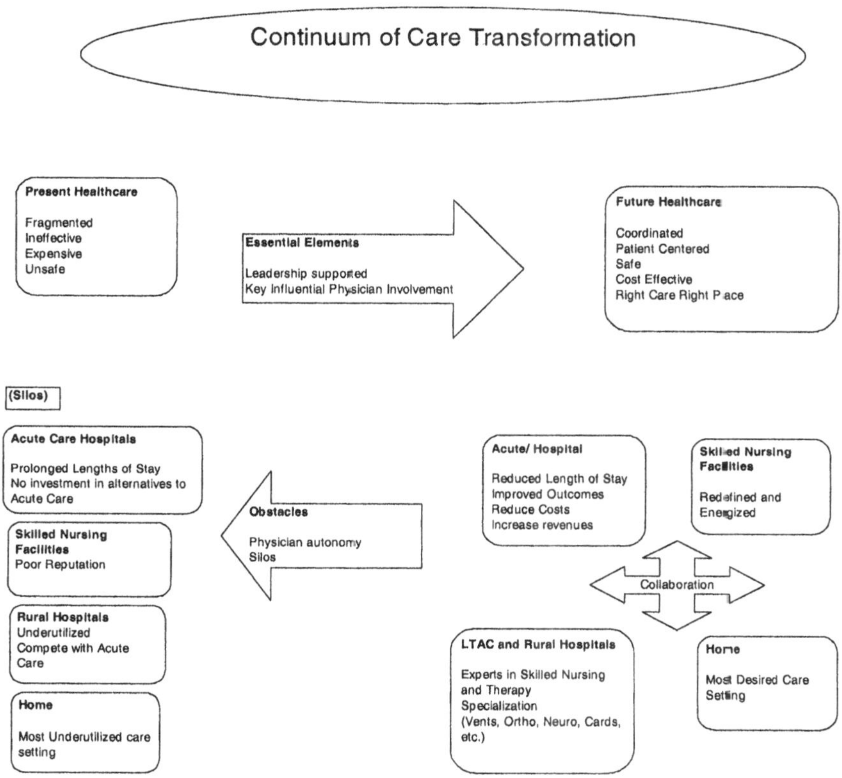

Figure 13-8. Transformation to the Continuum of Care Program

11.2 Case 2: Second Case in 24 Hours

Patient was admitted with COPD and an occipital stroke. The patient developed respiratory distress at 2 am. An arterial blood gas studies demonstrated hypercapnic respiratory failure with a pH of 7.26, pCO2 of 92. The patient was placed on the respiratory therapy directed NPPV protocol on the floor. Follow-up blood gas studies at 6 am were much improved with a pH of 7.39, pCO2 of 66. The patient was not transferred to the ICU.

Pearls

1. Cases 1 and 2 are two patients who were cared for in the same 24 hour period that were in respiratory failure. Both patients were started on NPPV protocol initiated by respiratory therapy.
2. Both patients not only avoided intubation but also avoided the ICU.
3. NPPV use reduces the need for intubation, improves outcomes, and avoids unnecessary ICU care and associated costs.
4. NPPV protocol also empowers respiratory therapy staff and improves job satisfaction.

11.3 Case 3: Best Practices Can Provide Very Effective "Pull Systems"

Patient with severe kyphoscoliosis and restrictive and obstructive lung disease. The patient was admitted to Luther Hospital for acute respiratory failure. The patient was hospitalized for several weeks and was transferred to the off-site nursing home ventilator unit. After several months, the patient was successfully converted to NPPV and discharged home. The Medical House Call advance practice provider participated on team rounds at the ventilator unit and provided home follow-up for several months post discharge. This patient has now been successfully cared for at home for more than 1 year without readmission.

Pearls

1. This case demonstrates the benefits of investing in each of the care settings. This patient had very high risk factors for readmission. The Nurse Practitioner who cared for the patient in the Nursing Home Ventilator Unit also cared for the patient at home.
2. This case also demonstrates the benefits of working with a single durable medical equipment provider who provided the equipment and supplies in the nursing home ventilator unit and the home supplies.
3. The ability to convert patients from mechanical ventilation to NPPV increases the likelihood of home discharge, maintains flow through the ventilator unit and acute care hospitals, and dramatically reduces the cost of care.

11.4 Case 4. Invest in all the Care Settings as Patients Transition from one Setting to the Next.

An octagenarian was admitted to Luther Hospital with pneumonia and myocardial infarction. He had a prolonged hospitalization and was transferred to the Osseo Transitional Care Unit where the patient received extensive rehabilitation. The patient was subsequently discharged home with follow-up from the Medical House Call advance practice provider.

Pearls

1. This case demonstrates the commitment of the Continuum of Care Program and the investment in each of the care settings.
2. The Transitional Care Unit has a much higher nursing ratio and collaborates with the Cardiovascular Surgery program at Luther.
3. The mortality rate for skilled nursing facilities caring for post CABG patients has been reported as high as 13%. The mortality rate for post CABG patients in the TCU program is very low.
4. The Medical House Call program saw the patient in the home setting 3 days after discharge from the TCU program.
5. Nurse Practitioner programs that have evaluated patients in the hospital with follow-up in the home have resulted in a significant reduction in readmissions and in one report a 50% reduction in Medicare dollars spent (Naylor and Brooten, 1999).

11.5 Case 5. Advance Directives and Advance Care Plans

Patient is an elderly male with cardiomyopathy and progressive deterioration of his health. The patient has had increasing dyspnea, need for multiple procedures to withdrawal fluid form his lung, and decreased mobility. The patient's daughter viewed a video called "Choices" that described the benefit of advance directives and advance care planning. The development of the video was a community effort to improve community education on advance directives, advance care planning and end of life care. As a result of watching the video, the daughter initiated discussion with her father regarding his wishes and an advance directive and care plan was discussed and implemented. Within a couple of weeks of filling out the advance directives, the patient was involved in a car accident and was brought to the emergency room. The daughter respected her father's wishes and no heroic measures were implemented. The daughter shared her sense of relief with the physician that she knew her father's wishes.

Pearls

1. This case demonstrates the importance of advanced directives and advance care planning, respecting patient wishes and the impact it has on allowing patients to have a dignified death and avoid unnecessary and costly intensive care in patients that have serious chronic illness.
2. The studies have demonstrated that the majority of patients with chronic illness have not filled out an advanced directive. The Continuum of Care Program would emphasize the importance of advanced directives and advance care planning. Best practices such as the LaCrosse effort that demonstrated the impact of a community educational effort would be encouraged.
3. Tools such as Luther Midelfort's "Choices Video" which educates patients and families on advance directives and advance care plan should be developed.

12. CONCLUSIONS

The Continuum of Care Program recognizes the importance of the shared opportunities through partnerships and collaboration, the investment in each of the care settings, and that the most cost-effective care will emphasize moving each patient to their highest level of independence in the most appropriate care setting. We must replace the word discharge from a particular care setting to continuity and collaboration across all care settings. Dashboards that provide transparency of patient-centered and clinical outcomes will help care teams work toward establishing best practices that are strong drivers. There is an opportunity with dedicated innovative leadership and strategic planning to successfully spread the strengths of this program across healthcare organizations. The Continuum of Care Program will be an instrumental partner to providing patients with the highest quality, safe, patient-centered, cost-effective healthcare. Importantly, acute care facilities, long-term acute care facilities, rural critical access hospitals, skilled nursing facilities, homecare agencies can aggressively participate in this model of care to improve patient care as well as positively impact their revenue streams.

It is important to acknowledge the commitment of Luther Midelfort leadership who has endorsed this program, especially Dr. Terry Borman who has provided strong support for the program growth and development. It is also important to recognize Dr. Wiechmann and the cardiovascular surgical team for their enthusiastic support and commitment to this program. Dr. Lokkesmoe, the leadership of the Continuum of Care Program components, the finance department, quality resources department and numerous other Luther Midelfort employees have provided significant contribution to the success of the program. It is important to conclude that the program is in the very early stages of development and the greatest opportunities and successes of this program have yet to be accomplished.

13. REFERENCES

Allen K, Hazelett S. (2004). Improving stroke outcomes: implementation of a post discharge care management model. *JCOM*. Nov 11(11):707-14.

American Health Care Association Analysis of 2002 long term care staffing. www.ahca.org

Ankrom MA, Barofsky I. (1998). What happens to patients in a Nursing Home-Based Chronic Ventilator Unit: A Five-Year Retrospective Review of Patients and Outcomes. *Annals of Long-Term Care*; 6(10):309-314.

Bagley PH, Cooney E. A (1997). Community-based regional ventilator weaning unit: development and outcomes. *Chest*. Apr;111(4):1024-1029.

Banazsak-Holl J, Hines MA. (1996). Factors associated with nursing home staff turnover. *The Gerontologist*; 36 (4): 512-517.

Bellomo R. Goldsmith D. (2004). Prospective controlled trial of effect of medical emergency team on postoperative morbidity and mortality rates. *Crit Care Med*; 32:916-21.

Callahan EH, Thomas DC. (2002). Geriatric hospital medicine. *Med Clin North Am.* 84 (4):707-29. Review

Carey JS, Parker JP. (2003). Hospital discharge to other healthcare facilities: impact on in-hospital mortality. *J Am Coll Surg*. 197(5):806-12.

Consensus Trial Study Group.(1987). Effects of enalapril on mortality in severe congestive heart failure. Results of the Cooperative North Scandinavian Enalapril Survival Study (Consensus). *N Engl J Med.* 316(23):1429-35.

Cook CH, Martin LC. (1999). Survival of critically ill surgical patients discharged to extended care facilities. *J Am Coll Surg*. Nov; 189(5): 437-41.

Decker FH, Gruhn P. Results of 2002 American Health Care Association Survey of Nursing Staff Vacancy and Turnover in Nursing Homes. www.ahca.org

Dodek PM, Raboud J. (2003). Explicit approach to rounds in an ICU improves communication and satisfaction of providers. *Intensive Care Med.* 29(9):1584-8.

Garibaldi R, Brodine S, et al. (1981). Infections among patients in nursing homes: policies, prevalence, problems. *N Engl J Med* 305: 731-735.

Gracey DR, Hardy DC, Koenig GE. (2000). The chronic ventilator-dependent unit: A lower-cost alternative to intensive care. *Mayo Clin Proc*. 75 (5), 445-449.

Greene J. (2002). Rural renewal. As momentum builds, critical access hospital program shows signs of success. *Hosp Health Netw*. 76(4):50-54, 2.

Institute of Medicine (1999). To Err is Human: Building a Safer Health System. Linda T. Kohn, Janet M. Corrigan, and Molla S. Donaldson, eds. Washington, D.C.: National Academy Press.

Institute of Medicine (2001). Crossing the Quality Chasm: A New Health System for the 21st Century. Linda T. Kohn, Janet M. Corrigan, and Molla S. Donaldson, eds. Washington, D.C.: National Academy Press.

Kalant N., Berlinguet M. (2000). How valid are utilization review tools in assessing appropriate use of acute care beds? *CMAJ* 162 (13).

Keenan SP, Sinuff T. (2004). Does noninvasive positive pressure ventilation improve outcome in acute hypoxemic respiratory failure? A systematic review. *Crit Care Med*, 32:2516-2523.

Kelley, L. (2001). *The Art of Innovation*. Doubleday.

Kollef M, Shapiro S. (1997). A randomized controlled trial of protocol –directed versus physician-directed weaning from mechanical ventilation. *Crit Care Med* 25: 567-574.

Koopman MM, Prandoni P. (1996). Treatment of venous thrombosis with intravenous unfractionated heparin administered in the hospital as compared with subcutaneous low molecular weight heparin administered at home. *N Engl J Med* Mar 14;334(11):682-687.

Law Watch, CMS Proposes expansion of post acute care transfer payment policy. www.foley.com.

Leape LL, Cullen DJ. (1999). Pharmacist participation on physician rounds and adverse drug events in the intensive care unit. *JAMA*. Jul 21; 282(3): 267-70.

Leff B, Burton JR. (1996). Acute Medical Care in the home. *J Am Geriatr Soc*. 44(5):603-5.

Leff B, Burton JR. (1999). Home Hospital Program: A pilot Study. *J Am Geriatr Soc*. 47(6): 697-702.

Liker, J. (2004). The Toyota Way. McGraw-Hill.

Lindsay ME, Bijwadia JS. (2004). Shifting care of chronic ventilator- dependent patients from the intensive care unit to the nursing home. *Jt Comm J Qual Saf.* 30(5) 257-65.

Lynne J, Goldstein NE. (2003). Advance care planning for fatal chronic illness: avoiding commonplace errors and unwarranted suffering. *Ann Intern Med*. 138(10):812-818.

Maier G. (2002). Career ladders: an important element in CNA retention. *Geriatr Nurs*. 23(4):217-219.

Malone DC, Shaban HM. (2001). Adherence to ATS Guidelines for Hospitalized Patients with Community –Acquired Pneumonia. *Ann Pharmacother*. 35:1180-5.

Marelich GP, Murin S. (2000). Protocol weaning of mechanical ventilation in medical and surgical patients by respiratory care practitioners and nurses: Effect on weaning time and incidence of ventilator-associated pneumonia. *Chest* 118:459-467.

McGlynn EA, Asch SM. (2003). The Quality of health care delivered to adults in the United States. *N Engl J Med* 26; 348:2635-45.

Minichiello TM, Auerback AD. (2001). Caregiver perceptions of the reasons for delayed hospital discharge. *Eff Clin Pract*. 4(6):250-5.

Morrison RS, Meier DE. (2004). Clinical practice. Palliative care. *N Engl J Med*. 17;3550(25):3582-90.

National Healthcare Expenditures: Centers for Medicare and Medicaid Services. www.cms.hhs.gov

Naylor MD, Brooten D. (1999). Comprehensive discharge planning and home follow-up of hospitalized elders: a randomized clinical trial. *JAMA*. Feb 17; 281(7):613-20.

Plant PK, Owen JL. (2000). Early use of non-invasive ventilation for acute exacerbations of chronic obstructive pulmonary disease on general respiratory wards: A multi-centre randomized controlled trial. *Lancet* 355:1931-1935.

Pfeffer MA, Braunwald E. (1992). Effect of captopril on mortality and morbidity in patients with left ventricular dysfunction after myocardial infarction. Results of the survival and ventricular enlargement trial. The SAVE Investigators. *N Engl J Med*. 327(10):669-677.

Private Equity Firms Target Long-Term Acute Care Hospitals. www.levin associates.com.

Rand Health. Research Highlights. The First National Report Card on Quality of Health Care in America. www.rand.org.

Resar R, Pronovost P. (2005). Using a bundle approach to improve ventilator care processes and reduce ventilator associated pneumonia. *Jt Comm J Qual Patient Saf.* 31 (5):243-8.

Ryden MB, Snyder M, Gross CR, et al. (2000). Value-added outcomes: the use of advanced practice nurses in long-term facilities. *Geront.* (6):654-662.

San Francisco Business Times (2005). Cost of building new hospitals. August 29. www.bizjournals.com

Scheinhorn DJ, Chao DC, Stern-Hassenpflug MA, LaBree LD, Hetsley DJ. (1997). Post-ICU mechanical ventilation: treatment of 1123 patients at a regional weaning center. *Chest* 111(6):1654-1659.

Smucker DR. (2004). Hospice and the continuum of primary care. *Clinics in Family Practice.* Vol. 6, Number 4.

Stewart S, Horowitz JD. (2002). Home-based intervention in congestive heart failure. *Circulation.* Jun 18;105(24):2861-6.

Stone RI, Reinhard SC. (2002). Evaluation of the Wellspring model for improving nursing home quality. Institute for the Future of Aging Services, American Association of Homes and Services for the Aging. August.

Umpierrez GE, Isaacs SD. (2002). Hyperglycemia: An independent marker of in-hospital mortality in patients with undiagnosed diabetes. *J Clin Endocrinol Medab* 87:978-82.

Van den Berghe G, Bouillon R. (2003). Optimal control of glycemia among critically ill patients. *JAMA.* Oct 15; 290 (15): 2041-7.

Weissman Charles. (2005). The enhanced postoperative care system. *J Clin Anesth.* Jun;17(4):314-22.

Wolosin Robert J (2003). Largest Study of Patients of Patient Satisfaction Ever Conducted. *Press Ganey*; Vol. VII, August.

Young MP, Gooder VJ, Oltermann MH, et al. (1998). The impact of a multidisciplinary approach on caring for ventilator-dependent patients. *Int J Qual Health Care.* 10(1):15-26.

Chapter 14

A LOGISTICS APPROACH FOR HOSPITAL PROCESS IMPROVEMENTS

Jan Vissers[1]

Institute for Health Policy and Management, Erasmus University Medical Centre, Rotterdam, Prismant institute for Health Management Development, Utrecht and Eindhoven University of Technology, Eindhoven, The Netherlands

Abstract: This chapter proposes a sustainable logistics approach for hospital process management as an alternative to traditional quality management. The underlying concepts are discussed and illustrated with material from case studies regarding cardiology patient flows. The distinctions between unit logistics, chain logistics and their combination network logistics are used to illustrate the focus of logistic improvement. A framework for hospital production control offers support for a systematic matching of supply and demand at different levels of planning and control. The concept of a focused factory and business unit is used to create a context for patient group management. These three concepts are used for a systematic and sustainable approach for hospital process improvement, as illustrated for an important patient flow in hospitals, i.e. cardiology.

Key words: Health operations management, patient flow logistics, patient group management, cardiology

[1] The author would like to thank his colleague Geerhard de Vries for his work on objective setting for process management in hospitals and the hospitals in which the projects on cardiology process improvement took place.

1. INTRODUCTION

How can service improvements be both realized and sustained in hospital processes? Over the years many improvements have been started successfully but did not survive the pilot phase. These efforts were often part of a quality management improvement program, and they demonstrated clearly that considerable gain is to be made in hospital process management. However, these improvements were not sustained for a number of reasons: the innovation concerned only an isolated process for a specific group of patients, no consideration was given to the interaction between processes and resources, and process monitoring and process management was lacking. To make improvements in process management sustainable, a more fundamental approach is required.

In general, hospitals do not manage the patient processes but rather manage departments or units such as outpatient clinics, diagnostic departments, operating theatres and wards. The process of the patient as such (referral, outpatient first visit to a specialist, diagnostic tests, second visit, admission to a ward, surgical procedure, rehabilitation, outpatient follow-up, referral back) is not yet mastered by hospital planning. One of the reasons is that no one is responsible for the whole trajectory of patients through the system. Therefore, no function assures that processes of individual patients are executed within the range of targets set for their patient groups.

This contribution will focus on an operations management approach to hospital process improvements, in which:

- Groups of patients are distinguished for which care delivery will be organized.
- Processes are described in main lines, using the expert knowledge of medical and other care professionals
- Care processes are organized in different ways, depending on their characteristics in terms of elective/acute, degree of predictability, use of bottleneck resources, etc.
- Responsibilities for process management are clarified, including objective setting for the performance of the process, and monitoring the performance of processes.
- Corrective measures are taken when processes are no longer within the bandwidth defined for its performance.

The chapter will describe these steps, illustrated with examples for cardiology. This description will be preceded with a section on principles of operations management, such as the distinction between logistics of units and chains and their combination, i.e. network logistics, and the systematic matching of demand and supply at different levels of planning, i.e. a framework for production control of hospitals.

2. AN OPERATIONS MANAGEMENT CONTEXT FOR HOSPITAL PROCESS IMPROVEMENT[2]

2.1. Unit, chain and network logistics

In our logistic approach we distinguish between unit logistics, chain logistics and network logistics. Units carry out the same types of operation for different types of patients whereas processes/chains represent a series of different operations (undertaken in different units) for the same type of patient. Network logistics combines both perspectives. Figure 14-1 illustrates these different logistical perspectives for a hospital setting. It describes a hospital as a representation of units and chains.

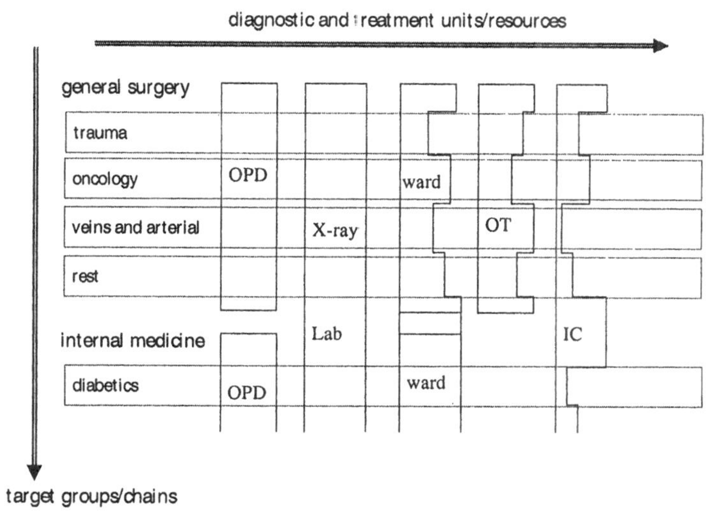

Figure 14-1. Unit, chain and network perspectives (OPD = outpatient department, OT = operating theatres, IC = intensive care)

[2] Based on Vissers and Beech (2005)

As can be seen from the example, general surgery has its own outpatient facilities that are not shared with, for instance, general medicine. Diagnostic departments, such as radiology and pathology, are shared by all patient groups and specialties. Wards are shared by the different patient groups within a specialty, with sharing of beds between specialties limited to overflow. In addition, not all patient groups use the ward at a similar level. All surgical patient groups share the operating theatre department, though some groups are treated without an intervention. The IC is again shared by all specialties, though the use of the IC differs much between patient groups.

The unit perspective is represented by the units: OPD, X-ray/lab, ward, OT and IC. Managers of these units are responsible for the running of the unit, for the level of service the unit offers to physicians requiring a service on behalf of their patients, and for the efficient use of the resources available. This is regarded as a total responsibility. The unit's concern is the total flow of all patients requiring a service of the unit, as this determines the prime objective of the unit, i.e. reaching a high but balanced use of resources without peaks and troughs in the workload during the hours of the day and days of the week. High occupancy level or use is seen as an important indicator of the 'efficiency' of the unit while balanced use is important not only for efficiency but also for the working climate of the personnel in the unit. Additional aims from the perspective of the unit are to produce the amount of output required with as less resources as possible or to produce as much output as possible with the amount of resources available (capacity management). The focus of unit logistics is therefore on the total flow of the patients using the unit, and on the effect of this flow on the use of resources and the workload of personnel.

The chain perspective is represented by patient groups, i.e. trauma patients, oncology patients, etc.. The focus of this perspective is on the total process of the patient, using different units on their journey through the hospital. The chain perspective strives to optimize this process according to some targets, which all relate to the time dimension. Typical targets are: short access time, short throughput time, and short in-process waiting times. Short throughput time can be reached by combining operations in one visit to the OPD, instead of having to come twice, or by having finished the diagnostic phase before the admission. The prime objective of the chain perspective is to maximize the service level for patients belonging to a certain patient group. As the focus is on the one patient group considered, it is difficult to look at the efficiency of the chain, in terms of use of resources. Resources are, in general, not allocated to patient groups, but to specialties. Therefore, efficiency issues can only be considered at the level of flows from all patient groups belonging to the specialty.

Network logistics combines the unit and the chain perspectives. It draws on the notion that optimization of the service in the chains needs to be balanced with efficiency in the use of resources in the units. A network logistics approach will make explicit any trade-off to be made between the service level provided in the chains and the utilization of resources in the units: for example, a desire to improve patient access to diagnostic services by making these services available for 24 hours per day might have a negative impact on the performance of diagnostic departments.

For a network logistics approach, ideally all chains and all units (i.e. the whole hospital) need to be included. However, this might be regarded as too complex, especially for a change to improve the performance of the process for a single patient group. There might be a desire to address such a change via a chain logistics approach. However, one should also strive for a network logistics approach by, for example, including all patient groups of the relevant specialty in the analysis. This would make it possible to look at the impact of the change on the use of resources available for both the specialty as a whole and for the other patient groups within it.

Consider a change that aims to improve patient access to physiotherapy by stroke patients. If there is a limited supply of physiotherapy services, improvements in the process of care for stroke patients might result in a reduced level of service for other patient groups both within neurology (the specialty that treats stroke patients) and within other specialties containing patient groups which require physiotherapy. These adverse consequences would go unnoticed if only a chain logistics approach is adopted. A network logistics approach therefore helps to avoid a situation where an improvement in one process goes unnoticed at the expense of a drawback for other processes.

The OM approach implies making explicit the choices to be made in a systems perspective. This serves also as a warrant for sub optimization, i.e. an improvement in one part of the system goes at the expense of the functioning of the system as a whole. Table 14-1 summarizes the main differences between the unit, chain and network logistics approach.

Table 14-1. Differences between the unit, chain and network logistics approaches

Perspective **Item**	**Unit logistics approach**	**Chain logistics approach**	**Network Logistics Approach**
Focus points	Resource utilization Workload control	Service level	Trade off between service level and resource utilization
Strong point	Capacity management	Process management	Combination
Weak point	Not process oriented	Not related to the use of resources	More effort
Suitable for	Efficiency analysis of OT's, OPD's, etc.	(Re)design of a process	Redesign and efficiency

2.2. A framework for hospital production control

A further feature of our approach is the distinction between the levels of logistic decision-making, i.e. operational, tactical and strategic. The framework we use as a reference in this contribution is a hierarchical framework for production control of hospitals that deals with the balance between service and efficiency, at all levels of planning and control. It shows analogies to frameworks used in industrial settings for manufacturing organizations. The framework is based on an analysis of the design requirements for hospital production control systems (De Vries, Bertrand and Vissers (1999)) and builds on the production control design concepts developed in Bertrand et al. (1990). The design requirements are translated into the control functions at different levels of planning required for hospital production control. This translation is built on notions of the hospital as a virtual organization with patient groups as business units and a focused factory approach for the production control per business unit. In short we can distinguish a number of production control functions, which can be positioned at different levels of planning in a framework (see Table 14-2).

Table 14-2. Production control functions distinguished in the planning framework for hospitals

	Decision Focus
1.	Range of services, markets and product groups, long-term resource requirements, centrally coordinated scarce resources; contracted annual patient volumes, target service levels
2.	Amount of resources available at annual level to specialties and patient groups, regulations regarding resource-use
3.	Time-phased allocation of shared resources, involving specialist-time detailed number of patients per period
4.	Urgency and service requirements, planning guidelines per patient group
5.	Scheduling of individual patients, according to guidelines at patient group level and resource-use regulations at resource level.

At the highest level decisions have to be made on the range of services provided, the markets one wants to operate in and the product groups for each market. Also decisions have to be made on the long term resource requirements of the hospital, which scarce resources are centrally coordinated, what level of annual patient volumes one wants to achieve, what service philosophy will be used and what level of service one wants to target for. These are all longer term strategic decisions, which essentially do not belong to the domain of OM, but which have impact on the management of operations at shorter terms.

The next level focuses on the amount of resources that is available annually to specialties and patient groups, to ensure that the contracted annual patient volume can be realized. At this level the rules for using the resources also need to be established to ensure that the target service and efficiency levels are achieved. At the third level, the focus is on the allocation of shared resources in time, taking into account the availability of specialists and seasonal developments. This requires more insight into the detailed numbers per patient group per period within the year. At level four, the urgency and service requirements per patient group need to be established, and the planning guidelines per patient group. The fifth level regards the scheduling of individual patients, according to the planning guidelines for the patient group and the resource-use regulations for the resources involved.

Though the planning framework seems to be working only top down, the need for each level and the requirements for coordination are established bottom-up. At the lowest level, individual patients are coupled to resources in the day-to-day scheduling. This level in the framework is called **patient planning and control**. The way patients are operationally scheduled needs to be governed by rules established at patient group level. Oncology patients, for instance, have different urgency and service requirements from patients with varicose veins. Therefore, operational scheduling of patients needs to be governed by what we called **patient group planning and control**. To allow for the planning of a patient group resources need to be allocated, taking into account the availability of specialists and personnel. This level is called **resources planning and control**, and includes also the time-phased allocation of resources. The level of resources required results from the annual patient volumes contracted, and the service and efficiency levels targeted for. This level is called **patient volume planning and control**. Finally, the volume level is governed by the strategic planning level, where, for instance, decisions are taken about which resources need to be shared or not. This level is called **strategic planning**. At this level there is no control involved.

These levels of planning can be further elaborated (Vissers, Bertrand and de Vries, 2001), resulting in the planning framework as shown in Figure 14-2. The framework shows that every level needs a horizontal control mechanism to match patient flows with resources and that vertical control mechanisms are required to set the targets for lower levels (feed forward) or to check whether activities develop within the boundaries set by higher levels (feedback).

The framework can be used as a reference for improving the capability of the hospitals to deal with process development within the wider context of the hospitals as a whole.

2.3. Iso-process patient groups as business units

An important third feature of our approach is that iso-processes are considered as basis for production control of hospital processes. Iso-process grouping is a way of classifying patients according to the trajectory that patients follow through their patient journey. There are different ways to classify hospital products, depending on the focus of the classification.

Given that processes or chains generate a service for a client, the focus for product classifications is driven by the requirements of the client. In particular, clients want a service that is efficient (for example, unnecessary delays in treatment are avoided) and effective (for example, evidenced based practices are used). In turn, the achievement of these goals is likely to increase levels of client satisfaction. Hence, in processes or chains, the operations manager wants a product classification that allows them to plan and monitor the efficient and effective delivery of products.

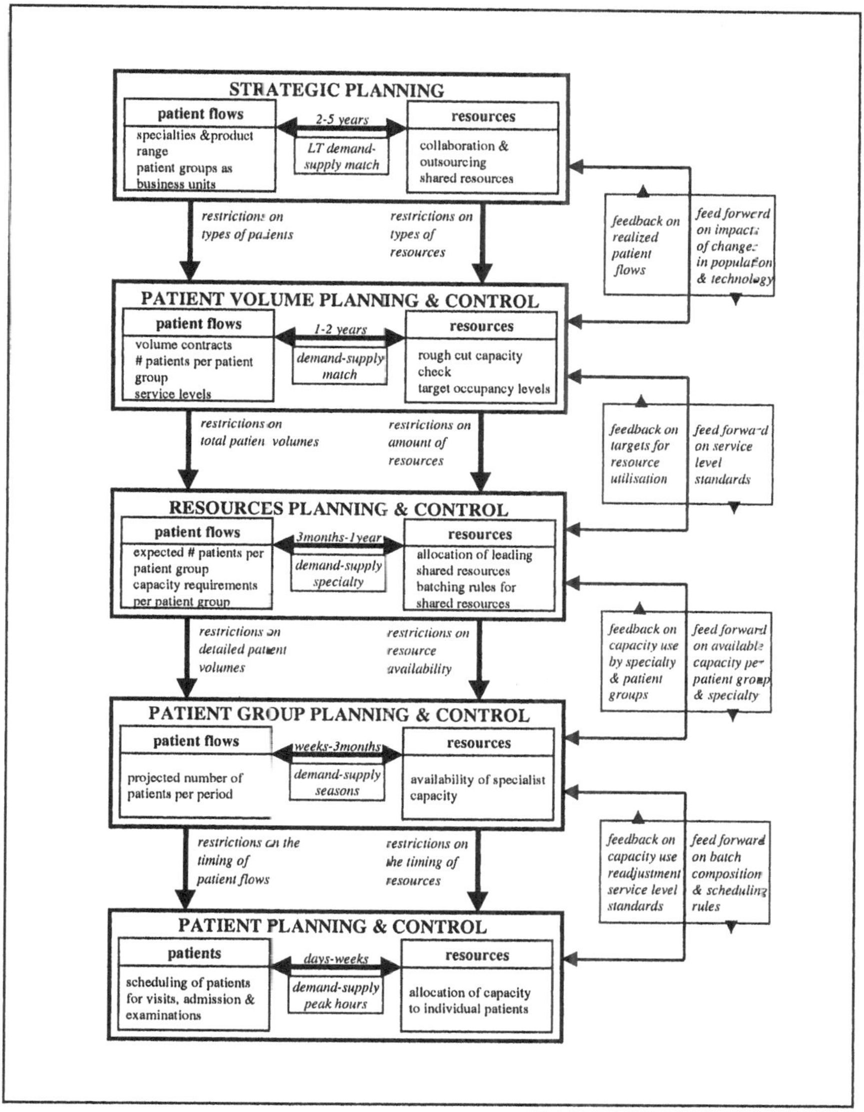

Figure 14-2. Framework for hospital production control

This means that an iso-process perspective is required. Patient group in an operations management perspective can include different products/subgroups that are homogeneous in terms of market performance and process. Homogeneity in terms of market performance implies similar criteria for urgency, acceptable waiting times, etc.. An example of such a sub grouping, based on market performance, could be that a product needs to be delivered on an emergency basis (e.g., process chain: attendance at emergency department, ward admission, outpatient follow up) or on a scheduled basis (e.g., process chain: referral to outpatient department, elective admission, outpatient follow up). The first subgroup will require a different planning approach then the second subgroup. Homogeneity in terms of process implies that the patients within the product group use the same constellation of resources. Patients requiring routine diabetes care (such as a one-off consultation) might be grouped with more complex patients who require more follow-up visits. This is because they are essentially using the same constellation of resources: for example, access to a clinician and a diabetic nurse. However, the overall amount of resources used by patients within the group may vary considerably, a fact that would need to be allowed for when planning capacity requirements. This iso-process grouping makes a logistics approach different from an economics approach (iso-resource grouping) and a medical approach (iso-diagnosis grouping).

The traditional way of classifying 'individual' patient products in the acute hospital is according to their complaint or diagnosis. Iso-diagnosis groupings of patients, for instance, are based on well accepted international classification schemes such as the ICD (International Classification of Diseases). These classification systems can be very extensive: for example, the ICD-9-CM version of 1979 counts 398 main groups and 7960 subgroups. However, such product classifications are mainly used for medical purposes. The number of patient groups that they generate, and the fact that some may generate very few admissions during a planning period, mean that it is difficult and usually undesirable to use them to plan and schedule care from an operations management perspective.

Acute hospitals also traditionally group patients by specialty: for example, general medicine patients, orthopaedic patients etc.. However, these groupings are too aggregated from an operations management perspective, as the constellation of resources used by patient types within specialties are likely to be very different. For example, patients diagnosed with asthma or stroke might both be grouped under the specialty general medicine but the care that they receive will be very different.

Hence, from an operations management perspective, a product classification somewhere between these two "traditional" approaches seems to be required. The first attempt to define hospital products from a managerial perspective can be credited to Fetter and his colleagues (Fetter, 1983). They developed the DRG-system (diagnosis related groups) to classify all diagnoses into groups of diagnoses that are recognisable for physicians and homogeneous in terms of use of resources. Up to then, x-rays, lab tests, medication, surgical procedures – in the DRG system seen as intermediate outputs – were considered as hospital outputs. Fetter developed 467 DRG's to describe the hospital's inpatient output.

Continuing lines of development have included Ambulatory Visit Groups (AVG's) for classifying ambulatory care products (Fetter and Averill, 1984), and a refinement of DRG's which take into account the stage of development of the disease with the patient (Fetter and Freeman, 1986). Another line of development in The Netherlands – with many parallels to the DRG approach - is to define hospital products as combinations of diagnosis and treatment (Baas, 1997). Similarly, in the United Kingdom, and again based on the DRG approach, Healthcare Resource Groups (HRGs) have been developed.

Product groupings such as DRGs were primarily developed to support the financial reimbursement of hospitals rather than to support the planning and management of health care chains. However, they have relevance to operations management as there will be a direct relationship between, for example, a hospital's DRG cost and the efficiency with which resources are used within a DRG. Hence, there are parallels between the analysis of DRG costs and the efficient planning of care within process chains.

Although specific groupings within, for example, the DRG system may be useful for operations management purposes, the overall number of groupings generated by such systems is again likely to be too large. In addition, products which use a similar amount of resources (iso-resource) will not necessarily use a similar constellation of resources (iso-process). For instance, a patient with a DRG/AVG profile of an admission of five days, five lab tests and three outpatient visits may represent a patient admitted on an emergency basis (with five tests during admission, and three outpatient visits to a specialist), as well as a patient admitted on a scheduled basis (with three preceding outpatient visits always using the same constellation of resources, i.e. the specialist, a specialised nurse and the lab). Finally, the boundaries of health care chains may stretch beyond, for example, DRG boundaries. For example, the care chain for a patient who has suffered a stroke will include follow-up care in the community. However, the DRG(s) to which such patients are assigned will only embrace their care within the acute hospital.

Alternatively, it might be possible to generate product groups because the care of the patients covered can be regarded as being delivered in a 'focused factory': a business unit concept. De Vries, Bertrand and Vissers (1999) specified the requirements for a 'focused factory': a clear relationship between the product group and the resources required; the volume of activity is large enough to allow the allocation of dedicated resources; and it is possible in advance to identify the level of specialization required.

Some 'focused factory' product groups might contain the same types of patient. For example, dedicated facilities and units for patients requiring treatment for cataracts have been established. In other 'focused factory' product groups, different types of patient might be clustered so that the volume of activity justifies the provision of dedicated resources. An example might be patients requiring day surgery. In the UK, the development of dedicated diagnostic and treatment centres will further increase the relevance of patient groups based upon the principles of a focused factory.

Finally, regardless of concerns about the volume of activity and clarity of resource requirements, client concerns about the continuity and co-ordination of existing services within a care chain might be the main driver for the creation of product groups. Such client concerns tend to be most evident for illnesses with a relatively long duration and/or which require contact with a range of professionals or agencies. Hence, in the UK, National Service Frameworks have been developed that map out the desirable care pathways and services required for patients receiving treatment for conditions such as diabetes and stroke. To some extent, product groupings driven by a desire to promote continuity and co-ordination mirror developments in clinical protocols and pathways. However, the variety of processes and agencies involved means that planning and controlling the care of patients within such multidisciplinary patient groupings is extremely complicated.

Although the above discussion has outlined a range of product classifications and groupings, it should be noted that there are some process characteristics that have a strong impact on the predictability of resource use by patients within product groups. An awareness of these characteristics is therefore helpful when developing product groups:

- Treatments for well-defined complaints with almost 100% certainty about the processes required and the outcome (e.g. a bone fracture) should be distinguished from treatments for ill-defined complaints with no routine treatment-path available and no certainty about results. We call these the routine and non-routine processes (see also Lillrank and Liukko, 2004).
- For routine processes, it is possible to define a treatment path, often based on a clinical guideline or protocol, which defines the different

operations in the process and their timing. Still the variability in resource use for these routine processes can be quite high due, for example, to practice variations, different modes of treatment, and the consequences of the interaction between doctor and patient. Nevertheless, process patterns can be recognized.

- For non-routine processes, the specialist will proceed in a step-by-step way, checking the patient's reaction on a treatment and deciding on the next step from there. There is no guarantee on the outcome, and there is no in advance layout of the process the patient will follow. Naturally, the predictability of resource use is much lower here than with routine processes.

Of course, these are the extremes on a continuous scale; there is much variation between specialties and within a specialty. However, the variation between specialties is dominant. For a surgical specialty with many protocol patients, such as orthopaedics, the number of routine processes may be very high but for a non-surgical specialty, such as internal medicine, it may be much less.

Using iso-process patient groups as business units implies that patient groups are distinguished fulfilling the criteria (homogeneous in terms of process and market performance), that the volume of the patient flow is sufficient to allow for a specific production control, that the trajectories within these groups are described, that production control for each of the patient groups is defined and that the responsibility for managing the patient group is clarified. These steps will be illustrated in the next section with data of an application of such an approach for cardiology.

3. STEPS IN AN OM APPROACH TO HOSPITAL PROCESS IMPROVEMENT

Based on the logistic concepts discussed in Section 2 we have performed a number of case studies with different specialties: cardiology, pulmonology, neurology, general surgery, orthopedics and dermatology. As the emphasis in these case studies is on process improvement, they can be positioned on the second level of the planning framework discussed in Section 2.2. The steps followed are:

- Defining the iso-process patient grouping
- Mapping and analyzing the patient processes
- Defining production control for each patient group
- Setting of objectives and monitoring performance

- Managing the process

These steps result in an organization of patient flows for patient groups that have each a production control fitting the characteristics of the process, and that are run as a business unit. We will illustrate these steps below with data from a case study with cardiology with six cardiologists in a medium sized hospital. They were interested to know how to improve their practice from the perspective of patient groups, and wanted to develop more insight into issues such as:

- How large are the patient flows per patient group?
- What are the average throughput times of patients?
- Do we have enough clinic capacity available for each patient group?

3.1. Iso-process patient grouping

The first step in an OM approach to hospital process improvement is the definition of patient groups fulfilling the criteria of being iso-process. Often these groupings already exist in the practice of clinics, i.e. general clinics and clinics for specific patient groups. Table 14-3 provides information on the main patient groups for cardiology.

Table 14-3. Patient groups for cardiology

Patient group	**average number of patients per week**	**percentage of total**
1. Chest pain	59.5	42.5
2. Short of breath	35.0	25.0
3. Heart rhythm	24.5	17.5
4. Heart murmurs	4.0	2.9
5. Risk analysis	7.0	5.0
6. Pre-operative screening	10.0	7.1
Total	140	100%

The average patient flow on a weekly basis counts 140 patients. Important to notice is that at the main level of patient groups complaint-based labels are chosen as to allow for a good linkage with referring general practitioners or physicians from another specialty. The next step is that within these main groups subgroups of patients are defined that follow a similar trajectory. Trajectories can be distinguished for invasive or non-invasive treatment paths, for simple or more complex problems, etc. Often at this level of the classification of patient groups it is possible to make the link with a medical diagnosis. It is also important to quantify the size of patient flows within patient groups and trajectories to be aware of the number of patients concerned. Table 14-4 shows the breakdown of the cardiology flow to the patient groups and trajectories.

The different trajectories can also be used for labeling a multidisciplinary collaboration with another specialty or a multi-site collaboration with a more specialized hospital where part of the treatment is performed. Therefore, the defining of patient groups and trajectories has a strategic dimension, as the patient groups and treatments offered need to fit within the strategic profile of the hospital.

The data shown regard mean weekly averages of number of patients flowing in each of these patient groups and distributing over trajectories. A week is chosen as time period of analysis as later on the match needs to be made with resources (outpatient clinic hours and staff, diagnostic department facilities, etc.) available to handle the flow of patients. The data are partly derived from administrative systems, and partly based on expert knowledge of professionals. These expert estimates on distribution of patients over trajectories will be used as a starting point as routine information systems will not be able to deliver these data. However, it is possible to check later on the distribution chosen by small tests with data from routine information systems.

3.2. Mapping and analyzing patient processes

The explicit description and mapping of the process is an extremely important step as this will allow exchanging the different views of medical specialists, nursing staff, clerical staff and patients. It is obvious that medical specialists play an important role in the describing of the process as it regards their core activities. There are more reasons that we resolve to use expert knowledge as the basis for describing processes. First of all, the data we need will not be available in routine information systems as these systems are most of the time based on departmental data collection and have no possibility to provide in a systematic way information on processes followed by patient groups. Of course, DRG's will be able to provide much of the data but not according to the more aggregated grouping chosen in our description for improving hospital processes. Also the information delivered by DRG's will not be able to provide the time dimension for the process description. DRG's contain the ingredients of the process (numbers of visits, diagnostic and therapeutic procedures, admissions, etc.) but not the process as such. For a description of a health care process we need to be able to follow the steps taken by patients in their journey through the hospital, which includes for instance:

Table 14-4. Patient groups and trajectories for cardiology (based on mean weekly averages)

Inflow Cardiology (per week)	Patient groups			Trajectories		
	Name	**Cases per week**	**% of total**	**Name**	**Cases per week**	**% in patient group**
140	chest pain	59.5	43%	a. no angina pectoris (ap)	6.0	10%
				b. stable angina pectoris	11.9	20%
				c. unstable ap (outpatient)	11.9	20%
				d. unstable ap (intervention)	3.0	5%
				e. acute coronary syndrom	26.8	45%
	short breath	35	25%	a. diagnostic test	7.0	20%
				b. heart failure	14.0	40%
				c. chronic condition	7.0	20%
				d. acute	7.0	20%
	heart rythm	24.5	18%	a. simple	7.4	30%
				b. serious	7.4	30%
				c. chronic	7.4	30%
				d. collaps	2.5	10%
	heart murmurs	4	3%	a. valve defect	3.6	90%
				b. valve procedure	0.4	10%
	risk analysis	7	5%	a. dislipidaemic	6.7	95%
				b. chronic dislipidaemic	0.4	5%
	pre-operative screening	10	7%	a. general	10.0	100%

- Time waited by patients for an appointment with a medical specialist (access time),
- Number and timing of visits to outpatient clinics and diagnostic departments in the diagnostic phase,
- Waiting time before admission or before a surgical procedure,
- Diagnostic and therapeutic procedures during admission,
- Number of follow up visits to outpatient clinics after discharge,

and the timing of all these steps.

The second reason to use expert knowledge is to involve the key players in the process of improvement. Often they have to get used to this way of looking at their practice, because it differs from the way they look as medical decision makers to the care process. Once they have appreciated the value of such a non-medical description of the process of the patient, they will be able to use it to improve their practice from the perspective of developing patient centered services.

We have developed a computer model 'processor' that allows us to describe and model the processes of the different patient groups within the patient flow of a specialty, in close interaction with the professionals involved in the process. The structure of the model - used for mapping the information on processes and resources - is illustrated in Figure 14-3.

Figure 14-3 shows the demand side of the model (upper part) and the supply side (lower part). The demand side starts with the inflow of new outpatients and the distribution over groups of patients that can be distinguished in the inflow and used for streamlining services and flows. Within these patient groups different treatment profiles are distinguished, representing the modes of treatment available for a patient group and the trajectories followed by patients. At the level of an individual trajectory, the process of the patients from this patient group following this trajectory is described, using input from the medical specialist and information on examinations and treatments. The inflow and distribution of patients over patient groups, combined with the treatment profiles, allows for a calculation of resource requirements in the outpatient department and the diagnostic departments.

The supply side consists of a description of the available capacity in the outpatient and diagnostic departments, in terms of rooms, personnel and equipment. In the results part of the model demand and supply are matched, which allows for visualizing throughput times of processes and calculation of resource utilisation.

We will now illustrate how the model is used for our case study setting of a cardiology practice with six cardiologists. The numbers of patients treated in 2001 are: 7000 first visits (including patients seen in the emergency department), 14.000 follow up visits, and 1300 inpatient admissions. Information on the clinics held each week is given in Table 14-5.

Each specialist has five sessions a week in which they see all types of patients. For each session the number of time slots reserved for first and follow up visits is given as well as the average time available for first and follow up visits. Apart from the clinics held by the six cardiologists there are a number of clinics held by nurse practitioners and other professionals dealing with patients with chronic conditions. To be able to determine the number of time slots available for each of the patient groups we need to know the mix of patients per clinic. Investigation of the type of patients seen in each clinic provided information on the mix of patients per type of clinic (see Table 14-6).

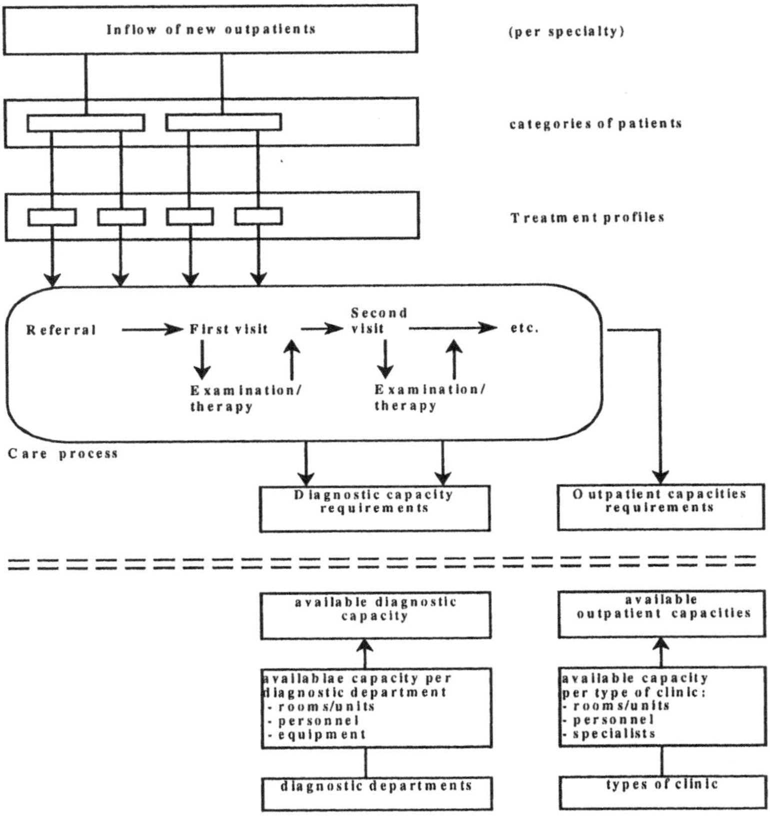

Figure 14-3.Structure of the demand-supply model for hospital processes

Table 14-5. Information on weekly clinic schedules

clinic	specialist	hours	first visits	duration first visit	follow up visits	duration follow up visit
general clinics by cardiologists	specialist 1	15.33	12	20	68	10
	specialist 2	15.33	12	20	68	10
	specialist 3	15.33	12	20	68	10
	specialist 4	15.33	12	20	68	10
	specialist 5	15.33	12	20	68	10
	specialist 6	15.33	12	20	68	10
	Total	**92**	**72**		**408**	
clinics by other professionals	lipid control	15	3	30	54	15
	heart failure	29	6	30	107	15
	after care	9	9	60		
	diagnostic service	6	8	30		
	pacemaker control	36			56	40
	Total	**95**	**26**		**217**	

Table 14-6. Mix of patients per type of clinic

Patient group Type of clinic	Chest pain	Short of breath	Valve defects	Heart murmurs	Risk analysis	Pre-operative screening
General	40%	22%	8%	5%	5%	5%
Lipids control					100%	
Heart failure		100%				
After care	100%					
Diagnostic service		100%				
Pacemaker control			100%			

As can be seen from Table 14-6, the mix of patients in a general clinic reflects the range of patients seen in the cardiology practice, while the other clinics have their dedicated patient group. So the amount of time available for each patient group is indeed not an obvious issue.

We have seen before that the average flow of patients in the practice is 140 each week, with about 85% of patients in the first three patient groups. Most patients enter cardiology practice via the outpatient department, but a considerable part enters also via the emergency department. Though it seems that we concentrate on the use of resources in the outpatient department, we have to take all the inpatient work of the specialists into account. Many people seen in emergency departments, or as inpatients, will continue as outpatients and want to use the time slots shown in Table 14-5. It demonstrates that even if the focus is the outpatient department, the complete workload of the cardiologists must be understood because of the links between the different strands of work and activity generated in OP departments. The six main patient groups are broken down into a number of subgroups that sometimes refer to a specific complaint or sometimes to a different treatment path. At this level a link can be made to the process of the patient. The processes of all these patient subgroups are described based on expert opinion from cardiologists. This information is structured with the help of the computer model that also returns the information to the specialists in the format of a process chart. Figure 14-4 shows one of these processes, i.e. a stable angina pectoris patient.

Figure 14-4 shows that the process for patients with stable angina pectoris consists of on average eight steps. All steps take place at the outpatient department. In the first step some diagnostic tests are performed (ecg, upward and downward arrow) and some tests require the patient to return at another occasion (e.g. ergometrics). After the first step everybody will return for a follow up visit at the outpatient department in 30 days time (not shown in this figure, but see Table 14-7). With step two 33% of all patients seen are discharged. In step three again 10% are discharged and 5% of patients have – depending on the results of tests – a chance to be admitted immediately. The rest of the patients are following a trajectory with annual follow up visits, with a chance of being discharged, admitted or referred for a PTCA. The information that is used to describe the different steps in the process is summarized in Table 14-7.

For each step in the process information is given on the content of the step (in this case, first and follow up visits, but it could also regard an admission or a procedure), the percentage of patients with diagnostics that are performed instantly (as a direct follow up of the encounter with the specialist) or with an appointment on another occasion, the next step in the flow (percentage of patients that will return for a next step, or require immediate admission, or continue in another profile, or are discharged), and the re-appointment interval for patients that return.

The diminishing patient flow by the chance of discharge in each step can be visualized by the model's output (see Figure 14-5). The model also provides insight into the match between available and required slots in outpatient clinics per patient group (see Table 14-8).

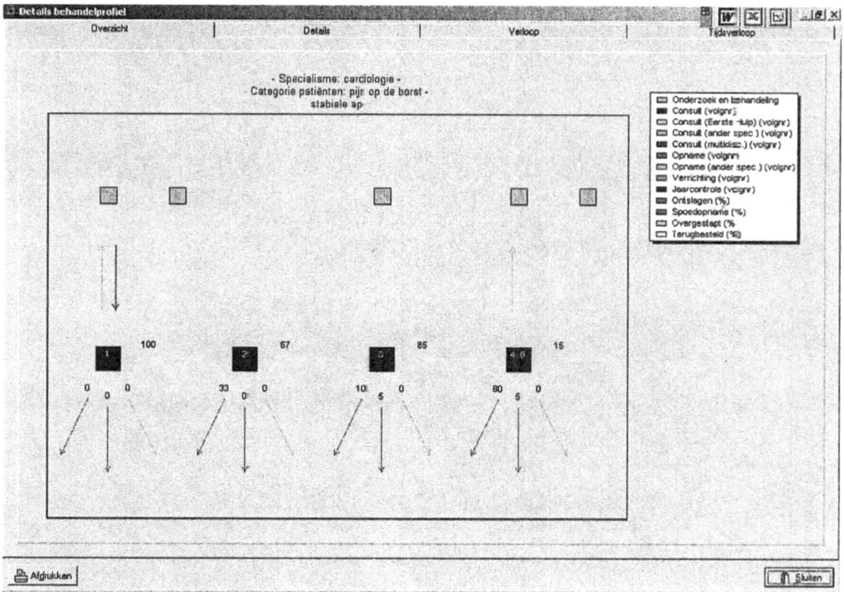

Figure 14-4.Graphical illustration care process 'stable angina pectoris' patient

Table 14-7.Summary of steps in the care process of stable angina pectoris patients

Patient Group: chest pain				Trajectory: stable angina pectoris				
Step	Content	Diagnostic/therapy		flow data				
		Direct	Appointment	Percentages				reapp. interval
				Continue	Urgent admission	Other trajectory	Discharge	
1	first visit	ecg (100%)	ergometrics (100%) lab tests (100%) CAG (10%) thallium test (10%)	100%				30
2	follow up visit			67%			33%	90
3	follow up visit	ecg (100%) lab (100%)		85%	5%		10%	180
4-8	follow up visit (5x)	ecg (100%) lab (100%)	PTCA (5%)	15%	5%		80%	360

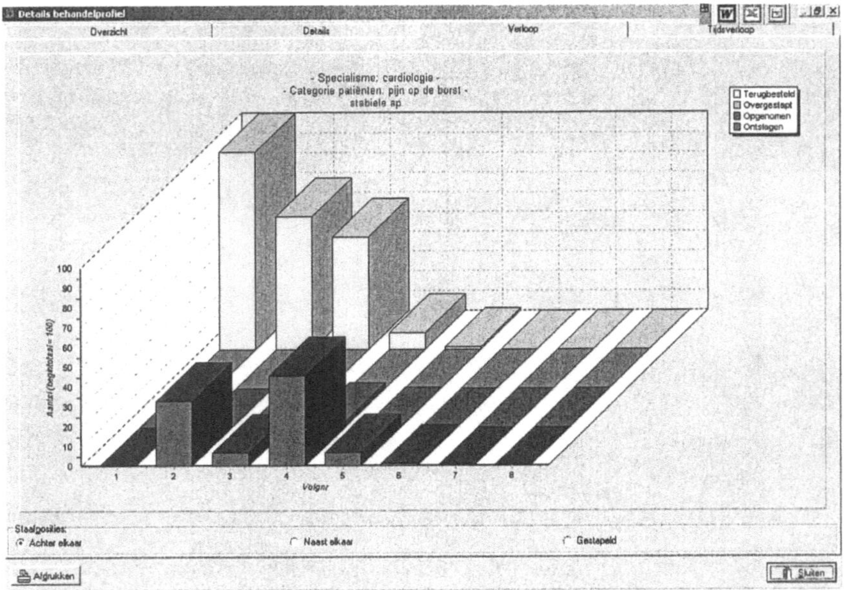

Figure 14-5.Graphical illustration of the diminishing patient flow in the care process 'stable angina pectoris' patients

Table 14-8.Match between demand for and supply of time slots in cardiology clinics

	First visits			Follow up visits		
Patient group	Demand	Supply	Occ..	Demand	Supply	Occ.
Chest pain	33	38	87%	117	163	72%
Short of breath	28	30	94%	243	197	123%
Valve defects	16	14	114%	63	89	71%
Heart murmurs	4	4	100%	12	20	56%
Risk analysis	7	7	100%	28	74	38%
Pre-operative screening	6	4	150%	10	20	49%
Total	98	87	112%	475	564	84%

Table 14-8 illustrates that the match at the level of the total of clinics is inadequate (too few slots for first visits, too many slots for follow up visits). Also the match at the level of individual patient groups can be improved. Another type of output is the throughput times of processes. Table 14-9 provides information on the number of activities per type and on the throughput times to complete all the steps in the process. For patient groups with a chronic condition, the process has been artificially cut off. The throughput times can also be visualised, as shown for the 'chest pain' patient group in Figure 14-6. The difference between the current throughput time and the 'minimum' throughput time shows the gain to be made by better planning of patients in relation to the diagnostic tests.

Table 14-9.Match between demand for and supply of time slots in cardiology clinics

Patient group	Trajectory	Visits cardiologists			Nurse visits	Admit	Admit other hospital	Through-put time
		first	Fol-low up	annual visits				
Chest pain	no ap	1	1					14
	stable ap	1	2	5				2100
	unstable ap (outpat.)	1	4	5				2145
	instable ap (intervention)	1	3	5			1	2071
	acute coronary syndrom	1	6			1		1039
Short of breath	diagnostic service	1			1			1
	heart failure	1	5		12			467
	chronic	1	8					610
	acute	1	3			1		312
Valve defects	simple	1	6		8	1		591
	serious	1	6			1		769
	chronic	1	9		7	1		1865
	collapse	1	1	4	9	1	1	1630
Heart murmur	valve defect	1	4					1454
	valve procedure	1	5				1	862
Risk analysis	Dislipidaemic	1			6			350
	chronic dislipidaemic	1			11			1970
Pre-operative screening	General	1	1					14

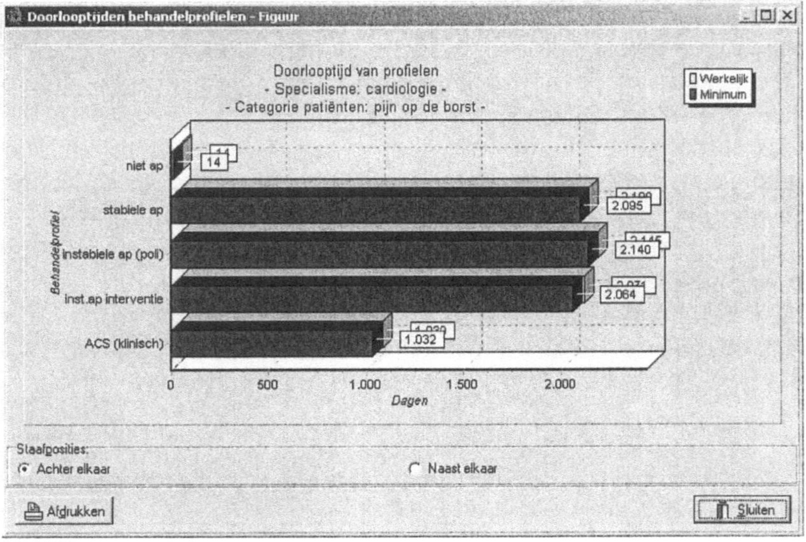

Figure 14-6.Graphical illustration of the throughput times for 'chest pain' patients

3.3. Defining production control

We now have insight into the different patient groups and trajectories, the size of the patient flows, the process of patients and their resource requirements. The next step in the OM approach to process improvement is to define production control for each patient group. To evaluate which type of control fits best with the process looked at, we need to know the characteristics of each of the processes. An evaluation of these characteristics is provided in Table 14-10. For this purpose some of the trajectories were combined, such as angina pectoris (ap) and heart failure (hf).

The characteristics considered are: number of steps in the process (whether it regards a short or a long process), the complexity of the process (due to diagnostic tests performed or due to consultation with other specialties), the chronicity of the process (whether it regards a chronic process with no defined end), the predictability of the process (regarding number of steps, duration of steps and the routing of steps), and the use of resources in the process (whether use is made of a shared resource or a bottleneck resource). For instance the patient group 'chest pain with ap' is characterized by a long process that is complex and chronic, with not good predictability of the process on duration and routing, and with use of a resource that is shared with other specialties (ergometric test).

Table 14-10. Characteristics of patient groups
(legend: -- not relevant at all, - not relevant, 0 hardly relevant, + relevant, ++ very relevant)

Patient group / Characteristics	Chest pain		Short of breath		Heart rhythm		Heart murmurs		Risk analysis	Pre-operative screening
	no ap	ap	no hf	hf	not relevant	relevant	not relevant	relevant		
Number of steps	--	+	-	+	--	0	--	+	-	-
complexity	--	+	-	+	--	0	--	0	--	--
chronic	--	+	-	+	--	+	--	+	-	-
Predictability										
-no of steps	++	+	-+	+	++	+	++	+	++	++
-duration	++	0	-+	+	++	+	++	0	++	++
-routing	++	0	-+		++	+	++	+	++	++
Use of resources										
-shared	--	0	++	++	-	0	0	0	0	0
-bottleneck	+	+	++	++	0	++	-	0	-	++

We now can use these characteristics to define a way of production control that fits the process considered. Though the best fit is a matter of tailor-made decision making for a specific patient group, the rules used to derive to a solution are:

- When predictability is high, and the process is not too long or complex, and there are no critical resources involved, the process can be scheduled with a longer planning horizon;
- When predictability is high, but the process is long or complex, and critical resources are involved, scheduling can be per phase, i.e. diagnosis, therapy, aftercare;
- When predictability is low, scheduling can only be performed on a short planning horizon, i.e. per step of the process.

For the example of the patient group 'chest pain', we would suggest a production control per phase of the process, i.e. scheduling all steps in phase in advance. This will create optimal conditions for creating the best service for the client (by combining visits and diagnostic tests) and advance scheduling of resources.

3.4. Objective setting and monitoring

Having defined the production control setting for each patient group we now have to set objectives for the performance of patient groups. We have distinguished four areas of performance:

- Quality: conformance to specification
- Delivery speed: time between the moment of demand and the moment of delivery
- Delivery reliability: degree of meeting the arrangements agreed
- Flexibility: degree of coping with unpredictable situations

These areas of performance are further operationalized with measures that are specified in Table 14-11. Tables 14-12 till 14-15 provide information on the scoring of these measures per patient group in the areas of the objectives. The scoring was based on the evaluation of these measures by the different cardiologists.

The overview of the performance on 'quality' measures in Table 14-12 provides insight into areas where improvement is required. Results that were evaluated as '0' or lower were regarded as indicators for quality that needs to be looked at. For the example of the patient group 'chest pain', action is required in these areas:

- Consistency between cardiologists in handling patients with angina pectoris: protocol for treatment of angina pectoris patients was discussed within the group of cardiologists to deal with the differences in treatment between them.
- Instruction and expertise: instruction material for guidance of angina pectoris patients improved and better qualified nursing staff were selected to deal with these problems.
- Inflow and outflow: problems in these areas required attention for the links with general practitioners. Improvement in the referral process and in the phase of aftercare could be realized by putting this patient group on the agenda for discussion in meetings with general practitioners.
- Tuning: Improvement of the tuning with other specialists dealing with the same patient group required discussion with other specialties on the multidisciplinary treatment of patients.

Table 14-13 also provides information on the scoring of 'delivery speed' performance by patient groups.

Table 14-11. Objectives and measures of performance (based on De Vries et al., 2004)

Objective	Measure	Description
1. Quality	Right at one go	no rework due to complications
	Consistency	no difference between different providers
	Adequacy	patients are treated adequately
	Instruction	patients receive adequate instruction
	Expertise	expertise of professionals is up to standard
	Inflow	correct referral and referral information
	Outflow	continuity of care with follow up providers
	Tuning	tuning with other professionals in multidisciplinary treatment
	Patient satisfaction	satisfaction of patient with treatment
2. Delivery speed	Access time	waiting time for patients to get access to cardiology services, for different levels of urgency
	Waiting list	waiting time on waiting list in case of elective admission
	Wait time in clinic	waiting time in the outpatient department
	Throughput time	lead time required for diagnosis, treatment and aftercare
	Consultation	availability of consultation by other specialists
	Diagnostics	availability of diagnostic facilities
3. Delivery reliability	Canceling Appointments	level of cancellation of appointment due to rescheduling of clinics
	Canceling Admissions	canceling of admissions due to, for instance, not availability of beds
	Output arrangements	levels of output required to fulfill contracts with purchasers
4. Flexibility	Service	time required to introduce a new type of service
	Mix	dealing with shifts in the mix of patient groups
	Volume	dealing with changes in the amount of patients in a patient group
	Delivery speed	dealing with changes in the arrangement for access of patient groups

Table 14-12. Objective 'quality': measures of performance per patient group
(legend: -- very bad, - bad, 0 not good, + good, ++ very good; na not applicable)

Items	Chest pain		Short of breath		Heart rhythm		Heart murmurs		Risk analysis	Pre-operative screening
	no ap	Ap	no hf	hf	not relevant	relevant	not relevant	relevant		
1. right at one	++	+	+	+	+	+	++	++	++	++
go	+	-	+	0	+	+	+	+	+	++
2. consistency	++	+	++	+	++	+	++	++	+	++
3. adequacy	0	0	0	0	0	+	+	+	+	+
4. instruction	0	0	0	+	0	0	+	+	+	+
5. expertise	0	0	0	0	0	0	0	0	+	+
6. inflow	+	0	0	0	+	+	+	+	+	+
7. outflow	na	0	na	0	na	na	+	+	0	--
8. tuning										
9. patient satisfaction	++	+	0	0	0	+	++	++	+	0

Table 14-13. Objective 'delivery speed': measures of performance per patient group
(legend: -- very bad, - bad, 0 not good, + good, ++ very good; na not applicable)

Items	*chest pain*		short of breath		heart rythm		heart murmurs		risc analysis	pre-operative screening
	no ap	ap	no hf	hf	not relevant	relevant	not relevant	relevant		
1.access time:										
• Acute	++	++	++	++	na	++	++	++	+	++
• Urgent	++	++	+	+	na	++	+	+	+	++
• (semi-) elective	++	++	0	0	+	+	+	+	+	++
2.waiting list	na	+	na	na	na	-	na	+	+	na
3.clinic wait	+	+	0	0	+	+	+	+	+	+
4.throughput time:										
• diagnosis	--	--	-	-	--	-	+	0	0	+
• treatment	na	0	na	-	na	-	na	+	+	+
• after care	na	-	na	+	na	+	++	+	+	++
5.consultation	na	+	na	+	na	na	+	+	+	++
6.diagnostics	0	-	0	-	0	0	+	+	+	+

From the information in Table 14-13 one can see where action is required to improve the performance on the speed of delivery of cardiology services to patients. For the example of 'chest pain' patients timely access for different urgency levels was OK, but the time required for a timely diagnosis was clearly indicated as an area where improvement was required. The low score on item 6 indicated that this was due to the availability of diagnostic facilities. Also the throughput time in the phase of treatment and aftercare could be improved.

Table 14-14 provides information on the scoring of 'delivery reliability' performance by patient groups, indicating where improvement is required in the reliability of the delivery of services, in terms of canceling appointment or admissions, and in terms of meeting the contract arrangements with the purchasers of hospital services, such as health insurance organizations. For 'chest pain' patients, attention was required for the fact that when clinics had to be cancelled due to non availability of a specialist, appointments for 'chest pain' patients had to be rescheduled at a short notice.

Table 14-14. Objective 'delivery reliability': measures of performance per patient group (legend: -- very bad, - bad, 0 not good, + good, ++ very good; na not applicable)

Items	Chest pain		Short of breath		Heart rythm		Heart murmurs		Risk Analysis	Pre-operative screening
	no ap	ap	no hf	Hf	not relevant	relevant	not relevant	relevant		
1.cancelling appointments	-	-	na	0	+	+	+	+	0	0
2.cancelling admissions	na	++	na	++	na	++	na	-	na	na
3. output volume										
-visits	+	+	+	+	+	+	+	+	+	+
-admissions	+	+	+	+	-	+	na	+	+	na

Table 14-15 provides information on the scoring of 'flexibility' performance by patient groups, giving insight into the performance of the organization of cardiology services to deal with unpredictable changes. For the patient group 'chest pain', no areas were found to require attention. The low scores on 'volume' and 'delivery time' flexibility for 'heart failure' patients referred to the capacity of diagnostic facilities to deal with unexpected larger patient flows or increased delivery speed.

Table 14-15. Objective 'flexibility': measures of performance per patient group
(legend: -- very bad, - bad, 0 not good, + good, ++ very good)

Items	chest pain		short of breath		heart rythm		heart murmurs		Risk Analysis	pre-operative screening
	no ap	ap	no hf	hf	not relevant	relevant	not relevant	relevant		
1.Service	+	+	+	+	0	0	+	+	+	+
2.Mix patients	+	+	0	0	+	+	+	+	+	+
3.Volume	+	+	-	-	+	+	+	+	+	++
4.Delivery time	+	+	-	-	+	+	+	+	0	+

3.5. Process management

We have shown in 3.4 that a number of indicators need to be monitored per patient group to assure that the performance of cardiology services is up to the agreed standards. It is very important that someone is responsible for and interested in the performance of processes. Unless the responsibility for process management is clearly defined, process improvements will not be sustained. Therefore it is necessary to discuss who will be responsible for process management in hospitals.

Process management involves a number of responsibilities. Most of them can be derived from the function process management fulfills in the framework for production control discussed in Section 2.2. Process management was discussed here under the heading of patient group planning and control. At the patient group level there must be a management function responsible for defining the market performance to be delivered (patient mix, urgency criteria, acceptable waiting times, etc.), the acquisition of the resources required for the patient group, the control of the patient flow and the utilization of resources by the patient group. The different tasks of patient group management in terms of planning and control are illustrated in Figure 14-7.

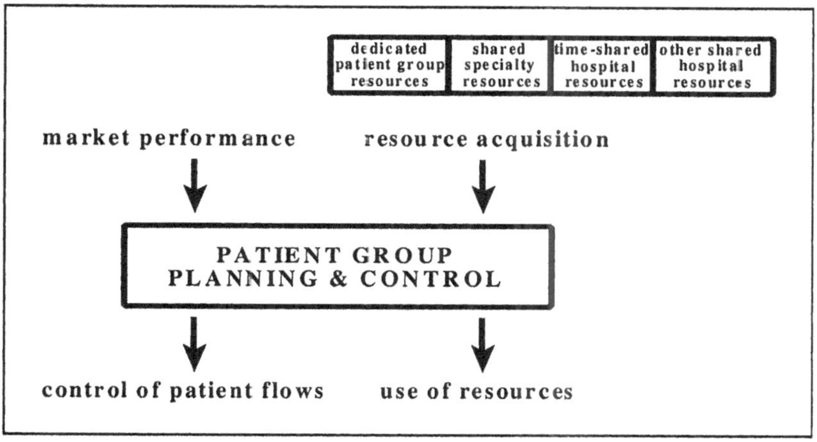

Figure 14-7. Responsibilities of patient group management

The detailed control at the level of the patient group involves checking that the day-to-day scheduling of patients is in line with the service requirements specified for the patient group as a whole and the regulations on resource use imposed on the patient group. We will concentrate first in Figure 14-7 on the resource acquisition and resource use regulations for the patient group. Some of these resources may be dedicated for use by the patient group only, some may be made available from the resources that are dedicated at the level of a specialty but shared by the patient groups served by the specialty, others must be contracted for specified periods as these are shared between specialties, and the remaining resources are supposed to be generally available for different patient groups. The four categories of resources distinguished in Figure 14-7 show a decreasing extent of influence that the management of the patient group can perform on their availability for the patient group.

In summary, the responsibilities of process management come down to defining the market performance to be delivered, acquiring the resources required for the patient group, controlling the flow of patients to assure that the process of individual patients fits within the bandwidth defined for the patient group considered, and controlling the efficient use of resources by the patient group.

Process management is clearly a managerial responsibility. Nevertheless, we would advocate a strong involvement of medical specialists in the running of patient groups. Ideally, a small management team should be defined for a patient group, consisting of a medical specialist, and for example possibly a nurse practitioner or other key professionals, supported by a manager. The medical specialist should be acting as the chairperson of the management team, with responsibilities for defining, monitoring and evaluating programs offered to patient groups. A nurse practitioner could assist in collecting the data required for the monitoring of the performance of the patient group. A manager could support the team by organizing the resources required for the patient group and by providing information on the use of resources. By putting the medical specialist in the position of chair of the management team for a patient group, we strive to make him/her the owner of the process organized for the patient group. Furthermore, running a patient group would also imply that he/she takes the lead in discussing medical practice with colleagues, if colleagues are performing outside the bandwidth agreed for the patient group.

We believe that this task can be very well performed in combination with clinical work, and would not require much time from medical specialists, as they receive many signals during each day if processes are running smoothly or not. Process management by medical specialists is a form of management participation by specialists that is much closer to clinical practice than the (co) responsibility of running a department. After all, professionals in health care want to spend more time on patients and less on managerial matters. The form of process management we are looking for will help them to have more influence on the way hospitals are organized to meet the demand of patients.

4. CONCLUSIONS AND FUTURE WORK

We have discussed in this chapter an operations management approach to hospital process improvement. First we have argued that a more fundamental approach for hospital process improvement should be used to make improvements sustainable and part of a new routine to be developed in hospitals, in which the process of patients is the basis for organizing hospitals. This is what operations management is about. We have introduced a few concepts that can be used to create such an operations management context for looking at hospital process improvement. The first concept is the distinction between unit and chain logistics and its combination i.e. network logistics. We also need to include unit logistics and chain logistics in our approach, because we want to avoid sub-optimization by only looking at an isolated process, and we want to account for the impacts of process improvements on the efficient use of resources. The second concept is a framework for production control of hospitals in which decisions regarding patient flows and resources are organized at different levels of planning. This will help to position process improvements in a wider context of production control of hospitals, and make those involved aware of the interactions between the different parts of the hospitals and the creation of conditions at higher levels of planning to make process improvement sustainable. The third concept is the definition of iso-process patient groups, based on the trajectory of the patient through the system and the use of similar constellation of resources. These patient groups can then be considered as business units that require a production control system fitting the characteristics of the process of the patient group. This will help to identify patient groups with a very predictable process that can be organized as a focused factory, and other patient groups with a less predictable process, which can be planned per phase of the process (diagnosis, therapy, aftercare) or at a more aggregate level of a program for patient groups.

The operations management approach to process improvement was then applied to the cardiology patient flow in hospitals. The different steps in the approach were elaborated and illustrated with cardiology patient flow examples. The first step was to identify iso-process patient groups, for which a specific organization of services is developed. Six patient groups were identified. Together with the different trajectories followed by patients within patient groups, a total of 18 processes were sufficient to describe the patient flow of cardiology. The second step was to describe these processes in a way that allows analysis of the service and resource use impacts of processes. We used a computer model developed for this purpose, which uses as a basis the expert knowledge of professionals on the characteristics of processes and the way processes are organized. The computer model helps to make the description more consistent and allows analysis of processes to improve the insight into specialty practice. The third step was to define a production control per patient group, taking into account the characteristics of the process considered. Characteristics taken into account are whether it regards a short or a long process, whether the process is complex due to diagnostic tests performed or due to consultation with other specialties, whether it regards a chronic process with no defined end, whether the process is predictable and whether the process makes use of a shared resource or a bottleneck resource. The fourth step involves the setting of objectives for the performance of the process to enable its monitoring. Objectives were defined for the quality of the service, the speed and reliability of delivery and the flexibility of the organization to meet changes of practice, such as an introduction of a new technology, a shift in the mix of patients, an increased volume of patients or a shorter access time for a patient group. The fifth step regarded the responsibility for process management in hospitals. We argued that medical specialists need to take up the responsibility for process management in order to make improvements in hospital processes sustainable.

Though we believe that we have come far in developing a comprehensive approach to hospital process improvement, a number of issues need to be looked at more fundamentally. We will list a few of these issues below.

The first issue is to improve the method of patient grouping based on the iso-process concept. This would require investigation of the variations in the process of a patient group, as well as the type of variation (more or less steps, longer or shorter duration of steps, variation in routings of steps), and identify what part of the variation has a structural cause and what part of variation is due to stochastic behavior of variables in the system. This will provide insight into the level of standardization that is possible in hospital business processes.

The second issue is to look more fundamentally at the characteristics of processes and to their importance in finding the best fit for production control of a patient group. Is predictability of the process the most important factor, and what role do the other characteristics play?

The third issue is how to construct from the massive data on patient encounters reliable process descriptions for patient groups. Can process mining, in which logs of data of patient encounters are used to construct process descriptions, help?

The fourth issue is how to define band widths for the performance of patient groups on the objectives for process management.

These are a few fundamental questions that can be put forward to provide better support for the steps taken in our operations management approach to hospital process improvement. But, above all, we need more experience in applying this approach to develop a hospital organization that puts patients in the centre by organizing processes in an effective and efficient way.

5. REFERENCES

Baas, L.J.C., 1996, Producttypering medisch-specialistische ziekenhuiszorg (Dutch). *Medisch Contact,* **51**: 356-358.

Bertrand, J.W.M., Wortmann, J.C. and Wijngaard, J., 1990, *Production Control: A Structural and Design Oriented Approach.* Elsevier, Amsterdam.

Fetter, R.B., 1983, *The new ICD-9-CM diagnosis-related groups classification scheme.* HCFA Pub. No. 03167. Health Care Financing Administration, Washington: U.S. Government Printing Office.

Fetter, R.B., Averill, A. a.c., 1984, Ambulatory Visit Groups: A Framework for Measuring Productivity in Ambulatory Care. *Health Services Research,* **19**: 415-437.

Fetter, R.B. and Freeman, J.L, Diagnosis Related Groups: Product Line Management within Hospitals. *Academy of Management Review,* **11:** 41-54.

Lillrank, P. and Liukko, M., 2004, Standard, routine and non-routine processes in health care. *International Journal of Quality Assurance,* **17**, no 1: 39-46.

Vissers, Jan and Beech, Roger (eds.), 2005, *Health Operations Management. Patient flow logistics in health care*, Routledge, London and New York.

Vissers, J.M.H., Bertrand, J.W.M. and Vries, G. de, 2001, A framework for production control in health care organisations. *Production Planning & Control,* **12**, no. 6: 591-604.

Vries, G. de, Bertrand, J.W.M and Vissers, J.M.H., 1999, Design requirements for health care production control systems. *Production Planning and Control,* **10**, no. 6: 559-569.

Vries, G.G. de, Buwalda, P. and Linde, M. van der, 2004, Besturing van patiëntengroepen in een zorginstelling. ***Kwaliteit in Beeld*, 2**: 8-11.

Chapter 15

MANAGING A PATIENT FLOW IMPROVEMENT PROJECT

David Belson, Ph.D.

Epstein Department of Industrial and Systems Engineering, University of Southern California, Los Angeles, California 9008-0193

Abstract: There are many opportunities for improvements in patient flow but a successful project to do so requires proper organization and execution. The professional project management tools used in many industries are relevant but the hospital environment places special demands that affect chances for success. A patient flow improvement project must have a well-understood scope and objective with measurable results. The project team must be multidisciplinary and ideas from staff members encouraged. Examples and specific relevant project management methods are discussed.

Key words: Project Management, patient flow

1. INTRODUCTION

In their attempt to reduce patient flow delays hospitals and other health care institutions invariably undertake a project as a way to accomplish the desired change. Projects are defined as unique and one-time endeavors such as a move to a new facility. (See PMI, 2000 and Grey, 2000.) Various situations may impel a project – such as the need to replace an information system or the necessity to change paperwork procedures. Executives frequently request their managers to undertake a "project" to correct some problem or to facilitate some objective and managers often assign their staff to undertake various projects. Thus, hospitals often have many projects underway at any point in time. However, the managers and staff involved may not be knowledgeable as to what it takes to assure a project's success.

Projects are also viewed as an opportunity. Staff may use them as a career opportunity to exhibit their skills to a range of people inside and outside the hospital. Projects can be a way to involve oneself in interesting new trends or to learn new skills or merely to socialize. Thus, projects may be an opportunity for growth and advancement for the individual.

Certainly projects are used to react to problems or crises. Few changes take place in a health care institution without a so-called project to organize the effort and to marshal the resources necessary to accomplish a goal that crosses organizational lines.

Projects go through a series of stages: start-up, planning, execution, and termination. The start-up stage may be long and includes development of the objectives and analysis of the situation. The planning phase is critical to success and is the subject of most of this chapter. The execution phase uses the most resources in executing the elements of the project. The termination phase is relatively brief and its role is often misunderstood.

Although projects are a commonplace activity in a hospital, few health care professionals have training in project management. This is unfortunate since there is clear body of knowledge regarding how to plan and execute a successful project. Project Management is one of the few fields where there is a comprehensive and universally agreed upon body of knowledge (Project Management Institute, 2000).

2. PROJECT MANAGEMENT METHODS IN HEALTH CARE

A project is a series of work tasks that have a definite beginning and an end and leads to an outcome (Verzuh, 1999). A successful project requires a clear plan with certain necessary components. The science of project management has existed for many years and the vast number of projects using these concepts has solidified the understanding of what is needed. Some the current project management tools were developed in the 1950's for large military and aerospace efforts (Kerzner, 2004). Many aspects of projects to improve patient flow are similar to projects in other industries, which have projects involving changing work practices or procedures. Projects in health care generally require a multidisciplinary team and a focus on effective communication among the members.

First among the requirements for a project management plan is the definition of a project's objective and its scope. A project objective is a concise description of what the project hopes to achieve. If possible, the objective is defined in measurable terms, such as a specific and quantifiable change in the average patient discharge time or an increase in the number of patients served per day in a particular department. Without a written objective, which can be measured after the project is complete – there is little chance for success.

A project's scope is a definition of the elements that are included in a project as well as what is not included. Defining what is not included is important because some people may assume that an aspect is included when it isn't. For example, a project to improve the patient flow through a radiology department may include speeding up the time patients spend at scanning equipment but not include speeding up the processing of scanning output data. By defining what is not included, as well as what is included, a project is less likely to disappoint the recipients of the project's results or disappoint the organization that is paying for the project.

	Example
Objective	The project will increase the total number of patients served per day in the hospital's CT function without increasing staffing costs or the number of machines in the unit
Scope	The project will redesign the work procedures in the department based on an analysis of the current patient flow and identified bottlenecks. Accelerating the handling of the patient scanning results is not part of this project.

2.1 Project Management Concepts for Patient Flow

Project Management, as it applies to the health care industry, can rely on the extensive body of knowledge regarding project management generally. PMBOK describes the area of expertise as involving managing the following aspects of projects:

1. Integration
2. Scope
3. Time
4. Cost
5. Quality
6. Human Resources
7. Communications
8. Risk
9. Procurement

In health care, each of these nine knowledge areas has a particular meaning and places specialized demands on the project manager.

1. **Integration** – it is necessary to coordinate the various elements of a project. In the case of a project to improve patient flow this can mean the need to coordinate an information system change to provide necessary reports while at the same time coordinate changes to clinical and administrative data entry procedures by the staff. The different organizational groups participating in a project may have individual priorities, which must be accommodated as a project progresses. For example, nursing may focus on patient convenience while administration may be more focused on costs and economic margins. Projects often require successful execution of diverse tasks including planning the project as well as its execution. Thus, the project manager must have the ability to deal with many different phases of a project, sometimes on a simultaneous basis.
2. **Scope** – often projects are ambitious. Hospitals wish to improve care and improve productivity, but with limited resources. Thus, the limitations of a project involving patient care must be clearly defined and the impact of potential changes well understood. Perhaps one of the most common causes of project failure is successive expansion to the initial project scope. Project team members or the project's client may want to accomplish more than was originally envisioned. "Project creep" is a common ailment. An effort to reduce outpatient's waiting times might expand into building construction, information systems and outsourcing. If a scope change is deemed necessary, the project management should document the change and the related changes to the project's budget and time schedule as well as approval of the change. A formalized scope change control is necessary and a documentation of any changes is needed.
3. **Time** – the timely completion of a project is often an organization's primary measure of a project's success. To assure a project's progress and meet time expectations, a number of items are necessary:
    a. Activity definition
    b. Activity duration estimation
    c. Activity sequence requirements
    d. Scheduling
    e. Schedule control

   If these are properly managed, then the project can be completed on time.
4. **Cost** – involves processes to assure that a project is completed within the planned budget. Sometimes hospitals will undertake a project without giving the project an explicit budget. This may seem to make the job of the project manager easier but it may rob the hospital of a

necessary control over its scarce resources. If a project is sufficiently large, the organization may institute project accounting whereby people working on the project report their time by task and project accomplishments are compared to costs.

5. **Quality** – involves making sure that a project meets the purpose for which it was undertaken. Health care is familiar with placing a high priority on quality and the same attitude should prevail in the execution of a project. Moreover, quality of care may be impacted by the changes generated by a project and there must be project resources allocated to verifying that no adverse impact has taken place.
6. **Human Resources** – involves making effective use of the people involved in a project. Ad hoc groups are often drafted to do projects in health care. The job of the project manager is to develop this team and focus its efforts. Team members must be motivated to act together and to rely on each other within the context of the project's scope. This may require so-called team building exercises to create a feeling of cohesion and a willingness to extend effort in support of the project.
7. **Communications** – involves the distribution of information regarding the project. Since health care organizations involve many different specialties and work groups, this can be a challenge. Differences in terminology, work schedules and reporting relationships are barriers. Moreover, regulatory authorities may have an interest in a project and information they need must be managed.
8. **Risk** – involves identifying and planning how to respond to project risks. The possibility of failure exists for patient flow projects. Tools are available to identify, quantify and respond to project risk.
9. **Procurement** – goods and services sometimes are required, as part of a project and the project must manage these as well as the use of internal resources.

The Project Management Institute (PMI) has long been a source for such knowledge. It publishes a body of knowledge book in order to clarify the scope and important ideas of the field. It also administers a widely recognized professional certification program. It also supports a special interest group (SIG) for health care. It includes subgroups interested in projects involving information systems, regulatory obligations, business process re-engineering and other areas.

Project managers should be aware that all projects involve conflicting interests. The so-called "triple constraint" of project management is the desire to minimize a project's costs, maximize results and accelerate the time taken to do the project. These three aspects tend to work in opposition to each other (MacGregor, 2005). For example, a project to conduct a patient flow analysis may want to minimize data collection in order to reduce its costs. However, better results may result from more data collection and more time taken to do the work. The best a project manager can do is to balance the achievement in each of the three constraints in regard to the expectations of the organization. A budget to approve the costs, an agreed upon timeline and a clear project objective and scope are the best way to deal with the problem of the triple constraint.

2.2 Project Management Tools

Projects can be made more effective through the use of the various software products made available to assist the project manager. Perhaps the most basic tool for the project manager is to develop a work plan using techniques such as a GANTT Chart or a PERT Diagram that provide a graphical picture of the project. These help clarify the relationships between activities and the relationship between activities and time. Scheduling a large project may prove impossible without such tools. They were, in fact developed specifically for large projects such as the Apollo space project and defense industry projects. Many computer software products are available for developing project plans by automating the charting and scheduling tasks. The most popular ones include:

1. **Microsoft Project**, the project management software with largest market share
2. **Open Workbench** an open source alternative to MS Project, formerly Project Workbench
3. **Primavera Project Manager,** popular for large scale projects such as construction and public works and SureTrak® Project Manager from Primavera for smaller projects
4. **Artemis 7** and **Artemis Views**
5. **FastTrack Schedule**
6. **CA Super Project**
7. **Low-cost tools** such as: *MinuteMan, Projcet Kickstart, TimeLine, PlanBee, ProjeX, Mission Manager, Intellisys Project Desktop.*

Such software facilitates revising the project schedule as the project progresses and can help facilitate team communications by sharing project plans electronically.

The Gantt Chart or Bar Chart was first popularized by H. L. Gantt, an Industrial Engineer, during World War I and it is useful for planning and describing a time schedule. Projects are broken down into activities and the duration of each of these is displayed against a timeline. The meaning of the resulting diagram is self-evident. Additional information can be displayed in the diagram to present task-by-task progress or the interrelationships between activities.

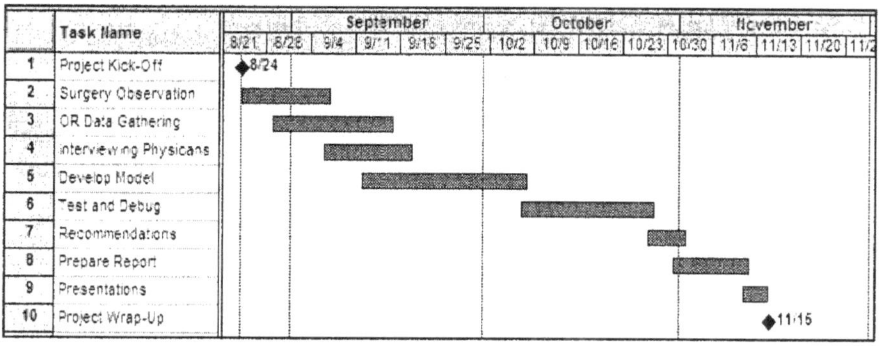

Figure 15-1. Typical Project Gantt Chart

As projects become larger it is necessary to do some "decomposition" – divide up the work into segments. Typically larger projects involve a work breakdown structure (WBS), numbering of tasks for accounting purposes. The numbered tasks are then used for the reporting of time spent and determining the extent to which planned work is completed. Some patient flow improvement projects may be relatively small and not require much measurement of their project. However, once a project becomes complex or requires a significant expense by the hospital, then project accounting and a formalized work breakdown structure becomes worthwhile.

The WBS serves as a helpful device to track costs and progress. Typically a hierarchical numbering scheme is used. It divides the project into various components and levels. For example, the project is divided at a high level into functional levels and within those levels into tasks, subtasks and work elements. Such as:

1 Data Gathering
1.1 Observing Daily Clinic Activities
1.1.1 Housekeeping of patient rooms
1.1.2 Admissions upon patient arrival
1.1.3 Security
1.2 Gathering Computer Reports
1.3 Gathering Patient Records
2 Interviewing Medical Staff
2.1 Interviewing Hospital Physicians
2.2 Interviewing Clinic Physicians
3 Identifying Computer Resources

The WBS is a tool to define the entire components of a project in an organized way, but it generally is not a tool to determine the sequence or duration of tasks.

Once the WBS is set, the project can use its structure to develop the project work plan by defining the sequence and duration of each task. In addition, the WBS numbering scheme can be used for project team members to report their progress and to allocate their work time. Progress can be reported in terms of the percent each task is complete as well as estimates of the amount of remaining time to complete each task. Thus, the project manager has the information to determine the status of a project regarding whether it is being completed according to the planned schedule or if it may not be finished at the time planned.

A useful measurement is to compute "earned value" as tasks are partially or totally completed. For example, a patient flow project may represent tasks that total 500 hours of work. Each task would have its individual hours also estimated as part of that total. As a task is completed, the completed or earned percentage can be completed. If 200 hours of tasks were completed then the project is reported as having a 40% earned value. If the project were planed to cost $10,000 then the earned value would be $4,000, which could be compared to the actual costs spent thus far on the project. Thus, administration can get a numerical picture of progress and cost as a project is underway.

A popular approach to conducting a patient flow improvement project is the six-sigma approach. This provides a standard sequence of activities. The methods discussed in this chapter apply to six-sigma as well as other improvement concepts. Among these is "lean thinking" which overlaps to some extent the six-sigma ideas. "Lean" places a focus on eliminating unnecessary work and utilizing successful productivity improvement concepts developed in Japan in recent decades.

Lean thinking projects generally follow an iterative approach with successive efforts to eliminate waste. (Womack, 2003) The basic sequence includes:

1. **Define Value**, focusing on the customer, concern only with what the patient needs
2. **Identify the Value Stream**, flowcharting is used with many approaches but in the case of Lean the focus is on those steps which add value, others can be eliminated
3. **Flow the Product**, wasteful steps are eliminated

4. **Institute Pull**, rather than pushing work through the system, a more efficient method is to have subsequent steps seek deliveries of patients or other elements
5. **Continuous Improvement**, recognize that there is always an opportunity to improve

Given the highly personal nature of health care services and the type of people it tends to involve, it is important to have good communications within the project and between the project team and the project's client. Many project managers have found the kick-off meeting to play a vital role. This is the initial meeting of the project, generally between the project team and the organization, which will be receiving the results of the project (the project's client). A kick-off event is a workshop type of meeting in which the beneficiaries of the project and the project team review the goals and objectives of the project, how it will be organized, etc. and who are then able to contribute to its planning, assignment of responsibilities, target dates, etc. (Weidman, 2002). A project to redesign the surgery scheduling system, for example, might have a kick-off meeting with the surgery leadership and with the entire surgery staff as well as the project team. The meeting might be part of a regular OR committee meeting or a special meeting set up for this purpose.

Several things should be accomplished in the kickoff meeting. All the participants should be introduced and how people can be contacted should be explained. Perhaps most important, the project's objectives and scope should be discussed and agreed upon and any differences resolved. Only if the objectives are known can support be expected from the recipients of the results of the project.

The kick off meeting can also accomplish other objectives. For example, at this time it may be appropriate to identify the resources that the project team will need, such as office space or access to medical staff.

2.3 Project Management Issues

Patient flow committees are common in hospitals. The Joint Commission on Accreditation of Healthcare Organizations (JCAHO) virtually requires it. However, do they contribute significantly to improvements? Do they ask the right questions? Frequently, hospitals create a committee to address patient flow issues and these groups initiate individual projects to institute a particular change.

The first step must be a clear definition of what the hospital intends. There are often a number of alternative objectives and each leads to a different improvement effort. Clarity is important. For example, a project to speed up patient discharge time may include the objective of a reduction in costs. Or, the objective of the same project may be to increase the number of patients served within the available resources. Still another objective might be to reduce average patient waiting time. Each of these objectives requires a different allocation of resources, different tasks and a different measure of success even if they are all projects to speed up patient discharge time. Thus, a first step is a clear definition of objectives and agreement by all of those involved.

Responsibilities in defining project objectives are also an important consideration. The setting of objectives may come from an outside agency, such as JACHO, or internally from the clinical staff. A successful project usually requires that a single individual, such as the hospital administrator, provide a formal approval of the project objectives.

Other project management planning steps, in addition to setting objectives, are:

- Define the project scope, including what you are not going to do. An explicit written scope becomes a contract between the project and the hospital. If the focus is on delays, then the scope should clearly define what particular delays are being addressed, which are not and to what extent are delays to be affected. The more this is clarified at the start – the better the chance for success. For example, a project may address waiting for an appointment but not address waiting after the patient arrives for the appointment.
- Secure the participation of the people who significantly influence the area being studied. This includes doctors, nurses and technicians. A variety of techniques exist to assure participation. (Gent, 1998 and Jones, 2000)
- Develop a project timeline based on estimates from the project's participants. The elapsed time for each major segment must be estimated so that the project's total time can be understood. If projects are regularly late, management's confidence in a project manager will be lost. This time estimation step also considers the sequence of tasks and determines the feasible final completion date. Staff in patient flow improvement committees may optimistically take on projects that are unrealistic, particularly regarding total project time. Projects often seem to always be late. However, that is not necessary with explicit planning. Some of the causes for late projects in health care include:
    - Forgetting to include tasks that delay the start up, such as the approval process, or tasks that delay the implementation of

results. Often implementation and experiencing the benefits of a project take longer than expected.

- Failure to consider the dependencies between tasks. Work on one task may depend on another, due to limited resources or the need for the output of one task to accomplish another. For example, IT may need to prepare a report before analysis of data can take place.
- All projects have a critical path. The critical path the subset of tasks that constitute the longest time for the project. These tasks are those that deserve the greatest attention to keep on time.
- Healthcare workers often are burdened with many responsibilities but willing to take on new projects. However, their availability to work on a project may be less than expected. Thus, the project manager must determine the time required from individual participants and if they cannot commit to the requirement – alternate plans must be made. If an individual is absolutely necessary for a project and is unavailable, the project must be rescheduled accordingly. Some project managers have found it helpful to get a signed commitment from project team members as to the amount of time they will devote to the project.
- By its interdisciplinary nature, health care projects often involve meetings with a large group of people – so that all interests are represented. Such meetings tend to be long and progress limited. It is often the responsibility of the project manager to monitor a meetings progress and take an active role to assure that the meeting is moving forward and addressing the proper topics.

- Develop a budget for the project. People cannot accomplish significant changes when a project is merely added to their current duties. The staffs in hospitals are already fully occupied and projects such as patient flow improvement will receive a low priority unless a specific budget is allocated. Even if the project is to be done without a separate financial accounting, it's a good idea to establish how much time and resources are to be allocated to the project. Otherwise, the naive assumption that a project can be squeezed among other duties will be assumed and the project will fail.
- Implementation of intra project communications. This may include regular meetings but periodic meetings are probably not sufficient. A project manager must regularly gather status from team members and report progress to stakeholders.

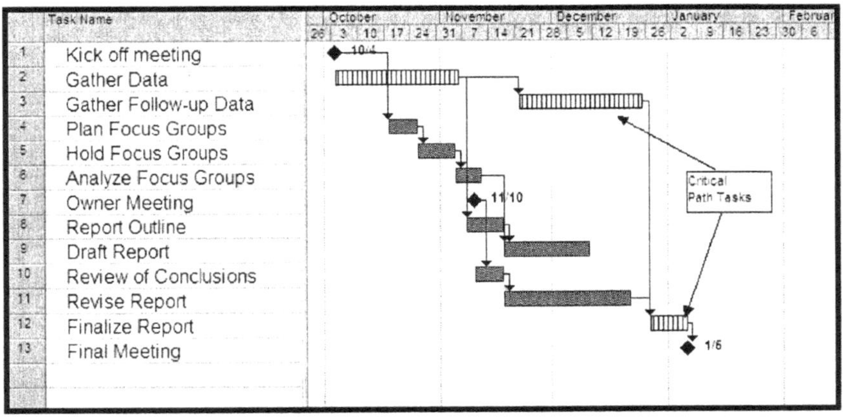

Figure 15-2. Project Gantt Chart with critical tasks identified

The Project Manager is a critical element in a project as the person who is responsible for the eventual successful execution of a project. If the project does not meet its objectives, the project manager is the person most responsible for any failure. The project manager is in a difficult position. In a sense, the project manager's fate is either a successful project whereupon he loses his job (because the project has ended) or an unsuccessful project where he also looses his job.

The project manager must play several roles:

- Communication with and among team. The team members may come from various departments or specialties, such as doctors, nurses, technicians or administrators. Each of these individuals has different backgrounds, training and priorities. Thus the project manager must understand their concerns as well as get them to work together as a team with a specific set of goals and objectives. Sometimes it becomes helpful to have a "kick-off" meeting. (see above)
- Communication with project's sponsors. Those interested in a project's results may include regulators, accrediting agencies and hospital administration. In some cases, patient's themselves need to be informed.
- Gathering resources needed to execute the project, such as a budget, authorization or information systems support.
- Monitoring project progress and reporting progress to management.

Depending on the requirements of a project, the project manager may not be responsible for completing particular work plan tasks but rather serve only the leadership role.

3. PATIENT FLOW PROJECTS

Patient flow improvement projects typically involve a sequence of phases to first understand the current processes, analyze them and then to determine opportunities for improvement. An equal amount of time may be involved in securing approval for the changes and implementing them. Also typically involved in patient flow projects is the need to measure and report on the ingoing impact of a project. There may be a tendency in a health care institution to revert to practices that were in place before the improvement project took place and this tendency must be managed until the improvement becomes permanent.

Completion is also an important phase of any project. A meeting may be held to review the results and to define any ongoing effects. In the case of patient flow projects, a successful project often means a change to past practices. Recommendations must be either approved and implemented or rejected. The success of a project should be determined regarding whether or not it made an improvement to patient flow commensurate with the cost of a project. A well-planned project would have been set up so such measurement of results is possible. For example, a project to improve radiology throughput should be able to point to the number of patients served per shift before the project was done and the number of patients served per shift after the project's recommendations were implemented. The so-called "bottom line" for a patient flow improvement project can be reported in specific measurable amounts, such as surgeries completed per day or average patient waiting time in a clinic.

3.1 Performance Measures in Patient Flow Projects

A key factor of success in any project is the ability to measure results. In the case of patient flow projects, here are a variety of choices. Many hospitals have found the concept of a "balanced scorecard" to be useful in determining performance measurement (Griffith, 2002; Hollingsworth, 1999). Such a scorecard incorporates financial, customer and internal performance information to measure the net results. In the case of patient flow the financial data might include utilization of resources, cost per patient or procedure and accuracy of billing details. Customer data might include patient satisfaction, wait times and appointments met. Other internal data might be procedures done per day or cost trends. All these measures should be compared to relevant benchmarks from other hospitals or organizations.

A project to improve patient flow for a particular radiology function might set a target at the outset, such as an increase of a specific percentage above current levels or a reduction of patient wait time by a specific amount of time. Measurement of targets aids the project team in identifying where they must focus their efforts. Measurement also rewards the team at the end of a project when they can point to specific accomplishments.

4. CASE STUDY: IDENTIFYING PATIENT FLOW BOTTLENECKS

A project was requested to study patient flow and identify related problems at a large county owned teaching hospital (LAC/USC), which was discussed in Chapter 1. The county's department of health services felt that they needed an outside review of their problems and a determination of where and how improvements in patient flow could be made using the tools of systems and industrial engineering.

As noted above, it's critical to have a clearly defined objective and scope. In this particular patient flow project they were:

> "To identify specific bottlenecks in the movement of patient flow in the General Hospital that could be improved by systems changes within the existing main facility and make specific recommended short-term and long-term actions. Excluded from the scope were information systems changes and clinical practices."

The project was then broken down into a group of tasks with sub tasks categorized in outline form. Normally a work breakdown structure (WBS) identifying accounting categories for the tasks would precede this. However, since the project was relatively small, involving four people, and no accounting of tasks costs was necessary, a formal WBS was unnecessary. A task-by-task timeline was developed with sufficient detail so that progress could be tracked and the likelihood of delays in completion determined. The initial Gantt chart for this project is shown in Figure 15-3.

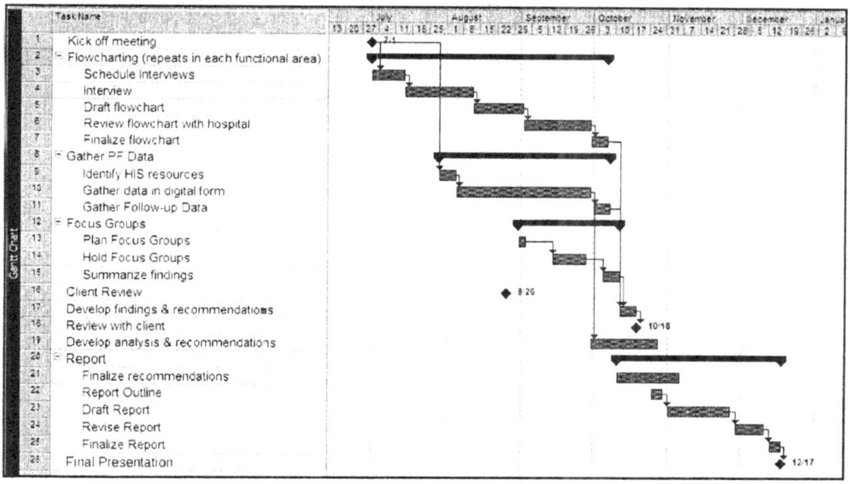

Figure 15-3. Patient Flow Project Bar (Gantt) Chart

During the course of the project, progress was tracked to assure that the agreed upon completion date would be met. There was an initial kick-off meeting before the project work began. This meeting was attended by the hospital's senior management (CEO, CMO and CNO), the county's head of health care services and members of the county's health care services department. The meeting identified individuals at the hospital that would serve as liaison and who would provide office resources to support the project. Thus, the project team knew how to get office space and services such as parking and telephones. It's not unusual for delays in such simple arrangements to delay a project's completion or reduce the quality of the results. The comprehensive nature of this initial meeting, particularly the discussion of roles and responsibilities, was critical to the project's eventual success.

The project proceeded by executing the individual tasks as planned. The most time consuming tasks were flowcharting the individual processes (summary task #2 in Figure 15-3) and extracting patient flow statistical data from the hospital's information system (task #10). The flowcharting tasks were demanding because of the wide diversity of the general hospital's services and the simple logistics of identifying and meeting with appropriate individuals from each department. In some cases the department head was the best source of workflow information but in many cases the best source was a nurse of technician who had years of familiarity with the department's activities. This step involved interviewing, flow chart diagramming, reviewing the initial diagrams with the department and revising the diagrams based on their feedback. Flowcharts were also helpful when discussing changes in the workflow since the chart provided an explicit description that everyone could view. We found the best approach when flowcharting a department, such as the pharmacy or surgery, to begin at a high level and then proceed to a more detailed set of charts. The initial flowchart may contain only a few overall processes, but when the department is fully charted there may be dozens or hundreds of processes worth noting.

The statistical data gathering at the hospital was problematic because the Hospital Information System (HIS) was not well suited to providing the quantitative patient flow data needed. The HIS was primarily used to track individual transactions for individual patients and summary statistics could only be provided with special programming. In the end, the project team wrote its own programs to analyze the HIS data externally through spreadsheets and graphs.

The patient flow information we desired was to quantify the numbers of patients moving from one area to another. This was done at a high level (Figure 15-4). This was a helpful in future follow-on projects by being able to know the relative volume of patients moving between areas.

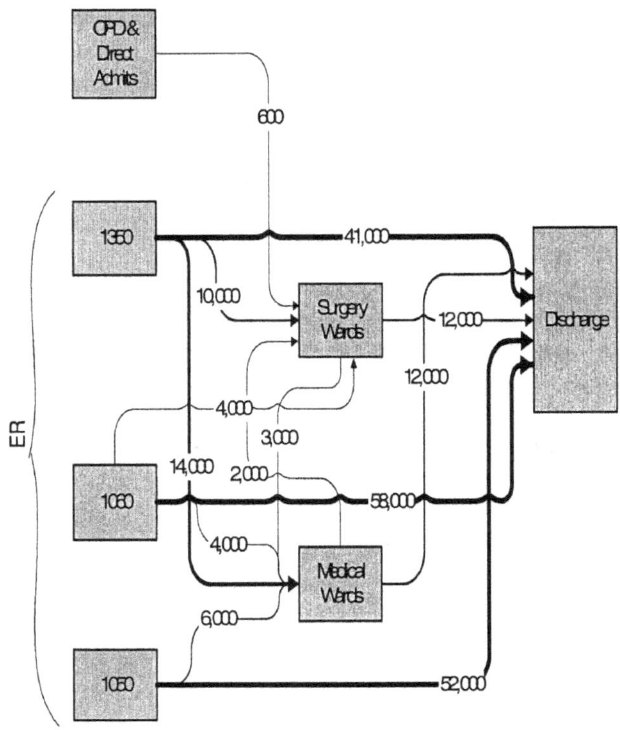

Figure 15-4. Patient flow between hospital areas.

Another portion of the project was gathering input from individual hospital staff. We found that a focus group discussion was particularly productive. This involved meetings with about 20 groups of people (5 to 15) who were involved directly in patient care (nurses, technicians, etc.). These group meetings were conducted on a confidential basis without anyone present from hospital administration or other management. The participants were given a formal document assuring their confidentiality and explaining the purpose of the meeting. The meetings were catered to create an informal and positive atmosphere. Resulting from the meetings was a wide variety of detailed suggestions to improve patient flow. Some of the time was spent on complaints about the environment but in each meeting there were a few individuals who had many useful ideas. These people proved to be good resources for future patient flow improvement work.

The last phase of the project involved developing recommendations, which grew from the analysis of the statistical data. The flow charts pointed to areas with the most severe bottlenecks and the data quantified the size of the problems. Brainstorming by the project team also produced many recommendations once the team had the background of the flowcharting, data analysis and focus group discussions. These recommendations were then reported back to the client, which constituted the people in the initial project kick-off meeting, as well as other interested individuals.

Findings of the project were recommendations that addressed the most serious delays and it identified where redesign of processes could be accomplished with little expense. As is the case with many local government owned hospitals, budget limitations were severe, so that only recommendations that did not add to staffing or require expensive new technology were practical. The recommendations included:

1. Implement improved radiology department procedures to reduce queues. Radiology proved to be a bottleneck, which contributed to an increased length of stay and total inpatient costs.
2. Expand the discharge waiting room to accelerate patient bed availability. By moving inpatients promptly from a hospital bed to a waiting area made it feasible to reduce queuing in the emergency department. This is an example of the interconnected nature of patient flow problems.
3. Formalize document control. A lack of document management led to duplicate and unnecessary paperwork.
4. Optimize patient transportation staffing. Delays here also contributed to the length of stay as well as delays in areas such as radiology and surgery.

5. Revise patient ID scheme. It turned out that patient status identification contributed to patient discharge process delays and also impacted the length of stay.
6. Bed management system. Due to the high bed utilization and the need to coordinate patient discharge and transportation a more powerful control system was needed.
7. Centralize appointment system. The hospital's outpatient clinics were numerous. Decentralized appointment processes resulted in underutilization of clinics and resulted in increased ER visits by patients who were unable to gain access to outpatient services.

Lessons learned and project documentation is also an important step in all projects. An organization should not have to relearn the experience. We prepared a formal report that documented this experience. Although the hospital was more interested in the immediate recommendations the project report will help future patient flow improvement efforts.

4.1 Case Study: Implementing the Findings of a Project

The aforementioned project identified bottlenecks in patient flow but real improvements require real implementation of changes with significant measurable results.

The initial project identified several hospital ancillary service areas where significant delays occurred. These were a particularly serious problem because they caused a costly increase in the patient's length of stay at the hospital. We had observed that patient wait times in radiology were long and unpleasant for many patients.

Radiology consisted of a variety of functions – too many to change all at once. In conjunction with managers of the radiology department we decided to focus on the CT (Computerized Tomography) function. It was important because many patients require the CT scans and the delays they experienced were long. Even with an appointment, outpatients regularly waited for four hours in the hospital to complete their scan. We therefore organized a project to address patient flow in the CT area in the hospital.

This project was intended to implement changes based on findings identified in the previous project. Patient flow through radiology could be quantified and the net effect of changes resulting from the project measured. The physical implementation of recommendations was to be the next step.

The first part of this project involved direct observation of the CT function by an engineering member of our team. CT is basically a simple process flow with patients queuing after arrival and being processed (scanned) by one of three identical machines. Our engineering oriented observation was done daily over one month period in order to get a clear understanding of the work procedures and to accurately measure the time taken for each step. A flow chart was prepared (Figure 15-5)and patient records were checked to compare to overall statistical reports generated by the department.

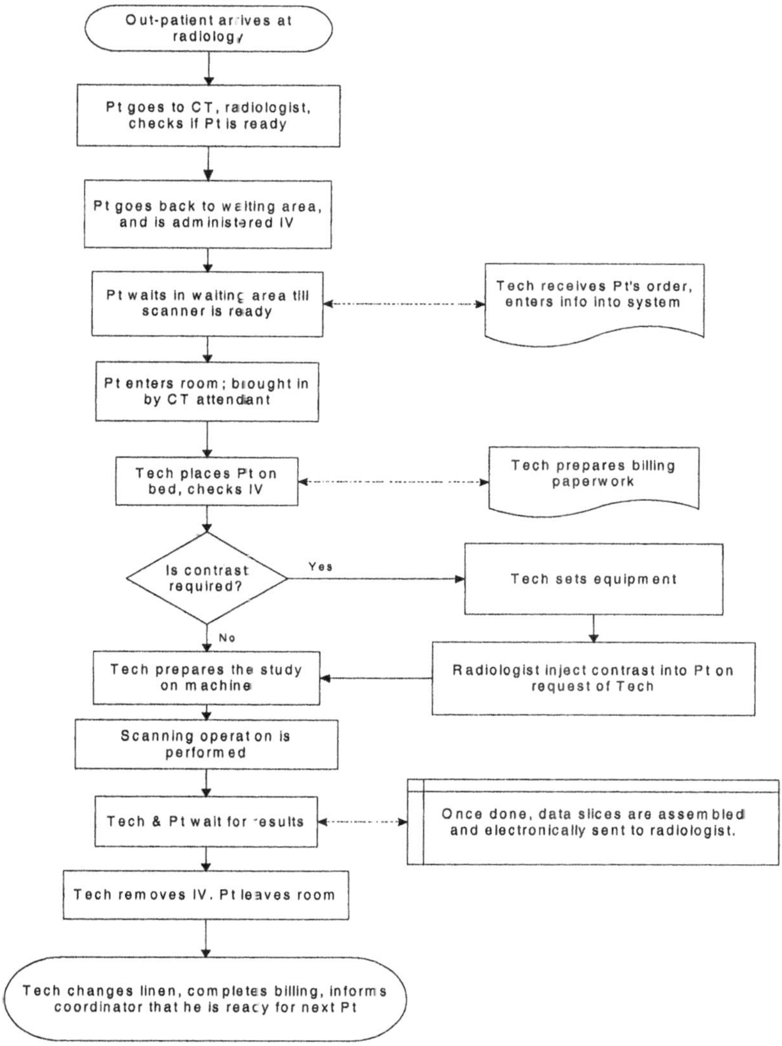

Figure 15-5. Radiology Flow Chart

The results of this sub project were:

- We developed a computer simulation of CT patient flow in order to test ideas and potential changes to the flow. The computer simulation allowed us to determine that total patient throughput could be doubled, increased by 100%. Of course, management was very interested in such a finding and had clear a incentive to act on our recommendations.
- We recommended specific operational changes to significantly increase the number of patients served daily without increasing costs. These included:
    - When the technologist is nearing completion of a scan, he should contact the coordinator who should bring up the next patient so that there is no delay between patients.
    - Patients should be seen in the order of their appointments, rather than first come first served. While this will not change the total throughput it will reduce the average patient waiting time.
    - Staffing shortages must be reduced. Frequently CT machines were not in use due to too few technicians available.
    - Accurate throughput data must be created and verified. Previously several systems were in use, which produced conflicting estimates of the number of patients served each day.
    - A CT leadership position must be created. Someone must be identified and assigned to assure that throughput is maximized. Previously no one person held that responsibility.
    - The CT technician duties could be relieved of certain paperwork preparation and filing. My spending more of their time on the scan process, more scans will be done because the availability of technicians was a bottleneck.
    - A CT function report card report should be established. This would include daily throughput measurement and comparisons to industry benchmarks. This report should be provided to management and the results compared to expectations.

4.2 Implementation Steps

These results were presented to hospital administration and a detailed report prepared. The management of radiology also reviewed the recommended changes and agreed with nearly all the changes suggested. Just circulating these recommendations seemed to have a beneficial effect. The hospital reported "dramatic" improvements resulting from awareness in the CT area of what must be done. Initially a reporting scheme was implemented which produced a daily report on the number of patients served. The calling up of patients by the coordinator seemed to accelerate and daily attendance was more closely monitored. This resulted in an increase in the number of patients served by about 30% within a few weeks of the publication of the study.

The hospital organized an implementation committee of radiology personnel, nurses and technicians, to proceed with all the changes. By involving the staff in planning the changes, it is more likely that the changes will be fully accepted by the direct care providers themselves.

The committee meets weekly to plan, design and implement changes. The first step was for the committee to develop its own flowchart of the process. This clarified their understanding of the patient flow. They also developed additional changes to improve patient flow. The committee decided that a separate waiting area was needed for CT patients. The hospital administration agreed to the construction budget as a sign of support for the change team. Thus changes not only included the recommendations from the patient flow project but additional changes that were developed during the implementation process. The net effect will probably result in an even greater improvement than the 100% forecasted by the initial study.

4.3 Report Cards to Measure Implementation

The measurement of results is an important ingredient in the implementation process. A report card provides a picture of the results of a patient flow project as well as a comparison to the target for which the project was intended. Quantitative measures provided tell the team whether the changes that they are making are actually leading to hospital improvements. It also tells management whether the project team is achieving the results they desire. The design of a "balanced scorecard" has been well established as a device to move an organization towards desired goals. (Kaplan, 1992) Balanced is achieved by considering several objectives, such as those of the patient as well as the hospital.

Many formats are possible for a report card as well as various possible individual measurements. Table 15-1 shows a report card for the CT patient flow improvement project. Both the patient's interest (wait time) and the hospital's objective (patients scanned per day) are included, along with modest targets. Initially, this report was done on a daily basis and senior management insisted on seeing the results each day. The reports were used as a basis for meeting with the CT department staff and management. All concerned agreed the report card was how they should be evaluated.

Table 15-1. CT Report Card

CT Report Card

Measure	Target value	Actual Average	Most recent measure
Days until next available appointment	23 days	36 days	35 days
Average outpatient wait at CT	0.5 hours	2.25 hours	2.3 hours
Average inpatient wait for CT	6 hours	28 hours	25 hours
Throughput, number of scans per day	150 scans	120 scans	135 scans

In the case of this scorecard, the report was first used to inform the team designing and implementing the changes what was the current patient flow in comparison to targeted values. Targets were developed from both industry standards and from what the clinical people in the department felt were reasonable. Many people were surprised initially at the low level of performance reported on the scorecard but this served as useful lever in motivating change.

Balanced scorecards can be used in nearly every type of project from improving an emergency room (Huang, 2004 and Cleverley, 2005) to hospital information systems. (Gordon, 1999)

5. SUMMARY AND CONCLUSIONS

Project management's methods provide resources to increase the likelihood of success in efforts to improve patient flow. Delays in health care services are a frequent concern for owners, managers, providers and users of health care. In an effort to reduce delays many projects are launched. However, only with proper project management methods do these projects have much chance for success in making significant improvements. Project management knowledge is available but those involved in reducing patient delays must familiarize themselves with the fundamentals before their projects begin.

Certain project management approaches seem particularly important in projects involving delays in patient flow. One suggestion is to keep projects as simple and focused as possible. Projects that involve all the many aspects of patient flow risk the danger of being bogged down in trying to change too many things at once. Another important idea is to make sure that each project is clearly defined and well thought out at the beginning. Objectives and scope must be clear and agreed to by management and the project team. By creating a written plan at the start gives the best possible opportunity for success. Such planning may uncover flaws or gaps in the undertaking that might not otherwise be known. There is always an opportunity for reducing delays, which can always be reduced by a well-managed project.

6. REFERENCES

Project Management Institute (2000). *A Guide to the Project Management Body of Knowledge (PMBOK)*, Newtown Square, PA.

Cleverley, William and Cleverely, James. "Scorecards and dashboards: using financial metrics to improve performance." *Healthcare Financial Management*. Jul 2005, 59, 7,64-70

Gent L., Parry A.E., Parry M.E. (1998) The high-cooperation hospital project team. *Team Performance Management*, Volume 4, Number 6, June 1998, pp. 253-268(16). Emerald Group Publishing Limited

Gordon, D., Geiger, G. "Strategic Management of an Electronic Record Project Using the Balanced Scorecard." *Journal of Healthcare Information Management*, 1999, 13, 113-123.

Gray, C. G. & Larson, E. W. (2000). *Project management: The managerial process*. New York, Irwin/McGraw Hill

Griffith, JR, Alexander, JA, Jelinek, RC (2002). Measuring Comparative Hospital Performance. *Journal of Healthcare Management*, 47(1), 41-57.

Hollingsworth, Bruce, Dawson, PJ, Maniadakis, N (1999). Efficiency Measurement of Health Care. *Health Care Management Science*, Sept., 1999. Vol. 2, (3), 161-172.

Huang. S. et. al. "Using a Balanced Scorecard to Improve the Performance of an Emergency Department." *Nursing Economics*. May/Jun 2004, 22, 140-147.

Jones, Katherine R. PhD, RN, FAAN; Redman, Richard W. PhD, RN (2000). Organizational Culture and Work Redesign: Experiences in Three Organizations. *Journal of Nursing Administration*. 30(12):604-610.

Kaplan, R. and Norton, D. "The Balanced Scorecard – Measures That Drive Performance." *Harvard Business Review*, 1992, 70, 71-79.

Kerzner, Harold (2004). *Advanced Project Management*, Hoboken, N.J.

Kerzner, Harold (2003). *Project Management, A Systematic Approach to Planning, Scheduling and Controlling*, 8th Ed., John Wiley, N.Y., 2003.

MacGregor, Steven P. (2005). Achieving Project Management Success, *Journal of Product Innovation Management*, Vol. 22(3), p 293.

Ozcan, Yasar A. (2005). *Quantitative Methods in Health Care*, 2005, Josey Bass, San Francisco, CA.

Rosenau, Milton D. (1998). *Successful Project Management*, John Wiley, N.Y.

Verzuh, E. (1999). *The Fast Forward MBA in Project Management*. New York City, N.Y.: John Wiley & Sons, Inc.

Wideman, Max (2002). Wideman Comparative Glossary of Common Project Management Terms v3.1, http://maxwideman.com/pmglossary/index.htm.

Womack, James P., Daniel T. Jones, Daniel Roos (1991). *The Machine That Changed the World : The Story of Lean Production*, Harper Reprint Edition.

Womack, James P., Daniel T. Jones (2003). *Lean Thinking: Banish Waste and Create Wealth in Your Corporation,* Revised and Updated, Free Press.

Young, Terry, et. al. (2004). Using industrial processes to improve patient care. *BMJ* 2004;328:162-164 (17 January).

Biographies

David Belson is a Senior Research Associate and Lecturer in the Epstein Department of Industrial and Systems Engineering, at the University of Southern California. He teaches a class at USC entitled *Improving Health Care Operations*. He previously was in management consulting with Tefen International and Ernst & Young. He served in executive positions with IBM and Universal Studios. He was the project manager on projects aimed at improving patient flow in the Los Angeles County Department of Health Services. He has worked with several hospitals in California regarding productivity improvement and information systems. Dr. Belson received his Ph.D. in Industrial Engineering from the University of Southern California.

Emilio Cerdá is Professor of Economic Analysis. He holds a Ph.D. in Mathematics. Areas of research include dynamic optimization, stochastic programming, and multiple criteria decision making, environmental and resource economics and health care management. He is currently Head of the Department of Foundations of Economic Analysis I at the Complutense University, Madrid, Spain.

Peter Congdon is a quantitative geographer with particular interests in spatial epidemiology, statistical modeling, and health service research. Since 2001 he has been a Research Professor in Geography at QMUL, and is also affiliated to the QMUL Centre for Statistics. He is the author of a range of articles and books, including the recent Wiley publications 'Bayesian Models for Categorical Data' and 'Applied Bayesian Modelling'. Dr. Congdon has been involved in several ESRC funded projects, including studies on the relationship between adolescent health and neighborhood context, influence of geographic setting on social differences in health, and locality-level mortality and socio-economic change. He has also been involved in a Department of Health Study of the public health workforce, and analysis of psychiatric need indicators for the New York Office of Mental Health. His professional activities include associate editorship of Biometrics and project review work for a number of research agencies (e.g. NHS Service Delivery and Organisation R&D Programme, Alberta Heritage Foundation for Medical Research, Arts and Humanities Research Board).

Maged M. Dessouky is a Professor in the Daniel J. Epstein Department of Industrial and Systems Engineering at the University of Southern California. Dr. Dessouky's research interests are in production and operations management, supply chain management, transportation, scheduling, simulation, and applied operations research. He is area editor of Planning and Scheduling for *Computers & Industrial Engineering* and area editor of Transportation Simulation & Methodology for *ACM Transactions on Modeling and Computer Simulation.* Dr. Dessouky received his B.S. and M.S. degrees in Industrial Engineering from Purdue University in 1984 and 1987, respectively. He received a Ph.D. in Industrial Engineering and Operations Research from the University of California, Berkeley, in 1992

Linda V. Green is the Armand G. Erpf Professor at Columbia Business School. She earned her doctorate in Operations Research from Yale University. Her research, which has focused on the development and application of mathematical models of service systems, has resulted in numerous publications in the major technical journals including *Operations Research, Management Science,* and *The Journal of Applied Probability* as well as prominent healthcare journals such as *Health Services Research, Inquiry* and *Academic Emergency Medicine.* Her current research is on identifying operational policies to improve the delivery of healthcare. Specific projects focus on improving emergency responsiveness, developing strategies for the efficient and effective use of major diagnostic equipment such as MRIs, and the development of a new nurse staffing methodology. She is a co-founder and co-director of the Columbia Alliance for Healthcare Management, a unique partnership of the College of Physicians and Surgeons, the Mailman School of Public Health and the Business School of Columbia University dedicated to promoting interdisciplinary research and education in healthcare management. In recognition of her professional achievements, Professor Green was elected a Fellow of INFORMS.

Randolph Hall is Vice Provost for Research Advancement, and a Professor in the Epstein Department of Industrial and Systems Engineering, at the University of Southern California. He previously served as the Principal Investigator for the Center for Risk and Economic Analysis of Terrorism

Events (CREATE) and the Director for the National Center for Metropolitan Transportation Research (METRANS), as well as the Chair of the Epstein Department, and Senior Associate Dean for Research in Engineering. He is the author of *Queueing Methods for Services and Manufacturing* and Editor for the *Handbook of Transportation Science*, and is the Principal Investigator on a pair of projects aimed at improving patient flow in the Los Angeles County Department of Health Services. Dr. Hall received his Ph.D. in Transportation Engineering from the University of California at Berkeley.

Shane N. Hall is a Captain in the United States Air Force and a PhD candidate in the Simulation and Optimization Laboratory, Department of Mechanical and Industrial Engineering at the University of Illinois at Urbana-Champaign. He has a B.S. in Mathematics from Brigham Young University and a M.S. in Operations Research from Air Force Institute of Technology. His dissertation research includes the formulation and analysis of discrete optimization models meant to address problems in pediatric vaccination.

Sheldon H. Jacobson is Professor, Willett Faculty Scholar, and Director of the Simulation and Optimization Laboratory in the Department of Mechanical and Industrial Engineering at the University of Illinois. He has a B.Sc. and M.Sc. (both in Mathematics) from McGill University, and a M.S. and Ph.D. (both in Operations Research and Industrial Engineering) from Cornell University. His research interests include the analysis and design of heuristics for discrete optimization problems, aviation security and health-care delivery systems. In 1998, he received the Application Award from the Institute of Industrial Engineers Operations Research Division. In 2002, he was named an Associate in the Center for Advanced Study at the University of Illinois, and was awarded the Aviation Security Research Award by Aviation Security International, the International Air Transport Association, and the Airports Council International. In 2003, he received the Best Paper Award in the IIE Transactions Focused Issue on Operations Engineering and was named a Guggenheim Fellow by the John Simon Guggenheim Memorial Foundation. His research has been published in a wide spectrum of journals, including *Operations Research, Mathematical Programming, INFORMS Journal on Computing, Operations Research Letters, Naval Research Logistics, IIE Transactions, and the Journal of the Operational Research Society*. He has received research funding from the National Science Foundation, the Air Force Office of Scientific Research, and the Federal Aviation Administration.

Hongzhong Z. Jia received his dual B. Eng degree in Mechanical Engineering and Industrial Management from Shanghai Jiao Tong University, China and then completed his M.Eng study at the Department of Mechanical Engineering, National University of Singapore (NUS) in 2001. He is currently a PhD candidate majored in Operations Research at the University of Southern California. His research interests include vehicle routing, manufacturing scheduling, agent-based systems, and product development. He is a member of INFORMS.

Linda Kosnik is the Chief Nursing Officer at Overlook Hospital, Atlantic Health System in Summit, NJ. Ms. Kosnik received her undergraduate degree from Columbia University and her MSN from Seton Hall University. She is currently a doctoral candidate in health science leadership also at Seton Hall University. Ms. Kosnik has lectured nationally and has published extensively on collaboration, quality improvement and process and performance management as applied to healthcare. She is a nationally recognized expert on reducing waits and delays, and in the overarching domain of improving patient-flow in hospitals, especially as it relates to demand and capacity management. Through the Institute for Healthcare Improvement (IHI) and other forums, Linda has successfully mentored hundreds of teams through improvement initiatives. Using a collaborative approach to leadership, she has established national recognition for Overlook Hospital, including receiving the New Jersey Governor's Award for Quality Improvement that is based on Malcolm Baldrige Criteria.

Lisa Kuramoto is a Statistical Analyst in the Centre for Clinical Epidemiology and Evaluation, a part of the Vancouver Coastal Health Research Institute in Vancouver. She holds an MSc in Statistics from the University of British Columbia. Her research interests are primarily in investigating surgical waiting times and their impact on patient outcomes.

Adrian R. Levy is Associate Professor in the Department of Health Care and Epidemiology at the University of British Columbia and is an investigator at St Paul's Hospital in the Centre for Health Evaluation and Outcome Sciences. He received his PhD from McGill University in epidemiologist and his academic interests are in health services research, specifically in the areas of access to care, pharmacoepidemiology, and economic evaluation. He has considerable experience using administrative databases and population registries for carrying out population-based health services research.

Mark Lindsay MD, MMM is the Department Chair of Pulmonary and Critical Care Medicine at Luther Midelfort, Mayo Health System. He is the Physician Chair of Luther's Continuum of Care Program and Utilization

Management, Medical Director of Wissota Ventilator Unit and the Medical Director of Luther's Medical House Call Program. He has been active in partnerships of acute care hospitals, with nursing homes, rural hospitals and home care programs to optimize patient care across care settings with an emphasis on the business case and clinical outcomes.

Pavan Murali is a doctoral student in Industrial Engineering at the University of Southern California (USC). He holds a Bachelor's degree in Mechanical Engineering from the Indian Institute of Technology, Madras, and a Master's degree in Operations Research from USC. His research interests mainly lie in the design and implementation of algorithms for combinatorial and non-linear optimization. He is currently working as a research assistant on a project involving simulation and mathematical modeling to improve health care operations in the radiology, surgery and bed management departments at the Los Angeles County Hospital

Fernando Ordóñez is an Assistant Professor in the Industral and Systems Engineering department at USC's Viterbi School of Engineering. His research focuses on convex optimization, robust optimization, complexity of algorithms, sensitivity analysis, condition number theory, and applications of optimization to engineering and management science. He received his BS and Mathematical Engineering degree, from the University of Chile in 1996 and 1997, respectively; and his Ph.D. in Operations Research from MIT in 2002.

Laura de Pablos is Head of the Department of Aplied Economics VI at the Complutense University, Madrid, Spain. She has published several papers and books about Public Economics. Areas of research include Budget Control, Evaluation and Control of Public Spending Policies, Analysis of the impact of Public Spending, Education Economics and Health Economics.

Roger Resar, MD, is Assistant Professor of Medicine at the Mayo Clinic School of Medicine and Change Agent for Luther Midelfort and Mayo Foundation. He shares his time between consulting within the Mayo System and the Institute for Healthcare Improvement where he is a Senior Fellow and functions as faculty and a founding member of the IHI Innovation Team. Dr Resar has contributed to the development and dissemination of key safety and improvement strategies, including Medication Reconciliation (which has been deemed a Joint Commission standard for 2006), a trigger tool methodology that is currently being used in hundreds of hospitals to measure adverse events, "bundle science", reliability concepts for design improvement work, and basic work in hospital flow. Dr. Resar is boarded in

Pulmonary and Critical Care Medicine and graduated from the University of Wisconsin Medical School in 1972.

María V. Rodríguez-Uría is a well known scientific expert in the MCDM field with numerous articles in the concerned literature. She is Professor and Head of the Department of Quantitative Economics at the University of Oviedo in Spain. She has also supervised several PhD Theses and she is responsible of the Multicriteria Decision Making Group of her University.

Sergei Savin is an Associate Professor of Decision, Risk, and Operations at the Graduate School of Business, Columbia University. Professor Savin holds PhD degrees in Physics from the University of Pennsylvania and in Operations and Information Management from the Wharton School. His research encompasses the areas of health care management, revenue management, marketing-operations coordination, E-business, and new product development. Professor Savin's works have been published in leading academic journals *Operations Research* and *Management Science* and have been supported by the grants from Columbia Health Alliance and Columbia Center for Excellence in E-Business. He serves as an Associate Editor for *Operations Research*, as a Senior Editor for *Production and Operations Management* and as an Editorial Board member for *Manufacturing and Service Operations Management*.

Zhihong Shen is currently a PhD student majored in Operations Research in the Industrial and Systems Engineering department at the University of Southern California. She received her BS in Electronics and Information Science and Technology and Bachelor of Economics from Peking University, China in 2000 and then completed her MS in High Performance Computing at Singapore-MIT Alliance in 2001. Her current research interests include vehicle routing, production and operations management, and applications of optimization.

Boris Sobolev is a Canada Research Chair in Health Services Research, Associate Professor at the University of British Columbia and a research scientist in the Centre for Clinical Epidemiology and Evaluation. He received PhD in Applied Statistics from the USSR Academy of Sciences. His research is focused on the development of statistical models for the analysis of waiting data in health services research. Dr. Sobolev also leads projects on healthcare simulation modeling and policy analysis using simulation. Recently he co-chaired the international conference on Modeling Healthcare Systems in Vancouver.

James R. Swisher is Director of Performance Improvement for Mary Washington Hospital (MWH). Mr. Swisher currently oversees MWH's quality, service, and industrial engineering programs. Upon his arrival at MWH in 1999, he established and has grown the industrial engineering function at MWH. He now works to leverage industrial engineering and operations research approaches to improving healthcare processes at MWH, particularly in the fields of clinical quality, patient satisfaction, and patient flow. Prior to joining MWH, he worked as Director of Analysis and Design for Biological & Popular Culture, Inc where he was responsible for management engineering. He holds a B.S. and a M.S. in Industrial Systems Engineering (Operations Research) from Virginia Tech and an M.B.A. from Mary Washington College. He is interested in the application of operations research techniques to complex business problems, particularly in field of health care. Mr. Swisher is a member of INFORMS, IIE, and Alpha Pi Mu.

Jan M.H. Vissers is professor in Health Operations Management at the institute for Health Policy and Management at Erasmus University Medical Centre Rotterdam at Rotterdam NL. He is also affiliated with the Department of Technology Management of Eindhoven University of Technology, Eindhoven. He is furthermore a senior management consultant at Prismant - institute for health care management development in Utrecht. Dr. Vissers Received his MSc Industrial Engineering and Management Science from EUT in 1975 and his PhD from EUT in 1994. He acts as current chairman of the European Working Group on Operational Research Applied to Health Services and is a member of the editorial board of Health Care Management Science. He received the 1995 Baxter Award for his thesis 'Patient Flow based Allocation of Hospital Resources' for its contribution to Health Care Management. Together with Roger Beech, he edited the book *Health Operations Management. Patient Flow Logistics in Health Care*, published in 2005 by Routledge. His research focuses on the analysis, design and control of operational health care processes and systems.

Michael Warner is Chairman and Chief Science Officer of AtStaff Incorporated, designing staff management systems for healthcare. Previously, he co-founded and was president of Atwork, Inc., a software company which he sold in 1995. Previous to Atwork, Warner was a faculty member at Duke University's Fuqua School of Business, Duke's Medical School, and the University of Michigan's School of Public Health. He is author of two textbooks in Health Administration, and numerous articles on the application of Operations Research to Health Administration. Dr. Warner received a BS in Math and a Masters in Health Administration from Duke University, and a Ph.D. in Operations Research from Tulane University.

Michael Williams is the president of The Abaris Group, a firm that specializes in emergency department and inpatient program patient flow and capacity building strategies. He has personally conducted greater than 350 hospital studies on improving performance, productivity and market share. He is a recognized expert on healthcare performance, benchmarking and financing having conducted 15 presentations during the past 24-months for organizations such as: American College of Emergency Physicians, California Hospital Association, Connecticut Hospital Association, American Trauma Society, Urgent Matters, The Zoll Corporation, The Coding Institute, and Beta. He is a frequent contributor to the Healthcare Advisory Board on a number of hospital and ED subjects. He is also a member of CAL/ACEP's Reimbursement Committee. He is also on the editorial board for *ED Management.* He is a senior faculty member for The Robert Wood Johnson Foundation's Urgent Matters Project (urgentmatters.org), which is a 10-hospital collaborative throughout the country and an instructor for Harvard University on their course on "Designing EDs for the Future."

Index

Early Titles in the
INTERNATIONAL SERIES IN
OPERATIONS RESEARCH & MANAGEMENT SCIENCE
Frederick S. Hillier, Series Editor, *Stanford University*

Saigal/ *A MODERN APPROACH TO LINEAR PROGRAMMING*
Nagurney/ *PROJECTED DYNAMICAL SYSTEMS & VARIATIONAL INEQUALITIES WITH APPLICATIONS*
Padberg & Rijal/ *LOCATION, SCHEDULING, DESIGN AND INTEGER PROGRAMMING*
Vanderbei/ *LINEAR PROGRAMMING*
Jaiswal/ *MILITARY OPERATIONS RESEARCH*
Gal & Greenberg/ *ADVANCES IN SENSITIVITY ANALYSIS & PARAMETRIC PROGRAMMING*
Prabhu/ *FOUNDATIONS OF QUEUEING THEORY*
Fang, Rajasekera & Tsao/ *ENTROPY OPTIMIZATION & MATHEMATICAL PROGRAMMING*
Yu/ *OR IN THE AIRLINE INDUSTRY*
Ho & Tang/ *PRODUCT VARIETY MANAGEMENT*
El-Taha & Stidham/ *SAMPLE-PATH ANALYSIS OF QUEUEING SYSTEMS*
Miettinen/ *NONLINEAR MULTIOBJECTIVE OPTIMIZATION*
Chao & Huntington/ *DESIGNING COMPETITIVE ELECTRICITY MARKETS*
Weglarz/ *PROJECT SCHEDULING: RECENT TRENDS & RESULTS*
Sahin & Polatoglu/ *QUALITY, WARRANTY AND PREVENTIVE MAINTENANCE*
Tavares/ *ADVANCES MODELS FOR PROJECT MANAGEMENT*
Tayur, Ganeshan & Magazine/ *QUANTITATIVE MODELS FOR SUPPLY CHAIN MANAGEMENT*
Weyant, J./ *ENERGY AND ENVIRONMENTAL POLICY MODELING*
Shanthikumar, J.G. & Sumita, U./ *APPLIED PROBABILITY AND STOCHASTIC PROCESSES*
Liu, B. & Esogbue, A.O./ *DECISION CRITERIA AND OPTIMAL INVENTORY PROCESSES*
Gal, T., Stewart, T.J., Hanne, T. / *MULTICRITERIA DECISION MAKING: Advances in MCDM Models, Algorithms, Theory, and Applications*
Fox, B.L. / *STRATEGIES FOR QUASI-MONTE CARLO*
Hall, R.W. / *HANDBOOK OF TRANSPORTATION SCIENCE*
Grassman, W.K. / *COMPUTATIONAL PROBABILITY*
Pomerol, J-C. & Barba-Romero, S. / *MULTICRITERION DECISION IN MANAGEMENT*
Axsäter, S. / *INVENTORY CONTROL*
Wolkowicz, H., Saigal, R., & Vandenberghe, L. / *HANDBOOK OF SEMI-DEFINITE PROGRAMMING: Theory, Algorithms, and Applications*
Hobbs, B.F. & Meier, P. / *ENERGY DECISIONS AND THE ENVIRONMENT: A Guide to the Use of Multicriteria Methods*
Dar-El, E. / *HUMAN LEARNING: From Learning Curves to Learning Organizations*
Armstrong, J.S. / *PRINCIPLES OF FORECASTING: A Handbook for Researchers and Practitioners*
Balsamo, S., Personé, V., & Onvural, R./ *ANALYSIS OF QUEUEING NETWORKS WITH BLOCKING*
Bouyssou, D. et al. / *EVALUATION AND DECISION MODELS: A Critical Perspective*
Hanne, T. / *INTELLIGENT STRATEGIES FOR META MULTIPLE CRITERIA DECISION MAKING*
Saaty, T. & Vargas, L. / *MODELS, METHODS, CONCEPTS and APPLICATIONS OF THE ANALYTIC HIERARCHY PROCESS*
Chatterjee, K. & Samuelson, W. / *GAME THEORY AND BUSINESS APPLICATIONS*
Hobbs, B. et al. / *THE NEXT GENERATION OF ELECTRIC POWER UNIT COMMITMENT MODELS*
Vanderbei, R.J. / *LINEAR PROGRAMMING: Foundations and Extensions, 2nd Ed.*
Kimms, A. / *MATHEMATICAL PROGRAMMING AND FINANCIAL OBJECTIVES FOR SCHEDULING PROJECTS*
Baptiste, P., Le Pape, C. & Nuijten, W. / *CONSTRAINT-BASED SCHEDULING*
Feinberg, E. & Shwartz, A. / *HANDBOOK OF MARKOV DECISION PROCESSES: Methods and Applications*
Ramík, J. & Vlach, M. / *GENERALIZED CONCAVITY IN FUZZY OPTIMIZATION AND DECISION ANALYSIS*
Song, J. & Yao, D. / *SUPPLY CHAIN STRUCTURES: Coordination, Information and Optimization*
Kozan, E. & Ohuchi, A. / *OPERATIONS RESEARCH/ MANAGEMENT SCIENCE AT WORK*
Bouyssou et al. / *AIDING DECISIONS WITH MULTIPLE CRITERIA: Essays in Honor of Bernard Roy*

Early Titles in the
INTERNATIONAL SERIES IN
OPERATIONS RESEARCH & MANAGEMENT SCIENCE
(Continued)

Cox, Louis Anthony, Jr. / *RISK ANALYSIS: Foundations, Models and Methods*
Dror, M., L'Ecuyer, P. & Szidarovszky, F. / *MODELING UNCERTAINTY: An Examination of Stochastic Theory, Methods, and Applications*
Dokuchaev, N. / *DYNAMIC PORTFOLIO STRATEGIES: Quantitative Methods and Empirical Rules for Incomplete Information*
Sarker, R., Mohammadian, M. & Yao, X. / *EVOLUTIONARY OPTIMIZATION*
Demeulemeester, R. & Herroelen, W. / *PROJECT SCHEDULING: A Research Handbook*
Gazis, D.C. / *TRAFFIC THEORY*
Zhu/ *QUANTITATIVE MODELS FOR PERFORMANCE EVALUATION AND BENCHMARKING*
Ehrgott & Gandibleux/ *MULTIPLE CRITERIA OPTIMIZATION: State of the Art Annotated Bibliographical Surveys*
Bienstock/ *Potential Function Methods for Approx. Solving Linear Programming Problems*
Matsatsinis & Siskos/ *INTELLIGENT SUPPORT SYSTEMS FOR MARKETING DECISIONS*
Alpern & Gal/ *THE THEORY OF SEARCH GAMES AND RENDEZVOUS*
Hall/*HANDBOOK OF TRANSPORTATION SCIENCE - 2nd Ed.*
Glover & Kochenberger/ *HANDBOOK OF METAHEURISTICS*
Graves & Ringuest/ *MODELS AND METHODS FOR PROJECT SELECTION: Concepts from Management Science, Finance and Information Technology*
Hassin & Haviv/ *TO QUEUE OR NOT TO QUEUE: Equilibrium Behavior in Queueing Systems*
Gershwin et al/ *ANALYSIS & MODELING OF MANUFACTURING SYSTEMS*

**** A list of the more recent publications in the series is at the front of the book ****

FSC
www.fsc.org
MIX
Papier | Fördert
gute Waldnutzung
FSC® C083411

Kolibri 360 GmbH
Ferdinand-Jühlke-Straße 7
99095 Erfurt, Deutschland
produktsicherheit@kolibri360.de